NORTHEASTERN ILLINOIS UNIVERSITY

3 1224 00517 4833

P9-CDA-364

WINDOWS XP

IN A NUTSHELL

WITHDRAWN
NORTHEASTERN ILLINOIS
UNIVERSITY LIBRARY

WINDOWS XP

IN A NUTSHELL

David A. Karp, Tim O'Reilly, and Troy Mott

O'REILLY®

Beijing • Cambridge • Farnham • Köln • Paris • Sebastopol • Taipei • Tokyo

Windows XP in a Nutshell

by David A. Karp, Tim O'Reilly, and Troy Mott

Copyright © 2002, 1999, 1998 O'Reilly & Associates, Inc. All rights reserved.
Printed in the United States of America.

Published by O'Reilly & Associates, Inc., 1005 Gravenstein Highway North,
Sebastopol, CA 95472.

O'Reilly & Associates books may be purchased for educational, business, or sales
promotional use. Online editions are also available for most titles (*safari.oreilly.com*). For
more information, contact our corporate/institutional sales department: 800-998-9938 or
corporate@oreilly.com.

Editor:	Tim O'Reilly
Production Editor:	Ann Schirmer
Cover Designer:	Hanna Dyer
Interior Designer:	Melanie Wang

QA
76.76
Q63
K37
2002

Printing History:

April 2002:   First Edition, *Windows XP in a Nutshell*.

Portions of this book have been previously published as follows:

June 1998:   *Windows 95 in a Nutshell*, by Tim O'Reilly and Troy Mott.

August 1999:   *Windows 98 in a Nutshell*, by Tim O'Reilly, Troy Mott, and Walter
Glenn.

Nutshell Handbook, the Nutshell Handbook logo, and the O'Reilly logo are registered
trademarks of O'Reilly & Associates, Inc. Many of the designations used by manufacturers
and sellers to distinguish their products are claimed as trademarks. Where those designations
appear in this book, and O'Reilly & Associates, Inc. was aware of a trademark claim, the
designations have been printed in caps or initial caps. The association between the image of
a climbing frog and the topic of Windows XP is a trademark of O'Reilly & Associates, Inc.

While every precaution has been taken in the preparation of this book, the publisher and
authors assume no responsibility for errors or omissions, or for damages resulting from the
use of the information contained herein.   10-28-02

ISBN: 0-596-00249-1
[C]   [6/02]

Ronald Williams Library
Northeastern Illinois University

Table of Contents

Preface

Windows XP is the latest product in a long line of operating systems from Microsoft. Although it's superficially similar to earlier versions of Windows, there's quite a bit new under the hood, and on the surface as well. A consumer-friendly, almost cartoonish interface sits on top of the most complex Windows version yet.

A graphical user interface, like the one in Windows XP, is not a substitute for good, thorough documentation. Naturally, colorful icons and animated interface elements make the interface more inviting and help uninitiated users stumble through the basics of opening programs and printing documents. There are only so many hours in the day, though, and spending most of them trying to figure out the new networking system, sorting through the thousands of settings in the Registry, discovering all of the hidden tools, or even learning to be productive with the new Windows Movie Maker, is really not good use of your time.

By taking the undocumented or otherwise hidden features and settings in Windows XP and placing them in context with more conspicuous and familiar components, this book provides the complete picture necessary to truly understand the operating system and what is involved in completing just about any task.

There are many books on Windows XP, but most of them get bogged down with elementary tutorials and the scrawniest tasks most of us could perform in our sleep. That's where this book comes in. *Windows XP in a Nutshell* provides a condensed but thorough reference to Windows XP, with an organization that helps you get right to the task at hand.

For example, there are literally hundreds of settings and features in Windows XP, scattered throughout dozens of dialog boxes. Some are plainly accessible through the Start menu or in the Control Panel, while others are hidden under layers of application menus. A few aren't apparent at all without knowledge of hidden features. In Chapter 5, all these settings are listed in the same place, sorted alphabetically from A–Z. So, instead of wading through menus and flipping through dialogs looking for a way to stop Windows from disconnecting your dial-up connection to the Internet (or for the setting that affects sounds in web pages) just look in Chapter 5, under "Dialing" and "Sounds," respectively.

Considerations and Scope

Our focus is on user applications, however, not on system or network administration. While we give you a basic understanding of these deeper levels and what's available, specific installation details and detailed configuration information for system and network administrators are largely beyond the scope of the book. There are also settings that depend on decisions made by your network administrator or Internet Service Provider (ISP), especially with networks systems. Whenever possible, we give you the information you need, but there are times when all we can tell you is where to go for additional information.

We have tried to speak universal truths about Windows XP, but sometimes we are forced to make assumptions about your settings or installed options. Microsoft gives so many configuration options that the truth is, for better or worse, that each user's machine represents a slightly different installation of Windows XP. Of all the code and data Microsoft ships on the Windows XP CD-ROM, only about half is used in any particular user's configuration. What we say about Windows XP may or may not be quite true about Windows XP as it's installed on your system.

For example, there's a setting in Control Panel → Folder Options that instructs Windows to open icons with either a double-click or a single-click, according to your preference. While most users tend to prefer the double-click option, and double-clicking is the default on most systems, your system might be different (it might even be the default, depending on the operating system you had installed previously). Although both setups are clearly defined in Chapter 2, some procedures elsewhere in this book will instruct you to double-click where you may only need to single-click. This "knowledge gap" is an unfortunate consequence of the malleable nature of the Windows operating system.

Consider another oddity in Windows XP: categories in Control Panel. This new addition in Windows XP (discussed further in Chapter 2) splits the components of the Control Panel into distinct categories, rather than simply listing them alphabetically, as in previous versions of Windows. What's more, the Control Panel can be accessed in any of three different ways, (as a menu in the Start menu, as a standalone folder window, or as an entry in the folder tree in Windows Explorer) and the category interface (which can be disabled completely, if desired) is used only in some cases. This means that it's difficult (and laborious) to predict when you'll need to open the "Appearance and Themes" category before you can get to the Display Properties dialog. We've compensated for this ambivalence by enclosing the category name in "maybe" brackets, like this: Control Panel → [Appearance and Themes] → Display Properties.

Also, for all the statements (from Microsoft and others) that Windows XP is "integrated" and "seamless," the fact is that the system is actually amazingly modular, customizable, and "seamy." This is a good thing. This book shows a lot of different ways to modify Windows XP to suit your needs, a theme that is expanded further in the Annoyances books (O'Reilly & Associates), also by David A. Karp. This almost infinite customizability and modularity of Windows XP means that many of our statements about the product—such as saying that the My Computer window has an icon for Control Panel, or that the Desktop corresponds to the *\Documents and Settings\Administrator\Desktop* folder, or that Windows XP is faster than Windows Me—may, strictly speaking, be false, or at least serious oversimplifications.

Basically, Windows XP is a platform and set of capabilities, not a single stable product with a fixed set of features. In this book, we give you the information you need to tap into all of Windows XP's capabilities, not just those that are showcased on Microsoft's web site or the Windows Desktop.

Organization of the Book

This book is divided into four parts.

Part I, *The Big Picture*

This part of the book is designed to give you the lay of the land and to introduce the concepts used throughout the rest of the book. It consists of two chapters:

Chapter 1, *The Lay of the Land*, gives a brief review of Windows XP, what's new in this release, and where it fits into the grand scheme of things.

Chapter 2, *Using Windows XP*, covers the basics of using Windows, such as starting applications, manipulating files, and getting around the interface. If you're familiar with any modern version of Windows, much of this is probably old hat.

Part II, *Alphabetical Reference*

This part of the book contains alphabetically organized references for each major element of Windows XP. Once you're at a given point in the system, what can you do there?

Chapter 3, *The User Interface*, is a thorough examination of the elements that make up the Windows XP graphical user interface. In addition to the basics of windows, menus, buttons, listboxes, and scrollbars, you'll learn about the new visual styles in Windows XP, how to make the most of the Taskbar, and how to use any component of Windows with only the keyboard.

Chapter 4, *Windows XP Applications and Tools*, is the comprehensive reference that covers all the programs that come with Windows XP, those listed in the Start menu and Control Panel, and as those available only if you know where to look. For GUI-based applications, we don't document every menu, button, and dialog box—the GUI is often self-evident. Instead, we focus on nonobvious features and provide helpful hints about power user features and things that will make your life easier. For command-line based programs, we cover every option, since these programs are not as obviously self-documenting (though many do support the conventional /? command-line option for help).

Chapter 5, *Task and Setting Index*, is the way to find that elusive setting or feature without having to know ahead of time where Microsoft has decided to hide it away. Every option in every dialog box, as well as many common tasks, are presented in a single, straightforward reference. Options that affect how Windows plays sounds, for example, are scattered in a half-dozen different dialogs; here, they're all under "S."

Chapter 6, *The Command Prompt*, provides complete documentation on this often overlooked and underestimated part of the operating system. In addition to learning the ins and outs of the Command Prompt application, you can look up any command and find exactly what options it supports. Batch files, a quick and easy way to automate repetitive tasks, are also covered.

Part III, *Advanced Topics*

This part, encompassing the final three chapters, covers the more advanced topics in Windows XP:

Chapter 7, *Networking*, is your one-stop shop for setting up home networking, connecting to the Internet, and everything in between. Furthermore, security is a genuine concern for home users and businesses alike, and is covered throughout the chapter as well.

Chapter 8, *The Registry*, describes the organization of the Windows XP Registry, the central configuration database upon which Windows and all of your applications rely to function and remember your settings. The Registry Editor, the primary interface to the Registry, is covered here, along with some of the more interesting entries scattered throughout this massive database.

Chapter 9, *The Windows Script Host*, describes the Windows Script Host (WSH), the built-in scripting subsystem that is surprisingly flexible and powerful. Use the scripting language of your choice to automate common tasks and access features not available elsewhere.

Part IV, *Appendixes*

This section includes various quick reference lists.

Appendix A, *Installing Windows XP*, covers everyone's least-favorite activity. In addition to documenting the various installers and options, the chapter includes a number of pitfalls and solutions that will apply to nearly every installation.

Appendix B, *Migrating to Windows XP*, presents some of the factors you should take into consideration before you upgrade to Windows XP, as well as some of the adjustments you'll need to make after you take the plunge. Among other things, you'll learn how to make Windows XP look and feel more like previous versions of Windows by turning off some of the most annoying bells and whistles.

Appendix C, *Keyboard Shortcuts*, gives a list of keyboard accelerators (also known as hotkeys or keyboard shortcuts) used in all parts of the Windows interface.

Appendix D, *Power Toys and TweakUI*, covers the add-on suite of tools Microsoft has provided for "power users" of Windows XP. TweakUI is easily the most important tool in the bunch. It provides many features and settings that should have been included in the operating system in the first place.

Appendix E, *Keyboard Equivalents for Symbols and International Characters*, explains how to type the symbols and international characters normally only accessible with Character Map (discussed in Chapter 4).

Appendix F, *Common Filename Extensions*, lists many file types and their descriptions. This appendix is useful when you're trying to figure out how to open a specific file and all you know is the filename extension.

Appendix G, *Services*, lists the background services that come with Windows XP and their respective filenames. If you need to find a service, or simply need to determine the purpose of a particular program shown to be running in the Windows Task Manager (see Chapter 4), this appendix will provide the answer.

Conventions Used in This Book

The following typographical conventions are used in this book:

Constant width
>   is used to indicate anything typed, as well as command-line computer output and code examples.

Constant-width bold
>   is used to indicate user input in code.

Constant-width italic
>   is used to indicate variables in examples and so-called "replaceable" text. For instance, to open a document in Notepad from the command line, you'd type notepad *filename*, where *filename* is the full path and name of the document you wish to open.

[Square Brackets]
>   Square brackets around an option (usually a command-line parameter) means that the parameter is optional. Include or omit the option, as needed. Parameters not shown in square brackets are typically mandatory. See "Path Notation," which follows, for another use of square brackets in this book.

Italic
>   is used to introduce new terms and to indicate URLs, variables in text, user-defined files and directories, commands, file extensions, filenames, directory or folder names, and UNC pathnames.

The following symbols are used in this book:

This symbol indicates a tip.

This symbol indicates a warning.

Path Notation

Rather than using procedural steps to tell you how to reach a given Windows XP user interface element or application, we use a shorthand path notation.

For example, we don't say, "Click on the Start menu, then click on Search, then For Files or Folders, and then type a filename in the Named: field." We simply say: Start → Find → Files or Folders → Named. We generally don't distinguish between menus, dialog boxes, buttons, checkboxes, etc., unless it's not clear from the context. Just look for a GUI element whose label matches an element in the path.

The path notation is relative to the Desktop or some other well-known location. For example, the following path:

> Start → Programs → Accessories → Calculator

means "Open the Start menu (on the Desktop), then choose Programs, then choose Accessories, and then click Calculator." But rather than saying:

> Start → Settings → Control Panel → Add or Remove Programs

we just say:

> Control Panel → Add or Remove Programs

since Control Panel is a "well-known location" and the path can therefore be made less cumbersome. As stated earlier in this preface, the elements of the Control Panel may or may not be divided into categories, depending on context and a setting on your computer. Thus, rather than a cumbersome explanation of this unfortunate design every time the Control Panel comes up, the following notation is used:

> Control Panel → [Performance and Maintenance] → Scheduled Tasks

where the category, "Performance and Maintenance," in this case, is shown in square brackets, implying that you may or may not encounter this step.

Paths will typically consist of clickable user interface elements, but they sometimes include text typed in from the keyboard (shown in constant-width text):

> Start → Run → `telnet`

or:

> Ctrl-Alt-Del → Shut Down

There is often more than one way to reach a given location in the user interface. We often list multiple paths to reach the same location, even though some are longer than others, because it can be helpful to see how multiple paths lead to the same destination.

The following well-known locations are used as starting points for user interface paths:

Control Panel

> Start → Control Panel (*if you're using the new Windows XP Start menu*)

> Start → Settings → Control Panel (*if you're using the classic Start menu*)

Explorer
> The two-pane folder view, commonly referred to as "Explorer:" Start → Programs → Accessories → System Tools → Windows Explorer

My Computer
> The My Computer icon on the Desktop (which may or may not be visible)

My Network Places
> The My Network Places icon on the Desktop (which may or may not be visible)

Recycle Bin
> The Recycle Bin icon on the Desktop

Start
> The Start button on the Taskbar

xxxx menu
> Menu *xxxx* in the application currently being discussed (e.g., File or Edit)

Command-Line Syntax

Further conventions used for representing command-line options and arguments are described in the introduction to Chapter 7.

We'd Like to Hear from You

Please address comments and questions concerning this book to the publisher:

> O'Reilly & Associates, Inc.
> 1005 Gravenstein Highway North
> Sebastopol, CA 95472
> 800-998-9938 (in U.S. or Canada)
> 707-829-0515 (international/local)
> 707-829-0104 (fax)

To comment or ask technical questions about this book, send email to:

> *bookquestions@oreilly.com*

For more information about our books, conferences, resource centers, and the O'Reilly Network, see the O'Reilly web site at:

> *http://www.oreilly.com*

Windows XP Resource Links

There is a web site for this book, which lists errata, examples, or any additional information. You can access this page at:

> *http://www.oreilly.com/catalog/winxpnut/*

or view David A. Karp's Windows resource on the Web at:

> *http://www.annoyances.org/*

Acknowledgments

This is the third *In a Nutshell* book covering a version of Microsoft Windows. Although this book has evolved substantially from its progenitors, *Windows 95 in a Nutshell* and *Windows 98 in a Nutshell* (as Windows itself has evolved), its existence is due to the hard work of those who worked on those earlier volumes.

Tim O'Reilly developed the original concept for the book; he and Troy Mott were the principal authors of the first edition. Andrew Schulman was also instrumental in helping get the first edition of this book off the ground, and it was he who insisted on the importance of the command line. Walter Glenn was a major contributor to the second edition. Thanks to John Fronckowiak, Stein Borge, and Ron Petrusha for their efforts, which formed the basis of the Windows Script Host chapter. This new edition was developed by David Karp and incorporates some material from his bestselling *Windows Annoyances* series. Tim O'Reilly was the editor of this new edition. He had help from Bob Herbtsman and Maeve O'Meara, who managed the day to day details of the project, and in Maeve's case, entered hundreds of last minute edits.

We are also indebted to the generosity of hundreds of Windows users who've shared tips, insights, and detailed documentation on particular aspects of the system they've uncovered, either through their own web sites, posts to the *Annoyances.org* discussion forums, or emails at 2:30 in the morning. We refer to some of these sites in the book, but many others have contributed to our understanding of Windows, taught us useful tips, or corrected our assumptions.

David adds: This book was a big job, much more so than I anticipated. But it was an important book for me to write, giving me a new perspective and appreciation for the attention and focus required to document such a complex and confusing product as Windows XP. I'd like to thank my friends and family, not only for keeping me grounded with their incessant computer questions as they were discovering Windows XP in their own highly individual and bizarre ways, but for distracting me when I needed it most with movies, food, cards, fresh air, Wei Qi, skiing, and of course, the Simpsons. D'oh!

The Big Picture

1

The Lay of the Land

In many ways, Windows XP is a bit of an anachronism. On one hand, it is technically only an incremental upgrade to Windows 2000, released only a year earlier.
On the other hand, it is the first consumer-level operating system based on a
powerful and robust platform previously available only to advanced users and
network administrators.

Windows XP is easily the most technically sophisticated operating system
Microsoft has ever released, but it is adorned with an almost cartoonish interface.
It has an advanced, scalable networking system built in, but networking is easier
to set up in Windows XP than in any other release. It has the heftiest system
requirements of any Windows to date, but given the same hardware, it ends up
outperforming its predecessors in almost every way. It also has more superfluous
bells and whistles than any other OS, but will likely be the OS of choice for most
power users for several years to come.

There's more to understanding Windows XP than simply knowing how to open
applications and manage your files effectively. In this chapter, we'll cover what's
new in this release and how Windows XP fits into the big picture. Move on to
Chapters 2 and 3 for some of the more basic aspects of day-to-day use of the operating system, or skip ahead to the later chapters for more of the meatier content.

The Big Picture

The first few releases of Microsoft Windows in the early 1980s were little more
than clunky graphical application launchers that ran on top of the Disk Operating System (DOS) (see Chapter 6 for details). Version 3.x, released in the late
1980's, gained popularity due to its improved interface (awful by today's standards, though) and ability to access all of a computer's memory. Being based on
DOS, however, it was not terribly stable, crashed frequently, and had very limited
support for networking and no support for multiple user accounts.

Soon thereafter, Windows NT 3.0 ("NT" for New Technology) was released. Although it shared the same interface as Windows 3.0, it was based on a more robust and secure *kernel*, the underlying code upon which the interface and all of the applications run. Among other things, it didn't rely on DOS and was capable of running 32-bit applications (Windows 3.0 could only run more feeble 16-bit applications).* Unfortunately, it was a white elephant of sorts, enjoying limited commercial appeal due to its stiff hardware requirements and scant industry support.

In 1995, Microsoft released Windows 95. Although based on DOS like Windows 3.x (it was known internally as Windows 4.0), it was a 32-bit operating system with a new interface. It was the first step in migrating the enhanced capability of the Windows NT architecture to the more commercially accepted, albeit less capable, DOS-based Windows line. Soon thereafter, Windows NT 4.0 was released, which brought the new Windows 95-style interface to the NT line. Both of these grand gestures were engineered to further blur the line between these two different Microsoft platforms. Although both operating systems sported the same interface, Windows NT still never garnered the industry support and commercial success of Windows 95.

As time progressed, the lineage of Microsoft Windows became even less linear. Windows 2000, despite its name, was *not* the successor to Windows 98 and Windows 95; Windows Me, released at the same time, had that distinction. Instead, Windows 2000 was the next installment of the NT line; it was actually known internally as Windows NT 5.0. Windows 2000 was particularly notable for being the first version of Windows NT to support plug-and-play, which was yet another move to combine the two platforms.

Then came Windows XP, known internally as Windows NT 5.1.† Although it's technically merely an incremental upgrade to Windows 2000, it has been positioned as the direct replacement to Windows Me, officially marking the end of the DOS-based Windows 9x/Me line. Windows XP is indeed the long-anticipated operating system designed to finally unify both lines of Windows, bringing the bullet-proof stability of NT to home and small business users, and the industry support of Windows 9x/Me to corporate and power users.

What's New in Windows XP

What you'll find new in Windows XP depends entirely on your perspective, or more specifically, the version of Windows you used last. As described earlier in this chapter, Windows XP is a more substantial upgrade for Windows 9x/Me users, but that doesn't mean there's nothing new for Windows 2000 users.

---

* A *bit*, or *binary digit*, is the smallest unit of information storage, capable of holding either a zero or a one. 32-bit operating systems like Windows NT and Windows 95 were capable of addressing memory in 32-bit (4 byte) chunks, which made them more efficient and powerful than a 16-bit OS like Windows 3.x.

† Type ver at any command prompt to see for yourself.

Although the following list of changes is not comprehensive, it does highlight some of the more interesting changes for users coming from both platforms.

What's New for Users of Windows 9x/Me

- As explained earlier in this chapter, the biggest change Windows 9x/Me users will notice is the dramatically improved stability of Windows XP. Although applications still crash in XP, they're much less likely to bring down the whole system.

- While Windows 9x/Me would slow down after only a few hours of use (requiring a reboot to bring it back to life), Windows XP can be left on for weeks without so much as a hiccup. The difference is the way system resources, an area of memory devoted to managing running applications and their interface elements, are handled: in Windows 9x/Me, this is a fixed (and rather small) area of memory, which can fill up fast. In Windows XP, system resources are allocated dynamically, which means you'll never run out.

- While Windows 9x/Me supported multiple users, this functionality was never more than a way for different users to have different color schemes and desktop icons. In Windows XP, multiple user management is much more sophisticated. If you're using Windows XP Professional (see the following section), a user will be able to securely encrypt files and folders so that other users can't read or modify them.

- Networking in Windows XP is much more powerful and secure than in Windows 9x/Me, but is substantially easier to set up and configure. The Network Properties window (see Chapter 7) actually makes sense now!

What's New for Users of Windows 2000

- Although nearly identical to Windows 2000 under the hood, Windows XP has some higher system requirements due to the increased overhead of all the extra bells and whistles. While Windows 2000 requires at least a 133-Mhz Pentium-class system with 64 Mb of RAM, Windows XP needs at least a 300 Mhz Pentium-II processor and 128 Mb of RAM.

- Given the same hardware, Windows XP should be substantially faster than Windows 2000. Among the areas particularly affected are startup time and hard drive data transfer. For example, a 30 megabyte file on my system took several seconds to copy from one hard drive to another in Windows 2000, but the same copy is nearly instantaneous in XP.

- Windows XP is now the de facto standard, which means gone are the days when new products won't be supported for your system. However, this doesn't mean that older product will necessarily be brought up to snuff; most likely, existing products not supported in Windows 2000 will be retired rather than updated to work with XP.

- While many games designed for Windows 9x would simply not run in Windows 2000, Windows XP has much better support for games, and it comes with more games than Windows 2000.

What's New, Regardless of Your Previous OS

- Windows XP has a new, more colorful and cheerful (some would say cartoonish) interface, although the classic interface can be easily selected to make XP look and feel nearly identical to Windows 2000 and Windows Me.

- A new copy-protection scheme known as Product Activation, designed to prevent a single copy of Windows XP from being installed on more than one machine at a time, is built into most versions of the operating system. This is one of the most controversial features of the system, since it requires you to provide personal information to Microsoft and allow them to remotely access your system.

- Windows XP has more bells and whistles, such as the Windows Movie Maker, built-in CD writer support, the Internet Connection Firewall, and Remote Desktop Connection.

See Appendix B for more issues that affect users upgrading to Windows XP from a previous version of Windows.

Windows XP Home and Professional Editions

Although only the Home and Professional editions of Windows XP are covered in this book, there are actually six editions of Microsoft Windows XP:

- Windows XP Home
- Windows XP Professional
- Windows XP .NET Standard Server
- Windows .NET Enterprise Server
- Windows .NET Datacenter Server
- Windows XP 64-bit*

Although all these editions of XP are similar, only the Home and Professional editions will be of interest to end users, while the others are intended for use in large corporations (Enterprise) as high-end server platforms.

The Home and Professional editions of Windows XP are nearly identical; the only differences are additional features found in the Professional edition that will appeal to power users and small businesses. The primary differences, aside from the price and the color of the packaging, are shown in Table 1-1.

Table 1-1. Differences between Windows XP Professional and Home editions

	Windows XP Home	Windows XP Professional
User accounts	All users are administrators, so there's no way to set up user accounts with limited privileges or protect files from other users.	Different user levels are supported. Administrators have unrestricted control, but each user's files can be encrypted and secured from other users.
Multiple processor support	None.	Yes. Systems with one, two, and four processors are supported.

---

* For more information on the 64-bit editions, see *http://www.microsoft.com/windowsxp/64bit/*.

Table 1-1. Differences between Windows XP Professional and Home editions (continued)

	Windows XP Home	Windows XP Professional
Networking	Built-in support for peer-to-peer networking.	Built-in support for peer-to-peer networking, plus support for joining a Windows NT domain.
Backup software included	No.	Yes, plus Automated System Recovery (ASR).
Dynamic Disk support	No.	Yes.

In addition, Windows XP Professional also includes the following tools and accessories (all documented in Chapter 4):

- Administrative Tools (in the Start menu and Control Panel)
- Boot Configuration Manager
- DriverQuery
- Group Policy Refresh Utility
- Multi-lingual User Interface (MUI) add-on
- NTFS Encryption Utility
- Offline Files and Folders
- OpenFiles
- Performance Log Manager
- Remote Desktop
- Scheduled Tasks Console
- Security Template Utility
- Taskkill
- Tasklist
- Telnet Administrator

There's nothing that Windows XP Home edition can do that the Professional edition can't do; in other words, the Professional edition is a superset of the Home edition.

Windows Update

Finally, I'd like to note the Windows Update feature in Windows XP. Since its initial release, Microsoft has made several updates to the software available on their web site. These updates range from simple bug fixes to patches for major security holes. It's highly recommended that you either run the Windows Update feature routinely or enable the Automatic Updates feature so that you'll never be without the latest and greatest fixes (and bugs). See "Windows Update" in Chapter 4 for more information.

2

Using Windows XP

This material in this chapter provides a quick overview of the features of the Windows XP user interface, which should be sufficient to help you get oriented and make the most of the system fairly quickly. If you're already familiar with the basic Windows interface, you may still find subtle differences between Windows XP and previous versions, making this chapter worth a quick read. If you're fairly new to Windows, you should definitely take the time to read this chapter. Concepts that advanced users might consider elementary should prove pretty enlightening. The most important thing is to get a sense of the continuity (or occasionally the lack thereof) in the Windows XP interface so that you can tackle any new Windows application with ease. Note, however, that if you are a very inexperienced user, you may prefer to start with a tutorial book on Windows XP, such as O'Reilly's *Windows XP: The Missing Manual*, by David Pogue. Even though this chapter is more introductory than the rest of the book, it still moves pretty quickly. Still, if you just take your time and try each feature as it's introduced, you may find that you don't need a step-by-step introduction after all.

The Desktop

Like most modern operating systems that use graphical user interfaces (such as the Mac, Unix, and earlier versions of Windows), Windows XP uses the metaphor of a Desktop with windows and file folders laid out on it. This Desktop metaphor is provided by a program called Windows Explorer (*explorer.exe*). Windows XP runs this program automatically every time you start Windows XP.[*]

---

[*] Occasionally, you may see the icons on your Desktop disappear and then reappear. This is caused by Windows Explorer crashing, and Windows relaunching it immediately thereafter. See "Taskbar" in Chapter 3 for more information.

Figure 2-1 shows the main features of the Windows XP Desktop. The callouts in the figure highlight some of the special-purpose icons and buttons that may appear on the Desktop. Each of these is described further in Chapter 3.

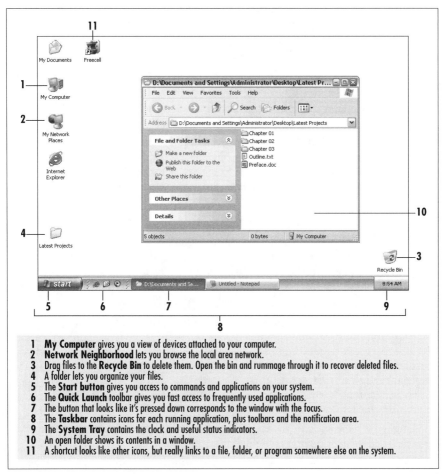

1 **My Computer** gives you a view of devices attached to your computer.
2 **Network Neighborhood** lets you browse the local area network.
3 Drag files to the **Recycle Bin** to delete them. Open the bin and rummage through it to recover deleted files.
4 A folder lets you organize your files.
5 The **Start button** gives you access to commands and applications on your system.
6 The **Quick Launch** toolbar gives you fast access to frequently used applications.
7 The button that looks like it's pressed down corresponds to the window with the focus.
8 The **Taskbar** contains icons for each running application, plus toolbars and the notification area.
9 The **System Tray** contains the clock and useful status indicators.
10 An open folder shows its contents in a window.
11 A shortcut looks like other icons, but really links to a file, folder, or program somewhere else on the system.

Figure 2-1. Windows XP Desktop features

Point and Click Operations

Windows XP offers several settings that affect the way the interface responds to mouse clicks. The default setting (the way it works when you first install Windows XP) will also be familiar to most users, as it is fairly consistent with the way most operating systems work.

Depending on your current settings, however, Windows may respond to mouse clicks differently. See the "Alternate Behavior" section that follows for differences. Later on, you'll see how to choose between the classic behavior and the alternate behavior.

If you are one of the few computer users who haven't used a graphical user interface before, here are some things you need to know:

- PCs usually come with a two- or three-button mouse (unlike the one-button mouse used with the Macintosh), although there are a variety of alternatives, such as touchpads (common on laptops), trackballs, and styluses.

- To *click* an object means to move the pointer to the desired screen object and press and release the left mouse button.

- *Double-click* means to click twice in rapid succession with the button on the left. (Clicking twice doesn't accomplish the same thing.)

- *Right-click* means to click with the button on the right.

- If your mouse has three or more buttons, you should just use the primary buttons on the left and the right, and read the documentation that comes with your pointing device to find out what you can do with the others. (You can often configure the middle button to take over functions like double-clicking, cut and paste, inserting inflammatory language into emails, and so on.)

Default Behavior

The default setting is consistent with most operating systems, including previous versions of Windows. You can tell if you have the default style if the captions under the icons on your Desktop are *not* underlined. The alternate behavior (sometimes called the Web View) is discussed in the subsequent section. Here is how Windows XP responds to mouse clicks by default:

- Double-click on any icon on the Desktop to open it. If the icon represents a program, the program is launched (i.e., opened). If the icon represents a data file, the file is opened by the associated program. (The associations between files and programs, called File Types in Windows, are discussed later in this chapter and in Chapter 8.) If the icon represents a folder (such as *My Documents*), a folder window appears, the contents of which are shown as icons within the window

- Single-click on an icon to select (highlight) it. A selected icon appears darkened and its caption text is highlighted.

- Single-click an icon, and then click again (but not so quickly as to suggest a double-click) on the icon's caption to rename it. Type a new caption, and then press the Enter key or simply click elsewhere to confirm the new name. You can also rename by clicking and pressing F2, or by right-clicking and selecting Rename.

- Right-click (click the right mouse button) on any icon to pop up a menu of other actions that can be performed on the object. The contents of this menu vary depending on which object you click, so it is commonly called the *context menu*. The context menu for your garden-variety file includes actions such as Open, Print, Delete, Rename, and Create Shortcut. The context menu for the Desktop itself includes actions such as Refresh and New (to create new empty files or folders). Nearly all objects have a Properties entry, which can be especially useful. See Chapter 4 for additional details.

- Click and hold down the left mouse button over an icon while moving the mouse to *drag* the object. Drag a file icon onto a folder icon or into an open folder window to move the file into the folder. Drag a file icon onto a program icon or an open application window (usually) to open the file in that program. Drag an object into your Recycle Bin to dispose of the object. Dragging can also be used to rearrange the icons on your Desktop. More drag-drop tips are discussed later in this chapter.

- By dragging a file with the right mouse button instead of the left, you can choose what happens when the file is dropped. With the release of the button, a small menu will pop up providing you with a set of options (Move Here, Copy Here, Create Shortcut(s) Here) to choose from. Although it is less convenient than left-dragging, it does give you more control.

- Click an icon to select it, and then hold down the Ctrl key while clicking on additional objects—this instructs Windows to remember all your selections so that you can have multiple objects selected simultaneously. This way, for example, you can select a group of files to delete and then drag them all to the Recycle Bin at once.

- Click an item and then hold down Shift while clicking a second item to select both items and all objects that appear between them. What ends up getting selected depends on the arrangement of items to be selected, so this method is more suitable for folder windows that have their contents arranged in a list format. You can use this method in conjunction with the Ctrl method (above) to accomplish elaborate selections.

- You can also select a group of icons without using the keyboard, as shown in Figure 2-2. Draw an imaginary rubber band around the objects you wish to select by clicking and holding on a blank area of the Desktop or folder window and dragging it to an opposite corner. Play around with this feature to see how Windows decides which items are included and which are ignored.

- Whether you have one icon or many icons selected simultaneously, a single click on another icon or a blank area of the Desktop abandons your selection.

- If you select multiple items simultaneously, they will all behave like a single unit when dragged. For example, if you select ten file icons, you can drag them all by just grabbing any one of them.

- Press Ctrl-A to select everything in the folder (or on the Desktop, if that's where the focus is). This corresponds to Edit → Select All. (See "Windows and Menus" later in this chapter if you don't know what we mean by the term *focus*.) See Appendix C for more keyboard shortcuts.

Alternate Behavior

In addition to the default style discussed in the previous section, Windows also provides a setting that makes the interface look and feel somewhat like a web page. Select Folder Options from Windows Explorer's Tools menu; if the "Single-click to open an item" option is selected (see Figure 2-3), you're using the settings described here. If you have this setting enabled on your system, clicking and double-clicking will work differently than described above, although dragging and right-clicking (as described in the previous section) will remain the same.

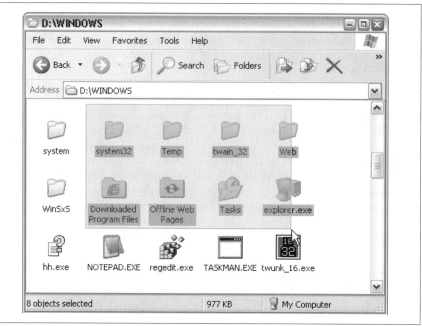

Figure 2-2. Select multiple files by dragging a "rubber band"

Here are the differences between the default and alternate behavior:

- The whole concept of double-clicking is abolished. Although double-clicking helps prevent icons from being accidentally opened when you're manipulating them, double-clicking can be confusing or awkward for some new users.
- To select an item, simply move the mouse over it.
- To activate (open) an item, click once on it.
- To rename an item, carefully float the mouse pointer over an icon and press F2, or right-click an icon and select Rename.
- You can still select multiple items using the Shift and Ctrl keys. However, instead of using Shift-click or Ctrl-click, hold the Shift or Ctrl keys down while moving the pointer over the desired items and don't click at all.

Since the default view is, by far, the setting used most frequently, most of the instruction in this book will assume it's what you're using. For example, if you see "Double-click the My Computer icon," and you're using the "Single-click to open" setting, remember that you'll simply be single-clicking the item.

Starting Up Applications

Windows XP has more ways to launch a program than just about any other operating system.

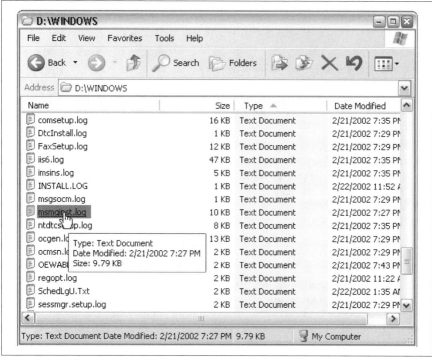

Figure 2-3. Folder options specify whether to use "web view"

You can:

- Double-click on a program icon in Explorer, on the Desktop, or in a folder window.

- Double-click on a file associated with an application to launch that application and open the file.

- Pick the name of a program from the Start menu. (See "Start Menu" in Chapter 3 for details.)

- Click on a program's icon in the Quick Launch Toolbar to start it. This Toolbar can include icons for any programs, although by default, it only has icons for Internet Explorer, Outlook Express, and MSN. See "Toolbars" in Chapter 3 for details.)

- Right-click on a file, executable, or application icon and choose Open.

- Select (highlight) an icon and press the Enter key.

- Type the filename of a program in the Address Bar, which can be displayed next to the Toolbar in any folder window, in Explorer, in Internet Explorer, or even as part of the Taskbar. You may also have to include the path (the folder and drive name) for some items.

- Select Run from the Start menu and type the filename of a program. You may also have to include the path (the folder and drive name) for some items.

- Open a command prompt window and type the name of the program at the prompt. Note that some knowledge of the command prompt (commonly known as DOS) is required—see Chapter 6 for details.

- Create shortcuts to files or applications. A shortcut is a kind of pointer or link—a small file and associated icon that point to a file or program in another location. You can put these shortcuts on the Desktop, in the Start menu, or anywhere else you find convenient. Double-click on a shortcut to launch the program. To launch programs automatically at startup, just place a shortcut in your Startup folder (\Windows\Start Menu\Programs\StartUp).

Some programs are really "in your face." For example, if you install AOL, it puts an icon on the Desktop, in the Office Shortcut Bar, on the Start menu (in two places, no less), and even shoehorns an icon into the System Tray, which is normally reserved for system status indicators. Other, less obtrusive programs may be more difficult to locate. In fact, you'll probably find several programs mentioned in this book you never even knew you had!

Styles and Consequences of Styles

Among the new interface changes in Windows XP is the configurable visual style with which all screen elements (windows, buttons, menus, the Start menu, etc.) are shown. Users of previous versions will immediately notice the default style in Windows XP, which has a more colorful, cartoony feel than the "classic" style more common to previous releases.

Unfortunately, many of the new interface changes in Windows XP, such as the new style, are turned on by default. This causes several problems. First, these changes widen the knowledge gap between novices, unaware of the ability or means to modify their environment, and experienced Windows users, who will most likely restore Windows XP to the "classic" interface within minutes of installation. Second, seasoned Windows users will avoid Windows XP for fear of being "stuck" with the new interface. Third, less-experienced users who read technical documentation, such as this book, may be confused by the reference to screen elements that do not appear on their systems.

A prime example is the Control Panel in Windows XP. The new default Control Panel interface (a consequence of the optional Web Content in Folders, as discussed in "Views through Folder Windows," later in this chapter) separates its contents into several categories. The category selection must therefore be included as an additional step to any discussion of the Control Panel.

For instance, to choose the style (explained at the beginning of this topic), double-click on the Display icon in Control Panel (short notation: Control Panel → Display). If, however, if you are using the Categorized view of Control Panel, you would click Appearance and Themes in Control Panel, and then click Display (short notation: Control Panel → Appearance and Themes → Display).

To make the Control Panel easier to use, turn off the categorized view by clicking "Switch to Classic View" in the lefthand pane. To turn off the lefthand pane altogether, go to Tools → Folder Options and select "Use Windows Classic Folders."

For simplicity, all subsequent discussion of the Control Panel in this book will assume you're using the classic view of the Control Panel.

For more information on the Control Panel, see Chapter 4. Details on changing the interface in Windows XP so that it more closely resembles the standard Windows look and feel are in Appendix B. More information on the Style setting and its consequences can be found in Chapter 3.

Windows and Menus

Any open window contains a frame with a series of standard decorations, as shown in Figure 2-4. To move a window from one place to another, click on the titlebar and drag.

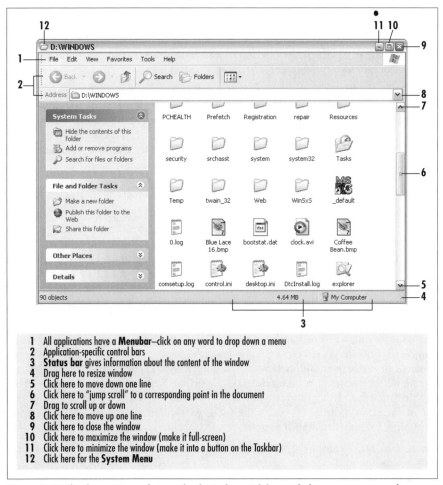

1 All applications have a **Menubar**—click on any word to drop down a menu
2 Application-specific control bars
3 **Status bar** gives information about the content of the window
4 Drag here to resize window
5 Click here to move down one line
6 Click here to "jump scroll" to a corresponding point in the document
7 Drag to scroll up or down
8 Click here to move up one line
9 Click here to close the window
10 Click here to maximize the window (make it full-screen)
11 Click here to minimize the window (make it into a button on the Taskbar)
12 Click here for the **System Menu**

Figure 2-4. The decorations of a standard window: titlebar, title buttons, menu, and a scrollable client area

Most types of windows are resizable, meaning that you can stretch them horizontally and vertically to make them smaller or larger. Just grab an edge or a corner and start dragging. There are two shortcuts that come in quite handy: maximize and minimize. If you click the maximize button (the middle button in the cluster in the upper right of most windows), the window will be resized to fill the screen. Maximized windows can't be moved or resized. If you minimize a window (the left-most button in the cluster), it is shrunk out of sight and appears only as a button on the Taskbar. Minimizing is handy to get windows out of the way without closing them.

Under certain circumstances, one or two scrollbars might appear along the bottom and far-right of a window. These allow you to move the window's view so that you can see all its contents. This behavior can be counterintuitive for new users because moving the scrollbar in one direction will cause the window's contents to move in the opposite direction. Look at it this way: the scrollbar doesn't move the contents; it moves the viewport. Imagine a very long document with very small type. Moving the scrollbars is like moving a magnifying glass—if you move the glass down the document and look through the magnifier, it looks like the document is moving up.

If multiple windows are open, only one window has the *focus*. The window with the focus is usually (but not always) the one on top of all the other windows, and it is usually distinguished by a border and title that are distinguished in some way from than the rest, usually appearing in a darker color. The window with the focus is the one that responds to keystrokes, although any window will respond to mouse clicks. To give any window the focus, just click on any visible portion of it, and it will pop to the front. Be careful where you click on the intended window, however, as the click may go further than simply activating it (if you click on a button on a window that doesn't have the focus, for example, it will not only activate the window, but press the button as well).

There are two other ways to activate (assign the focus to) a window. You can click on the Taskbar button that corresponds to the window you wish to activate, and it will be brought to the front. If it is minimized (shrunk out of sight), it will be brought back (restored) to its original size. The other way is to hold the Alt key and press Tab repeatedly, and then release Alt when the desired program icon is highlighted.

Just as only one window can have the focus at any given time, only one control (text field, button, checkbox, etc.) can have the focus at any given time. Different controls show focus in different ways: pushbuttons and checkboxes have a dotted rectangle, for instance. A text field (edit box) that has the focus will not be visually distinguished from the rest, but it will be the only one with a blinking text cursor (insertion point). To assign the focus to a different control, just click on it or use the Tab key (hold Shift to go backwards).

Often, new and veteran users are confused and frustrated when they try to type into a window and nothing happens—this is caused by nothing more than the wrong window having the focus. (I've seen skilled touch typists complete an entire sentence without looking, only to realize that they forgot to click first.)

Even if the desired window is in front, the wrong control (or even the menu) may have the focus.

 If you frequently find yourself mistaking which window has the focus, you can change the colors Windows uses to distinguish the active window by going to Control Panel → Display → Appearance → Inactive Title Bar.

Some windows can be configured to be *Always on Top*. This means that they will appear above other windows, even if they don't have the focus. Floating toolbars, the Taskbar, and some help screens are common examples. If you have two windows that are Always on Top, they behave the same as normal windows, since one can cover another if it is activated, but both will always appear in their own "layer" above all the normal windows.

The Desktop is also a special case. Although it can have the focus, it will never appear above any other window. To access something on the Desktop, you have two choices: minimize all open windows by holding the Windows logo key (not on all keyboards) and pressing the D key, or press the Show Desktop button on the Quick Launch toolbar (discussed in Chapter 3) to temporarily hide all running applications.

Most windows have a menu bar, commonly containing standard menu items like File, Edit, View, and Help, as well as application-specific menus. Click on the menu title to drop it down, and then click on an item in the menu to execute it. Any menu item with a small black arrow that points to the right leads to a secondary, cascading menu with more options, as shown in Figure 2-3. Generally, menus drop down and cascading menus open to the right; if there isn't room, Windows pops them in the opposite direction. If you wish to cancel a menu, simply click anywhere outside of the menu bar. See the next section, "Keyboard Accelerators," for details on navigating menus with keys.

 One thing that is often perplexing to new Windows XP users is the dynamic nature of its menus. For instance, menu items that appear grayed are temporarily disabled. (For example, some applications won't let you save if you haven't made any changes.) Also common are context-sensitive menus, which actually change based on what you're doing or what is selected.

Each window also has a *system menu* hidden behind the little icon on the left corner of the titlebar (see Item 12 in Figure 2-4). You can open the menu by clicking on the little icon, by pressing Alt-space, or by right-clicking on a button on the Taskbar. The System menu duplicates the function of the maximize, minimize, and close buttons at the right end of the titlebar, as well as the resizing and moving you can do with the mouse. Using this menu lets you move or resize the window without the mouse. (See ""Keyboard Accelerators," the next section, for details.) The system menu for folder windows also behaves like the icons for folder windows and can be a convenient way to delete an open folder. Finally, the system menu for command-line applications (such as the command prompt and

Telnet) provides access to the clipboard for cut, copy, and paste actions, as well as settings for the font size and toolbar (if applicable).

Keyboard Accelerators

Windows' primary interface is graphical, meaning that you point and click to interact with it. The problem is that repeated clicking can become very cumbersome, especially for repetitive tasks. Luckily, Windows has an extensive array of *keyboard accelerators* (sometimes called *keyboard shortcuts* or *hotkeys*) that provide a simple keyboard alternative to almost every feature normally accessible with the mouse. Some of these keyboard accelerators (such as F1 for help, Ctrl-C to copy, and Ctrl-V to paste) date back more than twenty years and are nearly universal, while others are specific to Windows XP or a given application.

Appendix C gives a complete list of keyboard accelerators. Some of the most important ones are described below:

Menu navigation

In any window that has a menu, press the Alt key or the F10 key to activate the menu bar, and use the cursor (arrow) keys to move around. Press Enter to activate the currently selected item or Esc to cancel.

You can also activate specific menus with the keyboard. When you press Alt or F10, each menu item will have a single character that is underlined (such the V in View); when you see this character, it means you can press Alt-V (for example) to go directly to that menu. Once that menu has opened, you can activate any specific item pressing the corresponding key (such as D for Details)—you don't even need to press Alt this time. The abbreviated notation for this is Alt-V+D (which means press Alt and V together, and then press D). You'll notice that it's much faster than using the mouse.

The other way to activate specific menu items is to use the special keyboard shortcuts shown to the right of each menu item (where applicable). For example, open the Edit menu in most windows, and you'll see that Ctrl+Z is a shortcut for Undo, Ctrl-V is a shortcut for Paste, and Ctrl-A is a shortcut for Select All. These are even faster than the navigation hotkeys described above. A few notes: not all menu items have this type of keyboard shortcut, and these shortcuts only work from within the application that "owns" the menu.

The special case is the Start menu, which can be activated by pressing the windows logo key (if your keyboard has one) or Ctrl-Esc, regardless of the active window. After that, it works pretty much like any other menu.

Note that once a menu has been activated, you can mix pointer clicks and keystrokes. For example, you could pop up the Start menu with the mouse, then type S for settings, and then click on Control Panel. Or you could type Ctrl-Esc, and then click Shut Down.

If there is a conflict and multiple items on a menu have the same accelerator key, pressing the key repeatedly will cycle through the options. You must press Enter when the correct menu item is highlighted to actually make the selection.

Window manipulation without the mouse

The system menu, described in the previous section, facilitates the resizing and moving of windows with the keyboard only. Press Alt-space to open the active window's system menu, and then choose the desired action. If you choose to move the window, the mouse pointer will change to a little four-pointed arrow, which is your cue to use the cursor (arrow) keys to do the actual moving. Likewise, selecting Resize will allow you to stretch any window edge using the cursor keys. In either case, press Enter when you're happy with the result, or press Esc to cancel the operation. If a window can't be resized or minimized, for example, those menu items will not be present. Note that system menus work just like normal menus, so you could press Alt-space+M to begin moving a window.

Editing

In most applications, Ctrl-X will cut a selected item to an invisible storage area called the Clipboard, Ctrl-C will copy it to the Clipboard, and Ctrl-V will paste it into a new location. Using the Delete key will simply erase the selection (or delete the file). There is a single, system-wide clipboard shared by all applications. This clipboard lets you copy something from a document in one program and paste it into another document in another program. You can paste the same data repeatedly until it's replaced on the Clipboard by new data. See Chapter 3 for more information on the Clipboard.

While you probably think of cut-and-paste operations as something you do with selected text or graphics in an application, the same keys can be used for file operations. For example, select a file on the Desktop and press Ctrl-X. Then move to another folder, press Ctrl-V, and Windows will move the file to the new location just as though you dragged and dropped it.

Ctrl-Alt-Del

Unlike Windows 9x/Me, simultaneously pressing the Ctrl, Alt, and Del keys opens the "Windows Security" window rather than a shutdown dialog. The Windows Security window provides access to several important features. The most useful is the Task Manager, which, among other things, allows you to close crashed applications. See Chapter 4 for details.

Alt-Tab and Alt-Esc

Both of these key combinations switch between open windows, albeit in different ways. Alt-Tab pops up a little window with an icon representing each running programs—hold Alt and press Tab repeatedly to move the selection. Alt-Esc has no window; instead, it simply sends the active window to the bottom of the pile and activates the next one in the row. Note that Alt-Tab also includes minimized windows, but Alt-Esc does not. If there's only one open window, neither keystroke has any effect. Also, neither method activates the Start menu (Ctrl-Esc) or the Desktop.

Tab and arrow keys

Within a window, Tab will move the focus from one control to the next; use Shift-Tab to move backwards. A control may be a text field, a drop-down list, a pushbutton, or any number of other controls. For example, in a folder window, Tab will switch between the drop-down list in the toolbar and the file display area. Use arrow keys in either area to make a new selection without moving the focus. Sometimes a dialog box will have one or more regions, indicated by a rectangular box within the dialog box. The arrow keys will cycle through buttons or fields only within the current regions. Tab will cross region boundaries and cycle through all the buttons or fields in the dialog box.

If there's only one control, such as in a simple folder window, Tab has no effect. In some applications, such as word processors and spreadsheets, Tab is assigned to a different function (such as indenting).

Common Controls

Many application and system windows use a common set of controls in addition to the ubiquitous titlebar, menubar, system menu, and scrollbars. This section describes a few of these common controls.

Figure 2-5 shows some of the common controls in Control Panel → Display → Screen Saver and the additional dialog box that pops up from its Settings button.

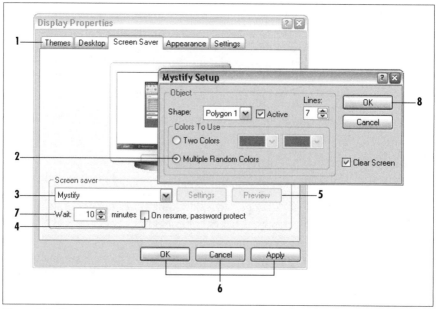

Figure 2-5. Common controls in Windows applications and dialogs

Some of these controls include:

(1) Tabbed dialogs

Settings may be grouped into separate tabbed dialog pages. For example, see Control Panel → System or Control Panel → Display. Click on any tab to bring that page to the front.

(2) Radio buttons

Radio buttons are used for mutually exclusive settings. Clicking on one causes any other that has been pressed to pop up, just like on an old car radio. The button with the dot in the middle is the one that has been selected. Sometimes you'll see more than one group of buttons, with a separate outline around each group. In this case, you can select one radio button from each group.

(3) Drop-down lists

Any time you see a downward-pointing arrow next to a text field, click on the arrow to drop down a list of other values. Often, a drop-down list contains a history of previous entries you've made into a text entry field. Pressing the first letter will often jump to that place in the list, as long as the list has the focus. The down arrow (or F4) will also drop down the currently selected list. The arrow keys will scroll through the stored entries, even if the list is not already dropped down. Microsoft sometimes calls these lists "Look In Lists." For an example, see Start → Find Files or Folders → Name & Location.

(4) Checkboxes

Checkboxes are generally used for on/off settings. A checkmark means the setting is on; an empty box means it's off. Click on the box to turn the labeled setting on or off.

(5) Grayed-out (inactive) controls

Any control like this one that is grayed out is disabled because the underlying operation is not currently available. In the dialog box shown in Figure 2-7, you need to click the "Password protected" checkbox before you can use the Change button.

(6) OK, Cancel, Apply

Most dialogs will have at least an OK and a Cancel button. Some also have Apply. The difference is that OK accepts the settings and quits the dialog and Apply accepts the changes, but doesn't quit. (This is useful in a dialog with multiple tabs, so that you can apply changes before moving to the next tab.) Cancel quits without making any changes. If you click Cancel after clicking Apply, your changes will probably already have been applied and will not revert to their original settings. But don't be surprised if some applications respond differently. Microsoft has never been clear with application developers about the expected behavior of these buttons.

(7) Counters

You can either select the number and type in a new value or click on the up or down arrow to increase or decrease the value.

(8) The default button

When a set of buttons is displayed, the default button (the one that will be activated by pressing the Enter key) has a bold border around it. The button or other area in the dialog box that has the additional dashed outline has the focus. You can move the focus by clicking with the mouse, typing the underlined accelerator character in a button or field label, or pressing the Tab or arrow keys.

In some dialog boxes, the default button (the button the Enter key presses) is *hardcoded*—it will always be the same (see Figure 2-6).

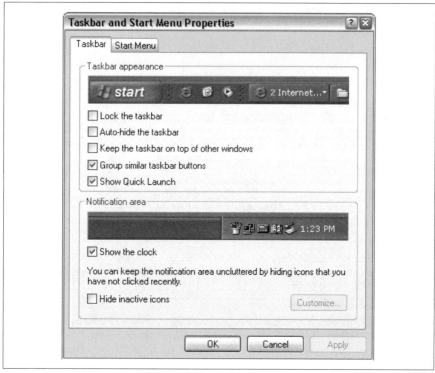

Figure 2-6. A tab containing a hardcoded default button

In others, the default button follows the focus from button to button, as in Figure 2-7. For example, right-click on the Taskbar and select Properties. The Taskbar Options tab has the OK button hardcoded as the default. Note that the bold border will stay on this button even when you move the focus among the checkboxes. The Start Menu Programs tab does not have a hard-coded default button. As you move the focus between buttons, the default button highlight moves with it. Regardless of which button is the default, pressing Esc always has the same effect as clicking the Cancel button: it cancels the dialog box.

For more information on these various UI features, see Chapter 3.

Files, Folders, and Disks

Files are the basic unit of long-term storage on a computer. Files are organized into folders, which are stored on disks. (In DOS, Unix, and earlier versions of Windows, folders were more often referred to as *directories*, but both terms are still used.) This section reviews fundamental filesystem concepts, including file- and disk-naming conventions and file types.

Figure 2-7. A tab without a hardcoded default button

Disk Names

Like every version of Windows that preceded it, Windows XP retains the basic DOS disk-naming conventions. Drives are differentiated by a single letter of the alphabet followed by a colon:

A:
> Represents the first "floppy" (usually 3.5-inch) disk drive on the system

B:
> Represents the second floppy disk drive, if present

C:
> Represents the first hard disk drive or the first partition of the first hard disk drive

D:
> Often represents a CD-ROM drive, but can represent an additional hard disk drive or other removable drive

E:–Z:
> Represent additional hard disk drives, removable cartridges such as Zip or Jaz drives, or mapped network drives

By default, driver letters are assigned consecutively, but it's possible to change the drive letters for most drives so that you can have a drive *N:* without having a drive *M:*.

Pathnames

Folders, which contain files, are stored hierarchically on a disk and can be nested to any arbitrary level.

The filesystem on any disk begins with the root (top-level) directory, represented as a backslash. Thus *C:* represents the root directory on the *C:* drive. Each additional nested directory is simply listed after its "parent," with backslashes used to separate each one. *c:\Windows\System\Color* means that the *Color* folder is in the *System* folder in the *Windows* folder on the *C:* drive. Thus a *path* to any given folder can be expressed as a single string of folder names.

A path can be absolute (always starting with a drive letter) or relative (referenced with respect to the current directory). The concept of a *current directory* is somewhat obsolete in Windows XP, with the exception of commands issued from the command prompt. Each command prompt window has an active folder associated with it, to which each command is directed. For example, if the current directory is *c:\windows*, and you were to type DIR (the directory listing command), you would get a listing of the files in that folder. If you were to then type CD cursors, the current directory would then become *c:\windows\cursors*.

The fact that the entire, absolute path was not needed after the CD command is an example of the use of a relative path.

A special type of relative path is made up of one or more dots. The names . and .. refer to the current directory and the parent of that directory, respectively (*c:\windows* is the parent folder of *c:\windows\cursors*, for example). Type CD .. while in *c:\windows*, and the current directory becomes simply *C:*. Additional dots (..., ..., and so on) move up more levels at a time (to the grandparent and great-grandparent, so to speak). The graphical equivalent of .. is the yellow folder icon with the curved arrow, found in common file dialogs.

The left pane in Windows Explorer (by default) contains a hierarchical tree-structured view of the filesystem. The tree structure makes it easier to navigate through all the folders on your system, since it provides a graphical overview of the structure. See Chapter 3 for more information on the tree and Chapter 4 for more information on the Explorer application.

Paths to Network Resources

Files on any shared network can be referred to via a Universal Naming Convention (UNC) pathname, which is very similar to a path (described in the previous section). The first element of a UNC pathname is the name of the computer or device that contains the file, prefixed by a double backslash. The second element is the device's share name. What follows is the string of folders leading to the target folder or file.

For example, the UNC path *\shoebox\o\hemp\adriana.txt* refers to a file named *adrianna.txt*, located in the *hemp* folder, located on drive *O:*, located on a computer named *shoebox*. For more information on UNC pathnames and sharing resources on a network, see Chapter 7.

Short Names and Long Names

DOS and Windows 3.1, the Microsoft operating systems that preceeded Windows 95 and Windows NT, only supported filenames with a maximum of eight characters, plus a three-character file type extension (e.g., *myfile.txt*). The maximum length of any path was 80 characters (see "Pathnames," earlier in this chapter, for more information on paths.) Legal characters included any combination of letters and numbers, extended ASCII characters with values greater than 127, and the following punctuation characters:

$ % ^ ' ` - _ @ ~ ! ( ) # &

Spaces were not allowed.

Windows XP supports long filenames (up to 260 characters), which can include spaces as well as the additional punctuation characters:

$ % ^ ' ` - _ @ ~ ! ( ) # & + , ; = [ ] .

For example, a file could be named *Picture of my Niece.jpg*, and could be located in a folder named *Family Photos*. Furthermore, extensions are no longer limited to 3 characters; for example, *.html* is perfectly valid (and distinctly different from *.htm*). For more information on file extensions, see the discussion of file types in Chapter 7.

The maximum length of any path in Windows XP depends on the filesystem you're using (NTFS, FAT32, etc.). For more information on filesystems, see Appendix A.

Windows XP's filesystem is case preserving, but also case insensitive. For example, the case of a file named *FooBar.txt* will be preserved with the capital F and B, but if you were to type FOObar in a file open dialog box, Windows would recognize it as the same file.

Long filenames are compatible with all modern versions of Windows, but to maintain compatibilty with DOS programs and applications written for Windows 3.x, Windows XP maintains a short counterpart to every long filename. The short name consists of the first six letters of the long name, a tilde, a number from 1 to 9 (the number is incremented to prevent two long filenames being linked to the same short filename; after ~9, those six characters are reduced to five), and the file type extension, if any. (If an extension is longer than three characters, only the first three characters appear.) Any spaces in the first six characters are removed.

The easiest way to investigate short filenames is to use the command prompt (see Chapter 6 for details). If, for example, you had a file named *Adrianna.html* and you typed DIR adrian~1.htm, you'd have a match. The same rules apply to folder names: *Program Files* becomes \PROGRA~1. For the most part, these short filenames are of little importance if you only use applications that are long filename-aware, but they may come up, for instance, if you share files with a user of an older computer.

File Types and Extensions

Most files have a filename extension, the (usually three) letters that appear after the last dot in any file's name. Here are some common file extensions:

.xls
> An Excel spreadsheet

.txt
> A text file (to be opened with Notepad)

.html
> A hypertext markup language file, commonly known as a web page

.jpg
> A JPEG image file, used to store photos

Although each of these files hold very different types of data, the only way Windows differentiates them is by their filename extension. How Windows is able to determine a given file's type is important for several reasons, especially because it is the basis for the associations that link documents with the applications that created them. For example, when you double-click on a file named *donkey.html*, Windows looks up the extension in the Registry (see Chapter 7), and then, by default, opens the file in your web browser. Rename the file to *donkey.jpg*, and the association changes as well. (The exception to this is a special, invisible link shared only by Microsoft Office documents. If you rename an Office 2000 document (say, *donkey.doc* to *donkey.stubborn*) and double-click it, Windows will still open it in Word. Unfortunately, this mechanism is not available for any non-Office file types.)

The lesson here is that filename extensions are not a reliable guide to a file's type, despite how heavily Windows XP relies on them. What can make it even more frustrating is that known filename extensions are hidden by Windows XP by default, but unfamiliar extensions are shown. Rename *donkey.xyz* (a unassociated extension) to *donkey.txt*, and the extension simply disappears in Explorer. Or, try to differentiate *donkey.txt* from *donkey.doc* when the extensions are hidden. To instruct Windows to show all extensions, go to Control Panel → Folder Options → View, and turn off the "Hide file extensions for known file types" option.

To see all the configured file extensions on your system, go to Control Panel → Folder Options → File Types. More information on File Types can be found in Chapter 4. Appendix F contains a list of common filename extensions and their descriptions.

Views Through Folder Windows

Double-click on a folder icon, and you'll see the contents of the folder. Look at the status bar (turn it on with the View menu if it's absent) for summary information, such as the number of items in the folder, the total size of the contents, and the amount of free disk space.

Depending on your settings, the icons may be shown in any of five different formats: Thumbnails, Tiles, Icons, List, or Details. If you're looking at a folder full of images, the Thumbnails settings (in the View menu) might be useful. The Icons setting resembles the way files and folders are shown on the Desktop, but the Details view shows the most information. To customize the columns in the Details view, use View → Choose Details. Figure 2-8 shows the Details view of a folder.

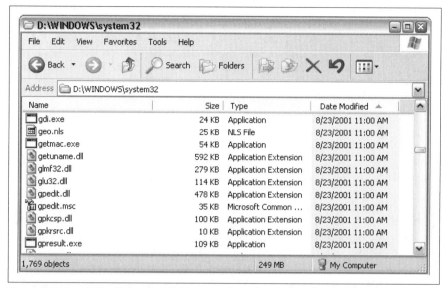

Using
Windows XP

Figure 2-8. Sort folder listings by clicking on column headers or change column widths by dragging boundaries between the headers

Windows XP will remember the view setting for each folder by default and will display it the same way the next time the folder is opened. (If a long time passes before you open a folder again, Windows will forget its settings.) You can turn this setting off by going to Control Panel → Folder Options → View → Remember each folder's view settings.

In addition to the icon styles, three other elements are of interest in Folder Windows: the Explorer Bar, the Web View, and the Explorer toolbar.

The first is the Explorer Bar, which usually contains the folder tree (called simply Folders). If you press Ctrl-F or F3, the folder tree disappears and a search box is put in its place. Use View → Explorer Bar to access the other things that can appear in that pane, or to hide it entirely. Note that the window icon changes to reflect the Explorer Bar setting, implying that the primary function of the window has changed. If you don't want the current state of the window to change, say, when you want to search for a file, you'll have to open a new folder window and search from there.

The second element is what is commonly known as the Web View, and in Windows XP, is more specifically known as Web Content in Folders. The Web View, first introduced in Windows 98, is intended to provide more information than is normally available in a bare folder window. Microsoft has changed the appearance and contents of the Web View in each successive release of Windows, although it has never proven to be especially useful. (For example, it provides little information that isn't already available in the Details view.) Unfortunately, the Web View in Windows XP is no different.

The "Common Tasks" feature replaces the Web View pane found in earlier versions of Windows, and can be turned on or off by going to Control Panel → Folder Options and selecting the "Show common tasks in folders" or "Use Windows classic folders" options, respectively. If the Common Tasks pane is visible, you can collapse and expand the boxes by clicking on the little arrows. Unlike the earlier Web View pane, however, the Common Tasks pane is not customizable. Although there is a Customize this Folder option in the Explorer View menu, it's only used for changing the icon of the currently selected folder.

The third element is the Toolbar. The Explorer Toolbar, like toolbars in most applications, provides quick access to some of the more frequently used features, all of which are otherwise accessible through the menus and with keyboard accelerators. Enable, disable, and customize the toolbar View → Toolbar. One of the components in the Toolbar, the Address Bar, is most useful with Internet Explorer, but can be of some use in ordinary folder windows. For example, you can type the path to a folder, press Enter, and the folder's contents will be shown in the current window. This can often be faster than navigating with the folder tree or using several consecutive folder windows. See Chapter 6 for details on using the Address Bar. Figure 2-9 shows the buttons on the Toolbar for a folder.

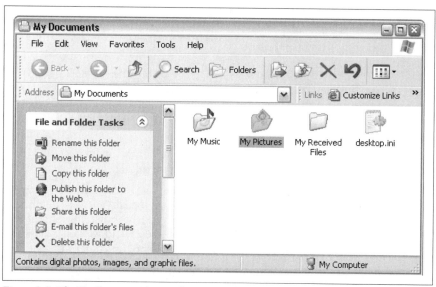

Figure 2-9. The Toolbar provides quick access to frequently used functions; the Status Bar shows additional information about selected icons

Although each new folder window you open will appear with Microsoft's default settings, it's possible to modify those defaults. Start by configuring a folder according to your preferences: choose the icon size, the sort order, etc. Then, go to Tools → Folder Options → View, and click Like Current Folder. The setting will then be used for each new single folder window that is opened.

If you click Windows Explorer in the Start menu, you'll get a folder window with the folder tree shown in the left pane (as opposed to a folder window opened by double-clicking on a folder icon). This window is commonly referred to simply as Explorer, and although the right pane looks just like a single folder window without the tree pane, Windows XP treats them slightly differently. For example, if you use the Like Current Folder button in a single folder window, as described above, Windows will use your preferences for all single folder windows, but not for Explorer. Likewise, saved settings in Explorer aren't reflected in single folder windows. Because of this, you may feel like you have to jump through several hoops in order to set your preferences in all the windows you use; unfortunately, there's no easier way.

Keyboard Accelerators in Folder Windows

Some keyboard accelerators are especially useful in Explorer and folder windows. These are used in addition to the various keys described in "Point and Click Operations," earlier in this chapter.

- Hold the Alt key while double-clicking on a file or folder to view the Properties window for that object.

- Hold the Shift key while double-clicking on a folder to open an Explorer window (with the tree view) at that location. (Be careful when using this because Shift is also used to select multiple files. The best way is to select the file first.)

- Press Backspace in an open folder to go to the parent (containing) folder.

- Hold Alt while pressing the left cursor key to navigate to the previously viewed folder. Note that this is not necessarily the *parent* folder, but rather the last folder opened in Explorer. You can also hold Alt while pressing the right cursor key to move in the opposite direction (i.e., forward); this is similar to the Back and Next buttons in Internet Explorer, respectively. The Windows Explorer toolbar also has Back and Next buttons.

- Hold the Shift key while clicking on the close button (the x in the upper right corner of the window on the menu bar) to close *all* open folders that were used to get to that folder. (This, of course, makes sense only in the single-folder view and with the "Open each folder in its own window" option turned on.)

- Press Ctrl-A to quickly select all contents of a folder: both files and folders.

- In Explorer or any single-folder window, press a letter key to quickly jump to the first file or folder starting with that letter. Continue typing to jump further. For example, pressing the N key in your \Windows folder will jump to NetHood. Press N again to jump to the next object that starts with N. Or, press N and then quickly press O to skip all the Ns and jump to *notepad.exe*. If there's enough of a delay between the N and the O keys, Explorer will forget about the N, and you'll jump to the first entry that starts with O.

Advanced Drag-Drop Techniques

Some of the basics of drag-drop are discussed in "Point and Click Operations," earlier in this chapter, but you can use some advanced techniques to have more control when you're dragging and dropping items. Naturally, it's important to be able to anticipate what will happen when you drag-drop an item before you actually do the dropping. The problem is that drag-drop is handled differently in various situations, so sometimes you'll need to modify your behavior to achieve the desired result. Here are the rules that Windows follows when determining how dropped files are handled:

- If you drag an object from one place to another on the same physical drive (*c:\docs* to *c:\files*), the object is moved.

- If you drag an object from one physical drive to another physical drive (*c:\docs* to *d:\files*), the object is copied, resulting in two identical files on your system.

- If you drag an object from one physical drive to another physical drive and then back to the first physical drive, but in a different folder (*c:\docs* to *d:\files* to *c:\stuff*), you'll end up with three copies of the object.

- If you drag an application executable (an EXE file), the same rules apply to it that apply to other objects, with the following exceptions:*

  — If you drag any file named *setup.exe* or *install.exe* from one place to another, Windows will create a shortcut to the file, regardless of the source or destination folder.

  — If you drag any file with the *.exe* filename extension into any portion of your Start menu or into any subfolder of your Start Menu folder, Windows will create a shortcut to the file. Dragging other file types (documents, script files, or other shortcuts) to the Start menu will simply move or copy them there, according to the previous rules.

- If you drag a system object (such as an item in the My Computer window or Control Panel) anywhere, a warning is displayed and a shortcut to the item is created. This, of course, is a consequence of the fact that these objects aren't actually files and can't be duplicated or removed from their original locations.

- If you drag system icons or items that appear within system folders, such as My Documents, Internet Explorer, or the Recycle Bin, any number of different things can happen, each depending on the specific capabilities of the object. For example, if you drag a recently deleted file from the Recycle Bin, it will always be moved, since making a copy of, or a shortcut to, a deleted file makes no sense.

If you have trouble remembering these rules, or if you run into a confusing situation, you can always fall back on the information Windows provides you while you're dragging, in the form of the mouse cursor. A small plus sign (+) appears

---

* The behavior in Windows XP is the same as in Windows Me and Windows 2000, but a little different from Windows 95, 98, and NT 4: in these releases, dragging an EXE file anywhere created a shortcut.

next to the pointer when copying, and a curved arrow appears when creating a shortcut. If you see no symbol, the object will be moved. This visual feedback is very important; it can eliminate a lot of stupid mistakes if you pay attention to it.

Here's how to control what happens when you drag-drop an item:

- To copy an object under any situation, hold the Ctrl key while dragging. If you press Ctrl before you click, Windows assumes you're still selecting files, so make sure to press it only after you've started dragging but before you let go of that mouse button. Of course, this won't work for system objects like Control Panel items—a shortcut will be created regardless. Using the Ctrl key in this way will also work when dragging a file from one part of a folder to another part of the same folder, which is an easy way to duplicate a file or folder.

- To move an object under any situation, hold the Shift key while dragging. Likewise, if you press Shift before you click, Windows assumes you're still selecting files, so make sure to press it only after you've started dragging but before you let go of that mouse button. This also won't work for system objects like Control Panel items—a shortcut will be created regardless.

- To create a shortcut to an object under any situation, hold the Ctrl and Shift keys simultaneously while dragging. If you try to make a shortcut that points to another shortcut, the shortcut will simply be copied (duplicated).

- To choose what happens to dragged files each time without having to press any keys, drag your files with the right mouse button and a special menu will appear when the files are dropped. This context menu is especially helpful because it will display only options appropriate to the type of object you're dragging and the place where you've dropped it.

The Command Line

Many of those who are new to computers will never have heard of the command line, also known as the command prompt or the Disk Operating System (DOS) prompt. (DOS was the operating system used by most PCs before Windows became ubiquitous. The command line in DOS was the only way to start programs and manage files.) Those who might have used older PCs may remember the command line, but may be under the impression that it's purely a thing of the past. Advanced users, on the other hand, whether they remember the old days of the DOS command line or not, have probably learned the advantages of the command-line interface, even when using Windows XP on a day-to-day basis.

Many tasks can be performed more quickly by typing one or more commands into the command prompt window. In addition, many of the programs listed in Chapter 4 are command-line based tools, and some familiarity with the command prompt is necessary if you plan to use them.

For full documentation on the command line and the Command Prompt application, see Chapter 6. Also see Chapter 3 for information on the Address Bar and Start → Run, two alternatives to the Command Prompt window.

Here are a few examples that show how the command line can be used as an alternative to the GUI:

- To create a folder called *sample* in the root directory of your hard disk, and then copy all the files from another folder into the new folder, for example, it can be quicker and easier to type:

  ```
  C:\>mkdir \sample
  C:\>copy d:\stuff\*.* \sample
  ```

  than it would to open Windows Explorer, navigate to your *d:\stuff* folder, select all the files, click File → Copy (or Ctrl-C), navigate to the new location, click New → Folder, type the folder name, open the new folder; and then click Edit → Paste (or Ctrl-V) to copy in the files. That's a heck of a sentence, and a heck of a lot of steps for what can be accomplished with the two simple commands shown above.

- Once you learn the actual filename of a program rather than its Start menu shortcut name (as described in Chapter 4), it's almost always quicker to start it from the Run prompt or the Address Bar (see below) than it is to navigate the Start menu hierarchy. Which is really easier? Clicking your way through four menus:

  Start → Programs → Accessories → System Tools → Character Map

  or typing:

  ```
  charmap
  ```

  into the Run prompt or Address Bar and pressing the Enter key? Typing a command is much faster than carefully dragging the mouse through cascading menus, where an unintentional slip of the mouse can get you somewhere entirely different than you planned.

- Finally, many useful programs don't appear on any menu in the Start menu. Once you know what you're doing, you can put shortcuts to such programs in the Start menu or on the Desktop—but once you know what you're doing, you might just find it easier to type the program name.

Online Help

Most windows have some degree of online documentation, in the form of a Help menu that you can pull down with the mouse or by typing Alt-H. In addition, you can press F1 at almost any time to display help. In some situations, pressing F1 will only display a tiny yellow message (known as a *tooltip*) with a brief description of the item with the focus; at other times, F1 will launch an online index to help topics. Sometimes, F1 will have no effect whatsoever.

Furthermore, if you hold the pointer over many screen objects (such as items on the Taskbar or a window's toolbar), a tooltip may appear. A tooltip may display nothing more than the name of the object to which you're pointing, but in other cases, it may provide additional information. For example, placing the pointer on the system clock pops up the date. You can turn tooltips off in the Windows interface by going to Control Panel → Folder Options → View and turning off the option "Show pop-up description for folder and Desktop items." Note that this won't necessarily turn off tooltips in other applications—only Explorer.

At the command prompt, you can get help on the available command-line options by typing:

```
commandname /?
```

Finally, Windows XP includes a number of readme files, which typically contain *release notes*—information about special handling required for specific applications or hardware devices. The file *c:\Windows\readme.txt* contains a list of all the other readme files on the system. Or, you can just look in the *Windows* directory for any file with the *.txt* extension. Use Notepad or any other ASCII text editor or word processor to read them.

Shutting Down

You shouldn't just turn off the power to a Windows XP machine, since it caches a lot of data in memory and needs to write it out before shutting down. See "Shut Down" in Chapter 3 for additional details.

Alphabetical Reference

3

The User Interface

One of the responsibilities of a graphical operating system like Windows XP is to provide a common set of interface controls not only for itself, but for all the applications that run on it. This chapter provides an alphabetical reference to the elements of the Windows XP user interface, how they're used, and what tricks can be performed with them. Also included are some of the building blocks of the Windows XP shell (commonly known as Explorer), such as the Desktop and the various toolbars, Chapter 4 provides a similar alphabetical reference to the individual programs and utilities that make up Windows, whether they are accessible through the graphical user interface or the command line. The alphabetical reference entries in this chapter are as follows:.

Address Bar	Labels	Shortcuts
Buttons	Listboxes	Shut Down
Checkboxes	Log Off	Start Menu
Clipboard	Menus	Status Bar
Combo Boxes	My Computer	System Tray
Context Menus	My Network Places	Tabbed Dialogs
Control Menus	Notification Area	Taskbar
Desktop	Progress Indicators	Text Boxes
Details	Properties	Title Bars
Dialog Boxes	Radio Buttons	Toolbars
Drop-Down Listboxes	Recycle Bin	Tray
File Open/Save Dialogs	Run	Trees
Icons	Scroll Bars	Turn Off Computer
Input Fields	Send To	Windows

In addition to imposing a certain level of user interface consistency, these common elements allow programmers to quickly piece together the interfaces for their applications with a "toolbox" of parts. While these interface elements are available to all applications, some application designers choose instead to implement their own custom controls and interface paradigms. Sometimes this can lead to an innovative and clever design, but more often than not, it just results in a mess. A poor result typically comes not so much from the choice not to use Windows common controls, but from a failure to follow the rules of good user interface design.

The following are a few guidelines that apply to all elements of the Windows interface, which should provide some understanding of why certain elements are designed the way they are in Windows XP.

Visual clues (perceived affordances)

One of the most basic advantages of a graphical operating system is that the elements of the interface contain visual clues on how they're used. For example, buttons have a 3D look, implying that you're supposed to push them in. Folder icons look like actual yellow folders you'd see in a file cabinet, reinforcing the notion that they are containers that hold your documents. They also light up when you're dragging items over them, signalling that they can accept dropped objects. Even the mouse pointer provides visual feedback, changing to a resize arrow when it's over the edge of the window, or changing to a circle with a line though it when you're dragging over an object that can't accept the object you're holding. (Don Norman, author of the book *The Design of Everyday Things* (Doubleday)), calls these *visual clues*, which are intended to recall the way the physical world affords opportunities to interact with objects, "perceived affordances.") These clues are present in nearly every aspect of the Windows interface; learn to recognize them, and you quickly find even the most unfamiliar interface more intuitive and easier to use.

Constraints

Many controls have limits, or *constraints*, that permit only certain values to be entered. Scrollbars have a maximum and minimum limit, for instance, so you can't scroll past the end of a document.

Grayed-out (inactive) controls

Any control that appears "grayed out" is disabled because the underlying operation is not currently available. For example, in the dialog box shown in Figure 3-1, you need to click the "Password protected" checkbox before you can use the Change button.

Gray items typically don't respond at all when clicked, and sometimes it's not obvious what action must be taken in order to "un-gray" a menu item. If you're stuck, try to imagine in what context the menu item is used, and then try to put the application in the correct state for that menu item to be appropriate. For example, some menu items in your word processor will be grayed out when graphics are selected, or if the spelling checker is open.

Ellipses (...)

You'll commonly see ellipses on menu items and command buttons, and occasionally on other interface elements. This notation implies that a new window will appear when the control is activated.

Figure 3-1. Some options are disabled (grayed-out) when unavailable or not applicable

Focus

The focus (explained in greater detail in Chapter 2) is the visual highlighting of a single control, identifying which element will receive input from keyboard. Since there's only one keyboard, only one control can have the focus at a time, and since only one window can be active at a time, you should always be able to determine what will happen when you press keys on the keyboard by simply looking for the focus. For example, if a button has the focus, a dotted line will appear around its inner parameter; if an input field has the focus, a blinking cursor will appear where text is to be typed (this is known as the "insertion point"). You can usually click an item to give it focus, or use the Tab key to move the focus from one control to another.

Style

A new concept in Windows XP is the user-selectable style of all your windows and interface elements. The cheerful, brightly colored style that is the default when Windows XP is first installed is known as "Windows XP style." As shown in Figure 3-2, you can choose another style, such as "Windows Classic style," by going to Control Panel → Display Properties → Appearance. Windows XP only ships with these two styles, but additional styles can be added with third-party utilities (available at *http://www.annoyances.org/exec/show/article02-001*). Using these tools, you can choose the look and feel of all of the controls documented in this chapter, including titlebars, buttons, scrollbars, and even the Start button and Taskbar.

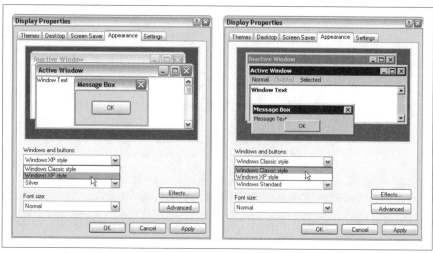

Figure 3-2. *The Display Properties dialog allows you to choose between the two visual styles available in Windows XP*

Don't confuse styles with themes. A theme is a collection of settings. Once you've chosen the style, specified colors, and selected a screensaver, go to Control Panel → Display Properties → Themes tab to "save" your settings under a single theme name. See "Display Properties" in Chapter 4 for more information on these settings.

Address Bar

The Address Bar (see Figure 3-3) is a special toolbar with an input field and (option-ally) a "Go" button. It appears in Internet Explorer, Windows Explorer, and on the Taskbar. When you type an Internet address, the name of a program, or the path of a folder, and then press Enter, the Address Bar will respond in one of many ways, depending on its location and your system's settings.

Figure 3-3. *The Address Bar, shown here on the Windows Taskbar, allows you to quickly open programs and web sites by typing their filenames and addresses, respectively*

The Address Bar is one of my favorite features in Windows. While its main purpose is to make it easy to type in a web address and point your browser to that address, it also can be used to type a command or application to launch, just like Start → Run. This means that you can easily choose between point and click and command-line opera-tions—whichever is easier for completing a given task. Because I keep the Address Bar visible in the Taskbar all the time as well as in each open folder window (which makes it easy to jump to any folder without having to hunt for it in the branches), it's become my primary command-line interface.

One major difference between the Run prompt and the Address Bar is how they treat an unknown address or command. The Address Bar assumes that any unknown text string is a web address. So, for example, typing oreilly in the Address Bar will launch your browser and start looking for *http://www.oreilly.com*. If you type the same string at the Run prompt, you'll get the message "Windows cannot find 'oreilly'. Make sure you typed the name correctly, and then try again. To search for a file, click the Start button, and then click Search." The Run Prompt's behavior is the reverse. It will treat a line beginning with *http://* or *www.* as a web address and launch the browser, but will assume that any other string is the name of an application or command.

Like the Run prompt, the Address Bar features a drop-down list containing the history of all recently entered URLs and command lines. Pick an item from the drop-down list to re-execute the command or revisit the specified web site.

Although it is useful for issuing commands, the Address Bar does have one drawback when used in this fashion. When you issue a command, the command is opened in a new window. Once the command has finished, that window closes instantly. If you are issuing a command that does not normally leave the Window open, but that you need to see a response (like *ping* or *dir*), you'll have to have very fast eyes. For these types of commands, you're better off using the Command Prompt. See the discussion of the Address Bar in "Command Prompt Choices" in Chapter 6 for more details on its use.

Buttons

Just click a button to make it do what its label says. In Figure 3-4, the Browse button is typically used to display a file dialog box. When you choose a file and click OK, the name and location (also known as the path) of the file is automatically entered into the text field. This synergy of controls is common, saves typing, and prevents typos. Some applications place a small folder icon next to a text field rather than the full-sized text field, but the usage is the same.

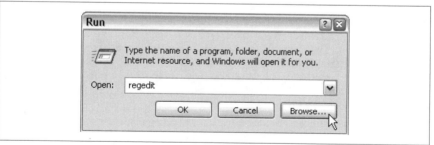

Figure 3-4. The Browse button is marked with ellipses (...), implying that another window will appear when it is clicked

If the button has the focus, press the spacebar to activate it. In dialogs with more than one button, often one of them has a thicker border than the rest (usually the OK button)—this is the "default" button and can be activated by pressing Enter, regardless of which control has the focus. Similarly, there is usually a cancel button (usually labeled "Cancel") that responds to the Esc key, but that has no visual distinction. If in doubt, use Tab to cycle through the buttons, and then press Space.

Figure 3-5 shows some special cases in which buttons work differently or have special meaning:

Figure 3-5. Toggle buttons, typically on application toolbars, allow you to turn options on or off by clicking

Toggle buttons

Some buttons, typically custom controls or buttons on toolbars, are used to change a setting, and will simply stay pushed in until clicked a second time. There's no rule that makes these buttons look different from standard buttons, so you'll have to rely on experience to determine which are "toggles." For example, the **B** or *I* buttons (corresponding to bold and italic, respectively) commonly found on word processor toolbars are toggles, but the Save and Print buttons are traditional buttons and are used to carry out a command rather than to change a setting.

The default button

When a set of buttons is displayed, typically at the bottom of a dialog box, one button will be the "default," meaning that it will be the one activated by the Enter key. It's identified by a thicker border (not to be confused with the dotted rectangle signifying the focus, discussed at the beginning of this chapter). Not all dialog boxes have a default button, but when it's there, it's usually the OK button.

The Cancel button

Much like the default button, a single button is often set as the Cancel button, meaning that it will be activated when the Esc key is pressed (regardless of which control has the focus). The Cancel button has no visual distinction from any other buttons.

OK, Cancel, Apply

Most dialogs will have at least an OK and a Cancel button, and many also have an Apply button. Typically, OK is the "default button," and Cancel is the "cancel button." Both the OK and Apply buttons accept whatever settings you've entered, but the OK button closes the window, while Apply leaves it open, allowing you to make more changes. Finally, Cancel closes the window without applying your settings. (See Figure 3-6.)

What may be confusing is what happens when you click Apply and then Cancel. The assumption is that the settings that were "applied" are not lost, but any that were made *after* Apply was clicked are ignored. Theoretically, the behavior should be the same as though you clicked OK, then reopened the dialog, and then clicked Cancel. But don't be surprised if some applications respond differently; Microsoft has never been clear with application developers about the expected behavior in this situation.

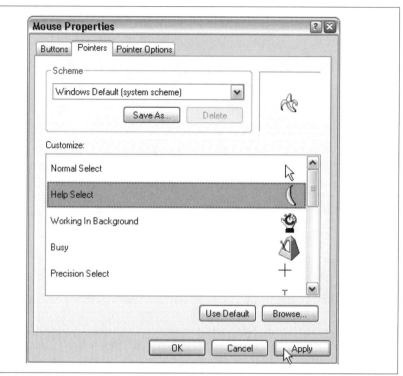

Figure 3-6. Click OK to accept your changes and close the dialog, Cancel to discard your changes, or Apply to accept your changes while leaving the dialog open for later changes

Checkboxes

Checkboxes are generally used for on/off settings. A checkmark means the setting is on; an empty box means it's off. Click on the box to turn the labeled setting on or off.

In some instances, the checkmark may be shown in a light gray color. This doesn't necessarily mean that the control is disabled (see "Grayed-out (inactive) controls," earlier in this chapter), but rather that the value is neither on nor off. Here's an example: select some files in Explorer or on your Desktop, right-click on one of them, select Properties, and you'll get a dialog similar to Figure 3-7. The checkmark is missing for the Read-only and Hidden attributes, but appears gray for the Archive attribute because some of the selected files have it enabled, and others don't.

Clipboard

A shared, system-wide storage area for temporarily holding and moving data.

To Open   Edit → Cut (Ctrl-X)
                       Edit → Copy (Ctrl-C)
                       Edit → Paste (Ctrl-V)

Figure 3-7. Checkboxes allow you to turn settings on or off

The Clipboard is an invisible portion of memory, used to temporarily hold data as it's moved or copied from one application to another. Although you won't ever "see" the clipboard, it's used every time you cut, copy, or paste something.

Using the clipboard is easy. Select a portion of text in your word processor, an image in your graphics program, or a file in Explorer, and then select Cut from the Edit menu; the selected object(s) will disappear and will be stored in the clipboard. (Use Copy instead of Cut if you don't want the original data erased.) Then, move to another location and select Paste from the Edit menu to place a copy of the object on the clipboard in that location. You can repeatedly paste the data as many times as you like.

Notes

- The Clipboard works like the penalty box in hockey; it holds only one item at a time. If you place new data in the clipboard, its previous contents are erased. If you never got around to pasting the previous data, it's lost for good.

- You can paste only data that an application is prepared to receive. For example, you cannot paste an image into some applications that recognize only text (such as the Command Prompt or Notepad).

- Even without an Edit menu, you can usually still access the clipboard using either keyboard shortcuts or the right mouse button. For example, web browsers have a Copy command in the Edit menu, but this command is used only for copying portions of the currently displayed web page to the clipboard. To cut, copy, or paste test in the Address Bar, just right-click on the text or use Ctrl-X, Ctrl-C, and Ctrl-V.

- You can use the Clipbook Viewer (discussed in Chapter 4) to view the data currently stored on the Clipboard or save it into a file or share it across a network.

- See Chapter 6 for help with copying and pasting data with the command prompt window.

- The keyboard shortcuts (Ctrl-X, Ctrl-C, and Ctrl-V) may not be intuitive at first, but when you consider that they appear all together on the keyboard and are located very close to the Ctrl key, the decision to use these keys becomes clear. As a holdover from earlier versions of Windows, Shift-Del, Ctrl-Ins, and Shift-Ins can also be used for Cut, Copy, and Paste, respectively.

- Also see "Clipbook Viewer" in Chapter 4

Combo Boxes

See "Listboxes."

Context Menus

In Figure 3-8, I've right-clicked on the Recycle Bin icon to display its context menu, which is a list of special actions or commands that affect only that object. The idea is that the options available for any given object in Windows depend upon the *context*, the set of circumstances under which you're operating. The "Empty Recycle Bin" option is shown here, since it is relevant to the context of the Recycle Bin, but since the Recycle Bin is currently empty here, the option is grayed out (disabled). Nearly all objects in Windows have their own context menus, almost always accessible with the right mouse button. See "Windows Explorer" in Chapter 4 for details on customizing the context menus for your files, folders, and certain Desktop items, and Chapter 8 for details on the way Windows stores file type information.

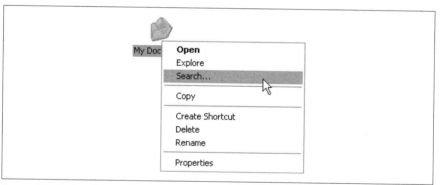

Figure 3-8. Right-click nearly any object to display its context menu, a list of actions that can be performed with the selected object

When a file or other object is selected (highlighted), press Shift-F10 to display the context menu. If you have a special Windows keyboard, there is a special key for this purpose, usually located to the right of the spacebar. The most frequently used item in most context menus is Properties, which can be more quickly accessed by pressing Alt-Enter. Other shortcuts for context menu items include Del, F2, Ctrl-X, Ctrl-C, and Ctrl-V for Delete, Rename, Cut, Copy, and Paste, respectively.

Notes

- The bold item (usually, but not always, at the top of any given context menu) is the default action, carried out when you double-click.

- Most new keyboards also include a context key (which looks like a menu with a pointer on it) that will open the context menu of any selected item.

Any program or command line on the system can be made into a new "verb" on a context menu using View → Options → File Types → Edit from any folder or Explorer window. (To create new verbs directly in the Registry, see O'Reilly's *Windows XP Annoyances*, by David Karp. Note that customizing the context menu for HKEY_CLASSES_ROOT*\shell lets you create verbs for all files; normally they'll apply to particular file types, based in turn on file extensions; objects—drive, folder, unknown, etc.; or URL prefixes—*http*, *ftp*, etc.)

- Context menus exist for all major interface elements—files, folders (including system folders like My Computer, Network Neighborhood, Recycle Bin, and My Briefcase), the Desktop, the Taskbar, the System Tray, and so on—but they often also exist for elements within an application window or dialog. If you're ever stuck, try right-clicking on a user-interface element and see if anything helpful pops up.

- Individual buttons or other user interface elements often have a context menu consisting of the single entry "What's This?", which gives a short description of what that element is used for. In other cases, the context menu is more extensive. For example, right-clicking on the files on your Desktop (or even on an empty area of the Desktop) provides access to the features that would otherwise be unavailable due to the absence of a standard menu. Of particular use is the New entry, which allows you to create a new Folder, Shortcut, or empty file.

- Right-clicking on the titlebar or the Taskbar button for an open application displays the context menu for the window, commonly known as the Control menu, also accessible by clicking on the upper-left icon (see "Windows," later in this chapter). Right-clicking in the body of the window gives you the context menu for the application or the selected element within the application, if one exists. Note that this is different from the context menu that you get by clicking on the program's shortcut icon when it is not running.

- See "Send To," later in this chapter, for details on the Send To command found in the context menu for files and folders.

Control Menus

See "Windows."

Desktop

The Desktop is the basis for the modern GUI paradigm. The Desktop is considered a container for all other resources on your computer, as well as a backdrop for your Windows workspace. The Desktop is always underneath any open windows—to access the Desktop if it's covered, you need to minimize or close any open windows (press the Windows logo key and D, or right-click on the Taskbar and select Minimize All Windows to accomplish this quickly)

As shown in Figure 3-9, the Desktop contains two types of icons; namespace icons and file icons.

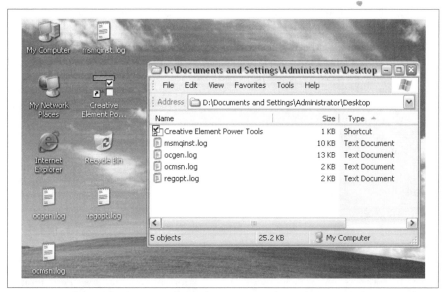

Figure 3-9. Of the icons shown on the Desktop, some are virtual objects and some are files; those that are actual files are also shown in your Desktop folder

File icons can be files or folders (actually located in your *Documents* and *Settings*\ *{username}**Desktop*\ folder on your hard disk)—you can drag-drop them to and from the Desktop as though it were any other ordinary folder. The Desktop is a good place to store newly downloaded files from the Internet, email attachments, items from floppies, and other files you're currently working on.

Namespace icons, on the other hand, such as My Computer, My Network Places, and the Recycle Bin, aren't files, but rather specific resources built in to Windows. All of these icons can be renamed or even hidden, although the process isn't always obvious. (See Chapter 5 for details specific to the object you wish to customize or remove.) The exception is that the Recycle Bin cannot be renamed, unless you have Norton Utilities or edit the Registry manually. (See directions at *http://www.annoyances.org.*)

As with most other components of the Windows interface, the Desktop has properties you can customize. Right-click on an empty portion of the Desktop and click Properties to change the wallpaper, color, screensaver, and settings for the display. (This is the same property sheet that you will get by opening Display Properties in Control Panel).

Notes

- The Arrange Icons By entry is also available in the Desktop's context menu. Icons can be arranged on the Desktop by type (system facilities, folders, and files, in that order), alphabetically by name, by date (with the most recent first), and by size (with the smallest first). Select AutoArrange if you want the icons to go into neat rows automatically; unselect it if you want to be able to drag them anywhere on the Desktop. When the Desktop is full, auto-arrange stops working.

- The Line Up Icons feature found here in earlier versions of Windows has been removed in Windows XP. In its place, Microsoft has added the Align to Grid option in the Arrange Icons By menu. Unfortunately, this is a toggle; to simply align the icons on your Desktop without restricting their future placement, you'll have to turn on the Align to Grid option and then turn it back off.

- The Quick Launch toolbar (see "Taskbar" and "Toolbars," later in this chapter) includes a Show Desktop button that instantly hides all open windows, thus allowing access to your Desktop. If you click the button a second time without opening any new items, all windows are restored to their original state.

- The "Active Desktop" functionality found in earlier versions of Windows has been taken out of Windows XP.

- Various options for customizing the Desktop, as well as the icons on it, are detailed in Chapter 5.

Details

See "Listboxes."

Dialog Boxes

Dialog boxes are temporary windows that applications use to request your attention or input. Dialog boxes usually don't have a resizable border (although File Open/Save Dialogs do), and they almost always have OK, Cancel, and Apply buttons. Dialog boxes are usually "modal," which means that when they're open, you can't use any other part of the owning application until they're closed. See "Windows," later in this chapter, for more information.

Drop-Down Listboxes

See "Listboxes."

File Open/Save Dialogs

There's a reason why File Open and File Save dialogs look the same in nearly all applications; they're common dialogs, provided by Windows. Strangely, one of the few applications that doesn't use these common dialogs is Microsoft Office, which instead employs custom dialogs that actually have more limited functionality then their standard, common counterparts.

The main part of the standard file dialog is really just a folder window as shown in Figure 3-10; you can even drag and drop items into and out of this window, as well as display the contents in the same Details, Icons, and List views found in Windows Explorer.

Another standard component in file dialogs is the gray stripe on the left side, called the Places Bar. Here, five (or more) shortcuts to special system folders are shown; click an icon to quickly jump to the corresponding location. However, most of the default entries will be of little use to the average user, so you may want to customize this area, a task possible only with the TweakUI add-on described in Appendix D.

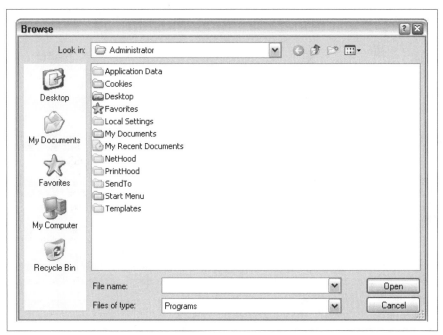

Figure 3-10. Standard File → Open, File → Save, and Browse dialogs like this one are used in many applications

Along the top of the window, you'll find the "Look in" list, and several buttons. The yellow folder icon with the curved arrow is used to jump to the parent folder, and the yellow folder icon with the star is used to create a new subfolder. The last button allows you to choose the way icons are shown in the main listing. Unfortunately, the full path of the current folder is not shown anywhere in this window (this has been a problem with Windows for years), but if you open the "Look in" list, you'll see the abbreviated hierarchy that reveals the location of the folder.

You can type any filename below, including the full path desired, to open or save. Finally, the "Files of type" list is used to filter the display of files in the main listing. This is often most confusing part of this window for new users, since, in most cases, only certain files are shown. If the file you're looking for does not match the file type selection, it won't show up at all. Typically, the last entry in this list is All Files (*.*); choose this item to turn off the filter and display all files, regardless of type.

Notes

- Like most dialog boxes, File Open/Save dialogs are modal, which means that they must be closed before you can use another part of the application.

- An alternative to opening an application and then using File → Open is to navigate to the folder containing your document and then double-click it to open it in its default application. (This default can be changed by going to the Tools → Folder Options → Files Types tab in Explorer.) You can also drag-drop a document icon into an open application window to open the file in that program.

In some applications, if you drop a file icon into an already-open document, the dropped icon will be inserted as an "object" into that document, rather than simply opening the document as you'd expect. The solution is to drop the icon onto the Application's titlebar.

Icons

Strictly speaking, an icon is any small picture used to symbolize an object or a function in the interface. Icons commonly appear in menus and on toolbars, but the term is most often used to describe the objects that represent files and folders on your Desktop and in Windows Explorer.

Chapter 2 covers the basic use of icons, especially in the way they can be opened, moved, copied, and deleted. Right-click any icon to display its context menu. (See "Context Menus," earlier in this chapter.)

The image used for a given icon depends on the type of object it represents, as does the procedure for customizing that icon. For example, the icons for My Computer, Recycle Bin and other Desktop "namespace" objects can be customized by right-clicking on an empty area of the Desktop and going to Properties → Desktop tab → Customize Desktop.

The icon used for a document depends on its type; all *.txt* files use the same icon, all *.jpg* files use the same icon, and so on. Icons for most file types can be changed by going to Tools → Folder Options → Files Types tab in Explorer (see Figure 3-11). The exceptions are application executables (*.exe* files), which have their own icons. All folders (except special folders, like My Documents and My Pictures) use the same icon, and cannot be changed without a third-party add-on like Microangelo (Version 5.5 or later; available from *http://www.impactsoftware.com/*).

You can change the icon for any Windows Shortcut or Internet Shortcut by right-clicking, and selecting Properties → Change Icon. By default, the Change Icon dialog box for a shortcut usually points to *\Windows\System\shell32.dll*, which contains over 200 different icons, including the standard icons for folders, disks, and so on. A browse button lets you search for other sources of icons, but where do you browse?

Icons can be stored in a variety of files, including *.exe* and *.dll* files (program components) and *.ico* files (standalone icon files). Even *.bmp* (Windows bitmap files) can be used for icons. Browsing for icons can be time consuming, though, since the Change Icon dialog can only look inside one file at a time. The alternative is to use Explorer: the standard file icon for *.ico* files is the actual icon it contains, making it easy to peruse an entire folder full of icon files (although you'll have to switch to the Thumbnails view to see your *.bmp* files).

Although other Windows files (such as *\windows\explorer.exe*) have additional icons, you may want to look on the Web for decent icons to decorate your workspace (and there's no end to web sites that contain freely downloadable icon libraries). Since I have a particular fondness for the NeXT interface from the 1980s, I've found the icons at *http://pcdesktops.emuunlim.com/* to be especially nice.

Notes

- On the Desktop, icons are shown in their full size, but in folder windows and in Windows Explorer, you can choose to display icons in a "list" or "details" view.

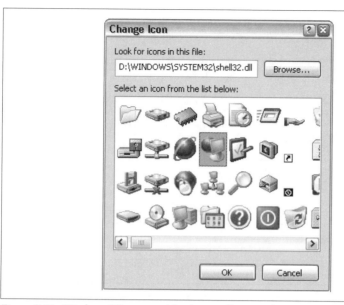

Figure 3-11. Windows XP comes with a large collection of images for your shortcuts

- Paint, the rudimentary image editor included with Windows XP (and every version of Windows since the 1980s), allows you to create and modify *.bmp* files, but it doesn't support *.ico* format. Furthermore, its tools for doing detail (essential when creating the tiny images used for icons) are pretty lousy. The Microangelo package, available from *http://www.impactsoftware.com/*, is about the best icon editor I've used.

Input Fields

As their name suggests, input fields are small controls (usually found in a dialog box that allows you to provide required information). (See Figure 3-12.) A textbox is one of the most common forms of input field. Essentially a mini word processor, the textbox is used for entering text. Most input fields allow only a single line of text (such as the Address Bar or the Filename field in File Open/Save dialogs), but some allow multiple lines. You can almost always right-click in a textbox to display a quick menu for Cut, Copy, Paste, and Undo (see "Clipboard," earlier in this chapter).

There are four common variations of input fields. The first type are the input fields made to look like labels (see "Labels," later in this chapter). The second are combo boxes (see "Listboxes," later in this chapter). The third are known as counters, which are simply input fields with up and down arrows to the right, allowing you increment or decrement a numeric value without typing (some even have a tiny divider between the arrows, allowing you to quickly "scroll" to any value). Finally, we have password fields (Figure 3-13), which look and act just like standard input boxes, except that their contents are masked with asterisks to hide them from prying eyes.

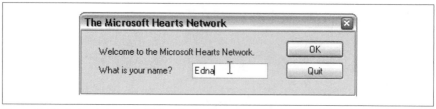

Figure 3-12. A simple input field (textbox) allows you to type a small bit of text; right-click to display Cut, Copy, Paste, and Select All commands

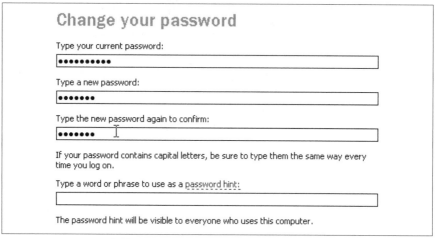

Figure 3-13. Password fields work like standard input fields, except that the characters you type are masked with round bullets

 Since the Tab key is used to shift the focus to the next control, you'll need to press Ctrl-Tab if you actually want to type a tab character into an input field. Likewise, Enter is often used to move between controls (or to press the default button; see "Buttons," earlier in this chapter), press Ctrl-Enter to insert a new line (multiline textboxes only). Hold Shift and use the arrow keys to select text without using the mouse (or Ctrl-A to select everything), and then use Ctrl-X, Ctrl-C, and Ctrl-V for Cut, Copy, and Paste, respectively. Press Ctrl-Z to undo.

Notes

- Right-click in an input field to display additional options. In addition to the clipboard operations (Cut, Copy, and Paste), you'll see Select All, Right to Left Reading order (to make the text right-justified), and two options for using Unicode characters (useful primarily for programmers).

- Some nonstandard input fields allow formatting (bold, italics, font selection, etc.). These "rich text" fields typically work the same as standard input fields, although they often have additional features specific to the application.

Labels

Labels are basically noninteractive pieces of text placed on dialogs used to describe a control (such as the slides shown in Figure 3-14) that doesn't have a place for a description. Clicking labels usually has no effect.

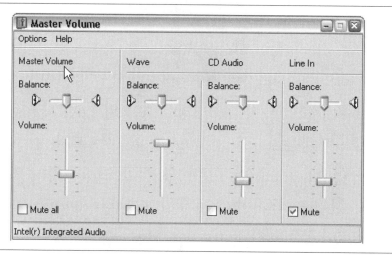

Figure 3-14. Labels are noninteractive captions for other controls (like these sliders) that don't have captions of their own

The important thing to note about labels is that they often contain a single underlined letter. Holding Alt and pressing the key for that letter will send the focus to the next control. This is useful because the input field in this example doesn't have a shortcut key of its own.

Notes

Some labels allow you to select and copy text and are distinguished because the mouse pointer changes to an "I-beam" when over the label. Strictly speaking, these are just standard input fields (without borders) that have been made to look like labels. Examples of this type of field can be seen by right-clicking on a file and selecting properties.

Listboxes

A listbox is a list of items from which you can choose one or many. There are four common types of listboxes:

Standard listbox

A simple listbox is a rectangular control that contains one or more entries. If there are more entries than can be displayed in the space allotted, scrollbars will appear as well. Click an entry to select it. If the listbox allows multiple items to be selected simultaneously, hold down the Ctrl key while clicking or pressing the spacebar to select additional items, one-by-one, or use Shift-click to select a range of items (see Figure 3-15).

Figure 3-15. This listbox shows the bitmap files in your Windows folder, from which you can choose one to be your Desktop background image

Use the arrow keys to move up and down the list. Type a letter to jump to the first entry that begins with that letter; if there are a lot of items, you can type several letters, quickly in succession, to jump to the first item the begins with those letters.

Drop-down listbox

A drop-down listbox (see Figure 3-16) works much like a standard listbox, except that only the currently selected entry is shown. Click the down arrow to open the list and choose another item. Drop-down listboxes never allow multiple selections.

Shortcuts

With the focus on a drop-down listbox, press the down arrow key to open the list, the arrow keys to navigate, and then the Tab key to jump to the next control, which will close the list automatically (press Esc to close the list without selecting a new item). If you press Enter to commit your selection, though, it might activate the default button (see "Buttons," earlier in this chapter).

Combo box

A combo box is a hybrid between an input field and a drop-down listbox. You can type just like in an ordinary input field, or you can click the down arrow to choose an item from the list. If you click an item, that item's caption will be placed into the text field, at which point you can edit or move on. Often, a drop-down list contains a history of previous entries you've made into a text entry field; the Address Bar is essentially a glorified combo box.

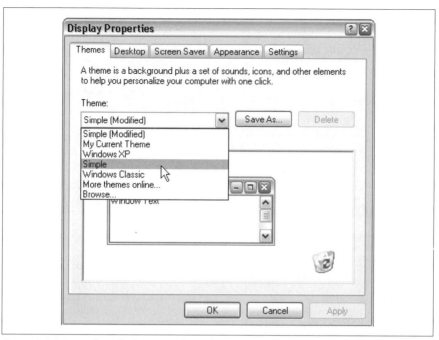

Figure 3-16. Drop-down listboxes work much like standard listboxes, except that they consume less screen real estate

The keyboard shortcuts are the same as for drop-down listboxes, shown above, and input fields (discussed earlier in this chapter). Additionally, you can begin typing, and then press the down arrow, and the first entry in the list that matches what you've typed (if any) will be selected automatically.

ListView (commonly known as Details)

An enhanced version of the standard listbox, the ListView control is what appears in folder windows and File Open/Save dialogs. It's commonly used to display lists of files, but it's not unusual to see this presentation for other types of data as well. (See Figure 3-17.)

The main advantage of this control is that it supports multiple, resizable columns, each of which has a header that can usually be clicked to sort the contents of the list (click again to reverse the sort order). Drag the lines dividing the headers to resize the width of columns or drag the headers to rearrange them. Double-click on column header separators to size columns automatically to the widest contents.

See Chapter 2 for more information on working with the folder window. Since folders use the common ListView control, almost anything that works with a folder will work with other ListView controls. For example, in addition to selecting multiple items with Ctrl and Shift, as described for standard listboxes, above, you can usually select multiple items by drawing a rubber band with your mouse as well.

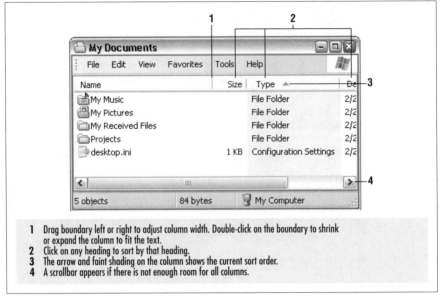

1   Drag boundary left or right to adjust column width. Double-click on the boundary to shrink
    or expand the column to fit the text.
2   Click on any heading to sort by that heading.
3   The arrow and faint shading on the column shows the current sort order.
4   A scrollbar appears if there is not enough room for all columns.

*Figure 3-17. ListView controls, like the one used for Explorer's Details View, are enhanced
listboxes with multiple columns of information*

Log Off

Logs off the current user.

To Open   Start → Log Off *{username}*
                     Ctrl-Alt-Del → Log Off

See "User Accounts" in Chapter 4 for more information on logging on, logging off, and
managing multiple users.

Menus

The menu is a place where you can cram all the functionality of a program. Rather
than littering your screen with all available commands, they are categorically arranged
into cascading lists, as shown in Figure 3-18. Modern applications have become so
elaborate, however, that menus are often very complex, making it a pain to have to sift
through them all to find the command you want. Thus, designers invented toolbars
(discussed later in this chapter) as shortcuts for the items we actually use. It makes us
wonder, then, why we need menus in the first place?

If you ever get lost, menus tend to be pretty consistent across applications. For
example, you can almost always find Open, Save, Print, and Exit in the File menu, just
as Cut, Copy, Paste, and Undo are always in the Edit menu.

See Chapter 2 for more information on using menus. See "Context Menus," earlier in
this chapter, for details on the menu that appears when you right-click on something.

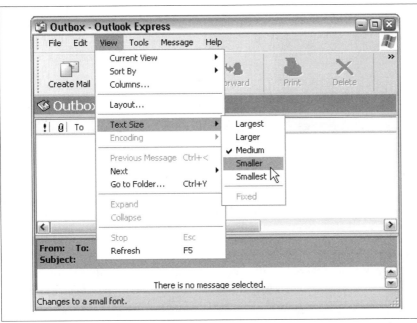

Figure 3-18. Nested (cascading) menus provide access to all options and features of an application

Press F10 or Alt (by itself) to enter the menu, use the cursor keys to navigate, and press Enter to select an item. Once you're in the menus, press the underlined letter of a menu item to quickly jump to that item, or if no letter is underlined, press the first letter of the item's caption. You can also jump right to a specific menu from anywhere else in the application by pressing the key of the underlined letter while holding Alt. Look to the right of many menu items for additional keyboard shortcuts. For example, open the Edit menu in most applications, and you'll see Ctrl-X, Ctrl-C, and Ctrl-V alongside the Cut, Copy, and Paste commands, respectively.

My Computer

See "Windows Explorer" in Chapter 4.

My Network Places

See "My Network Places" in Chapter 4.

Notification Area

The notification area, commonly known as the *Tray*, is the small area at the far right (or bottom) of the Taskbar, which, by default, holds the clock and the tiny, yellow speaker icon. With the exception of the clock, the purpose of the tray is to hold status icons (see Figure 3-19) placed there by Windows and other running applications. Hold the mouse cursor over the clock to see the date temporarily or right-click on an empty area of the Taskbar and click Properties to turn the clock on or off and change other settings. (Sorry, no permanent date is available without a third-party utility—see *http://www.annoyances.org/*.)

Figure 3-19. The Notification Area (Tray), located on the far end of your Taskbar, holds the clock and icons for some running processes

The Tray can be a convenient place for applications to display information and quick access to certain features, but there is little standardization among Tray icons. Some icons are clicked, others are double-clicked, others require a right-click, and some don't get clicked at all. Some flash, some don't. Most icons can be disabled, but some just won't go away. Most support tooltips, so you can find out what each icon does by holding the mouse over it for a second or two.

The only way to turn the notification area off completely is to hide each of the icons (and the clock) individually. However, you can selectively hide icons by going to Control Panel → [Appearance and Themes] → Taskbar and Start Menu → Taskbar tab → Customize. See "Taskbar and Start Menu Properties" in Chapter 4 for more information, and See Chapter 5 for additional settings that affect the Taskbar, the notification area, and the icons that routinely appear there.

Notes

- Right-click or double-click on the clock when it is displayed to adjust the system date and time. (You can also get there by opening the Date and Time properties in the Control Panel.)

- The System Tray is available to any application that chooses to use—or misuse—it. For example, both AOL and RealPlayer install a startup icon in the System Tray (as well as just about anywhere else they can put one)—a clear abuse of the intended purpose.

- The language indicator is useful only if multiple keyboard layouts are enabled. Click on the indicator to display a pop-up menu that lets you switch between available keyboard layouts.

- The power status indicator is generally useful only on laptops. It shows a plug when the system is connected to AC power, and a battery when the system is running on the battery. The height of the color in the battery gives a rough idea of how much power is left; to get a more precise estimate, hold the pointer over the indicator until a Tooltips bubble pops up showing the percentage of the remaining charge.

- The PC card indicator gives you a quick way to get to the Control Panel → PC Card property sheet. This indicator is useful if you will be taking PC cards in and out of your system frequently, since the system prefers to be notified before you do so.

- The "Super-Fast User Switcher" is a notification area-based tool that allows you to switch between configured users simply by clicking on its tray icon; see Appendix D for details.

Progress Indicators

The progress indicator is a linear gauge that graphically shows the completion of a particular task, allowing you to roughly estimate the time to completion (see Figure 3-20). The annoying part is that the accuracy of progress indicators is typically not very good; the value (zero to 100 percent) displayed by an indicator is based entirely on approximations made by the application. What's worse is that some programs, especially application installers, often have several, consecutive progress indicators; unfortunately, these only display the progress of a particular task rather than the entire process, which obviously is not terribly helpful.

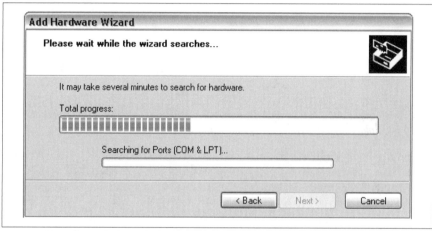

Figure 3-20. Often a dialog will show two progress indicators: one showing the completion of the current task and one showing the progress of the entire job

Properties

The Properties window (sometimes called the Properties sheet) is a dialog box that serves a very specific purpose: to display and allow changes to the settings associated with a file, folder, or other object in Windows. Most objects have Properties sheets, almost always accessible by right-clicking and selecting Properties, as shown in Figure 3-21. (You can also display Properties by holding Alt and double-clicking, or if the item is already highlighted, by pressing Alt-Enter.) Many items in the Control Panel can be quickly accessed by right-clicking on various interface elements and selecting Properties; for example:

- My Network Places icon → Properties points to Network Connections
- Empty portion of the Desktop → Properties points to Display Properties
- My Computer icon → Properties points to System Properties
- Taskbar or Start button → Properties points to Taskbar and Start Menu Properties
- Clock (in the notification area) → Properties points to Time and Date Properties

At minimum, most Properties sheets will have a General tab, but most have more. Note that the particular information and settings available depend entirely on the object that was clicked.

Figure 3-21. Right-click an item and select Properties to display the item's Properties dialog, often a good place to find extra features and settings

Notes

- Folders, printers, and disk drives have a second property tab called Sharing. See Chapter 7 for details. Shortcuts to MS-DOS and command-line-based programs have additional settings for legacy support.

- To see the amount of disk space used by a group of files, select them and then view the Properties entry for the selected list. On the first tab, you'll see the size of the whole group. Change any of the attributes, and the change will be applied to all of the files in the selected group. (Unfortunately, if any of the files in the selected group has a different attribute from other files in the group, the checkbox for that attribute will be grayed out, so this does not work in all cases. This poor user interface design was discussed in "Combo Boxes," earlier in this chapter.)

- Certain types of files, such as Microsoft Word files, will have additional property pages that are generated by the application that created them. Word files, for example, have pages that let you summarize and view the statistics for documents.

- Among the settings in a Properties sheet for files are the Attributes (Read-only, Hidden, and Archive). See "Attrib" in Chapter 4 for details.

- In previous versions of Windows, the Properties sheet also contained the "MS-DOS name," the eight-character "short filename," plus a three-character extension. Since Windows XP has better support for long filenames, it's assumed that this information is no longer necessary. If you need a short filename for a file or folder, type dir /x at a command prompt (see Chapter 6 for details).

Radio Buttons

Radio buttons are used for mutually exclusive settings. Clicking on one causes any other that has been pressed to pop up, just like on an old car radio. The button with the dot in the middle is the one that has been selected. Sometimes you'll see more than one group of buttons, with a separate outline around each group. In this case, you can select one radio button from each group. Functionally, a group of radio buttons works like a standard listbox. (See Figure 3-22.)

Figure 3-22. Two radio buttons are used to allow you to choose only one of the available Start menu styles

Navigating radio buttons with the keyboard can be confusing. When using the Tab key to jump between controls, Windows considers a group of radio buttons to be a single control. When the Tab key places the focus on a single radio button, you'll need to use the arrow keys to select a different one; otherwise, another press of the Tab key will jump to a different control, seemingly skipping a whole bunch of radio buttons.

Recycle Bin

In the early days of computing, once you deleted a file, it was gone. An unerase tool (available as part of Norton Utilities) was commonly used to recover accidentally deleted files, and can even be used in Windows XP to recover items emptied from the Recycle Bin. Thus, the Recycle Bin was implemented—a feature that gives nearly every file a second chance, so to speak.

Drag any item from the Desktop to the Recycle Bin icon to delete it, as shown in Figure 3-23. File → Delete on the menubar of a folder also moves items to the Recycle Bin, as does selecting the item and then pressing the Delete key. By default, files are not deleted immediately, but are stored until the Recycle Bin runs out of space, at which point they are deleted, oldest first, to make space. Until that time, they can be retrieved by double-clicking on the Recycle Bin icon, browsing through the contents of the Recycle Bin window, and dragging or sending the file elsewhere.

Figure 3-23. Drag nearly any icon onto your Recycle Bin to delete it; subsequently open the Recycle Bin folder to retrieve it

Use the Delete key to move any selected files to the Recycle Bin. To access the Recycle Bin with the keyboard, it's easiest to simply open Windows Explorer and navigate to your *\Recycled* folder (there's one on each drive, if you have more than one).

 Files dragged to the Recycle Bin (or that are otherwise deleted) from floppies, network drives, or other external drives such as Zip drives will not be stored in the Recycle Bin. They are simply deleted.

The following settings are available in the Recycle Bin's Properties window:

- A slider allows you to specify how much of each drive can be allocated to the Recycle Bin. The default is 10 percent. You can specify the same value for all drives or set a separate value for each drive. Keep in mind that on today's huge drives, 10 percent can be a lot: 10 percent of a 40 gigabyte disk is 4 full gigabytes of stored junk. The amount of space actually used by the files in the Recycle Bin is displayed in the Bin's status bar when you open it.

- A checkbox allows you to specify that deleted files are not to be stored in the Recycle Bin, but removed immediately from the disk. Check this box if you don't want to have to remember to empty your Recycle Bin to delete files, although it can be rather dangerous if you're careless with the Del key.

- A checkbox asks if you want to display a delete confirmation dialog. Unlike some earlier versions of Windows, it's possible to have the delete confirmation turned off at the same time that the "Do not move files to the Recycle Bin" setting is turned on. This means that it's possible to permanently delete files without any warnings at all.

 To delete a single file without sending it to the Recycle Bin, use Shift-Delete or the *del* command at the command prompt.

Notes

- With the Details view (the default), you can sort the contents of the Recycle Bin by name, by original location (useful in case you want to put something back where it was), by the date deleted, by type, or by size. Click on any of the headings to sort contents by that heading. Click again on the same heading to reverse the order of the sort.

- You can delete the entire contents of a floppy disk by dragging the disk icon to the Recycle Bin. You will be prompted for confirmation. You cannot drag a hard disk (such as C:) to the Recycle Bin, however, nor can you drag key components of the user interface, such as the My Computer, the Control Panel, or My Network Places to the Recycle Bin. (Well, you can drag them there, but they won't go in.) Note that some of these Desktop items can be removed by right-clicking and selecting Delete. See Chapter 5 for more ways to control what appears on your Desktop.

Run

The Start menu lists many common Windows XP applications and accessories, plus any third-party applications you've installed. It is far from complete, though, and navigating to the program you want is often fairly tedious.

Ironically, the increasing complexity of the system pushes even the most graphically oriented user back in the direction of the command line. Just about the quickest way to run any program that isn't already on your Desktop is to type the name of the program at the command line. Windows XP offers three different command lines: the Address Bar, the Run dialog, and the command prompt window.

If you keep an Address Bar visible at all times (see "Address Bar," earlier in this chapter), it is by far the most convenient of the three command lines. The Run Dialog is a close second. However, if you are a heavy user of command-line utilities, you may still find a command prompt window most useful. The command prompt window has an advantage in that it provides useful file management commands such as *dir*, *del*, *copy*, and so on.

For the most part, though, you can use the three command lines interchangeably. If you type the name of a Windows GUI application, it will launch in its own window. If you type the name of a text-based program (for example, *ping*) it will display its output in the current command prompt window, or, if issued from the Address Bar or Run dialog, will launch its own command prompt window, which will last only as long as the command itself executes.

Notes

- You'll only be able to launch a program using the Run command if that program's *.exe* file is in a folder listed in the system path. See Chapter 6 for details.
- One important difference between the one-line prompts (Address or Run) and a command prompt window is the context in which commands run. A command interpreter, or shell, always has a particular context, or environment, in which it runs. This environment can create significant differences in the results when you type a command name.
- There are a number of commands you can issue only at a command prompt window (documented in Chapter 6), all of which are unavailable from the Run prompt or Address Bar.

See Also

See "Address Bar," earlier in this chapter, and Chapter 6.

Scroll Bars

A scrollbar is a vertical or horizontal bar on a window with a little box inside it (called the slider or "thumb") that can be dragged along it with the mouse. Applications use the scrollbar not only to set the position of something (such as the text cursor in a textbox or the currently displayed page of a word processor document), but to give us visual feedback of where we are and how much stuff we can't see. The thumb shows us where we are in the entire piece of text, and the size of the thumb shows us what percentage we're viewing. (A large thumb means that most of what's there is visible and a small thumb means that there's a lot we can't see.) The scrollbar usually becomes disabled (grayed-out) if there's no scrolling to be done.

Click the up or down arrows to move the scroll bar incrementally, or drag the thumb with the mouse to move to the desired position. You can also click in the gray areas between the arrows and the thumb to move up or down a page at a time.

It is possible to use the cursor keys and PgUp/PgDn keys to control the scrollbar if it has the focus. If the scrollbar is part of another control, such as the textbox shown in Figure 3-24, then it cannot receive the focus to receive keyboard input directly. Instead, use the cursor keys to navigate in the listbox or input field with which the scrollbar is associated. The thumb blinks if it has the focus.

Figure 3-24. Use scrollbars to view all of the items in a folder when the folder window is not sufficiently large

Send To

Send a selected item to a program, disk drive, or folder.

To Open   File or folder's context menu → Send To

Right-click on any file or folder and select Send To to send it to one of the shortcuts in your *SendTo* folder. The result is the same as though you drag-dropped the icon onto the shortcut (see Figure 3-25).

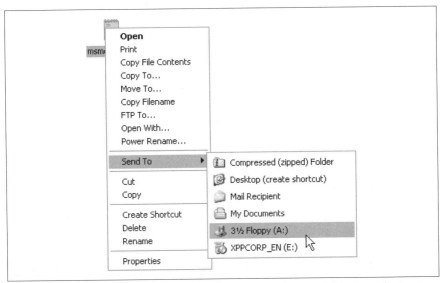

Figure 3-25. Right-clicking any file or folder, selecting Send To, and choosing a destination has the same result as dragging and dropping the item to the destination, but Send To is often more convenient

For example, if the destination is an application, the application will be started and the selected file(s) will be opened. If the destination is a folder or a drive, the item(s) will be copied or moved (depending on several circumstances described in Chapter 2).

Notes

- The options that appear in the Send To menu are determined by the contents of the *\Documents and Settings\[username]\SendTo* folder. To add another Send To recipient, create a shortcut in that folder. For example, if you put a shortcut to *notepad.exe* into that folder (which I find extremely handy), you could easily open any file in Notepad, regardless of the file type.

 Send To works a bit differently, depending on the destination. Sending to a folder (including the Recycle Bin) actually moves the file there or copies if the source and destination are on different drives; sending to a program simply opens the file. You can use Send To on shortcuts with impunity, but when you use it on an original file, remember that you may actually be moving the file.

- If you place a shortcut to your *SendTo* folder in your *SendTo* folder, you can create new Send To destinations simply by sending them to the *SendTo* folder! (Say that five times fast.)

- Place shortcuts to folders in Send To for an easy way to organize your files. You can work on files on the Desktop then use Send To to move them to their storage location when you're done. You can even create shortcuts to shared folders on other machines.

- If you want to have a lot of Send To locations, create subfolders in \Windows\ SendTo. They will show up as cascading submenus on the Send To menu.

Shortcuts

A Shortcut is a link to a program, file, folder, drive, system object, printer, or URL. Shortcuts are actually small files that come in two flavors: Windows Shortcuts (.lnk) and Internet Shortcuts (.url). (See Figure 3-26.)

My Documents   Shortcut to My
               Documents

Figure 3-26. A standard shortcut icon is distinguishable from other icons by the little curved arrow

While you can start a program or open a folder by double-clicking on its icon on the Desktop or selecting its icon in the Start menu, odds are that application is stored elsewhere and you're using a shortcut only to access the application executable. If you find that there's a program, document, folder, or web site you use often, it's easy to create a shortcut to the object.

There are several ways to create a shortcut:

- Use the Explorer to navigate to the directory where the program's executable (.exe) is stored; if the program is a Windows component (listed in Chapter 4), it's executable is probably in the \Windows\System32 folder. Otherwise, the executable is probably located in a subfolder of \Program Files. Once you've located the .exe file, use the right mouse button to drag it to the location of your choice (typically the Desktop or the Start menu) and select "Create shortcut here" from the context menu that appears. The same procedure works for folders, drives, and documents, as well. In some earlier versions of Windows, dragging an .exe file with the left mouse button (in most situations) automatically created a shortcut, regardless of the destination. This feature, which nobody liked, has been removed in Windows XP. More information on right-dragging can be found in Chapter 2.

- Right-click on an empty area of the Desktop (or any folder), and select New → Shortcut. This four-page wizard prompts you for only two pieces of information: the full path of the object and the name of the resulting shortcut. This procedure is more laborious than the others listed here, but it does have the advantage of allowing you to create a shortcut to a program with command-line parameters.

- A quick way to create a shortcut to a folder (or drive) is to open the folder and then drag the control icon (the small icon in the upper-left of the window) onto the Desktop or other destination.

- Right-click any file, system object (such as an item in Control Panel or the Printers and Faxes folder), and select Create Shortcut. A shortcut to the selected object will be created in the same folder; if the folder is a "virtual folder" (like Control Panel) and does not allow new items, you'll be prompted to create the shortcut on the Desktop. Once the shortcut has been created, it can be moved anywhere you like.

- Open any web page in Internet Explorer, Netscape, or Mozilla and drag the little icon in the Address Bar (immediately to the left of the *http://*) onto the Desktop or other destination, as shown in Figure 3-27.

Figure 3-27. Quickly create an Internet Shortcut by dragging the icon from the Address Bar to your Desktop or Favorites menu

Shortcuts are commonly placed on the Desktop and Start menu for quick access to programs and documents, but can really be placed anywhere. One of the purposes of having a central My Documents folder is to enforce the notion that documents and personal files should be arranged by project, not by application. This means that Internet Shortcuts and Windows Shortcuts might be placed in the same folder as WordPerfect and Excel documents, making it easy to group all the resources for a particular project together and decreasing the time spent repeatedly trying to locate files and data.

You can also create a shortcut to a local or network printer. Dragging a file onto the shortcut sends that file to the printer without requiring you to open the associated program, which is handy if you do a lot of printing. Putting printer shortcuts in your Send To menu lets you conveniently send files to printers other than your default printer.

Shortcut properties

You'll notice that the names of shortcuts, by default, begin with the phrase "Shortcut to...," and their icons have a small curved arrow superimposed on the lower left. This arrow helps distinguish shortcuts from the files to which they're linked, but it is not set in stone. To change the default visual characteristics of shortcuts, use TweakUI (see Appendix D). There's also a feature in Windows that is supposed to automatically stop adding "Shortcut to" to the your shortcut names if it sees you removing it manually several times in a row, but I've never been able to get this feature to work reliably. TweakUI is much more direct and much less hassle.

To get more information about a shortcut, go to its Properties sheet (right-click it and select Properties). Figure 3-28 shows an example of the second page of a shortcut's properties.

Target
> This field appears in the Properties sheet of Windows Shortcuts (see the URL below for its counterpart in Internet Shortcuts). If the shortcut is to an executable with a command-line equivalent (including, but not limited to, command prompt programs), or even to a folder, the full command line required to activate the target is specified here.

Figure 3-28. View the Properties of a Windows Shortcut to view or change its target, choose a new icon, or assign a hotkey to it

If it's a shortcut to Notepad, you'll just see *Notepad.exe* here. If it's a shortcut to Adobe Photoshop, it'll look like *c:\Program Files\Adobe\Photoshop\Photoshop.exe*. Note that the full path is required for Photoshop, but not for Notepad because Notepad is already in a folder in the system path (described in Chapter 6).

This field is also convenient for adding command-line parameters that are typically used to pass options to the target program, so you don't have to do it manually every time it's started. For example, instead of creating an ordinary shortcut to *Explorer.exe*, create a shortcut to Explorer.exe /n,/e,/select,c:\ to launch Explorer rooted at My Computer with drive *C:* selected. See "Windows Explorer" in Chapter 4 for details on this syntax.

Start in

If the shortcut is to a program, this option specifies the working folder in which the program will first look for files to open or save.

Shortcut key

You can map a keyboard sequence to open or execute the shortcut (sometimes called a keyboard accelerator), allowing you to activate the shortcut without having to hunt for the shortcut icon. For instance, you might want to map the keys Ctrl+Alt+E to a shortcut to Explorer.

Press any key on the keyboard here and you will see Ctrl+Alt+key appear as the shortcut key sequence. Type that sequence to launch the shortcut without clicking on it. You should check Appendix C to make sure you aren't creating conflicts with any existing keyboard accelerator.

Bug alert: If you delete a shortcut with a keyboard accelerator configured, Windows may not release the accelerator, which means it
might warn you if you then try to use that accelerator in another
shortcut. To avoid this problem, clear a shortcut's keyboard accelerator before deleting the shortcut.

Run

A drop-down list allows you to specify whether the target application should run
in its normal window, be maximized, or be minimized. The Minimized option
can be useful for applications you'd like to have started automatically when
Windows starts (see Notes, below). The Maximized option can be useful for
applications you'd like to run in full-screen mode, but don't automatically
remember their window state from session to session.

Find Target

Click this button to open the folder containing the original file to which this
shortcut is a link. The original file will be selected in the folder window.

Change Icon

By default, the icon used for the shortcut is the same as its target; in the case of
Internet Shortcuts, the icon is simply an Internet Explorer logo. See "Icons,"
earlier in this chapter, for more information on customizing icons.

URL

The URL field is the Internet Shortcut counterpart to the Target field, described
above. It simply contains the full address (URL) of the page to which it's linked.

Make this page available offline

This option, available only with Internet Shortcuts, instructs Windows to download web pages to your hard disk so they can be viewed when you're not online. I
find this feature most useful for saving web sites I'm concerned won't be available the next time I check. See "Offline Files" in Chapter 4 for more information.

Compatibility tab

The Compatibility tab appears only in Windows Shortcuts and is not available for
Windows components or applications Windows knows to be fully compatible
with Windows XP. Generally, you'll never need to mess with these settings,
unless you're using an older Windows or DOS program that behaves strangely in
Windows XP. You'll probably need to experiment with these settings, or possibly
contact the manufacturer of the application for suggestions, to get the program to
work most reliably.

Options, Font, Layout, and Colors

Shortcuts to Command Prompt applications have four additional tabs—Options,
Font, Layout, and Colors—all used to control the options of the Command
Prompt environment in which the program will run. This applies to older DOS
programs as well as the newer Windows XP command prompt programs, such as
Telnet (see Chapter 4). The settings in these extra tabs are described in Chapter 6
and are also available from the control menu of the command prompt window.

Notes

- Since shortcuts are merely links to applications and not the applications themselves, shortcuts can be deleted without fear of any permanent damage. If you
  wish to actually delete an application, use Add or Remove Programs, and the
  associated shortcuts will probably be removed as part of the uninstall process.

- To have one or more shortcuts launched automatically when Windows starts, place them in your Start → Programs → Startup menu. See "Start Menu," later in this chapter for details.

Shut Down

Shut down the system, restart the computer, or put it in power-saving mode.

To Open   Start → Turn off Computer (or Start → Shut Down)
Ctrl-Alt-Del → Shut Down

A Windows XP machine should never be simply turned off because the system caches data in memory and needs time to write it out to disk before it is turned off. Always use Shut Down before you turn off the power.

Depending on your settings, you may see "Turn off Computer" or "Shut Down" at the bottom of your Start menu. Both do the same thing, but the interface is slightly different. "Shut Down" displays the Shut Down dialog found in earlier versions of Windows, allowing you to Log off, Shut down, Restart, or Stand by. "Turn off Computer" displays the same choices, except as new Windows XP-style buttons instead of a drop-down listbox. To choose between these two Shut Down dialog styles, go to Control Panel → User Accounts → Change the way users log on or off. Turn off the "Use the Welcome screen" option to use the classic Shut Down dialog, or turn it on to use the new XP-style dialog. Keep in mind that this option also affects the logon dialog; when you use the Welcome screen, an icon is shown for each user. When you use the classic logon dialog, you'll need to type the username to log on.

The classic logon dialog may not be as friendly as the Welcome screen, but it offers better security because any user must know both the username and password to log on. Furthermore, the classic logon dialog is the only way to log into the Administrator account, which is not shown at all in the Welcome screen.

Notes

- If Windows displays the "It is now safe to turn off your computer" message instead of simply cutting power automatically, your computer is not properly set up for APM (Advanced Power Management). There are two requirements for auto-power off: your computer must have an ATX-compliant power supply and APM support must be enabled in your system BIOS. Check with your system or motherboard documentation for details.
- Windows XP also has a new option that, at least in theory, will go through the proper shutdown procedure when you press the power button on your computer. Go to Control Panel → Power Options → Advanced tab, and change the "When I press the power button on my computer" option to "Shut down." Whether this works or not depends on how APM-compliant your motherboard is.

Start Menu

The central location for your application shortcuts and many Windows features.

To Open   Desktop → Start
Press the Windows logo key, if you've got one
Ctrl-Esc

The Start menu was one of Microsoft's answers to the growing size and complexity of the Windows operating system when it was introduced in Windows 95. Since then, other features have been introduced to compensate for the Start menu's inadequacies, such as the QuickLaunch toolbar and the new Windows XP-style Start menu. (See the discussion of "Style" at the beginning of this chapter).

Here is a quick rundown of the items you'll find in the Start menu. Note that some of these items may be hidden as a result of settings described in Chapter 5. (Also see Figure 3-29.)

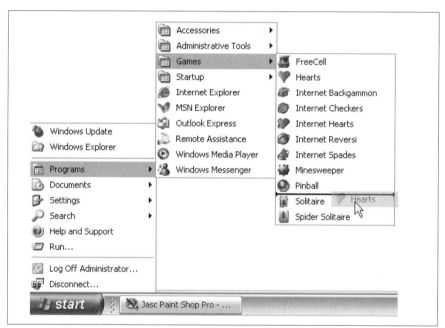

Figure 3-29. Start menu items can be rearranged by dragging and dropping

Programs (or All Programs)
    While the Desktop is commonly used to hold icons for the most frequently used programs, the Programs menu (or All Programs menu, with the new Windows XP style Start menu) is designed to hold icons for every program installed on your computer. See "Shortcuts," earlier in this chapter, for details.

Programs (or All Programs) → Startup
    To have a program run automatically when Windows starts, place a shortcut to the program in this special folder. If you have more than one user set up on your

computer, you'll want to control whether the program starts up automatically for just you or for all users, so instead of dropping it right in your Start menu, open Explorer and navigate to either *\Documents and Settings\{username}\Start Menu\ Programs\Startup* or *\Documents and Settings\All Users\Start Menu\Programs\ Startup*.

Documents

The Documents menu is a list of automatically generated links to the last dozen or so documents that were opened. Click the links to open the documents in their default applications.

The shortcuts in this menu are stored in the *\Documents and Settings\{username}\ Recent* folder. To clear this menu, delete the shortcuts in the Recent folder, or go to Control Panel → Taskbar and Start Menu → Start Menu tab → Customize, and click Clear (or Clear List, if you're using the Windows XP style Start menu).

For security reasons, you may wish to disable this menu; see Appendix D for information on TweakUI, which has a feature to clear this list every time Windows is shut down, or even to hide the Documents menu entirely.

Favorites

This is a mirror of the current user's Favorites folder (*\Documents and Settings\ {username}\Favorites*) and the All Users' Favorites folder (*\Documents and Settings\All Users\Favorites*). Although this is the same menu you'll see in Windows Explorer and Internet Explorer, the shortcuts in this menu will launch whatever browser is currently registered as the default.

Internet, E-mail (Windows XP style Start menu only)

These two items are user-customizable links to your favorite web browser and email program, respectively. By default, they're set to Internet Explorer and Outlook Express, but can be replaced with any programs properly registered as web browsers and email clients. See Chapter 5 for details on choosing your own programs here.

Shut Down

See "Shut Down," earlier in this chapter.

Log Off

See "Log Off," earlier in this chapter.

Run

See "Run," earlier in this chapter.

Search

See "Windows Explorer" in Chapter 4.

Settings (classic Start menu only) or Control Panel (Windows XP style Start menu only)

See "Control Panel" in Chapter 4.

Notes

- If you want to place a new shortcut in your Start menu, remove an existing shortcut from your Start menu, or rearrange your Start menu shortcuts, you can drag-drop shortcuts in your Start menu almost as easily as you can in Explorer or on your Desktop. When you start dragging, an insertion line will appear where you can drop the shortcut; if the mouse pointer changes to a circle with a line through it, you're over a portion of the Start menu that can't be customized. To drag new shortcuts into the Start menu, start dragging and hover the mouse cursor over the Start button for a second or two; it will open automatically, allowing you to complete your drag. Finally, you can right-click any shortcut in your Start menu, allowing you to delete it, change its properties, or even rename it in place. I frequently use this feature to make certain application shortcuts more accessible by placing items on the Desktop that otherwise would be buried many menus deep.

- When you first install Windows XP, the shortcuts in your Start menu will be sorted alphabetically. Any subsequent items added to your Start menu will appear at the end of the menu, and will not be sorted automatically. To sort any single menu, right-click on one of its entries and select Sort by Name. To sort all folders in your Start menu, go to Control Panel → Taskbar and Start Menu → Start Menu tab → Classic Start menu → Customize, and click Sort. (Note that this feature is only available in the Customize dialog for the Classic Start menu, so if you're using the new Windows XP-style menu, you'll need to temporarily switch to the classic menu to sort all the folders at once. (See Chapter 8 for another solution.)

- You can also add programs and folders to the top level of the Start menu by dragging and dropping their icons onto the Start button, or by waiting until the Start menu is open and then dropping items onto the space above the built-in entries (see Figure 3-30).

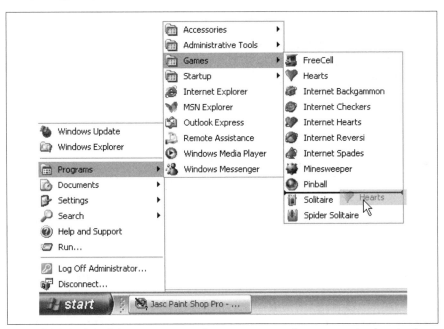

Figure 3-30. Drag and drop items in your Start menu to re-order or reorganize them in place

This will place a shortcut directly into the \Documents and Settings\[username]\ Start Menu folder, as opposed to \Documents and Settings\[username]\Programs. You should do this only for programs that you use fairly often. Good programs to add there might be the Explorer and the Command Prompt (DOS). Adding folders at this level is a great way of organizing all of your programs into categories. Once you have created new folders, you can move the program short-cuts from the Start Menu → Programs folders into your own folders and leave all the other shortcuts (uninstalls, readmes, etc.) behind.

- By default, dragging any files or other objects directly into the Start menu will create shortcuts to those items, which is inconsistent with the way Windows handles drag-drop elsewhere (see Chapter 2). If you're dragging an existing shortcut or a folder full of shortcuts into the Start menu, hold the Shift key to force Windows to move (or the Ctrl key to copy) the items, rather than create shortcuts to them.

- Start → Programs can get fairly cluttered, since most programs add shortcuts to this menu as part of their installation process. Don't be afraid to rearrange and consolidate your shortcuts here; most of them are probably never used anyway.

- If you want programs in the Startup folder to run in a particular order, instead of putting in shortcuts to each program, create a single batch file (see Chapter 6) or a WSH Script (see Chapter 9) that launches the applications in the desired order.

- To bypass the programs in the Startup folder, hold down the Shift key while the system is booting. Keep holding it down until the Desktop has completely loaded.

- In addition to the Startup folder, there are other ways programs can be configured to run at Startup. Services (see Chapter 4) lists many background programs that are run, even if no user has logged on; the Startup folder, since it's a per-user setting, launches programs only after the user has logged in. Other locations include the Registry key, HKEY_LOCAL_MACHINE\Microsoft\Windows\CurrentVersion\Run.

- If you're migrating from Windows 95 or Windows NT 4.0, you may have become accustomed to the way menus are split into multiple columns when there are too many shortcuts. In Windows 98/Me, Windows 2000, and now Windows XP, the default is scrolling menus, which tends to be awkward. This setting can be changed by going to the Start menu, and then to Control Panel → Taskbar and Start Menu → Start Menu tab → Customize and turning off the Scroll Programs option. (It's in the Advanced tab if you're using the Windows XP-style Start menu.)

- Shortcuts that appear in Start → Programs and Start → Favorites are saved for the currently logged-on user, as noted several times throughout this section. If you have more than one user configured on your machine and you want any of these items to appear for all of those users (as everyone may wish to use the installed word processor, for example), open Explorer and navigate to the \Documents and Settings folder. There's a folder for each configured user, as well as an All Users folder, and a Default User folder (a template for subsequently added users). You may wish to delegate shortcuts to these various folders, depending on their use. Note that if a shortcut is listed in a user's personal Start Menu folder as well as the All Users Start Menu folder, it will appear twice in that user's Start menu. The same goes for the Desktop and Send To folders (both discussed earlier in this chapter).

Status Bar

The Status Bar is a panel at the bottom of each window (part of the same frame that contains the titlebar) that gives information about the contents of the window. The standard status bar shown in Figure 3-31 has several sections, each of which is used to show a relevant statistic or setting.

Figure 3-31. The Status Bar often shows useful information; in Windows Explorer, the free disk space or the combined size of the selected objects is shown

Some elements of the status bar respond to clicks and double-clicks, although there's no standard for any user interaction. If an application has a status bar, it can usually be hidden or made visible as an entry in the View menu. Some programs even let you configure the status bar with the information that is important to you. (Try right-clicking on the status bar for configuration options.)

The Status Bar in the Windows Explorer, for example, shows the number and combined size of the selected files, as well as the amount of free space on the drive. And when you're navigating through menus, you'll see a tip for the currently selected menu item in the Status Bar. One especially useful tip is the one that appears for Edit → Undo, as it shows exactly which file operation(s) will be undone.

System Tray

See "Notification Area."

Tabbed Dialogs

Tabs are used in dialog boxes when there are too many settings to fit on the same page. (See Figure 3-32.)

Activate a tab by clicking on it. The active tab (or page) is visibly more prominent than the rest, and the displayed settings typically fall within the category depicted by the caption of the selected tab.

The rule, when changing settings in a dialog box, is that all settings behave as though they were all on the same page. That is, if you change a setting under one tab, switch to another tab and change a setting there, and then click OK, both settings will be implemented. Unfortunately, some application developers don't follow these rules. Sometimes the tab selection itself is a setting; in the example above, this means that only one of these settings would be implemented and the other would be lost. The other problem occurs when settings are saved when you flip between taps.

Press Ctrl-Tab to move to the next tabbed page or Shift-Ctrl-Tab to move in reverse.

Taskbar

The Taskbar, shown in Figure 3-33, contains the Start Menu button, buttons representing all open application windows, the notification area (also known as the Tray, discussed earlier in this chapter), and any optional toolbars (see "Toolbars," later).

The User Interface

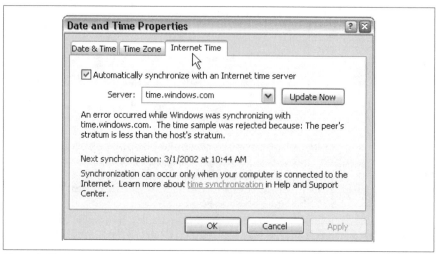

Figure 3-32. Settings in dialog boxes like this one are often divided into separate Tabs; the OK and Apply buttons apply to all tabs simultaneously

Figure 3-33. In addition to your Start button and the notification area, a Taskbar button appears for each open window; click a button to activate the window

The Start button isn't terribly complicated: just click on it to open the Start menu (discussed earlier in this chapter). There are two choices for the look of the Start button, each part of the currently selected style (see "Style," at the beginning of this chapter). Unfortunately, there's no way to customize the look of the Start button without a third-party add-on.

You can keep tabs on all running applications by looking in the portion of the Taskbar between the Start button and the notification area (Tray). Nearly every currently open window is represented by a button on your Taskbar. Click the button of a corresponding window to bring that window to the top (if it happens to be obscured) and shift focus to that window. If the window is currently active, clicking its Taskbar button will minimize (hide) it. The currently active window appears pushed in, while any others (if any) appear as normal buttons. If a window has been minimized (see "Windows," later in this chapter), it will also appear as a normal button, indistinguishable from those for visible windows. Right-click on a Taskbar button to access the window's control menu (see "Windows"), allowing you, among other things, to close a window without first having to restore it.

 If an application is busy, clicking a Taskbar icon sometimes won't activate the window. If this happens, try right-clicking on the Taskbar icon and selecting Restore. If an application has crashed and you're unable to shut it down gracefully, you can often close it by right-clicking its Taskbar button and selecting Close. Although this doesn't always work, it is much quicker and more convenient than using the Windows Task Manager (discussed in Chapter 4).

By default, the Taskbar appears at the bottom of the screen, but it can be dragged to the top or either side by grabbing any empty portion of the Taskbar with the mouse (unless it's locked—see below). You can also resize the Taskbar by grabbing its edge.

Right-click on an empty area of the Taskbar to pop up its context menu.

Toolbars
Show or hide any of the Taskbar toolbars (discussed later in this chapter) or the Address Bar (discussed earlier in this chapter).

Cascade Windows
Arrange all windows (except those that are minimized) so that they appear "cascaded:" the window on the bottom of the pile will be moved to the upper-left of your Desktop, the next will appear just slightly lower and to the right, and so on.

Tile Windows Horizontally, Vertically
Arrange all windows (except those that are minimized) so that they don't overlap and that, together, they fill the screen. Horizontal tiling results in wider windows and vertical tiling results in taller, narrower windows.

Show the Desktop
Bring the Desktop to the top of the pile, covering all open windows. This has the same effect as minimizing all open windows, except that you can then use Show Open Windows to quickly drop the Desktop back down to the bottom and restore all windows to their previous states. Note that the "Minimize all Windows" option found here in previous versions of Windows has been removed in Windows XP, but you can still quickly minimize all open windows by holding the Windows logo key and pressing D.

Task Manager
Open the Windows Task Manager (see Chapter 4).

Lock the Taskbar
If you lock the Taskbar, you won't be able to move or resize it, nor will you be able to move or resize any Taskbar toolbars that happen to be docked. If you find yourself accidentally messing up the Taskbar, locking it will eliminate the problem. Most toolbars in Windows can be locked in this way. Note also that locking the toolbar will hide the resize handles, giving you a little more Taskbar real estate for your task buttons.

Properties
This is the same as Control Panel → Taskbar and Start Menu, which is the same as Start → Settings → Taskbar and Start Menu and as right-clicking the Start button and selecting Properties. See "Taskbar and Start Menu Properties" properties in Chapter 4 for details on these settings, as well as "Style," at the beginning of this chapter.

Notes

- To activate the Taskbar buttons with the keyboard, first press Ctrl-Esc to show the Start menu, then Esc to close it, and then Tab to send focus to the task buttons. Use the cursor keys to navigate, and press the spacebar to activate a window or Shift-F10 to display it's control menu. It's usually preferable to simply use Alt-Tab (or Shift-Alt-Tab to go in reverse) to cycle through the open windows rather than this elaborate procedure. While we're at it, you can also press Alt-Esc to send a window to the bottom of the pile (an alternative to minimizing it).

- From time to time, Explorer (the application responsible for the Taskbar, Desktop, and Start menu) will crash, and the Taskbar and all your Desktop icons will disappear. Now there's a built-in safeguard that relaunches Explorer automatically if such a crash is detected, but it doesn't always work as it's designed. For example, if you have a separate Windows Explorer window open and the "Launch folder windows in a separate process" option (Control Panel → Folder Options → View tab) is enabled, and the Taskbar disappears, Windows will mistakenly open another Windows Explorer window instead of reinstating your Taskbar and Desktop. If this happens, you'll need to close all visible Windows Explorer windows. Then, press Ctrl-Alt-Del, and click Task Manager. In the Windows Task Manager application that appears, go to File → New Task (Run), type explorer, and click OK.

- Some applications have icons in the Notification Area (or Tray, discussed earlier in this chapter) instead of Taskbar buttons. A few applications have both and some have neither. If an application window has no Taskbar button, it will not be accessible when you press Alt-Tab (used to switch between running applications).

- By default, the Taskbar "groups" similar task buttons together. But what does this mean? Most applications are capable of opening several documents simultaneously without having several separate instances of the application, a design known as multiple document interface (MDI). This not only saves memory and screen real estate, but it makes comparing documents side by side and sharing information between multiple documents much easier. In Office 2000, and now Office XP, Microsoft has unfortunately tried to abolish MDI in favor of separate single document interface (SDI) windows.* The consequence was increased clutter on the Taskbar, so Microsoft came up with task button grouping, which consolidates all of the open documents of an SDI application into a single button. To enable or disable this option, go to Control Panel → Taskbar and Start Menu → Taskbar tab.

- See "Taskbar and Start Menu Properties" in Chapter 4 for more settings that affect the Taskbar. Among the more useful are the "Auto-hide the Taskbar" and "Keep the Taskbar on top of other windows" options.

Text Boxes

See "Input Fields."

Title Bars

See "Windows."

---

* Their reason for this change is reportedly due to confusion among new users regarding the use of the MDI interface. Unfortunately, in my opinion, their cure was much worse than the disease. Most third-party application developers have not instituted this design. Furthermore, Office 2000 and Office XP both have the option of using the MDI interface. See *http://www.annoyances.org/exec/show/article08-805* for details.

Toolbars

Toolbars are used to provide quick access to frequently used functions in a program. Windows comes with several toolbars, including those found in Windows Explorer, Internet Explorer, Wordpad (and other applications), and the Quick Launch toolbars on the Taskbar (see Figure 3-34).

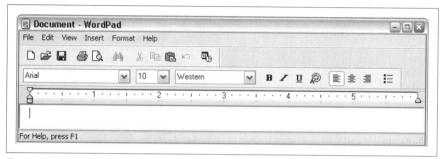

Figure 3-34. Wordpad's toolbar provides access to eleven of the most commonly used functions, such as Open, Save, Print, and Find

Usually, the buttons in a toolbar don't provide any functionality that isn't otherwise accessible through the menus or via a keystroke or two. Toolbars are almost exclusively mouse oriented, so a toolbar that works with the keyboard is a rare occurrence.

The toolbars in most modern applications are configurable; that is, you can rearrange the tools to your liking, add new items, and remove the ones you don't use. It's definitely worth taking a few minutes to configure the toolbar with the features that you use the most, especially since the default toolbars in most applications are set up to showcase the most marketable features of the product rather than to make the program easier to use.

The configuration and features of a particular toolbar is typically the responsibility of the application that owns it, although most modern applications use Microsoft's toolbar controls, which afford a good degree of consistency.

You can often right-click on an empty portion of a toolbar to change its properties or to add or remove buttons. Toolbars can usually be "docked" to the top, bottom, or sides of an application, or they can float. Play around with toolbars to get a feel for how they respond to being dragged and resized; there's no substitute for 30 seconds of fooling around. Some newer toolbars can be "locked" so that they can't be accidentally moved, resized, or closed. I can't tell you how many phone calls I've gotten from frantic friends and relatives telling me that they've lost their toolbars! Locking is a welcome feature, indeed.

Many larger applications, such as WordPerfect Office and Microsoft Office, support multiple toolbars, including custom toolbars you can create as needed. These toolbars can typically be rearranged by dragging them around, although you may not get any visual feedback until you let go. To hide a toolbar, try right-clicking on it, or just drag it (if it's docked) so that it floats and then click the close button in the toolbar's titlebar.

A quick way to customize the buttons on toolbars is to hold the Alt key while dragging or right-clicking (to move a button or changes its properties, respectively). Pressing the Alt key puts the toolbar into "edit" mode temporarily; in fact, you can even drag buttons from one toolbar to another with this method. Note that Taskbar toolbars (see below) are always in edit mode, so the Alt key is not needed.

Toolbars on the Taskbar

In addition to the Desktop and Start menu, shortcuts to frequently used programs can also be placed in configurable toolbars that are either docked on the Taskbar (discussed earlier in this chapter) or are allowed to float.

By default, there are four Taskbar toolbars. Right-click an empty area of the Taskbar and select Toolbars to show or hide any of them. The four toolbars are as follows:

Address
   The Address Bar on the Taskbar is the same as the one in Windows Explorer and Internet Explorer and works very much like Start → Run. See "Address Bar," earlier in this chapter, for details.

Links
   The Links toolbar is designed to hold your favorite Favorites, or, more specifically, links (Internet Shortcuts) to your favorite web sites. This is the same toolbar as the Links toolbar in Internet Explorer (see "Internet Explorer" in Chapter 4). Shortcuts displayed on this toolbar are stored in *\Documents and Settings\ {username}\Favorites\Links*.

Quick Launch
   The Quick Launch toolbar works very much like the Programs menu in the Start menu: it shows any number of shortcuts to your most frequently used programs.

   The Quick Launch toolbar, as well as any other custom toolbars you create (except Desktop, discussed below) are mirrors of folders on your hard disk. For example, the contents of the Quick Launch toolbar are stored in *\Documents and Settings\ {username}\Application Data\Microsoft\Internet Explorer\Quick Launch*. You can get there quickly by right-clicking on an empty portion of the Quick Launch toolbar and selecting Open Folder (see below for other items on this menu).

One of the niftiest icons on the Quick Launch Toolbar is the Show Desktop icon: . Don't delete this one—it's not a shortcut, but rather a Windows Explorer Command (*.scf*) file. It has the same effect as right-clicking on the Taskbar and selecting Show Desktop (see "Taskbar," earlier in this chapter, for details); it pops the Desktop on top of all other windows, allowing access to Desktop icons without having to minimize anything. I find this icon far superior to displaying the Desktop Toolbar.

You can create your own custom toolbars by right-clicking on the Taskbar and selecting Toolbars → New Toolbar. Simply specify an existing folder whose contents you want made into a toolbar (such as Control Panel, Dial-Up Networking, or one of the folders in your Start menu), or click Make New Folder if you want to start with a blank toolbar.

One of the limitations of custom toolbars is that if they're ever closed, Windows won't display them on the list of available toolbars, as with the preconfigured toolbars discussed here. If you ever close a custom toolbar, you'll have to start over and go through the New Toolbar process to get it back (though all your shortcuts will still be there). For a more sophisticated toolbar launcher, go to *http://www.creativelement.com/software/route1.html*

Desktop

The Desktop Toolbar was intended as a handy way to get at the contents of your Desktop when it's covered with open windows. It's really just another custom toolbar (like Quick Launch, discussed above), except that it mirrors the contents of your Desktop folder. Of course, if you have a lot of things on your Desktop, this toolbar can itself get pretty unwieldy, so I don't find it too useful. Your mileage may vary. You'll probably prefer to just use Show Desktop (either the button in the Quick Launch toolbar or the entry on the Taskbar's context menu) for quick access to items on your Desktop.

Once a toolbar is enabled, you can right-click on an empty portion to display a context menu with several options. (Right-clicking one of the toolbar buttons is the same as right-clicking the corresponding shortcut in Explorer.) In addition to the standard entries on the Taskbar context menu (see "Taskbar," earlier in this chapter), you'll find the following:

View → Large Icons, View → Small Icons

Allows you to display either large (32 × 32) or small (16 × 16) icons. Neither choice is perfect; small icons can be very difficult to see and distinguish and large icons take up too much space and offer little advantage over Desktop icons. Choose whichever icons best suit your needs.

Open Folder

Opens the folder to which the toolbar is linked. When customizing a toolbar, it's often easier to deal with the actual shortcuts in a real folder than it is to mess with the buttons on the Toolbar.

Show Text

Displays a text label next to each icon. This is useful if you have a toolbar containing icons of the same type, and if you've got room on your Taskbar to spare. It's the default setting for the Links toolbar, but not for the Quick Launch toolbar.

Show Title

Shows the name of the toolbar when it is docked on the Taskbar; this option has no effect when the toolbar is floating. It's really a waste of space for the standard toolbars, but perhaps it is useful if you set up a lot of custom toolbars. The title can also be used as a handle.

Close Toolbar

Closes the Toolbar. You can also drag the toolbar off the Taskbar and then click the close button to get rid of it. As stated above, closed custom toolbars do not remain on the Toolbars list.

Notes

- Taskbar toolbars can be docked on the Taskbar simply by dragging them there. You can also dock these toolbars along the sides or top of your Desktop, regardless of the position of the Taskbar.

- If a Taskbar toolbar doesn't seem to allow dragging or resizing, right-click on an empty portion of the Taskbar and turn off the "Lock the Taskbar" option.

Tray

See "Notification Area."

Trees

Many different parts of the Windows XP interface are represented by hierarchical trees, like the one in Figure 3-35. This collapsible tree interface can be found in Explorer (representing drives and folders), the Registry Editor (representing Registry Keys), and Device Manager (representing installed devices).

Figure 3-35. The Folder Tree is an efficient and useful way to visualize and navigate the hierarchy of your filesystem

In most cases, displaying all entries in all branches of a tree would take too much time, and would certainly be unwieldy. Instead, branches are "collapsed" and only the top levels are shown; you can expand any branch by clicking the plus sign (+), and then collapse any branch by clicking the corresponding minus sign (-). You can also double-click any branch to expand it, and again to collapse it. If no plus sign (+) appears, then the entry has no "children" and cannot be expanded further.

Navigating trees with the keyboard is often more convenient than using the mouse. As with listboxes (discussed earlier in this chapter), you can jump to any branch by typing the first letter (or first few letters) of its name. This works regardless of the depth of the entry, but only on entries that are currently visible. Use the right arrow key to expand the currently selected branch, or the left arrow key to collapse it; if the branch is already collapsed, the left arrow key jumps to the parent. The Backspace key also jumps to the parent, but it never collapses branches. Finally, the asterisk key (*) expands all branches from the current location.

Turn Off Computer

See "Shut Down."

Windows

The window is the basis for the graphical user interface. Xerox developed the first graphical windowing user interface. This style of interface was first popularized by Apple and later by Microsoft, but Xerox developed the first graphical windowing operating system more than a decade before the first Mac or Windows computer ever saw daylight.

Most windows are rectangular, but irregular shapes are allowed too. (See "Windows Media Player" in Chapter 4 for an example.) Standard windows have a titlebar across the top, which, in addition to identifying the window and the currently open document (if applicable), is used as a handle with which to move the window around the screen (see Figure 3-36). The titlebar also shows which window is currently active; depending on your color settings (set through Control Panel → Display → Appearance tab → Advanced), the titlebar of active window will typically appear darker than the others. (Small floating toolbars in some applications ignore this rule, always appearing either inactive or active.)

Figure 3-36. A garden-variety window, complete with title, menu, and client area

The elements commonly found on window titlebars are described below (any or all might be missing, depending on the type of window).

Control Menu

Click the icon on the upper-left corner of a window or press Alt-Spacebar to display the control menu, which duplicates the Minimize, Maximize, and Close buttons and provides Move and Resize options (see below). Double-click the control menu icon to close the window.

Dialog boxes typically don't have control menu icons, but the menu is still there and can be accessed with Alt-Spacebar. The standard entries in the control menu are present to make it possible to move, resize, minimize, maximize, and close the window with the keyboard. For example, press Alt-Space and then S to resize a window with the cursor keys.

Some windows have additional functions in this menu, especially if those applications don't have full-blown menus. Good examples are the control menus of Windows Explorer and single-folder windows, which are the same as the context menus of the icons that open them. Navigate to *c:\My\Stuff* and click the control menu, and you'll get the same options as though you right-clicked on the Stuff icon in the *c:\My* folder. This, for example, lets you delete a folder without having to first open its parent. You can also drag the control menu icon to move or copy the folder as though you were dragging the folder's icon.

If you see two control menus, one on top of the other, you're using an application (such as a word processor) that can have one or more document windows open simultaneously; see the description of Multiple Document Interface below.

Minimize

Click Minimize to hide a window so that only its task button on the Taskbar is visible. See "Taskbar," earlier in this chapter, for details.

Maximize/Restore

Maximize a window to have it fill the screen. Click the maximize button again to restore it to its free-floating position and size. You can also double-click the titlebar to maximize and restore a window.

Close

Close a window. This is usually the same as selecting File → Close or File → Exit, or at least it's supposed to be. Double-clicking the control menu icon also closes windows, as does Alt-F4.

Most, but not all, windows can be resized by grabbing any edge with the mouse and dragging. Some windows have an additional resize handle on the lower-right corner, which can be a little easier to get a purchase on than the edges.

Multiple Document Interface (MDI) applications have windows within windows, usually allowing multiple documents to be open simultaneously. The MDI parent window, the container of the document windows, usually has a Window menu, which allows you to switch to any open documents and provides some features to arrange the documents visually (Cascade, Tile, etc.). Some applications (Corel's WordPerfect and Qualcomm's Eudora, to name a few) have incorporated a clever Taskbar for their MDI applications, making it easy to manage several document without having to use the somewhat awkward Window menu.

See "Taskbar," earlier in this chapter, for more information on MDI applications and how some newer Microsoft applications are abandoning this design.

Here are some keyboard shortcuts for working with windows:

- Alt-Tab switches between open application windows. Hold Shift to go in reverse.

- Ctrl-Tab (or Ctrl-F6) switches between open documents in an MDI application window. Again, hold Shift to go in reverse.

- Alt-Esc sends the current window to the bottom of the pile and activates the next one in line.

- Alt-F4 closes the current application window. Ctrl-F4 closes the current document in an MDI application window.

- If a window has multiple panes (such as Windows Explorer), use F6 or Ctrl-Tab to switch between them.

Notes

- Some more stylish (read "weird") windows without Taskbars can usually be moved by clicking on any empty area of the window.

- Technically, the Desktop is a window, although it's always at the bottom of the pile (called the Z-order). Conversely, some windows (and even the Taskbar) can be set to "always on top," which means that they're always on top of the pile and can't be covered by other windows (except by other "always on top" windows).
- Also see "Menus" and "Taskbar."

4

Windows XP Applications and Tools

This chapter provides an alphabetical reference to all of the useful components that make up Windows XP: an encyclopedia of everything you can do with Windows out of the box. Some of the more prominent applications and utilities that come with Windows XP are available through shortcuts on the Start menu, but many useful tools aren't as conspicuous—available only to those who know where to look. What you'll undoubtedly find interesting is the large number of applications that aren't listed in the Start menu or documented in the manual or in most books.

At the beginning of each entry, you'll find all the different methods of launching (or opening) these components, including their locations in the Start menu (if applicable), their executable filenames for starting them from the command prompt, or any other means of accessing the component. See Chapter 2 for an overview of all the ways to launch programs in Windows XP.

Using the Command Prompt

You may need to use the command prompt to run some of the programs listed in this chapter (see Figure 4-1). In addition to the command prompt application, *cmd.exe*, two other elements in Windows XP can also be used as command prompts. The Address Bar, typically found at the top of the Internet Explorer window, is where you type a web site address to instruct IE to open the corresponding web page. The Address Bar can also be used as a rudimentary command prompt, where you can type application filenames, document filenames, and even folder names to open them. The Address Bar can appear at the top of any Internet Explorer or Windows Explorer window, and can even be placed on the Taskbar. The other alternative to the command prompt is the Run entry in the Start menu, which behaves nearly identically to the Address Bar. To start an instance of the Command window, select Start → *.cmd* or type cmd ·in the Address Bar of any window.

```
C:\WINDOWS\System32\cmd.exe                                    _ □ ×
Microsoft Windows XP [Version 5.1.2600]
<C> Copyright 1985-2001 Microsoft Corp.

C:\Documents and Settings\Administrator>ipconfig

Windows IP Configuration


Ethernet adapter Local Area Connection:

        Connection-specific DNS Suffix  . : mshome.net
        IP Address. . . . . . . . . . . . : 192.168.0.97
        Subnet Mask . . . . . . . . . . . : 255.255.255.0
        Default Gateway . . . . . . . . . : 192.168.0.1

C:\Documents and Settings\Administrator>_
```

Figure 4-1. Some tools can be used only at the Command Prompt, such as the Windows IP Configuration utility

Applications and Tools

Note that some of the components listed in this chapter are purely command-line based. That is, rather than having interactive windows of their own, they rely on the command prompt application to receive commands and display information. Many of these types of programs (often called console applications) simply close when they've completed their task. This means that if you launch one of these programs from the Start menu or Address Bar, it will simply appear and disappear before you know what happened. To use one of these components, you must first open a command prompt window (*cmd.exe*) and type the command there.

Chapter 6 provides more detail on how to use the command prompt and explains the more subtle differences between the command prompt application and the Address Bar. Chapter 3 documents the Address Bar further.

Alphabetical Reference to Windows Components

The following reference lists all the useful, discrete components that come with Windows XP, sorted alphabetically by their common names (e.g., Minesweeper would be found under "M," not "W" for *winmine.exe*).

Note that some components are not installed by default. The set of components included with a basic Windows XP installation depends on the method by which Windows XP was installed, whether it was installed fresh, or over an older version of Windows. Any of the following components that appear to be missing can be added easily by using Add or Remove Programs (discussed later in this chapter) and clicking the Add/Remove Windows Components button.

Table 4-1 provides an easy cross reference between the common name and the executable filename of an application or other component. Unlike previous editions of this book, control panel options are included in this chapter. For these items, the corresponding command line varies (and is documented more completely in the Control Panel section in this chapter), but usually consists of the *.cpl* filename, as specified in Table 4-1.

Table 4-1. Executable filenames of the applications and tools in Windows XP

Common application name	Executable filename / command line	Professional edition only
Accessibility Options	*access.cpl*	
Accessibility Wizard	*accwiz.exe*	
Activate Windows	*msoobe.exe*	
Active Connections Utility	*netstat.exe*	
Add Hardware Wizard	*hdwwiz.cpl*	
Add or Remove Programs	*appwiz.cpl*	
Address Book	*wab.exe*	
Administrative Tools	n/a	✓
At	*at.exe*	
Attrib	*attrib.exe*	
Backup	*ntbackup.exe*	✓
Boot Configuration Manager	*bootcfg.exe*	✓
Cabinet (CAB) maker	*makecab.exe, diantz.exe*	
Calculator	*calc.exe*	
Character Map	*charmap.exe*	
Chkdsk	*chkdsk.exe*	
Chkntfs	*chkntfs.exe*	
Clipbook Viewer	*clipbrd.exe*	
Command Prompt	*cmd.exe*	
Component Services (console)	*dcomcnfg.exe*	
Computer Management	*compmgmt.msc*	
Connection Manager Profile Installer	*cmstp.exe*	
Control Panel	*control.exe*	
Create Shared Folder	*shrpubw.exe*	
Date and Time	*timedate.cpl*	
DDE Share	*ddeshare.exe*	
Device Manager	*devmgmt.msc*	
DirectX Diagnostic Tool	*dxdiag.exe*	
Disk Cleanup	*cleanmgr.exe*	
Disk Defragmenter	*defrag.exe*	
DiskPart	*diskpart.exe*	
Display Properties	*desk.cpl*	
Dr. Watson	*drwatson.exe, drwtsn32.exe*	
Driver Verifier Manager	*verifier.exe*	
DriverQuery	*driverquery.exe*	✓
Event Viewer (console)	*eventvwr.exe*	
FAT to NTFS Conversion Utility	*convert.exe*	
Fax Console	*fxsclnt.exe*	
Fax Cover Page Editor	*fxscover.exe*	
File Compare (comp)	*comp.exe*	

Table 4-1. Executable filenames of the applications and tools in Windows XP (continued)

Common application name	Executable filename / command line	Professional edition only
File Compare (fc)	*fc.exe*	
File Expansion Utility	*expand.exe*	
Files and Settings Transfer Wizard	*migwiz.exe*	
Finger	*finger.exe*	
Folder Options	*control.exe folders*	
Font Viewer	*fontview.exe*	
Fonts	*control.exe fonts*	
ForceDOS	*forcedos.exe*	
Format	*format.com*	
FreeCell	*freecell.exe*	
FTP	*ftp.exe, tftp.exe*	
Game Controllers	*joy.cpl*	
Group Policy Refresh Utility	*gpupdate.exe*	✓
Hearts	*mshearts.exe*	
Help and Support Center	*helpctr.exe*	
HyperTerminal	*hypertrm.exe*	
IExpress	*iexpress.exe*	
Internet Backgammon	*bckgzm.exe*	
Internet Checkers	*chkrzm.exe*	
Internet Explorer	*iexplore.exe*	
Internet Hearts	*hrtzzm.exe*	
Internet Options	*inetcpl.cpl*	
Internet Reversi	*rvsezm.exe*	
Internet Spades	*shvlzm.exe*	
Java Command Line Loader	*jview.exe, wjview.exe*	
Keyboard	*main.cpl keyboard*	
Label	*label.exe*	
Local Security Policy	*secpol.msc*	
Logoff	*logoff.exe*	
Microsoft Chat	*winchat.exe*	
Microsoft Magnifier	*magnify.exe*	
Microsoft Management Console	*mmc.exe*	
Microsoft Netmeeting	*conf.exe*	
Minesweeper	*winmine.exe*	
Mouse Properties	*main.cpl*	
Msg	*msg.exe*	
MSN Explorer	*msn6.exe*	
MSN Gaming Zone	*n/a*	
Narrator	*narrator.exe*	
Net	*net.exe*	

Table 4-1. Executable filenames of the applications and tools in Windows XP (continued)

Common application name	Executable filename / command line	Professional edition only
Network Connections	ncpa.cpl	
Network Setup Wizard	n/a	
New Connection Wizard	icwconn1.exe	
Notepad	notepad.exe	
NSLookup	nslookup.exe	
NTFS Compression Utility	compact.exe	
NTFS Encryption Utilitiy	cipher.exe	✓
Object Packager	packager.exe	
ODBC Data Source Administrator	odbcad32.exe	
On-Screen Keyboard	osk.exe	
OpenFiles	openfiles.exe	✓
Outlook Express	msimn.exe	
Paint	mspaint.exe	
Pentium Bug Checker	pentnt.exe	
Performance Log Manager	logman.exe	✓
Performance Logs and Alerts	perfmon.msc	
Phone and Modem Options	telephon.cpl	
Phone Dialer	dialer.exe	
Pinball	pinball.exe	
PING	ping.exe	
Power Options	powercfg.cpl	
Printers and Faxes	control.exe printers	
Private Character Editor	eudcedit.exe	
Program Manager	progman.exe, grpconv.exe	
Query Process	qprocess.exe	
Regional and Language Options	intl.cpl	
Registry Console Utility	reg.exe	
Registry Editor	regedit.exe	
Remote Assistance	rcimlby.exe	
Remote Copy	rcp.exe	
Remote Desktop Connection	mstsc.exe	
Route	route.exe	
Rundll32	rundll32.exe	
Run As	runas.exe	
Scanners and Cameras	wiaacmgr.exe	
Scheduled Tasks	n/a	
Scheduled Tasks Console	schtasks.exe	✓
Security Template Utility	secedit.exe	✓
Send a Fax	fxssend.exe	
Services	services.msc	

Table 4-1. Executable filenames of the applications and tools in Windows XP (continued)

Common application name	Executable filename / command line	Professional edition only
Shutdown	*shutdown.exe*	
Signature Verification Tool	*sigverif.exe*	
Solitaire	*sol.exe*	
Sound Recorder	*sndrec32.exe*	
Sounds and Audio Devices	*mmsys.cpl*	
Speech	*control.exe speech*	
Spider Solitaire	*spider.exe*	
SQL Server Client Network Utility	*cliconfg.exe*	
Subst	*subst.exe*	
Synchronization Manager	*mobsync.exe*	
System Properties	*sysdm.cpl*	
System Configuration Editor	*sysedit.exe*	
System Configuration Utility	*msconfig.exe*	
System Information	*winmsd.exe, msinfo32.exe*	
System Restore	*rstrui.exe*	
Task Manager	*taskmgr.exe*	
Taskbar and Start Menu	n/a	
Taskkill	*taskkill.exe*	✓
Tasklist	*tasklist.exe*	✓
Telnet	*telnet.exe*	
Telnet Administrator	*tlntadmn.exe*	✓
Tracert	*tracert.exe*	
User Accounts	*nusrmgr.cpl*	
Utility Manager	*utilman.exe /start*	
Volume Control	*sndvol32.exe*	
Windows Explorer	*explorer.exe*	
Windows File Checker	*sfc.exe*	
Windows Help System	*winhlp32.exe, hh.exe, winhelp.exe*	
Windows IP Configuration	*ipconfig.exe*	
Windows Media Player	*mplay32.exe, wmplayer.exe*	
Windows Messenger	*msmsgs.exe*	
Windows Movie Maker	*moviemk.exe*	
Windows Picture and Fax Viewer	n/a	
Windows Script Host	*cscript.exe, wscript.exe*	
Windows Update	*wupdmgr.exe*	
WordPad	*wordpad.exe*	

Applications
and Tools

Accessibility Options

\windows\system\access.cpl

Provides options for the accessibility tools in Windows XP

To Open   Control Panel → [Accessibility Options] → Accessibility Options
Command Prompt → access.cpl

Description

Accessibility is Microsoft's term for the collection of tools and settings designed to make a computer easier to use for those with poor eyesight, hearing, or some other physical challenge. The settings in this dialog are shown on the following five tabs:

Keyboard

StickyKeys allows you to use keyboard combinations, such as Shift-Y and Alt-F4, without having to hold down more than one key simultaneously.

FilterKeys lets you configure Windows' behavior when a key is held down, such as how long a key must be held down before it starts to repeat and how fast it repeats once it starts (settings are also available in Control Panel → [Printers and Other Hardware] → Keyboard → Speed). However, FilterKeys also lets you disable keyboard repeat completely.

ToggleKeys instructs the Windows to play sounds whenever you press Caps Lock, Num Lock, or Scroll Lock.

Sounds

SoundSentry lets you substitute visual warnings (e.g., flashing the titlebar or the entire screen) for sounds normally made for the system.

ShowSounds lets you substitute captions for speech and other sounds in programs that support this feature (unfortunately, not many do).

Display

High Contrast is a quick way to choose a color scheme with more contrasting colors, which may make text and other screen elements easier to see. These settings are also available through Control Panel → [Appearance and Themes] → Display → Appearance tab, but this feature also lets you toggle between high contrast and standard colors with a hotkey.

The Cursor Options allow you to adjust the settings of the insertion point (text cursor) so that it is easier to see. To make the mouse pointer easier to see, use large pointers or enable Mouse Trails (which leaves a ghost track when you move the pointer) by going to Control Panel → [Printers and Other Hardware] → Mouse and using the Pointers and Motion tabs, respectively.

Mouse

MouseKeys lets you use keys on the numeric keypad to move the pointer around the screen (see Figure 4-2).

Move the pointer to an object and press Ins to start dragging. Press Del to end the drag. Press the – key to switch "clicking" to the right button. That is, – then 5 to right-click or – then + to right double-click. "Right-click" mode remains enabled until you press / to switch back to left-clicking. Hold down Shift while using the arrow keys to move the pointer pixel by pixel; hold down Ctrl to move in big jumps.

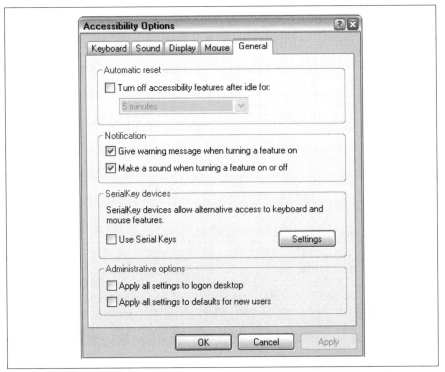

Figure 4-2. The Accessibility Options dialog allows you to enable or disable specific Accessibility tools you want

The Settings dialog box lets you control how fast the pointer moves and how quickly it speeds up when you hold down a key. Higher Top speed and a lower acceleration settings here will make your pointer easier to control. The "Use MouseKeys when Num Lock is [on/off]" option allows you to use MouseKeys without giving up your numeric keypad for cursor movement or numeric entry, whichever you use more.

General

Automatic Reset instructs Windows to automatically turn off all accessibility features after a certain period of inactivity, a useful feature if several people use the same computer and you don't want to have to remember to turn off the features every time you're done using it.

Notification lets you specify whether messages or sounds should be used to let you know when an accessibility option is turned on or off.

SerialKey devices enables the use of special alternative input devices attached to a serial port, allowing you to take the place of your keyboard or mouse with a more appropriate device.

Notes

- All of the settings in this dialog are also covered in Chapter 5.
- As an alternative to the settings found here, the Accessibility Wizard can be used to help you choose which settings are right for you, one-by-one.

See Also

"Accessibility Options," "Control Panel"

Accessibility Wizard

\windows\system32\accwiz.exe

A step-by-step interface designed to help choose accessibility options

To Open   Start → Programs → Accessories → Accessibility → Accessibility Wizard
              Command Prompt → `accwiz`

Description

The Accessibility Wizard is simply an alternate interface to the settings provided in the Accessibility Options dialog (see Figure 4-3). Accessibility is Microsoft's term for the collection of tools and settings designed to make a computer easier to use for those with poor eyesight, hearing, or some other physical challenge. The advantage of the Wizard interface here is that it will walk you through the available options, one-by-one, lending assistance where you may not know which options you need. For example, you can change the font size with predetermined settings based on your needs or disability, rather than by simply changing a numeric value.

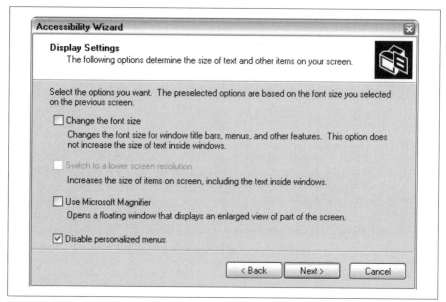

Figure 4-3. The Accessibility Wizard asks questions and sets Accessibility options accordingly

---

Notes

In addition to the settings and utilities normally found in the Accessibility Options window, the Accessibility Wizard also makes it easy to turn off "personalized menus," a feature found in later versions of Windows that shows or hides menu items based on how frequently they're used. Since personalized menus can make Windows more difficult to use, you may want to disable this feature, whether or not you need the other accessibility options.

See Also

"Accessibility Options"

Activate Windows

\windows\system32\oobe\msoobe.exe

The copy protection scheme in Windows XP (see Figure 4-4).

To Open   Start → Settings → Activate Windows
Command Prompt → \windows\system32\oobe\msoobe /A

Description

Product activation is a new and somewhat controversial feature in Windows XP. Intending to curb software piracy, Microsoft now requires that each installed copy of Windows XP be *activated*. This involves contacting Microsoft, either over the Internet or with a telephone call, to obtain a special key to unlock Windows. If Windows is not activated within a certain period, it will expire and refuse to load.

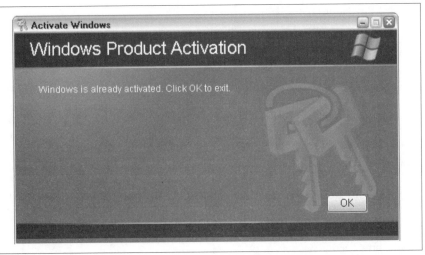

Figure 4-4. Once you've activated Windows XP, you probably won't ever need to again

The sequence of steps to install and activate Windows is as follows:

1. During the installation of Windows, type the 25-character CD Key provided with the Windows XP installation CD. The CD Key distinguishes one end-user license of Windows from another.

2. Windows then generates a 20-digit product ID based on the CD Key and the Windows version.

3. You, the user, transmit the "Installation ID," comprised of the 20-digit product ID plus an 8-digit hardware ID, to Microsoft. The hardware ID, a unique number based on values obtained from hardware in your computer (see below), distinguishes one computer from another.

4. Microsoft responds with a 42-digit Confirmation ID, which is fed into Windows to activate it.

5. Since the confirmation ID is based upon the unique CD key and the unique hardware ID, it represents a single, unique system. If someone attempts to activate Windows with the same CD Key and a different hardware key (representing the same copy of Windows being installed on more than one computer), the copy protection will kick in and the product activation will fail.

Notes

- The Hardware ID is based on a *hardware hash*, a long sequence of numbers based on a information found in your computer's hardware. The specific devices used are as follows:

  - Display adapter (video card)
  - SCSI adapter (if available)
  - IDE adapter
  - Network adapter MAC address (if available)
  - RAM amount range
  - Processor type
  - Processor serial number
  - Hard drive
  - Hard drive volume serial number
  - CD-ROM, CD-RW, or DVD-ROM

- In theory, you should be able to upgrade one or two of these components without causing a problem. However, if you replace the motherboard or upgrade several components at once, the hardware ID will change significantly. Since Windows XP compares the confirmation ID against the hardware ID every time Windows is started, a change in the hardware ID will probably void the activation, and you'll have to reactivate Windows.

- It probably goes without saying that the automated activation will probably fail at this point, meaning that you'll have to speak with a Microsoft representative and explain that you're merely reinstalling and not pirating the software. It remains to be seen how much hassle reactivation will be; those who upgrade often will bear the brunt of that hassle.

- If a virus attacks or your computer crashes and you're forced to format your hard disk and reinstall Windows, you'll have to activate Windows again. However since the hardware will probably not have changed, there should be no problem.

- Aside from the hassle involved, the primary focus of the controversy lies in the process by which Microsoft gathers information about users' hardware configurations and how they monitor subsequent alterations. Although Microsoft insists that the online activation is benign, you may want to stick with the tedious telephone activation procedure to be on the safe side.

- Many users may not be confronted with product activation at all. Systems purchased with Windows XP preinstalled may be preactivated as well, in one of two possible ways. Either the manufacturer may choose to activate Windows using the method described above, or by a separate mechanism called System Locked Pre-installation (SLP). SLP ties the hardware ID to the system BIOS, rather than the discrete components listed above. The resulting system may be upgraded more freely, but if the motherboard is replaced or the BIOS is upgraded, the owner will have to reactivate windows as described above. The other exception is the version of Windows XP sold with a volume license, usually to large businesses, which doesn't include the product activation feature at all.

See Also

"Fully Licensed WPA Paper" at *http://www.licenturion.com/xp/*

Active Connections Utility

\windows\system32\netstat.exe

Displays protocol statistics and current TCP/IP network connections.

To Open   Command Prompt → netstat

Usage   netstat [-a] [-e] [-n] [-o] [-p *proto*] [-r] [-s] [*interval*]

Description

Type netstat by itself to list the active incoming and outgoing network connections. This can be useful, for example, to determine exactly what is being transmitted or received across the network at any given time.

The Active Connections Utility accepts these options:

-a

   Display all connections and open ports (see Notes).

-e

   Display Ethernet statistics; it can be combined with -s.

-n

   Display addresses and ports in a numerical format (e.g., 192.168.0.1:88).

-o

   Display the process that owns each listed connection.

-p *proto*

   Show the connections corresponding to the protocol; the protocol can be IP, IPv6, ICMP, ICMPv6, TCP, TCPv6, UDP, or UDPv6.

-r

   Display the routing table (see "Route," later in this chapter).

-s

   Display statistics for each protocol. By default, statistics are shown for all protocols, but this display can be filtered with the -p option.

interval

Repeatedly run `netstat`, pausing *interval* seconds between each display. Press Ctrl-C to stop the display at any time. If omitted, `netstat` will display the current statistics once and then quit.

Information is displayed in the following columns:

Proto

The protocol—usually TCP for the TCP/IP protocol used on the Internet and most local networks

Local Address

The name of the local machine, followed by a colon, and then the process ID of the application that has initiated the connection

Foreign Address

The name or IP address of the remote machine, followed by a colon, and then the port number

State

Shows whether the connection is established or broken

Notes

- You must have an open command prompt window to use netsat; otherwise, the window closes before you can read the program's output.

- The the -a parameter is especially useful, as it lists all currently open ports. Open ports can sometimes compromise security, so it's best to know about any back doors. See Chapter 7 for more information.

- Type `netstat /?` at the command prompt for a description of the command-line options.

See Also

"OpenFiles"

Add Hardware Wizard

\windows\system\hdwwiz.cpl

Detect non-plug-and-play devices and install the appropriate drivers.

To Open   Control Panel → Add Hardware
Command Prompt → `hdwwiz.cpl`

Description

When you turn on your computer, Windows automatically scans for any newly added plug-and-play (PnP) devices and installs drivers for any that are found. If you're trying to install a device that isn't detected automatically, you'll need to run the Add Hardware Wizard (see Figure 4-5).

When you start the Add Hardware Wizard and click Next, it goes through the following steps:

1. The wizard scans your system for any newly attached PnP devices. If one or more devices are found, the appropriate drivers are located and installed. This process happens every time Windows is started.

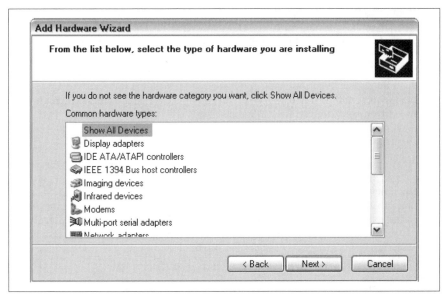

Figure 4-5. If Windows doesn't detect your newly installed hardware automatically, you'll need to use the Add Hardware Wizard

2. If no new devices are found in Step 1, you'll be asked if the device has been connected to the system yet. If you choose no, the wizard quits.

3. The next step, assuming you selected yes in Step 2, displays a list of all of your existing devices. If you select one of the devices and click Next, the wizard will quit. Instead, scroll to the bottom of the list and select "Add a new hardware device" and click Next.

4. Your next choice is between having Windows search for and install your new hardware, or having it present a list from which you can manually select a driver. Choose the first option, "Search for and install..." if you don't already have a driver. Otherwise, choose the second option, "Install the hardware...," and click Next.

5. Chose the category of the device, or just select Show All Devices if you're feeling lazy, and click Next.

6. If you have the drivers for the device, either on a floppy, a CD, or on your hard disk, click Have Disk at this point. Otherwise, choose the manufacturer of the device from the list on the left and then the specific model number from the list on the right. If your device doesn't show up here, then drivers for it aren't included with Windows XP.

7. The last steps involve copying and installing the drivers, and then prompting you to restart (if applicable).

Notes

• When Windows discovers new hardware, either during startup or when using the Add Hardware Wizard, you'll usually be prompted to specify a driver. The "Install Software Automatically" option is usually the best choice, as it will attempt to use one of Window's built-in drivers. If no compatible driver can be found, you'll be prompted to insert a disk or point to a folder containing appropriate drivers, either shipped with the hardware product or downloaded from the manufacturer's web site, respectively.

- When installing some drivers, Windows XP may complain that the driver is not digitally signed. This confusing and rather harsh message simply informs you that the manufacturer of the driver you're installing hasn't added a digital signature to the driver software, which, in most cases, will pose no problem. Just click Continue Anyway to proceed. See the "Signature Verification Tool," later in this chapter, for more information on driver signing.

- See "Control Panel," later in this chapter, for information on finding Add Hardware when using the Control Panel in Category View.

- Some new devices, especially printers and USB peripherals, have specific installation procedures that must be followed. For example, you may need to install the included software first, and then connect the device. When Windows detects the device, the drivers are already in place and installation proceeds without a hitch. Make sure you review the installation instructions before you resort to the Add Hardware Wizard.

See Also

"Control Panel"

Add or Remove Programs

\windows\system32\appwiz.cpl

Uninstall applications and add or remove Windows XP components.

To Open   Control Panel → Add or Remove Programs
Command Prompt → `appwiz.cpl`

Description

The Add or Remove Programs window has three sections:

Change or Remove Programs

A list of all your installed applications, or at least those applications that were registered for uninstallation, is displayed here. The Add or Remove Programs dialog doesn't actually perform any software removal; rather, it launches the uninstall utility that was registered when the application was originally installed. Some uninstallers have the capability to selectively add or remove components of the application, while others simply delete all the files that were copied during installation.

Select an application by clicking its name. Note that this listing can take a little getting used to, as the entries change size when they're selected. If the application has provided such information, you'll see the amount of disk space consumed by the installation, as well as how often the program is used. Click Change/Remove to launch the uninstaller for the selected program.

Uninstaller programs vary widely, but most will display a progress indicator and explain what they're removing, what they're not removing, and whether or not you need to restart your computer. Along the way, though, you may be prompted to remove shared files. Each shared file is registered with Windows, along with a numeric counter; applications that use the file increase the counter when they're installed and decrease the counter when they're removed. When the counter reaches zero, uninstallers assume the files are no longer needed and prompts for their removal; unless you specifically know that a file should not be deleted for some reason, just answer yes (see Figure 4-6).

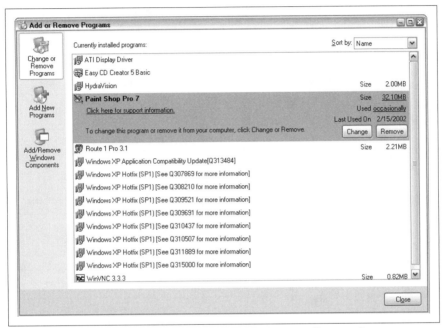

Figure 4-6. The Add or Remove Programs dialog lets you uninstall any application on your computer

Add New Programs
There's not much point to this section. The first button simply looks for the file, *setup.exe*, in your floppy drive and CD drive, and if found, launches it. The second button launches Windows Update (discussed later in this chapter).

Add/Remove Windows Components
The Windows Components Wizard lets you add or remove any of the optional programs that come with Windows XP. Select a category and click Details to selectively install or remove any particular component. Note the Description below the list for a one-line explanation of the component, or refer to the corresponding section in this chapter for more information.

Notes

- You can remove entries from the Change or Remove Programs list without actually uninstalling the corresponding applications using TweakUI (see Appendix D).

- Applications are registered in Add or Remove Programs with keys in the Registry key, `HKEY_LOCAL_MACHINE\SOFTWARE\Microsoft\Windows\CurrentVersion\Uninstall`.

See Also
"Control Panel"

Address Book
\program files\outlook express\wab.exe

A database containing names, addresses, and other contact information, used by Outlook Express and other Windows applications

To Open   Start → Programs → Accessories → Address Book
Start → Search → For People
Outlook Express → Tools menu → Address Book
Command Prompt → wab

Description
The main window in the Address Book is set up somewhat like Explorer, with a hierarchical view of folders in the left pane and a list of addresses contained in the currently selected folder in the right pane, as shown in Figure 4-7.

Figure 4-7. The Address Book lets you organize your contacts and is used primarily with Outlook and Outlook Express

To add a new entry to your address book, select New Contact from the File menu, or right-click an empty area of the right pane, and select New, and then New Contact. In the window that appears, type all the relevant information about this contact in the spaces provided. If you're setting up an entry simply for emailing, it's only necessary to enter the name and an email address. (Be sure to click the Add button after you've typed the email address but before you click OK.)

Notes
- Contacts can be divided into folders, either to differentiate one user's contact list from another's or to organize contacts into categories. It's important to understand the distinction between folders and groups. A group is a single address book entry intended to contain multiple email addresses. For example, if you frequently find yourself sending messages to the same collection of people, create a group entry that lists all of those people. Specifying that group name as the single recipient of a message will send the message to all members of the group.

- The Address Book is linked to the applications that use it in two different ways. First, you can open the address book, select a name, and then choose the appropriate program from the action list (accessible either through the Action button

---

on the Toolbar, or through the Tools menu). Second, when it comes time to enter a contact in your communications program (such as the recipient in an email message), there's often a button that allows you to easily select an entry for the address book. Note that not all applications that use addresses are designed to work with the Address Book application; naturally, you can simply copy and paste information as needed with any application.

- You can also access entries in your Address Book without opening the Address Book application. Select Search and then "For People" from the Start menu to look up a name (see Figure 4-8). Furthermore, you can use any of several online directories to obtain a new contact information. To configure the list of online directory services, open Address Book and select Accounts from the Tools menu. These services are typically free, sponsored by advertising, and based on information already made publicly available in phonebooks and other sources. Privacy advocates may wish to investigate their own inclusion in these lists and take appropriate actions, such as contacting these services to have personal information removed.

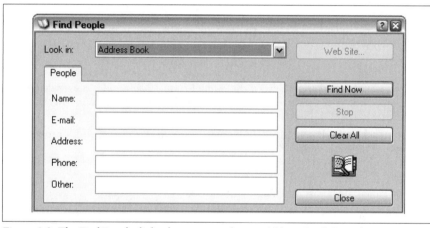

Figure 4-8. The Find People dialog lets you search your Address Book from the Start menu

- Note that some viruses use your Address Book to duplicate themselves by sending harmful attachments to everyone in your contact list via Outlook Express. Aside from not opening email attachments without first scanning them with antivirus software, you can avoid this problem by using a different program for your email and contact list.

See Also

"Microsoft NetMeeting," "Outlook Express," "Phone Dialer"

Administrative Tools

Shortcuts for several important administrative utilities in Windows XP Professional. (The Administrative Tools folder is included with Windows XP Professional only.)

To Open   Control Panel → [Performance and Maintenance] →
Administrative Tools
Command Prompt → `control admintools`

Description

The Administrative Tools entry in Control Panel is nothing more than a standard Start Menu folder full of shortcuts to programs listed elsewhere in this chapter. The folder is stored in *\Documents and Settings\All Users\Start Menu\Programs\Administrative Tools*, and the shortcuts included in this folder, by default, are:

- Component Services
- Computer Management
- Data Sources (ODBC)
- Event Viewer
- Local Security Policy
- Performance
- Services

Since this is a standard folder, you can remove any of these items or add any of your own shortcuts as you see fit.

Notes

- Like other Start menu folders, if the *Administrative Tools* folder is ever deleted or renamed (or if any of its contents are deleted or modified), Windows will not recreate it.
- See "Taskbar and Start Menu Properties," later in this chapter, for an option to show or hide this item in the Start menu.

See Also

"Control Panel," "Microsoft Management Console"

At
\windows\system32\at.exe

Schedules commands and programs to run on a computer at a specified time and date.

To Open   Command Prompt → at

Usage   at [\\computer] time [/interactive] [/every:date] "command"
at [\\computer] [id] [/delete] [/yes]

Description

At is the command-line interface to the Scheduled Tasks feature, discussed later in this chapter. Given the somewhat tedious wizard interface used to create new tasks in the Scheduled Tasks window, At is a refreshing and user-friendly alternative.

To use At, you can simply type something like:

    at 11:15 /interactive notepad

---

which would instruct Windows XP to launch Notepad at 11:15 AM today. When you enter the command and press Enter, At responds with something like:

```
Added a new job with job ID = 1
```

and a corresponding entry appears in the Scheduled Tasks window. The ID is used only to subsequently delete tasks with At (using the second Usage, shown above), like this:

```
at 1 /delete
```

The following options extend the usefulness of At:

\\computer

Specify the name of a remote computer on the network to add the new task to that computer's scheduled tasks list, rather than that of the local computer.

time

The time of day to run the task, specified in 24-hour (military) time. Type 5:20 for 5:20 in the morning, 17:20 for 5:20 in the afternoon, 12:00 for noon, and 0:00 for midnight.

/interactive

If you omit the /interactive option, the task will be run invisibly in the background. For example, if you were to launch Notepad with the example above without specifying /interactive, there would be no visible evidence that Notepad is running, except for its listing in the processes tab of the Task Manager (discussed later in this chapter). You may want to run an application in the background if you do not want to interfere with any foreground applications. Use caution when starting background processes, however, since won't be able to interact with them at all, other than closing them with Task Manager.

/every:date, /next:date

By default, At creates one-time tasks, executed only on the date when they were created; if you were to type the example above at 4:00 in the afternoon, for example, the task would never run. To specify the day or a range of days, use the /every or /next options.

For example, to run Disk Defragmenter at 11:15 PM every Thursday, type:

```
at 23:15 /every:thursday dfrg.msc
```

To run Disk Defragmenter at 11:15 AM on the 21st day of every month, type:

```
at 11:15 /every:21 dfrg.msc
```

To specify multiple days, separate them with commas. To run Solitaire at 3:45 in the afternoon (note the mandatory use of 24-hour time) on both Tuesdays and Thursdays, type:

```
at 15:45 /interactive /every:tuesday,thursday sol
```

The /next option works similarly, although /every and /next should not be used together. To run Chkdsk at 6:33 PM next Saturday, type:

```
at 18:33 /next:saturday chkdsk
```

/delete

Use /delete to remove one or all tasks. Specify the task ID (described earlier in this section) to end that task, or omit the ID to delete all tasks. If you try to delete all tasks, At will ask you to confirm; use the optional /yes option to bypass the prompt. Only tasks originally created with At can be deleted in this way; all other tasks will be left alone.

/yes

Include /yes to bypass the prompt that appears when you try to delete all tasks.

Notes

- The Schedule service must be running to use At. To see if it is running, open the Scheduled Tasks window and select the Advanced menu. If the first menu item is "Stop using Task Scheduler," the service is active; click the item to turn the service off. Conversely, click "Start using Task Scheduler" to turn the service back on.

- To choose the user account under which tasks created with the At command are run, open the Scheduled Tasks window and select At Service Account from the Advanced menu.

- The Scheduled Tasks Console, discussed later in this chapter, is intended to replace At. Although the Scheduled Tasks Console is a little more full featured, At is much easier to use.

See Also

"Scheduled Tasks"

Attrib   \windows\system32\attrib.exe

Change or view the attributes of one or more files or folders.

To Open   Command Prompt → attrib

Usage   attrib [+r|-r] [+a|-a] [+s|-s] [+h|-h] [filename] [/s [/d]]

Description

Attrib allows you to change the file and folder attributes from the command line—settings otherwise only available in a file's or folder's Properties window. The attributes can be thought of as switches, independently turned on or off for any file or group of files. The individual attributes are as follows:

R (read-only)

Turn on the read-only attribute of a file or folder to protect it from accidental deletion or modification. If you attempt to delete a read-only file, Windows will prompt you before allowing you to delete it. Different applications handle read-only files in different ways; usually you will not be allowed to save your changes to the same filename.

A (archive)

The archive attribute has no effect on how file is used, but it is automatically turned on when a file is modified or created. It is used primarily by a backup software to determine which files have changed since a backup was last performed; most backup programs turn off the archive attribute on each file that is backup.

S (system)

Files with the system attribute are typically used to boot the computer. There's little reason ever to modify a file with the system attribute, or to ever turn on or off the system attribute for any file. If you turn off the system attribute of an important file, it may stop the file from working. See Notes, below, to display or hide system files.

H (hidden)

To hide any file or folder from plain view in Explorer or on the Desktop, turn on its hidden attribute. See Notes, below, to display or hide hidden files.

Examples

To hide a file in Explorer, right-click on it, select Properties, and turn on the hidden option. To hide the same file using the command line, type:

    attrib +h *filename*

where *filename* is the full path and filename of the file to change. To specify multiple files, include a wildcard, such as *.* (for all files) or *.txt (for all files with the *.txt* filename extension). Note the use of the plus sign (+) to turn on an attribute; use the minus sign (-) to turn it off. For example, to turn off the hidden attribute and simultaneously turn on the archive attribute, type:

    attrib -h +a *filename*

To display the attributes of a file or a group of files in Explorer, select Details from the View menu. Then, select Choose Details from the View menu and turn on the Attributes option. To display the attributes of a file or a group of files on the command line, type:

    attrib *filename*

where *filename* is the full path and filename(s) of the files you wish to view. Omit *filename* to display the attributes of all the files in the current folder. If *filename* is not used, or if it contains wildcards (in other words, if the command is intended to act on more than one file), you can use the /s option to further include the contents of all subfolders of the current folder. The /d option instructs Attrib to act upon folders as well as files, but only has meaning if it is used in conjunction with the /s parameter.

Notes

- By default, files with the system or hidden attributes are not shown in Explorer. To display system and hidden files, go to Explorer → Folder Options → View and select "Show hidden files and folders." If hidden and system files are shown, they will appear with faded icons.

- Attrib allows you to change the system attribute, something you can't do by right-clicking and selecting Properties. Attrib does not, however, let you change the Advanced attributes, such as those concerned with indexing, compression, or encryption. Note that the "File is ready for archiving" option in the Advanced Attribute window (right-click → Properties → Advanced) is the same as the Archive attribute just discussed (see Figure 4-9).

See Also

"Backup"

Backup

\windows\system32\ntbackup.exe

Backup (copy) files from your hard drive to a tape drive, second hard drive, or other removable storage device for the purpose of safeguarding or archiving your data. (Backup is included with Windows XP Professional only.)

Applications and Tools

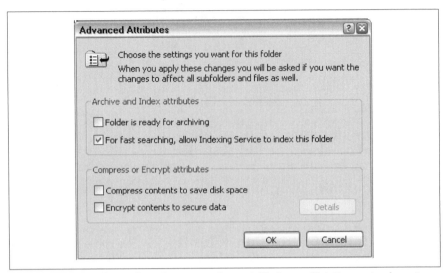

Figure 4-9. These advanced attributes are only available from a file's Properties sheets in Windows Explorer

To Open   Start → Programs → Accessories → System Tools → Backup
Command Prompt → ntbackup

Description

Microsoft Backup works by creating a backup set—a collection of selected files to be backed up to a removable storage device. This backup set, along with all the selected options available in Backup (e.g., data compression, password protection, error report listing, etc.) are known collectively as a backup "job."

To begin creating a backup job, choose the Backup tab and use the familiar Explorer-like two-pane view to navigate through your folders. Click on the checkbox next to a file to select it for backup; click the checkbox next to a folder to select it and all of its contents for backup (see Figure 4-10). A blue checkmark appears next to each folder or file to be backed up; a gray checkmark appears next to each folder name with only some of its contents selected.

When you're done selecting files, choose Job → Save Selections to save your selections into a *.bks* file.

Next, choose a Backup destination from the list below the folder tree. If you have more than one backup device, choose the desired drive here. If you have no dedicated backup hardware, the only option will be "File," which is used to back up to your hard disk. If you choose File, the "Backup media or filename" field is used to specify the name of the single file in which to store the backed up data (usually a *.bkf* file).

Finally, select Options from the Tools menu, and then choose the Backup Type tab to choose how files are backed up. The different backup types are as follows:

Normal
Backs up all the selected files. The archive attribute (see "Attrib," earlier in this chapter) is automatically turned off for each file that is backed up.

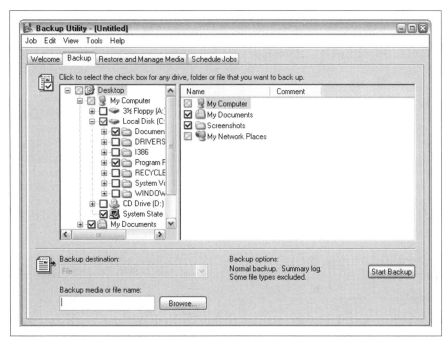

Figure 4-10. Choose the drives, folders, and files you wish to back up by placing checkmarks next to them in the Backup Utility

Copy

The same as normal, above, except that the archive attribute is left alone.

Differential

Backs up only the files with a Last Modified date that is more recent than the last backup performed with the Backup application. This backup type affords a quicker backup, but since it relies on previous backups, it may not be the best choice when backing up important data.

Incremental

Backs up only those files with the archive attribute turned on. This option really only makes sense when used after a "Normal" backup, described above, as it relies heavily on the archive attribute. Like the differential backup, it is quicker than the Normal backup, but since it relies on previous backups, it may not be the best choice when backing up important data.

Daily

Backs up only those files with a Last Modified date the same as today's date. This option is useful only if you run backup every single day, or are only concerned with backing up files modified in the last few hours.

Note that the *.bks* file only saves the file selections; the other options are saved as defaults in the Backup program and must be changed manually every time if you need different options for different backup jobs.

When you're ready, click the Start Backup button to begin the backup process. If you've turned on the "Compute selection information" option (Tools → Options → General tab), Backup will count up the sizes of all the selected files so that it can provide an accurate estimate of the time to completion. If you've chosen to "Verify data after the backup completes," Backup will compare the backed-up files against the originals on your hard disk; this will double the time taken for the backup job, but you'll be more certain that the backup contains a valid, complete copy of your data

Choose the Restore tab to restore some or all of the files you've previously backed up. Backup keeps a catalog of all backed-up files, so you don't have to wait for Backup to read your tape or other media before you see a list of files you can restore. The catalogs are displayed in the left pane of the Restore window, arranged first by backup media, then by backup job, then by original location (see Figure 4-11). For example, if you've backed up a folder called *My Stuff* to a tape last Monday, you would open the tape drive branch and then open the branch dated last Monday. You would see the familiar folder hierarchy with the backed up files and folders. Simply place a checkmark next to those files and folders you wish to restore (like when you backed up originally) and click Start Restore when you're ready (see Figure 4-12).

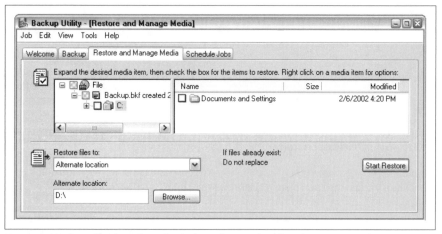

Figure 4-11. Once files have been backed up, they are listed in the Restore and Manage Media tab for easy retrieval

Notes

- Files with the *.bks* extension are not associated with the Backup application by default. This means that you cannot double-click a *.bks* file to start the backup without first configuring your File Types. Go to Explorer → Tools → Folder Options → File Types tab. Click New, type BKS, and click OK. Then click Advanced and type Backup Set for the name of the file type. Click New, type Backup in the Action field, and type something like:

  ```
  ntbackup.exe backup "@%1" /f "c:\mybackup.bkf"
  ```

  which will open Backup and begin backing up the files specified in the *.bks* file (represented here by %1). In this example, the target is a backup file (*c:\mybackup. bkf*). Type ntbackup /? at the command prompt to see a list of the available command line parameters and some examples of how they're used so you can form a command line appropriate to your needs and hardware.

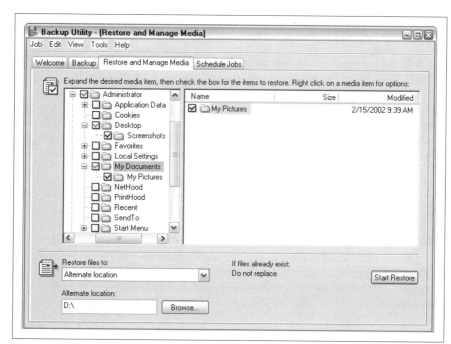

Figure 4-12. Place checkmarks next to the items you wish to restore using an interface very similar to Explorer

- In addition to the drives shown in the folder tree, you'll see an additional item called "System State." Place a checkmark next to the System State entry to back up the Registry, Boot files, special System files that are under Windows File Protection, and several other databases. Although you could back up the Registry by backing up the hives (see Chapter 7), for example, backing up the System State is a more graceful solution, especially since it makes restoration much easier. If you're backing up the drive on which Windows is installed, you should also back up the System State.

- Go to Tools → Options → Restore to choose whether the restored file will overwrite an existing file, overwrite an existing file only if it's older than the backed up file, or prompt you before overwriting.

- Tools → Options → Exclude Files lets you exclude specific files or groups of files from the backup. By default, Backup is set to exclude nearly twenty different files or file types, such as the swap file (*pagefile.sys*) and the file responsible for the Internet Explorer cache (*index.dat*).

- The Wizards available under the Welcome tab provide step-by-step walkthroughs of the backup and restore processes, but don't offer any special options or features.

- The Automated System Recovery Wizard helps create a special boot disk, allowing you to more easily restore your system if there's a disk crash or some other serious problem that requires the drive to be reformatted.

- Before you become complacent about your backups, make sure you've worked through the steps required to restore all the data you've gone to so much trouble to back up.

- There are wizards for performing a backup and restore: Tools → Backup Wizard and Tools → Restore Wizard, respectively.

Boot Configuration Manager   *\windows\system32\bootcfg.exe*

Configure and view entries in the *boot.ini* file, used by the Windows XP Boot Manager. (Boot Configuration Manager is included with Windows XP Professional only.)

To Open   Command Prompt → bootcfg

Usage   bootcfg /*command* [*parameters*]

Description

The Windows XP Boot Manager, responsible for supporting multiple operating systems on the same system, is installed when Windows XP is installed. If there is more than one boot entry, a menu appears before Windows is loaded, allowing the user to choose an operating system to load. The entries in the menu are configured in a file called *boot.ini*, located in the root directory of your boot drive. *Boot.ini* is a plain text file and can be edited with Notepad. However, the syntax can be complex, so the Boot Configuration Manager can be used to add, remove, or configure entries and options.

Unfortunately, the Boot Configuration Manager doesn't have an interface to speak of. Rather, commands are issued by typing them at the command prompt, like this:

    bootcfg /query

There are eleven primary commands, each with its own set of parameters. To list all the available commands, type:

    bootcfg /?

To see the usage of any particular command, type the command followed by /?, like this:

    bootcfg /query /?

Notes

- Among the commands available to the Boot Configuration Manager, the most interesting are the /copy, /delete, and /query commands, used to add, remove, and view the entries in *boot.ini*, respectively. The /query command is the default; if you simply type bootcfg with no command, it's the same as typing bootcfg /query.

- *Boot.ini* is a hidden file; see "Attrib," earlier in this chapter, for details on hidden files.

- Some of the aspects of the boot menu (e.g., settings in the *boot.ini* file) can also be set by going to the Control Panel → [Performance and Maintenance] → System → Advanced tab, and clicking Settings in the Startup and Recovery section. The options in the System Startup section allow you to choose the default operating system and the timeout before the default is selected. (These settings duplicate the /default and /timeout commands, respectively.) Finally, click Edit to open the *boot.ini* file in Notepad.

- The obvious advantage of this utility is the ability to modify the boot menu with a batch file or WSH script.
- The BOOT.INI tab of the System Configuration Utility, discussed later in this chapter, also provides access to several boot preferences not otherwise available.

See Also

Windows Me Annoyances by David A. Karp (O'Reilly), Chapter 3, for a discussion of *.ini* files; "Control Panel," "System Configuration Utility"

Cabinet (CAB) Maker

\windows\system32\makecab.exe; diantz.exe

Cabinet file (*.cab*) compression utility

To Open   Command Prompt → makecab

Usage
```
makecab [/v[n]] [/d var=value] [/l dir] source [destination]
makecab [/v[n]] [/d var=value] /f directive_file
```

Description

A cabinet file is a compressed archive commonly used to package application installation files. Cabinets are similar to *.zip* files, although there are added features such as a rudimentary script system intended to install and register application components.

There are two ways to use the Cabinet Maker. First, you can compress one or more files directly, like this:

```
makecab \windows\greenstone.bmp greenstone.cab
```

which compresses the file, *greenstone.bmp*, into the *greenstone.cab* archive. The new cabinet file, *greenstone.cab*, is created automatically in the current directory; if it already exists, it is replaced with the new archive. Unfortunately, wildcards (*.*) aren't allowed in the source, so you can only specify one file at a time. This is where the second usage of the Cabinet Maker comes in: instead of specifying options and files directly, a single plain text file, called a directive file (*.ddf*) is used. The simplest directive file lists all the files to include. A line beginning with a semicolon is treated as a comment.

Assuming the lines:

```
;Example directive file
c:\windows\greenstone.bmp
c:\windows\rhododendron.bmp
```

are saved into a file called *test.ddf*, the Makecab command would then look like this:

```
makecab /f test.ddf
```

Multiple directive files can be specified in the same command, listed one after another.

Notes

- Diamond Cabinet Builder (*Diantz.exe*) is identical to *makecab.exe*; it's included only for legacy support.
- There are two ways to open Cabinet files and extract their contents. The easiest way is to double-click on any *.cab* file in Explorer to display a folder view of the contents. You can then drag files out of the *.cab* file (items cannot be added here, however). The other way is to use the File Expansion Utility (*expand.exe*).

- WinZip (*http://www.winzip.com*) can also be used to open *.cab* files, but it's not compatible with all variants of the *.cab* format, and thus won't open every *.cab* file you encounter.

- More complicated directive files, including the use of *.inf* installation routines, are possible with the Cabinet Maker. See *http://msdn.microsoft.com/* for details, including the use of the /v and /d parameters.

See Also
"File Expansion Utility," "IExpress"

Calculator
\windows\system32\calc.exe

Numerical scientific and nonscientific calculator.

To Open   Start → Programs → Accessories → Calculator
Command Prompt → calc

Description
By default, the Calculator starts in Standard mode, containing only the numeric keypad and some basic functions (add, subtract, invert, square root, etc.). Select Scientific from the View menu to use the calculator in Scientific mode, useful for more advanced functions, such as logarithmic, logical, trigonomic, and base functions (see Figure 4-13). Each time you subsequently open the calculator, it will appear in the previously used mode.

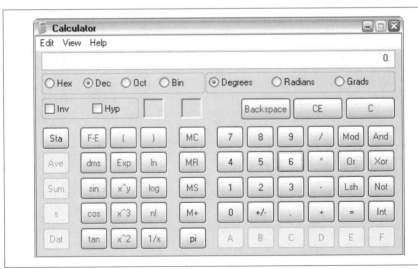

Figure 4-13. The scientific view of the Calculator provides access to many more functions than the standard view

Entering data and performing calculations

Data can be entered by clicking the buttons or by pressing keys on the keyboard. All keys have keyboard equivalents; key mappings that are not quite obvious (such as log) are documented in Table 4-2. Note that many of the functions below are only available in Scientific mode.

Table 4-2. Calculations and keyboard equivalents

Calc button	Keyboard key	Action
C	Esc	Clear all calculations
CE	Del	Clearthe last entry
Back	Backspace	Clear the last digit
MR	Ctrl-R	Display the number stored in memory
MS	Ctrl-M	Store the current value in memory
M+	Ctrl-P	Add the current value to the number stored in memory
MC	Ctrl-L	Clear the memory
+/-	F9	Change the sign (negative)

When in Hex mode, hexadecimal values A–F can be entered from the keyboard or by using the A-F buttons on the calculator. Number systems and keyboard equivalents can be seen in Table 4-3. Table 4-4 and Table 4-5 show binary mode keyboard equivalents and bitwise (logic) functions and keyboard equivalents, respectively.

Table 4-3. Number systems and keyboard equivalents

Calc Button	Keyboard key	Action
Hex	F5	Hexadecimal (base 16)
Dec	F6	Decimal (base 10)
Oct	F7	Octal (base 8)
Bin	F8	Binary (base 2)

Table 4-4. Binary mode keyboard equivalents

Calc button	Keyboard key	Action
Qword	F12	64-bit value
Dword	F2	32-bit value
Word	F3	16-bit value (low order bit)
Byte	F4	8-bit value (low order bit)

Table 4-5. Bitwise (logic) functions and keyboard equivalents

Calc Button	Keyboard key	Action
Mod	%	Modulus
And	&	Bitwise AND
Or			Bitwise OR

Table 4-5. Bitwise (logic) functions and keyboard equivalents (continued)

Calc Button	Keyboard key	Action
Xor	^	Bitwise exclusive OR
Lsh	<	Left shift (right shift via Inv + Lsh or >)
Not	~	Bitwise inverse
Int	;	Integer (remove the decimal portion)

When in Decimal mode, the Deg, Rad, and Grad radio buttons switch between degrees, radians, and gradients (see Table 4-6).

Table 4-6. Decimal mode keyboard equivalents

Calc button	Keyboard key	Action
Deg	F2	Calculate trigonomic functions in degrees
Rad	F3	Calculate trigonomic functions in radians
Grad	F4	Calculate trigonomic functions in grads

Statistical functions

To perform a statistical calculation, start by entering the first data, then click Sta to open the Statistics Box, click Dat to display the data in the Statistics Box, and then continue entering the data, clicking Dat after each entry. When you've finished entering all the numbers, click the statistical button you want to use (Ave, Sum, or S). The buttons available in the Statistics Box are listed in Table 4-7.

Table 4-7. Statistics Box buttons

Calc button	Action
RET	Returns the focus to the calculator
LOAD	Displays the selected number in the Statistics Box in the Calculator display area
CD	Clears the selected number (data)
CAD	Clears all numbers (data) in the Statistics Box

Scientific calculation

Scientific calculations buttons and keyboard equivalents are shown in Table 4-8.

Table 4-8. Scientific calculations buttons and keyboard equivalents

Calc button	Keyboard key	Action
Inv	i	Sets the inverse function for $sin, cos, tan, Pl, xy, x^2, x^3, Ln, log, sum$, and s.
Hyp	h	Sets the hyperbolic function for sin, cos, and tan.
F-E	v	Turns scientific notation on and off. Can only be used with decimal numbers. Numbers larger than 10^{15} are always displayed with exponents.
( )	( )	Starts and ends a new level of parentheses. The maximum number of nested parentheses is 25. The current number of levels appears in the box above the) button.

Table 4-8. Scientific calculations buttons and keyboard equivalents (continued)

Calc button	Keyboard key	Action
dms	m	If the displayed number is in degrees, convert to degree-minute-second format. Use Inv + dms to reverse the operation.
Exp	x	The next digit(s) entered constitute the exponent. The exponent cannot be larger than 289. Decimal only.
Ln	n	Natural (base e) logarithm. Inv + Ln calculates *e* raised to the *n*th power, where *n* is the current number.
sin	s	Sine of the displayed number. Inv + sin gives arc sine. Hyp + sin gives hyperbolic sine. Inv + Hyp + sin gives arc hyperbolic sine.
x^y	y	*x* to the *y*th power. Inv + x^y calculates the *y* th root of *x*.
Log	l	The common (base 10) logarithm. Inv + log yields 10 to the *x* th power, where *x* is the displayed number.
Cos	o	Cosine of the displayed number. Inv + cos in gives arc cosine. Hyp + cos in gives hyperbolic cosine. Inv + Hyp + cos in gives arc hyperbolic cosine.
x^3	#	Cubes the displayed number. Inv + x^3 gives the cube root.
n!	!	Factorial of the displayed number.
tan	t	Tangent of the displayed number. Inv + tan gives arc tan. Hyp + tan gives hyperbolic tan. Inv + Hyp + tan gives arc hyperbolic tan.
x^2	@	Squares the displayed number. Inv + x^2 gives the square root.
1/x	r	Reciprocal of displayed number.
Pi	p	The value of *pi* (3.1415...). Inv + Pi gives 2 × pi.

Notes

- If you convert a fractional decimal number to another number system, only the integer part will be used.

- Those serious about calculators will probably notice that there is no Reverse Polish Notation (RPN) mode. Fortunately, there are literally dozens of freely available alternatives on the Web (try the Aepryus Calculator from *http://www. aepryus.com/* or the Trig+ PC Calculator from *http://www.web-ee.com/*). Also see "Powertoy Calc," part of Microsoft's Power Toys package described in Appendix D.

Character Map
\windows\system32\charmap.exe

Display all the characters and symbols in a particular font. This provides access to symbols not easily accessible with the keyboard

To Open   Start → Programs → Accessories → System Tools → Character Map
Command Prompt → charmap

Description

Character Map displays a visual map of all the characters in any font, making it easy to paste them into other documents (see Figure 4-14).

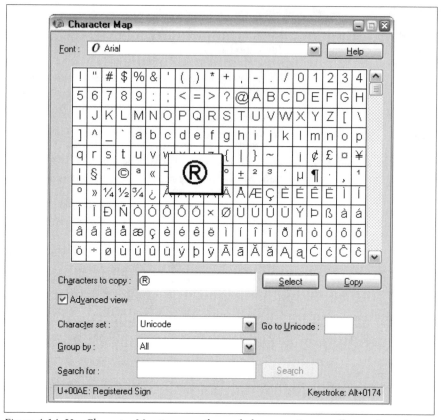

Figure 4-14. Use Character Map to access the symbols you can't normally type from the keyboard

To use Character Map:

1. Select a font from the Font drop-down list. If you're inserting a character into an existing document, you should select the same font that is used in the document.

2. Find the character you wish to use; click once on any cell to magnify its character. If you can't find the desired character, remember to scroll down. If the selected font doesn't have the character you want, try another font.

3. Double-click the character you want (or click once and then click the Select button) to place the character in the "Characters to copy" box. You can place as many successive characters as you want in this box.

4. Click Copy to copy the character(s) to the Windows clipboard.

5. Switch to your other application, click where you want the character(s) to appear, and paste (using either the Edit menu or Ctrl-V).

6. If the font in the target application isn't the same as the one you've selected in Character Map, you'll need to highlight the newly inserted character(s), and then change them to the same font you used in Character Map. If the character in your document doesn't look as it did in Character Map, it's because the wrong font is being used.

Notes

- Effective use of Character Map relies on correct font selection, especially when you're pasting characters into applications that don't support multiple fonts. For example, the default font used in Notepad is Lucida Console (changed by going to Notepad → Format → Font), and the default font used in most text boxes is Tahoma (changed by going to Control Panel → [Appearance and Themes] → Display).

- Character Map is helpful not only for selecting extended characters in standard fonts, but also for accessing dingbats, such as those found in the Webdings, Wingdings, Symbol, and Marlett fonts.

- Character Map is useful for finding out what key combination will produce a nonstandard character in any given font. This can eliminate the need to repeatedly go back to Character Map to retrieve the same character. Select a character in any cell and see the corresponding character code in the status bar. For example, the Yin-Yang symbol in Wingdings is character code 0x5B. Now, this is a hexidecimal code, so you'll need to use Calculator to convert it to a decimal number. In Calculator's scientific mode, click Hex, type the code (not including the 0x prefix - 5B in this case), and then click Dec to view the decimal equivalent (91 in this case). To then insert the character into an application using the keyboard, hold the Alt key, and type the code using the numeric keypad (the numbers above the letters won't work). In the case of the Yin-Yang, type Alt-91. Appendix E lists some of the most useful character codes.

See Also

"Fonts Folder," "Calculator," "Private Character Editor"

Chat

See "Microsoft Chat."

Chkdsk

Check the disk for errors and fix any that are found (replaces Scandisk).

To Open   Command Prompt → chkdsk

Usage   chkdsk [drive[filename]] [/f] [/r] [/x] [/i] [/c] [/v]

Description

Chkdsk scans the disk surface, checks the integrity of files and folders, and looks for lost clusters (among other things), correcting any problems that are found and sometimes even freeing disk space consumed by unusable fragments of data.

If you run Chkdsk with no command-line parameters, it will check the current drive for errors. Or, specify a drive letter to check a specific drive, like this:

```
chkdsk e:
```

However, Chkdsk run this way will only report problems—it won't correct them. The report you'll get looks something like this:

```
The type of the file system is NTFS.
Volume label is Hard Disk.


WARNING!  F parameter not specified.
Running CHKDSK in read-only mode.

CHKDSK is verifying files (stage 1 of 3)...
File verification completed.
CHKDSK is verifying indexes (stage 2 of 3)...
Index verification completed.
CHKDSK is verifying security descriptors (stage 3 of 3)...
Security descriptor verification completed.
Correcting errors in the Volume Bitmap.
Windows found problems with the file system.
Run CHKDSK with the /F (fix) option to correct these.

   29302528 KB total disk space.
    2997136 KB in 19467 files.
       5132 KB in 1320 indexes.
          0 KB in bad sectors.
      94368 KB in use by the system.
      65536 KB occupied by the log file.
   26205892 KB available on disk.

       4096 bytes in each allocation unit.
    7325632 total allocation units on disk.
    6551473 allocation units available on disk.
```

The report starts with a warning about the /f parameter (see below), followed by descriptions of the stages of the scan. Note that an error has been found, but according to the report, it wasn't fixed. Next comes the summary of the total disk space, used space, and other statistics, which are fairly self-explanatory.

To use Chkdsk effectively, you'll need to use the following optional parameters:

/f

Fix any errors found. If /f is omitted, errors are merely reported and no changes to the disk are made.

/r

Locates bad sectors and recovers readable information. Using the /r parameter implies /f (see above). Think of the /r parameter as a beefed-up version of /f. Keep in mind that bad sectors represent physical errors on the disk surface, and safe recovery of the data residing in those areas is not guaranteed. Only use the /r option if you have reason to believe you have one or more bad sectors, either because Chkdsk is reporting this problem or if you encounter another symptom, such as your computer crashing or freezing every time you attempt to access a certain file.

/x

Forces the volume to dismount before the scan is performed. Using the /x parameter implies /f (see above). This effectively disconnects the drive from Explorer and all other programs, closing any open files stored on the drive, before any changes are made. You may wish to use this option when checking or repairing a shared drive used frequently by the several users on a network; otherwise, access to the drive might interrupt Chkdsk, or even corrupt data further.

/i

Performs a less vigorous check of index entries. The /i option can be used only on NTFS disks, as index entries only exist on NTFS volumes. Typically, you'll probably never need this option, although you may choose to use it to reduce the amount of time required to check the disk.

/c

Skips checking of cycles within the folder structure. Like /i, the /c option can be used only on NTFS disks. Likewise, you'll probably never need this option either, although you may choose to use it to reduce the amount of time required to check the disk.

/v

Use of the /v parameter abandons Chkdsk's primary purpose, and instead simply displays a list of every file on the entire hard disk (in no particular order). Note that the /v parameter can be used only on a disk with a FAT or FAT32 file system; it has no meaning on an NTFS disk.

Notes

- Chkdsk can also be used to check a single file or a specific group of files for fragmentation (see "Disk Defragmenter," later in this chapter), but only on FAT or FAT32 disks. To do this, specify the full path and filename (or use wildcards, such as *.*, to specify multiple files) instead of the drive letter on the command line.

- In Windows 9x/Me, regular usage of Scandisk was recommended, but that's not necessarily the case with Chkdsk and Windows XP. Whenever Windows isn't properly shutdown, or when Windows detects a potential problem during startup, Chkdsk is run automatically during the boot process. Additionally, given the added stability of Windows XP, you may not ever need to run Chkdsk manually unless you suspect a problem.

- When Chkdsk is launched during Windows startup, it is preceded by a message and a 10-second delay, giving you the option of skipping the scan. While Chkdsk is running, either during Windows startup or any other time, it can be corrupted by pressing Ctrl-C.

- During normal use of Chkdsk, you'll see references to various terms describing problems on your hard disk. Among the more popular players are lost clusters (pieces of data no longer associated with any file), bad sectors (actual flaws in the disk surface), cross-linked files (two files claiming ownership of the same chunk of data), invalid file dates and filenames, and a few other more secure errors.

- The /v parameter is a funny option, especially considering it has very little to do, at least in terms of results, with the other functions of this program. However, when used in conjunction with pipe operators (see Appendix C), this feature can generate filtered reports of the contents of a drive.

- If you wish to schedule Chkdsk at regular intervals to help ensure a healthy disk, you can configure the Task Scheduler (discussed later in this chapter) to run Chkdsk, say, every Friday at 3:30.

See Also
"Chkntfs"

Chkntfs

Display or change the checking of a disk (using Chkdsk) at Windows startup

To Open   Command Prompt → chkntfs

Usage   chkntfs [drive | /d | /t:time | /x drive | /c drive]

Description

Chkdsk, described earlier in this chapter, is run automatically during Windows startup, either if the previous session was not ended gracefully (the computer was turned off without shutting down) or if errors are detected. Chkntfs is used to modify this behavior for one or all of your drives.

If you run Chkntfs with only a drive letter (e.g., chkntfs c:), you get a somewhat cryptic report, like this:

```
The type of the file system is NTFS.
C: is not dirty.
```

The identification of the filesystem type on the first line is fairly self-evident. The "not dirty" report implies that the drive was properly "cleaned up" the last time the system shut down. In other words, the system shut down properly. If the system isn't shut down properly, any drives in use (drives containing one or more files that were open when the computer lost power, for example) are marked "dirty," and those drives are scanned the next time Windows starts. To change this behavior, use one of the following options. Note that all options, including the specification of the drive letter above, are exclusive; only one can be used in any time.

/d

> Type chkntfs /d to restore the default behavior of the entire machine; all drives automatically check to boot time, and any drives found to be "dirty" are checked with Chkdsk.

/t:time

> Used to change the countdown before this scan is started, during which time the user can press the Spacebar to skip the scan. Time is simply any number, in seconds: chkntfs /t:5 configures Windows to wait five seconds before running Chkdsk.

/x drive

> Excludes a particular drive from those checked at startup. For example, type chkntfs /x e: to exclude drive E: from the auto-check.

/c drive

> Includes a particular drive in those checked at startup; /c is the opposite of /x. For example, type chkntfs /c e: to instruct Windows to check drive E: during startup, and if found "dirty," to run chkdsk e: /f.

See Also
"Chkdsk"

Clipbook Viewer

View the contents of the Clipboard, manage clipboard data, and share data with other users.

To Open   Command Prompt → `clipbrd`

Description

The Clipboard is merely a place in memory; it's where data is stored when it is cut or copied from most Windows applications. It's not a discrete application and has no interface of its own to speak of. However, the Clipbook Viewer is provided as a "window" into the clipboard, so to speak, as it allows you to view whatever has been placed in the Clipboard without disrupting or interfering with it any way.

Furthermore, you can save data into special *.clp* files, making retrieval at a later time—without having to open the original application—easy. This effectively affords us multiple clipboards.

When you first start Clipbook Viewer, it contains a single document called "Clipboard," which displays the current contents of the clipboard at any time. In fact, you can leave open and watch the contents change as you copy and paste items from various programs. For example, if you cut or copy a file in Explorer, you'll see the full path and filename of the object listed in the Clipboard document window. The same goes for plain text, rich text, images, spreadsheet cells, or most other types of data.

Although Clipbook Viewer won't be able to display all types of data accurately, it does correctly preserve the format of the data, so you can safely save and retrieve your clipboards without altering the data. To save the data in the clipboard, select Save from the File menu, type a filename (with the *.clp* extension), and click OK. Then, at a later time, open the file using the Clipbook Viewer (or by double-clicking the *.clp* file in Explorer). You'll be asked whether or not you wish to clear the contents of the clipboard; if you answer yes, the contents of the clipboard will be replaced with the data stored in the file you've opened. Otherwise, the operation is canceled.

Sharing, a mechanism by which clipboard data can be transferred between computers on a network, is not an automatic process. Instead, you must manually paste data to be shared into the Local Clipbook window, a document that should appear alongside the Clipboard document window in the Clipbook Viewer. The security menu allows you to set permissions for your shared data so that only authorized users can get access to it. To access the data on another computer's Local Clipbook, select Connect from the File menu.

Notes

- If the Local Clipbook window does not appear in the Clipbook Viewer, the Clickbook Viewer is unable to establish a connection with another computer on your network. Make sure sharing is enabled and properly configured on all computers involved.

- Note that some applications use an "internal" clipboard, allowing information to be copied and pasted only within the application. Data originating from these applications will not show up in the ClickBook Viewer.

Command Prompt

\windows\system32\cmd.exe

The Windows XP command line interface, commonly known as a DOS box.

To Open   Start → Programs → Accessories → Command Prompt
              Command Prompt → cmd

Usage   cmd [/q][/d] [/a|/u] [/e:on|off][/f:on|off][/v:on|off] /t:*fg*
              [[/s][/c|/k] *string*]

Description

The Command Prompt (see Figure 4-15) is a simple application in which you type commands rather than pointing and clicking. While the Command Prompt is sparse and may be somewhat intimidating to new users, it carries out several very important functions in Windows XP, including access to otherwise inaccessible programs and utilities and even some advanced file management functions. Appendix C fully documents the command prompt, its commands, and the related Address Bar.

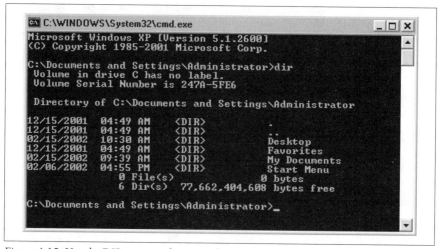

Figure 4-15. Use the DIR command to view the contents of the current directory in the Command Prompt

Cmd accepts the following parameters:

string
    When used with /c or /k, specifies a command to be carried out when the command prompt window is first opened. Multiple commands can be specified here if they're separated by &&, and *string*, as a whole, is surrounded by quotation marks. *String* must be the last parameter on the command line. See Chapter 6 for more information on the types of commands that can be typed at the command prompt.

/c   Carries out the command specified by *string* and then stops.

/k   Carries out the command specified by *string* and continues.

/s   Strips any quotation marks in *string*. Type cmd /? for details.

/q   Turns the echo off; see "echo" in Chapter 6.

/d   Disables execution of AutoRun commands. Without /d, any programs or commands listed in the Registry keys, HKEY_LOCAL_MACHINE\Software\Microsoft\ Command Processor\AutoRun and HKEY_CURRENT_USER\Software\Microsoft\Command Processor\AutoRun are executed every time a command prompt window is opened.

/a   Formats all command prompt output so that it is American National Standards Institute (ANSI)-compliant.

/u   Formats all command prompt output so that it is Unicode-compliant.

/e:on|off
      Enables or disables command extensions (the default is on). Turn off command extensions to disable certain advanced features of the commands discussed in Chapter 6.

/f:on|off
      Enables or disables file and directory name completion (the default is off). Type cmd /? for details.

/v:on|off
      Enables or disables delayed environment variable expansion (the default is off). Type cmd /? for details.

/t:fg
      Sets the foreground and background colors (f and g, respectively) of the command prompt window. The single-digit values for f and g are as follows: 0=Black, 1=Blue, 2=Green, 3=Aqua, 4=Red, 5=Purple, 6=Yellow, 7=White, 8=Gray, 9=Light blue, A=Light green, B=Light aqua, C=Light red, D=Light purple, E=Light yellow, and F=Bright white.

Notes

- Also included with Windows XP is *command.com*, the command prompt used in Windows 9x/Me. It's used similarly to *cmd.exe*, but has limited support of long filenames and other XP features. *Command.com* is included for legacy purposes only and should be avoided; *cmd.exe* is the preferred Command Prompt in Windows XP.

- Refer to the beginning of this chapter for more information on how the command prompt is used to access those programs that don't have Start menu entries.

See Also

Chapter 6

Component Services
\windows\system32\dcomcnfg.exe

See "Microsoft Management Console."

Computer Management
\windows\system32\compmgmt.exe

See "Microsoft Management Console."

Connection Manager Profile Installer

\windows\system32\cmstp.exe

An automated connection profile installation utility.

To Open   Command Prompt → cmstp

Description

The Connection Manager Profile Installer is used to automate the installation (or removal) of connection profiles. For example, an Internet service provider or network administrator may build an *.inf* file containing all the necessary information to connect to another computer or service, and then use the Connection Manager Profile Installer to integrate the information into a particular computer. Type cmstp at any prompt for information on its usage.

Control Panel

\windows\system32\control.exe

The central interface for most of the preferences, hardware configuration, and other settings in Windows XP.

To Open   Start → Control Panel (when using the new Windows XP Start menu)
Start → Settings → Control Panel (when using the classic Start menu)
Windows Explorer → navigate to the *Desktop\My Computer\Control Panel* folder
My Computer → Control Panel*
Command Prompt → Control

Usage   control [*filename.cpl*] [*applet_name*]
control [*keyword*]

Description

The Control Panel has no settings of its own; it's merely a container for any number of options windows (commonly called applets or Control Panel extensions), most of which can be accessed without even opening the Control Panel folder. Unfortunately, the Control Panel can look vastly different from one computer to another, based on preferences scattered throughout several dialog boxes. Furthermore, the default settings vary (depending on how Windows XP was installed) (see Figure 4-16). In order to simplify notation in this book, I'm making certain assumptions about your preferences. It's best to familiarize yourself with the various options described below so that you won't be confused when a setting in the Control Panel is referenced.

There are several different ways to access the Control Panel and its contents:

Start menu
    The way the Control Panel appears in the Start menu depends on several different settings, resulting in no fewer than five different possibilities.

---

* Control Panel only appears in the My Computer window if the "Show Control Panel in My Computer" setting is enabled in the Control Panel → [Appearance and Themes] → Folder Options → View tab. Regardless of this setting, however, Control Panel appears under the My Computer branch in Explorer.

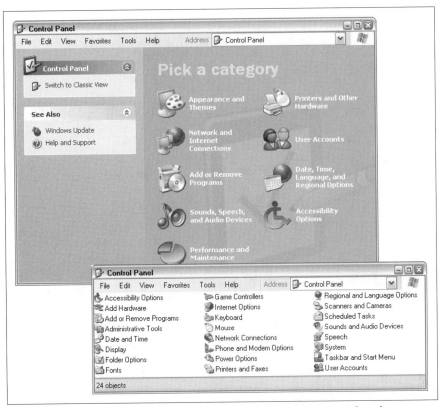

Figure 4-16. The category view of the Control Panel (top) is more inviting but also more cumbersome than the standard Control Panel (bottom)

If you're using the new Windows XP-style Start menu, right-click on the Start button and select Properties. Click Customize, and then choose the Advanced tab. In the Start menu items list, there are three possibilities for the display of the Control Panel: "Display as a link," which opens the Control Panel folder when clicked, "Display as a menu," which skips the folder and displays the contents as menu items, and "Don't display this item," which hides it from the Start menu altogether. If enabled, the Control Panel entry appears in the second column in the Start menu (see Figure 4-17).

If you're using the Classic Start menu (a simpler, cleaner layout, resembling earlier versions of Windows), go to Start → Settings → Taskbar and Start Menu → Start Menu tab, and click Customize. By default, the Control Panel entry, which also appears in the Settings menu, opens the Control Panel folder. If, instead, you want a menu to appear, turn on the "Expand Control Panel" option in the list of "Advanced Start menu options."

Explorer

The Control Panel appears as another folder under the My Computer branch. Whether or not the Control Panel icon is configured to be displayed in the My Computer window, it will appear here. Select the folder to display its contents.

Figure 4-17. The Control Panel can be accessed through the Start menu; you'll never see categories here

My Computer

    Double-click the My Computer icon on your Desktop; if it's not there, select My Computer from the Start menu. If the Control Panel icon does not appear in the My Computer window, it can be added: go to Tools → Folder Options → View tab and turn on the "Show Control Panel in My Computer" option.

Command prompt

    At any command prompt, type control to open the Control Panel. See "Command-line usage," below, for information on opening specific Control Panel applets from the Command Prompt.

Shortcuts

    In addition to accessing a particular entry by first opening Control Panel, it's possible to open a specific applet directly, either with a standard Windows shortcut, or with one of the many links built into the Windows interface. For example, "Folder Options" is also available in the Tools menu of Windows Explorer, and "Internet Options" is available in the Tools menu of Internet Explorer. To make a standard Windows Shortcut to a Control Panel applet, simply drag the desired icon from the Control Panel folder onto your Desktop or into any folder. Then double-click the icon to open the applet, skipping the Control Panel folder altogether.

Categories

A new, optional feature in Windows XP divides the contents of the Control Panel into discrete categories. Unfortunately, these categories are used only under certain circumstances. In other words, depending on how you access the Control Panel (see above), you may or may not have to make a category selection before you can open the desired applet.

If you have Explorer's "Show common tasks in folders" option turned on (Explorer → Tools → Folder Options → General tab), a separate pane will appear to the left of the contents of any folder, containing links and some summary information. In the case of the Control Panel folder, the first entry in the tasks pane (named either "Switch to Classic View" or "Switch to Category View") allows you to turn categories off or on, respectively. If, on the other hand, the "use Windows classic folders" option is selected (as opposed to the "common tasks" option, above), categories will never appear in the Control Panel. Furthermore, regardless of these settings, categories will never appear when the Control Panel is viewed as a menu through the Start menu.

In addition to containing the icons for most of (but not all) the standard Control Panel applets, the categories have additional links based on the task to be performed. Essentially, these links point to the same icons, only using different language. For a more comprehensive task index than is possible with categories, see Chapter 5.

Since categories are simply an extra, and basically unnecessary, step, you may wish to turn off the category view. This makes the Control Panel easier to use (since you won't have to hunt for applets), allows you to access all Control Panel settings, and ensures that the applets are presented consistently, no matter how you open the Control Panel. See Table 4-9 for the categories in which each applet can be found (where applicable). Note also that two applets, Fonts and Add Hardware, are not found in any category; see Notes, below, for details.

Regardless of the setting you prefer, it's important understand the notation adopted throughout this book. For example, the following instruction shows the category name in square brackets (commonly used to denote an optional step or parameter):

Go to Control Panel → [Appearance and Themes] → Display

If you are using Control Panel categories, include the step in brackets; if you have categories turned off, ignore the bracketed step.

Command-line usage

This section explains how to use *control.exe* from the command line, most notably for creating Windows shortcuts to specific Control Panel applets. Note that most, but not all, applets can be launched from the command line; see Notes for a workaround. *Control.exe* supports two command-line methods (see Usage, at the beginning of this section), but no method covers all applets. *Control.exe* accepts the following parameters:

filename.cpl

The filename of the *.cpl* file (found in *\Windows\System32*) containing the applet you wish to open. For example, type:

```
control main.cpl
```

to open the Mouse Properties dialog. If there's more than one Control Panel applet contained in treflistvhe *.cpl* file, and the one you want is not the default, you'll need to specify the *applet_name* (see below) to open it.

applet_name ,tab

The formal name of the applet you want to launch, spelled and capitalized exactly as described in the table below. This parameter is necessary only if there's more than one applet contained in a given *.cpl* file. If you omit *applet_name*, the default applet in the specified *.cpl* file will be used. For example, type:

```
control main.cpl Keyboard
```

to open the Keyboard Properties dialog. Note that the *main.cpl* file is the same file as the one in the previous example, but the use of *applet_name* allows applets other than the default to be opened.

For some tabbed dialogs (but not all), you can also specify the specific tab to open by including a space and then a comma after the *.cpl* filename (the preceding space is required), and then a number. Specify 0 for the first tab (or omit the tab completely), 1 for the second, and so on. For example, type control.exe sysdm. cpl ,3 to open the System Properties window to the Advanced tab.

keyword

Keyword is an alternate way of opening a specific Control Panel applet from the command line. Instead of using *filename*.cpl and *applet_name*, simply include one of the following names: admintools, color, date/time, desktop, folders, fonts, international, keyboard, mouse, netconnections, printers, schedtasks, telephony, or userpasswords.

See Table 4-9 for a list of all available Control Panel applets, the category in which they can be found, and how to open them directly from the command line.

Table 4-9. Control panel applets

Applet name	Category	Command line
Accessibility Options	Accessibility Options	control access.cpl
Add Hardware	n/a (see Notes)	control hdwwiz.cpl
Add or Remove Programs	Add or Remove Programs	control appwiz.cpl
Administrative Tools	Performance and Maintenance	control admintools or explorer "\Documents and Settings\All Users\Start Menu\Programs\ Administrative Tools"
Date and Time	Date, Time, Language, and Regional Options	control timedate.cpl or control date/time
Display	Appearance and Themes	control desk.cpl or control desktop or control color (opens the Appearance tab automatically)
Folder Options	Appearance and Themes	control folders

Table 4-9. Control panel applets (continued)

Applet name	Category	Command line

Fonts	n/a (See Notes)	`explorer "\windows\fonts"`
		 or
		 `control fonts`

Game Controllers	Printers and Other Hardware	`control joy.cpl`
Internet Options	Network and Internet Connections	`control inetcpl.cpl`

Keyboard	Printers and Other Hardware	`control main.cpl Keyboard`
		 or
		 `control keyboard`

Mouse	Printers and Other Hardware	`control main.cpl`
		 or
		 `control mouse`

Network Connections	Network and Internet Connections	`control ncpa.cpl`
		 or
		 `control netconnections`

Phone and Modem Options	Printers and Other Hardware	`control telephon.cpl`
		 or
		 `control telephony`

Power Options	Performance and Maintenance	`control powercfg.cpl`
Printers and Faxes	Printers and Other Hardware	`control printers`

Regional and Language Options	Date, Time, Language, and Regional Options	`control intl.cpl`
		 or
		 `control international`

Scanners and Cameras	Printers and Other Hardware	n/a

Scheduled Tasks	Performance and Maintenance	`control sticpl.cpl`
		 or
		 `control schedtasks`

Sounds and Audio Devices	Sounds, Speech, and Audio Devices	`control mmsys.cpl`
Speech	Sounds, Speech, and Audio Devices	`control speech`
System	Performance and Maintenance	`control sysdm.cpl`
Taskbar and Start Menu	Appearance and Themes	n/a

User Accounts	User Accounts	`control nusrmgr.cpl`
		 or
		 `control userpasswords`

All of the applets mentioned here are discussed elsewhere in this chapter. Additionally, all the settings in all Control Panel applets that come with Windows XP are documented in Chapter 5 (arranged alphabetically). Rather than being listed by their location in the interface, settings are arranged alphabetically. That way, you'll be able to find the setting you need without having to figure out where Microsoft decided to place it.

Notes

- Those items with "n/a" in the Command line column of Table 4-9 can't be launched from the command line using *control.exe*. However, it's still possible to launch these (and any other) applets from the command line using a Windows shortcut. Simply drag the desired icon onto your Desktop or into a folder to create a shortcut. Then, to launch the shortcut from the command line, just type its full path and filename, including the *.lnk* filename extension. For example, to launch a shortcut named "Taskbar and Start Menu" (presumably linked to the applet of the same name), stored in your *Stuff* folder, type the following to open it:

      \stuff\printers and faxes.lnk

- Three Control Panel applets are not in categories, but appear on the top level: Accessibility Options, Add or Remove Programs, and User Accounts.

- Neither Fonts nor Add Hardware are listed in any category, and if you're viewing the Control Panel in Windows Explorer, there's no way to activate either applet without disabling the category view altogether. However, if you have the "Show common tasks in folders" option turned on (Control Panel → [Appearance and Themes] → Folder Options → General tab), and you're viewing Control Panel in a single folder window (no folder tree on the left), Fonts and Add Hardware appear as one of the tasks on the common tasks pane in the "Appearance and Themes" and "Printers and Other Hardware" categories, respectively.

- In previous versions of Windows, *control.exe* had a *property_tab* parameter, which allowed you to jump to a specific tab in a tabbed dialog. This parameter appears to be ignored in Windows XP, although you may find some older third-party applets that still support it.

- If you've configured Control Panel to open as a menu in the Start menu, you can open the Control Panel folder by right-clicking on Control Panel and selecting Open or Explore.

- Some applications, software drivers, and hardware drivers come with their own applets, so you may have additional applets in your Control Panel not listed here. Also, depending on your version of Windows XP (Home or Professional), as well as any installed optional components (via Control Panel → Add or Remove Programs), some of the items listed here might not be present in your Control Panel. See the specific entries, elsewhere in this chapter, for details on each of the applets mentioned here.

- Selective Control Panel icons can be hidden with TweakUI (see Appendix D).

- If you've upgraded from an earlier version of Windows and several Control Panel applets appear to be missing, open the Registry Editor, navigate to HKEY_CURRENT_ USER\Control Panel and delete the don't load key entirely:

See Also

Chapter 5

Create Shared Folder
\windows\system32\shrpubw.exe

Share a folder with other users on the network, either locally or remotely.

To Open   Command Prompt → shrpubw

Usage   shrpubw [/s *computer_name*]

Description

The easiest way to begin sharing a folder or drive is to right-click on its icon in Explorer, select Sharing and Security, and turn on the "Share this folder on the network" option. However, this procedure only allows you to share local folders. If you need to access an unshared folder on a computer on the other side of the building, for example, you would have to walk over to that computer and enable sharing for the folder while sitting in front of it.

The Create Shared Folder utility not only provides an alternative interface for sharing folders, it also lets you enable sharing of a folder on the remote computer (see Figure 4-18). Create Shared Folder can almost be thought of as a "back door," enabling access to computer where no such access has been explicitly defined. Naturally, if you don't have administrative rights on the target computer, you won't be able to do anything. (See Notes, below.)

Figure 4-18. The Create Shared Folder dialog provides an alternate way to share any folder on your hard disk with other computers on your network

If you run Create Shared Folder with no arguments, it will only let you share resources on the local computer. To share resources on a remote computer, use the /s parameter, like this:

    shrpubw /s lenny

When Create Shared Folder starts, the computer named Lenny will appear in the Computer field, and you'll be able to enable the sharing of any available resources on that computer.

Regardless of the computer being manipulated with Create Shared Folder, the interface is extremely simple. Below the Computer field (which can't be changed once the program has started), there are three other fields:

Folder to share

Enter the full path of the folder you wish to begin sharing (e.g., c:\my stuff\) or click Browse to navigate the folder tree.

Share name

Enter the name under which the folder will be known on the network (e.g., my stuff).

Share description
> The description is optional, but a quick note, describing the purpose of the folder, can be very helpful, especially in large organizations. For example: Lenny's Stuff.

When you're done, click Next to view the second and final page. Here, you can specify the security options for the share, such as which users will be able to read and/or modify the data in the shared folder. Click Finish when you're done, and the new shared folder will appear in the My Network Places folder.

Notes

- Based on the type of network you're using, administrative rights may be a little confusing. For example, on a peer-to-peer network, there is no central database of user accounts and passwords. In this case, you would need an identical username and password on each machine, and that user account must have administrative privileges to be recognized as an administrator.

- Obviously, this utility redefines security on a network. Just because you haven't explicitly shared a folder doesn't mean someone else can't get access to it. A word to the wise: if your computer resides in a networking environment, which can include ordinary Internet access, you need to be very careful about how you configure user accounts on your system. A further security hazard is the fact that all user accounts in Windows XP Home Edition have administrative privileges.

See Also

Chapter 7, "User Accounts"

Date and Time Properties
\windows\system\timedate.cpl

Set your system's clock, choose a time zone, and enable Internet time synchronization (see Figure 4-19).

To Open   Control Panel → [Date, Time, Language and Regional Options] → Date and Time
Double-click on the clock in the notification area (Tray)
Command Prompt → timedate.cpl
Command Prompt → control date/time

Description

The Date and Time dialog is pretty straightforward. Set your system's clock with the Date & Time tab and your time zone with the Time Zone tab.

The Internet Time tab allows you to synchronize your PC's clock with one of several Internet time servers automatically. If you turn on the "Automatically synchronize with an Internet time server" option, Windows will synchronize your clock once a week. Naturally, you must be connected to the Internet for this option to work; if you're not connected when Windows attempts to connect to the time server, it will just try again next week. Also, your time zone and daylight savings settings must be set properly; otherwise, the time synchronization will set the wrong time.

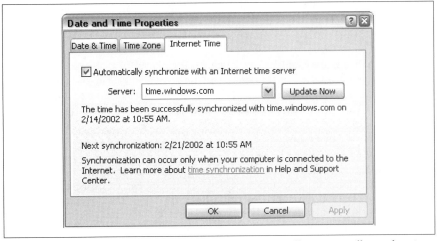

Figure 4-19. A new feature in Windows XP, Internet Time, will automatically synchronize your PC's clock with Microsoft time

Notes

- All settings in this dialog are covered in Chapter 5.
- The default Internet time server, *time.windows.com*, is Microsoft's own server for Internet time synchronization, but it is not your only choice. You can type the address of any time server here, which is useful if your connection to Microsoft's server is slow or if you get errors when you try to synchronize your PC's clock. There are literally hundreds of time servers on the Internet. To find one that is geographically close to you, find an Internet Time Server list, such as the one at *http://www.eecis.udel.edu/~mills/ntp/clock1.htm*.

See Also

"Control Panel"

DDE Share

\windows\system32\ddeshare.exe

Facilitates Dynamic Data Exchange (DDE) communication over a network.

To Open   Command Prompt → ddeshare

Description

Dynamic Data Exchange is a mechanism that allows one application to send instructions to another. DDE Share extends this functionality by facilitating this communication across a local network, using the NetDDE protocol. NetDDE is a cross-platform tool, capable of communicating with applications on Windows, DOS, OS/2, Solaris, VMS, and HP/UX systems.

When you start DDE Share, you'll see a simple window with a menu and two unlabeled icons. The two icons correspond to the first two entries in the Shares menu: double-click the icon with the hand holding the blank window to display the DDE

Shares window, or double-click the icon with the hand holding the "checked" window to display the DDE Trusted Shares window.

Notes

- The NetDDE service must be running on both machines. (See the "Microsoft Management Console," later in this chapter, for more information on services.)

- One of the two computers assumes the role of server, and the other assumes the role of client. On the server machine only, DDE shares must be created; these shares work similarly to shared folders and printers (see Chapter 6), where a particular resource is given a "share name." In the case of Microsoft Chat, this is already done (shared as Chat$).

  If the required entries are not present, you'll need to create them. Unfortunately, DDE conversations are proprietary; that is, the commands involved are decided by the application developer, so you'll have to refer to the documentation that comes with a particular application you're using to determine what type to use in the DDE Share dialogs.

- Once the shares have been established, the client machine must be set up to use the share from the server. For example, if you're using Chat and the server machine is named Karl, the service/topic pair would be \\Karl\NDDE$ and Chat$, respectively.

Device Manager

\windows\system32\devmgmt.msc

Configure all hardware installed in or attached to a computer.

To Open   Start → Programs → Administrative Tools → Computer Management → Device Manager

Control Panel → [Performance and Maintenance] → System → Hardware tab → Device Manager

Command Prompt → devmgmt.msc

Keyboard shortcut: Windows logo key + Pause/Break

Description

Device Manager is the central interface for gathering information about and making changes to all the hardware installed in a system. Device Manager has an Explorer-style tree listing all of the various hardware categories, as shown in Figure 4-20; expand any category branch to display all installed devices that fit in that category. For example, expand the Network adapters branch to list all installed network cards in the system. Right-click any device and choose one of the following actions:

Update Driver

If you have a newer driver than what is currently installed (find out by using Properties), select Update Driver to locate and install the new driver. This is the preferred way to update drivers in Windows XP, though some devices may have proprietary installation programs and don't support their drivers being updated in this way.

Note that if you've got a driver disk or have downloaded updated drivers for a device, choose the second option, "Install from a list or specific location" on the first page of the Hardware Update Wizard (see Figure 4-21). If you choose the first option, "Install the software automatically," you won't be able to specify the location of the newer driver files.

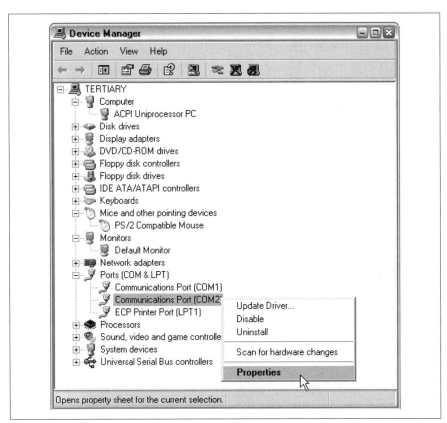

Figure 4-20. Device Manager lets you view and change the settings for nearly any hardware device attached to your system

Disable

Select Disable to effectively turn off this device, usually releasing hardware resources it normally consumes. This can be very handy when attempting to resolve hardware conflicts; if you removed the device using Uninstall, discussed below, Windows XP would simply reinstall the device the next time Windows starts.

Disable plays an important role in the use of Hardware Profiles (Control Panel → [Performance and Maintenance] → System → Hardware tab → Hardware Profiles), with which you can set up multiple hardware configurations, each with its own set of enabled devices. For example, say you're using a laptop with a built-in touchpad; when you're on the go, the touchpad is your primary pointing device. However, in your office, your docking station has a mouse attached to it. You could set up two hardware profiles—one that loads the driver for the touchpad and disables the one for the mouse and one that enables the mouse (and other devices attached to the docking station) and disables the touchpad. You may not need to go through all this trouble for situations like this, but in the case of the touchpad, you may prefer to have it turned off when you don't need it, as touchpads can sometimes interfere with frequent typing.

Figure 4-21. The Hardware Update Wizard walks you through the process of choosing a new driver for an already-attached device

Uninstall

Uninstall is more useful than it might seem on the surface. When you uninstall a device from Device Manager, it completely removes the driver from the system and erases all the corresponding configuration settings for that device. In addition to using Uninstall when you're physically removing a device from your system, it's also very handy when you're experiencing a problem with the device. When you remove a device from Device Manager and restart your computer, Windows will redetect the device and install it as though it were plugged in for the first time; this can be a very useful tool for repairing corrupt installations and fixing all sorts of problems with devices and their drivers.

Note that Uninstall is not the way to force Windows to stop recognizing the uninstall device, since Windows will just reload the driver the next time it starts. Instead, use Disable for this purpose.

Scan for hardware changes

Highlight a device and select "Scan for hardware changes" to force Windows to rescan the device, checking to see it has been removed, turned on, turned off, or reconfigured in some way.

Highlight a category and select "Scan for hardware changes" to not only scan for changes in the installed hardware, but to force Windows to look for new devices in this category as well. Typically, you'd use Add Hardware Wizard to install new devices. However, this procedure is useful for reattaching devices that have already been installed, such as USB devices or removable hard disks that are attached and reattached repeatedly. Likewise, highlight the root (the entry at the top of the tree, named for your computer) and select "Scan for hardware changes" to scan all categories for newly attached, recently changed, or recently disconnected devices.

Properties

The Properties sheet for any device contains lots of information about the device's driver, the status of the device, and several troubleshooting features (including those mentioned previously). Information and settings are divided into the following tabbed pages, some of which may or may not be present, depending on the device (see Figure 4-22).

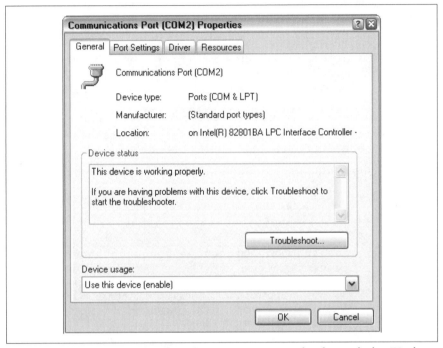

Figure 4-22. The Properties sheet for a device on your system also shows whether Windows thinks the device is working

The General tab shows the name, type, and physical location of the device (if applicable). Selecting "Do not use this device" from the Device usage list is the same as selecting Disable, as described previously. The Device status box shows relevant messages stating whether or not the driver is installed properly or whether the device is functioning. The Troubleshoot button only displays on interactive help documents (see "Help and Support Center," later in this chapter) relevant to the category in which the device appears, but does not have any specific troubleshooting information for your particular device. Instead, you should check the manufacturer's web site for an updated driver, updated firmware, or more specific troubleshooting information.

The Advanced tab contains settings specific to the device. For example, the Advanced tab for network adapters contains several settings that select which connector type to use (and some other options).

The Driver tab displays several pieces information about the currently installed driver, such as the provider (which corresponds to the distributor, not the manufacturer, of the software), the driver date and version, and whether or not the driver has a digital signature (used to verify the integrity of the driver, available only on drivers designed especially for Windows XP). Click Driver Details to see the individual files that make up the driver, or click Roll Back Driver to uninstall the current driver and replace it with the previously used driver (available only if the driver has been updated since Windows was installed). The Update Driver and Uninstall buttons have the same effect as the actions of the same name, described above.

Finally, the Resources tab lists all the hardware resources consumed by the selected device. Most devices use one or more of the following: a range of memory (expressed as a hexadecimal address), an I/O range (again, expressed as a hexadecimal address), a direct memory access line (DMA) or an interrupt request line (IRQ). Use information on this page to help diagnose hardware conflicts, where two or more devices try to use the same address or IRQ.

Notes

- Open the View menu to rearrange the devices by type (the default) or connection. (Group all PCI devices together and all USB devices together, for example.) You can also arrange devices by the resources they consume. This is useful for resolving conflicts. See the discussion of the Resources tab, under "Properties," above, for more information.

- The Show hidden devices entry in the View menu is used to display all currently installed drivers, including those for some of the more obscure "Non-Plug and Play Drivers."

 When you remove a drive, card, or other piece of hardware from your computer, Windows does not automatically remove the corresponding drivers, but deactivates them. To remove the drivers for a device you don't plan on reinstalling later on, you should locate the device in Device Manager, right-click, and select Uninstall before you physically disconnect the device.

- Device Manager is a Snap-in, used with the Microsoft Management Console, discussed later in this chapter.

- While Device Manager can be used to configure and remove installed devices, and even add devices by using "Scan for hardware changes," the preferred way to add new hardware is to use the Add Hardware Wizard.

- All branches in Device Manager are collapsed by default; to expand the branches, highlight the root entry and press the asterisk (*) key.

DirectX Management Tool

\windows\system32\dxdiag.exe

Test, diagnose, and tweak DirectX drivers.

To Open   Command Prompt → dxdiag

Description

DirectX is the system that allows applications, usually games, to directly access graphic, audio, and input devices to maximize performance. Unless you're experiencing a problem with DirectX or a program that uses DirectX, you should never need to use the DirectX Management Tool. If you do indeed encounter a problem, such as poor performance, an apparent glitch in a game, an error message, or some other compatibility problem, use the following steps to diagnose and treat the condition:

1. DirectX relies on hardware drivers, so the first thing you should do whenever you encounter problems with DirectX is make sure you have the latest drivers for your display adapter, sound card, and game controller (if applicable).

2. Next, go to *http://www.microsoft.com/directx/* and see if there's a more recent version of DirectX than the one installed on your system. To determine the currently installed version of DirectX, open the DirectX Management Tool and read the DirectX Version of the bottom of the System tab. The initial release of Windows XP ships with DirectX 8.1.

3. If you're experiencing problems only with a certain application or game, check with the manufacturer of that software to see if there's an update or compatibility issue with your specific hardware. Often, manufacturers will post workarounds, patches, or other fixes on their web sites.

4. If you wish to start exploring troubleshooting options, choose the appropriate tab (e.g., display, sound, etc.) in the DirectX management tool and try running the tests. Some of the pages have options that can be turned on or off. You may wish to try disabling certain DirectX features to see if it solves the particular problem you're having.

5. Choose the More Help tab to try one of the interactive troubleshooters, each a series of questions designed to help diagnose and solve DirectX-related problems.

Disk Cleanup
\windows\system32\cleanmgr.exe

Reclaim disk space by removing unwanted files from your hard drive.

To Open   Start → Programs → Accessories → System Tools → Disk Cleanup
Command Prompt → `cleanmgr`

Description

Disk Cleanup summarizes the disk space used by several predefined types of files, such as Temporary Internet Files and items in the Recycle Bin. If you have more than one hard drive, Disk Cleanup prompts you to choose one (see Figure 4-23).

The main window presents a list of file categories from which desired items can be checked to have the corresponding files deleted. The approximate space to be reclaimed by any categories, shown to the right. Here are descriptions of the various categories:

Downloaded Program Files
> This folder contains mostly ActiveX and Java applets downloaded from the Internet. If you clean out this folder, these components will simply be down-loaded again when you revisit the sites that use them.

Temporary Internet Files
> Temporary Internet Files, commonly known as the browser cache, are web pages and images from recently visited web sites, stored in your hard disk for the sole purpose of improving performance when browsing the Web. Deleting the files will have no adverse effects other than requiring that they be downloaded again the next time the corresponding web sites are visited.

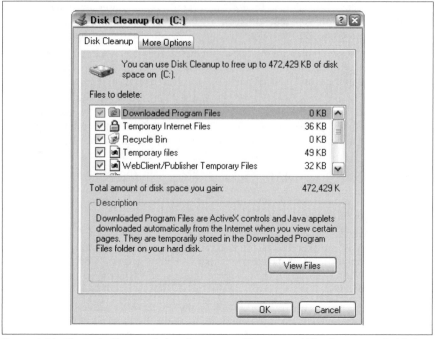

Figure 4-23. The Disk Cleanup dialog shows several locations of files that can probably be safely deleted

You can set the maximum size of this folder using Control Panel → [Network and Internet Connections] → Internet Options → General → Settings → Amount of disk space to use. Note that copies of cookie files (regularly stored in \Windows\ Cookies\) for IE4 are also stored in this folder, but are not deleted along with other Internet files.

Recycle Bin

By default, files that are deleted aren't really deleted; they are simply moved to the recycle bin for deletion at a later time. You can empty the Recycle Bin at any time by right-clicking the Recycle Bin icon on your Desktop and selecting Empty Recycle Bin. Right-click the Recycle Bin and select properties to change the maximum amount of disk space allocated to the storage of deleted files (or to disable the Recycle Bin and have files permanently erased immediately).

Temporary Files

Many applications open files to store temporary data, but aren't especially meticulous about deleting those files when they're no longer needed. Application crashes and power outages are other reasons why temporary files might be left behind. The disk space consumed by temporary files, especially after several weeks without maintenance, can be several megabytes.

WebClient/Publisher Temporary Files

These files are essentially the same as the Temporary Internet Files, kept around only for performance reasons, and can be safely deleted as well.

Temporary Offline Files, Offline Files

Temporary offline files are local copies of recently used documents normally stored on remote computers, and marked "Offline." If you take advantage of the "Offline Files" feature in Windows XP, you may wish to examine the files in these folders before you indiscriminately delete them with this utility.

Compress old files

A feature of the NTFS filesystem is that files can be selectively compressed in place. This is a much more advanced version of DriveSpace (the disk compression utility included with Windows 9x/Me), and somewhat more transparent than *.zip* files. One of the features of NTFS compression is that "old" files can be compressed automatically to save disk space; the downside is a slight performance hit. Turn on this option to enable compression of all files; don't bother if you don't need the disk space. Click Options to specify the age past which a file is considered "old." See the "NTFS Compression Utility," later in this chapter, for more information.

Catalog files for the Content Indexer

The indexing service speeds up file searches by maintaining an index of some files on your hard disk. The index files can be safely deleted and rebuilt automatically.

In addition to the aforementioned categories, the More Options tab provides access to three other tools that can also reclaim disk space:

Windows components

Click Clean up to selectively add or remove optional Windows components; this is the same as Control Panel → Add or Remove Programs → Add/Remove Windows Components.

Installed programs

Click Clean up to selectively add or remove installed applications; this is the same as Control Panel → Add or Remove Programs.

System Restore

This tool allows you to "roll back" your system to an earlier state (say, three weeks ago) before you installed those last seven applications. Although technically, use of this feature can result in reclaimed disk space, it is not an appropriate measure to take simply to increase the amount of free disk space, and should be used with extreme caution.

Disk Defragmenter

\windows\system32\dfrg.msc

Reorganize the files and pieces of files on a disk to optimize disk performance and reliability.

To Open   Start → Programs → Accessories → System Tools → Disk Defragmenter
         Command Prompt → dfrg.msc

Description

As files on your hard disk are created, modified, and deleted, they become fragmented (so that a single file is physically stored on the disk surface in several noncontiguous pieces). As more files become fragmented, reliability and performance of the drive both diminish. Disk Defragmenter reorganizes the files and folders on any drive so that not only are the files stored contiguously, but free space is also contiguous (see Figure 4-24).

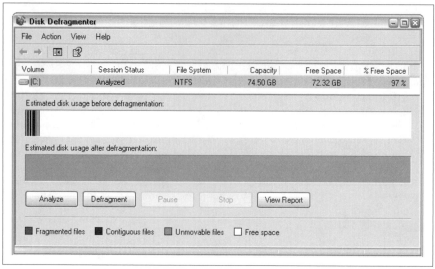

Figure 4-24. Disk Defragmenter rearranges the data on your hard disk for quicker, more reliable operations

Use of Disk Defragmenter is extremely simple. At the top of the window, you'll see a list of the hard drives installed on your system (on many systems, only one drive, *c:*, will be shown). Highlight a drive and click Defragment to begin the defragmentation process. Or, click Analyze to view a fragmentation report and a recommendation; note that Disk Defragmenter will claim that defragmentation is unnecessary if the percentage of fragmented files in the drive is lower than about 3 percent.

Note the map, signifying the files on your disk; refer to the legend of the bottom of the window for the meanings of the various colors. Defragmentation can take anywhere from 15 seconds to an hour, depending on the speed of your drive, the level of fragmentation, and the amount of data to move.

Notes

- Disk Defragmenter is a "snap-in," a component used with the Microsoft Management Console (discussed later in this chapter). You can open it via its icon on the Start menu, by launching *dfrg.msc*, or by opening MMC and installing the Disk Defragmenter snap-in.

- You can run other programs while Disk Defragmenter runs in the background, but this is not recommended for several reasons. Not only will writing to the disk interfere with Disk Defragmenter, causing it to restart repeatedly, but defragmenting a drive can slow system performance substantially.

- With Scheduled Tasks, you can run Disk Defragmenter when you're away from your system (for example, every Sunday night).

See Also

"Chkdsk," "Scheduled Tasks"

DiskPart

Prepare and partition a hard disk.

To Open   Command Prompt → `diskpart`

Description

DiskPart is a full-featured program used to prepare hard disks and, optionally, divide them into two or more partitions. It's a command-line program and has no interface to speak of. When you start DiskPart, you'll see a simple prompt: `DISKPART>`. Type `help` and press Enter to view a list of all the available commands:

`add`
> Add a mirror to a simple volume (Windows XP Server / Advanced Server only).

`active`
> Activate the current basic partition so that it can be used as a boot disk; using it is not necessary if there's only one partition in the volume.

`assign`
> Assign a drive letter or mount point to the selected volume. Note that it may be easier to use the Disk Management tool; see the Microsoft Management Console for details.

`break`
> Break a mirror set (undoes the `add` command).

`clean`
> Clear the configuration information, or all information, off the disk; this effectively erases the disk.

`convert`
> Convert between different disk formats; most users will never need this command.

`create`
> Create a volume or partition; this is the first step in preparing a hard disk.

`delete`
> Delete an object (undo the `create` command).

`detail`
> Display details about an disk, partition, or volume. Note that you'll need to use `select` first.

`exit`
> Exit DiskPart (Ctrl-C also works).

`extend`
> Extend a volume.

`import`
> Import a disk group.

`list`
> Print out a list of object; similar to `detail`.

`online`
> Change the status of the disk from offline to online.

remove
> Remove a drive letter or mount point assignment (undo the assign command). Note that it may be easier to use the Disk Management tool; see "Microsoft Management Console" for details.

rescan
> Rescan the computer looking for disks and volumes.

retain
> Place a retainer partition under a simple volume.

select
> Choose a disk, partition, or volume to view or modify. Even if you have only one disk or partition, you'll still need to select the object before carrying out any other commands. Use list to obtain object numbers for use with select, and then use detail to get more information.

Each of these commands (with the exception of exit) has one or more subcommands. For example, if you simply type detail at the prompt, you'll get a list of the subcommands for use with the list command: disk, partition, and volume. So, to display a list of all the disk volumes on the system, you would type:

    list volume

and you'll get a report that looks look something like this:

```
Volume ##  Ltr  Label        Fs     Type       Size     Status    Info
---------  ---  ----------   -----  ---------  -------  -------   ----
Volume 0    D   XPPCORP_EN   CDFS   CD-ROM      492 MB
Volume 1    C   Hard Disk    NTFS   Partition   28 GB   Healthy   System
```

From the report, is clear that drive C: is Volume 1; the next step is to select the volume, like this:

    select volume 1

Subsequent commands will then apply to the currently selected volume.

Notes

- Disk partitioning is tricky business and unless you're preparing a new drive, you'll probably never need to use DiskPart. If you need to repartition a drive that you're currently using, DiskPart is not the way to go, as it will erase any drive you attempt to repartition. A better choice is to use PartitionMagic by PowerQuest (*http://www.powerquest.com/*), which allows you to add, remove, and resize partitions without destroying the data they contain.

- DiskPart replaces the Fdisk utility found in Windows 9x/Me.

See Also

"Microsoft Management Console"

Display Properties

Change the appearance of the Desktop and most application windows, choose a screensaver, and change the settings of your display adapter and monitor.

To Open   Control Panel → [Appearance and Themes] → Display
Right-click on an empty portion of your Desktop → Properties
Command Prompt → `desk.cpl`
Command Prompt → `control desktop`
Command Prompt → `control color`*

Description

The Display Properties window allows you to configure a wide variety of settings that affect the Desktop, display, and appearance of just about anything on the screen (see Figure 4-25).

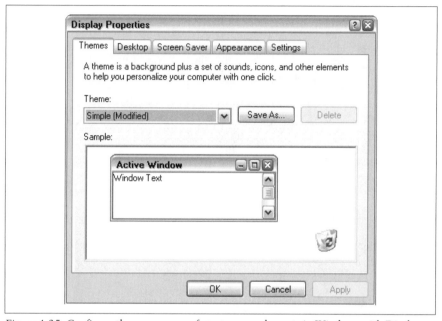

Figure 4-25. Configure the appearance of most screen elements in Windows with Display Properties

Settings are divided into the following tabs:

Themes

A theme is a name under which a collection of display settings is saved. After you've selected the preferences in the other tabs in this dialog, click Save As to create a new theme. Then, if you ever make a subsequent change, you can easily revert back to your saved preferences by selecting the desired theme from the Theme list. Don't confuse themes with styles (available in the Appearance tab).

Saving your theme is a good idea, as it will allow you to restore your settings easily if they're ever changed. It also allows you to quickly switch between multiple groups of settings, which is useful, for example, if you use two different monitors. When you click Save As, you'll be prompted to enter a filename with

---

* This opens the Display Properties window and automatically switches to the Appearance tab.

the *.theme* filename extension. However, the default folder for these files is My Documents, which is not where Windows looks for themes when it populates the Theme drop-down listbox. To have your theme listed in the Theme list, save your *.theme* file in the \Windows\Resources\Themes folder.

Due to a strange quirk in the way Windows XP handles themes, several other Control Panel settings will be reset whenever you change the theme. Preferences like your mouse pointers (see "Mouse Properties"), sound scheme (see "Sounds and Audio Devices"), and your Media Player skin (see "Windows Media Player") will all revert to their defaults. What's even more confusing is that while these settings appear to be linked to the Themes setting in Display Properties, none of them are actually saved with your theme when you click Save As.

Desktop

The Desktop tab allows you to select a background image. If no background image is selected, a solid color is used (set by the Color option here or by Appearance → Advanced). The background image (also called wallpaper) can be centered (displayed actual size in the middle, surrounded by the background color if it's not big enough), tiled (repeated so it fills the screen), or stretched (displayed once, but enlarged or shrunk so it fits the screen exactly).

Click Customize Desktop to selectively show or hide the My Documents, My Computer, My Network Places, and Internet Explorer icons on the Desktop (see Figure 4-26). You can also change the icons for My Computer, My Documents, My Network Places, and the Recycle Bin. The Desktop cleanup section helps remove less frequently used Desktop icons.

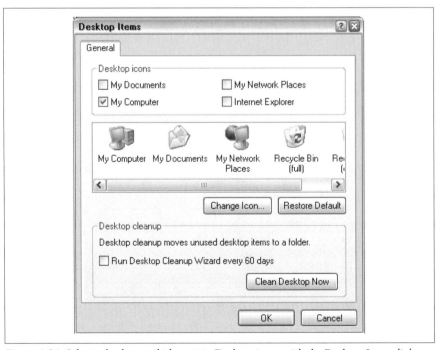

Figure 4-26. Selectively show or hide certain Desktop icons with the Desktop Items dialog

Note that most items on the Desktop are merely shortcuts and other files, stored in the folders \Documents and Settings\[username]\Desktop and \Documents and Settings\All Users\Desktop. See "Desktop" in Chapter 3 for details.

Screen Saver

Years ago, monochrome monitors, when left on for long periods of time, would be ruined when the images displayed would get "burned in." So, screensavers were invented, which blanked the screen after a certain period of inactivity. It wasn't long before screensavers started showing animations instead of just a blank screen.* Today, the concept of monitor burn-in is obsolete, but screensavers are still fun and can even provide security from prying eyes by obscuring the screen when you walk away from your computer. Choose from one of the available screensavers here and click Settings to configure it or Preview to see it in action (see Figure 4-27).

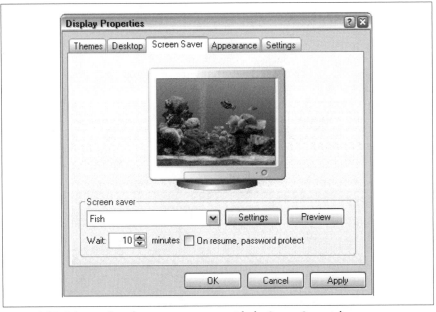

Figure 4-27. Select and configure a screensaver with the Screen Saver tab

Choose the length of inactivity before the selected screensaver is activated. A computer is considered inactive if no mouse or keyboard entry is received; updates to the screen, such as progress indicators or animations don't count and won't stop a screensaver from being invoked. Use the "On resume, password protect" feature to lock up access to the computer once a screensaver has been invoked.

Third-party screensavers are plentiful; one of my favorites is Jim Sachs' fabulous SereneScreen Aquarium (*http://www.serenescreen.com/*), of which a scaled-down

---

* At one time, the After Dark screensaver (made by Berkeley Systems, famous for their "Flying Toaster" animation) was the bestselling software program in the world. For some reason, the screensaver frenzy appears to have died down.

version is included in the Microsoft Plus! add-on for Windows XP, and even comes preinstalled with some copies of Windows XP.

Note that the screensaver can interfere with some programs, so you may want to temporarily disable it if you're experiencing a problem backing up to tape or burning a CD, for example.

Any particular screensaver can also be started from the command line or from Windows Explorer by launching the corresponding *.scr* file.

Appearance

The following settings are available in the Appearance tab:

Windows and buttons

See the discussion of Styles at the beginning of Chapter 3.

Color scheme

Save your color selections into a scheme, which is a subset of the theme selection (see the Themes tab, above).

Font size

If you're having trouble reading the text on your screen, try adjusting the font size here. Better yet, click Advanced and choose the typeface and size for each screen element independently.

Effects

Choose visual goodies, such as animation, fading, and shadows. These settings are really just eye candy and can significantly slow down your system (see Figure 4-28). See "System Properties," later in this chapter, as well as TweakUI in Appendix D, for additional related options.

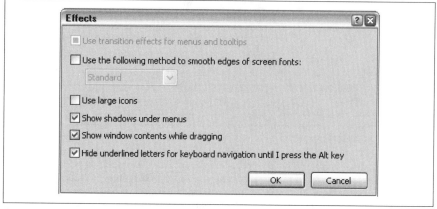

Figure 4-28. You can make Windows seem faster and more responsive by turning off some of the visual effects

Advanced

This window allows you to choose the colors and fonts for all of the various screen elements. Choose the desired element from the Item list and change any available options to your liking. In addition to colors and fonts, you can also change the spacing of Desktop icons, the thickness of titlebars and menus, and even the colors of buttons (see Figure 4-29).

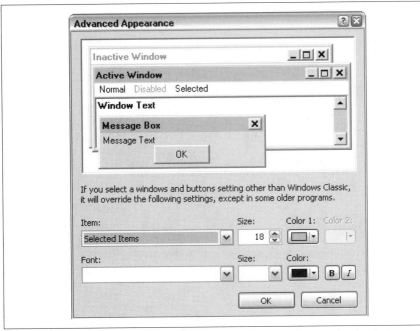

Figure 4-29. Even though the preview here always shows the classic style, this dialog can be used to configure some aspects of the new Windows XP style as well

Although the preview in the Advanced dialog is shown using the "Classic" style, most settings will apply regardless of the selected style. For example, you can shrink down the huge titlebars that are the default in the Windows XP style by choosing "Active Title Bar" from the Item menu and changing Size to something more reasonable, such as 20. Note, however, that you can't change any of the colors when using the Windows XP style (other than using the "Color scheme" listbox under the Appearance tab, discussed above), a limitation that will hopefully be lifted in subsequent versions of Windows.

Settings

Last, but not least, comes the Settings tab, which allows you to change your display hardware settings (see Figure 4-30). Here, you can choose the resolution and color depth of your screen. There are two limitations of your video card that may affect the settings here. First, the amount of memory on your video card dictates the maximum color depth and resolution you can use. The memory required by a particular setting is calculated by multiplying the horizontal size times the vertical size times the bytes per pixel. If you're in 32-bit color mode, then each pixel will require 32 bits, or 4 bytes (there are 8 bits/byte). At a resolution of 1024×768, that's $1024 \times 768 \times 4$ bytes/pixel, or about 3.14MB. Therefore, a video card with 4MB of video memory will be able to handle the display setting, but a card with only 2MB will not.

As you adjust your color depth, Windows may automatically adjust other settings depending on your card's capabilities. If you increase your color depth, your resolution might automatically decrease; likewise, if you raise the resolution, your color depth might go down.

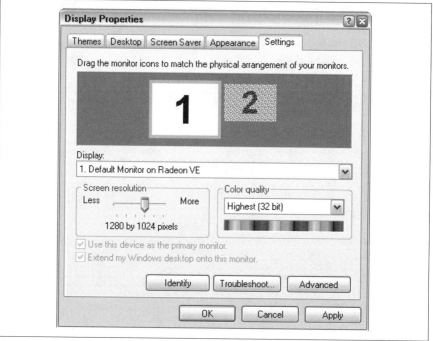

Figure 4-30. Choose your screen resolution, color depth, and multiple monitor setup with the Settings tab

The other limitation that may affect your available settings is the refresh rate that your card will be able to generate. Although the maximum refresh rate does not depend on the amount of your card's memory, you may have to lower your resolution to achieve the desired rate. Windows should automatically adjust your refresh rate to the highest setting your card supports, but this is not always the case. If you notice that your display appears to be flickering, especially under fluorescent lights, you'll need to raise your refresh rate, either by adjusting the refresh rate setting directly or by lowering your resolution or color depth. (Note that this does not apply to flat-panel or laptop displays, which never flicker.) Consequently, if you hear a slight whine from your monitor, it means your refresh rate is too high. The minimum refresh rate you should tolerate is 72 Hz. People with corrective lenses seem to be more sensitive and might require a higher setting to be comfortable. Most cards available today support refresh rates of 75 Hz and higher, so this is usually not a problem. Click Advanced → and choose the Adapter tab. If your display driver supports it, you can adjust your refresh rate with the Refresh Rate setting. If the setting is not there, you'll either need to obtain a more recent video driver, reduce your resolution or color depth, or get yourself a better video card.

If you have more than one monitor, either using two separate video cards or a single video card that supports two monitors, all configured screens will be shown in the preview area. Click any screen icon to activate it; the settings below apply only to the selected monitor. You can even drag-drop monitor icons to rearrange them so that, for example, a different monitor assumes the role of the upper left. Click Identify, below, if you're not sure which monitor is #1 and which is #2.

The Advanced button allows you to view the hardware properties for your video adapter(s) and monitor(s). You'll really never need to adjust these settings unless you're updating a driver for your monitor or display adapter, adjusting your refresh rate (see above), or configuring color profiles (for matching the color output of your printer with your scanner and monitor).

Notes

- All of the settings in this dialog are also covered in Chapter 5.
- A bug in Windows' handling of themes may cause your sound scheme and mouse pointer schemes to revert to their defaults whenever you change the display theme. However, neither the sound nor mouse schemes are saved with the display theme.
- No piece of hardware inside or attached to your computer is more important, in my opinion, than your monitor (with the possible exception of the keyboard and pointing device). A bad monitor can give you headaches, not to mention neck and back pain. I strongly recommend one of the newer flat-panel displays, if you can afford them; in addition to consuming less desk space and power, the better ones actually provide superior image quality and color reproduction than any CRT.

See Also

"Control Panel," Chapter 3

Dr. Watson
\windows\system32\drwatson.exe; drwtsn32.exe

Records system error information when a system error occurs.

To Open   Command Prompt → drwatson *(start daemon)*
Command Prompt → drwtsn32 *(change settings)*
Start → Programs → Accessories → System Tools → System Information
   → Tools menu → Dr Watson *(change settings)*

Description

Dr. Watson is a diagnostic tool that records information on the internal state of Windows when a system error occurs. It collects information such as system details, running applications, startup applications, kernel drivers, and user drivers. Although the reports that Dr. Watson produces are of little use to most users, they diagnostic information that may be helpful to developers and Microsoft support technicians for diagnosis of the problem.

If activated, Dr. Watson waits invisibly in the background until a system error occurs, at which time a dialog box appears, asking for comments on the activities prior to the error. The comments you type will be added to a file as long as you select File → Save or File → Save As from the dialog. The two available formats include Dr. Watson log files (*.wlg*) and plain text files (*.txt*). The default is a *.wlg* file, and is recommended if you want to subsequently use the Dr. Watson application to view a GUI version of the information.

If Dr. Watson detects a fault that might not be fatal, you'll have the opportunity to ignore the fault or close the application. If you choose to ignore the fault, Windows continues without performing the faulting instruction. You might be able to save your work in a new file at this point, but you should then restart Windows.

See Also

"System Properties," (Specifically, the topic of error reporting in the Advanced tab).

Driver Verifier Manager

\windows\system32\verifier.exe

A tool for monitoring Windows kernel-mode drivers and graphics drivers.

To Open   Command Prompt → `verifier`

Description

Driver Verifier Manager is included with Windows XP (primarily for hardware manufacturers to test their drivers to ensure that drivers are not making illegal function calls or causing system corruption).

Notes

For more information on using the Driver Verifier Manager, see *http://www.microsoft.com/hwdev/Driver/Verifier.htm*.

DriverQuery

\windows\system32\driverquery.exe

Display a list of the installed device drivers and their properties. (DriverQuery is included with Windows XP Professional only.)

To Open   Command Prompt → `driverquery`

Usage   `driverquery [/fo] [/nh] [/si] [/v] [/s [/u [/p]]]`

Description

Although Device Manager (see "Microsoft Management Console") displays a hierarchal view of all of the devices attached to the system, only Driver Query provides a comprehensive list for every installed driver, either on a local machine or on any remote computer on the network.

Run DriverQuery without any options to print out the basic list, or use one of the following options:

/fo format

Specify the format of the display: type /fo table (the default) for a formatted table, /fo list for a plaint text list, or /fo csv for a comma-separated report, suitable for importing into a spreadsheet or database.

/nh

If using the /fo table or /fo csv format (above), the /nh option turns off the column headers.

/v

Display additional details about driver other than signed drivers.

/si

Display additional details about signed drivers.

/s system

Connect to a remote system, where *system* is the name of the computer.

/u user

Specify a user account (include an optional domain before the username) under which the command should execute.

/p password

Specify the password for the user account specified with the /u parameter; prompts for the password if omitted.

Notes

Refer to Appendix C for information on redirecting the output of this program to a text file, making it easy to save or import into a spreadsheet or database application.

Event Viewer
\windows\system32\eventvwr.exe

See "Microsoft Management Console."

Explorer

See "Windows Explorer."

FAT to NTFS Conversion Utility
\windows\system32\convert.exe

Convert a drive using the File Allocation Table (FAT) filesystem to the more robust NT File System (NTFS).

To Open   Command Prompt → convert

Usage   convert volume /fs:ntfs [/v] [/cvtarea:fn] [/nosecurity] [/x]

Description

The filesystem is the invisible mechanism on any drive that is responsible for keeping track of all the data stored on the drive. Think of the filesystem as a massive table of contents, matching up each filename with its corresponding data stored somewhere on the disk surface. The File Allocation Table (FAT) file system first appeared in DOS, and has been the basis for each successive version of Windows, including Windows 95, Windows 98, and Windows Me. A slightly improved version of FAT, called FAT32, was introduced in Windows 95 OSR2 and included support for larger drives and smaller cluster sizes.

Meanwhile, the Windows NT/2000 line of operating systems also supported the newer and more robust NTFS filesystem. Among other things, NTFS provides much more sophisticated security than FAT or FAT32 does, as well as encryption and compression. However, NTFS and FAT/FAT32 are not compatible with each other, and since Windows 9x/Me doesn't support NTFS, you'll need to stick with FAT or FAT32 if you intend to have a dual-boot system. Furthermore, if you've upgraded from Windows 9x/Me, your drive probably still uses the FAT or FAT32 filesystem. This tool is used to convert a FAT or FAT32 drive to an NTFS drive without damaging the data stored on it. To convert drive *c:*, for example, type the following:

```
convert c: /fs:ntfs
```

The following options are also available:

/v

>   Run the Conversion Utility in verbose mode (provide more information).

/cvtarea:*filename*

>   Specify a contiguous file in the root directory as the placeholder for NTFS system files.

/nosecurity

>   Include this parameter if you want the initial security privileges for all files and folders on the newly converted volume to be set so the files and folders are accessible by everyone.

/x

>   Force the volume to dismount first—if necessary, closing any opened files on the volume. Use this option if you're on a network and concerned that other users may disrupt the conversion by accessing your drive during the process.

Notes

To determine the filesystem currently used on any drive, right-click the drive icon in My Computer or Explorer, and select Properties.

See Also

"Chkntfs," "DiskPart"

Fax Console

\windows\system32\fxsclnt.exe

Manage incoming and outgoing faxes using the Microsoft Fax service.

To Open   Start → Programs → Accessories → Communications → Fax → Fax Console
Command Prompt → fxsclnt

Description

The Fax Console is the central interface for sending, receiving, and managing faxes using the Microsoft Fax service (see Figure 4-31). The Fax Console is set up like Outlook Express, with folders shown in a hierarchal tree in the left pane and the contents of the currently selected folder shown in the right pane.

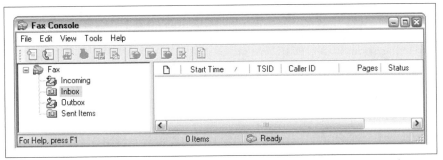

Figure 4-31. View and manage all incoming and outgoing faxes with the Fax Console

The first time you run Fax Console, the Fax Configuration Wizard will appear, which will ask for your personal contact information, primarily for use with cover pages. All of the fields are optional and can be left blank. This information can be entered later by going to Tools → Sender Information.

There are two ways to send a fax using the Microsoft Fax service. The first, using File → Send a Fax (which is the same as running *fxssemd.exe* or selecting Start → Programs → Accessories → Communications → Fax → Send a Fax), walks you through selecting a document and then creating a corresponding fax job.

The preferred method of sending a fax, though, is to start the application used to create the original document (e.g., your word processor or spreadsheet) and print to your fax printer. Indeed, the fax is really only a remote printer connected with a phone line. After your application has sent the document to the fax printer driver, a new Wizard appears and asks you for the recipient name and phone number, as well as any queuing options (useful if you wish to postpone sending the fax until off-peak hours).

Start the Fax Monitor (Tools → Fax Monitor) to automatically answer incoming calls and receive faxes. If you don't want the Microsoft Fax service to automatically answer incoming calls, you can selectively receive faxes by going to File → Receive a fax now.

Notes

- Not surprisingly, if you don't have a modem, you won't be able to send or receive faxes. However, Fax Console will let you view and export fax documents you may have already stored on your hard disk; use File → Import to view faxes created in previous versions of Windows and File → Save As to export them to a more usable format.

- If you wish to receive faxes but don't have a modem, or if you just don't want to leave the Microsoft Fax service running all the time, there are Internet-based fax services (such as *http://www.efax.com*), some of which are completely free, that send incoming faxes to you as email attachments.

- An alternative to using faxes is to email documents and scans. A program like Adobe Acrobat (*http://www.adobe.com*) is especially useful for preserving fonts and formatting in computer-generated documents, and can even accommodate scanned pages, making it easy for the recipient to view or even print them. Not only will this result in higher quality documents and lower phone bills, but it might save a few trees.

- To send a fax on the fly, place a shortcut to the Fax icon in your Printers and Faxes folder in your Send To menu. Then right-click any file and select Send To → Fax to quickly fax the document. Note that this won't work for all document types, so a little experimentation may be required.

See Also

"Fax Cover Page Editor," "Windows Picture and Fax Viewer"

Fax Cover Page Editor

\windows\system32\fxscover.exe

Create and modify cover pages for use with the Microsoft Fax service.

To Open   Start → Programs → Accessories → Communications → Fax → Fax Cover Page Editor

Fax Console → Tools → Personal Cover Pages → New (or) Open

Command Prompt → fxscover

Description

The Fax Cover Page Editor works like an ordinary drawing/layout program, in that you can indiscriminately place text, shapes, and images on a blank page. Pages created with the Cover Page Editor are used automatically when sending faxes with the Microsoft Fax service.

What makes the Cover Page Editor different from other drawing/layout programs to which you might be accustomed is its support for fields. Naturally, it wouldn't do you much good to create a custom cover page for only a single recipient; rather, it is desirable to create a single cover page (or series of cover pages) that can be used with any number of recipients. Use the Insert menu to place text fields on the page; fields are divided into the following three categories (menus):

Recipient
> Place the name or phone number fields on your cover page and Microsoft Fax will insert those details of the recipient on each fax that is sent out.

Sender
> The information in the Sender menu does not change from fax to fax; rather, it is set in the Fax Console application (discussed earlier in this chapter) by going to Fax Console → Tools → Sender Information. Note that it's generally preferred to use fields rather than static text, even if the information contained therein is the same for all faxes—it not only makes it easier to change later on, but means that your cover pages can be used easily by others.

Message
> Like items in the Recipient menu, above, Message details the message change from fax to fax, such as the subject, time, date, and number of pages.

When you've created or modified the cover pages desired, you must save it into a Cover Page (.cov) file, stored, by default, in *\Documents and Settings\[username]\My Documents\Fax\Personal Coverpages*. Then, when sending a fax, simply specify the desired Cover Page file, and it will be used as the first page in your outgoing fax.

You may wish to preview outgoing faxes immediately after creating or modifying a cover page to make sure information is inserted into the fields properly.

See Also
"Fax Console"

File Compare (comp)

Compare the contents of two files (or sets of files) byte-by-byte and display the differences between them.

To Open   Command Prompt → comp

Usage   comp [file1] [file2] [/n=number] [/c] [/offline] [/d] [/a] [/l]

Description

File Compare (*comp.exe*) compares two files (or more, using wildcards), and reports whether or not the files are identical. If the files are identical, *comp.exe* will report Files compare OK. If the files are the same size but have different contents, *comp.exe* displays the differences, character-by character, by reporting Compare Error at OFFSET *n* (where *n* is byte offset—the location of the difference, in characters, from the beginning of the file). If the files are different sizes, *comp.exe* reports Files are different sizes, and the comparison stops there.

Here are the options for *comp.exe*:

file1, file2
> Specify the filenames of the files to compare. For any files that aren't in the current directory, you'll need to include the full path. If *file1* includes a wildcard, all matching files are compared to *file2*. Likewise, if *file2* includes a wildcard, each matching file is compared to *file1*. If one or both of these parameters are omitted, *Comp.exe* will prompt you for the files to be compared.

/n=*number*
> Include the /n option to compare only the first specified number of lines in the files, or omit to compare the entire files. For example, specify /n=5 to check on the first five lines in each file.

/c
> Disregard the case of ASCII characters; upper and lower case letters are treated as identical.

/offline
> *Comp.exe* normally skips files marked as "offline." Specify /offline (or just /off) to include offline files as well. (See "Synchronization Manager," later in this chapter for more information on offline files.)

/d
> Displays differences in decimal format.

/a
> Displays differences in ASCII characters. The /a option is the default, so specifying it has no effect.

/l
> Include line numbers in any output.

Notes

- Windows XP actually comes with two file comparison utilities, *comp.exe* (this one) and *fc.exe* (discussed in the next section). *Comp.exe* performs a character-by-character comparison, but only displays differences if the files are exactly the same size. *Fc.exe* performs a line-by-line comparison and works regardless of the file sizes. For most users, *fc.exe* will be the tool of choice, as it displays the differences between the files and doesn't have any prompts, so it can be used from a WSH script or batch file.

- Regardless of the outcome of the comparison, *comp.exe* will ask if you want to perform another comparison. There's no way to disable this prompt, but you can use the input redirection character (see Appendix C), like this:

      comp file1 file2 <n

which "types" the letter n at the prompt automatically, disabling the prompt.

File Compare (fc)

\windows\system32\fc.exe

Compare the contents two files (or sets of files) line by line and display the differences between them.

To Open   Command Prompt → fc

Usage

      fc file1 file2 [/a] [/c] [/lbn] [/n] [/t] [/w] [/offline] [/nnn]
         [/l]
      fc /b filename1 filename2

Description

File Compare (*fc.exe*) compares the contents of two files (or more, using wildcards) and displays the differences (if any). If the files are identical, *fc.exe* will report FC: no differences encountered. If the files are different, *fc.exe* lists the differing lines. Here's an example of how *fc.exe* is used:

Start with an ordinary text file, say, *Bill.txt*. Open it in Notepad, change one line, and save it into a new filename, say, *Marty.txt*. Then open a command prompt window, make sure you're in the same directory as the two files, and type the following:

      fc bill.txt marty.txt

The output will look something like this:

      Comparing files Bill.txt and Marty.txt
      ***** Bill.txt
      Way down Louisiana close to New Orleans
      Way back up in the woods among the evergreens
      There stood a log cabin made of earth and wood
      ***** Marty.txt
      Way down Louisiana close to New Orleans
      Way back up in the woods among the antihistamines
      There stood a log cabin made of earth and wood
      *****

For each line or sequence of lines that is found to differ in the two files, *fc.exe* prints out a pair of excerpts from each of the files. The first and last line in each excerpt are what the two files have in common and are included for context. The lines in between (only a single line in this example) show the differences. The report will include one pair of excerpts for each difference found; if there are three nonconsecutive differing lines, there will be six excerpts. Here are the options for *Comp.exe*:

file1, file2

Specify the filenames of the files to compare. For any files that aren't in the current directory, you'll need to include the full path. If *file1* includes a wild-card, all matching files are compared to *file2*. Likewise, if *file2* includes a wildcard, each matching file is compared to *file1*. Both parameters are required.

/a

Display only first and last lines for each set of differences, as opposed to the default of every different line. This option is only applicable if a single sequence of differing lines (resulting in a single excerpt pair) is three lines or longer; other-wise, /a has no effect.

/c

Disregards the case of ASCII characters; upper- and lowercase letters are treated as identical.

/lbn

Specify the maximum consecutive mismatches; /lb17 will list only the first 17 differing lines. If omitted, the default is 100 maximum mismatches.

/n

Include line numbers in the report.

/t

Preserve any tabs in the files being compared. By default, tabs are treated as spaces with 1 tab = 8 spaces.

/w

Compress whitespace (tabs and spaces) to a single space for comparison. Possibly useful when comparing *.html* files, as web browsers will eliminate redundant tabs in spaces as well.

/offline

Fc.exe normally skips files marked as "offline." Specify /offline (or simply /off) to include offline files as well. (See "Synchronization Manager," later in this chapter, for more information on offline files.)

/nnn

Specify the number of consecutive lines that must match after a mismatch. For example, if you specify /4, a mismatched line followed by 3 matching lines, followed by one or more mismatched lines, is treated as though it were a single sequence of mismatched lines in the report.

/l

Treat the files as ASCII (plain text). Since /l is the default, it has no effect.

/u

Treat the files as unicode text.

/b

Treat the files as binary and perform the comparison on a byte-by-byte basis (similar to *comp.exe*, the other file comparison utility). Instead of the pairs of excerpts explained above, differing bytes are displayed in parallel columns. A binary comparison is typically only appropriate for files of the same sizes, but

Applications and Tools

unlike *comp.exe*, the comparison will still be performed if they are different sizes. The /b option can't be used in conjunction with any of the other options.

Notes

- Windows XP actually comes with two file comparison utilities, *comp.exe* (discussed in the previous section) and *fc.exe* (this one). *comp.exe* performs a character-by-character comparison, but only displays differences if the files are exactly the same size. *fc.exe* performs a line-by-line comparison and works regardless of the file sizes. For most users, *fc.exe* will be the tool of choice, as it displays the differences between the files and doesn't have any prompts, so it can be used from a WSH script or batch file.

- *Fc.exe* is most useful when comparing two different, but similar, text files. For example, you can compare two Registry patches (since *.reg* files are plain text files) made at two different times to see what changes have been made. See Chapter 8 for more information on Registry Patches.

- Although *fc.exe* can compare two binary files, if you try to compare two word processor documents (*.doc* and *.wpd* files are binary files), the results won't be terribly helpful. Try converting the documents to an ASCII-based format, such as *.rtf* or *.html*, and then perform an ASCII comparison. Naturally, most modern word processors have their own document comparison tools, but they can often be limited; while word processors may miss subtle formatting changes, *fc.exe* will catch every single difference.

File Expansion Utility

\windows\system32\expand.exe

Extract one or more compressed files from a cabinet (*.cab*) file.

To Open   Command Prompt → expand

Usage
```
expand -d source.cab [-f:files]
expand [-r] source.cab [destination]
expand source.cab -f:files destination
```

Description

A cabinet file is a compressed archive commonly used to package application installation files. The File Expansion Utility is used to extract files embedded in these cabinet files and takes the following options:

source.cab

   The name of the cabinet (*.cab*) file from which to extract the files.

destination

   The name of the folder in which to place the extracted files, a new filename to use for the extracted files, or a combination of the two. If using the -f option, *destination* is mandatory and must include a filename (with or without wildcards).

-d

   Display (list) the contents of the specified cabinet file.

-r

Specify -r (recursive) without *destination* to extract all the files contained in the specified cabinet file. For example:

```
expand -r package.cab
```

Specify -r along with *destination* to rename the files according to the file specification included in *destination*. For example, the following extracts all the files in *package.cab* and renames their file extensions to *.txt*:

```
expand -r package.cab *.txt
```

-f:*files*

Use the -f option to specify one or more files to extract; use this if you don't want to extract all the files from the cabinet file. For example, the following extracts the file *uno.txt* from *package.cab*:

```
expand package.cab -f:uno.txt uno.txt
```

Note that the *destination* parameter is mandatory when using the -f option and is used to specify the target filename. In this example, as well as most times this program will be used, *files* and *destination* will be the same.

Notes

The easiest method for extracting files from cabinets is to simply double click the *.cab* file in Explorer and then drag the desired file(s) out. Since *expand.exe* is a command-line program, it is better suited for use with WSH scripts and batch files. It can also be used when installing or repairing Windows XP when Explorer isn't available.

See Also

"Cabinet (CAB) Maker," "System Configuration Utility"

File and Settings Transfer Wizard

\windows\system32\usmt\migwiz.exe

Helps you transfer files and settings from one computer to another.

To Open   Start → Programs → Accessories → System Tools → File and Settings Transfer Wizard
Command Prompt → \windows\system32\usmt\migwiz

Description

The File and Settings Transfer Wizard is a step-by-step guide that walks you through the process of transferring your personal documents, contents of your Favorites folder, Internet Explorer and Outlook Express settings, Desktop and display preferences, dial-up connections, and other settings from one computer to another (see Figure 4-32). The wizard is intended to assist the migration of these files and settings from an "old" computer to a "new" computer, but could be used to duplicate a configuration across several computers just as easily, or even to assist you in upgrading your hard disk.

The first question the wizard asks is whether the computer being used is the "new computer" (the machine to receive the files and settings) or the "old computer" (the machine on which the files and settings are currently stored). Although you can begin the process from either computer, it makes more sense to start off from the old computer (unless the old computer is not running Windows XP).

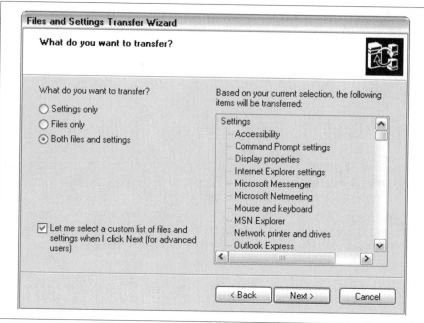

Figure 4-32. The File and Settings Transfer Wizard helps you migrate your personal documents and preferences to a new computer

If you choose "Old Computer," the next step is a choice between the following:

Direct cable

A direct cable connection uses a cable, commonly known as a null modem cable or LapLink cable, to connect two computers for the purpose of the transfer of data. Although it's much cheaper to set up than a network, the speed is glacial by comparison.

Home or small office network

This option uses a Microsoft Windows peer-to-peer network to transfer data between the two machines. Note that this choice may be disabled if another Windows XP system is not found on the network or if the network does not have all the required protocols installed. If this option is unavailable, you can still utilize your network using "Other," below.

Floppy drive or other removable media

If you have a zip drive, writable CD drive, writable DVD drive, removable hard disk, or some other removable cartridge drive, the wizard will place the necessary files on the media for later use on the new machine. Note that either the target (new) computer must also have the same drive or you'll need to transfer the drive to the new system.

Other

Use this option to simply specify a path in which to place the files. This can be a network path, a path to a removable drive, or a folder on your hard disk.

If you choose "New Computer," the next step is a choice between the following:

I want to create a Wizard Disk

> Select this option to use your floppy drive to transfer the wizard program to the old computer, which is useful if the old computer is running earlier version of Windows. The wizard works on Windows 95/98/Me, Windows NT 4.0, Windows 2000, and Windows XP.

I already have a Wizard disk

> This option simply quits the wizard and instructs you to use the wizard disk you already have on the old computer.

I'll use the wizard from the Windows XP CD

> This option also quits the wizard and instructs you how to use the wizard located on the Windows XP installation CD on the old computer.

I don't need the Wizard disk

> This is the only option of the four on this page that is used if you've already run the wizard on the old computer, as it will simply prompt you to locate the files and settings that have been packaged by the wizard.

Once you've chosen an option, follow the prompts on the screen to complete the process.

Notes

- Naturally, you can simply use Explorer and an active network connection or removable drive to transfer the files manually. Furthermore, using carefully selected registry patches, you can transfer many Windows settings and files from one machine to another. While this wizard will make the migration of documents, and especially settings, pretty easy, it may not end up being as flexible or complete as a manual migration.

- Another option is to use Backup (discussed earlier in this chapter) to transfer some or all of your files from one system to another.

Finger
                                                \windows\system32\finger.exe

Display information about a user account.

To Open   Command Prompt → `finger`

Usage   `finger [-l] [user][@host]`

Description

The Finger client uses a standard protocol to retrieve publicly available information from any networked computer. Let's say you want to find out about a username "Woodrow" on your own system; you would simply type:

    finger woodrow

Finger accepts the following options:

user

> The username you wish to query. Omit to list all the users currently logged in on the specified host.

@host

> The target machine containing the user account(s) you wish to query. Omit to query the local machine (localhost).

-l

> Displays information in a long list format

The finger protocol has been around for long time and is supported by all versions of Windows NT, Windows 2000, Windows XP, Unix, Solaris, and other platforms. The output from a Finger request varies widely (if you get a response at all); it depends on the operating system running on the specified host and the specific settings imposed by that machine's administrator.

Finger, when it works, commonly retrieves a report that looks something like this:

```
Login: woodrow                      Name: Gordie Howe
Directory: /usr/local/home/woodrow  Shell: /bin/csh
Never logged in.
New mail received Mon Oct  1 23:35 2001 (PDT)
     Unread since Wed Nov 20 11:54 1996 (PDT)
No Plan.
```

Although most the information included in this simple report is self-evident, the last line makes mention of a *plan*. The plan is a text file to be shown when one's account is fingered. It might contain contact information, office hours, personal statistics, or anything else the user wants. My plan file, for example, has several of my favorite quotes, including my favorite poem by Robert Creeley, "I Know a Man."

Notes

- The Finger daemon is the service responsible for responding to finger requests. This service is disabled by default, but can be enabled or otherwise configured using the services component of the Microsoft Management Console. Note that enabling the service on your computer may pose a security hazard, allowing outsiders to gain some information about one or more users on your system.

- As more users and administrators become security savvy, you'll find fewer occasions when a finger request actually gets a response. Typically, you'll receive a "connection refused" message.

Folder Options

Control the way folders appear in Explorer and configure file type associations.

To Open   Control Panel → [Appearance and Themes] → Folder Options
Windows Explorer → Tools → Folder Options
Command Prompt → `control folders`

Description

The Folder Options window has four tabs:

General

> Of the three settings on this page, the one that may not be entirely self-explanatory is the Tasks section (see Figure 4-33). Microsoft has removed the highly criticized Web View found in earlier versions of Windows and added an optional

feature called Common Tasks. When enabled, a common tasks pane appears along the left side of folder listings in Explorer and single-folder windows, which contains information and links related to the currently selected folder. Those new to Windows might appreciate the extra information, although advanced users will probably prefer to turn off Common Tasks to reduce screen clutter.

Figure 4-33. Among other things, the General tab lets you turn off the common tasks pane shown in many single folder windows

Of note in the Common Tasks pane is the feature to turn on or off the category view in Control Panel (covered earlier in this chapter), an otherwise unavailable setting.

View

After you've selected all your preferences in the General and View tabs, as well as Explorer's View menu, click Apply to All Folders to make your settings the default. Otherwise, all your settings will be lost as soon as you switch to a different folder (see Figure 4-34).

The Advanced settings here are actually quite important, as many of their default values can actually end up making Windows more difficult to use. Many of these settings are self-explanatory; some of the more interesting ones are as follows:

Display the simple folder view in Explorer's Folders list

This rather oddly named option simply shows or hides the dotted lines shown in the collapsible folder tree (see "Trees" in Chapter 3) in Windows Explorer. The default is on, but if turned off, the tree appears more like it did in earlier versions of Windows. In my opinion, the lines make the tree a little clearer and easier to use, so I recommend turning this option off.

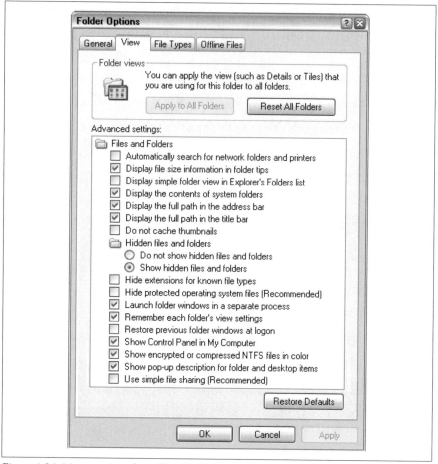

Figure 4-34. Many settings that affect the display of folders and files are located in the Folder Options' View tab

Display the contents of system folders

Turn this option on to eliminate the warning that appears when you attempt to view the contents of certain folders, such as *C:* and *\Windows*. The default is off.

Display the full path in the Address Bar / titlebar

By default, both of these settings are disabled, which, to me, is utterly baffling. For example, when viewing the folder, *c:\Documents and Settings\ Bubba\Documents\Stuff* in Windows Explorer, only "Stuff" will appear in the titlebar and Address Bar. This can be extremely confusing, especially when you also have a *d:\Additional Files\Latest\Stuff* folder. I strongly recommend enabling both "full path" options.

Hidden files and folders

Windows does not show hidden files by default in Explorer. Change this option if you need to access hidden files; see "Attrib," earlier in this chapter, for details on hidden files.

Hide extensions for known file types

In one of Microsoft's biggest blunders, this option has been turned on, by default, since Windows 95. See the discussion of the File Types tab, below, for why it should be turned off.

Launch folder windows in a separate process

Turn on this option to start a new instance of the Windows Explorer application every time you open a new folder window. Although this takes slightly more memory, it means that if one Explorer window crashes, they won't all crash.

Remember each folder's view settings

If this option is enabled and you use Explorer's View menu to alter the display of a particular folder, those settings will be saved with that folder for the next time it's opened. If you're looking for a way to save your View settings as the default for all folders, this option won't do it—instead, use the Apply to All Folders button (see Figure 4-34).

Use Simple File Sharing

Despite the "Recommended" note here, it is strongly recommended that this option be disabled for security purposes. See Chapter 7 for more information on sharing resources over a network.

File Types

The term *file types* describes the collection of associations between documents and the applications that use them (see Figure 4-35). For example, Windows knows to run Notepad when you double-click on a file with the *.txt* extension.

Launching the correct program for a particular file begins with file extensions, the letters (usually three) that follow the period in most filenames. For example, the extension of the file *Readme.txt* is *.txt*, signifying a plain text file; the extension of *Resume.wpd* is *.wpd*, signifying a document created in WordPerfect. By default, Windows hides the extensions of registered file types in Explorer and on the Desktop, but it's best to have them displayed (turn off the "Hide extensions for known file types" option under the View tab).

File extensions allow you to easily determine what kind of file you're dealing with (because icons are almost never descriptive enough). They also allow you to change Windows' perception of the type of a file by simply renaming the extension. Note that changing a file's extension doesn't actually change the contents or the format of the file, only how Windows interacts with it.

By hiding file extensions, Microsoft hoped to make Windows easier to use—a plan that backfired for several reasons. Because only the extensions of registered files are hidden, the extensions of files that aren't yet in the File Types database are still shown. What's even more confusing is that, when an application finally claims a certain file type, it can appear to the inexperienced user as though all of the old files of that type have been renamed. It also creates a "knowledge gap" between those who understand file types and those who don't. (Try telling someone whose computer still has hidden extensions to find *Readme.txt* in a directory full of files.) Other problems have arisen, such as trying to differentiate

Excel.exe and *Excel.xls* in Explorer when the extensions are hidden; one file is an application and the other is a document, but they may have the same icon.

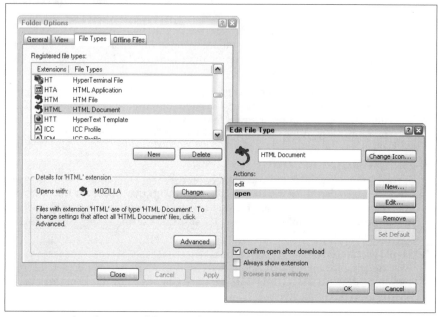

Figure 4-35. The File Types tab lets you change the associations between documents and the programs that open them

In the File Types window, all registered file extensions and their descriptions are shown in the list.

Here's how to customize a file type:

1. Select the desired file type from the list and click Advanced. (The Change button only displays the limited Open With dialog box.) You can sort the entries by filename extension or file type description to make any given file type easier to find.

2. Keep in mind that some file types may be claiming more than one extension. For example, the *.htm* and *.html* extensions are most likely associated with the same file type. If you are editing such a file type, it won't matter which extension you select.

3. The Actions list box contains a list of the customizable context menu items. Each one has a name and a command line (the application filename followed by command-line parameters, if applicable).

   A typical command line (the one for the *.txt* file type) might look like this: notepad /p "%1". This line tells Windows to launch Notepad with the /p parameter (see "Notepad," later in this chapter) when you double-click on a *.txt* file.

   The %1 is where you want Windows to insert the name of the clicked file, and is actually optional. However, the quotation marks, which ensure compatibilty with any spaces in the filenames, are not used by default in Windows; if you want to be able to double-click on any file with a space in its filename, add "%1" to the end of the command line here. If you double-clicked on a file called *stuff.txt*, located in the folder, *e:\things*, this file type action would result in the following command being executed: notepad /p "e:\things\stuff.txt".

4. Some actions have dynamic data exchange (DDE) commands, which are used only by certain applications—you probably won't have to bother with this setting. You can also change the icon for all the files of a particular type by clicking Change icon. See "Icons" in Chapter 3 for more information.

5. The bold item is the default action, also shown in bold at the top of the context menu. If there's no bold item, and therefore no default, double-clicking a file of that type will do nothing. To make "no action" the default, you'll have to delete the current default (bold) action. If you don't want to remove any actions, just add a new, temporary action, make it the default, and then delete it.

6. Click OK when you're done. The changes should take effect immediately; your Desktop and any open Explorer or single-folder windows will automatically refresh within a few seconds.

Offline Files

See "Synchronization Manager," later in this chapter, for more information on Offline Files.

Notes

All of the settings in this dialog are also covered in Chapter 5.

See Also

"Control Panel," "Windows Explorer"

Font Viewer

\windows\system32\fontview.exe

Display a preview and summary of any supported font file.

To Open   Control Panel → Fonts → Double-click any font file

Usage   fontview [/p] *filename*

Description

Font Viewer is most easily used by double-clicking on a font file (see Figure 4-36). You can view any font formats normally supported by Windows XP, including TrueType fonts (*.ttf*), bitmap fonts (*.fon*), and Type 1 fonts (*.pfm*).

In addition to the font name and summary information displayed at the top of the report, a preview of the font is shown with the full alphabet in upper- and lowercase, the full set of numbers, a few symbols, and the phrase "the quick brown fox jumps over the lazy dog. 1234567890" in several different sizes.

To run Font Viewer from the command line, you must specify the full path and filename of the font file, including its extension (such as *.fon* or *.ttf*). To send the report to the printer, use the /p option (which is the same as clicking the print button in the Font Viewer window).

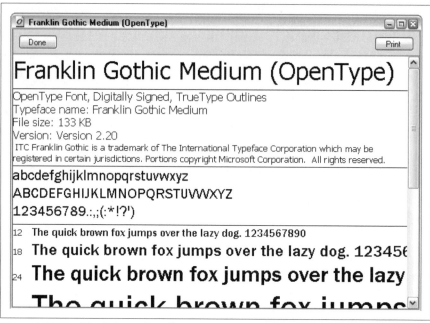

Figure 4-36. Double-click any font file to view a preview like this

Notes

- Windows XP typically keeps its installed font files in \Windows\Fonts, which is most easily accessible by going to Control Panel → Fonts. File Viewer can also be used to view fonts before they're installed, simply by double-clicking them in Explorer.

- Although Adobe Type 1 fonts are actually stored in the font binaries (.pfb), Font Viewer works only with the font metrics (.pfm).

- Font Viewer does not display every character in the font, only the predefined subset described above. To display every character in the font, use Character Map. (However, Character Map only works on installed fonts.)

See Also

"Fonts Folder," "Character Map"

Fonts Folder

Displays all the installed fonts.

To Open   Control Panel → Fonts*

Command Prompt → control fonts

Command Prompt → explorer \windows\fonts

---

* See "Control Panel," earlier in this chapter, for information on finding fonts using the Control Panel in Category View.

Description

The Fonts folder is merely a folder on your hard disk (specifically, \Windows\fonts). However, when viewed in Explorer, it's configured to display a list of installed fonts instead of a list of the contents of the folder. (The two aren't necessarily the same thing.) Select View → Details for more the most useful listing, which, among other things, allows you to match up a font name with the file in which it's stored (see Figure 4-37).

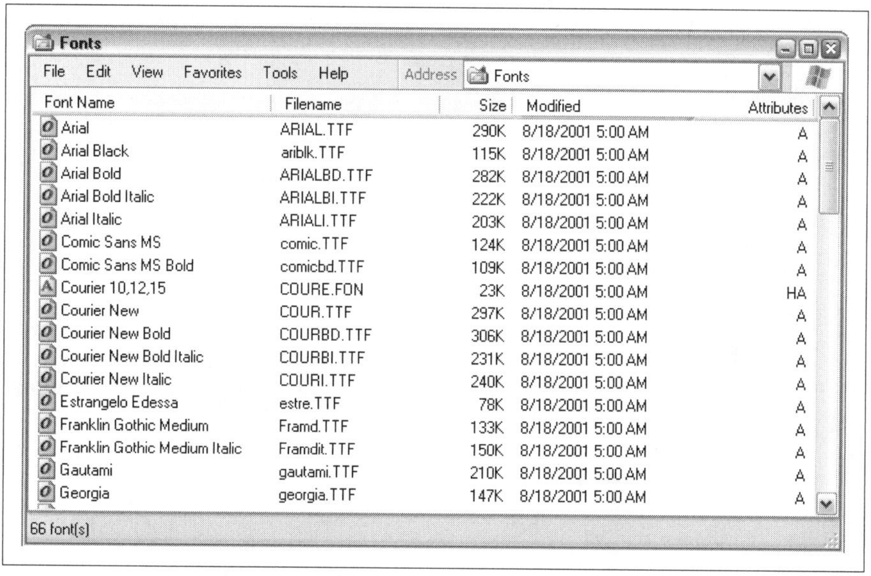

Font Name	Filename	Size	Modified	Attributes
Arial	ARIAL.TTF	290K	8/18/2001 5:00 AM	A
Arial Black	ariblk.TTF	115K	8/18/2001 5:00 AM	A
Arial Bold	ARIALBD.TTF	282K	8/18/2001 5:00 AM	A
Arial Bold Italic	ARIALBI.TTF	222K	8/18/2001 5:00 AM	A
Arial Italic	ARIALI.TTF	203K	8/18/2001 5:00 AM	A
Comic Sans MS	comic.TTF	124K	8/18/2001 5:00 AM	A
Comic Sans MS Bold	comicbd.TTF	109K	8/18/2001 5:00 AM	A
Courier 10,12,15	COURE.FON	23K	8/18/2001 5:00 AM	HA
Courier New	COUR.TTF	297K	8/18/2001 5:00 AM	A
Courier New Bold	COURBD.TTF	306K	8/18/2001 5:00 AM	A
Courier New Bold Italic	COURBI.TTF	231K	8/18/2001 5:00 AM	A
Courier New Italic	COURI.TTF	240K	8/18/2001 5:00 AM	A
Estrangelo Edessa	estre.TTF	78K	8/18/2001 5:00 AM	A
Franklin Gothic Medium	Framd.TTF	133K	8/18/2001 5:00 AM	A
Franklin Gothic Medium Italic	Framdit.TTF	150K	8/18/2001 5:00 AM	A
Gautami	gautami.TTF	210K	8/18/2001 5:00 AM	A
Georgia	georgia.TTF	147K	8/18/2001 5:00 AM	A

66 font(s)

Figure 4-37. The Details view of the Fonts folder shows the relationships between your font names and font filenames

Right-click a font file and select Properties to see bunch of additional information pertaining to the font, such as hinting and font smoothing properties, copyright information, font vendor information, and whether such fonts can be embedded.

To view a preview of an installed font, just double-click its name; see "Font Viewer," earlier in this chapter, for more information. To delete a font, delete it as you'd delete any file (press the Del key or drag-drop it into the Recycle Bin).

To install a font (as long as it's one of the supported types), just drag-drop it into the Fonts folder. Supported typeface formats include TrueType (*.ttf*), Adobe Type 1 (*.pfm* and *.pfb*), OpenType (also known as TrueType v2), and ugly old raster fonts (*.fon*) used in early versions of Windows.

Notes

- If a font file icon has a shortcut arrow (see "Shortcuts" in Chapter 3), it means the font is installed, but not actually stored in the \Windows\Fonts folder.

- Unlike some earlier versions of Windows, Windows XP comes with built-in support for Adobe Type 1 fonts, so a product like Adobe Type Manager is no longer needed.

- The View → List Fonts by Similarity feature, while a good idea in principle, rarely provides any useful information.

- If you're sharing documents with other users, you may need to send them copies of the font files you've used as well. If you drag-drop the desired files from the fonts folder onto, say, your Desktop, make sure to hold the Ctrl key (or drag with the right mouse button and select Copy Here) so the font file is copied and not moved (which would uninstall it). Keep in mind that some fonts are commercial products and copying them constitutes software piracy and copyright violation.

- Use a program like Adobe Acrobat (not the free reader application, but the full version available at *http://www.adobe.com/*) to share documents without having to share the fonts used.

- If the Fonts folder appears to be displaying an ordinary list of files rather than the specialized font listing, it can be fixed with TweakUI (see Appendix D).

- Any non-font files, that, for whatever reason, have been stored in the Fonts folder, will not show up at all, nor will they appear in any search results. To display a normal listing of the files in the Fonts folder, use the dir command in the Command Prompt (See Chapter 6.)

- Thousands of freeware fonts are available for download on the Internet, from such sites as *http://www.pcfonts.com/* and *http://www.microsoft.com/typography/*. You can also create your own fonts with an application like Fontographer (*http://www.macromedia.com/*).

- Fonts for icons, menus, and other screen elements are selected by going to Control Panel → [Appearance and Themes] → Display → Appearance tab.

See Also

"Control Panel"

ForceDOS   *\windows\system32\forcedos.exe*

Force a misbehaving DOS application to run in MS-DOS mode.

To Open   Command Prompt → forcedos

Usage   forcedos [/d directory] filename [parameters]

Description

Use the ForceDOS utility when Windows XP fails to recognize a DOS program and is unable to start or run it reliably. ForceDOS accepts the following options:

filename
: The filename of the executable to launch; include the full path if necessary.

/d *directory*
: Use the /d option to specify the working directory, necessary for many DOS programs that access files.

Parameters
: Specify any parameters here to be passed on to the launched program.

Format

Prepare floppy diskettes, hard disks, and some removable media for use.

To Open   Command Prompt → format.com

Usage   format volume [/q] [/c] [/x] [/v:label] [/fs:file-system] [/a:size]

Description

Before data can be stored on a floppy disk, hard disk, or many removable media disks (like Zip disks), the disk must be formatted. This process creates various low-level data structures on the disk, such as the filesystem (FAT, FAT32, NTFS, etc.). It also tests the disk surface for errors and stores bad sectors in a table that will keep them from being used. If there's any data on the disk, it will be erased.

The options for Format are:

volume

> The drive letter, followed by a colon, containing the media to be formatted. For example, to format the floppy in drive A:, type:

>> format a:

> If the specified drive is a hard disk, you'll be prompted to verify that you actually want to erase the disk.

/q

> Performs a "quick" format, a process that only wipes out the file table, resulting in an empty disk. This option does not check for bad sectors, nor does it rewrite the filesystem. Also, it does not write over data on the disk, meaning that files could potentially be recovered or "undeleted." The advantage of the /q option is that you can erase a disk in a few seconds.

/c

> Files created on the new volume are compressed by default (NTFS volumes only).

/x

> Forces the volume to dismount first, if necessary. All opened handles to the volume would no longer be valid. This effectively disconnects the drive from Explorer and all other programs, closing any open files stored on the drive, before any changes are made.

/v:*label*

> Specifies the volume label, an arbitrary title you assign to any disk. It can be up to 11 characters and can include spaces. The volume label will show up next to the drive icons in Explorer (hard disks only) and at the top of dir listings (see Appendix C). See "Label," later in this chapter, for more information. If the /v option is omitted, or the label isn't specified, a prompt for a volume label is displayed after the formatting is completed. If a label is specified with /v and more than one disk is formatted in a session, all disks will be given the same volume label.

/f:*size*

> Specifies the size of the floppy disk to format (such as 160, 180, 320, 360, 720, 1.2, 1.44, 2.88). *format* size (specified with the /f option) must be equal to or less than the capacity of the disk drive containing the disk to be formatted. For example, a

1.44MB capacity drive will format a 720K disk, but a 720K drive will not format a 1.44MB disk.

/fs:*filesystem*

Specifies the type of the filesystem; can be fat, fat32, or ntfs.

/a:*size*

Overrides the default allocation unit size, which, when multiplied by the number of clusters, equals the final capacity of the disk. Allowed values for *size* depend on the filesystem:

- NTFS supports 512, 1024, 2048, 4096, 8192, 16K, 32K, and 64K.
- FAT and FAT32 supports 512, 1024, 2048, 4096, 8192, 16K, 32K, 64K, (and 128K and 256K for sector size > 512 bytes).
- Note that the FAT and FAT32 filesystems impose the following restrictions on the number of clusters on a volume:
  - FAT: Number of clusters <= 65,526
  - FAT32: 65,526 < Number of clusters < 4,177,918
- NTFS compression is not supported for allocation unit sizes above 4096.

Notes

- The /f, /t, and /n parameters are also available for use with Format, but are essentially obsolete. Type format /? for more information.
- If formatting an ordinary 3.5" floppy diskette, the disk will always be formatted to a capacity of 1.44MB. The DMF diskette format, which squeezes about 1.7MB on a standard floppy, is not directly supported by Format. If formatting a pre-formatted DMF diskette, use the /q parameter to preserve the format and only erase the files. To create new DMF diskettes, you'll need the WinImage utility (Version 2.2 or later), which can be downloaded from *http://www.annoyances.org*.
- The easiest way to format a disk is to right-click on the drive icon in Explorer or My Computer and select Format. However, using Format from the command line is more flexible, and in some cases, faster.

See Also

"FAT to NTFS Conversion Utility," "Label"

FreeCell   *\windows\system32\freecell.exe*

A solitaire card game, considered by many users to the more addictive than traditional Solitaire (Klondike).

To Open   Start → Programs → Games → FreeCell
                  Command Prompt → freecell

Description

FreeCell is a solitaire card game (see Figure 4-38), but is played differently from the traditional Klondike game (see "Solitaire," later in this chapter). The object of the game is to move all the cards to the home cells.

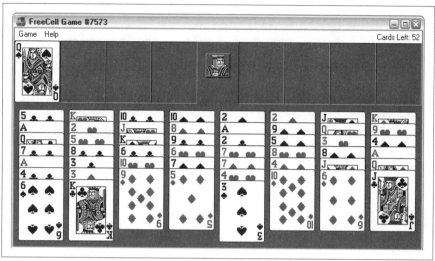

Figure 4-38. Some people buy their computers just to get the FreeCell game

Like Klondike, cards are rearranged by placing cards of descending value and alternating color (the 4 of clubs can be placed on the 5 of hearts or the 5 of diamonds). Click a card to highlight it and click another card to move the highlighted card. Multiple cards can be moved, but only those that are arranged accordingly. Cards can also be moved to one of the four "free cells," temporary storage slots that fill up fast.

FreeCell is somewhat like a cross between Klondike and the Towers of Hanoi puzzle.

Notes

In FreeCell, cards are not dealt randomly. Rather, there are 32,000 distinct numbered games, each representing a different predetermined deal of the cards. According to the help, "It is believed (although not proven) that every game is winnable." In fact, it has been proven that game #11982 is indeed not winnable.

See also

"Solitaire," "Spider Solitaire"

FTP

\windows\system32\ftp.exe

File Transfer Protocol; transfer files between two computers, typically across the Internet.

To Open Command Prompt → ftp

Usage
```
ftp url
ftp [-v] [-d] [-i] [-n] [-g] [-s:filename] [-a] [-A] [-w:size]
    [host]
```

Description

FTP is used to transfer files to and from a remote computer, typically on the Internet. Like many Internet applications, FTP is a client application that requires a corresponding FTP server to work. When you start FTP, you are connecting to a remote host and then issuing commands to instruct the host to send or receive files, display directory listings, and so on.

Although each FTP session requires a username and password, there's a very common workaround that allows anonymous connections. Typically, one enters anonymous as the username and an email address (or, frankly, any bogus text) as the password to log in (assuming anonymous access is allowed on the server at all).

Once you've logged in, commands are issued by typing in the prompt; the complete list of FTP commands is documented later in this section. The exception is when FTP is run in noninteractive mode using the *url* option.

Command-line parameters for FTP are as follows:

url

A web-style address (URL) to a specific file located on an anonymous FTP server, which looks something like this:

```
ftp://server.com/path/file
```

If you specify a complete URL, FTP will download the file and then quit automatically, rather than going into interactive mode.

host

Specify the hostname or IP address of the remote host (server) to which to connect. If omitted, it can be entered once FTP has started by using the open command. Example:

```
ftp ftp.microsoft.com
```

Note the common ftp. prefix, while not mandatory with FTP, is merely a hostname that signifies a specific machine, often solely devoted to serving FTP requests.

-v

Suppress the display of remote server responses to commands—useful if you're running FTP from a script.

-n

Suppress auto-login upon initial connection. To connect, you'll need to use the user command once FTP is running.

-i

Turn off interactive prompting during multiple file transfers when using the mget and mput FTP commands.

-d

Enable debugging, displaying all FTP commands passed between the client and server (for troubleshooting purposes).

-g

Disable filename globbing, which permits the use of wildcard characters in local file- and pathnames. (See the FTP glob command.)

-s:*filename*

Specify an FTP script, a plain text file containing sequential FTP commands, one per line. The commands are issued as though they were typed at the keyboard.

-a

Use any local interface when establishing a connection.

-A

Login as anonymous (note capital A). This is the same as logging in normally and manually typing in anonymous as the username and an email address as the password.

-w:size

Override the default transfer buffer size of 4096. Change only if you encounter performance problems.

Note that you can start FTP without any command-line parameters to enter interactive mode, but you won't be able to use most of the commands until you log in with the open command (see below).

FTP commands

The following list shows the commands available once FTP is running. Most require that a connection has been established and not all will work with every FTP server. The most important commands to know are put, get, mput, mget, cd, lcd, dir, and bye. If you are transferring binary files across platforms (from a Unix host to a Windows-based client, for example), be sure to use the binary command first, or the files may be corrupted in transit.

! [command]

Run the specified command (e.g., cd) on the local computer, as though you temporarily jumped out of FTP, ran a command, and then jumped back in—all without disconnecting. Naturally, you could just open a second command prompt window, but some contextual commands, such as cd (see Appendix C) require the use of the ! command to be effective. Type ! by itself to start a mini-DOS session in which you can type multiple commands; type EXIT to return to the active FTP session.

? [command]

Same as help.

append

Append a local file to a file on the remote computer.

ascii

Set the file transfer type to ASCII (plain text), the default (except in noninteractive mode). ASCII mode is the default and is useful if you're transferring plain text files between Unix and Windows systems, as minor translation must be performed on these types of files. Note that this translation can corrupt binary files, so you should use the binary command if you're not transferring ASCII files.

bell

Turn on or off the beep after each file transfer command is completed. By default, the bell is off.

binary

Set the file transfer type to binary, a crucial step for transferring nontext files (such as *.zip*, *.gif*, and *.doc*) between Unix and Windows-based machines. Although it's not necessary if the server is also a Windows system, it's a good idea to get into the habit of typing binary (or simply bin) every time you use FTP. Note that binary is the default in noninteractive mode, when used with the *url* command-line parameter. See also "ascii."

bye

End the FTP session, and if necessary, disconnect from the remote computer. The standard DOS *exit* and *quit* commands won't work here.

cd [*directory*]

Change the working directory on the remote computer (to cd on the local machine, use ! cd or lcd).

close

Disconnect from the remote computer without exiting FTP. Use open to connect to a different FTP server or bye to exit FTP.

debug

Toggle debugging. When debugging is on, each internal command sent to the remote computer is displayed, preceded by the string --->. By default, debugging is off.

delete *remote_file*

Delete a file on the remote computer. Only a single file can be deleted at a time with delete (no wildcards are allowed); use mdelete to delete multiple files at once.

dir

Display a list of the contents of the working directory on the remote computer, with details. Use ls for a simple listing. Occasionally, directory listings for anonymous users may be disabled, in which case dir will not work; if you wish to download, you'll need to know the particular filename(s) beforehand.

disconnect

Same as close.

get *remote_file* [*local_file*]

Transfer *remote_file* from the server to the local machine. If *local_file* is not specified, the local file will be given the same name as the original. The file will be placed in the local working directory; to choose a different destination, use lcd. Only a single file can be downloaded at a time with get (no wildcards are allowed); use mget to delete multiple files at once. If transferring binary (nontext) files, use the binary command first.

glob

Toggle filename "globbing." Globbing permits use of wildcard characters in local file or pathnames. By default, globbing is on. Globbing can also be disabled with the -g command-line parameter.

hash

Turn on or off FTP's crude progress bar for file transfers. A hashmark (#) character is displayed for each 2k of data transferred, so large files will have longer progress bars than small files. By default, hashmark printing is off.

help [*command*]

Display all the available commands. Include *command* to get help with a single command (e.g., help get). Same as ?.

lcd [*directory*]

Change the working directory on the local computer. Enter a full path as directory (e.g., *c:\downloads*) to effectively instruct FTP to place downloaded files there. Omit directory to simply display the current working directory. By default, the working directory is in use when FTP is started is used; if FTP is opened from Start → Run, the working directory is *c:\documents and settings\{username}*.

---

literal *command_line*
> Send so-called "arbitrary" commands to the remote FTP server (such as retr, stor, pasv, and port). A single FTP reply code is expected in return. Typical use of FTP does not involve using literal, but it can provide access to some advanced functions; among the more interesting is the ability to transfer files between two remote computers without having to first transfer them to the local machine.

ls
> Display an abbreviated list of a remote directory's files and subdirectories. This is useful when a directory contains a lot of files. Type ls -l (or use dir) to show the "long" listing, including file details. Occasionally, directory listings for anonymous users may be disabled, in which case ls will not work; if you wish to download, you'll need to know the particular filename(s) beforehand.

mdelete [*files*]
> Delete multiple files on remote computers. Unlike delete, wildcards can be used (e.g., *.txt for all *.txt* files).

mdir *remote_files local_file*
> Store a listing of the remote working directory's contents (with details) into a file; both parameters are required. The *remote_files* parameter is used to modify the listing, either by specifying a wildcard (use * to list all files) or by specifying the name of another directory. *local_file* is the target filename in which the directory listing is stored.

mget *remote_files*
> Transfer one or more remote files to the local computer. Unlike get, wildcards can be used (e.g., *.txt for all *.txt* files). You will be asked to confirm each transfer unless you turn off prompting with the prompt command. Local files will be given the same names as their remote counterparts. If transferring binary (nontext) files, use the binary command first.

mkdir *directory*
> Create a remote directory. Note that anonymous users are usually not permitted to create directories on remote systems.

mls *remote_dir local_file*
> Same as mdir, except that a short listing (no details) is stored.

mput *local_files*
> Transfer one or more local files to the remote computer. Unlike put, wildcards can be used (e.g., *.txt for all *.txt* files). You will be asked to confirm each transfer unless you turn off prompting with the prompt command. Remote files will be given the same names as their local counterparts. If transferring binary (nontext) files, use the binary command first.

open *hostname or IP address*
> Connect to the specified FTP server. This is the same as specifying a server in the FTP command line; use open if you omitted the host parameter. Open can be used whenever there's no current connection, either if you disconnected using disconnect or close or if the initial connection attempt was unsuccessful.

prompt
> Turn on or off prompting for multiple file transfers. When you use the mput or mget commands, FTP will prompt you before transferring each file. By default, prompt is turned on; type prompt before using mput or mget to transfer multiple files without being prompted.

Applications and Tools

put *local_file* [*remote_file*]

Transfers *local_file* from the server to the local machine. If *remote_file* is not specified, the remote file will be given the same name as the original. The file will be placed in the remote working directory; to choose a different destination, use cd. Only a single file can be uploaded at a time with put (no wildcards are allowed); use mput to delete multiple files at once. If transferring binary (nontext) files, use the binary command first.

pwd

Print Working Directory (PWD) displays the remote working directory; use cd to change to a different remote directory.

quit

End the *ftp* session with the remote computer and exit *ftp*.

quote [*command_line*]

Same as literal.

recv *remote_file* [*local_file*]

Same as get.

remotehelp [*command*]

Display help for remote commands supported by the server. This is probably similar to the commands available on the client, but may not be identical. As with ? and help, supplying no arguments returns a list of command names. Use remotehelp *command* to get more info on each command.

rename *from_name to_name*

Rename a remote file. Note that anonymous users are usually not permitted to rename files on remote systems.

rmdir *remote_directory*

Delete a remote directory. Note that anonymous users are usually not permitted to delete directories on remote systems.

send *local_file* [*remote_file*]

Same as put.

status

Display the current status of the connection and the current settings of options like prompt, verbose, and ascii|binary.

trace

Turn on or off packet tracing, which displays the route of each packet when executing an FTP command. By default, trace is off.

type [*type*]

Display whether transfers are performed in binary or ascii mode. Use type binary (or just binary) to transfer binary files.

user *username* [*password*]

Specify the username on the remote computer; if no password is specified, you will be prompted for one. Typically, FTP prompts for the username and password when a connection is first established; however, if you type an incorrect username and password, you can try again with the user command without having to reconnect.

verbose

Turn on or off verbose mode. If verbose is on (the default), all FTP responses are displayed, such as when a file transfer completes and any statistics regarding the efficiency of the transfer.

Examples

To copy the file *preface.doc* from the directory */pub/nutshell* on a remote computer to \temp\docs on your local computer, once you're logged on to a server, you would perform the following from the DOS prompt (note that cd within *ftp* is for the remote computer):

```
C:\>cd \temp\docs
C:\temp\docs>ftp remote_computer
username
password
ftp>binary
ftp>cd /pub/nutshell
ftp>get preface.doc
```

Run a script containing *ftp* commands:

```
C:\>ftp -s:myfile.scr
```

This will load *ftp* and run *myfile.scr*, executing any *ftp* commands in the file.

Notes

- Most web browsers support the *ftp://* protocol, which provides limited FTP functionality without having to use an FTP client. For example, you can retrieve a single file from an anonymous FTP server by opening this address in any web browser: *ftp://server.com/path/filename.ext*.

- Furthermore, you can specify a username and (optionally) a password, like this: *ftp://username:password@server.com/path/filename.ext*.

- Some browsers will even let you upload files when connected to an FTP server (assuming the server permits you to do so). In Netscape 4.x, select "Upload File" from the File menu. In Internet Explorer, you can simply drag-drop files into an FTP window as though it were a folder on your hard disk.

- All *ftp* command names can be abbreviated to the first four letters; sometimes fewer.

- If any nonoptional arguments are omitted from most FTP commands, you'll be prompted for them.

- When using the get or mget commands, transferred files will be placed in whatever directory was the working directory when you launched FTP. Once an FTP session has begun, you can change the working directory with the lcd command: to switch from the local *C:* to the *A:* drive, for example, you would type:

  ```
  C:\>lcd a:/
  ```

- In FTP, to maintain consistency with its Unix heritage, you must use the forward slash (/) instead of the backslash (\) when specifying pathnames. Furthermore, directory and filenames are case sensitive when connecting to a Unix FTP server; *readme.txt* is a different file than *Readme.TXT*.

- Many FTP servers impose an "idle timeout" on FTP connections; that is, if you open an FTP connection and let it sit for several minutes without typing any commands, the FTP server will disconnect you.

Game Controllers

Configure any joysticks, steering wheels, and game pads attached to your system.

To Open   Control Panel → [Printers and Other Hardware] → Game Controllers
Command Prompt → control joy.cpl

Description

Before a joystick or other game controller can be used with Windows-based games, its driver must be installed here. If your game controller doesn't appear in this list, click Add (see Figure 4-39). If your device doesn't show up on the list and the manufacturer doesn't provide native Windows XP drivers, try Custom to set up a rudimentary configuration for the device.

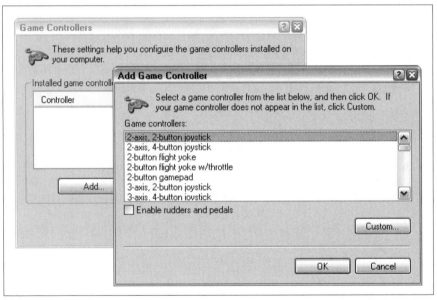

Figure 4-39. Windows supports many types of joysticks, gamepads, steering wheels, and flight yokes for your games

Notes

Not all game controllers have settings that can be changed, so the Properties button may be grayed out.

See Also

"Control Panel"

Group Policy Refresh Utility

Refresh group policies and settings. (Group Policy Refresh Utility is included with Windows XP Professional only.)

To Open   Command Prompt → gpupdate

Usage   gpupdate [/target] [/force] [/wait] [/logoff] [/boot] [/sync]

Description

Type gpupdate at the command prompt to refresh group policy settings. The Group Policy Refresh Utility accepts the following options:

/target:computer *or* /target:user
    Refresh only user or only computer policy settings; by default, both are refreshed.

/force
    Reapply all policy settings—by default, only policy settings that have changed since the last refresh are applied.

/wait:*value*
    Wait a specified number of seconds for policy processing to finish before being returned to the command prompt. The default is 600 seconds; specify 0 (zero) not to wait at all, or 1 (one) to wait indefinitely.

/logoff
    Log off the current user after the Group Policy settings have been refreshed.

/boot
    Restart Windows after the Group Policy settings have been refreshed.

/sync
    Cause the next foreground policy application (occurring at computer startup and user logon) to be done synchronously. If /sync is specified, /force and /wait parameters will be ignored.

Hearts

A card game played with three opponents.

To Open   Start → Programs → Games → Hearts
    Command Prompt → mshearts

Description

Hearts is a trick-based game, like Spades or Wizard™, but the object is to have the lowest score at the end of each hand. The online help tells you how to play the game and provides strategy and tips (see Figure 4-40).

Notes

- Normally, the object of Hearts is to stick your opponents with as many points (hearts) as possible. However, if one player takes all the points in a hand, it's called "shooting the moon": that player gets zero points and everyone else gets 26 points.

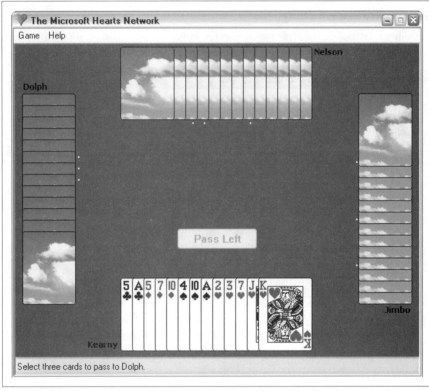

Figure 4-40. Hearts lets you play the classic card game against artificial opponents or other people on your network

- In previous versions of Windows, Hearts was a network game that allowed you to play against other players on a network. This functionality has been removed from the Windows XP-version of Hearts; however, a new version of the game, Internet Hearts, has been added.

Help and Support Center   \windows\pchealth\helpctr\binaries\helpctr.exe

The primary online documentation for Windows XP.

To Open   Start → Help and Support
              Command Prompt → `helpctr`

Description

Rather than a standard help file, Help and Support Center is more like a web site, providing documentation for some of the components included in Windows XP, a collection of tips and tricks, some troubleshooting information, and rudimentary walk-throughs for such tasks as keeping your computer up to date and adding hardware and software (see Figure 4-41).

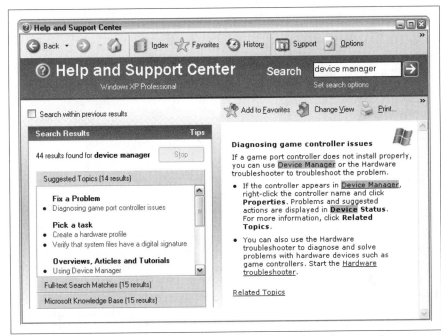

Figure 4-41. The search tool in the Help and Support Center shows the most relevant information in the included documentation and in Microsoft's online knowledge base

While Help and Support Center does have some minimal troubleshooting content, it's mostly simple solutions to common problems (i.e., if you can't print, check to see if your printer is turned on and is loaded with paper). However, if you're connected to the Internet, the Search tool at the top of the window will also search the Microsoft Knowledge Base, an immense database of troubleshooting information, frequently asked questions, bug reports, compatibility lists, and other technical support issues. In fact, since I access the Microsoft KB frequently, I find this built-in interface to be faster and more convenient then using the search function on Microsoft's web site! To view the results from searches other than the standard help content, click the gray bar above or below the displayed results (in the case of the KB, you would simply click Microsoft Knowledge Base). This is a terrific feature and can even be customized by going to Options → Set search options; you may want to increase the default of 15 results per provider (the Microsoft KB counts as a provider).

Notes

- If your job description involves supporting other computers, including those running other versions of Windows, the Help and Support Center can be augmented with documentation from other editions of Windows XP by going to Options → Install and share Windows Help. Furthermore, you can share your help content with others for precisely the same reason.

- From time to time, you'll find an especially useful page in the Help and Support Center window, either part of Windows' built-in documentation or a page on Microsoft's support web site. When available, click the Add to Favorites button to bookmark the page you're viewing; then, open Favorites (not the same as your main Favorites folder) and click the bookmark at any time to return to that page.

- If you need help with a specific Windows component, such as WordPad or Explorer, use that application's Help menu, rather than the more general Help and Support Center.

HyperTerminal
\Program Files\windows nt\hypertrm.exe

Terminal access to remote computers, typically via a modem; also a substitute for Telnet.

To Open Start → Programs → Accessories → Communications → HyperTerminal
Command Prompt → hypertrm

Description

With HyperTerminal and a modem, you can connect to a remote computer that supports terminal access, sends and receives files, and so on. HyperTerminal is useful for connecting to computer bulletin boards (popular in the 1970s and '80s); however, this type of terminal access has largely been replaced by the Internet.

When HyperTerminal is first started (or when you use File → New), it prompts you to name your connection and choose an icon, the first of two steps necessary to initiate a connection. The name is arbitrary and can be anything; it's really useful only if you intend to save your connection settings for use at a later time, but you have to enter something to proceed.

Next comes the Connect To dialog. The first option you should set is ironically the last one: in the Connect using list, choose either TCP/IP (Winsock) to initiate a session over your Internet connection, or choose a COM port (usually COM1) to use your modem (if installed). If you choose TCP/IP, HyperTerminal will be used as a Telnet client (see "Telnet," later in this chapter, for more information), and you'll be asked for a Host address (server name or IP address) and a Port number (use 23 for normal Telnet access). If you choose a COM port, you will be prompted for an area code and phone number used to place the subsequent phone call. If the Phone number field is disabled, the selected COM port either doesn't have a modem attached to it or your modem is not properly set up.

Once you've established a connection, HyperTerminal is merely a portal through which you can type commands and view information. The specific commands and information depend on the type of connection you're using and what the host computer supports.

All the options in HyperTerminal deal with managing connection profiles (saved as .ht files) and configuring the display (e.g., choosing fonts, colors, etc.). The transfer menu is used to help transfer files with the remote computer and is used only with terminal access. To transfer files with computers accessed with Telnet, use FTP.

Notes

For support and upgrades to HyperTerminal, go to *http://www.hilgraeve.com/*.

IExpress

Create a self-extracting/self-installing package, used to distribute files and install applications.

To Open   Command Prompt → iexpress

Usage   iexpress.exe [/n [/q] [/m]] *file* [/o:overide *file,section*]

Description

A self-extracting/self-installing package is actually an application, commonly known as an installer or setup program, that is used to install one or more files onto a Windows system and, optionally, to execute a setup script. IExpress is an interactive program that helps you create these packages, making it easy to, among other things, distribute files to other computers (see Figure 4-42).

Figure 4-42. The IExpress Wizard lets you package up a collection of files for easy distribution

Say you wish to put together a collection of documents that can be sent to another user, either via email, or by using a floppy disk or CD. Rather than simply sending the files separately or compressing them into a *.zip* file, both of which would require additional instructions, not to mention a reasonably knowledgeable and patient recipient, you can make a full-featured, professional-looking installer with IExpress.

When you start IExpress, the IExpress Wizard guides you through the steps to creating a self-extracting package. The first step prompts for a Self Extraction Directive (*.sed*) file, a file that contains all the options and files to include. If you don't have one, select "Create new Self Extraction Directive file" and click Next.

The next page, "Package purpose," asks what you want the installer to do with the files on the target computer when the package is opened by its recipient. If you select the first option, "Extract files and run an installation command," the files will be copied to a temporary folder and a separate installer program that you provide will be launched. If you don't have a separate installation program, choose "Extract files only" and click Next. The last option, "Create compressed files only," is used by application developers to assist in the distribution of application components and is of little use to most users.

The subsequent steps allow you to specify a package title, type welcome and "finished" messages, and even include a license agreement. When you reach the "Packaged files" page, use the Add button to select one or more files to be included in the package; you can choose as many files as you like, and they can be any format. In fact, IExpress will compress the files so that they take up less space (like *.zip* files). Then, IExpress will ask you to specify a package name, which is the path and filename of the package (*.exe*) to be created. IExpress will also optionally save your choices into a Self Extraction Directive (*.sed*) file, making it easy to recreate this package without having to answer all the above prompts again.

When the process is complete, you'll end up with a new *.exe* file that can then be run on any Windows system. This package can now be emailed, FTP'd, distributed on a CD a floppy, or even posted on a web site; the recipient won't need any special tools or elaborate instructions to extract the files from the package.

IExpress also has an automated, noninteractive mode for advanced users who wish to skip the somewhat cumbersome wizard interface and instead, create a package using the following command line parameters:

file
> The full path and filename of a Self Extraction Directive (*.sed*) file. If you don't have a *.sed* file, you'll have to use the wizard interface to create one.

/n
> Build package now (*file* must be specified). If you omit /n, IExpress will open in the interactive wizard interface.

/q
> Quiet mode (no prompts); used only with /n.

/m
> Use minimized windows; used only with /n.

/o
> Override.

If you've already created a *.sed* file (say, *c:\stuff\thing.sed*), and you wish to generate the corresponding package without walking through the wizard or being bothered with any prompts, type the following at a command prompt:

```
iexpress /n /q c:\stuff\thing.sed
```

The filename of the resulting package will be as specified in the *.sed* file.

Notes

Self Extraction Directive (*.sed*) files are just plain text files, similar in format to Configuration Files (*.ini*), and can be edited with a plain text editor, such as Notepad. The easiest way to get started with *.sed* files is to use the IExpress Wizard to create one and then edit (if necessary) to suit your needs.

See Also

"Cabinet (CAB) Maker"

Internet Backgammon

\program files\msn gaming zone\windows\bckgzm.exe

See "MSN Gaming Zone."

Internet Checkers

\program files\msn gaming zone\windows\chkrzm.exe

See "MSN Gaming Zone."

Internet Explorer

\program files\internet explorer\iexplore.exe

A web browser used to view web content.

To Open   Start → Programs → Internet Explorer
Use the Internet Explorer icon on the Desktop or on the QuickLaunch
    Toolbar
Command Prompt → iexplore

Usage   iexplore [-nohome] [*url*]

Description

Internet Explorer (IE) is a full-featured web browser that can be used to navigate the web, as well as view web content on your local network or hard drive. Web content is typically in the form of web pages (*.html*), but can also be images (*.gif* and *.jpg*), FTP sites, or even streaming video or audio (via the Windows Media Player) (see Figure 4-43).

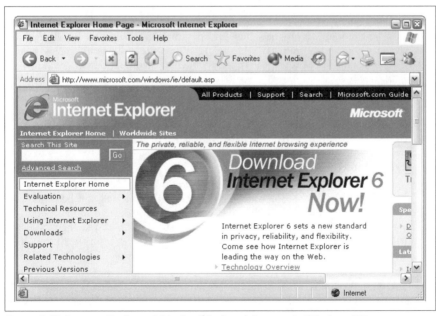

Figure 4-43. Internet Explorer 6.0 is the default web browser in Windows XP

Navigation in IE is accomplished by clicking hyperlinks in web pages or by typing addresses in IE's Address Bar. Frequently visited sites can be "bookmarked" by creating Internet Shortcuts (similar to Windows Shortcuts), stored in your Favorites folder, your Desktop, or anywhere else on your hard disk.

Use the Back and Next buttons (Alt-left arrow and Alt-right arrow, respectively) to navigate through the history, which is empty in each new IE window that is opened. Use the Stop button (or press ESC) to stop the loading of a page, and use the Refresh button (or press F5) to reload the page, displaying any changes that might have been made or displaying an updated version of a dynamically generated page.

The Home button loads the currently configured *home page* into the browser window. The home page is merely a shortcut to a single web site and can be changed by going to Tools → Internet Options. Finally, the Media button opens the Media Explorer bar, a pane on the left side of the window that displays advertising and entertainment from Microsoft's *WindowsMedia.com* site.

If you start IE from the command line, you can use either of the following options:

-nohome

> Start IE without loading the home page (blank). You can also configure Internet Explorer to use a blank page (*about:blank*) as its homepage, effectively causing Internet Explorer to always start without loading a home page.

url

> The Uniform Resource Locator—the address of a page to load. If you omit *url*, IE will display the home page.

Here are descriptions of some of the features of Internet Explorer:

Windows Update

> Updates to Internet Explorer are frequently made available on the Windows Update site. The initial release of Windows XP comes with Internet Explorer 6, but subsequent versions will add support for new standards, new features, bug fixes, and probably a few new bugs. If upgrading to a new version, always take advantage of the feature that saves the old system files, allowing the new version to be uninstalled in case you run into a problem or incompatibility.

AutoComplete

> IE has an autocompletion feature, which encompasses several features to help reduce typing. While you're typing web addresses, IE checks your browser history for any matches and displays them below the Address Bar. The more characters you type in the Address Bar, the narrower the list of suggestions will be, until the list disappears. To choose a URL from the list, just use the arrow keys on your keyboard and press Enter, or use your mouse.
>
> You can also type an address without the *http://* prefix, the *.com* extension, and even *www* (if applicable) in your addresses, and the site will still be found and loaded, as long as the site is in the *.com*, *.edu*, or *.org* domain. To add new domains to be included in AutoComplete, use the Registry Editor to add them to HKEY_ LOCAL_MACHINE\SOFTWARE\Microsoft\Internet Explorer\Main\UrlTemplate (see Chapter 7).
>
> AutoComplete goes further to remember usernames, passwords, and even some form data. Be careful when having IE "remember" sensitive data, as others will be able to access it as well. For example, don't store your bank PIN or credit card

number if others have access to your computer. The AutoComplete options can be configured by going to Tools → Internet Options → Content → AutoComplete.

The AutoSearch feature extends AutoComplete by allowing you to initiate web searches (using your favorite search engine) from the Address Bar. To use AutoSearch, start by typing a keyword into the Address Bar (such as bozo), and when Search for "bozo" appears in the AutoComplete box, click it. To configure or disable AutoSearch, go to Tools → Internet Options → Advanced and choose Desired Option from the Search From the Address Bar section. You may wish to experiment with these settings until you find one you can live with. Unlike Netscape 6 or Mozilla, IE doesn't allow you to choose the search engine used to perform these searches; IE can only use MSN search (*http://search.msn.com*).

Offline Files

You can make any entry in your Favorites menu available offline (when you're not connected to the Internet) by right-clicking it and selecting the "Make available offline" option. This launches a wizard that walks you through the following options:

1. Make other linked pages available offline. If yes, choose between 1 and 3 links deep, but be careful because this can take up a lot of disk space.

2. Select synchronization options. The default option allows synchronization only when chosen from the Tools menu. You can create your own schedule, which will take you to a dialog where you can set the synchronization between 1 and 99 days, set the time, and be given the option to automatically connect if you aren't connected to the Internet.

3. Set a password for synchronization. You can require a password to be given before the site can be viewed offline by entering a username and password.

When you're ready to work offline (a formal step that must be taken regardless of the status of your Internet connection), select File → Work Offline. You can then view any of your offline pages from the Favorites folder (they have the red dot on the corner of the icon). To work online again, just select File → Work Offline again. See "Synchronization Manager," later in this chapter, for more information.

Cookies

Cookies, first introduced by Netscape, allow a web site to store specific information on your hard disk. For example, if you visit an online store that has a shopping cart, that web site will be able to keep track of who you are by storing one or more cookies on your computer. This allows thousands of people to simultaneously access a site, yet have a separate and distinct shopping cart for each user. Cookies are often the target of privacy advocates, since it's possible for web site administrators to use cookies to track which pages certain visitors view at their site. However, cookies are only available to the sites that assign them (a cookie defined at Amazon.com cannot be read by any other web site), so the actual risk is minimal. You can adjust how Internet Explorer handles cookies by going to Tools → Internet Options → Privacy tab.

Notes

• If IE is the default browser, you can also go to Start → Run and type any web address to open the pages that addressed in IE. However, any browser can be set as the default. Typically, during installation of another browser, such as Netscape (*http://www.netscape.com/*), Mozilla (*http://www.mozilla.org/*), or Opera (*http://*

Applications and Tools

www.opera.com/), there will be an option to make that browser the default. Once one of these other browsers is installed, the procedure to make them the default varies. In Internet Explorer, go to Tools → Internet Options → Programs tab, and turn on the "Internet Explorer should check to see whether it is the default browser" option. Then, after closing all open Internet Explorer Windows, open a new Internet Explorer window; when prompted, verify that you try to make Internet Explorer the default.

- Go to Tools → Internet Options (see "Internet Options," later in this chapter) to set the various options relating to the display of web pages, security on the Internet, related Internet applications, and other, more technical Internet-related settings. All settings are fully documented in Chapter 5.

- The Forward and Back buttons have a drop-down list feature (see Figure 4-44) that lets you quickly jump several sites forward or backward, skipping over sites you don't want to load.

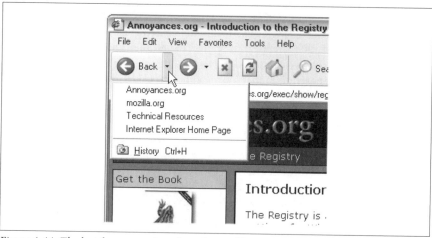

Figure 4-44. The last few pages viewed can be quickly accessed with the Back button's drop-down list

- The files that make up web pages, *.html* files, are simply plain text files, and can be viewed or modified with a plain text editor, such as Notepad. In fact, if you select View → Source, IE will display the code for the current page in a new Notepad window.However, if you're not familiar with HyperText Markup Language (HTML) code, you can use any modern word processor to create and modify web pages. Most Internet Service Providers will even host your pages for you, effectively giving you your own web site.

- When you type the name of a folder on your hard disk into IE's Address Bar, the IE window will be replaced with a standard folder window and the contents of the folder will be displayed. Likewise, if you type an Internet address into the Address Bar of an Explorer window or a single folder window, the window will be replaced with IE and the page will load.

- From any web page, you can select the Tools → Show Related Links option, which will open the Search pane and fill it with a list links compiled by a centralized database at *http://www.alexa.com/*.

- If you find the text size on any page to be too small, go to View → Text Size and enlarge (or shrink) the text size to your liking.

- From time to time, and depending on the Internet Explorer features you use and the web sites you visit, you may be prompted to sign up for a Microsoft .NET Passport account. Unfortunately, this has caused some confusion among many users. A Passport account is absolutely not required for any feature of Windows, with the exception of the MSN Explorer and Windows Messenger components. Passport is an optional service (and Microsoft has been widely criticized for making it appear otherwise). Unless you wish to use MSN, Messenger, or the Hotmail service, you'll most likely have no use for a Passport account.

See Also

"Internet Options," "Network Connections," "Windows Explorer"

Internet Hearts
\program files\msn gaming zone\windows\hrtzzm.exe

See "MSN Gaming Zone."

Internet Reversi
\program files\msn gaming zone\windows\rvsezm.exe

See "MSN Gaming Zone."

Internet Options

Change the settings that affect Internet Explorer and your dial-up Internet Connection.

To Open   Control Panel → [Network and Internet Connections] → Internet Options
Command Prompt → `control inetcpl.cpl`
Internet Explorer → Tools → Internet Options

Description

The Internet Options dialog is a densely packed dialog with about every conceivable option for Internet Explorer. Settings are divided into the following tabs:

General
>   The Home page section allows you to choose the page that loads automatically whenever an Internet Explorer window is opened, as well as the page linked to the Home button on the toolbar.
>
>   Temporary Internet files, also known as your browser cache, is a folder on your hard disk that stores copies of recently visited web pages for quicker access the next time they're visited. The Temporary Internet Files folder is located at *\Documents and Settings\[username]\Local Settings\Temporary Internet Files* by default. Cookies, a feature unrelated to Temporary Internet files, are pieces of information stored on your computer to allow certain web sites to remember your identity or preferences; click Delete Cookies to clear all cookies stored on your computer. To selectively remove cookies, open the *\Documents and Settings\[username]\Cookies* folder in Windows Explorer. See the Privacy tab for more Cookie settings.

Internet Explorer keeps track of pages you've visited and displays links to those pages in a different color (purple, by default, as opposed to the standard blue for links to pages you haven't yet visited). Items in your History are also accessed with the AutoComplete feature discussed in "Internet Explorer," earlier in this chapter. The History section controls how long before pages are removed from Internet Explorer's history (see Figure 4-45).

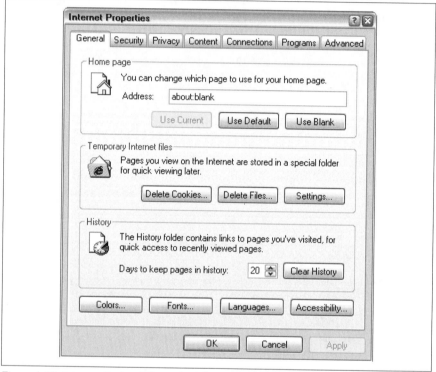

Figure 4-45. Internet Options' General tab lets you choose a default home page, manage cookies, and clear out your browser history

The remaining buttons allow you to control the default colors, fonts, and languages with which pages are shown. The Accessibility button essentially limits the control web pages have over their appearance.

Security

Lets you specify the security settings for different predefined zones of Internet content. There are four basic zones: Internet, Intranet, Trusted, and Restricted. By default, all sites are placed into one of the first two zones. All sites found on your local network are placed into the Intranet zone. All other sites are placed into the Internet Zone. You can manually add sites to the Trusted and Restricted zones. Security settings for each zone are preset, but you can change these settings if you wish. For each zone, you can specify High, Medium, Low, or Custom security settings. Security settings govern such things as whether ActiveX controls, Java applets, and JavaScript programs are used, how files are downloaded, and how user authentication takes place.

Privacy

The Privacy tab essentially controls when and how Internet Explorer accepts cookies. Play around with the slider to choose between six different preconfigured privacy policies, or click Advanced to choose your own settings. The Medium or Low policies should be suitable for most users. You can also click Edit in the Web Sites section to selectively choose which web sites can store and retrieve cookies, and which can not. You can view the cookies currently stored on your hard disk by opening the *Documents and Settings\[username]\Cookies* folder in Windows Explorer.

Content

The Content tab contains a number of functions that allow you to control what can and can't be viewed by IE. Many of the features here are not widely used and still have a few kinks to be worked out.

Content Advisor

Lets you use an Internet ratings service to screen out potentially offensive content. The first time you use this function, you will be asked to define a supervisor-level password that will later be used to change any of the content ratings.

By default, the only content advisor installed is the Recreational Software Advisory Council Internet advisor (RSACi). RSACi depends on voluntary ratings by sites as to the amount of violence, nudity, sex, and profanity they contain. While this may seem silly, sites with potentially objectionable content (such as porn sites) are embracing such "self-regulation" to forestall more stringent government regulation.

The rating system is fairly self-explanatory—you choose one of four levels for each of four types of "objectionable" content (Language, Nudity, Sex, or Violence); by default, every slider is set to the lowest level. One problem with this system is that the browser expects a rating from every site and requires a password to access sites with no ratings. Since few sites have RSACi ratings, this can become quite a hassle.

Ratings services publish their ratings in files of type *.rat*. A source for additional rating service files is *http://www.classify.org/pics.htm*. Download the *.rat* file for a given service, save it in *\Windows\System*, then go to the Advanced tab → Ratings Systems button to add the ratings file to the Content Advisor → Ratings tab.

Certificates

It's fairly easy for one site to masquerade as another. Digital certificates, which use cryptography to create unique identifiers that can't be forged, can be used by sites that want to prove their identity to you. Here, you can identify which certificate authorities (certificate issuers) you want to trust. If IE receives a certificate by an authority it doesn't know about, it will either display a warning or will not display the associated web page at all, depending on your settings here. Companies sometimes self-certify their pages, especially in an Intranet context.

Personal Information

Microsoft Profile Assistant is used to store personal information, such as your name and email address, that is often required by forms on web sites. Web sites that support the use of the Profile Assistant can automatically draw this information from the assistant.

Right now, very few sites make full use of the functionality provided by the Profile Assistant. This may change in the future, but for now, these tools can still be useful as just a convenient location to store these types of information. Due to privacy concerns, however, you may understandably not feel comfortable doing this.

See "Internet Explorer," earlier in this chapter, for more information on the Auto-Complete feature.

Connections

The Connections tab allows you to choose to have your dial-up connection dialed automatically. If you're not using a dial-up connection, but rather using DSL, cable, or a direct LAN connection, most of this page will be of no use to you. The exception is the LAN Settings dialog, which lets you configure your proxy (if you have one).

If you have one or more dial-up connections, they will be listed here. If you have two or more connections and you want to use the Auto Dial feature, choose one and click Set Default. Then, click either "Dial whenever a network connection is not present" or "Always dial my default connection," whichever you prefer.

Select a connection and then click Settings → Advanced to choose how many times Windows will dial before giving up and whether it should disconnect automatically if it detects that the connection is no longer needed.

It's a bit dangerous to use the automatic idle disconnect feature if you are using Internet applications other than IE, since IE doesn't recognize activity in other applications (such as Telnet). This can cause connections to close unexpectedly.

The Setup button starts the New Connection Wizard, discussed later in this chapter. See Chapter 7 for more information on setting up new Internet connections.

Programs

The settings in the Programs tab let you choose the default programs to use for sending mail, reading Internet news, placing Internet calls, viewing calendar scheduling, and viewing contact information (see Figure 4-46). For example, if you click a "mailto" link in a web page, Internet Explorer will activate the email program specified here. If your favorite applications don't appear in these lists, you may have to reinstall them or obtain updates from the respective manufacturers.

If the "Internet Explorer should check to see whether it is the default browser" box is checked, any time you start up IE (as long as it isn't already your default browser), it will ask you whether you want to make it your default browser. Thus, this setting is really just a shortcut to change file/program associations; see Control Panel → [Appearance and Themes] → Folder Options → File Types tab. Unless you're fond of what has come to be called "nagware," I recommend leaving this box unchecked.

Advanced

Advanced contains additional security settings in a hierarchical tree (see Figure 4-47). Many of these settings are rarely used and most are self-explanatory. Useful settings include:

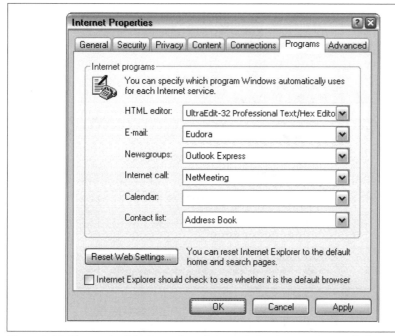

Figure 4-46. Choose the default email application and web page editor with the Programs tab

Notify when downloads complete
    Normally, a message pops up when a download is complete, interrupting whatever you are doing. Disabling this feature is particularly helpful when you perform multiple downloads at once.

Use Smooth Scrolling
    Specifies whether a page slides gradually when you click the scrollbar, a feature than can be especially distracting.

Underline Links
    Specifies whether links on pages should be underlined always, never, or only when you hover your mouse pointer over them.

Multimedia
    Multimedia can be a great part of the Web experience, but it can also slow down the delivery of web pages. The multimedia section lets you control whether certain multimedia elements, such as pictures, videos, and sounds, are downloaded for display. Thankfully, all those awful sounds in web pages can be silenced for good!

Printing
    Enables or disables the printing of background colors and images when you print a web page. Print speed can be increased considerably with this option disabled. The settings that control Java, JavaScript (found under the Advanced tab in some earlier versions of Windows), can be found in Security → Custom Level.

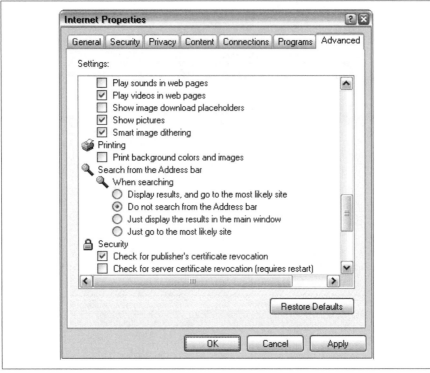

Figure 4-47. The Advanced tab contains many settings that affect all aspects of web browsing with Internet Explorer

Notes

- All of the settings in this dialog are also covered in Chapter 5.
- Only the settings in the Connections tab affect your dial-up Internet Connection (if you have one), which affects all your Internet applications. All the other tabs affect only the Internet Explorer application. Settings that control the security and privacy features of other browsers, such as Netscape or Mozilla, can be found in those applications' options windows.

See Also

"Control Panel," "Internet Explorer"

Internet Spades *\program files\msn gaming zone\windows\shvlzm.exe*

See "MSN Gaming Zone."

Java Command-Line Loader *\windows\system32\jview.exe; wjview.exe*

Run Java programs without using a web browser.

To Open   Command Prompt → jview
                Command Prompt → wjview

Usage   jview [options] *filename* [arguments]
                wjview [options] *filename* [arguments]

Description

Java is a programming language that allows developers to create programs that can run on any platform, including Windows, Unix, and MacOS. Since Java applications (*.class* files) aren't formal Windows programs, they can't be opened by themselves; rather, you must use the Java Command-Line Loader to run them. The exceptions are so-called Java applets, which are Java programs included in web pages and run internally by your web browser.

Windows XP comes with two Java command-line loaders, *jview.exe* and *wjview.exe*. Both versions do the same thing and accept exactly the same parameters (see below). The difference is that *jview.exe* is a command-line-based program and *wjview.exe* is a Windows-based program. The Java Command-Line Loader takes the following options:

classname
> The full path and filename of the *.class* file to be executed.

/a
> Executes AppletViewer.

/d:*<name>*=*<value>*
> Defines a system variable to be used by the Java program.

/n *<namespace>*
> The namespace in which to run.

/p
> Pauses before terminating if an error occurs.

/v
> Verifies the Java program before executing it.

arguments
> The command-line arguments to be passed onto the Java program.

/vst
> Prints verbose stack traces (requires debug classes).

/cp *classpath*
> Sets the class path.

/cp:a *path*
> Appends *path* to the class path.

/cp:p *path*
> Prepends *path* to the class path.

Notes

- The Java Command-Line Loader uses Microsoft's version of the Java Virtual Machine (JVM), which is very fast, since it uses Just-In-Time compiler technology.

- Unfortunately, there is not an option or Registry setting that enables Java logging. However, you can redirect the output (see Appendix C) when invoking an application, as in the following example:

```
C:\>jview main > javalog.txt
```

- When you run a Java application using the Java Command-Line Loader from within the Microsoft Developer Studio IDE, the command prompt window closes immediately after the Java application terminates. To prevent the MS-DOS window from closing immediately, you can have an input statement as the last statement in your Java application.

  For example:

  ```
  system.in.read( );
  ```

- A second option is to run your Java application externally (outside the Developer Studio environment).

- For the Microsoft SDK containing the latest Java compiler and Virtual Machine for using Java with the WIN32 API only, go to *http://www.microsoft.com/java/download.htm.*

Keyboard Properties

Change the keyboard repeat rate and text cursor blink rate.

To Open   Control Panel → [Printers and Other Hardware] → Keyboard
Command Prompt → `control main.cpl Keyboard`
Command Prompt → `control keyboard`

Description

The Keyboard Properties dialog controls the way characters are repeated when keys are held down, as well as how quickly the text cursor (insertion point) blinks. Tip: move the Repeat rate slider all the way to the right (towards Fast) and your computer will actually seem faster (see Figure 4-48).

The Hardware tab simply provides access to the Properties sheet for your keyboard (the same one you'll get in Device Manager, discussed earlier in this chapter).

Notes

- All settings in this dialog are also covered in Chapter 5.

- Additional features that affect the keyboard repeat rate and text cursor can be found in Accessibility Options, discussed earlier in this chapter.

- Some keyboards, especially those with additional function buttons (such as web links and CD player controls), come with their own software. Some of this software includes hardware drivers and is absolutely necessary for operation, while other software is purely optional, adding only trivial features. Given the potential compatibility problems with Windows XP, it's best only to install such software if it's necessary or if it provides features you can't live without.

See Also

"Control Panel"

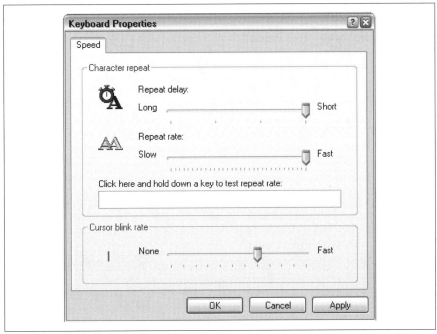

Figure 4-48. Move both sliders all the way to the right in Keyboard Properties to make your computer seem faster

Label

\windows\system32\label.exe

Change the label of any hard disk, floppy disk, or removable media.

To Open   Command Prompt → label

Usage   label [*drive:*] [label]

Description

Every disk has a label, the name shown in Explorer next to the drive letter (except for floppies). To change the label for any disk, right-click on its icon in Explorer (or the My Computer window), select Properties, and type a new name in the unlabeled field at the top of the properties window. The Label tool duplicates this functionality from the command line. For example, to change the label of drive *c:* to "shoebox," type:

    label c: shoebox

If you omit *label*, you will be prompted to enter a new label. If you omit *drive*, label will use the current drive.

Notes

A disk's label has no effect on the operation of the disk; for hard disks, it's purely decorative. For CDs and other removable media, it's used to quickly identify what's in the drive.

Local Security Policy

See "Microsoft Management Console."

Logoff

Log out the current user (or another user).

To Open   Command Prompt → `logoff`

Usage   `logoff [session | id] [/server:name] [/v]`

Description

Among other things, Logoff is the quickest way to log off the current user, rather than selecting "Shut Down from the Start Menu," choosing "Log off" from the list, and clicking OK. In fact, you can create a shortcut to Logoff on your Desktop and simply double-click it to enter current session.

Logoff can also be used to end the session of a remotely connected user, either through terminal services or through the Telnet daemon. For example, if someone has connected to a Windows XP computer using Telnet, you can disconnect them, either from another Telnet session or from the command prompt, by using Logoff and the following options:

session
> The name of the session to end; use either `session` or `id` to end a session, but not both.

id
> The ID of the session to end; use either `session` or `id` to end a session, but not both.

`/server:name`
> Specifies the terminal server containing the session to end; the default is current.

`/v`
> Displays additional information about the actions being performed.

See Also

"Shutdown," "Shut Down" in Chapter 3

Microsoft Chat

Conduct a text-based chat session with another user over a network.

To Open   Command Prompt → `winchat`

Description

Microsoft Chat is a simple chat program that allows two users to have a text-based conversation using two computers connected over a network (see Figure 4-49). It's similar to the Unix `talk` command, where the screen is split in two panes and each user types and watches as the other types. Both screens are updated in real time, so you can see letters as they are typed by your partner.

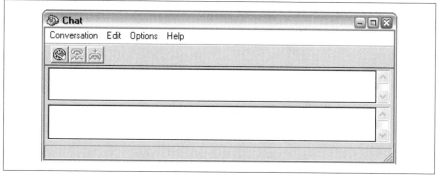

Figure 4-49. The Chat tool is used to facilitate text conversations between two users on a network

To initiate a chat session, click the Dial button on the toolbar or select Dial from the Conversation menu, select the target computer from the list (other computers in your workgroup will be shown here), and click OK. Then the user of the computer that has been dialed will see a Chat button in their Taskbar; that user must click the button to "answer" the call.

Notes

- If you're looking for the comic-strip style graphical IRC chat client included with some earlier versions of Windows (*cchat.exe*), this application is not included with Windows XP. However, there are several third-party alternatives that can be obtained from the Internet, such as LeafChat (*http://www.leafdigital.com/*) and mIRC (*http://www.mirc.org/*).

- To receive a Microsoft Chat call, you'll either need to have Chat running or have the Network DDE service started (see "Microsoft Management Console" for more information on services).

See Also

"Microsoft NetMeeting," "Msg," "DDE Share"

Microsoft Magnifier

\windows\system32\magnify.exe

Show an enlarged version of the area of the screen near the mouse cursor.

To Open   Start → Programs → Accessories → Accessibility → Magnifier
Command Prompt → `magnify`

Description

The Microsoft Magnifier is used to assist those with the visual impairments by magnifying a portion of the screen. When you start Magnifier, the top 15 percent of the screen turns into an automatic magnifying glass, which follows the mouse cursor around screen. If you have trouble seeing something on the screen, just float the cursor over it to magnify it (see Figure 4-50).

Figure 4-50. The Magnifier tool can follow your mouse cursor, enlarging any portion of the screen you point to

The Magnifier can be resized or moved with the mouse. Furthermore, when Magnifier is first opened, the Magnifier settings window appears, allowing you to change magnification level and choose whether or not Magnifier follows the mouse cursor, keyboard focus, or the text cursor. To hide the settings window, just minimize it; if you close it, Magnifier will close.

Notes

Magnifier can also be very handy for application developers and web site authors, who may need to see pixel detail in their work.

See Also

"Narrator," "On-Screen Keyboard," "Utility Manager"

Microsoft Management Console

\windows\system32\mmc.exe

A single interface for dozens of administrative tools in Windows XP.

To Open   Start → Programs → Administrative Tools → Computer Management
Command Prompt → mmc

Usage   mmc *filename* [/a] [/64] [/32]

Description

The Microsoft Management Console (MMC) is a host for most of the administrative tools that come with Windows XP (see Figure 4-51). Each of the tools that works with MMC is called a *Snap-in*; Several Snap-ins can be shown in MMC at any given time and appear as entries in the Explorer-style tree in the left pane.

Figure 4-51. The Microsoft Management Console houses many important troubleshooting and system-maintenance tools

A collection of one or more Snap-ins can be saved into a Console (*.msc*) file, which is a small file that simply lists Snap-ins to display in the Console window. Double-click any *.msc* file to open it in MMC. Windows XP ships with more than a dozen predefined Console files, and you can modify them (or even create your own) by adding or removing snap-ins or creating custom Taskpad Views—pages with lists of shortcuts to programs or other snap-ins.

There are about two dozen Snap-ins included in Windows XP. To add a Snap-in to the current Console file (select File → New to start a new Console), go to File → Add/Remove Snap-in, and click Add (see Figure 4-52). Then, choose one of the available Snap-ins (note that not all Snap-ins described here are available in all versions of Windows XP), and click Add to add it to the list in the previous Window. A wizard or other dialog may appear when certain items are added, used to configure this instance of the Snap-in being added; any preferences set here are saved into the Console file. You can continue to add additional items as needed; when you're done, click Close. Note that it's possible to add the same Snap-in more than once, so you may want to position the Windows side-by-side so you can see what has been installed.

Here are the Snap-ins included with Windows XP; most of the following are documented further in the Microsoft Management Console online help. Note that all

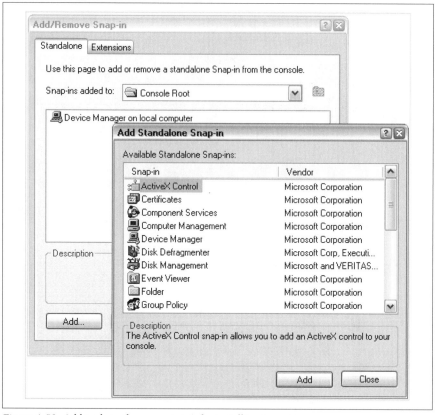

Figure 4-52. Add tools to the current view by installing Snap-ins

Console (*.msc*) files mentioned are in the *windows\system32* folder unless otherwise mentioned.

ActiveX Control

Use this Snap-in to add an ActiveX control to your console file. Although Windows XP ships with many ActiveX controls, most of them aren't appropriate for MMC. More advanced users may wish to use this feature to create custom Snap-ins. Most users are likely to find the System Monitor Control to be the only useful ActiveX Snap-in included with Windows XP.

Certificates

Installed by default in *certmgr.msc*.

Browse all the security certificates used by Internet Explorer and IIS, the web server included with Windows XP (Professional only).

Component Services

Installed by default in *windows\system32\com\comexp.msc*.

Manage installed component object model (COM) components.

Computer Management

Installed by default in *compmgmt.msc*.

Computer Management doesn't have any functionality by itself; rather, it is a collection of the following thirteen Snap-ins: Event Viewer, Shared Folders, Local Users and Groups, Performance Logs and Alerts, Device Manager, Removable Storage, Disk Defragmenter, Disk Management, Services, WMI Control, Indexing Service, Message Queuing, and Internet Information Services.

Device Manager

Installed by default in *devmgmt.msc* and *compmgmt.msc*. See "Device Manager," earlier in this chapter.

Disk Defragmenter

Installed by default in *drfg.msc* and *compmgmt.msc*. See "Disk Defragmenter," earlier in this chapter.

Disk Management

Installed by default in *diskmgmt.msc* and *compmgmt.msc*.

The Disk Management Snap-in lists all the installed drives, including hard disks, CD drives, and other removable storage devices (floppies are not included). Right-click on any drive (except the one on which Windows is installed) to change its drive letter. Go to View → Top and View → Bottom to choose whether drives are viewed as disks (physical devices), volumes (local drives, including partitions), and disks using a graphical view. Disk Management also has the ability to create and delete partitions (see also "DiskPart," earlier in this chapter), but cannot make any modifications that affect the volume on which Windows is installed. PartitionMagic (*http://www.powerquest.com/*) allows more complete control over the creation and modification of partitions.

Among the features of the Disk Management console is the ability to change drive letters of your CD or DVD drive, removable cartridge drive, and even hard disk partitions. Just right-click a volume in the upper pane (for hard disk partitions) or one of the large buttons on the left side of the lower pane (for CD drives and the like) and select Change Drive Letter and Paths. Then, click Change to choose a new drive letter. If there's a drive letter conflict, you may have to click Remove first, resolve the conflict, and then return to the Change Drive Letter and Paths dialog and click Add to choose a drive letter.

Event Viewer

Installed by default in *eventvwr.msc* and *compmgmt.msc*.

Views the three system event logs: Application, Security, and System. The Application log lists every application crash, status reports and warnings generated by services (see "Services," below), and other events logged by some applications. The Security log records events such as valid and invalid logon attempts, as well as events related to the use of shared resources. The system log contains events logged by Windows XP system components, such as driver failures and system startup errors.

A computer running Windows configured as a domain controller records events in two additional logs, Directory service and File Replication service. A computer running Windows configured as a Domain Name System (DNS) server records events in an additional log, DNS server.

Event Viewer logs contain five types of events: Errors (driver and service failures), Warnings (indications of possible future problems), Information entries (the successful operation of an application, driver, or service), and Success Audits and Failure Audits (audited security access attempts that succeed and fail, respectively).

Folder

A folder is used to organize Snap-ins in the tree display. To use a folder, first add it using the procedure explained above. Then, close the Add Standalone Snap-in dialog, select the new folder from the "Snap-ins added to" list, and click Add again; this time, added items will appear in the new folder. Unfortunately, you can't drag-drop items from one folder to another, so the only way to move an item is to remove it from one folder and then add it to another. Folders can be renamed only from the main MMC window.

FrontPage Server Extensions

This Snap-in is used to manage the various FrontPage Server extensions and their settings.

Group Policy (also known as Local Computer Policy)
Installed by default in *gpedit.msc*.

A collection of policy settings, controlling startup and shutdown scripts, security settings for Internet Explorer, and user account policies. Group Policy replaces the System Policy Editor found in earlier versions of Windows. See Chapter 3 for documentation on the settings in this Snap-in.

Indexing Service
Installed by default in *ciadv.msc* and *compmgmt.msc*.

The Indexing Service collects information from the documents on your hard disk and compiles a database used to enhance searches. The Indexing Service indexes *.html* files, *.txt* files, Microsoft Office documents, Internet mail and news, and any other document for which a document filter is available. The Indexing Service Snap-in allows you to manage the directories that are routinely scanned and query the database catalog.

Internet Information Services
Installed by default in *compmgmt.msc* and *\windows\system32\inetsrv\iis.msc*.

IIS is the Web/FTP/SMTP server built into Windows XP, and the Internet Information Services Snap-in allows you to administer the various functions associated with the server service. For example, you can configure how CGI scripts are running from web pages posted on the server.

IP Security Monitor

Monitor the IP Security status; see "IP Security Policy Management," below, for more information.

IP Security Policy Management

Manage Internet Protocol Security (IPSec) policies for secure communication with other computers. IPSec can be thought of as a minimalistic firewall, allowing and disallowing certain communication over an Internet connection.

Link to Web Address

The Link to Web Address Snap-in allows you to insert, not surprisingly, the web site as an entry in the tree. For example, you may wish to include a link to a software downloads site, an HTTP-based administration page for a web site, or another troubleshooting web site, such as *http://www.annoyances.org/*.

Local Computer Policy

See "Group Policy (also known as Local Computer Policy)," above.

Local Users and Groups
Installed by default in *lusrmgr.msc* and *compmgmt.msc*.

This plug-in provides more advanced settings, using a simpler and more direct interface, then Control Panel → User Accounts. Here, you can set preferences relating to the expiration of passwords, the assignment of certain users to groups, logon scripts, location of a user's home folder, and other advanced options.

Performance Logs and Alerts
Installed by default in *perfmon.msc* and *compmgmt.msc*.

Performance Logs and Alerts allow you to collect performance data automatically from certain applications, and then create logs that can be exported then analyzed. The applications, designed to generate performance logs, are typically associated with web servers when an administrator would need to know exactly how the system resources are being utilized at any given time. See Help for more information on setting up performance data.

Removable Storage Management
Installed by default in *ntmsmgr.msc* and *compmgmt.msc*.

The Removable Storage Management Snap-in enables you to the view all the devices that support removable media, such as CD and DVD drives, CD and DVD writers, tape drives, Zip drives, flash memory readers, and other similar devices. Removable Storage labels, catalogs, and tracks media and stores this information into libraries. Media Pools, collections of removable media to have the same management policies, are used to organize these libraries. For example, the catalogs in the Backup component rely on Removable Storage Management.

Resultant Set of Policy
Installed by default in *rsop.msc*.

This Snap-in allows you to view and change the policy settings for a particular user. See "Group Policy (also known as Local Computer Policy)," above, for more information.

Security Configuration and Analysis
This Snap-in is used to view and manage security databases for computers using Security Templates (see below) and is especially helpful for tracking changes to security.

Security Templates
Installed by default in *secpol.msc*.

Security Templates are used to create a security policy for computers. They are used mostly by administrators for Windows XP-based servers. See Help for detailed information.

Services
Installed by default in *services.msc* and *compmgmt.msc*.

A service is a program that runs invisibly in the background, usually started when Windows starts. You can set up any program to run automatically when Windows starts by placing a shortcut in your Startup folder, but such a program would only be run when you log in. A service is run when Windows starts and is already running when the login prompt is shown. Windows XP comes with nearly 80 preinstalled services, some of which are active by default (called "Started" in the Services window), and some of which are not.

Double-click any service in the list to view its properties, such as its status (Started or Stopped), whether or not it's started automatically, under which user accounts it is enabled, what actions to take if the service encounters a problem,

Applications and Tools

and which other components the service depends on (if any). Common services include the plug-and-play manager, the task scheduler, the print spooler, automatic updates, an FTP server, a web server, a mail server, and many other programs responsible for keeping Windows XP running. You can start or stop any service by right-clicking on it and selecting Start or Stop, respectively. Stopping unnecessary services will not only increase system performance, but will close potential security "backdoors" that could be used to break into a computer. Naturally, you should use caution when disabling any enabled service, but most home users won't need the "mail server" service to be running all the time.

See Appendix G for a list of the default services in Windows XP, their corresponding filenames, and their descriptions.

Shared Folders

Installed by default in *fsmmgmt.msc* and *compmgmt.msc*.

As described in Chapter 7, any folder or drive can be shared, allowing access to it from another computer on the network. The Shared Folders Snap-in lists all of the shared resources in one place, as well as any open connections to those resources from other computers. Rather than "sharing and forgetting," this tool allows you to keep a more active watch on how shared resources are being used.

One thing to note is the existence of administrative shares, those items listed in the Shares portion of the Shared Folders Snap-in, denoted by a dollar sign ($) at the end of the share name. Administrator shares cannot be disabled, and when used in conjunction with Create Shared Folder (discussed earlier in this chapter), can even be a security risk, in which someone else with your username and password can access to any file or folder on your computer without ever sitting in front of it. Suffice it to say, if you're on a network, or even an Internet connection, you should investigate the security settings in your computer and try to close as many back doors as you can without disabling functions that you still need. If you're concerned about security, you may wish to use Windows XP's built-in firewall (see Chapter 7) or invest in third-party firewall software (such as Norton Personal Firewall (*http://www.symantec.com/*), each of which actively helps prevent unauthorized access your computer.

WMI Control

Installed by default in *wmimgmt.msc* and *compmgmt.msc*.

WMI (Windows Management Instrumentation) is set of standards for accessing and sharing management information over an enterprise network. WMI will be of little use to most users; for more information, see Help.

One of the most interesting features of the Microsoft Management Console is its ability to access most of these tools remotely. For example, you can use it to run Device Manager on a machine other than the one you're using. Naturally, this would be most useful to an administrator, who can now configure and maintain a whole group of computers from a single machine. However, as home networks become more common, ordinary users are being turned into administrators. For instance, if you were responsible for setting up a network between the two or three computers used by the members of your family, you'd be able to run Disk Defragmenter on all the machines without having to jump around between them. Nevertheless, it provides more power than is normally available via My Network Places.

Connecting to another computer with MMC depends on the particular Snap-in you're using. Most Snap-ins that support remote administration will prompt you when you first add them, asking whether the Snap-in should be used with the current computer or with another on the network. In the case of Computer Management (*compmgmt. msc*), just right-click on the Computer Management root entry of the tree, select "Connect to another computer," and type the name of the computer in the box that appears. When connected to another computer, the root entry will be named Computer Management (*computername*).

The Microsoft Management Console also has a few command-line options:

/a

> Some Console (*.msc*) files have been configured so that the Snap-in tree normally shown is not only hidden, but inaccessible. Furthermore, you may not have access to the standard MMC menus, meaning that you will not be able to add or remove Snap-ins as desired. The /a option opens MMC in "author" mode, allowing you to treat any saved Console file as though you created it, giving you power to modify the Console by adding or removing Snap-ins.

/s

> The /s parameter is included with some shortcuts to *.msc* files in the Start menu, but it does not appear to have any effect.

/32 or /64

> Run MMC in 32-bit or 64-bit mode, respectively; it is only available on 64-bit systems.

Notes

- Eventually, you'll probably want to create your own Console file with the Snap-ins you use most. While it can create a new Console file from scratch, it may be easier to modify one of the supplied *.msc* files and then save it with a new name. To modify a saved Console file, start MMC with the /a switch, as described above.

- Programmers who wish to learn how to create custom Snap-ins can find more information at *http://msdn.microsoft.com/*.

Microsoft NetMeeting

\program files\netmeeting\conf.exe

Voice and video conference application.

To Open   Start → Programs → Accessories → Communications → NetMeeting
Command Prompt → conf

Description

NetMeeting allows videoconferencing (videophone) and voice conferencing (net phone) over a network or Internet connection (see Figure 4-53). The connection is made via either a central directory service (Microsoft provides several) or directly to another user's IP address.

All you need to initiate a voice conference (audio only) is an Internet connection and a sound card, speakers, and a microphone on each end. For video conferencing, all you need in addition are two videoconferencing cameras (USB cameras are surprisingly cheap). As you might expect, videoconferencing requires more bandwidth than voice conferencing alone. Make sure your Internet connection and all your sound and video hardware are properly installed before you try to use them with NetMeeting.

Figure 4-53. NetMeeting facilitates voice and video conferencing over an Internet or LAN connection

The first time you start NetMeeting, you'll be asked several questions about your iden-tity. If privacy is a concern, you don't have to fill out all the fields, but the email address will help others find you if they don't have your IP address (using a directory server).

The next page in the setup wizard allows you to choose how you'll use directory services. For NetMeeting to establish a connection between two computers, one user must call another; and in order for that to happen, the caller must either know the recipient's IP address or must specify the recipient's email address. Since a user's IP address can change every time that user connects to the Internet (only with dynamic IP assignment), a directory server can be used to automatically look up a user's IP address by supplying only the user's email address.

If you choose to "Log onto a directory server when NetMeeting starts," NetMeeting will update the directory server with your current IP address every time you start a session; turn this option off if you have a static (unchanging) IP address or if you wish to manu-ally inform prospective callers of your IP address every time you need to use NetMeeting. If you choose to use a directory server, you can use Microsoft's default (Microsoft's Internet Directory) or specify your own server (see Notes). Unless you wish to have strangers calling you, you'll probably want to place a checkmark next to the "Do not list my name in the directory" option. After that, you will be asked to specify the speed of your connection and whether or not you what to create a Desktop icon. Next, you'll be walked through the Audio Tuning Wizard, the tool that will help you adjust the levels of your microphone and speakers so that NetMeeting will work properly. If you make any changes to your sound hardware, you can run the Audio Tuning Wizard again by going to Tools → Audio Tuning Wizard.

Using NetMeeting is not hard. To start a conference, one user must call another; if you're the caller, type the recipient's email address or IP address into the text field at the top of the window and press enter or click the little telephone button. The recipient must also be running NetMeeting; when a call is placed, the recipient's copy of NetMeeting will "ring" and the recipient will be given the chance to accept or ignore the incoming call. Hang up any call by clicking the Hang Up button or by selecting Hang Up from the Call menu.

The "Windows NetMeeting" box in the middle of the NetMeeting window is for the video of the other person in the conversation and can be turned off with View → Data Only. The Play/Pause button underneath is used to start and stop the video portion of the conference. If you are videoconferencing, you'll probably want to select My Video from the View menu to see what your partner is seeing.

In addition to facilitating a person-to-person conference, NetMeeting allows you to set up a meeting in which any number of users can join and video or voice conference. Rather than placing calls, however, the meeting is initiated when one user decides to host a meeting (Call → Host Meeting). Furthermore, several collaboration tools are made available with meetings:

Sharing
Also called "Remote Desktop Sharing," this feature is a basic remote control program, in which you can see another user's Desktop and control it as though you were sitting in front of it. Alternatives to Remote Desktop Sharing include pcAnywhere (commercial software, *http://www.symantec.com/*), VNC (freeware, *http://www.uk.research.att.com/vnc/*), and Remote Desktop Connection (included with Windows XP Professional and discussed later in this chapter).

Whiteboard
The NetMeeting Whiteboard is not unlike a real whiteboard: it allows users to collaborate by using drawing tools on blank white page. All members of the meeting see the same whiteboard and can watch as others draw.

Chat
Like Microsoft Chat, the Chat feature in NetMeeting allows users to communicate by typing. While it may seem archaic, it's really an easy way to share short pieces of text, such as web addresses, phone numbers, or excerpts from documents.

File Transfer
What communication tool would be complete without a way to share files? NetMeeting allows you to send and receive files with those who have joined your meeting by going to Tools → File Transfer → Send File. You can also send a file to all members by simply dragging the file into the call window; once a file is sent, recipients can individually accept or decline the transfer. Note that, unless you have an exceptionally fast connection, the transfer of files during a meeting will significantly slow down your connection and the quality of the video and sound will go down. Naturally, you can also send and receive files via email or FTP.

To join the meeting in progress, place a call to the user hosting the meeting as you would when initiating a one-on-one conference, as described above.

Notes

- To use a video camera or other video source with NetMeeting, the driver must be compatible with either the H.261 or H.263 compression/decompression (codec) protocols.
- If you don't wish to use the directory service, you can have others connect to you by providing your IP address. To find out what your IP address is, select About from

NetMeeting's Help menu or use the Windows IP Configuration, described later in this chapter. If you have a dynamic IP address, you can use a service like DynIP (*http://www.dynip.com*) or HomeIP (*http://www.homeip.org*) to associate a domain with your IP address, a link that is updated every time you connect to the Internet.

- There are circumstances when others will not be able to connect to you, usually because of a problem with your IP address or because of a firewall. For example, if you're using computer connected to the Internet through Internet Connection Sharing (see Chapter 6), you may not have a valid IP address. Likewise, a firewall, which is designed to prevent certain types of network communication, can easily interfere with NetMeeting. The solution, if you encounter one of these problems, is for you to place the call and for your partner to answer.

- While NetMeeting is designed to facilitate conferencing over the Internet, it also supports local area networks. If you wish to call another NetMeeting user on your local network, simply type that user's computer name instead of the IP address or email address.

- Microsoft Internet Directory is a dedicated directory server that allows users to host meetings and allows other users to view a directory of all users on the server, similar to the way a chat server works. You can browse the directory of users and join any meetings they are hosting. ILS 2.0 is part of Microsoft Site Server and is also available for free download from *http://www.microsoft.com/*, if you are interested in running your own server on the Internet or a local network. When you first run NetMeeting, you can choose from a list of popular ILSs to which to connect (most are run by Microsoft). Once connected, the NetMeeting directory view lists users that are hosting meetings on the server.

- If you want NetMeeting to run automatically when you start Windows, select Tools → Options → General → Run when Windows starts. This will also set NetMeeting to alert you of incoming calls. The other thing you may wish to do is set NetMeeting to automatically log onto a directory server by going to Tools → Options and turning on the "Log onto directory server when NetMeeting starts" option. This turns NetMeeting into a "messenger" or "buddy list" application.

- When using Netmeeting, you may be prompted to sign up for a Microsoft .NET Passport account. Unfortunately, this has caused some confusion among many users. A Passport account is absolutely not required for any features of Windows, with the exception of the MSN Explorer and Windows Messenger components. Passport is a totally optional service (and Microsoft has been widely criticized for making it appear otherwise), and unless you wish to use MSN, Messenger, or the Hotmail service, you'll most likely have no use for a Passport account.

See Also

"Microsoft Chat," "Msg," "Phone Dialer"

Minesweeper

\windows\system32\winmine.exe

A silly little game relying on the process of elimination.

To Open   Start → Programs → Games → Minesweeper
                  Address → winmine

Description

The object of Minesweeper is to uncover "safe" areas on a playing field without hitting on any landmines. Start by clicking a square with the left mouse button to uncover it; if it's a mine, the game is over. Otherwise you'll either see a number, corresponding to the number of mines immediately adjacent to the clicked square, or the square will be blank, meaning that there are no adjacent mines. If you click a square with no adjacent mines, all the connecting squares are automatically uncovered until a numbered square is reached. Use the numbers as hints to where the mines are located; use the process of elimination to uncover all the squares that aren't mines. Use the right mouse button to mark uncertain squares, which has the added benefit of preventing them from being clicked accidentally (see Figure 4-54).

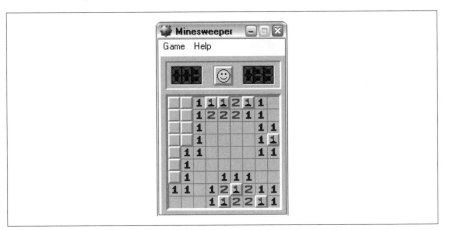

Figure 4-54. Try to clear the mine field without upsetting the little smiley guy

Notes

- The beginner game uses an 8 × 8 grid with 10 mines; intermediate uses a 16 × 16 grid with 40 mines; expert uses a 30 × 16 grid with 99 mines. You can also create custom games, such as an easy 30 × 30 grid with only 10 mines, or a difficult 8 × 8 grid with 60 mines.

- If a number appears on a square, it specifies how many mines are in the eight squares that surround the numbered square.

Mouse Properties

Change settings that affect the behavior of your pointing device and the appearance of the mouse cursor.

To Open   Control Panel → [Printers and Other Hardware] → Mouse
Command Prompt → control main.cpl
Command Prompt → control mouse

Description

The Mouse Properties dialog controls the buttons and motion of your pointing device and the appearance of the various mouse cursors, such as the arrow and hourglass. Settings are distributed into the following sections:

Buttons

> The three settings on this page allow you to switch the left and right mouse buttons (useful for southpaws or those with unusual pointing devices), change the speed at which items respond to double-clicks, and control the ClickLock feature (which enables dragging without having to hold down any buttons).

Pointers

> The Pointers tab lets you choose how your mouse pointer looks. This affects not only the standard arrow cursor, but the hourglass, the arrow/hourglass combination, all of the resize arrows, and even the hand cursor used in Internet Explorer. Cursors that ship with Windows are stored in the *\Windows\Cursors* folder and additional cursors are available on the Internet from such web sites as *http://www. anicursor.com/*. You can also get a cursor editor, allowing you to create your own static and animated mouse pointers (try AX-Cursors, at *http://www.axialis.com/ axcursors/*, or Microangelo, at *http://www.impactsoftware.com/)*(see Figure 4-55).

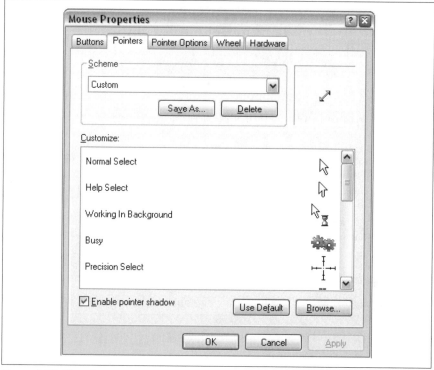

Figure 4-55. Choosing custom mouse pointers can go a long way to improving your sanity when sitting in front of a computer

The pointer shadow is actually kind of cool, but it isn't compatible with all display drivers.

Pointer Options

These settings are used to adjust how the mouse pointer responds to the physical motion of your pointing device. A fast pointer speed makes the cursor more sensitive. The Enhance pointer precision option enables minor mouse acceleration and deceleration, which moves the pointer more slowly when you move only a short distance.

Wheel

The mouse wheel, present on some mice and trackballs, is intended to aid scrolling. Just roll the wheel to scroll up or down in a listbox, document, or web page instead of controlling the scrollbar directly with the mouse pointer. If your pointing device doesn't have a wheel, these settings are ignored.

Hardware

Finally, the Hardware tab simply lists the pointing devices attached to the system. Note that the Properties page is the same one you'll get in Device Manager (discussed earlier in this chapter). The Troubleshoot button simply opens up a Help and Support Center window with a step-by-step troubleshooting tutorial.

Notes

- All settings in this dialog are also covered in Chapter 5.

- Many pointing devices come with their own software. Some of this software includes hardware drivers and is absolutely necessary for operation, while other software is purely optional, adding only trivial features. Given the potential compatibility problems with Windows XP, it's best to install such software only if it's necessary or if it provides features you can't live without.

See Also

"Control Panel"

Msg

\windows\system32\msg.exe

Send a text message to one or all local users.

To Open   Command Prompt → msg

Usage   msg *recipient* [/server:*name*] [/time:*sec*] [/v] [/w] [*message*]

Description

Msg is used to send a text message to a user currently logged onto the local computer; it can also be used to send a message simultaneously to all logged-in users.

Note that Msg is not intended to send messages to other computers, but to users remotely logged onto your computer. The exception is a user on another machine currently logged into your machine (or the machine specified by /server), assuming that machine is set up as a Terminal Server. To send a message to another computer, use Microsoft Chat (or just send an email).

Msg accepts the following options:

message

> The text message to send. If omitted, Msg prompts for it. Also can read from stdin; see Appendix C.

recipient

> *Recipient* can be a username, a session name, a session ID, or a filename (pointing to a file containing a list of usernames, session names, or session IDs). Or, specify an asterisk (*) to send a message to all sessions on the specified server.

/server:name

> Specifies */server:name* to send the message to users on another machine, where *name* is the name of a Terminal Server (see "Services" in "Microsoft Management Console," earlier in this chapter).

/time:sec

> Indicates the amount of time, in seconds, to wait for the recipient to acknowledge the message being sent.

/v

> Verbose mode; displays additional information about the actions being performed.

/w

> Waits for a response from the recipient, useful with /v.

See Also

"Microsoft Chat," "Microsoft NetMeeting"

MSN Explorer

\program files\msn\msncorefiles\msn6.exe

The graphical interface to the MSN online service.

To Open   Little butterfly icon in the quicklaunch toolbar
Command Prompt → msn6

Description

The MSN online service, in addition to providing basic Internet access, supplies online content, somewhat like American Online (AOL). The MSN Explorer is an integrated web browser, email program, and messenger ("buddy list") for use with the MSN service (see Figure 4-56).

You don't have to be a subscriber to MSN to use MSN Explorer, but you to have to complete the initial signup wizard. Although it's free, it does require several pieces of personal information, such as your geographic location, birthdate, and occupation. Once you complete the sign-in process, the MSN Explorer window resembles the Internet Explorer web browser, except the menu is gone, the toolbar is simplified, and an additional task pane is shown on the left.

Notes

- The MSN Explorer offers very little functionality above and beyond Internet Explorer. It is merely a friendlier, less intimidating interface designed to appeal to novices and children. One potential advantage is the total lack of knowledge required to get up and running with MSN Explorer; for example, most features

Figure 4-56. The MSN online service works like Internet Explorer, but has more brightly colored icons and is linked up with Microsoft's Passport service

on the toolbar are automatically configured for the currently logged-in user, so all one needs to do is click the buttons.

- The toolbar buttons, images, and default pages are all rather large. The minimum recommended resolution to use MSN Explorer is 800 × 600, and that's only appropriate if the window is maximized.

- The Email button is essentially a shortcut to Hotmail, Microsoft's free web-based email client. Likewise, the Online Buddies, the People & Chat, and the Money buttons all are shortcuts to corresponding web sites at *http://www.msn.com/*.

- When you close MSN Explorer, it remains in memory. To sign out of MSN and shut down the MSN Explorer completely, right-click on the MSN icon in the Tray (next to the clock) and select Exit MSN Explorer.

- In order to use MSN Explorer or Windows Messenger, you'll need to set up a Microsoft .NET Passport account. There has been some confusion regarding Passport among many users, however. A Passport account is absolutely not required for any other features of Windows; in fact, Microsoft has been widely criticized for making it appear otherwise.

See Also

"Internet Explorer," "Outlook Express," "MSN Gaming Zone"

MSN Gaming Zone

A collection of games that can be played with other users over the Internet.

To Open   Start → Programs → Games → Internet Backgammon
Start → Programs → Games → Internet Checkers
Start → Programs → Games → Internet Hearts
Start → Programs → Games → Internet Reversi
Start → Programs → Games → Internet Spades

Description

Windows XP ships with eleven games, five of which are part of the MSN Gaming Zone and support play with other users over the Internet. All five games, while different in gameplay, work similarly. When you first start one of the games, you are automatically connected to a gaming server provided by Microsoft that is designed to post the communication between all of the different users. In addition to allowing collaborative play, a simple chat session is initiated in which the players can type text messages to communicate. Consult Help in any game window for playing tips.

Notes

- The MSN Gaming Zone randomly assigns players to games, so you never know who you're up against. By default, the selected skill level is beginner, which unfortunately pits you against other users who're most likely just goofing around, probably trying these games for the first time. Your best bet to find a more serious opponents is to select an Intermediate or Advanced skill level by going to Game → Skill Level.

- If the gaming server can't find a human opponent at any given time, one or more computer opponents will be used. However, there is no way to specify a computer opponent. Whether you've been assigned a computer or a person as an opponent, you can have a new one assigned to you by going to Game → Find New Opponent.

- None of the MSN Gaming Zone games can be played without an Internet connection, so if you don't wish to play against a human opponent, you'll need to obtain a non-network version of the particular game. (Hundreds of downloadable, single-player games are available on the Internet.)

See Also

"MSN Explorer," "Hearts," "Microsoft Chat"

My Computer

See "Windows Explorer."

My Network Places

See "Windows Explorer."

Narrator
\windows\system32\narrator.exe

A text-to-speech program intended for use by visually impaired users.

To Open   Start → Programs → Accessories → Accessibility → Magnifier
Command Prompt → narrator

Description

The Narrator is used to assist those with the visual impairments by using a voice synthesizer and your computer's sound hardware to read aloud text and the titles of screen elements (see Figure 4-57). Narrator reads the following types of text:

Events on screen

Check the "Announced events on screen" option to have Narrator speak messages that appear, the titles of Windows when they are activated, and the captions of many types of screen elements.

Typed characters

Narrator can optionally speak each letter and number as its corresponding key is pressed on the keyboard.

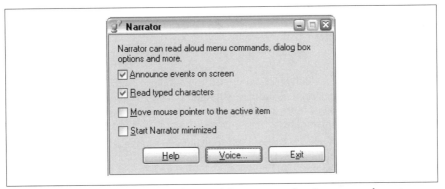

Figure 4-57. The Narrator uses speech to read the captions of various screen elements over your speakers

In addition to these functions, the following keyboard shortcuts can be used to read additional items:

- To read an entire window, click the window and then press Ctrl-Shift-Spacebar.
- To read the caption of the control with the focus, or to read the contents of a text field, press Ctrl-Shift-Enter.
- To get a more detailed description of an item, press Ctrl-Shift-Insert.
- To read the titlebar of a window, press Alt-Home.
- To read the status bar of a window, press Alt-End.
- To silence the speech, press the Ctrl key by itself.

Notes

- Narrator is supported only in the English version of Windows XP.
- A far more impressive, related technology is that used in speech recognition software, in which the computer will take dictation, translating anything spoken into a microphone into text on the screen. Although initially developed for physically challenged users, speech recognition has become very popular among all types of users, partly because of the novelty, partly because of the speed (some can type up to 160 words per minute), and partly to help reduce repetitive stress injuries. In fact, some of this book was dictated with the assistance of Dragon NaturallySpeaking (*http://www.dragonsys.com/*). Microsoft Office XP also comes with a new voice recognition feature, although it's not nearly as sophisticated as NaturallySpeaking or IBM's ViaVoice (*http://www.ibm.com/speech*).

See Also

"Microsoft Magnifier," "On-Screen Keyboard," "Utility Manager"

Net
\windows\system32\net.exe

Display, modify, and troubleshoot your current workgroup settings.

To Open   Command Prompt → net

Usage   net command [parameters]

Description

Net is a general purpose diagnostic tool used to configure, control, and troubleshoot the networking settings on a Windows XP system. The Net tool is largely obsolete, although it may appeal to more advanced users or those who need to control network settings from the command line.

To use Net, you must specify one of the following 22 commands, followed by any of the applicable parameters. To get more information about any of these commands, use the help command, like this:

    net help command

Here are the commands used with Net:

accounts

Use net accounts to update the user accounts database and modify password and logon requirements for all accounts. If used without parameters, the current settings for password, logon limitations, and domain information are displayed.

computer

Use net computer to add or delete computers from a domain database; only available on Windows XP Server and Advanced Server.

config

The net config command displays configuration information about the workstation or server service. See Examples, below.

continue

Type net continue to reactivate a Windows service that has been suspended by net pause.

file

Closes a shared file and removes any file locks. When used without options, net file lists the open files on a server (see "OpenFiles," later in this chapter). The listing includes the ID number, location, number of locks, and the user currently accessing the file.

group

Adds, displays, or modifies global groups on servers. When used without options, net group displays a list of the groups on the server.

help

Displays more information about any command. When used without options, net help displays all the available commands.

---

helpmsg

The net `helpmsg` command displays information about error, warning, and alert messages relating to a Windows network. For example, type net `helpmsg 2181` to display an explanation of error #2181 and any possible remedies.

localgroup

Modifies local groups on computers. When used without options, net `localgroup` displays a list of the groups on the server.

name

The net name command adds or deletes a messaging name, an alias to which messages are sent (via net send). When used without options, a list of names accepting messages at the computer is displayed.

pause

Use net `pause` to temporarily suspend a Windows service or resource and use net `continue` to reactivate it when you're ready.

print

The net print command displays print jobs and shared printer queues.

send

Sends messages to other users, computers, or messaging names (see net `name`) on the network. You can use net `send` to send a message only to a name that is active on the network; if the message is sent to a username, that user must be logged on and running the Messenger service to receive the message.

session

Net session lists or disconnects sessions between the computer and other computers on the network.

share

The net share command makes a server's resources available to network users. When used without options, it lists information about all resources being shared. See also "Create Shared Folder," earlier in this chapter.

start

Use net `start` to start a service. When used without options, it lists services that have already been started.

statistics

Displays the statistics log for the local workstation or server service. Used without parameters, net `statistics` displays the services for which statistics are available.

stop

Use net stop to stop a service that has been started with net `start`. Note that stopping some services will cause others to be stopped, and some services cannot be stopped at all.

time

Probably the most interesting command in the bunch, net time is used to synchronize the computer's clock with that of another computer or domain. You can also use net `time` to set the NTP timeserver for the computer.

use

The net use command connects (or disconnects) a computer to a shared resource (shared with net share). When used without options, it lists the computer's active connections.

user

Creates and modifies user accounts. When used without options, net user lists the user accounts for the computer. The user account information is stored in the same user accounts database used by Control Panel → User Accounts; see "User Accounts," later in this chapter.

view

Net view displays a list of resources being shared on a remote computer. When used without options, it displays a list of computers in the current domain or network.

Examples

To display your computer's current workgroup settings:

```
C:\>net config

Computer name                      \\WHISTLER
Full Computer name                 whistler
User name                          Administrator

Workstation active on
        NetbiosSmb (000000000000)
        NetBT_Tcpip_{50127698-1089-4C0F-A969-96B844756D47} (00105A1E5108)

Software version                   Windows 2002

Workstation domain                 WORKGROUP
Workstation Domain DNS Name        (null)
Logon domain                       WHISTLER

COM Open Timeout (sec)             0
COM Send Count (byte)              16
COM Send Timeout (msec)            250
The command completed successfully.
```

See Also

"Network Connections," Chapter 7

Netstat

See "Active Connections Utility."

Network Connections   \windows\system\ncpa.cpl

Manage connections to varying network resources.

To Launch   Control Panel → [Network and Internet Connections] → Network Connections

Start → Settings → Network Connections*

---

* This only appears when you're using the Classic Start menu, and then only sometimes.

Right-click the My Network Places icon → Properties
Command Prompt → ncpa.cpl
Command Prompt → control netconnections

Description

The Network Connections folder is used to connect your computer to the Internet, to another computer on a local area network, and to many other types of network resources (see Figure 4-58). See Chapter 7 for a comprehensive discussion of the Network Connections window and the networking features built into Windows XP.

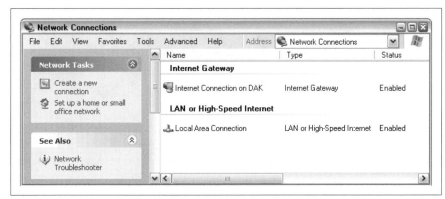

Figure 4-58. The Network Connections window allows you to connect your computer to a local network or to the Internet

Network Setup Wizard

Automatically configure your Internet connection and local network settings based on one of several predefined scenarios.

To Open   My Network Places → Network Setup Wizard
Start → Programs → Accessories → Communications → Network Setup Wizard
Control Panel → [Network and Internet Connections] → Network Connections → Network Setup Wizard*
Command Prompt → rundll32 hnetwiz.dll,HomeNetWizardRunDll

Description

The Network Setup Wizard walks you through some basic networking settings and is intended to make it easy to set up Windows to work with your Internet connection or to gain access to other computers on your network (see Figure 4-59).

The first page of the Network Setup Wizard implies that the wizard will set up a network for you, help you set up Internet connection sharing, install a firewall, and share files and printers. In fact, it will do none of these things; rather, it will simply

---

* If you have the "Show common tasks in folders" option turned on (see "Folder Options"), click the "Set up a home or small office network" link to start the Network Setup Wizard.

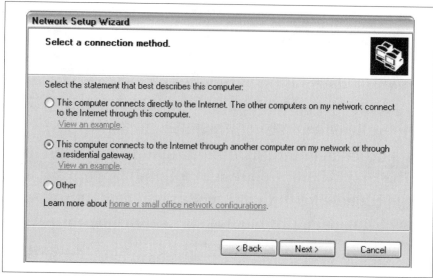

Figure 4-59. The Network Setup Wizard asks you a few networking questions and configures your network settings accordingly

ensure that some of the necessary protocols are installed and properly configured for the type of network to which you plan on attaching your computer. Before you use the Network Setup Wizard, you'll need to make sure all of your networking hardware is properly installed, as described in Chapter 7.

The "Select a connection method" page asks you to define a role for the computer, in so much as how the computer is to be connected to the Internet. Note that if you choose the second option, which specifies that the computer is to connect to the Internet through another computer or a gateway, you still have to set up that other computer or gateway to provide the Internet connection. If neither of the first two options presented applies to your system, choose Other to display three other scenarios.

One of the nice things about the Network Setup Wizard is that it controls settings that relate both to your Internet connection and to your connection to your local network (if applicable). While it can't recognize and set up every possible configuration, it is programmed to recognize when your selections are not compatible with the hardware it detects.

Continue to answer questions until the summary page is displayed, and if you have no objections, click Finish to apply the settings. Naturally, you can always run the wizard again or modify the settings manually to get it to work.

Notes

- If the Network Setup Wizard prompts you to create a setup disk for use on other computers, answer "Just finish the wizard," as the disk is of little use.

- The Network Setup Wizard won't help you set up an Internet connection, but the New Connection Wizard (discussed later in this chapter) will.

- The Network Setup Wizard replaces the Home Networking Wizard found in Windows Me.

See Also

Chapter 7

New Connection Wizard   *\Program Files\Internet Explorer\Connection Wizard\icwconn1.exe*

Set up

a new network connection.

To Open   Control Panel → [Network and Internet Connections] → Network
                 Connections → New Connection Wizard*
                 Start → Programs → Accessories → Communications → Connection
                 Wizard
                 Command Prompt → icwconn1

Description

Windows XP handles network and Internet access with distinct "connections," listed
in the Network Connections window (discussed earlier in this chapter). The New
Connection Wizard will guide you through the process of setting up a new connection; the following four types, presented on the first page of the wizard, are available:

Connect to the Internet

Use this option to set up a new Internet connection (see Figure 4-60). The next
page shows three options. Most users want to pick the second, "Set up my
connection manually," as it will set up a basic connection, compatible with most
Internet service providers. The first option, "Choose from a list...," is used only if
you wish to sign up for MSN (Microsoft's online service) or if you want to cruise
Microsoft's list of service providers (see Notes). The third option, "Use the CD I
got from an ISP," merely starts the setup program on whatever CD is inserted in
the drive.

Connect to the network at my workplace

This option helps set up a remote connection to a business network, either
through a dialup connection or through Virtual Private Networking (VPN). Note
that your business network must be set up to accept such connections; contact
your administrator for specific instructions.

Set up a home or small office network

Choose this option to close the New Connection Wizard and run the Network
Setup Wizard (explained earlier in this chapter).

Set up an advanced connection

The last option on this page lets you set up other types of connections, such as
those that use a single serial or parallel cable (called "Direct Cable Connection" in
previous versions of Windows) or those that communicate wirelessly with an
infrared port. While these types of connections aren't strictly network connections, Windows XP treats them as such—not only in this wizard, but in Explorer
(after they've been set up) as well. There is one tangible difference with this type of

---

* If you have the "Show common tasks in folders" option turned on (see "Folder Options"), click
the "Create a new connection" link to start the New Connection Wizard.

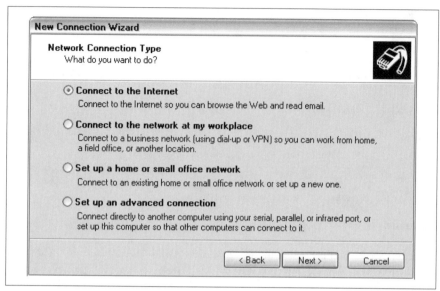

Figure 4-60. Add an Internet connection with the New Connection Wizard

connection, at least concerning this wizard: one computer must be first set up to "accept incoming connections" before another computer can be connected to it.

You may notice that there's no way to add a standard Ethernet connection. This is because a new connection icon is automatically added for each network interface card installed in your computer; install two network cards, and you'll see two connection icons here.

The first thing you may wish to do after creating a new connection is to rename it so that it is easier to identify later on and easier to distinguish from the other connections. To make any other changes to the new connection, right-click on it and select Properties. See Chapter 7 for more information on the various protocols and settings in these properties sheets necessary for setting up a network.

Notes

- All the choices made in this wizard result in the creation of a new connection icon in the Network Connections window; no changes to any other connections are made (except where new hardware has been added). This means that, even after completing this wizard, you can undo your changes simply by deleting the new connection.

- The New Connection Wizard is designed to create a new connection, not to modify an existing one. See "Network Setup Wizard," discussed earlier in this chapter, if you're having trouble configuring your network or Internet connection, or if you can't get Internet Connection Sharing to work.

- The New Connection Wizard replaces the Internet Connection Wizard found in earlier versions of Windows.

See Also

Chapter 7

Notepad

\windows\notepad.exe

A rudimentary plain text editor.

To Open   Start → Program → Accessories → Notepad
Command Prompt → notepad

Usage   notepad [/p] [*filename*]

Description

Notepad is one of the simplest, yet useful tools included with Windows XP. Those familiar with word processors may find Notepad to be laughably limited at first glance, as it has no support for even the simplest formatting. However, the fact that it supports only text in the documents that it creates is an absolute necessity for many of the tasks for which it is used on a daily basis (see Figure 4-61).

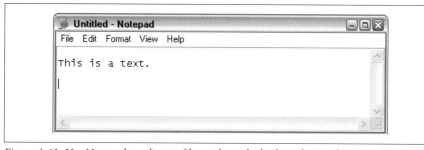

Figure 4-61. Use Notepad to edit text files without the bother of a word processor

Among the file types Notepad can edit are *.txt* files (plain text files), *.reg* files (see registry patch files in Chapter 7), *.bat* files (see batch files in Appendix C), *.ini* files (configuration files), *.html* files (web pages), and any other ASCII text-based file type.

Notepad is the default application for *.txt* and *.log* files and is set up as the Edit context menu action for *.bat*, *.inf*, and *.reg* files, among others. Furthermore, via the /p command-line parameter, Notepad is used to print most text-based file types via the Print context menu action.

Notes

- In some previous versions of Windows, Notepad had a limit as to the size of documents it could open. The Windows XP version of Notepad has no such limit, and can be used to open a file of any size.

- Notepad has no intrinsic formatting of its own, so any file that is opened in Notepad is displayed exactly as it is stored on the hard disk, with the proviso that only visible characters will be shown. This means that you can open any file, text-based or otherwise, in Notepad; if you try to open a binary file, however, you'll see mostly gibberish. There are times, though, when this can be useful; if you

Applications and Tools

suspect that an image file or a movie file has the wrong extension, you can open it in Notepad to verify its contents. (Naturally, some experience is required to correctly identify different types of files.)

- The Word Wrap feature (Edit → Word Wrap) will break apart long lines of text so that they are visible in the Notepad window without horizontal scrolling. However, no permanent changes will be made to the file, so you can use the Word Wrap feature without fear of damaging the integrity of the document.

- If you type the text, .LOG (in uppercase and including the period) as the first line in a text file, Notepad will automatically place the time and date at the end of the file (with the cursor right below it) every time you open it, forming a simple log file. Furthermore, you can use the F5 key to manually place a date/time stamp at the current cursor location while editing any file.

- Notepad is a simple program, but by no means a full-featured text editor. UltraEdit (*http://www.ultraedit.com/*) is a much more sophisticated text editor, and can also be used as a hex (binary) editor.

See Also
"WordPad"

NSLookup
\windows\system32\nslookup.exe

Perform a Domain Name Server (DNS) lookup, used to convert domain names to IP addresses, and vice-versa.

To Open   Command Prompt → nslookup

Usage   nslookup *address*

Description

When you type a web address into a browser's address bar and press Enter, Windows looks up the server name to determine the corresponding IP address. Then the IP address is used to initiate communication with the server. If the lookup fails, either because the name servers (the machines containing the DNS lookup tables) are down or because the specified domain does not exist, the connection attempt will fail as well.

NSLookup is a simple tool that allows you to look up the IP address of any domain name or server name, as well as find the server name associated with any particular IP address. To use NSLookup, just specify the domain name at the prompt, like this:

```
c:\> nslookup annoyances.org

Name:    annoyances.org
Address: 209.133.53.130
```

Likewise, you can specify an IP address and NSLookup will report the associated domain (called a reverse lookup):

```
c:\> nslookup 209.204.146.22

Name:    www.oreilly.com
Address: 209.204.146.22
```

Notes

- Every time you initiate communication with a server, there will be a delay while Windows performs an NSLookup. To eliminate the delay, use NSLookup to determine the IP address and then replace the reference with the IP address. This is especially useful with applications that frequently access the same server; for example, use an IP address as the mail server in your email program (or as the server name in your web browser homepage) for the best performance.

- Most Internet service providers employ at least two name servers, which are used for lookups for all of their customers. If one goes down, the other takes up the slack. However, if both name servers are down for some reason, or even just performing poorly, it can disable most Internet communication. If, however, you use IP addresses as described in the previous note, you eliminate your susceptibility to this problem.

- Since NSLookup, as well as the automatic lookups performed behind the scenes, all depend on your ISP's name servers, they are susceptible to receiving outdated information. If you're having trouble accessing a particular server, you can use an NSLookup gateway to double check your findings. An NSLookup gateway is simply a web-enabled version of NSLookup. It can also be used to perform lookups; however, if the gateway site is outside your Internet service provider, it will use its own name servers and therefore may provide more up-to-date information. To find such a site, perform a web search for "NSLookup gateway."

- NSLookup also performs a lookup of the IP address of your local computer and displays it before performing the requested look up. In many cases, though, it will fail, which means that you may see an error message every time you run NSLookup (such as "Can't find server name..."). However, this won't interfere with NSLookup's primary function.

- Windows caches some lookups, which means that you may see outdated information. To flush the cache, type `ipconfig /flushdns` at the command prompt. See "Windows IP Configuration," later in this chapter, for more information.

See Also

"Ping," "Tracert," "Windows IP Configuration"

NTFS Compression Utility

\windows\system32\compact.exe

View or configure the automatic file compression on NTFS drives.

To Open   Command Prompt → compact

Usage   `compact [/c | /u] [/s[:dir]] [/a] [/i] [/f] [/q] [filename]`

Description

One of the features of the NTFS filesystem (see "FAT to NTFS Conversion Utility," earlier in this chapter) is its support for automatic compression of individual files; older files can be optionally compressed to take up less disk space at the expense of speed to access them.

Right-click on any file or folder, select Properties, and then click the Advanced button. The "Compress contents to save disk space" option is used to instruct Windows to compress the selected item. If a folder is selected, all of its contents will be compressed (you'll be prompted about any subfolders); furthermore any files added to that folder will be automatically compressed as well.

The NTFS Compression Utility is the command-line equivalent of this setting, useful for automating the compression or decompression of several files with the help of a WSH script or batch file. The NTFS Compression Utility takes the following options:

filename

> Specifies a file, folder, or group of files (using wildcards) to compress or uncompress.

/c

> Compresses the specified file(s). If a folder is specified for *filename*, the folder will be marked so that subsequent files added to the folder will be compressed automatically. Include the /s parameter to compress files already in the folder.

/u

> Uncompresses the specified file(s). If a folder is specified for *filename*, the folder will be marked so that subsequent files added to the folder will not be compressed automatically. Include the /s parameter to uncompress files already in the folder.

/s

> If a folder is specified for *filename*, the /c and /u parameters will act only on new files added to the folder. Include the /s parameter as well to compress or uncompress files already in the folder. If *filename* is omitted, use the /s option to act on all files in the current folder.

/a

> Includes files with hidden or system attributes set; otherwise, ignored by *compact.exe*.

/i

> Ignores errors; otherwise, *compact.exe* will stop when the first errors are encountered.

/f

> Forces compression on all specified files; otherwise, files that are already compressed will be skipped.

/q

> Quiet mode; use this option to report only the most essential information.

If you run the NTFS Compression Utility without any options, it will display the compression settings for the current directory and all of its contents.

Notes

- This type of file compression is supported on NTFS drives only. If you wish to compress files on a non-NTFS drive, you can either upgrade to NTFS or use a third-party compression utility (such as WinZip).

- Go to Control Panel → [Appearance and Themes] → Folder Options → View tab and turn on the "Show encrypted or compressed NTFS files in color" option to visually differentiate such files from unencrypted, uncompressed files.

- For tangible proof that a given folder or file is actually compressed, right-click on it in Explorer and select Properties. If the "Size on disk" value is less than the "Size" value, then the item is compressed.

See Also

"FAT to NTFS Conversion UtilityFAT," "Compress old files" in "Disk Cleanup," "NTFS Encryption Utility"

NTFS Encryption Utility
\windows\system32\cipher.exe

View or configure the automatic file encryption on NTFS drives. (NTFS Encryption Utility is included with Windows XP Professional only.)

To Open   Command Prompt → cipher

Usage
```
cipher [/e|/d] [/s] [/a] [/i] [/f] [/q] [/h] [filename]
cipher /k
cipher /r:efs_file
cipher /w:dir
cipher /u [/n]
```

Description

Encryption is used to prevent unauthorized access to your data, and one of the features of the NTFS filesystem (see "FAT to NTFS Conversion Utility," earlier in this chapter) is its built-in support for automatic encryption of files and folders using "public key cryptography." NTFS encryption is invisible and encrypted files are opened as easily as decrypted files. The difference is that other users, either those who access your computer remotely (via My Network Places, Telnet, or FTP) or those who also log into your computer under a different user account, will not be able to open or read encrypted files on your system.

Right-click on any file or folder, select Properties, and then click the Advanced button. The "Encrypt contents to secure data" option is used to instruct Windows to encrypt the selected item. If a folder is selected, all of its contents will be encrypted (you'll be prompted about any subfolders); furthermore, any files added to that folder will be automatically encrypted as well.

The NTFS Encryption Utility is the command-line equivalent of this setting, but it adds several powerful features not normally available through Explorer. It's also useful for automating the encryption or decryption of several files with the help of a WSH script or batch file. The NTFS Encryption Utility takes the following options:

filename
> Specifies a file, folder, or group of files (using wildcards) to compress or uncompress. Omit *filename* to act on the current directory.

/e
> Encrypts the specified file(s). If a folder is specified for *filename*, the folder will be marked so that subsequent files added to the folder will be encrypted automatically. Include the /a parameter to encrypt files already in the folder and the /s parameter to act on subdirectories as well.

/d
> Decrypts the specified file(s). If a folder is specified for *filename*, the folder will be marked so that subsequent files added to the folder will be decrypted automatically. Include the /a parameter to decrypt files already in the folder and the /s parameter to act on subdirectories as well.

/s

By default, if *filename* is a directory, the /e or /d options act on the specified directory, but not on any subdirectories. Include /s to include all subdirectories as well. Use the /a option to encrypt the files stored in these directories.

/a

Operates on files as well as folders. If folders and files are not *both* marked to be encrypted, it's possible for an encrypted file to become decrypted when it is modified if its parent folder is not encrypted

/i

Ignores errors; otherwise, *cipher.exe* will stop when the first errors are encountered.

/f

Forces encryption on all specified files; otherwise, files that are already encrypted will be skipped.

/q

Quiet mode; use this option to report only the most essential information.

/h

Includes files with hidden or system attributes set; otherwise, ignored by *cipher.exe*.

/k

Generates and displays a new file encryption key (certificate thumbprint) for the current user. The /k option cannot be used with any other options.

/r:*efs_file*

Generates an Encrypting File System (EFS) recovery agent key and certificate, and then writes them to *efs_file.pfx* (containing the certificate and private key) and *efs_file.cer* file (containing only the certificate). Since the /r option will automatically add the appropriate file extensions, all you need to specify is the path and file prefix for *efs_file*. See Notes for more information.

/w:*dir*

"Wipes" the drive containing directory *dir*. When a file is deleted in Windows, only that file's entry in the filesystem table is deleted; the actual data contained in the file remains on the hard disk until it is overwritten with another file. Wiping a drive writes over all unused portions of the disk, possibly containing deleted files so that previously deleted data cannot be recovered. The /w option does not harm existing data, nor does it affect any files currently stored in the Recycle Bin. This is an extreme form of data security and should be used on a regular basis if security is a big concern.

/u

Updates all encrypted files on all local drives. /u is used to ensure that your file encryption key or recovery agent key are current. The /u option cannot be used with any other options, except for /n.

/n

Modifies /u so that encrypted files are only listed, not updated. Type cipher /u / n to list all the encrypted files on your system. The /n option can only be used in conjunction with /u.

If you run the NTFS Encryption Utility without any options, it will display the encryption settings for the current directory and all of its contents.

Notes

- Windows supports placing encrypted files in nonencrypted folders, but you'll be warned, by default, if you try to do so. The reason for this is that, when modifying a file, some applications delete the file and then re-create it, and if the folder is not marked to encrypt new files, the once-encrypted file will become decrypted without warning.

- If you encrypt some or all of the files on your drive and your hard disk crashes, or you encounter some other program that requires Windows to be reinstalled, you may not be able to access your previously encrypted files (assuming they're still intact). You can avoid this by using the /r parameter to generate a "recovery agent key," a cryptographic key that can be used to unlock files in the event of an emergency. You should be able to use this key to subsequently gain access to your encrypted files when necessary. For more information, go to Start → Help and Support and search for "cryptography."

- The /w option, used to wipe unused data on a drive, isn't strictly a form of encryption and can be used whether or not you employ Windows XP's built-in encryption.

- NTFS drives support both encryption and compression, but a given file cannot be compressed and encrypted at the same time. If you attempt to encrypt a compressed file, Windows will first uncompress the file.

- This type of file encryption is supported on NTFS drives only. If you wish to encrypt files on a non-NTFS drive, you can either upgrade to NTFS or use a third-party file encryption utility (such as Encryption Plus Folders, a freeware program available at *http://www.pcguardian.com/*).

- Go to Control Panel → [Appearance and Themes] → Folder Options → View tab and turn on the "Show encrypted or compressed NTFS files in color" option to visually differentiate such files from unencrypted, uncompressed files.

See Also

"FAT to NTFS Conversion Utility," "NTFS Compression Utility"

Object Packager
\windows\system32\packager.exe

Create "packages" for insertion into documents.

To Open   Command Prompt → packager

Description

Many larger applications support the dragging and dropping of data from one program to another. For example, you can highlight a dozen cells in Microsoft Excel, drag them into a Microsoft Word document, and Word will insert the dropped data as a new table. Furthermore, under certain circumstances, there will be an active link between the two applications so that you could make a change to one of the spreadsheet cells and the change would be reflected in the Word document immediately.

As you might expect, there's more going on behind the scenes to make all this possible than might be immediately apparent. Indeed, Windows creates a "package" containing the selected data and then inserts that package into the target document. Microsoft has given many names to this technology, but their first, Object Linking and Embedding (OLE), is the one that has stuck in many users' minds

Object Packager is a tool used to create such a package manually, useful if you need more flexibility than is achieved with drag-and-drop.

The Object Packager window has two panes: the Appearance pane displays the icon that will represent the package and the Content pane displays the name of the file that contains the information you want to package. To choose an icon, click the Insert Icon button. To choose a file, go to File → Import.

When you're done, go to Edit → Copy Package to prepare the package. The last step is to switch to the target application and paste the newly prepared package into your document. Once the package icon appears in the target document, you can activate the package by double-clicking it, which will open the packaged file according to your Files Types settings. For example, if the packaged file is a bitmap, activating the package will open that bitmap in Paint (discussed later in this chapter).

This preservation of the original file's format, and its associated application, is the whole point of Object Packager. Otherwise, pasting a bitmap into a document would be a one-way procedure; if you needed to update the bitmap at a later time, you would most likely need to delete the bitmap from the target document and then repaste it.

Another advantage of Object Packager is its ability to override the default association for the inserted file. Go to Edit → Command Line to enter any new application filename or other command to be executed when the package is activated.

ODBC Data Source Administrator
\windows\system32\odbcad32.exe

Add, remove, or configure sources of database management system data.

To Open   Start → Programs → Administrative Tools → Data Sources (ODBC)
                 Command Prompt → odbcad32

Description

Open Database Connectivity (ODBC) is a system that connects ODBC-enabled applications to the database management systems that provide the data. The ODBC Data Source Administrator is used to configure your applications so that they can get data from a variety of database management systems. For example, if you're using an application that accesses data in an SQL database, the ODBC Data Sources Administrator lets you connect that application to a different data source, such as a Microsoft Excel spreadsheet or a Paradox database.

In the ODBC Data Source Administrator, the different sources of data are called "data providers." To add a new provider, click Add under the User DSN, the System DSN, or the File DSN tab. A list of the available drivers is listed under the Drivers tab; new drivers can be installed separately. The Tracing allows you to log the communication between applications and the ODBC data sources they use. The Connection Pooling tab is used to improve performance with ODBC servers. Finally, the About tab is used to check the versions of the installed ODBC components.

On-Screen Keyboard
\windows\system32\osk.exe

A full, onscreen keyboard controlled by the pointing device.

To Open   Start → Programs → Accessories → Accessibility → On-Screen Keyboard
Command Prompt → osk

Description

Among the tools provided with Windows XP to assist those with physical disabilities is the On-Screen Keyboard. Intended to be used by those who are unable to comfortably use a keyboard, the On-Screen Keyboard allows any key normally available on the keyboard to be pressed with click of the mouse, or whatever pointing device is currently being used (see Figure 4-62).

What makes the On-Screen Keyboard especially appropriate as a primary input device is that you can click keys when another application has the focus. For example, open the On-Screen Keyboard, and then open your word processor; the keyboard will float above the word processor, allowing you to click any key to "type" it into your document.

Configuring the On-Screen Keyboard is straightforward. Use the Keyboard menu to change the layout of the keys, or Settings → Font to change the font of the key labels. Go to Settings → Typing Mode to choose how keys are pressed; by default, each key must be clicked, but you can set it up so that you can hover over keys to select them, or even use a joystick to control the keyboard.

Figure 4-62. The On-Screen Keyboard lets you type by pointing and clicking

Notes

Also included with Windows XP is the Character Map (discussed earlier in this chapter), which allows access to symbols and other characters not normally available on a standard keyboard. However, only the On-Screen Keyboard is designed to be a primary input device.

See Also

"Microsoft Magnifier," "Narrator," "Utility Manager," "Character Map"

OpenFiles   \windows\system32\openfiles.exe

List all currently open files, either shared and accessed by other users on a network or (optionally) opened locally. (OpenFiles is included with Windows XP Professional only.)

To Open   Command Prompt → openfiles

Usage
```
openfiles /local [ on | off ]
openfiles /query [/s system [/u user [/p [pass]]]]
    [/fo format] [/nh] [/v]
openfiles /disconnect [/s system [/u user [/p [pass]]]]
    {[/id id] [/a accessedby] [/o openmode]} [/op openfile]
```

Description

The OpenFiles tool lets you view a list of all the shared files that are currently open across the network and, optionally, files that are opened locally. This prevents, say, one user deleting a document that another user is working on.

Type openfiles without any options to display a report like this:

```
Files Opened Remotely via local share points:
----------------------------------------------
ID    Accessed By   Type        Open File (Path\executable)
===== ============= ========== ======================================
98    LOU           Windows    C:\Stuff to Eat\frittatas.txt
101   EDDIE         Windows    C:\Stuff to Drink\milkshakes.txt
107   CLANCY        Windows    C:\Stuff to Eat\pork chops.txt
```

OpenFiles accepts one of three primary commands, each of which has a range of parameters:

/local [parameters]
> Turn on or off the inclusion of local files in reports. Type:
>
> ```
> openfiles /local on
> ```
>
> to turn on the 'maintain objects list' global flag; this setting is turned off by default and requires Windows to be restarted when changed. Note that turning on this setting may slightly reduce performance.

/query [parameters]
> Display a list of opened files and folders; specify /query for more flexibility than using openfiles without any options, such as the ability to connect to a different machine. Type openfiles /query /? for more information on the available parameters.

/disconnect [parameters]
> Selectively disconnect files and folders that have been opened remotely. When viewing the list of open files, each entry has an ID; that ID can be used to close open files. Type openfiles /disconnect /? for more information on the available parameters.

Notes

OpenFiles is available only to a user with administrator privileges.

See Also

"Net"

Outlook Express

\program files\outlook express\msimn.exe

An Internet email client and newsgroup reader.

To Open   Start → Programs → Outlook Express

Double-click the Outlook Express icon on the Desktop
Quick Launch Bar → "Launch Outlook Express"
Command Prompt → `msimn`

Description

Outlook Express is the email client included with Windows XP (see Figure 4-63). Outlook Express uses a familiar Explorer-like tree interface to manage the folders into which email messages are organized. Highlight any folder name to display its messages; the currently highlighted message is then shown in the preview pane. Double-click the message to open it in a new window for easier reading and other options.

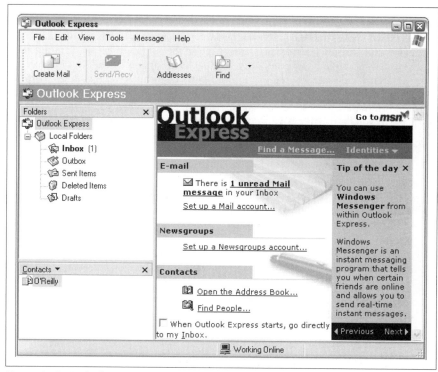

Figure 4-63. Outlook Express is the rudimentary email application that comes with Windows

Newly received messages are stored in the Inbox folder. Files queued to be sent are stored in the Outbox folder, and are then moved to the Sent Items folder when they have been sent. The Deleted Items folder is like the Recycle Bin because it stores deleted messages until it is emptied manually. The Drafts folder stores messages as they're being composed. To add a new folder, select Local Folders in the tree and go to File → New → Folder. Messages can be moved from folder to folder by dragging and dropping.

The first time you open Outlook Express, a wizard walks you through setting up your first account. An account in Outlook Express is not actually an email account, but rather an entry in the Tools → Accounts → Mail tab that corresponds to an existing email account. Outlook Express uses either the Post Office Protocol 3 (POP3) or the Internet

Message Access Protocol 4 (IMAP4) Internet mail protocols to receive mail and the Simple Mail Transfer Protocol (SMTP) to send mail. Nearly all Internet Service Providers and many online services (like AOL and MSN) use POP3 and SMTP for mail transfer.

In addition to mail accounts, you can set up Directory Service accounts, which allow you to look up contact information using any of several online global contact lists. Outlook Express also functions as a newsreader for participating in Internet newsgroups; you'll need to add a News Account to Outlook Express before you can read any newsgroups (contact your ISP for details).

Much of Outlook Express is fairly intuitive, and given that it would require more space than we have here to cover Outlook Express in its entirety, the following sections highlight only some of the most useful and interesting aspects of the program.

Accounts (Tools → Accounts)

As stated above, the Accounts window stores information about all of your email, news, and Directory Service accounts. Choose the All tab to list them all together. You can modify any account entry by double-clicking it. To add a new account entry, click Add and choose the account type. Unfortunately, the only way to set up an account entry is to use the cumbersome wizard; there's no way to skip ahead and use the Properties window to enter information. When you're done with the wizard, you'll probably have to use the Properties window anyway to set some of the more advanced options, such as whether or not to automatically check mail from this account, whether to leave copies of your mail on the server, or whether to use a different email address when replying to messages sent to this account.

Most problems encountered when sending or receiving email are caused by improper settings in this window.

If you have more than one mail account, you can choose the default by highlighting it and clicking Set as Default. Thereafter, that account will be used as your return address when sending outgoing email (unless you change it on a per-message basis).

The Set Order button, which lets you choose the search order when looking up contacts in your Directory Services, may be a little confusing at first. Since only an entry is shown, there's nothing to rearrange; to include more entries in Set Order, double-click each entry and turn on the "Check names against this server when sending mail" option (see Figure 4-64).

Address Book (Tools → Address Book)

The Address Book is used to store names and contact information for people to whom you send email on a regular basis. See "Address Book," earlier in this chapter, for more information.

Options (Tools → Options)

Specify options that govern the behavior of Outlook Express and apply to all mail and news accounts. This is where you control things like how often Outlook Express checks for mail when it's running and whether it is the default email program. The Dial Up tab lets you specify whether a connection is dialed automatically when you start Outlook Express, whether it should hang up after getting your messages, and whether it should dial automatically when you do a Send and Receive.

Identity Management (File → Identities → Manage Identities)

In addition to its support of multiple email accounts, Outlook Express supports multiple identities, a feature that lets more than one person use Outlook Express

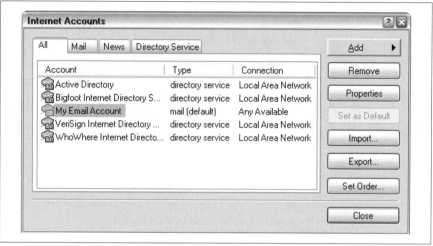

Figure 4-64. Configure multiple email accounts with the Internet Accounts dialog

on the same machine. Each identity has its own set of accounts, settings, and mail. The preferred approach is to forget the Identities feature, and instead set up multiple users in Windows XP (Control Panel → User Accounts), wherein each user would have his/her own Desktop, Start menu, and Explorer settings, as well as separate accounts and mail in Outlook Express. The Identity feature in Outlook Express is for people who don't want to go to the trouble of dealing with multiple Windows users, which would require a second user to log out and then log back in in order to check your mail (see Figure 4-65).

It's tempting to use Identities if you want to send out mail using more than one persona; but this really isn't what the feature is designed for. Instead, you should set up multiple accounts, one for each "persona" you wish to assume.

Say you have three different email addresses— one for work, one for personal email, and one left over from a previous job—all of which are still being used to receive email. You'd like to retrieve all your mail at once and store it all in the same place. In addition, you want to preserve both your work and personal email addresses, so when you respond to messages sent to either address, the return address and "real name" are set appropriately. In this case, you would set up three accounts in Outlook Express, but only one Identity.

To add a new identity, go to File → Identities → Add New Identity. You can then enter the name of the new user and select a password, if needed. To switch identities at any time, select File → Switch Identity. Note that the first time you use a new identity, Outlook Express will act as though it's the first time you've started the program, prompting you for personal contact information and account settings. The identity in use at any given time will be shown in the titlebar of the main Outlook Express window.

Figure 4-65. If more than one person needs to access their email on the same machine, use the Manage Identities dialog to switch between them

To share contacts in your Address Book between identities, open the Address Book and select View → Folders and groups. Contacts, by default, are only made available to the user that created them, but they can be shared by moving (or copying) them into the Shared Contacts folder.

Message Rules (Tools → Message Rules)

Outlook Express can be set up to automatically handle incoming mail in a number of different ways. For example, you can set up rules instructing Outlook Express to store all email retrieved from your business account in a certain folder, all email retrieved from your personal account in a different folder, and all junk mail (spam) in the trash. Furthermore, you can have Outlook Express automatically respond to certain messages and mark some messages as urgent and others as potentially annoying.

Go to Tools → Message Rules → Mail to view the mail rules currently in effect. If you haven't yet set up any rules, you would be prompted to do so now; otherwise, click New to create a new rule. Each rule is set up as follows:

1. *Select the conditions for your rule.* Choose one or more conditions that, when met, will instruct Outlook Express to take the desired action. For example, to create a rule that applies to all email from Grandma, Place a checkmark next to "Where the From line contains people."

2. *Select the actions for your rule.* After you've chosen one or more conditions (above), these options allow you to decide what to do with messages that meet those conditions. For example, you may wish to place all of Grandma's email in a certain folder, in which case you would place a checkmark next to

"Move it to the specified folder." On the other hand, if Grandma drives you nuts, you may wish to place a checkmark next to "Delete it."

3. *Rule description.* The third box displays a summary of the conditions and actions you've chosen, and allows you to input the specifics. For example, if you've chosen to move all of Grandma's email into a certain folder, the phrase "contains people" will be underlined and hyperlinked, as will the word "specified." Before you can complete this rule, you must click each of these links; in the case of "contains people," you would type Grandma's email address. Likewise, in the case of "specified," you would select the image of the folder in which to store Grandma's email.

4. *Name of the rule.* Finally, choose a label for the rule; although the name makes no difference, it will allow you to easily identify and differentiate the rules.

Don't expect to get all your rules right the first time. For example, after setting up several rules to delete spam, you may find that some legitimate messages are being inadvertently deleted as well. After creating a new rule, scrutinize its performance as new mail is retrieved.

You can also create new rules on the fly, using some of the context-based tools in Outlook Express. Start by opening a message, and then go to Message → Create Rule from Message. Here, the familiar rule dialog box is shown, but some fields have been filled in with information from the selected message. Likewise, you can go to Message → Block Sender to place the sender on the Blocked Sender List (Tools → Message Rules → Blocked Sender List), which causes subsequent email from the sender to be deleted automatically. While not technically a new rule, the Blocked Sender List does have a similar effect and is easier to implement and manage.

Be sure to read the message that pops up right after you add a sender to the Blocked Senders List. Selecting the Yes button will automatically move every message in any folder from this sender into the Deleted Items folder. This is especially dangerous (if you select Yes by mistake) if you've checked the Tools → Options → Maintenance → "Empty messages from the Deleted Items folder on exit" box.

Message → Flag Message

This does exactly what it sounds like. Select one or several messages and click the Flag Message command to add a little flag in a column (as long as the column is activated at View → Columns) near the message to remind yourself that the message needs a follow-up. You can also just click in the flag column to add a flag to a message. To remove the flag, select the message(s) and click the command again, or just click on the flag itself. You can sort the messages by this column to group all the flagged messages for later review.

Conversations (Message → Watch Conversation, Message → Ignore Conversation)

A conversation is a continuous series of email or newsgroup messages, often called a thread. For example if you were to write an email with the subject "Propane Elaine," it might spark a series of messages between you and the recipient, all of which would have the subject, "Re: Propane Elaine." This thread of messages is called a "conversation" in Outlook Express, and there are tools included for dealing with conversations.

You can "watch" a conversation that is of interest to you by highlighting a message and going to Message → Watch Conversation. Likewise, you can "ignore" a conversation by going to Message → Ignoring Conversation. Either of these will place an icon in the Watch/Ignore column: sunglasses or a red circle with a line through it, respectively. Click the icon to toggle between Watch, Ignore, and nothing.

For the most part, this is merely a decorative setting; it doesn't affect the way Outlook Express handles these messages. However, you can choose to highlight Watched conversations and hide Ignored conversations, as follows. You can customize the color of messages in watched conversations by going to Tools → Options → Read tab → Highlight watched messages. To hide all messages in a conversation marked as Ignored, go to View → Current View → Hide Read or Ignored Messages. Then, go to View → Current View → Customize Current View, place a checkmark next to "Where the messages watched or ignored," and click the links (see above) so that description reads: "Where the message is ignored, Hide the message."

Finally, if you select View → Current View → Group Messages by Conversation, messages in conversations will be grouped in expandable branches, like the folders in Explorer.

Signatures and Stationary

A signature is a bit of text that is automatically placed at the end of every outgoing message you write. Go to Tools → Options → Signature tab (see Figure 4-66) to create and edit signatures. Make sure you turn on the "Add signatures to all outgoing messages" option. You can have as many signatures as you want and you can even have a different default signature for each account; just click Advanced and choose the account with which the current signature should be associated. To use a signature on a per-message basis, go to Insert → Signature in the message composition window.

Stationery is just as you expect; it imposes a visual style on your message, including colors and even images. Stationary files are just *.html* files (web pages), stored by default in *\Program Files\Common Files\Microsoft Shared\Stationary*. They can be edited with any web page editor or plain text editor. To create new stationery or to use one of the supplied templates, go to Tools → Options → Compose tab. Click Create New to start a wizard to build a new stationery file for you. Place to checkmark next to Mail or News, and then click Select to choose an *.html* file to set as the default stationery. Unfortunately, you can't set default stationery for each account (something Eudora lets you do), but you can choose stationary on a per-message basis by going to Format → Apply Stationary in the message composition window.

Both signatures and stationery are shown in your message as you write, so you can modify them as needed without disrupting the permanent signature or stationary file. To make a template, useful when repeatedly sending messages that are similar, open a stationary file in a web page editor (or plain text editor, if you're familiar with HTML) and type whatever text content you need.

Notes

- Alternatives to Outlook Express include the popular Eudora Email (*http://www.eudora.com*) by Qualcomm, the web-based Hotmail email service (*http://www.hotmail.com*) by Microsoft, and PINE for those die-hard Unix users.

Figure 4-66. Use signatures to add a footer to every email you send

- Since it is an integrated component of Windows, Outlook Express is often the target of virus and Trojan horse attacks. Many of the recent widespread virus infestations have exploited the vulnerabilities in Outlook Express to replicate themselves, sometimes by sending a virus-infested attachment to everyone in your contact list. The same applies to Outlook, OE's big sister, which is included with Microsoft Office. To protect yourself, you should consider installing antivirus software, or even using a different email program.

- If you have more than one account setup in Outlook Express, only one account can be the default at any time. Although you can choose a From account each time you compose outgoing mail, the default account is the one that is used if you don't make a choice. Unfortunately, there's no way to set up a Message Rule (see above) to change the default account used when responding to incoming messages; for that, you'll need a more full-featured email program like Eudora.

- The filename *msimn.exe* gives a taste of the history of this program. Originally called Microsoft Internet Mail and News, it was renamed Outlook Express to position it as the "lite" version of Microsoft's Outlook application. In fact, the two programs share nothing but the name.

- By default, Outlook Express automatically compacts your mail and news files when it detects that 20 percent of your storage space is being wasted. You can adjust this percentage using Tools → Options → Maintenance → "Compact files when...". You can also click Clean Up Now here to perform the compression whenever you want.

- If you want to use Outlook Express when you're not connected to the Internet, go to File → Work Offline. If you are using a dial-up connection, you may even want to further reduce online time by configuring Outlook Express to hang up after sending and receiving messages. To do this, go to Tools → Options → Connection tab and turn on the "Hang up after sending and receiving" options. If autodial is enabled, Outlook Express will reconnect automatically when you go to Tools → Send and Receive.

- If you access the same account from two different computers, you may wish to set up one computer to download messages, but not delete them from the server. Set up your other system to delete messages after downloading them. This way, one system always has a complete set of messages. Do this by using Tools → Accounts → *any account* → Properties → Advanced tab → Leave a copy of messages on server.

- If you have multiple accounts set up and do not want one included when you click Send and Receive, go to Tools → Accounts → *any account* → Properties → General tab, and deselect "Include this account when receiving mail or synchronizing."

- To send a file along with an email message, go to Insert → File Attachment in the message composition window, or just drag the file from your Desktop or Explorer into the body of message. If Outlook Express is your default email program, you can also send a file as an email attachment by right-clicking it and selecting Send To → Mail Recipient. This opens a new, blank message with the file attachment included.

- Outlook Express supports rich text email, which adds fonts, color, images, and other formatting to otherwise plain text-based email. There is a drawback, however, in that users of older email programs may not be able to read rich text email, instead seeing only gibberish. You can configure or turn off the support for rich text email by going to Tools → Options → Send tab. Also note when you send an attachment with a rich-text email message, recipients who view messages in plain text will often not receive your attachments intact. If you are have that problem, you can either disable Outlook Express's support for rich text email or simply change the format for an individual message using that message window's Format menu.

- It can be annoying to wade through the thousands of messages that can exist in a single newsgroup. Custom views work like Rules (above) and let you weed out some of the extraneous messages. For example, you can hide messages written by certain users (in Usenet parlance, this is referred to as a "bozo filter"), contain certain words in the subject, are over a certain length, or are over a certain age. Go to View → Current View → Customize Current View to set your preferences.

Paint
\windows\system32\mspaint.exe

A rudimentary image editor, used to create and modify *.bmp*, *.jpg*, *.gif*, *.tif*, and *.png* image files.

To Open   Start → Programs → Accessories → Paint
Command Prompt → mspaint

Description

Paint is a basic image editor (often called a "paint program") capable of creating and modifying most Windows Bitmap (*.bmp*), Joint Photographic Experts Group (*.jpg*), Compuserve Graphics Interchange Format (*.gif*), Tagged Image File Format (*.tif*), and Portable Network Graphics (*.png*) image files. In essence, Paint is to image files as Notepad is to text files (see Figure 4-67).

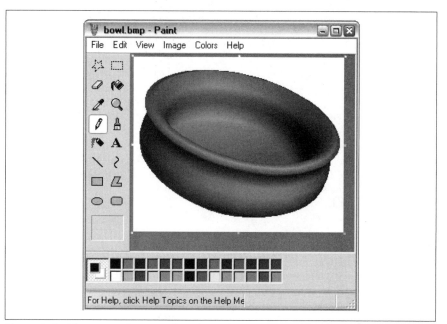

Figure 4-67. The Paint utility provides a few rudimentary tools for working with image files

The first time you start Paint, you'll get a blank (white) image, 400 × 300 pixels in size. Depending on the size of the Paint window, you may see the entire canvas, surrounded by a gray border. To change the size of the image, go to Image → Attributes, and type new values. The default units are pixels, but if you choose inches or centimeters, the size of the image will be calculated using the resolution displayed at the top of the window. For example, if you specify an image size of 8" × 11" at 64 dots per inch (1 dot = 1 pixel), the resulting image dimensions will be 8*64 × 11*64, or 512 × 640 pixels. The pixels are the only thing that is important if the image is to be displayed on the screen or in a web page; the dimensions in inches or centimeters are only important if you're printing the image.

At the bottom of the window, you'll see a color palette; the leftmost box shows the currently selected foreground and background colors. Choose a new foreground color by left-clicking on any color in the palette; choose a new background color by right-clicking. The roles of the foreground and background colors depend on the currently selected tool (see below). For example, if you draw a filled-in ellipse (choose the ellipse tool and then select the second variation), the foreground color will appear as the border and the background color will be used to fill the ellipse. You can mix your own colors by going to Colors → Edit Colors.

To the left of the document area is a simple toolbox. Each tool has a different function used to manipulate the image in some way. The first two tools are used to select portions of the image: the star selects an irregular shape and the rectangle selects a rectangle. The eraser tool works like a paintbrush, except that it paints with the background color. The paint bucket is used to fill a bounded area with a solid color. The eyedropper is used to set the foreground or background colors to an area in the image. The magnifying glass zooms in and out; left-click to zoom and right-click to zoom out. The pencil icon draws single-pixel-width lines, and the paintbrush draws with a variety of brush sizes, chosen in the brush palette beneath the toolbox; the left mouse button draws with the foreground color, and the right mouse button draws with the background color. The spray can draws by splattering random dots. The A tool is used to add text to an image, although once text has been applied, it becomes part of the image and can't be changed. The line tool is used to draw a straight line between two points; choose the squiggly line tool to first draw a straight line, and then distort the line with a third click. The last four tools are shapes; choose the shape, and then choose whether or not it will be filled or have a border by using the brush palette below.

In addition to these basic tools, there are some other goodies. Go to File → Set as Background (Tiled or Centered) sets the current image as the Windows Desktop wallpaper (it only works if the file has been first saved as a *.bmp* file). Use View → View Bitmap to temporarily fill the screen with the image; click or press any key to go back. Entries in the Image menu let you perform some extra functions, such as flipping, rotating, and stretching the image.

Notes

- If you're creating an image file to be used on a web page, that file must be saved using the *.jpg* or *.gif* format, a selection that is made in the File → Save As box. *.bmp* files, while visible in some versions of Internet Explorer, are not a suitable file format for web pages, mostly because most web browsers will not be able to read them. Note that it is not enough to simply rename a file to a different format; you must open it and save it as the new format.

- If you paste an image into MSPaint that is larger than the bitmap you currently have open, you are prompted and can choose to have the bitmap enlarged.

- If you'd like the Explorer to show miniature previews (icons) of *.bmp* files in Explorer and on your Desktop, make the following changes to your Registry:

  1. Open the Registry Editor (see Chapter 7 for details).

  2. Navigate to HKEY_CLASSES_ROOT\Paint.Picture\DefaultIcon .

  3. Double-click the Default value and change the value data to '%1' (with the quotes).

  4. Close the Registry Editor when you're done.

- To change the icon to its default, repeat the above steps, instead typing mspaint. exe,1 for the value data in Step 3.

- For a more advanced image editing and image format conversion tool, download the shareware version of Paint Shop Pro from *http://www.jasc.com/*.

See Also

"Windows Picture and Fax Viewer"

Pentium Bug Checker

Check your processor for the Floating Point Division Pentium bug.

To Open   Command Prompt → pentnt

Description

Back in 1994, a bug was discovered in a certain number of Intel Pentium processors in which certain mathematical operations would yield an incorrect result. The bug was fixed in all Pentium processors produced after 1994. In the unlikely event that you're running Windows XP on a computer that old, open a command prompt and type pentnt to test your processor for the bug.

Notes

For more information on the FDIV bug, go to *http://www.ukans.edu/cwis/units/IPPBR/ pentium_fdiv/pentgrph.html.*

Performance Log Manager

Manage the "Performance Logs and Alerts" service for creating and managing Event Trace Session logs and Performance logs. (Performance Log Manager is included with Windows XP Professional only.)

To Open   Command Prompt → logman

Usage   logman *command collection_name* [*options*]

Description

The Performance Log Manager is a command-line utility used to manage Performance Logs and Event Trace Session logs. Commands can be any of the following (type logman *command* /? for help with each one):

create
: Creates a new collection.

start
: Starts an existing collection and sets the begin time to manual.

stop
: Stops an existing collection and sets the end time to manual.

delete
: Deletes an existing collection.

query
: Queries collection properties. If *collection_name* is omitted, all collections are listed.

update
: Updates the properties of an existing collection.

Notes

The Performance Log Manager is largely replaced by the "Performance Logs and Alerts" Console (*perfmon.msc*); see "Microsoft Management Console," earlier in this chapter, for details.

Performance Logs and Alerts

\windows\system32\perfmon.msc

See "Microsoft Management Console."

Phone and Modem Options

\windows\system\telephon.cpl

Configure your modem and telephony devices and choose dialing preferences.

To Open   Control Panel → [Printers and Other Hardware] → Phone and Modem Options
Command Prompt → `telephon.cpl`
Command Prompt → `control telephony`

Description

Although DSL and cable Internet access are rapidly making modems obsolete, they're still used by more users than any other type of device to connect to the Internet and send computer-based faxes. These settings affect how Windows uses your modem(s):

Dialing Rules

Assuming your modem is properly installed (see the Modems tab), Windows will use these settings to determine how to dial. Click Edit to change the dialing rules for the selected location (see Figure 4-68). Multiple locations can be configured if you have a portable computer and need to dial out from within different area codes or from varying phone numbers with different dialing requirements.

As you undoubtedly know, if you dial a phone number in your own area code, you usually don't need to include the area code. For this reason, Windows needs to know which area code it's in, as well as any special numbers that are required to dial outside lines, place international calls, place calling-card calls, or disable call waiting (so you won't get interrupted by incoming calls).

Modems

Before a modem can be used with Network Connections (which replaces Dial-Up Networking, found in earlier versions of Windows) or with Microsoft's fax service, it must be configured here. The items listed here are the same as those listed in the Modems branch in Device Manager (discussed earlier in this chapter), so if Windows has detected your modem through plug-and-play, for example, there's probably nothing left to do here. If your modem doesn't show up in the list, it's probably not plug-and-play compliant; click Add to start the Add Hardware Wizard (discussed earlier in this chapter) to scan your system and install the appropriate drivers.

Select your modem from the list and click Properties to view the device's Properties sheet, which is the same as the one in Device Manager. Of special interest here is the Diagnostics tab, which will communicate with your modem and provide troubleshooting data, and the Advanced tab, which allows you to specify a modem

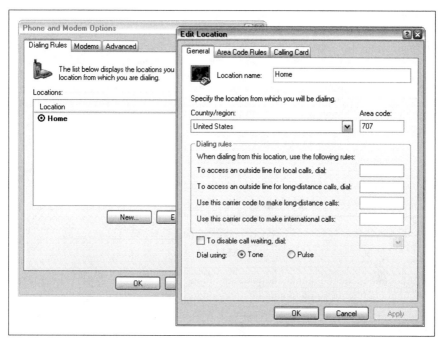

Figure 4-68. If you use a portable computer, you may want to configure multiple locations for dialing

initialization string (refer to your modem's documentation). Don't waste your time trying to get an old modem to work with Windows XP; brand-new plug-and-play PCI modems are ridiculously cheap and extremely easy to install.

Advanced

The Advanced tab lists the telephony drivers currently installed on your system. Drivers can be added, removed, or configured here. Note that unless you use a telephony application, you'll never need to touch these settings.

Notes

All of the settings in this dialog are also covered in Chapter 5.

See Also

"Control Panel"

Phone Dialer

\program files\windows nt\dialer.exe

Make voice calls, video calls, and conference calls using a phone line or Internet connection.

To Open   Start → Programs → Accessories → Communications → Phone Dialer
Command Prompt → dialer

Description

Phone Dialer is a surprisingly complete program, given that most people don't even know it exists. The primary Phone Dialer window is essentially a contact list, which allows you to initiate a call or conference with one or more people (see Figure 4-69). To place a call, click the Dial button or select Phone → Dial; if no contact is selected (from either the Speed Dial folder or from one of the Internet Directories folders), you'll be prompted to enter the other party's contact information. Another Phone Dialer user can be contacted in one of the following ways (specified either in the Dial window or when editing a Speed Dial entry):

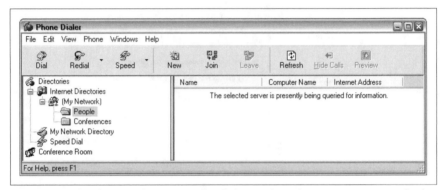

Figure 4-69. The Phone Dialer is not used to dial your phone, but to initiate voice and video conferences over a network

Phone Call
> Choose this option to use your modem to call another user's modem over standard telephone lines. Naturally, it's simpler to just pick up the phone and place an old-fashioned phone call; and while Phone Dialer supports video, few analog modems are fast enough to accommodate two-way video communication.

Internet Call
> Whether you're connecting over the Internet or over a local network, choose Internet Call to initiate a call. If you're connecting over the Internet, enter the other user's IP address; if you're connecting over a local network, enter the other user's computer name (without the \\ prefix).

For the call to go through, the other user must also have Phone Dialer open. When a call is received, the recipient can accept or reject the incoming call.

A conference, as opposed to call, allows you to communicate with several users at once. To start a conference, click New in the toolbar or go to Phone → New Conference. Then, other users call you to join the conference.

Notes

- Like Microsoft NetMeeting, discussed earlier in this chapter, Phone Dialer lets you use your computer as a telephone, initiating and conducting voice and video conversations over an Internet connection (or even using standard phone lines, although I fail to see the point). Of the two, NetMeeting has more features and is easier to use, but Phone Dialer is the only one that works over phone lines.

- The hardware requirements for voice and video calls with Phone Dialer are the same as those with Microsoft NetMeeting. However, NetMeeting and Phone Dialer are not compatible with one another; calls placed with NetMeeting can't be answered by Phone Dialer, and vice versa.

- Phone Dialer is nothing like the utility of the same name included in Windows 9x/Me, which was only a telephone autodialer. It is, however, identical to the Phone Dialer included with Windows 2000.

- Although the main Phone Dialer window looks suspiciously like the Address Book (discussed earlier in this chapter), it does not share contacts or any other information with the Address Book.

See Also

"Microsoft NetMeeting"

Pinball

\program files\windows nt\pinball\pinball.exe

A "Space Cadet 3D Pinball" game.

To Open   Start → Programs → Games → Pinball
Command Prompt → pinball

Description

The ball is launched by holding the Spacebar for a second or two to pull back the plunger and letting go. By default, the left and right flippers are controlled with the Z and / keys, respectively. You can change the keys use play the game by going to Options → Player Controls (see Figure 4-70).

Notes

- If the game is paused, none of the above keys will work until you press F3 to resume the game.

- Select Options → Full Screen or press F4 to play Pinball in full-screen mode. Press F4 again to revert back to the normal display. Note that full-screen mode will temporarily change the resolution of your display and may not work on all display adapters.

- The "boss" key is Esc; press it to quickly minimize the game in case your boss walks by.

Ping

\windows\system32\ping.exe

Test the "reachability" of another computer on the network or across the Internet.

To Open   Command Prompt → ping

Usage
```
ping target [-t] [-a] [-n count] [-l size] [-f] [-w timeout]
     [-r count] [-s count] [-j host_list | -k host_list]
     [-i ttl] [-v tos]
```

Figure 4-70. Although it hardly duplicates the thrill of a real metal ball bouncing in a box, the 3D Pinball game is fun to look at

Description

The primary function of Ping is to see if another computer is "alive" and reachable. Ping works on local networks and across Internet connections. For example, type the following at a command prompt:

    ping oreilly.com

and you'll get a report that looks something like this:

    Pinging oreilly.com [209.204.146.22] with 32 bytes of data:

    Reply from 209.204.146.22: bytes=32 time=78ms TTL=238
    Reply from 209.204.146.22: bytes=32 time=31ms TTL=238
    Reply from 209.204.146.22: bytes=32 time=15ms TTL=238
    Reply from 209.204.146.22: bytes=32 time=78ms TTL=238

    Ping statistics for 209.204.146.22:
        Packets: Sent = 4, Received = 4, Lost = 0 (0% loss),
    Approximate round trip times in milli-seconds:
        Minimum = 15ms, Maximum = 78ms, Average = 50ms

Here, Ping sent out four pings (the default), reported the time it took for them to return (in milliseconds), and then displayed various statistics about the session. Ping is especially useful if you're having trouble contacting a server and you want to see if the server is alive (running and accepting connections). If the server does not reply (meaning that it is down or the connection has been severed), you'll see Request timed out. Ping accepts the following options:

target
> The machine to ping; it can be the name of a computer on your network, an IP address (e.g., 209.204.146.22), or an Internet address (e.g., *oreilly.com*).

-t
> Normally, Ping sends out four pings and then quits. Include the -t option to ping continually until Ping is interrupted by pressing Ctrl-C. Press Ctrl-Break to display statistics without interrupting.

-a
> Resolve addresses to hostnames.

-n *count*
> The number of pings to send; the default is four.

-l *size*
> The size of the packets to send, in bytes; the default is 32 bytes.

-f
> Turn on the "Don't Fragment" flag in packet.

-w *timeout*
> The amount of time to wait, in milliseconds, before Ping gives up and displays Request timed out; the default is 500 milliseconds (1/2 second).

-r *count*
> Display the route taken to reach the server (see "Tracert," later in this chapter). The count is the maximum number of hops to record, and can range from 1 to 9.

-s *count*
> Display a time stamp for *count* hops.

-j *host_list*
> Impose a "loose" route (see the -r option) along which to ping.

-k *host-list*
> Impose a "strict" route (see the -r option) along which to ping.

-i *ttl*
> Specify the Time To Live (TTL); valid range is from 0 to 255.

-v *tos*
> Specify the Type of Service (TOS); valid range is from 0 to 255.

Notes

The name "ping" comes from submarine lingo, when sonar was used to detect nearby objects, such as ships and other submarines. Pulses of sound were sent through the water; those that returned indicated the existence of an object off which the pulses were reflected. *ping.exe* works very similarly, except it sends packets instead of sonic pulses.

See Also

"Tracert," "NSLookup"

Power Options   \windows\system\powercfg.cpl

Control Windows' support for Advanced Power Management (APM).

To Open   Control Panel → [Performance and Maintenance] → Power Options
Command Prompt → powercfg.cpl

Applications and Tools

Description

Advanced Power Management relies on cooperation between your computer's BIOS and operating system. APM covers everything from your computer's power switch to the power-saving features that reduce power consumption or extend the life of your computer's battery (see Figure 4-71).

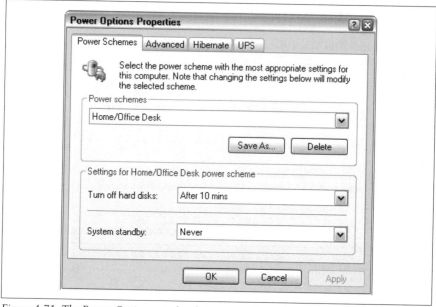

Figure 4-71. The Power Options window lets you configure the various power-saving features of your computer

Before you mess with any settings here, make sure that APM support is enabled in your system BIOS. For best results, enable the main "APM support" option, but disable all APM options in your BIOS. Refer to the documentation that came with your computer or motherboard for details. Settings in this window are divided into the following tabs:

Power Schemes

The Power schemes listbox allows you to save your power management settings into one or more schemes, much like Themes (see "Display Properties") and Sound Schemes (see "Sounds and Audio Devices"). Click Save As to create a new scheme or Delete to remove the currently selected scheme.

The Settings below allow you set timed power-saving features for the currently selected scheme. Note that not all computers support the System standby and System hibernates features; even those that claim to may not do it very well. If your computer crashes coming out of standby or hibernation mode (see "Hibernate," below), or simply doesn't come out at all, check with your computer or mother-board manufacturer for a BIOS update.

Advanced

The settings on this page are pretty self-explanatory. See "Hibernate," below, for details on the hibernation feature.

Hibernate

Hibernation, also known as "Instant On," allows you to completely shut off your computer and then turn it back on later (and resume work in seconds as though it was never shut off). It does this by saving an image of your system's memory into a file called *hiberfil.sys*, located in the root directory of your windows drive (usually *C:*); when the computer comes out of hibernation, the file is read back into memory and your previous session is restored, all without having to reload Windows or any of your applications.

UPS

Windows XP includes built-in support for Un-interruptible Power Supplies (UPSs), which keep your computer running in the event of a power outage or other disruption. Depending on the capacity of your UPS, you may have anywhere from a few minutes to a half hour to save your work and shut down your computer gracefully. A UPS is a good investment if you live in a stormy climate or other area where power interruptions are frequent.

Although a UPS doesn't really have to interact with Windows at all, support configured through this dialog enables some advanced features, such as monitoring tools that alert you when a power outage has occurred and inform you of how much power is left in the UPS battery.

Notes

All settings in this dialog are also covered in Chapter 5.

See Also

"Control Panel"

Printers and Faxes

Manage local and network printers.

To Open   Start → Settings → Printers and Faxes (Classic Start menu only)
Control Panel → [Printers and Other Hardware] → Printers and Faxes
Command Prompt → control printers

Description

The Printers and Faxes folder contains icons representing your installed printers and fax devices. Once a printer is installed here, you can print to it from within your applications, drag documents to the its icon to print them, or double-click on the printer icon to see or change the status of current print jobs (see Figure 4-72).

The Add Printer wizard helps you select the appropriate printer driver for a local or network printer. The context menu for each printer, among other things, allows you to select that printer as the default printer—the one that appears, by default, in all your applications' print dialogs.

File → Print is the standard way to print for most applications. Right-clicking on a file then selecting Print from its context menu allows you to send a file to the printer without opening it first, although this can have mixed results. You can also create a shortcut to a printer on the Desktop and then drag-and-drop a file on the printer icon.

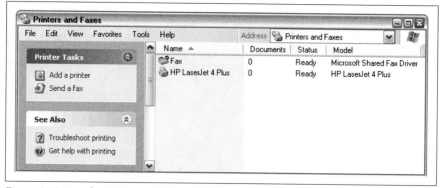

Figure 4-72. Use the Printers and Faxes folder to add, configure, and troubleshoot your printers

 If you drag more than one file to a printer icon, the system will open a separate copy of the application for each file. This may be OK for text files and a small application like Notepad, but drag a group of Word or Excel files to the printer, and it may bring your system to its knees.

Double-click on any printer icon for a view of the printer's job queue. You'll see the document name, status (printing, paused, and so on), the owner of the job, progress (in number of pages printed), and when the job was started. You can drag your own jobs up and down to change their priority. Use the Printer menu to pause the printer or purge all print jobs. Use the Document menu to pause or cancel (delete) any selected documents.

Notes

- To have more than one computer print to the same printer, just connect the printer directly to one of the computers. After it has been installed, right-click its icon, select Sharing, and click the Share this printer option. Once a printer has been shared, it can be installed as a network printer on all the other computers on the network (see Figure 4-73). See Chapter 7 for more details.

- You can choose whether print spooling ("offline printing") should be enabled for any printer. If offline printing is selected, you can print to a network printer even when you aren't connected, or to a local printer when it is turned off. When the printer then becomes available, you will be asked whether to print any files in the queue.

See Also

"Control Panel"

Private Character Editor
\windows\system32\eudcedit.exe

Create special characters, such as logos or symbols, that can be inserted into ordinary documents.

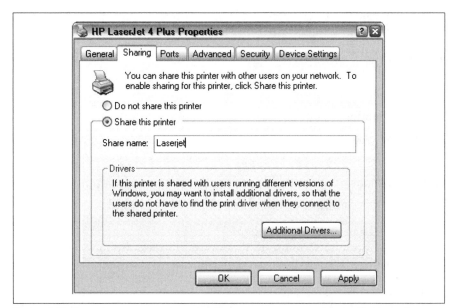

Figure 4-73. Let others on your network print to your computer with the Sharing tab

To Open   Command Prompt → `eudcedit`

Description

The Private Character Editor is like a small-image editor (see "Paint," earlier in this chapter), except that the images created with it are used like symbol fonts, making it easy to insert any custom logo or symbol into your documents.

When you first start the Private Character Editor, you'll be presented with a rather confusing Select Code window. This is used to associate the new (or existing) character you'll be editing with a particular slot, and is somewhat akin to the main Character Map window. Select any slot and click OK to proceed.

The main window contains the character editor and a simple set of drawing tools (like those found in Paint, discussed earlier in this chapter). Each character is a 50 × 50 black and white bitmap. Draw in black with any of the available tools and the left mouse button; draw in white with the right mouse button. You can copy and paste bitmap selections between the Private Character Editor and other image editing programs, such as Paint.

When you're done, save your work into the slot you chose in the first screen by going to Edit → Save Character (Ctrl-S). Or, save it into a different slot by going to Edit → Save Character As. At any time, you can choose a different slot to edit with Edit → Select Code, or with View → Next Code (Ctrl-N) and View → Prev Code (Ctrl-P). As you choose slots in which to place your new characters, you can use another font as a reference to decide the most convenient slots to use. Select Window → Reference to view the orientation of an existing font on your computer.

To use your new character in another application, open Character Map (*charmap.exe*) and choose "All Fonts (Private Characters)" from the top of the list. If this entry is not present, you didn't save your work. See "Character Map," earlier in this chapter, for more information on pasting characters into other applications.

See Also
"Character Map"

Product Activation

See "Activate Windows."

Program Manager   *\windows\system32\progman.exe*

The obsolete Program Manager interface, found in Windows 3.x and Windows NT 3.x.

To Open   Command Prompt → progman

The Program Manager is a simple icon-based menu system used in Microsoft Windows 3.x and Windows NT 3.x. All of the more modern releases of Windows have abandoned Program Manager (with good cause) in favor of the Start menu and other features of Windows Explorer. Program Manager is still included for legacy purposes. Of course, a simple folder filled with Windows Shortcuts serves the same purpose and does a much better job of it, too.

See Also
"Windows Explorer"

Query Process   *\windows\system32\xd5 process.exe*

Display a list of running processes.

To Open   Command Prompt → qprocess

Usage   qprocess [*target*] [/server:*computer*] [/system]

Description
Query Process is a simple, command-line utility used to display a list of the running processes. A process is essentially any program running in the foreground or running invisibly in the background. "Task Manager," discussed later in this chapter, does the same thing, but is much easier to use.

Query Process takes the following parameters:

target
> Target can be any of the following: Specify a username to display the processes started by that user. Specify a session name or number (via /id:*sessionid*) to display all the processes started in that session. Specify a program name to display all the processes associated with that program. Specify an asterisk (*) to list all processes. Finally, omit target to display all the processes started by the current user.

/server:*computer*

> Query a remote computer, where computer is the network name of the machine. Omit to display processes for the local computer.

/system

> Include system processes. Type qprocess * /system to display all the currently running processes.

See Also

"Task Manager," "Taskkill," and "Tasklist"

Regional and Language Options   \windows\system\intl.cpl

Language and localization settings affecting the display of numbers, currency, times, and dates.

To Open   Control Panel → [Date, Time, Language, and Regional Options] → Regional and Language Options
Command Prompt → intl.cpl
Command Prompt → control international

Description

Numbers, times, dates, and currency are displayed differently in different parts of the world, and the Regional and Language Options dialog (see Figure 4-74) allows you to choose your display preferences in painful detail.

This dialog has the following tabs:

Regional Settings

> Select your language from the list and click Customize to start choosing your preferences. The settings in this dialog are fairly self-explanatory, although it's important to realize that the entries in the language list are not "themes." That is, if you customize your settings and then change the language in the list, those customized settings will be lost.

Languages

> Click Details if you wish to change the desired language or to add support for additional languages. If more than one language is installed, the Language Bar and Key Settings features will be available, which can be used to easily switch between the installed languages with a Desktop bar or keyboard shortcut, respectively.

Advanced

> Most programs should be able to detect the preferred language, and if supported, adjust their interfaces accordingly. The "Language for non-Unicode programs" option is used to add support for older programs that don't recognize the settings made in the Languages tab.

> The Code page conversion tables, when installed, can be accessed in word processors and web browsers, enabling the display of foreign language content. Most users won't have a need to alter these settings, although you may need to if a particular document or web page isn't being displayed correctly.

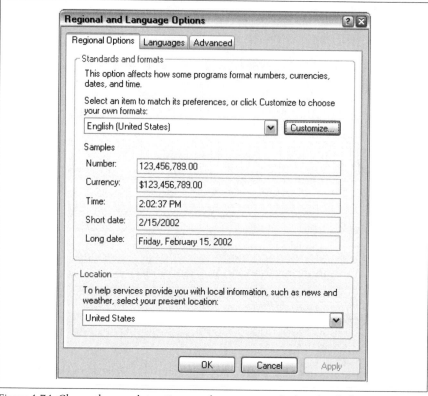

Figure 4-74. Choose the way dates, times, and currency are displayed with the Regional and Language Options dialog

Notes

All of the settings in this dialog are also covered in Chapter 5.

See Also

"Control Panel"

Recycle Bin

See "Windows Explorer."

Registry Console Utility

\windows\system32\reg.exe

A command-line utility to access and modify portions of the Windows Registry.

To Open   Command Prompt → reg

Usage   reg *command* [*options*]

Description

The Registry Console Utility performs all of the functions of the Registry Editor, discussed later in chapter and in Chapter 8, but can be used from the command line. It also does a few things Registry Editor can't do, such as making a duplicate of a registry key (via copy, below). To use the Registry Console Utility, type reg, followed by one of the following commands and any applicable parameters:

query *keyname* [/v *valuename* | /ve] [/s]

Displays the data stored in a Registry value, where *keyname* is the full path of a registry key and *valuename* is the name of the value to query. Omit /v *valuename* to display list of all the values in *keyname* or specify /ve to query the (Default) value. Include /s to query all subkeys and values as well. Valuename can also specify the remote computer like this: query computer\keyname.

add *keyname* [/v *valuename* | /ve] [/d data] [/t typ] [/s sep] [/f]

Adds a new value. The *keyname*, /v, and /ve options are the same as with query, above. The /d option assigns data to the new value; if omitted, the new value will be empty. Use /t to specify the data type for the value; if omitted, a string value (REG_SZ) will be added. Use the /s option to specify a separator, used if you're creating a REG_MULTI_SZ value. If the value being added already exists, you'll be prompted to overwrite, unless the /f parameter is specified.

delete *keyname* [/v *valuename* | /ve | /va] [/f]

Deletes an existing value. All options are the same as with add, above. The /va parameter instructs the Registry Console Utility to delete all values in the specified key.

copy *keyname1 keyname2* [/s] [/f]

Duplicates a key and all its values, where *keyname1* is the full path of the source key and *keyname2* is the full path of the new key. Specify /s to include all subkeys and their values and use the /f option to force the copy without first being prompted.

save *keyname filename*

Saves a portion of the registry into a file, where *keyname* is the full path of the key to save, and *filename* is the name of the new hive file. Note that this command does not create a registry patch (*.reg*) file, but a binary hive file that can only be read with restore, below. Note also that the root key in keyname must be a four-letter abbreviation (e.g., HKLM, HKCU, HKCR, HKU, or HKCC).

restore *keyname filename*

Reads a hive file (created with save, above) into the Registry. Note that *keyname* doesn't have to be the same as the key from which the file was originally created. See the notes for save for details. Only works on the local machine.

load *keyname filename*

Installs a hive file (created with save, above) onto the Registry. Load is similar to restore, above, except that any changes to the loaded keys or values are stored back into the hive file specified by *filename*. With restore, on the other hand, the new keys are added to a pre-existing hive.

unload *keyname*

Uninstalls a key, *keyname*, that has been installed with load, above.

compare *keyname1 keyname2* [/v *valuename* | /ve] [/s] [*output*]

Compares two keys or values. The *keyname1* and *keyname2* options are the same as with copy, above. The /v, /ve, and /s options are the same as with add, above. The

Applications and Tools

output option can be /oa (output all differences and matches), /od (output only differences), /os (output only matches), or /on (no output); when omitted, /od is assumed. See reg compare /? for more information.

export *keyname* *filename*

Creates a registry patch (*.reg*) file, *filename*, from the key at *keyname*. Registry patches can be imported with import, below, or by double-clicking in Explorer (via Registry Editor).

import *filename*

Imports a registry patch (*.reg*) file, *filename*, created either with export, above, or with Registry Editor.

Notes

- All of the concepts in terms discussed here are explained in Chapter 8.
- Many of the functions discussed here can only be accomplished with the Registry Console Utility and are not possible with Registry Editor. Among them are the copy, save, restore, load, unload, and compare commands.

See Also

"Registry Editor," Chapter 8

Registry Editor

\windows\regedit.exe

View and modify the contents of the Registry.

To Open   Command Prompt → regedit

Description

Registry Editor provides a means to view and modify the contents of the Windows Registry, the master database that stores configuration settings for Windows XP and many of the applications on your computer. However, don't confuse Registry Editor with the Registry; Registry Editor is merely an application, like any other. See Chapter 8 for more information on the Registry and the use of Registry Editor. See Chapter 5 for many of the settings that can also be changed in the Registry.

See Also

"Registry Console Utility"

Remote Assistance

\windows\system32\rcimlby.exe -LaunchRA

Allow others to connect to your computer using Remote Desktop Connection.

To Open   Start → Programs → Remote Assistance
Command Prompt → rcimlby -LaunchRA

Description

Remote Assistance is a page in the Help and Support Center (discussed earlier in this chapter) that works with several other Windows components to allow another user to

---

connect to your computer. The idea is that you would invite a technical support representative, a friend, or co-worker, to help you with a computer problem by allowing them to connect to your computer as though they were sitting in front of it (see Figure 4-75).

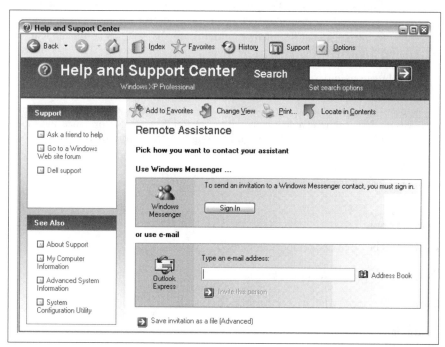

Figure 4-75. Use Remote Assistance to invite another person to connect to your computer with Remote Desktop Sharing

The first step involves inviting another user to connect. While it may seem like an unnecessary formality, it takes care of the very important step of transmitting your IP address to the other user. You can either use Windows Messenger (discussed later in this chapter) to send an instant message or Outlook Express (discussed earlier in this chapter) to send an email. Once the invitation has been received, that user will have enough information to connect to your computer via Remote Desktop Connection (discussed later in this chapter).

Notes

- Both users must be running Windows XP to use Remote Assistance.

- Remote Assistance is a very interesting use of integration, where several seemingly disparate components can work together to accomplish a single task.

- Either Outlook Express or Windows Messenger are required to send an invitation, which means that at least one of these programs must be set up with your account information prior to using Remote Assistance. Note that you can skip this step if you wish to 1) transmit your IP address to the other user, and 2) set up your computer to accept connections via Remote Desktop Connection.

- Remote Assistance opens several back doors to your computer, potentially allowing unwanted access to your computer and data. Be sure to take advantage of the features in Remote Assistance to help protect your computer, such as requiring a password and allowing only remote connection within the next hour.

- When you send an invitation via email, the recipient receives a link to *http://windows.microsoft.com/RemoteAssistance/RA.asp*, as well as a file attachment (*rcBuddy.MsRcIncident*) with your connection information. The information stored in the file attachment is not easily readable; the recipient simply opens the attachment to initiate a connection.

- If you get the error "Your current system settings prevent you from sending an invitation," it means that the Remote Assistance feature has been disabled for security reasons. You can re-enable it by going to Control Panel → [Performance and Maintenance] → System → Remote tab and turning on both options on this page.

See Also

"Remote Desktop Connection"

Remote Copy   *\windows\system32\rcp.exe*

Copies files between two remote computers.

To Open   Command Prompt → rcp

Usage   rcp [-b] [-h] [-r] *source destination*

Description

Remote Copy is a little tool you can use to copy one or more files from one remote computer to another remote computer without first transferring the files to your own computer. Remote Copy takes the following parameters:

source, destination
> The full network path of the source file and destination, respectively. See the examples below for syntax. Specify a folder name for *source* to transfer that folder and all of its contents. You can specify wildcards here (to transfer multiple files at once), but only with an escape character (e.g., apple.* becomes apple.*).

-b
> Transfers the files with binary mode; the default is ASCII mode. See the discussion of ASCII and binary modes in "FTP," discussed earlier in this chapter.

-h
> Include the -h parameter to transfer hidden files.

-r
> When copying a folder, include all the subfolders and their contents.

Examples

The following command transfers the file, *c:\docs\rings.txt*, from the computer called *cooder* to the *c:\stuff* folder in the computer called *spud*:

    rcp -b \\cooder\c\docs\rings.txt \\spud\

The following command does the same thing, but using IP addresses (when accessing computers on the Internet) instead of on a local network.

Note how the usernames (mandatory with IP addresses) are specified:

```
rcp -b 192.168.0.1.cooder:c\docs\rings.txt 192.168.0.1.spud:c\stuff
```

Notes

- Both the source and destination computer must be running the RCP service.

- The username must be specified if the host (either in the source or destination) is an IP address.

See Also

"FTP"

Remote Desktop Connection

\windows\system32\mstsc.exe

Access another computer remotely, as though you were sitting in front of it. (Remote Desktop Connection is included with Windows XP Professional only.)

To Open   Start → Programs → Accessories → Communications → Remote Desktop Connection

Command Prompt → `mstsc`

Description

Remote Desktop Connection allows you to connect to another computer (or allows someone else to connect your computer) and use it as though you were sitting in front of it. Much more than simply a Telnet connection, Remote Desktop Connection allows you to see a full Desktop, complete with icons and the Start menu, and even run programs on the remote computer (see Figure 4-76).

To configure a computer to accept incoming connections via Remote Desktop Connection, go to Control Panel → [Performance and Maintenance] → System → Remote tab, and turn on the "Allow users to connect remotely to this computer" option. By default, the administrator always has access, but you can enable access for other users as well by clicking Select Remote Users.

Once a computer has been set up, you can connect to it by opening Remote Desktop Connection and typing that computer's name (if connected on a local network) or that computer's IP address (if connected to the Internet). Click Options to specify a username, password, domain (only for Windows NT domains), and even to save your connection settings to a file so you can connect more easily later. The Display tab lets you choose between full-screen mode and windowed mode. The Local Resources tab lets you choose whether sounds generated by the remote computer are played locally (which can slow the connection), whether certain keystroke combinations are interpreted locally or sent to the remote computer, and whether to automatically connect you to the remote computer's disks, printers, or serial ports. Choose the Programs tab to set up a program to start automatically when a connection has been established. Finally, the Experience tab allows you to turn on or off features that will affect performance; depending on your connection, for example, you may wish to enable or disable the remote computer's background wallpaper.

Figure 4-76. Use another Windows XP computer as though you were sitting in front of it with a Remote Desktop Connection

You can save the connection profile for a particular connection by clicking Save As. This will create an Remote Desktop Profile (*.rdp*) file, which can then be double-clicked to start the connection without having to retype the connection information. Right-click any *.rdp* file and select Edit to return to the Properties dialog for the profile.

Notes

- Currently, both computers involved in a Remote Desktop Connection must be running Windows XP, although Microsoft may release Remote Desktop Connection clients for other versions of Windows in the future.

- Alternatives to Remote Desktop Connection include pcAnywhere (commercial software, *http://www.symantec.com/*), VNC (freeware, *http://www.uk.research.att.com/vnc/*), and the Remote Desktop Sharing feature of Microsoft NetMeeting (discussed earlier in this chapter). Unlike Remote Desktop Connection, these alternatives work on all modern versions of Windows. Furthermore, VNC works on Unix and Macintosh systems as well.

- Remote Desktop Connection replaces the Terminal Services client found in Windows NT and Windows 2000.

See Also
"Remote Assistance," "Telnet"

Route

Manipulate the TCP/IP routing table for the local computer.

To Open   Command Prompt → route

Usage
```
route [-f] [-p] [command] [destination] [gateway]
      [mask netmask] [metric metric] [if interface]
```

Description

Routing tables provide information necessary to connect to other computers on a network or the Internet. Route accepts the following options:

command

Specifies one of four commands:

print

Prints a route (similar to netstat -r). The route print command is useful if you are having a problem (e.g., "Host Unreachable" or "Request timed out") with the routes on your computer, since it will display all the different fields in the active route (see the example).

add

Adds a route to the routing table; used until the computer is shut down (unless the -p option is specified).

delete

Deletes a route from the routing table.

change

Modifies an existing route in the routing table.

destination

The remote computer that is reachable via *gateway*.

-f

Frees (clears) the routing tables of all gateway entries. If this is used in conjunction with one of the commands listed above, the tables are cleared prior to running the command.

-p

When used with the add command, -p makes a route persistent across boots of the system. If you don't specify -p, any route you add will be valid only until the computer is restarted. The -p option has no effect on other commands, as they're all persistent.

gateway

The gateway computer to be used for traffic going to *destination*. It is possible to use a hostname for the gateway, but it is safer to use an IP address, as a hostname may resolve to multiple IP addresses. For example, you might type the following:

```
route add 0.0.0.0 10.0.0.200
```

mask *netmask*

> Specifies the subnet mask for a *destination*. If not specified, a mask of 255.255. 255.255 is used (i.e., a "host route" to a single host, not a network).

metric *metric*

> Specifies the metric or "hop count" for this route. The metric indicates which route is preferred when multiple routes to a destination exist and signifies the number of hops or gateways between the local computer and the gateway. The route with the lowest metric is used unless it is unavailable, in which case the route with the next lowest metric takes over.

if *interface*

> Specifies the interface number for the specified route.

If you type route print at the command prompt, you'll get something that looks like this:

```
Active Routes:
Network Address Netmask Gateway Address Interface Metric
0.0.0.0 0.0.0.0 172.16.80.5 172.16.80.150 1
127.0.0.0 255.0.0.0 127.0.0.1 127.0.0.1 1
172.16.80.10 255.255.255.0 172.16.80.150 172.16.80.150 1
172.16.80.150 255.255.255.255 127.0.0.1 127.0.0.1 1
172.16.80.200 255.255.255.255 172.16.80.150 172.16.80.150 1
224.0.0.0 224.0.0.0 172.16.80.150 172.16.80.150 1
255.255.255.255 255.255.255.255 172.16.80.150 0.0.0.0 1
```

The fields in this printout are as follows:

Gateway Address

> The IP address of the gateway for the route. The gateway will know what to do with traffic for the specified network address.

Interface

> The IP address of the network interface that the route will use when leaving the local computer.

Metric

> The hop count or number of gateways between the local computer and the gateway.

Netmask

> The mask to be applied to the network address. If all ones (255.255.255.255), the route is a host route and refers to a single machine, not a network.

Network Address

> Any network matched by this address should use this route. The default route is all zeros and is used if no other route is found.

Notes

If the command is print or delete, wildcards may be used for the destination and gateway or the gateway argument may be omitted.

See Also

"Tracert"

Rundll32

Run a single routine in a DLL file from the command line.

To Open   Command Prompt → rundll32

Usage   rundll32 *filename,function_name* [*function_arguments* . . .]

Description

Rundll32 provides "string invocation," which lets you execute a command buried in a Dynamic Link Library (DLL) file.

Rundll32 accepts the following options:

filename
> The filename of a DLL (*.dll*) file.

function_name
> The case-sensitive name of a function in the DLL file.

function_arguments
> Any parameters used by *function_name*; refer to the function's documentation for details. Note that any string parameters are case sensitive.

Examples

The following example starts the "Network Setup Wizard" (note that no parameters are required for this one):

    rundll32.exe hnetwiz.dll,HomeNetWizardRunDll

This batch file allows you to display an "Open As" dialog box for unknown file type *.xyz* without actually having a file of type *.xyz* handy (see Appendix C for more information on batch files):

    echo blah blah blah > foobar.%1
    rundll32 shell32.dll,OpenAs_RunDLL foobar.%1

Then type the following at a command line:

    C:\>openas xyz

Notes

Rundll32 provides dynamic linking to functions exported from 32-bit Dynamic Link Libraries. *Rundll*, the 16-bit equivalent found in earlier versions of Windows, is not included in Windows XP.

Run As

Run a program under a different user's account.

To Open   Command Prompt → runas

Usage   runas [/noprofile] [/env] [/netonly] /user:*username program*
    runas [/noprofile] [/env] [/netonly] /smartcard
        [/user:*username*] *program*

Applications and Tools

Description

Windows XP is a multiuser environment. When you open an application, Windows runs that program in a "user context," which means that the settings and capabilities imposed upon an application are those associated with your user account. Use Run As to instruct Windows to open an application in another user's context. This is especially useful when running services or other background applications, where you can't always assume which user will be logged on at any time, but you want to make sure the settings and permissions are correct.

Run As takes the following parameters:

program

> The full path, filename, and optional command-line parameters for the *.exe* file to run.

/user:*username*

> The username under which to run *program*; *username* should be of the form *user@domain* or *domain\user*.

/noprofile

> Specifies that the user's profile should not be loaded. This causes the application to load more quickly, but can cause those applications that rely on settings stored in the HKEY_CURRENT_USER registry key to malfunction.

/env

> Uses the current environment instead of *username*'s.

/netonly

> Specifies that the credentials specified are for remote access only.

/savecred

> Uses credentials previously saved by the user. This option is not available on Windows XP Home Edition and will be ignored.

/smartcard

> Specifies that the credentials are to be supplied from a smartcard.

Notes

Scheduled Tasks, discussed later in this chapter, also lets you run programs under different user accounts.

Scanners and Cameras

Install drivers to access the pictures on a digital camera through Explorer.

To Open   Control Panel → [Printers and Other Hardware] → Scanners and Cameras
Command Prompt → wia acmgr *(to open installation wizard)*

Description

The Scanners and Cameras window (see Figure 4-77) lists any digital cameras or scanners attached to the system.

This window is designed to work with the following device types:

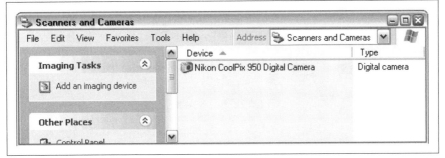

Figure 4-77. The Scanners and Cameras folder lets you retrieve images from your digital camera or scanner

Digital still cameras

Any devices, typically digital still cameras, whose pictures need to be manually transferred to the computer, can be configured as drives so that they're accessible through Windows Explorer. Although most cameras come with their own software for transferring pictures, accessing them through Explorer is especially slick and painless.

Note that you can also get USB-based card readers that will turn CompactFlash, SmartMedia, and MultiMediaCard media into virtual drives, with the added benefit of not having to repeatedly hook up special cables to your camera.

Right-click on the icon for any configured camera and select either Get pictures (to transfer images to your hard disk) or Properties (to change how pictures are accessed).

Scanners

Most scanners come with their own dedicated scanning software, so it's not strictly necessary to configure scanners in this window. However, it may add more flexibility than the scanner's proprietary software. For example, it's possible to program any buttons on the scanner itself to launch whichever program you choose to do the actual scanning (see Figure 4-78).

Right-click on the icon for any configured scanner, select Properties, and choose the Events tab to choose what happens when your scanner's buttons are pressed. Note that depending on your scanner, certain options may be unavailable.

The Scanner and Camera Installation Wizard is used to add new cameras to the Scanners and Cameras folder. If the common tasks pane is visible, click "Add an imaging device"; otherwise, double-click the Add Device icon. (You can also run *wiaacmgr.exe*.) Follow the steps to complete the installation. Note that only cameras can be added with the Scanner and Camera Installation Wizard; to add a scanner to the Scanners and Cameras folder, you'll need to install the scanner software according to the manufacturer's instructions. (Many manufacturers, especially those of older scanners, don't support the Scanners and Cameras folder at all.)

Notes

Many newer digital cameras and scanners won't be supported by this tool. Refer to the documentation that comes with your device for information on connecting it to your

Figure 4-78. Use the Properties sheet to control how (or if) Windows responds to the buttons on your scanner

computer and installing the appropriate software and drivers, or contact the camera's manufacturer for updated drivers that support this feature of Windows XP.

See Also

"Control Panel"

Scheduled Tasks

Run a program or script at a specified time.

To Open   Control Panel → [Performance and Maintenance] → Scheduled Tasks

Start → Programs → Accessories → System Tools → Scheduled Tasks

Description

The Scheduled Tasks feature is fairly simple, allowing you to schedule any program or WSH script (see Chapter 8) to run at a specified time or interval (see Figure 4-79).

To create a new scheduled task, open the Scheduled Tasks folder and double-click Add Scheduled Task to start the Scheduled Task Wizard. You'll then be prompted to choose a program and specify when and how often to run it.

Unfortunately, there's no way to skip the cumbersome wizard, but you can repeatedly click Next until you reach the last page, where you'll see an option to open "advanced

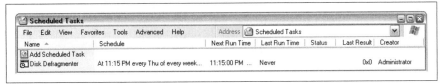

Figure 4-79. Scheduled Tasks lets you run programs at predetermined times or intervals

properties for this task." The Properties window, also accessible by right-clicking on any existing task and selecting Properties, is a simpler and more straightforward way to configure a task (see Figure 4-80).

The Task tab allows you to specify the command line, the full path and filename of the application, or the script to run. You can also choose the default folder and the user under which to run the program (see "Run As," earlier in this chapter).

The Schedule tab lets you choose when and how often to execute the task. Choose the Show multiple schedules option to allow more flexibility, such as running a task at 3:01 PM next Thursday only and every Saturday morning at 10:43.

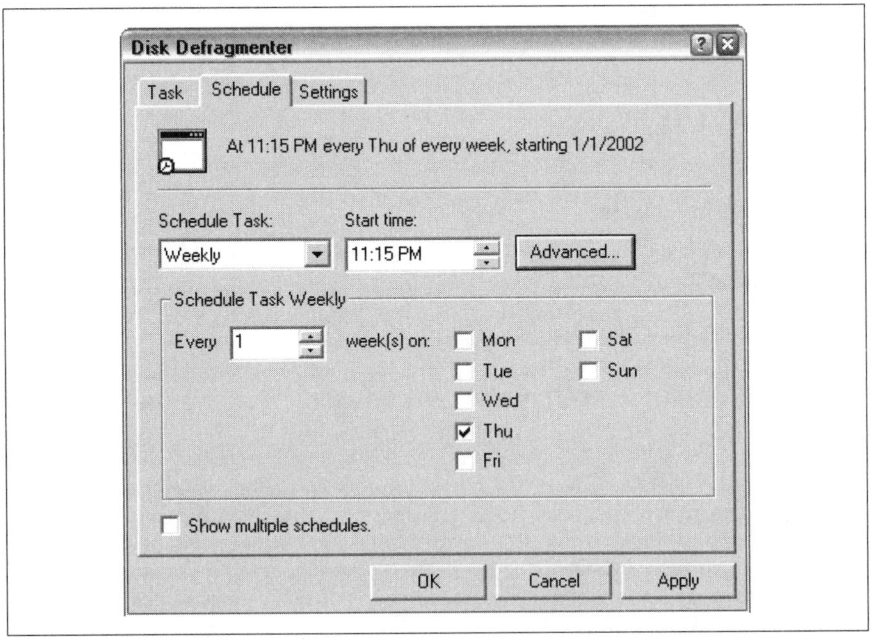

![Disk Defragmenter Properties dialog showing the Schedule tab. At 11:15 PM every Thu of every week, starting 1/1/2002. Schedule Task: Weekly. Start time: 11:15 PM. Advanced button. Schedule Task Weekly: Every 1 week(s) on: Thu checked. Show multiple schedules unchecked. OK, Cancel, Apply buttons.]

Figure 4-80. The Properties dialog for this task lets you choose when a task is run

Finally, the Settings tab allows you to set various preferences, many of which can be important and none of which are set by the wizard. For example, you can have Scheduled Tasks delete the task after it has run, stop the task if it appears to have crashed, or run the task only if the computer isn't currently being used. Note that, by default, tasks won't be run if your computer is running on batteries, a setting you may want to change if you need the task performed regardless of your computer's power source.

In the main Scheduled Tasks window, use Advanced → Stop Using Task Scheduler to disable the Schedule Tasks service; use Advanced → Start Using Task Scheduler to enable it again. The service remains stopped (or started) even when the computer is restarted. To temporarily disable the service or have it restart when the computer is restarted, use Advanced → Pause Task Scheduler/Continue Task Scheduler.

Notes

- The logging option is limited and only tells you if a given task was started. It can be hard to tell whether a scheduled task has actually been performed successfully unless you specifically implement logging in a script.

- Also, any scheduled tasks will not be performed if you've selected the Stop Using Task Scheduler option, if your computer is turned off, if Windows isn't running, or if your portable computer is running off its battery. These mistakes may be obvious but they can be easy to forget and Windows won't tell you if you missed any tasks.

- Unlike previous versions of Windows, there's no icon in the tray to tell you that Task Scheduler is working.

- The At utility, discussed earlier in this chapter, and the Scheduled Tasks Console, discussed later in this chapter, both allow you to create new tasks from the command line.

See Also

"At," "Scheduled Tasks Console"

Scheduled Tasks Console

\windows\system32\schtasks.exe

Control the Task Scheduler from the command line. (Scheduled Tasks Console is included with Windows XP Professional only.)

To Open   Command Prompt → schtasks

Usage   schtasks /*command_name* [*arguments*]

Description

The Scheduled Tasks Console is the command-line equivalent of Scheduled Tasks, discussed earlier in this chapter. Although it doesn't do anything not already possible with the Scheduled Tasks window, it can be convenient for automating the creation and management of tasks. The Scheduled Tasks Console accepts one of six options. To find out more about any of the commands, type schtasks /*command_name* /?:

/create [/s *system* [/u *user* [/p *password*]]] /ru *user* [/rp *password*]] /sc *schedule* [/mo *modifier*] [/d *day*] [/i *idletime*] /tn *taskname* /tr *taskrun* [/st *starttime*] [/m *months*] [/sd *startdate*] [/ed *enddate*]

Creates a new scheduled task on the local computer or a remote system.

/delete [/s *system* [/u *user* [/p *password*]]] /tn *taskname* [/f]

Deletes one or more scheduled task(s).

/query [/s *system* [/u *user* [/p *password*]]] [/fo *format*] [/nh] [/v]

Displays all scheduled tasks on the local computer or a remote system.

/change [/s *system* [/u *username* [/p *password*]]] [/ru *runasuser*] [/rp *runaspassword*]
[/tr *taskrun*] /tn *taskname*
> Changes some of the properties of an existing task, such as the program to run or the username and password.

/run [/s *system* [/u *user* [/p *password*]]] /tn *taskname*
> Runs a scheduled task immediately.

/end [/s *system* [/u *user* [/p *password*]]] /tn *taskname*
> Stops a currently running scheduled task.

Notes
The Scheduled Task Console is intended to replace At, discussed earlier in this chapter. Although the Scheduled Tasks Console is a little more full featured, At is much easier to use.

See Also
"Scheduled Tasks"

Security Template Utility
\windows\system32\secedit.exe

Create and apply security templates and analyze system security. (Security Template Utility is included with Windows XP Professional only.)

To Open   Command Prompt → secedit

Usage   secedit /*command* [*arguments*]

Description
Security Templates are used by administrators for Windows XP-based servers to create a security policy for a computer. The Security Template Utility is a command-line tool used to create and apply these templates. Although there isn't room here to go into all the details of Security Templates, you can type secedit without any options to display a help window with more information on this tool (and Security Templates in general).

See Also
"Security Templates" in "Microsoft Management Console"

Send a Fax
\windows\system32\fxssemd.exe

See "Fax Console."

Services
\windows\system32\services.msc

See "Microsoft Management Console."

Shutdown
\windows\system32\shutdown.exe

Shut down a computer from the command prompt or remotely via Telnet.

To Open   Command Prompt → shutdown

Usage   shutdown [-*command*] [-f] [-m *computername*] [-t *xx*]
           [-c "*comment*"] [-d [*u*][*p*]:*xx*:*yy*]

Description

Shutdown is used to perform a graceful shut down of the computer from the command line; it is useful if you wish to automate the shutdown of computer or if you need to shutdown and you don't have access to the Start menu. This tool can be used to shut down the computer with a Windows shortcut, from a script or batch file, via Scheduled Tasks, or remotely using a Telnet client.

Shutdown uses the following command-line parameters:

-*command*

    Command can be one of the following:

    -i

        Displays the same Shut Down window used by going to Shart → Shut Down. If the -i option is specified with other options, it must be the first option.

    -l

        Logs off (cannot be used with -m option). Whether a logon window is shown depends on system preferences.

    -s

        Shuts down the computer.

    -r

        Restarts the computer.

    -a

        Aborts a system shutdown in progress; only applicable if using a timed shutdown and there's enough time to type shutdown -a.

-m *computername*

    Shuts down a remote computer; works with all commands except for -l. Note that you must have administrator privileges on the remote computer.

-*t xx*

    Sets a timed countdown before the shutdown is performed. This command gives other users who are currently logged in time to save their work and log out. The default is 30 seconds; specify 0 (zero) to skip the countdown.

-c "*comment*"

    Specifies a text message to be shown to other currently logged-on users while the countdown commences; *comment* must be enclosed in quotes and can be a maximum of 127 characters long.

-f

    Forces running applications to close without warning. Normally, all running applications are notified of a shutdown and are allowed to close gracefully (prompting users to save their work, for example). The -f option will result in a quicker shutdown, but some data loss may occur.

-d [*u*][*p*]:*xx*:*yy*

    Specifies the reason code for the shutdown, where *u* is the user code, *p* is a planned shutdown code, *xx* is the major reason code (a positive integer less than 256), and *yy* is the minor reason code (a positive integer less than 65536). Some applications use these codes to perform certain cleanup operations and even to reject shutdowns under certain circumstances.

If you type shutdown without any arguments, you'll see a brief help page. To perform a simple shutdown after a 30-second warning, type shutdown -s. To restart the computer without any countdown, type shutdown -r -t 0.

Notes

Using the -1 command with Shutdown (to log off) may produce undesired effects, such as some services stopping unexpectedly. Make sure you test this feature before using it in the field.

See Also

"Shut Down" in Chapter 3

Signature Verification Tool
\windows\system32\sigverif.exe

Verify digital signatures in device drivers.

To Open   Start → Programs → Accessories → System Tools → System Information
            → Tools menu → File Signature Verification Utility
      Command Prompt → sigverif

Description

Microsoft digitally signs device drivers shipped with Windows so you can verify that they have not been modified since testing. Drivers developed by third-party manufacturers are submitted to Microsoft for testing and, once those drivers pass the hardware standards testing, they are signed as well. The Signature Verification Tool (*sigverif.exe*) lets you manually verify that your installed drivers have not been modified in any way since testing.

Click Start to scan your system for unsigned drivers; if any are found, you'll be notified. Click Advanced to search files other than drivers and to enable logging.

Notes

Windows automatically checks every driver installed through traditional channels (such as the Add Hardware Wizard) for a digital signature. If one is found, it is displayed; if no such signature is found, a warning message is shown instead.

Solitaire
\windows\system32\sol.exe

The traditional Klondike solitaire card game.

To Open   Start → Programs → Games → Solitaire
      Command Prompt → sol

Description

Solitaire, the simple card game included with every version of Windows since Windows 3.0, is a single-player game that follows the traditional Klondike rules (see Figure 4-81). The object of the game is to organize all the cards by suit and place them

Solitaire

in order (starting with the ace) in the four stacks at the top of the window. Cards are moved by placing them on the seven piles in sequential descending order, alternating color. For example, place a black four on a red five, or a red Jack on a black Queen. The game is over when all the cards have been moved to the top stacks.

Figure 4-81. The original Solitaire (Klondike) game is a great way to waste time at work

You can choose a new look for the deck by going to Game → Deck (note that some are animated). Go to Game → Options to choose whether one or three cards are drawn from the deck at a time, which type of scoring to use, and whether the game is timed.

If you start a game drawing three cards at a time, trying to switch to Game → Options → Draw One will start a new game. Press Ctrl-Alt-Shift while you draw to draw a single card in a Draw-3 game.

Notes

- I often use Solitaire as a teaching tool for those just learning to use a mouse. It's a great way to learn clicking, double-clicking, and dragging, and best of all, the student often becomes addicted to the lesson!

- Additional decks (chosen in Game → Deck) can be downloaded from a variety of sources, including *http://www.solitairecity.com/*, *http://www.solitairecentral.com/*, and *http://www.goodsol.com/*.

- When Windows 3.0 was first released in the late 1980's, the most flattering thing that some critics had to say about Microsoft's latest and greatest operating system was that it was a "great solitaire game."

See Also

"FreeCell" (the deterministic version of Solitaire), "Spider Solitaire"

Sound Recorder

\windows\system32\sndrec32.exe

Record and play sound (.wav) files.

To Open   Start → Programs → Accessories → Entertainment → Sound Recorder
Command Prompt → sndrec32

Usage   sndrec32 [play] [/close] [*filename*.wav]

Description

Sound Recorder is used to record simple sound clips and play them back. It supports standard sound (.wav) files used in Control Panel → [Sounds, Speech, and Audio Devices] → Sounds and Audio Devices and hundreds of other applications (see Figure 4-82).

Figure 4-82. Use Sound Recorder to create short audio clips (.wav files)

Its controls are just like those you'd find on a VCR or tape deck, including the standard rewind, fast forward, play, stop, and record. The slider lets you set the position the "playback head" anywhere within the sound file. Both the total length of the sound clip in seconds and your position in the file are shown above. A waveform display gives a visual readout of the sound as it plays.

When running Sound Recorder from the command line, you can use the following options:

filename
    The name of the sound file to load.

/play
    Plays the specified sound file immediately. Without this option, the file will be loaded but not played.

/close
    Closes Sound Recorder when finished playing the sound clip; otherwise, the Sound Recorder window remains open.

Go to File → New to create a new, blank sound file (.wav). If your computer has a microphone or auxiliary input, you can use these blank files to record your own audio. Here are some of the limited features available with Sound Recorder:

- The Effects → Increase Volume and Effects → Decrease Volume options work by increasing or decreasing the amplitude of the recorded sound wave data. When you decrease the volume level of the recorded wave, you risk losing signal clarity, thus giving less audio detail and creating distortion. Increasing the volume of an ordinary speech file shouldn't affect the quality, but music files are less forgiving due to their wider dynamic range.

- The Effects → Increase Speed and Effects → Decrease Speed options are similar to the volume options, except that you deal with the speed in which the sound is being played rather than the volume at which it's being played.

- The Effects → Reverse option reverses the order in which the *.wav* samples contained in the file are played.

- The Effects → Add Echo is fun to use, but the only way to remove the echo is to select Revert before you save the file.

- To mix sound files, move the slider to the place you want to overlay the second sound file, use Edit → Mix With File, and select the *.wav* file you want to mix.

Notes

- Really big *.wav* files take a long time to open in Sound Recorder because it must read the whole file before playing it. The preferred sound player is the Windows Media Player, discussed later in this chapter.

- You can only modify an uncompressed *.wav* file. If you don't see a green line in the waveform area of the window, the file is compressed and you can't change it.

See Also

"Windows Media Player"

Sounds and Audio Devices   \windows\system\mmsys.cpl

Configure the sounds and sound devices used in Windows.

To Open   Control Panel → [Sounds, Speech, and Audio Devices] → Sounds and Audio Devices
Command Prompt → `mmsys.cpl`

Description

Settings affecting the sounds Windows generates are divided into the following sections:

Volume

Your sound card's volume is typically controlled with the Volume Control (covered later in this chapter and accessible by clicking Advanced in the Device volume section); this volume control is redundant (see Figure 4-83).

Options that affect your speakers are found under the second Advanced button in the Speaker settings section, although most users will find little use in changing these settings. In the Advanced Audio Properties dialog, choose between the available speaker setups (used only by some games that support environmental audio) on the Speakers tab, and if you experience any audio-related problems, play around with the settings on the Performance tab.

Sounds

Formerly its own Control Panel applet, the Sounds dialog allows you to associate short clips of sounds with various system events and messages. Select an event

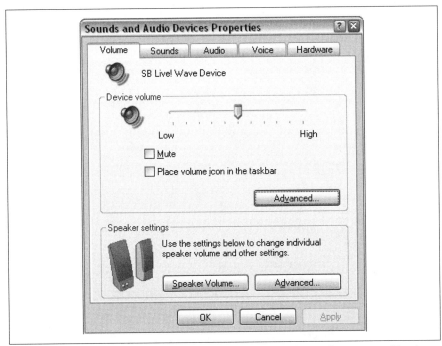

Figure 4-83. Choose whether the volume control appears in the notification area (Tray) with the Volume tab

from the list and then choose a sound (.*wav*) file to associate with it. When you're done, save your choices into a Sound scheme for easy retrieval later on (see Figure 4-84).

Audio, Voice

The Audio and Voice tabs allow you to choose the primary devices for each of which devices handle each of the available channels, including sound playback, sound recording, MIDI music playback, voice playback, and voice recording. Although most computers have only a single sound card, many sound cards provide different types of services for each channel. For example, a particular sound device might offer both standard MIDI playback and wavetable synthesis. Note that some other devices, such as voice-capable modems and video capture cards, will also show up here; if you're not getting sound even though everything appears to be hooked up correctly, check these two tabs for any incorrect settings.

Hardware

Finally, the Hardware tab displays a summary of all the installed audio devices and CD/DVD drives. Select any item and click Properties to change the hardware settings or update the driver for a device. Note that the Properties page is the same you'll get in Device Manager (discussed earlier in this chapter). The Troubleshoot button simply opens up a Help and Support Center window with step-by-step troubleshooting tutorial.

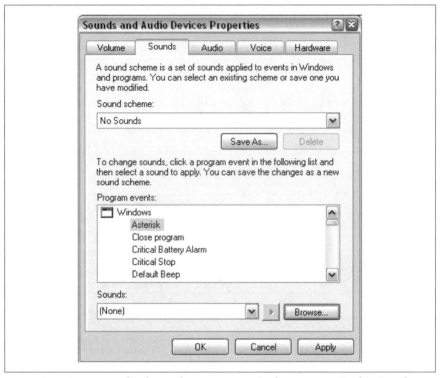

Figure 4-84. Associate audio clips with certain events (such as starting Windows) or choose the No Sounds scheme to keep things quiet

Notes
All settings in this dialog are also covered in Chapter 5.

See Also
"Control Panel," "Volume Control"

Speech Properties

Controls the text-to-speech translation (speech synthesizer) feature in Windows XP.

To Open   Control Panel → [Sounds, Speech, and Audio Devices] → Accessibility
           Options
           Command Prompt → control speech

Description
Text-to-speech translation is used in conjunction with the Narrator utility. The Speech Properties dialog is used to adjust the tone and speed of the "voice" that is used. Try different voices and speeds, using Preview Voice to test them out, until you've found the best combination.

Notes

All of the settings in this dialog are also covered in Chapter 5.

See Also

"Control Panel," "Narrator"

Spider Solitaire

\windows\system32\spider.exe

A variation on the Solitaire card game, using eight piles.

To Open Command Prompt → spider

Description

Spider Solitaire (see Figure 4-85) is a simple card game, similar to Solitaire, which was discussed earlier this chapter. The object is to arrange the cards sequentially and by suit. Cards are moved by placing them on the eight piles in descending order, following suit. For example, place the Jack of Spades on the Queen of Spades, or the Two of Hearts on the Three of Hearts. When you complete an entire suit, King to Ace, it is removed from the board. The game ends when all cards have been removed.

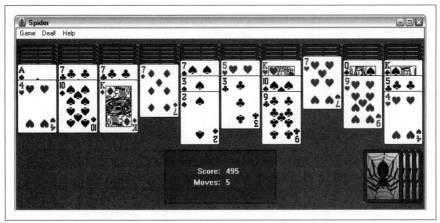

Figure 4-85. Spider Solitaire isn't nearly as addictive as Klondike or FreeCell, but if you like arachnids...

The game is always played with 52 cards, but easier skill levels (chosen at the beginning of the game) reduce the number of suits; for example, the easiest skill level uses all Spades. Go to Game → Options to choose your preferences, such as whether or not your game is saved when you exit.

See Also

The cards in Spider Solitaire will overlap unless you're using a screen resolution of at least 800 × 600 and the window is maximized.

See Also

"Solitaire," "FreeCell"

SQL Server Client Network Utility   *\windows\system32\cliconfg.exe*

Connect to an SQL server and display information about any installed network libraries.

To Open   Command Prompt → cliconfg

Description

SQL Server Client Network Utility is a graphical tool that allows you to manage networking connections to Structured Query Language (SQL), pronounced "sequel") servers, used with corporate database applications. It also lets you view information about the currently installed network libraries. Most users won't have any use for this utility; it's used mostly by network administrators and those setting up or trouble-shooting applications that access an SQL Server. See Help for more information.

See Also

"ODBC Data Source Administrator"

Start Menu

See "Windows Explorer," later in this chapter, and "Start Menu" in Chapter 3.

Subst   *\windows\system32\subst.exe*

Create a new drive letter that is linked to a folder on your hard disk.

To Open   Command Prompt → subst

Usage   subst [*drive*:] [*path* | /d]

Description

Subst is a neat little utility that creates a new drive letter and actively links it to an existing folder on your hard disk. For example, type:

```
subst z: c:\my documents\downloaded music\led zeppelin
```

to create a new drive letter, *z:*, and link it to the folder *c:\my documents\downloaded music\led zeppelin*. When you open drive Z: in Explorer, you'll see the contents of the linked folder; this is very useful if you access a particular folder frequently but find Windows Shortcuts too limiting. For example, a drive created with Subst allows you to access a file in the folder, like this: *z:\stairway.mp3*. To disconnect a Subst'd drive, type:

```
subst z: /d
```

Notes

Any drive letters created with Subst are forgotten when the computer shuts down. To have drives re-Subst'd every time you turn on your computer, write a batch file or WSH script (see Appendix C and Chapter 8, respectively) and place it in your Startup folder.

Synchronization Manager

Synchronize offline files and prepare remote files for offline use.

To Open   Start → Programs → Accessories → Synchronize
Internet Explorer → Tools menu → Synchronize
Command Prompt → mobsync

Description

Using a network, you can open and edit files stored on remote computers. However, if your network connection is not always present, such as on a laptop that is connected to the network only when it's in its docking station, you may choose to work with "offline files." Offline files allow you to open files remotely, work on them when you're disconnected, and then update them at a later time when the connection has been re-established.

Naturally, you could just save remote files on your own hard disk manually, edit them, and then transfer them manually to their original locations, replacing older versions where necessary. However, Windows XP's support for offline files is much more convenient and is made possible with the Synchronization Manager (see Figure 4-86).

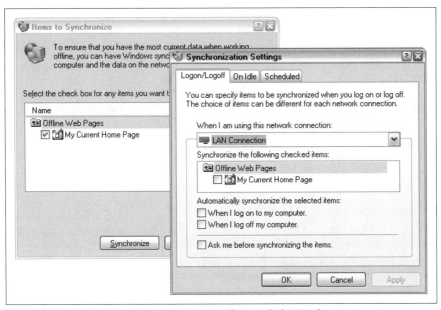

Figure 4-86. Help reduce document version conflicts with the Synchronization Manager

The main window, entitled Items to Synchronize, lists the files and folders currently set up for offline use. However, you can't add new files to this list here. Instead, use Explorer to navigate to a remote folder shared on another computer. Then, right-click on the file(s) or folder(s) you wish to use offline and select Make Available Offline. This will start the Offline Files Wizard, which will guide you through the rest of the process, including whether or not files will be automatically synchronized. The final result is that the files or folders you've selected will show up as a new entry in the Offline Files folder and will also appear in the Items to Synchronize window. Once the desired files and folders have been set up for offline use, you can use the Synchronization Manager to synchronize offline items manually, as well as choose the synchronization preferences. Here's how synchronization works:

1. A file is placed in a shared folder.

2. The user on another computer makes that file available offline (using procedure explained above).

3. The remote user then begins to edit the file and continues to edit the file after being disconnected from the network.

4. The next day, the user reconnects to the network and uses the Synchronization Manager to update the remote file with the one that has been edited.

5. If the Synchronization Manager finds that the file has been modified by another user since it was made available offline, a warning appears. This prevents two users from inadvertently editing the same file, which of course, would result in someone's work being lost.

Notes

- The Synchronization Manager also allows you to schedule synchronizations, either whenever the computer is idle or at predetermined times.

- The Offline Files Folder is also found on the Desktop; it can be turned on or off from the Offline Files Wizard and accessed when you make files available offline.

- The Offline Web Pages folder can be found in *c:\windows\Offline Web Pages*.

System Properties
\windows\system32\sysdm.cpl

View and modify many general Windows settings.

To Open   Control Panel → [Performance and Maintenance] → System
right-click on the My Computer icon → Properties
Command Prompt → control sysdm.cpl

Description

The System Properties window contains settings that affect hardware, system performance, networking, and other Windows features. The tabs in this dialog are as follows:

General

This information-only tab displays the current Windows version, the edition (Home, Professional, Server, Advanced Server), the registered user, the speed of the processor, and the amount of installed memory (see Figure 4-87).

Computer Name

These settings affect how your computer is identified on your network, such as the computer's name and whether or not you're connected to a Windows NT domain system (referred to as a business network here). The Computer description field is for entering a comment only; it has no effect on any networking settings. See Chapter 7 for more information.

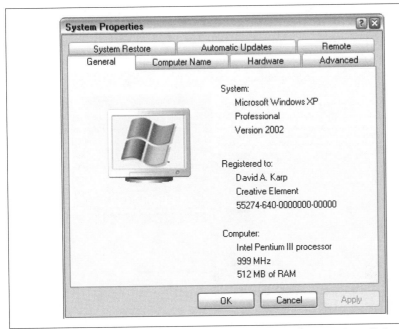

Figure 4-87. Get a quick overview of your Windows version, amount of installed memory, and registered user with the General tab

Hardware

The Add Hardware Wizard and Device Manager are discussed elsewhere in this chapter. The Driver Signing Options dialog allows you to instruct Windows to accept or deny unsigned device drivers; see the Signature Verification Tool, discussed earlier in this chapter, for details.

Finally, the Hardware Profiles dialog allows you to set up multiple configurations of hardware, each with its own set of enabled and disabled devices. Use this feature if you're unable to get two devices working at the same time or if you use a laptop with a docking station (and several devices may be unavailable at any given time).

Advanced

In this tab, you'll find a bunch of important Windows settings covering a wide variety of areas.

Performance → Settings → Visual Effects tab

Selectively disable several enhanced display features, such as shadows under menus and the animation of several screen elements. Depending on your system, especially the capabilities of your display adapter (video card), the disabling of some of these items may substantially improve system performance. It's certainly worth experimenting with these settings, not only to make Windows more responsive, but to enable some of the cooler features that are disabled by default.

Performance → Settings → Advanced tab

In most cases, you'll want both the Processor scheduling and Memory usage options set to "Programs." However, if your computer is used as a web server, for example, you may experience better performance if you change these settings (see Figure 4-88).

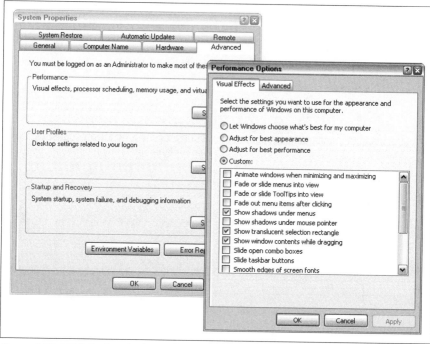

Figure 4-88. Click Settings in the Performance section of the Advanced Tab to turn off some of the annoying eye candy that can slow down your computer

Click Change in the Virtual Memory section to adjust how Windows uses virtual memory, commonly known as your swap file. When Windows has used up all of your physical memory (RAM) with programs and data, it stores some of that data on your hard disk to make room for other running programs. Since your hard disk is much slower than your RAM, this process (known as paging or swapping) can significantly impair system performance, which is why adding more memory to your system (up to a point) will make it faster. In most cases, you'll want to leave these settings alone, but if you're running out of disk space, you may want to limit how much of it is used as virtual memory. If, on the other hand, you have plenty of disk space, you might realize better performance if you click Custom size and then set the Initial size and Maximum size to the same value, thereby eliminating a potential delay when Windows resizes the swap file.

User Profiles → Settings

This dialog displays a summary of configured user accounts. See "User Accounts," later in this chapter, for more information.

Startup and Recovery → Settings

The System startup section allows you to change settings in the *boot.ini* file, which contains the configuration for the Boot Manager. The Boot Manager is used when you have more than one operating system installed on the same system and wish to choose which one to use whenever you turn on your computer. Most users will have no use for this section.

The System failure section lets you control what happens when Windows encounters a serious error (known as the blue screen of death). Unless you're trying to diagnose such a problem, you'll probably never need to change these settings.

Environment Variables
See Chapter 6 for more information on the environment.

Error Reporting
Whenever a program crashes, whether it's a Microsoft application, a component of Windows, or a third-party application, a window appears, prompting you to send a "report" to Microsoft. Use this page to completely or selectively disable this feature.

System Restore
The settings in this tab allow you to selectively disable the System Restore feature for the drives in your computer. See "System Restore," later in this chapter, for details.

Automatic Updates
Windows can automatically and routinely activate the Windows Update feature (in the background) to see if any updates to Windows XP exist, and optionally, install them without prompting. See "Windows Update," later in this chapter, for details.

Remote
These settings control the Remote Desktop feature (discussed earlier in this chapter). Unless you specifically want others to be able to connect to your computer using Remote Desktop, it's strongly recommended that you disable both options on this page.

Notes

- All settings in this dialog are also covered in Chapter 5.

- If you're looking for the Device Manager tab found in some earlier versions of Windows, it's now a separate application; see "Device Manager," earlier in this chapter. There's also a shortcut in the Hardware tab.

- The Advanced tab → Environment Variables dialog allows you to set the default values for the system environment. This feature effectively replaces the *autoexec.bat* file used in Windows 95/98.

See Also

"Control Panel"

System Configuration Editor

\windows\system32\sysedit.exe

Obsolete; quick editor for *system.ini*, *win.ini*, *config.sys*, and *autoexec.bat*.

To Open   Command Prompt → sysedit

Description

The Systems Configuration Editor is essentially a special version of Notepad used to provide convenient access to a few configuration files used in previous versions of Windows. When you start it, the four following files are opened: *system.ini*, *win.ini*, *config.sys*, and *autoexec.bat*. Since none of these files are actively used in Windows XP (except for legacy application support), this tool has very little use. It's included for legacy purposes only and should not be used.

See Also

"Notepad"

System Configuration Utility

\windows\pchealth\helpctr\binaries\msconfig.exe

Selectively enable or disable several startup options for diagnostic/troubleshooting purposes.

To Open Command Prompt → `msconfig`

Description

The System Configuration Utility allows you to selectively enable or disable various settings that affect system startup (see Figure 4-89). For the most part, this tool was designed for an earlier version of Windows and therefore isn't too useful in Windows XP. However, it does provide a few options not available elsewhere:

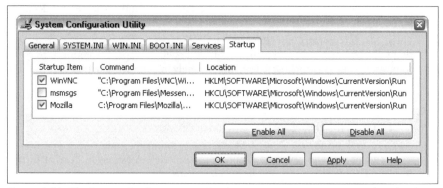

Figure 4-89. The System Configuration Utility lets you stop certain programs from loading automatically when Windows starts

General tab → Expand File
> Provides a graphical interface to the File Expansion Utility (*expand.exe*), discussed earlier in this chapter.

SYSTEM.INI and WIN.INI tabs
> These two tabs let you turn on or off any settings in either the *system.ini* or *win.ini* files, respectively. Note that these files aren't actually used by Windows XP and are only kept around to support old Windows applications.

BOOT.INI tab
> Displays the contents of the *boot.ini* file, used to display the startup menu in a multiple-boot environment, as well as several options that affect the boot menu. For example, if there is more than one operating system installed on your computer, you can use the Set as Default button to choose the default OS and the Move Up button to rearrange the menu items. Some of these options here are also available by going to Control Panel → [Performance and Maintenance] → System

→ Advanced tab, and clicking Settings in the Startup and Recovery section. However, the System Configuration Utility has several boot options not otherwise available without having to manually edit the *boot.ini* file.

Click Check All Boot Paths to scan all of the entries in *boot.ini* and remove any menu items that point to invalid partitions or operating systems. This is very useful if, for example, you've installed to operating systems, and then deleted one of them, yet still are bothered by the boot menu every time you turn on your computer.

For more information on *boot.ini*, see Help or take a look at the "Boot Configuration Manager," earlier in this chapter, for details.

Services tab

Displays system services. The preferred interface for viewing and controlling services is the Services Snap-in (*services.msc*) of the Microsoft Management Console, discussed earlier in this chapter.

Startup tab

This tab shows some of the programs that are configured to run automatically when Windows starts. Although most startup programs are configured by placing Windows Shortcuts in the Startup folder in the Start menu, the Start tab shows only those seemingly hidden entries specified in the Registry (see Chapter 8) at `HKEY_LOCAL_MACHINE\SOFTWARE\Microsoft\Windows\CurrentVersion\Run`.

System Information

\windows\system32\winmsd.exe
\program files\common files\microsoft shared\msinfo\msinfo32.exe

Collect and display information about your computer.

To Open   Start → Programs → Accessories → System tools → System Information
Command Prompt → `winmsd`
Command Prompt → `msinfo32`

Description

Microsoft System Information is a reporting tool used to view information about hardware, system resources used by that hardware, software drivers, and Internet Explorer settings (see Figure 4-90). Information is arranged in a familiar Explorer-like tree. Expand or collapse branches with the little plus (+) and minus (-) signs, and click any category to view the corresponding information in the right-hand pane.

The "Components" view of your hardware is similar to Device Manager, except that Device Manager also allows modification and removal of the devices. Likewise, the "Hardware Resources" view can also be duplicated in Device Manager with View → Resources by type. One advantage Microsoft System Information has over Device Manager is its ability to show history of changes, using View → System History.

The information displayed in Software Environment category is also available in bits and pieces through other utilities (such as DriverQuery, discussed earlier in this chapter), but only here is it presented all in one place.

Notes

- Rather than wading through all of the categories, jump right to the item you want by using the "Find what" field at the bottom of the window.

Applications and Tools

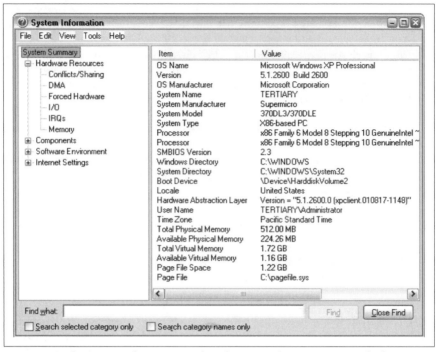

Figure 4-90. The System Information window shows an exhaustive amount of information about your system

- Like Device Manager, you can also connect to another computer and view information about that system. Go to View → Remote Computer and enter the name of the remote machine.

- The Tools menu provides access to several diagnostic utilities, all of which are documented elsewhere in this chapter.

- System Information can also be used to view reports and logs generated by other utilities, such as Dr. Watson (*.wlg* files), Windows Report Tool (*.cab* files), and even *.txt* files.

- You can print a report with System Information, but you can only print the entire system information collection, which usually comes out to more than 75 pages. If you want to print only sections of the system information, copy it to Notepad and print it from there.

- If information appears to be incorrect, out-of-date, or missing altogether, try View → Refresh or press F5.

- *winmsd.exe* and *msinfo32.exe* have the same features, except that *msinfo32.exe* accepts command-line parameters, all of which are documented at *http://support. microsoft.com/support/kb/articles/Q255/7/13.ASP*.

See Also

"Microsoft Management Console"

System Restore

\windows\system32\restore\rstrui.exe

Roll back your computer's configuration to an earlier state, with the intention of undoing a potentially harmful change.

To Open   Start → Programs → Accessories → System Tools → System Restore
System Information → Tools menu → System Restore
System Configuration Utility → Launch System Restore
Command Prompt → \windows\system32\restore\rstrui

Description

System Restore is a feature that runs invisibly in the background, continuously backing up important system files and registry settings. The idea is that at some point, you may wish to roll back your computer's configuration to a time before things started going wrong (see Figure 4-91). By default, System Restore is turned on, using up to 12 percent of your computer's hard disk space.

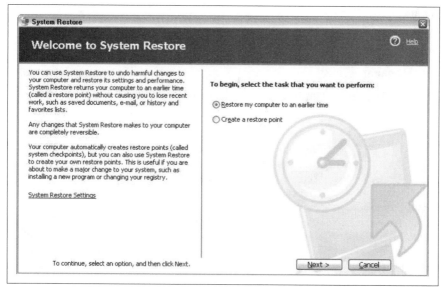

Figure 4-91. Use System Restore to roll back your computer's configuration to a time before a specific problem occurred

Normally, you'll never need to use System Restore. In fact, if you back up your entire system often (see "Backup," earlier in this chapter), you could easily disable the System Restore feature altogether. However, if you install an application that turns out to wreak havoc, or if your system is attacked by a virus, you may be glad you had System Restore.

To configure System Restore, click "System Restore Settings" in the main System Restore window or go to Control Panel → [Performance and Maintenance] → System → System Restore tab.

Here you can turn off the feature, change the amount of disk space that is used, and view the status of the System Restore service. If you decrease the disk space made available to

System Restore (which is understandable, as 12 percent is a lot), you'll be reducing the number of available "restore points," theoretically reducing the effectiveness of this tool.

 System Restore indiscriminately replaces files installed in your computer with potentially earlier versions, resets registry preferences, and in some cases, uninstalls software. While the intention is to solve some problems, it can inadvertently cause others. If you suspect that a particular application is causing a problem, your best bet is to uninstall that single application rather than attempting a System Restore. Use System Restore as a last resort only.

Start the System Restore application if you wish to restore an earlier configuration or create a restore point. Restore Points are packages containing files and settings, created at regular intervals. To roll back your computer's configuration, simply choose a date when a restore point was created. You can also create a restore point at any time to "lock in" today's configuration.

See Also

"Backup"

Task Manager

\windows\system32\taskmgr.exe

Display currently running programs, background processes, and some performance statistics.

To Open   Ctrl-Alt-Del → Task Manager
Right-click on empty portion of Taskbar → Task Manager
Command Prompt → taskmgr
keyboard shortcut: Ctrl+Shift+ESC

Description

Task Manager is an extremely useful tool, but is strangely omitted from the Start menu. In its simplest form, it displays all running applications, allowing you to close any that have crashed or stopped responding. The main window is divided into the following four tabs:

Applications
Shows all foreground applications as well as the status of each one (see Figure 4-92). The Status can be "Running" or "Not responding." You can switch to any running application by double-clicking it, which makes it similar to the Taskbar in this respect. Click New Task or go to File → New Task (Run) to start a new program (which has the same effect as going to Start → Run).

Select any item and click End Task to close the program. Although it is preferred to use an application's own exit routine, this function is useful for those programs that have crashed or have stopped responding.

Processes
A process is any program running on your computer, including foreground applications shown in the Applications tab and any background applications that might be running (see Figure 4-93). Like the End Task button in the Applications

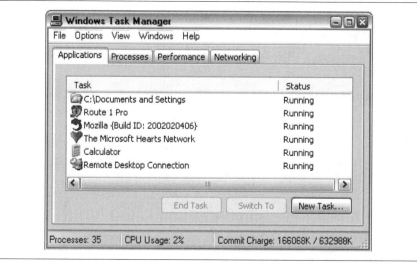

Figure 4-92. The Applications tab shows the currently open windows, but not all running programs

tab, the End Process button is used to close unresponsive programs. Additionally, however, it allows you to close background applications that otherwise have no window or other means of exiting gracefully.

Right-click on any running task to display a list of options, including End Process (see above), End Process Tree (similar to End Process, but ends all "child" processes as well), and Set Priority. The Set Priority menu allows you to increase or decrease the priority of a program; higher-priority processes may run better and are less likely to be interrupted or slowed down by other processes, and lower-priority processes are more likely to yield CPU cycles to other processes. Note that changing a process's priority may have unpredictable results. It should be used only if that process or application explicitly supports running at higher or lower priorities.

Performance

The Performance tab shows several graphs, all updated in real time, used to monitor the performance of the system. The refresh rate of the graphs can be changed by going to View → Update Speed.

The CPU Usage is expressed as a percentage, in which an average idling computer will take about 3 to 7 percent of a processor's clock cycles, and a computer running a graphics-intensive game (such as one of my favorites, Black & White) might take 80 to 90 percent. Don't be alarmed if your CPU Usage appears to be unusually high, although you may wish to investigate running processes for crashed programs or even tasks that may have been started by unauthorized intruders. (See "Active Connections Utility," discussed earlier in this chapter.) The CPU Usage History is a running history of the last few minutes of CPU Usage readings; it can be very interesting to see what happens to the CPU Usage History when you start a particular program or just move the mouse around the screen. To change how Windows handles multitasking, go to Control Panel → [Performance and Maintenance] → System → Advanced tab, click Settings in the Performance section, and choose the Advanced tab. If you have a multiprocessor

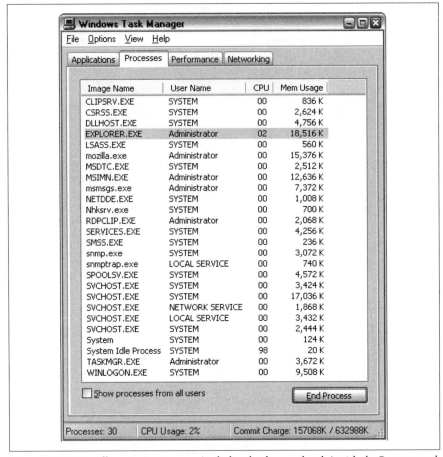

Figure 4-93. View all running programs (including background tasks) with the Processes tab

system, you'll see a separate graph for each processor, which can be very useful to see how your processors are being utilized (see Figure 4-94).

The Page File Usage and Page File Usage History work the same as CPU Usage, described above, except that they report on the performance of the virtual memory. Virtual memory is the portion of your hard disk used to store data when Windows has used up all of your installed RAM. To change virtual memory settings, go to Control Panel → [Performance and Maintenance] → System → Advanced tab, click Settings in the Performance section, choose the Advanced tab, and click Change.

Also shown in the Performance tab are several performance-related statistics, such as the amount of total and available memory, or even the number of active handles (unique identifiers to resources, such as menu items, Windows, registry keys, or anything else Windows has to keep track of).

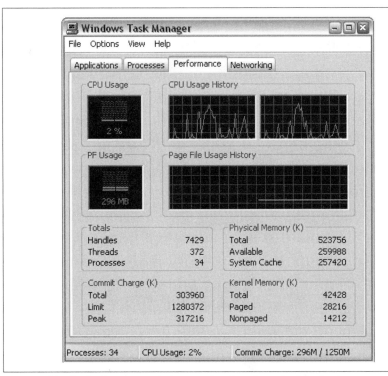

Figure 4-94. The Performance tab shows a time-based graph of the load on your processor and virtual memory

Networking

Similar to the Performance tab, above, the Networking tab shows real-time graphs depicting the performance of your network connections. You'll see a graph for each network connection currently in use. See Chapter 7 for more information.

The Options and View menus can be used to set several preferences; note that the options available in these menus change depending on the currently selected tab. For example, if you want to leave the Task Manager open all the time, you may wish to turn off the "Always On Top" option so that you can see other running applications.

Notes

Task Manager replaces the Close Program box found in Windows 9x/Me (via Ctrl-Alt-Del). However, instead of being a system-modal dialog (meaning that when it is visible, all other applications are frozen and inaccessible), it's just another application that can be left open all the time.

See Also

"Query Process," "Taskkill," and "Tasklist"

Taskbar and Start Menu Properties

Change the appearance and behavior of the Taskbar, notification area, and Start menu (see Figure 4-95).

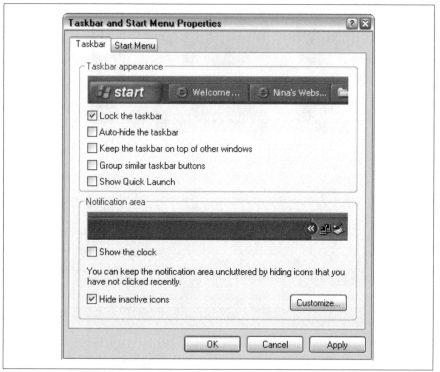

Figure 4-95. Use Taskbar and Start Menu Properties to specify your preferences for your Start menu, Taskbar, and Notification Area (Tray)

To Open   Control Panel → [Appearance and Themes] → Taskbar and Start Menu
                 Right-click on an empty portion of the Taskbar → Properties
                 Right-click on the Start button → Properties
                 Start → Settings → Taskbar and Start Menu (Classic Start menu only)

Description

The Taskbar is the bar, typically appearing along the bottom edge of your screen, that holds the Start button, the notification area (commonly known as the Tray), and the task buttons (one for each open application window). The settings in this dialog are as follows:

Lock the Taskbar

Lock the Taskbar to prevent it from being accidentally (or intentionally) resized or moved or to prevent resizing or removal of any Taskbar toolbars. See "Taskbar" in Chapter 3 for details.

Auto-hide the Taskbar

Enable this feature to have the Taskbar drop out of sight when it's not being used. Move the mouse to the bottom of the screen (or the sides or top, if that's where you have your Taskbar) to make the Taskbar pop up. You can also press Ctrl-Esc (or the Windows logo key, if you have one) to pop up the Taskbar and open the Start menu.

Keep the Taskbar on top of other windows

Enable this feature to prevent other windows from covering the Taskbar. Although similarly named features appear in some other applications (such as the Task Manager), this one is somewhat different because in addition to having the Taskbar appear "always on top," this option actually shrinks the Desktop and space available for applications. For example, if you maximize an application, its outer edge will become flush with the Taskbar. See "Windows" in Chapter 3 for more information.

Group similar Taskbar buttons

See "Taskbar" in Chapter 3 for more information on task button grouping.

Show Quick Launch

See "Toolbars" in Chapter 3 for more information on the Quick Launch toolbar.

Show the clock

Displays or hides the clock in the notification area. Hold the mouse pointer over the clock for a second or two to temporarily display today's date. Double-click the clock to open Date and Time Properties (discussed earlier in this chapter).

Hide inactive icons

Windows keeps a history of the status icons various applications display in the notification area. Turn on the Hide inactive icons option and then click Customize to display the Customize Notifications dialog, which allows you to selectively show or hide icons that are currently displayed—or have ever been displayed—in the notification area (see Figure 4-96). Here the term "Inactive" means currently not displayed.

If you want to hide an icon, try the settings in the application that owns the icon first. Only if there is no such setting, or if the setting doesn't work, should you resort to the Customize Notifications dialog. If there are no icons shown in the notification area and if the clock is disabled (see above), the notification area disappears entirely. If one or more icons is hidden with the Customize Notifications dialog, however, a small arrow appears, allowing you to show or hide any such icons.

Start Menu tab: Start menu versus Classic Start menu

This setting changes the arrangement of the items in your Start menu. The Classic Start menu is a single-column menu, similar to the one found in Windows 2000 and Windows 9x/Me. All of your installed programs are listed in the Programs menu (see Figure 4-97).

The Start menu is a more complex, double-column menu with all the same options as the Classic Start menu, plus links to the most frequently used applications, as well as your favorite web browser and email program. All of your installed programs are listed in the All Programs menu.

Note that this setting has no effect on the "style" of the Start button or Taskbar. Use Control Panel → [Appearance and Themes] → Display → Appearance tab to change the style. Unfortunately, there's no way to change the color or appearance of the big, green Start button when using the new Windows XP style with a

Applications and Tools

Figure 4-96. Selectively hide unwanted Tray icons with the Customize Notifications dialog

third party add-on (see *http://www.annoyances.org/exec/show/article02-001*). See the beginning of this chapter and the beginning of Chapter 3 for more information on styles in Windows XP.

Don't be alarmed if some of your Desktop icons may disappear when you switch between the Start menu and the Classic Start menu; for some reason, whether these icons are shown or hidden is saved with the Start menu selection (go to Control Panel → [Appearance and Themes] → Display → Desktop tab → Customize Desktop for more options). The default for the Classic Start menu is to have the My Computer, My Network Places, and Recycle Bin icons shown; the default for the new Start menu is to have only the Recycle Bin icon shown.

Customize

The Customize button, available with either Start menu type, allows you to selectively show or hide certain items in the Start menu. See "Start Menu" in Chapter 3 for more information (see Figure 4-98).

Notes

All settings in this dialog are also covered in Chapter 5.

See Also

"Control Panel," "Taskbar" in Chapter 3

Figure 4-97. Choose between the new Windows XP style Start menu and or the simpler "Classic" Start menu

Applications and Tools

Taskkill

\windows\system32\taskkill.exe

End one or more running processes, either on a local or remote system. (Taskkill is included with Windows XP Professional only.)

To Open   Command Prompt → taskkill

Usage   taskkill [/s system [/u username [/p [password]]]]
              { [/fi filter] [/pid pid | /im image] } [/f] [/t]

Description

Taskkill is used to end one or more running processes from the command line. Taskkill works together with Tasklist, discussed later in this chapter, to provide command-line equivalents to the functionality provided by the Processes tab in Task Manager. For more information on processes, see "Task Manager," discussed earlier in this chapter.

Taskkill takes the following command-line parameters:

/s system
    Specifies the remote system to which to connect.

/u [domain\]user
    Specifies the user context under which the command should execute.

/p [password]
    Specifies the password for the user specified by \u; prompts for input if omitted.

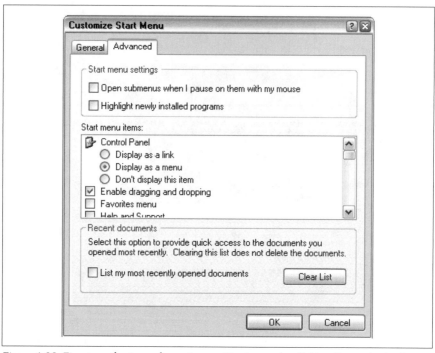

Figure 4-98. Fine-tune the items shown in your Start menu by clicking Customize in the Taskbar and Start Menu Properties window

/f

Specifies to forcefully terminate process(es).

/fi *filter*

Displays a set of tasks that match a given criteria specified by the filter. Use Tasklist for more display options.

/pid *process_id*

Specifies the process ID of the process to be terminated. To obtain the process IDs, use Tasklist (later in this chapter).

/im *image_name*

Specifies the image name of the process to be terminated; specify * to terminate all image names.

/t

Terminates the specified process and process tree, which includes any child processes that were started by it.

See Also

"Tasklist," "Task Manager"

Tasklist

Display a list of running applications and processes running on either a local or a remote system. (Tasklist is included with Windows XP Professional only.)

To Open   Command Prompt → packager

Usage   tasklist [/s *system* [/u *username* [/p [*password*]]]]
          [/m [*module*] | /svc | /v] [/fi *filter*] [/fo *format*] [/nh]

Description

Taskkill is used to list running processes from the command line. Tasklist works together with Taskkill, discussed earlier in this chapter, to provide command-line equivalents to the functionality provided by the Processes tab in Task Manager. For more information on processes, see "Task Manager," discussed earlier in this chapter.

Taskkill takes the following command-line parameters:

/s *system*
> Specifies the remote system to which to connect.

/u [*domain*]*user*
> Specifies the user context under which the command should execute.

/p [*password*]
> Specifies the password for the user specified by \u; prompts for input if omitted.

/m [*module*]
> Lists all tasks that have DLL modules loaded that match the pattern, *module*. If *module* is not specified, /m displays all modules loaded by each task.

/v
> Verbose mode; display all available information.

/fi *filter*
> Displays a set of tasks that match a given criteria specified by the filter. Use Tasklist for more display options.

/fo *format*
> Specifies the format of the display: type /fo table (the default) for a formatted table, /fo list, for a plain text list, or /fo csv for a comma-separated report, suitable for importing into a spreadsheet or database.

/nh
> If using the /fo table or /fo csv format (above), the /nh option turns off the column headers.

See Also

"Taskkill," "Task Manager," "Query Process," "OpenFiles"

Telnet

Create an interactive, text-based terminal session on a remote computer.

To Open   Command Prompt → telnet

Usage   telnet [-a] [-e *esc*] [-f *file*] [-l *user*] [-t *term*] [*host*]

Description

Telnet is used to connect to a remote computer. A Telnet session works very much like a command prompt window, except that commands entered are executed on the remote machine. What you do in Telnet depends on the platform of the remote machine; for example, if connecting to a Unix host, you'll get a standard terminal window. If you connect to a Windows host, you'll get a DOS command-prompt window.

The following options can be used with Telnet:

host

> The name or IP address of the remote computer. If you omit host, Telnet will start with a standard Microsoft Telnet> prompt, at which point you can type any of the commands listed below (such as open).

port

> Specifies a port number to use for the connection; if omitted, the default Telnet port (23) is used.

-l *user*

> Specifies the username with which to log in on the remote system. If omitted, you'll be prompted to enter a username at the remote system's login. The -l option only works if the remote system provides support for the Telnet ENVIRON option.

-a

> Attempts an automatic logon using the username and password of the currently logged-on user.

-e *esc_character*

> Defines the escape character for the Telnet session; by default, escape is set to Ctrl-]. Type the escape character during a Telnet session to temporarily jump to the internal Telnet command prompt (see below).

-f *filename*

> Specifies a file in which to store a log of the session.

-t *term*

> Specifies the terminal type; can be vt100, *vt52*, vtnt, or ansi (the default).

If a connection has been established, commands typed at the prompt will be interpreted by the remote host. However, if a connection has not yet been established, or if you press the escape character (by default, Ctrl-]), you can use one of the following internal Telnet commands:

close

> Closes the current connection.

display

> Displays settings for the current session, such as the terminal type and escape character. Use set, below, to change an option for the current session; use a command-line parameter, above, to change an option for the next session.

open *host*

> Connect to a remote computer, where *host* is the same as the command-line option of the same name, described above.

quit

> Closes the current connection (if applicable) and exits Telnet.

set *variable* [*value*]

> Sets *variable* to *value*. In the case of ntlm, local_echo, and crlf, use set to turn them on or unset (below) to turn them off. In the case of term, type set *value*, where *value* can be vt100, vt52, vtnt, or ansi.

status

> Displays the status of the current connection.

unset

> Turns off an option previously turned on with set, above.

Notes

- The local_echo variable causes everything you type to be displayed in the Telnet window; some remote hosts require this; others don't. If you can't see what you type, turn local_echo on; if you see two of each character, turn it off.

- Setting the terminal type to vt-100 or ansi will serve your purposes in most cases, unless the remote host instructs you differently when you log in. If you need to emulate a terminal type that Telnet doesn't support, you'll need to get a different Telnet client.

- Since Telnet is a command-line application, you can change settings such as the color and buffer size by clicking on the control box and selecting Properties. Note that a large buffer will allow you to scroll up and see several pages of past commands. For more information on the command prompt window, see Appendix C.

- Another way to launch Telnet is through a URL, like this: telnet://*server:port*. If typed into the Address Bar of a web browser, or if a telnet:// link in a web page is clicked, it will start a common sessions using the default Telnet client.

- To accept incoming Telnet sessions, open Services (*services.msc*), right-click Telnet in the list and select Start. To configure the Telnet service to start automatically with Windows, right-click on it and choose Automatic from the Startup type list.

- Telnet, as a protocol, is slowly being phased out, primarily because there is no encryption. If you log onto a remote server, for example, your password as typed into the window is transmitted in plain text, which means that it could be observed by a third-party monitoring tool. For better security, use SSH instead of Telnet (on both the client and server sides). Good SSH clients for Windows XP include SSH Secure Shell (*http://www.ssh.com/*) and PuTTY (*http://putty.bhni.net/*).

See Also

"Telnet Administrator"

Telnet Administrator

\windows\system32\tlntadmn.exe

Control active Telnet sessions. (Telnet Administrator is included with Windows XP Professional only.)

To Open   Command Prompt → tlntadmn

Usage   tlntadmn [*host*] [*options*] command

Description

The Telnet Administrator lets you manage current Telnet sessions. Most users will never need the Telnet Administrator; it's typically only used by network administrators to manage servers that receive a large quantity of incoming Telnet connections, and full documentation of this tool is beyond the scope of this book. For more information on the Telnet Administrator, type tlntadmn /? at a command prompt.

See Also

"Telnet," "Microsoft Management Console"

Tracert

\windows\system32\tracert.exe

Trace the route of communication across the Internet.

To Open   Command Prompt → tracert

Usage   tracert [-d] [-h *max_hops*] [-j *list*] [-w *timeout*] *target*

Description

The Internet is a decentralized interconnection of computers. This means that there is rarely, if ever, a direct connection between two computers on the Internet. Instead, information is transferred across several, if not dozens, of computers to make it from one place to another. The further the geographical distance between two machines, the greater the likelihood that there will be more hubs and other intermediate computers along the way. Tracert is used to list all the computers encountered on the journey from one computer to another.

Type the following at a command prompt (while connected to the Internet) to trace the route from your computer to *microsoft.com*:

    tracert microsoft.com

Tracert accepts the following options:

target
     The name or IP address of the computer to contact.

-d
     If you specify an IP address, Tracert will attempt to resolve the host name (using NSLookup). Include the -d option to skip this step.

-h *max_hops*
     Specifies the maximum number of "hops" (servers along the route) to display before giving up; the default is 30 hops.

-j *list*
     Loosely imposes a route to follow, where *list* is a list of hosts.

-w *timeout*
     Sets the amount of time to wait (in milliseconds) for each reply.

Notes

Tracert has many uses, but probably the most valuable on a day-to-day basis is for troubleshooting. For example, if you are trying to contact a web server, email server, or any other machine on the Internet, and it does not appear to be responding, you can perform

---

a Tracert to see if it is the fault of the actual machine or one of the hosts along the way. If it turns out to be one of the hosts along the way, your network administrator or Internet service provider may be able to use your Tracert report to help solve the problem.

See Also

"NSLookup," "Ping"

User Accounts

\windows\system32\nusrmgr.cpl

Add or remove user accounts and change the privileges of existing users.

To Open   Control Panel → User Accounts
Command Prompt → `control nusrmgr.cpl`
Command Prompt → `control userpasswords`

Description

Windows XP fully supports multiple users, each with his or her own Start menu, Desktop, My Documents folder, color and display theme preferences, application settings, and other odds and ends. Each user has a password and a home directory (located in *\Documents and Settings\{username}*), under which all of the user's personal files and folders are stored.

If you have the Home edition of Windows XP, support for multiple users basically ends there. However, Windows XP Professional edition has a more advanced and comprehensive system for managing user accounts.

In Windows XP Professional, some users can be more privileged than others. Administrators have complete control over the system and can run any program, install or remove hardware and software, change any setting, and create, remove, and modify other user accounts. You can also set up "Limited" user accounts, such as the Guest account, which allow others to use your computer without being able to read or modify any of your password-protected files (see Chapter 7) or make any changes to the system. In Windows XP Home edition, all users are considered Administrators.

The User Accounts window is extremely simple and all features are fairly self-explanatory. The main window displays all of the configured users (see Figure 4-99).

It also has three options:

Change an account
Use this to change your password or picture (the icon shown next to your user account on the Welcome screen). If a user account has no password defined, you'll see "Create Password" here instead of the standard "Change Password." Administrators can change any account, but nonadministrators can only make changes to their own accounts.

Create a new account
Adds a new account to the system. If you have several people in your home or office who share the same computer, create a separate account for each person. If you don't really care about security, make them all Administrators (which is the only option in Windows XP Home edition); otherwise, choose "Limited" and follow the prompts on the screen.

Applications and Tools

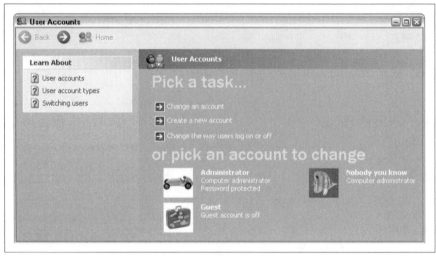

Figure 4-99. All configured users are shown in the User Accounts window

Usernames can be anything, as long as they're not the same as pre-existing user-names. If you're connecting two or more computers over a standard peer-to-peer network and would like to be able to share files and printers between them, you'll need to create accounts that match the currently logged on user on each machine. For example, if a user named Seymour, using a Windows 98 machine, wishes to connect to a Windows XP machine on the network, a user account named "Seymour" (with the same password) must exist on the Windows XP machine.

Windows XP Professional also has a preconfigured "Guest" account. This extremely limited account is perfect for one-time users because there's no setup and no password is required. The Guest account can be turned off or on with the "Change an account" link, shown above.

Change the way users log on or off

Turn off the "Use the Welcome screen" option (the default is on) if you want the classic logon screen, similar to the one found in Windows 2000 (see Figure 4-100). The Welcome screen allows users to log on by simply clicking their icon and, if applicable, typing a password. The classic logon screen, however, is considered more secure because users must type their username as well as the password to log on. Click "Logon options" in the "Learn About" section for a preview.

Note also that the Welcome screen/classic logon screen option also changes the style of the Shut Down screen. If the Welcome screen is used, the last entry on your Start menu will be "Turn off the Computer," with three choices: Stand By, Turn Off, and Restart. If the classic logon screen is used, the last entry in the Start menu will be "Shut Down," with five options: Log Off, Shut Down, Restart, Stand By, and Hibernate.

The "Use Fast User Switching" option, available only if the "Use the Welcome screen" option is enabled, speeds up the process of switching between users by not closing applications when a user logs out. Thus, unless the computer is shut down, any applications and documents that were open the last time you used the computer would still be open when you logged back in.

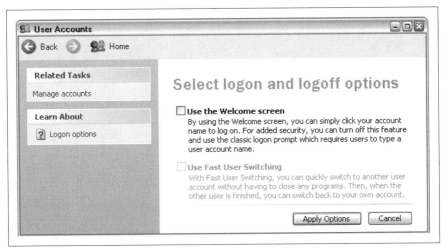

Figure 4-100. Turn off the Welcome screen to use the older Shut Down and Logon screens found in earlier versions of Windows

Notes

- All the settings in this dialog are also covered in Chapter 5.

- More user account options can be found in the Local Users and Groups console (*lusrmgr.msc*; see "Microsoft Management Console," earlier in this chapter).

- If you want to configure Windows to start up without asking for a username and password each time, you'll need TweakUI (see Appendix D); choose Autologon from the Logon category and type your username and password into the fields provided.

- If you have multiple users configured and switch between them frequently, you might appreciate the Fast User Switcher (see Appendix D).

- Go to Control Panel → [Performance and Maintenance] → System → Advanced tab and click Settings in the User Profiles section to view additional information about active user accounts. See "System Properties," earlier in this chapter, for details.

- If you have only a single Administrator account, it's called something other than "Administrator," and you try to create another account, a bug in the User Accounts program causes it to think there is currently no Administrator and it will only allow you to create a new Administrator account.

See Also

"Control Panel"

Utility Manager *\windows\system32\utilman.exe*

Manage the various accessibility tools that come with Windows XP.

To Open   Windows logo key + U
Start → Programs → Accessories → Accessibility → Utility Manager
Command Prompt → `utilman /start`

Description

The Utility Manager application allows you to control the Magnifier, Narrator, and On-Screen Keyboard—all of which are discussed earlier this chapter—from one central location (see Figure 4-101). Use the Utility Manager to start or stop the accessibility tools, or configure Windows to start any or all of them automatically when you log in, when you lock your Desktop, or when the Utility Manager starts.

Figure 4-101. Use the Utility Manager to control Magnifier, Narrator, and On-Screen Keyboard from a single window

Notes

- As the warning states the first time you try to open Utility Manager from the Start menu, some features will be disabled if it is not started using the keyboard hotkey (Windows logo key + U).

- If you have an older keyboard that does not have a Windows logo key on it, and if you must start Utility Manager from the Start menu or command line, you won't be able to set the automatic starting of accessibility tools from within Utility Manager.

See Also

"Microsoft Magnifier," "Narrator," "On-Screen Keyboard"

Volume Control   \windows\system32\sndvol32.exe

Control the master volume, volume level, and the balance of the system's sound devices.

To Open   Start → Programs → Accessories → Entertainment → Volume Control
                Tray → Double-click yellow speaker icon (if it's there)
                Command Prompt → sndvol32

Description

Volume Control displays volume and balance adjustments for all of the different sound devices, such as the audio CD volume, microphone volume, and line-in volume. To choose the controls that are shown, or to hide those you never use, go to Options

→ Properties and select any of the following (note that different sound drivers may omit some of these, or add additional entries):

Volume Control
This is the master volume control—the same control that pops up when you single-click the volume icon in the System Tray (see Figure 4-102).

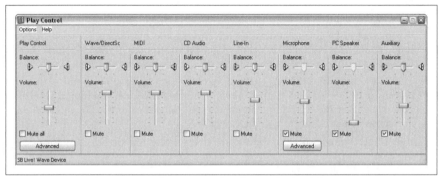

Figure 4-102. Configure your Volume Control to show only the sliders your use

Wave
Sound generated by Windows, including MP3 players, Windows Media Player, most games, Sound Recorder, and many other applications.

MIDI
Synthesized music generated by your sound card's MIDI synthesizer or wavetable feature.

CD Audio
Control the volume of audio CDs played with CD player applications. Note that your CD drive must be connected directly to your sound card with a special three-conductor audio cable.

Line In
Control the volume of the Line-In or Aux input of your sound card, often used to record audio from an external device, such as a stereo.

Microphone
Control the volume of the microphone input of your sound card, usually used with a microphone or voice dictation headset.

PC Speaker
Control for the system's built-in speaker, which is the only control not directly affiliated with your sound card (in most cases).

Alternatively, choose Recording in the "Adjust volume for" section to show and adjust volume controls for the recording of audio. All available controls are the same as those described above, except "Recording Control," which is the recording counterpart to the master volume control.

Notes

- Also in the Properties dialog, you'll be able to choose the mixer device if you have more than one sound card or other sound hardware (such as a voice modem or video capture card). If you wish to use more than one sound device simultaneously, your best bet is to connect the outputs of all your sound devices (except one) to the line-in (or auxilary) inputs of your primary sound card.

- Click Advanced in the main Volume Control window to adjust the bass and treble settings. When recording, you can also enable the microphone gain control.

- To turn on or off the volume control on the Taskbar, go to Control Panel → [Sounds, Speech, and Audio Devices] → Sounds and Audio Devices → Volume tab and turn on the "Place volume icon in the Taskbar" option.

- If you want to be able to control both recording and playback volume at the same time, launch two instances of Volume Control and choose Options → Properties → Recording for one, and Options → Properties → Playback for the other.

- The most common problem encountered while trying to play sound is that the particular device is either turned down or muted. Likewise, a common recording problem is that the recording volume is turned down or muted (or the requested device isn't enabled in the Volume Control).

- If you find that any or all of the volume controls are too sensitive, try turning up the external volume knob on your speakers or amplifier (if available); this effectively gives Volume Control a broader range.

See Also

"Sound Recorder," "Windows Media Player"

Windows Explorer   *\windows\explorer.exe*

The default Windows interface, including the Start menu, the Desktop, the Taskbar, the Search tool, the Windows Explorer window, and all folder windows.

To Open   Start → Programs → Accessories → Windows Explorer
              Command Prompt → explorer
              Double-click My Computer or any folder icon on the Desktop or in any
                folder window

Usage   explorer.exe [/n] [/e] [,/root,*object*] [[/select],*subobject*]

Description

The Explorer is the default Windows shell (see Figure 4-103). It creates the Desktop, Taskbar, and the Start menu the first time it is run. Running it thereafter (without any command-line parameters) opens a two-paned window (commonly referred to simply as "Explorer") in which you can navigate through all of the files, folders, and other resources on your computer.

See Chapter 2 for basic navigation and file management principles and Chapter 3 for discussions of the visual elements.

Explorer accepts the following command-line options (note the mandatory commas):

/n

Forces Explorer to open a new window (even if the specified folder is already open somewhere).

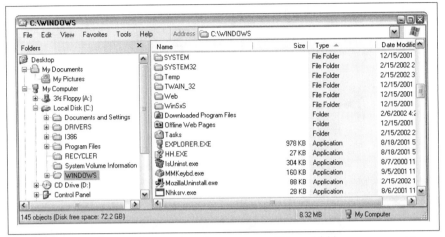

Figure 4-103. Windows Explorer is the primary means of file and folder management in Windows XP

/e

Instructs Explorer to display the Folders Explorer Bar (commonly known as the tree) rather than the default single-folder view. In most cases, you'll want to use /n and /e together.

[/select],*subobject*

Include *subobject* to specify the file or folder to be initially highlighted or expanded when the folder is opened. If *subobject* is a folder, it will be expanded in the tree. If you also include the /select parameter (not valid without *subobject*), the parent of the specified folder is highlighted on the tree, no branches are initially expanded, and *subobject* will be highlighted in the right pane.

,/root,*object*

By default, Explorer opens with the Desktop as the root folder. Use ,/root,*object* to specify a different root. The *object* parameter can be a folder name or a class ID (see Chapter 7).

For example, if you want Explorer to open to the My Computer folder so that no drive branches are initially expanded (handy if you have several drives), type the following:

```
explorer.exe /n, /e, /select, c:\
```

To open an Explorer window rooted at the My Documents folder, type:

```
explorer.exe /e,/root,c:\Documents and Settings\{user}\My Document where
{user} is the username of the owner of the My Documents folder.
```

CD burning

Windows XP is the first version of Windows to include support for CD writers built into the operating system (or more specifically, into Windows Explorer and Windows Media Player) (see Figure 4-104). It's quite easy to use, but it doesn't offer the flexibility of most third-party CD burning applications.

If you have a CD recorder, follow these steps:

1. Open Explorer, right-click on the drive icon for your CD recorder, and select Properties.

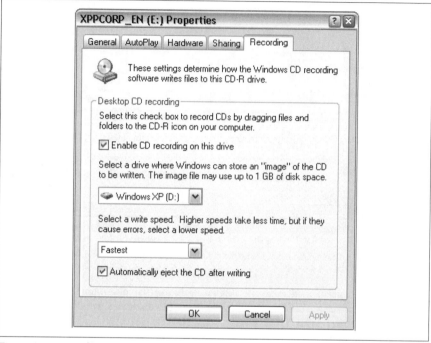

Figure 4-104. Configure Windows XP's built-in support for CD writers with the Properties window for your CD recorder

2. Choose the Recording tab and make sure the "Enable CD recording on this drive" option is turned on. Set any other options here as desired and click OK.

3. Drag-drop files onto the drive as though it were just another hard disk. You can even create folders and rearrange files by dragging and dropping.

4. When you're done, right-click the drive icon (or the Files Ready to Be Written to the CD note above the file listing) and select Write these files to CD.

5. The CD Writing Wizard appears (see Figure 4-105), which allows you to specify a label for the disk (a task that is unavailable elsewhere). Follow the instructions here to complete the process.

This procedure will write data CDs that can be read by nearly all CD drives, regardless of the operating system. See "Windows Media Player," later in this chapter, for details on making audio CDs.

Notes

- Press Ctrl-F or F3 in any open folder or Explorer window to begin a file search from that location. If the folder tree is shown, it will be replaced with the search pane.

- Most options for Explorer are located in Folder Options, which is accessible through Explorer's Tools menu or through Control Panel. The options are documented in Chapter 5.

- The built-in CD burning feature might interfere with some third-party CD recording applications. If you have trouble getting your CD recording software to

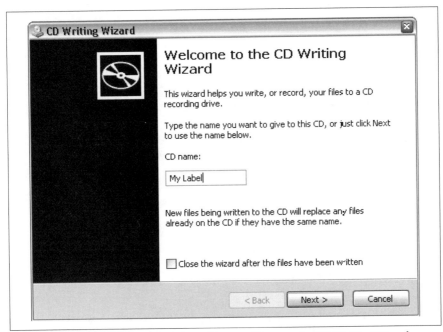

Figure 4-105. When you're ready to burn files to a CD, open the CD Writing Wizard

work with Windows XP, check with the manufacturer of the software (and possibly the drive) for updates.

See Also
"Internet Explorer," "Folder Options," Chapter 2, Chapter 3 (specifically, "Shortcuts" and "Start Menu")

Windows File Checker
\windows\system32\sfc.exe

Verify the existence and integrity of some Windows files.

To Open   Command Prompt → sfc

Usage   sfc [/scannow] [/scanonce] [/scanboot] [/revert]
                [/purgecache] [/cachesize=x]

Description
Windows File Checker scans your system for corrupt, changed, or missing files, as long as those files are specified in a predetermined list of important system files. By default, Windows File Checker automatically scans your system every time Windows is started. Use the Windows File Checker utility to perform a manual scan or change the automatic settings. The Windows File Checker takes the following options:

/scannow
    Performs an immediate scan of all protected system files.

/scanonce

Instructs Windows to scan all protected system files the next time Windows is started.

/scanboot

Instructs Windows to scan all protected system files every time Windows is started.

/revert

Returns Windows File Checker settings to their defaults.

/purgecache

Purges the file cache; essentially empties a folder on your hard disk devoted to storing backup copies of protected system files.

/cachesize=x

Sets the amount of hard disk space to allocate to the file cache folder.

Windows Help System

\windows\winhlp32.exe; winhelp.exe; hh.exe

Online Help system and viewer of WinHelp and HTML files.

To Open   Start → Help and Support
Explorer → Help → Help and Support Center
Select Help or press F1 in nearly any application
Double-click any *.hlp* or *.chm* file.
Command Prompt → helpctr (Help and Support Center)
Command Prompt → winhlp32 (*.hlp* file viewer)
Command Prompt → hh (*.chm* file viewer)
Command Prompt → help (command prompt help)

Description

The Windows Help System is actually a collection of utilities and viewers that provide help in Windows XP. The first, Help and Support Center (accessible through the Start menu), is a distinct application and is documented earlier in this chapter. Most other applications, including many of the components discussed in this chapter, use one of the following two help formats:

.hlp

The traditional help file format, introduced in Windows 3.0. Old applications, and even some new ones, use this format for online documentation. Help pages look and feel somewhat like Web pages, with hyperlinks and embedded graphics. However, *.hlp* files are somewhat limited compared with HTML Help files, discussed below.

.chm

HTML Help is a newer format, introduced originally in Windows 98 and supported on any Windows system running Internet Explorer 3.0 or later. HTML Help-based files are actually collections of web pages (*.html*) that have been compiled into a single *.chm* package. HTML Help does everything that *.hlp* files do, add support for Web links (linked pages are even displayed right in the help window), and have shortcuts to individual pages (see Figure 4-106).

To create a shortcut to an individual page in a HTML Help file, right-click on the link to the page, drag-drop the link onto your Desktop, or right-click on an empty area of the page and select Properties. The URL syntax for this is:

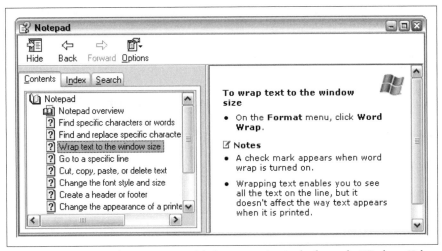

Figure 4-106. Most applications come with documentation in the form of a Windows Help or HTML Help document

> mk:@MSITStore: .chm file location ::/.htm page name

Notes

- *Help.exe*, the command prompt help, is documented in Appendix C.
- For more information about HTML Help, see *http://msdn.microsoft.com/ workshop/author/htmlhelp/*.

See Also

"Help and Support Center"

Windows IP Configuration

\windows\system32\ipconfig.exe

Display the current IP address(es) of the active connection(s).

To Open   Command Prompt → ipconfig

Usage   ipconfig [*/command*] [*adapter*]

Description

The Windows IP Configuration tool, used without any options, displays your computer's current IP address, subnet mask, and default gateway. Knowing your computer's IP address is important for many reasons, such as allowing other users to connect to you using Remote Desktop Connection or calling you with Microsoft NetMeeting.

Windows IP Configuration takes the following parameters:

adapter

Used with some of the commands listed below, *adapter* specifies the name of a network connection (see "Network Connections," earlier in this chapter) on

Applications and Tools

which to act. *Adapter* can contain wildcards, such as *. Omit *adapter* (if allowed) to act on the default connection.

`/all`

Displays all available configuration information.

`/release [adapter]`

Releases the IP address(es) for the specified connection, effectively disconnecting that connection from all network communication. Use `/renew` to re-establish communication.

`/renew [adapter]`

Renews the IP address for the specified adapter, effectively reestablishing communication for the connection.

`/flushdns`

Purges the DNS Resolver cache. See "NSLookup," discussed earlier in this chapter, for details. See see `/displaydns` to show the contents of the DNS cache.

`/registerdns`

Refreshes all DHCP leases and reregisters DNS names

`/displaydns`

Displays the contents of the DNS Resolver Cache (see `/flushdns`).

`/showclassid adapter`

Displays all the DHCP class IDs allowed for *adapter*.

`/setclassid adapter [classid]`

Modifies the DHCP class id for *adapter*.

Notes

- The IP address of any given network connection is also shown in the connection's Status window, viewed by double-clicking the connection in the Network Connections window. See "Network Connections," earlier in this chapter, for details.

- Figure 4-1, at the beginning of this chapter, shows an example of how the Windows IP Configuration utility is used in the Command Prompt window.

Windows Media Player

\program files\windows media player\wmplayer.exe;
\windows\system32\mplay32.exe

Play back video and audio media files, such as *.mpg* movies, *.mp3* songs, audio CD tracks, and *.asf* streaming media.

To Open Start → Programs → Accessories → Entertainment → Windows Media Player
Double-click on any associated media file
Command Prompt → `wmplayer` (version 8)
Command Prompt → `mplay32` (version 5)

Description

Windows Media Player is the default application used to open and play most of the types of video and audio media supported by Windows XP (see Figure 4-107). Although you can open Windows Media Player from the Start menu, it makes the

---

most sense to simply double-click on a supported media file or click on a link in a web page to open that video or audio clip and play it.

Figure 4-107. Windows Media Player is used to play video and audio clips

Windows XP actually comes with two different versions of the media player. The main application, Windows Media Player 8 (*wmplayer.exe*) is the default for all supported media file types, and is the one that is launched from the Start menu. Windows Media Player 5 (mplay32.exe) has a far more modest interface and even supports multiple instances (two or more videos playing at once), but uses the same media player subsystem, so its support for all the different media formats is identical to Windows Media Player 8. Try both to see which one you like better.

The rest of the Windows Media Player (either version) is fairly straightforward, with the standard VCR-like controls (e.g., Play, Stop, etc.).

Windows Media Player 8 supports several additional "gee whiz" features, such as visualizations, which are graphical displays that react to audio. In addition to the visualization *plug-ins.com* with Windows Media Player 8, you can download additional plug-ins for all sorts of visual effects. Also supported are "skins," which are used to make Windows Media Player look more exotic or interesting. Like visualizations, additional skins can be downloaded and installed (see Figure 4-108).

The Radio Tuner in Windows Media Player 8 allows you to listen to radio broadcasts over the Web. Although no special radio hardware is required, a fast Internet connection certainly helps.

CD burning

Windows XP is the first version of Windows to include support for CD writers built-into the operating system (or more specifically, into Windows Media Player and Windows Explorer). The interface is a little awkward, and it doesn't offer the flexibility of most third-party CD burning applications, but it works.

If you have a CD recorder, follow these steps:

1. Open Explorer, right-click on the drive icon for your CD recorder, and select Properties.

Figure 4-108. Lots of "skins" help you dress up the Windows Media Player window

2. Choose the Recording tab and make sure the "Enable CD recording on this drive" option is turned on. Set any other options here as desired and click OK.

3. Open the Windows Media Player and go to View → Taskbar → Media Library.

4. In the tree on the left, navigate to Media Library → Audio → All Audio (if you're not already there).

5. Drag-drop any *.mp3* or *.wav* files into this window in the desired order. Songs can't be rearranged here, but they can be after the next step.

6. When you're done, click the "Copy to CD or Device" button on the left (or go to Media Library → Audio → Copy to CD or Device) (see Figure 4-109).

7. The songs to be written to the CD are shown on the left, and the songs already on the CD (if any) are shown on the right. The songs in the playlist can be reorganized by right-clicking and selecting Move Up or Move Down.

8. When you're ready, click the Copy Music button in the upper right. Any *.mp3* files are temporarily converted to *.wav* format, and then all tracks are written to the CD.

This procedure will write audio CDs that can be played by nearly all CD players (with the exception of some older DVD drives). See "Windows Explorer," earlier in this chapter, for details on making data CDs.

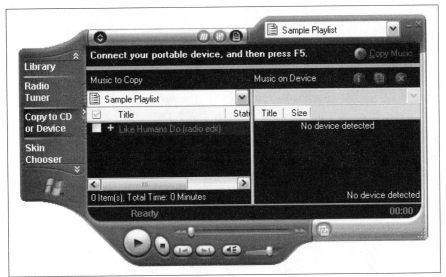

Figure 4-109. Use Windows Media Player's built-in support for CD writers to burn your own music CDs

Notes

- Although it doesn't come with many of the goodies found in the newer version, Windows Media Player 5 is much simpler to use, loads faster, and takes up less screen real estate.

- If you encounter a video or audio file that Windows Media Player doesn't understand, you can usually add support for it by downloading the appropriate codec (compression/decompression driver). Right-click on the media file, select Properties, and choose the Summary tab to view the name of the required codec (if available). Then, use an Internet search engine (such as *http://www.google.com*) to locate the codec installer.

- Use the Windows Update feature, discussed later in this chapter, to install the latest drivers, codecs, and updates to the Windows Media Player.

- The CD Player application found in earlier versions of Windows has been removed in Windows XP, and the Windows Media Player has assumed its role in playing audio CDs. To play an audio CD or DVD, just put it in the drive. If a disk is already inserted, you can eject it and reinsert it, or start Windows Media Player and go to Play → DVD or CD Audio.

- To choose the program that plays audio CDs automatically when they're inserted (or to disable autoplay entirely), right-click on your CD drive icon in Explorer, select Properties, and choose the AutoPlay tab. Choose Music CD from the list and choose the desired action below.

Windows Messenge

\program files\messenger\msmsgs.exe

Maintain an open connection with a directory server, allowing others to contact you.

To Open   Start → Programs → Windows Messenger
                Command Prompt → msmsgs

Description

Windows Messenger allows users to send each other quick text messages over the Internet by maintaining an open connection to a central directory server (see Figure 4-110). That server links a user's "screen name" with their IP address (which can change every time that user connects to the Internet). The IP address is necessary for establishing direct communication between two computers, such as when using Microsoft's NetMeeting or Remote Desktop Connection.

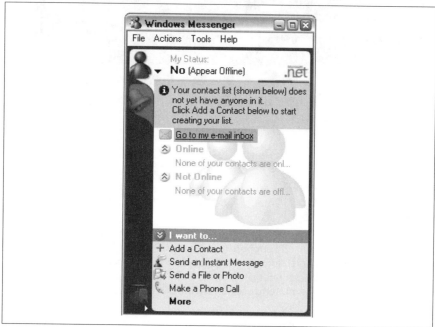

Figure 4-110. Windows Messenger lets you send text messages to other Windows Messenger users on the Internet

Windows Messenger is similar to AOL Instant Messenger and Yahoo Messenger. Although they're similar, they're all totally incompatible, so it would not be unusual to see two or three of them running simultaneously on the same machine.

The first time you start Windows Messenger, you are given the opportunity to sign in. If you already have an account at one of Microsoft's online services (such as Hotmail or MSN), you can use that same login here.

When you're signed in, other users only need to know your screen name to send you an instant message, invite you to connect to their computer, or play an online game (see "MSN Gaming Zone," earlier in this chapter).

Notes

- Windows Messenger, by default, is started every time Windows is started, regardless of whether or not you use it or even have an account. To disable Windows Messenger, use the Registry Editor (see Chapter 7) and remove the corresponding entry from HKEY_LOCAL_MACHINE\SOFTWARE\Microsoft\Windows\CurrentVersion\Run. You can also use the Start tab of the System Configuration Utility, discussed earlier in this chapter.

- In order to use Windows Messenger or MSN Explorer, you'll need to set up a Microsoft .NET Passport account. There has been some confusion regarding Passport among many users, however. A Passport account is absolutely not required for any other features of Windows; in fact, Microsoft has been widely criticized for making it appear otherwise.

See Also

"Remote Assistance," "Microsoft Chat," "Microsoft NetMeeting"

Windows Movie Maker
\program files\movie maker\moviemk.exe

Capture, edit, and convert video clips.

To Open   Start → Programs → Accessories → Windows Movie Maker
Command Prompt → moviemk

Description

A new feature in Windows XP, the Windows Movie Maker allows you to edit and convert video clips, and if you have video capture hardware or a digital video camera, you can even create your own video clips (see Figure 4-111). Windows Movie Maker (and most video editing software) can be quite complex, so we will only include an introduction here.

Video editors don't work like most other applications. Instead of opening files, making changes to them, and then saving them, a typical video editing session works something like this:

1. Start a new project by going to File → New → Project.

2. Add one or more existing video files to the project by going to File → Import. Windows Movie Maker supports many different video formats (see Notes). If necessary, Windows Movie Maker may need to prepare the clips for editing, which may take several minutes.

3. All imported videos are then shown in the Collections pane; click a video filename to display "clips," arbitrary divisions in the file intended to make it easier to work with (see Notes, below). Depending on the length of the video, it might be divided into one or dozens of clips .

4. Next comes the fun part: editing consists of cutting apart your video and splicing other portions or even other videos together to make a single movie.

   The actual video project consists of clips inserted into the timeline (shown at the bottom of the window), not those simply listed in the Collections pane. The timeline is like a storyboard, showing what the final video output will look like in a

Figure 4-111. The new Windows Movie Maker lets you edit video clips

long a linear display. To add a clip to the timeline, drag it from the Collections pane and drop it at the desired location.

5. Using the magnify controls to the left of the timeline, you can zoom in for more precise work or zoom out to see more of the timeline at once.

Above the magnify controls is the storyboard/timeline button: click it to switch between the default Storyboard view (where each clip is the same size) and the more sophisticated Timeline view (where clips are sized relative to their duration). I find the Timeline (the view with the numbers across the top) to be much more intuitive and easier to use, as it shows a more accurate view of the project and allows more precise control when splitting. You can also select the desired view with View → Storyboard and → Timeline.

6. The video preview, shown in the upper right, allows you to view the video project as it will appear when you're done. Click the Play button, or simply drag your mouse across the timeline to view any portion of the video project.

When you reach a point in your video when you'd like to cut out footage or insert additional footage, go to Clip → Split (or press Ctrl+Shift+S) to break apart the current video clip into two discrete clips. Once you've split a clip, you can delete a segment by highlighting it and pressing Del, or drag-drop a segment of video from another part of the timeline (or even another video) from Collections into the timeline.

7. Once you're happy with the video constructed in the timeline, go to File → Save Project. Note that this only saves the project, it doesn't actually create the final video.

8. Use File → Save Movie to create a new video file based on your work in the timeline. No changes to any of the source videos are made. Saving a movie file can take a long time, so you probably will not want to take this step until you're happy with your editing. If you save your project (see the previous step), you can close Windows Movie Maker and then open it up again later and resume your work; it's not necessary to save the movie each time.

Notes

- Windows Movie Maker supports a variety of video formats, allowing you to import videos from a number of different sources into your projects. Among the supported formats are *.asf*, *.avi*, *.wmv*, *.mpg* movies, *.wav* and *.snd* audio files, and *.bmp*, *.jpg*, and *.gif* still image files (see below). Windows Movie Maker is currently the only video editor in existence that can read *.asf* streaming video files. Previously, Microsoft would not allow any other application to read these files. Even if you prefer not to use Windows Movie Maker to edit your video, it is a great tool for converting *.asf* files into a more usable format.

- You can also insert still image files into your videos—not only to have a portion of still videos, but to combine a series of video stills into a crude motion video. This is useful, for example, with some still digital cameras that can shoot short video clips, yet store the clips as a series of still images.

- By default, Windows Movie Maker divides imported videos into discrete "clips." Theoretically, one clip ends and another clip begins when the scene changes dramatically. For instance, if the video is of two people talking and the camera alternates between the two participants, each head shot would be its own clip. However, in practice, the clip-making process ends up being completely arbitrary; sometimes you'll only get one clip, and other times, clips will begin and end in the middle of scenes. Go to View → Options and turn off the "Automatically create clips" option to disable this feature. Not only will Windows Movie Maker import video files much more quickly when clips aren't used, but you'll be able to choose where cuts occur (which is really the whole point of the program).

- Imported items added to My Collections are common to all Windows Movie Maker projects and act somewhat like an ordinary folder full of shortcuts. Note that when you delete items from My Collections, it does not affect the original source files.

- Almost immediately after the initial release of Windows XP, an update to Windows Movie Maker was made available (see "Windows Update," later in this chapter) that upgraded it to Version 1.2 and fixed several bugs. It is recommended that everyone obtain this patch.

Windows Picture and Fax Viewer

Simple image viewer, capable of displaying *.bmp*, *.emf*, *.gif*, *.jpeg*, *.png*, *.tif*, and *.wmf* files.

To Open   Double-click any *.emf*, *.gif*, *.jpeg*, *.bmp*, *.png*, or *.tif* file

Usage   rundll32 C:\WINDOWS\System32\shimgvw.dll,ImageView_Fullscreen
            filename

Description

The Windows Picture and Fax Viewer isn't a standalone application in the traditional sense, but rather a simple viewer window. When Windows XP is first installed, it is the default viewer for the following file types:

.emf
> Enhanced Meta File

.gif
> Compuserve Graphics Interchange Format

.jpeg
> Joint Photographic Experts Group

.bmp
> Windows Bitmap

.png
> Portable Network Graphics

.tif
> Tagged Image File Format

.wmf
> Windows Meta File

 An unfortunate design in the Windows Picture and Fax Viewer becomes evident when you use the File Types dialog (see "Folder Options," earlier in this chapter) to try to change the default application for any of the above image file formats. The Windows Picture and Fax Viewer will still be opened when you double-click on any image file. Furthermore, the only way to fix this is to edit your Registry. To do this, open the Registry Editor (described in Chapter 8), navigate to HKEY_CLASSES_ROOT\ SystemFileAssociations\ image\ ShellEx\ ContextMenuHandlers, and delete the ShellImagePreview key entirely. Close the Registry Editor when you're done; the change will take effect immediately.

Notes

The Windows Picture and Fax Viewer is really a poor image viewer; just about any substitute would be preferred. For a better image viewer, try ACDSee-32 (*http://www. acdsee.com/*) or Paint Shop Pro (*http://www.jasc.com/*). You could even associate image files with Internet Explorer (or another web browser), or even Paint.

See Also

"Paint," "Fax Console"

Windows Script Host   *\windows\system32\wscript.exe; cscript.exe*

Runs WSH scripts.

To Open   Command Prompt → `wscript`
                Command Prompt → `cscript`

Usage   `wscript filename [options] [arguments]`
                `cscript filename [options] [arguments]`

Description

The Windows Script Host runs WSH script files you create and edit. Of the two executables, *wscript.exe* is used to run Windows-based scripts, and *cscript.exe* is for running command-prompt based scripts. For more information on the Windows Script Host, see Chapter 8.

Both executables take the following options (note the use of double slashes to distinguish them from ordinary arguments passed onto the script):

`//b`

> Batch mode: suppresses script errors and prompts from displaying.

`//d`

> Enables active debugging.

`//e:engine`

> Uses *engine* for executing the script; the default depends on the filename extension of the script file.

`//h:cscript`

> Changes the default script host to *cscript.exe*, the command-prompt-based host.

`//h:wscript`

> Changes the default script host to *wscript.exe*, the Windows-based host (the default).

`//job:xxxx`

> Executes a WSF job.

`//nologo`

> Prevents the display of the banner logo at execution time.

`//s`

> Saves current command line options as the default for this user.

`//t:nn`

> Timeout in seconds: the maximum time a script is permitted to run.

`//x`

> Executes script in debugger.

`//u`

> Uses Unicode for redirected I/O from the console.

Windows Update   *\windows\system32\wupdmgr.exe*

Use Internet Explorer to download updates to Windows XP over the Internet.

To Open   Start → Windows Update
                Internet Explorer → Tools menu → Windows Update
                Internet Explorer → open *http://www.windowsupdate.com*
                Command Prompt → `wupdmgr`

Description

The Windows Update feature allows Microsoft to make updates to Windows XP available publicly. It also allows Windows XP users to download and install those updates quickly and easily.

When you open the Windows Update site in Internet Explorer, it looks like any other web site on the surface. In addition to links to other portions of the Microsoft web site, including a similar Office Update site, the main link of interest here is "Scan for updates." When you initiate the scan, Internet Explorer retrieves a list of all available updates from the Microsoft web site, and then compares it to a list of already-installed updates. Any new updates are shown in the window, from which you can select items to download and install (see Figure 4-112).

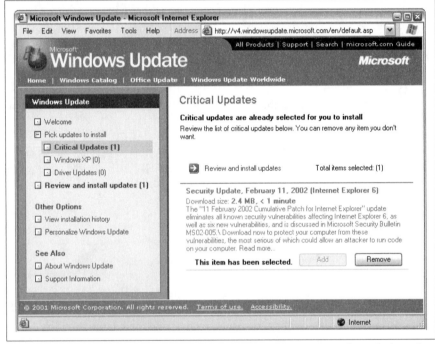

Figure 4-112. Use the Windows Update tool frequently to make sure you have the latest bug fixes and security patches

There are three categories of updates: Critical Updates, which are typically new versions of shared files that fix problems and patch security holes; Critical Updates typically don't contain newer versions of software, so it's generally safe to install them. The Windows XP category contains new versions of some of the components discussed in this chapter, such as Internet Explorer and Windows Media Player, and are typically considered optional. The last category, Driver Updates, compares your installed drivers with the ones that Microsoft has on file (see Notes).

Windows XP also has an automatic update feature, where the Windows Update site is routinely checked for critical updates; if any are found, they are automatically downloaded and installed. To change your preferences regarding automatic updates, go to Control Panel → [Performance and Maintenance] → System → Automatic Updates tab.

Notes

- Windows Update requires Internet Explorer, and unfortunately will not work with any other web browser.

- By default, updates are installed only on the computer accessing the site. However, if you have a slow connection or have several computers to update, you may wish to "package" the updates so that they can be repeatedly installed without being repeatedly downloaded. Click About Windows Update for more information.

- One of the features in Windows Update is its ability to update some of the hardware drivers in your system (the Driver Updates category). This category is unlike the others, as these updates may or may not be applicable. In fact, Windows Update often recommends that you update a driver when, in fact, the driver is totally wrong for your system. Your best bet here is to update drivers only for Microsoft products, such as their mice and game controllers. Drivers for all other products should be downloaded from the manufacturer's web site. Naturally, if you see an update available here, it's only prudent to check with the manufacturer see if a new driver is indeed available; but don't be alarmed if there's a new driver available at Windows Update, but not on your manufacturer's web site.

- Updates to Windows can be numerous and time consuming to download, especially over a slow connection. If you have several computers, you may find it handy to download the updates once and then install them manually on all your systems. You can also put the updates on a CD so that Windows machines without Internet connections can be updated as well. On the Windows Update site, click the "Personalize Windows Update" link under "Other Options," turn on the "Display the link to the Windows Update Catalog under See Also" option, and then click Save Settings. Then click "Windows Update Catalog" to view the listing of downloadable updates and any applicable instructions. You can also go to *http://corporate.windowsupdate.microsoft.com/*.

- If you've used Windows Update before, you can click View installation history to see a list of the previously installed updates.

See Also

"Internet Explorer"

WordPad   *\program files\windows nt\wordpad.exe*

A simple word processor.

To Open   Start → Programs → Accessories → WordPad
                Command Prompt → wordpad

Description

Although WordPad lacks many of the features that come with full-blown word processors such as Wordperfect or Microsoft Word, it has enough features to create and edit rich-text documents. WordPad is the default editor for *.rtf*, *.doc*, and *.wri* files (unless Microsoft Word is installed). WordPad can also be used to edit plain text files (*.txt*),

Applications and Tools

although Notepad (discussed earlier this chapter) is the default and is more appropriate for this task (see Figure 4-113).

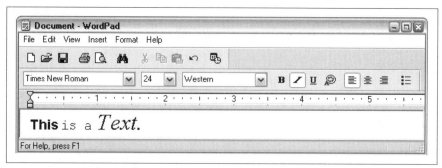

Figure 4-113. Wordpad is the rudimentary word processor that comes with Windows XP

Depending on the type of file opened, WordPad may or may not display its formatting toolbar and ruler. When you use File → New, WordPad prompts you to choose a document type, including "Rich Text Document" (formatted text, such as word processor documents), "Text Document" document (plain ASCII text), and "Unicode Text Document" (plain text using the Unicode character set). Once a file is open, however, you can turn on or off the formatting bar and ruler and even apply formatting to plain text documents. If you try to save a text document with formatting, though, WordPad will warn you that your formatting will be lost (since text files don't support formatting).

WordPad has several advantages over the simpler Notepad application. Among other things, WordPad lets you choose from a wide selection of fonts and font sizes, use colors in your documents, set tab stops, use rulers, and even insert objects (e.g., images, some clips, etc.). Although not a full-featured word processor, WordPad does enough to create simple formatted documents that can then be printed, emailed, or faxed.

Notes

- You can open Microsoft Word documents with WordPad, but you might lose some formatting if you save the file (which will prompt WordPad to warn you).

- Beware of the following when dragging a file onto WordPad: be sure to drop the file icon onto the WordPad titlebar if you want to view it or edit it, or drop it onto the middle of the document if you want to embed the icon as an object into the currently open document.

- To prevent WordPad from overwriting your file extensions and adding its own when you save a file, place quotation marks around the name of the file you want to save (e.g., "read.me") and click Save. Otherwise, you'll get *read.me.doc*

- Like Notepad, WordPad does not allow you to open more than one document at a time. If you want to view multiple WordPad documents simultaneously, you'll need to open multiple instances of the WordPad application.

See Also

"Notepad"

5

Task and Setting Index

After a quick assessment of Windows XP, it should become apparent that there are literally hundreds of settings, features, and displays of information. Finding all these items in the interface can sometimes be a challenge.

In Chapter 4, all of the components of Windows XP were listed alphabetically. This chapter provides the other end of the spectrum; a comprehensive listing of settings and tasks that can be performed with the components described in Chapter 4, but sorted alphabetically by their function rather than by their location in the operating system interface. The following index contains nearly 700 entries, all of which are accessible with components listed in Chapter 4. Headings show major functional groupings (like "Accessibility" or "Cookies") interspersed with purely alphabetical headings (like "Br-Ca") that group miscellaneous entries up until the next functional grouping.

Note that Registry settings (see Chapter 8) are typically not included here, not only because of their complexity and relative obscurity, but because most of the more common settings have corresponding options in the interface that, of course, are listed here. The remaining Registry "goodies" are introduced in Chapter 8 and are documented more fully in a reference like *Windows XP Annoyances* (forthcoming from O'Reilly).

Under certain circumstances, the contents of the Control Panel are divided into categories. For the sake of simplicity and brevity, these categories have been omitted in this chapter. See "Control Panel" in Chapter 4.

Accessibility

A collection of settings and features designed to make Windows XP easier to use for those with visual, hearing, and physical impairments. See Figure 5-1.

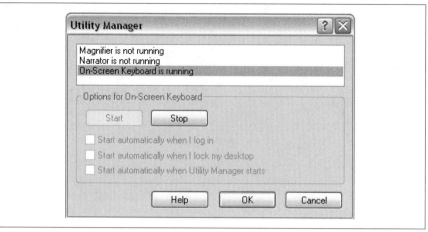

Figure 5-1. The Utility Manager lets you control several accessibility features from one window

Accessibility, additional settings for web pages
> Control Panel → Internet Options → General tab → Accessibility

Accessibility, enable / disable warnings and notifications
> Control Panel → Accessibility Options → General tab

Accessibility, magnify a portion of the screen
> See "Microsoft Magnifier" in Chapter 4.

Accessibility, make Alt Key "sticky"
> Control Panel → Accessibility Options → Keyboard tab → Use StickyKeys

Accessibility, manage startup options
> See "Utility Manager" in Chapter 4.

Accessibility, move Magnifier with focus change in web pages
> Control Panel → Internet Options → Advanced tag → Accessibility → Move system caret with focus/selection changes

Accessibility, read screen text out loud
> See "Narrator" in Chapter 4.

Accessibility, type with the mouse
> See "On-Screen Keyboard" in Chapter 4.

Address Bar

A text field, available in Windows Explorer, Internet Explorer, and the Taskbar that allows you to type an address or folder name to open.

Address Bar, Go button
> See "Go button, show in Address Bar."

Address Bar, history settings
> Control Panel → Internet Options → General tab → History section

Address Bar, search settings
> Control Panel → Internet Options → Advanced tag → Search from the Address Bar

Address Bar, show in Explorer
> Explorer → View → Toolbars → Address Bar

Address Bar, show on Taskbar
> Right-click on empty area of Taskbar → Toolbars → Address

Address Bar, show the full path of current folder
> Control Panel → Folder Options → View tab → Display the full path in the Address Bar

Address Book, make the default contact list
> Control Panel → Internet Options → Programs tab → Contact list

Address Book, profile assistant (enable / disable)
> Control Panel → Internet Options → Advanced tag → Security → Enable Profile Assistant

Address Book, set default profile for AutoComplete
> Control Panel → Internet Options → Content tab → My Profile

Administrative Tools

A Start Menu folder providing links to several administrative programs, all of which are documented in Chapter 4.

Administrative Tools, show in Start menu (Classic Start menu only)
> Control Panel → Taskbar and Start Menu → Start Menu tab → Customize → "Advanced Start menu options" section → Display Administrative Tools

Administrative Tools, show in Start menu (XP Start menu only)
> Control Panel → Taskbar and Start Menu → Start Menu tab → Customize → Advanced tab → "Start menu items" section → System Administrative Tools

Advanced Power Management (APM)

The collection of power-saving features in Windows XP that work together with your APM-compatible hardware.

Advanced Power Management, additional settings
> Your computer's BIOS setup (typically accessible by pressing Del or F2 after turning on system but before beep—refer to your computer's documentation for details.)

Advanced Power Management, effect on offline files
> Explorer → Tools → Synchronize → Setup → On Idle tab → Advanced → Prevent synchronization when my computer is running on battery power

Advanced Power Management, effect on Scheduled Tasks
> Control Panel → Scheduled Tasks → right-click task → Properties → Settings tab → Power Management section

Advanced Power Management, enable/disable
> Control Panel → Power Options → APM tab → Enable Advanced Power Management support

Task and Setting Index

Animation

The animated movement of interface elements intended to make Windows XP more visually appealing (see Figure 5-2).

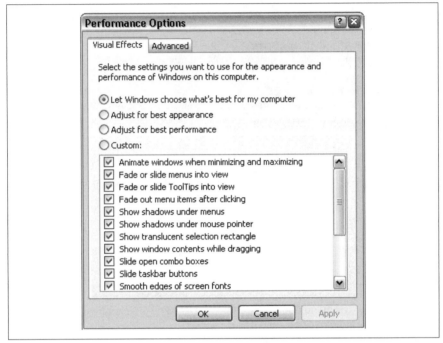

Figure 5-2. Some of the animation in Windows can be disabled to improve performance using the Performance Options dialog

Animation, enable / disable selectively
> Control Panel → System → Advanced tab → Performance section → Settings → Visual Effects tab → Custom

Animation, fading between web pages
> Control Panel → Internet Options → Advanced tag → Browsing → Enable page transitions

Animation, show animated GIFs in web pages
> Control Panel → Internet Options → Advanced tag → Multimedia → Play animations in web pages

Animation, smooth scrolling of web pages
> Control Panel → Internet Options → Advanced tag → Browsing → Use smooth scrolling

Applications

Settings and features that affect running applications.

Applications, ending
Task Manager (*taskmgr.exe*) → Applications tab

Applications, ending background processes
Task Manager (*taskmgr.exe*) → Processes tab

Applications, list loaded DLLs
System Information (*winmsd.exe*) → Software Environment → Loaded Modules

Applications, list running processes from command line
See "Query Process" in Chapter 4

Autocomplete

The "history" associated with various text boxes, where web addresses and other text are filled in automatically based on what you typed previously. See Figure 5-3.

Figure 5-3. Autocomplete lets you choose among the most frequently accessed web sites so you don't have to type them every time

AutoComplete, edit data
Control Panel → Internet Options → Content tab → My Profile

AutoComplete, enable / disable
Control Panel → Internet Options → Advanced tag → Browsing → Use inline AutoComplete

AutoComplete, Profile Assistant (enable / disable)
Control Panel → Internet Options → Advanced tag → Security → Enable Profile Assistant

AutoComplete, settings
Control Panel → Internet Options → Content tab → AutoComplete

Autodial

See "Dialing."

Task and
Setting Index

Automatic Windows Update

Automatically run Windows Update at regular intervals.

Automatic Windows Update settings
Control Panel → System → Automatic Updates tab

Background

The look of the Desktop, including wallpaper and colors. See also "Desktop."

Background, create and modify
Paint (*mspaint.exe*) → save as *.bmp* in Windows folder

Background, select and configure
Control Panel → Display → Desktop tab

Br-Ca

Browser, set default
Control Panel → Internet Options → Programs tab → Internet Explorer should check to see whether it is the default browser

Button color
Control Panel → Display → Appearance tab → Advanced → choose "3d Objects" from the "Item" list

Calendar, default application
Control Panel → Internet Options → Programs tab → Calendar

Calling
See "Dialing."

Cascading Style Sheets
See "Style sheets, impose a single style sheet for all web pages."

CD Drive

Settings that affect CD and DVD drives.

CD drive, autoplay enable / disable
Explorer → right-click CD drive icon → Properties → AutoPlay tab

CD drive, change drive letters
Disk Management (*diskmgmt.msc*); see "Microsoft Management Console" in Chapter 4.

Certificates

Used by Internet Explorer to verify the identity of secure web sites, certificates facilitate secure web transactions.

Certificates, check for revocation in Internet Explorer
Control Panel → Internet Options → Advanced tag → Security

Certificates, Internet Explorer settings for secure sites
Control Panel → Internet Options → Content tab → Certificates section

Certificates, manage
Certificates (*certmgr.msc*); see "Microsoft Management Console" in Chapter 4.

Certificates, warn about invalid certificates in Internet Explorer
Control Panel → Internet Options → Advanced tag → Security → Warn about invalid site certificates

Cl-Co

Clock, show on the Taskbar
Control Panel → Taskbar and Start Menu → Taskbar tab → Show the clock

Code page conversion table
Control Panel → Regional and Language Options → Advanced tab → Code page conversion tables

Color Profiles

Color profiles (*.icm* files) are used for color matching between scanners, cameras, monitors, and color printers.

Color profiles, associate with device
Right-click on *.icm* file → Properties → Associate Device tab

Color profiles, management
Control Panel → Display → Settings tab → Advanced → Color Management tab

Colors

Colors make Windows XP prettier or uglier, at your option.

Colors, change for all display elements
Control Panel → Display → Appearance tab → Advanced

Colors, in web pages
Control Panel → Internet Options → General tab → Colors

Colors, increase or decrease number of supported colors (color depth)
Control Panel → Display → Settings tab → Color Quality

Colors, show high contrast screen colors
Control Panel → Accessibility Options → Display tab → Use High Contrast

Com-Con

Combo boxes, enable / disable animation
Control Panel → System → Advanced tab → Performance section → Settings → Visual Effects tab → Custom

Compressed NTFS files, differentiate with a different color

Control Panel → Folder Options → View tab → Show encrypted or compressed NTFS files in color

Contact list, default

Control Panel → Internet Options → Programs tab → Contact list

Control Panel

These settings affect the way the Control Panel (discussed in Chapter 4) appears and the way its contents are accessed. The settings in the various Control Panel applets are documented throughout this chapter.

Control Panel, security policies

Group Policy (*gpedit.msc*) → User Configuration → Administrative Templates → Control Panel

Control Panel, show / hide categories

Control Panel → Tools → Options → General tab → Show common tasks in folders → OK → Switch to Classic View or Switch to Category View

Control Panel, show as menu in Start menu (Classic Start menu only)

Control Panel → Taskbar and Start Menu → Start Menu tab → Customize → "Advanced Start menu options" section → Expand Control Panel

Control Panel, show as menu in Start menu (XP Start menu only)

Control Panel → Taskbar and Start Menu → Start Menu tab → Customize → Advanced tab → "Start menu items" section → Control Panel

Control Panel, show in My Computer

Control Panel → Folder Options → View tab → Show Control Panel in My Computer

Cookies

Cookies are pieces of information used by Internet Explorer to store information for various web sites. Other browsers store cookies independently.

Cookies, change settings (block, allow, prompt)

Control Panel → Internet Options → Privacy tab → Advanced → Override automatic cookie handling

Cookies, change settings for specific web sites (block, allow, prompt)

Control Panel → Internet Options → Privacy tab → Edit

Cookies, delete all

Control Panel → Internet Options → General tab → Temporary Internet Files section → Delete Cookies

Country

Settings that allow Windows XP to conform to your Country's standards. See also "Language."

Country, choose for dialing preferences
Control Panel → Phone and Modem Options → Dialing Rules tab → select location → Edit → Country/region

Country, choose for localized information
Control Panel → Regional and Language Options → Regional Options tab → Location section

Cr-Da

Crashes, send reports to Microsoft
Control Panel → System → Advanced tab → Error Reporting

Critical Update Notification
Control Panel → System → Automatic Updates tab

Ctrl Key, make it "sticky"
Control Panel → Accessibility Options → Keyboard tab → Use StickyKeys

Ctrl-Alt-Del window, settings
Group Policy (*gpedit.msc*) → User Configuration → Administrative Templates → System → Ctrl+Alt+Del Options

Currency, customize display
Control Panel → Regional and Language Options → Regional Options tab → Customize → Currency tab

Cursor, mouse cursor
See "Mouse."

Cursor, text cursor
See "Text Cursor."

Date, customize display
Control Panel → Regional and Language Options → Regional Options tab → Customize → Date tab

Date, set
Control Panel → Date and Time → Date & Time tab

Daylight Savings, enable / disable
Control Panel → Date and Time → Time Zone tab

Desktop

The Desktop is the "window" that appears behind all other windows. The icons that appear on the Desktop are stored in *\Documents and Settings\[username]\Desktop*.

Desktop, color
Control Panel → Display → Desktop tab → Color

Control Panel → Display → Appearance tab → Advanced → choose "Desktop" from the "Item" list

Desktop, icons
See "Icons."

Desktop, refresh
Click on an empty portion of the Desktop → press F5

Desktop, restrict installation of items

Control Panel → Internet Options → Security tab → Custom Level

Desktop, security policies

Group Policy (*gpedit.msc*) → User Configuration → Administrative Templates → Desktop

Desktop, show contents without minimizing applications

Right-click on Taskbar → Toolbars → Show Desktop

Right-click on Taskbar → Toolbars → Show Open Windows (to restore)

(Also, you can simply open the Desktop folder in Explorer.)

Desktop Cleanup Wizard, enable / disable

Control Panel → Display → Desktop tab → Customize Desktop → General tab → Run Desktop Cleanup every 60 days

Desktop web pages, add / remove / hide

Control Panel → Display → Desktop tab → Customize Desktop → Web tab

Desktop web pages, allow moving and resizing

Control Panel → Display → Desktop tab → Customize Desktop → Web tab → Lock Desktop items

Desktop web pages, automatic download of linked pages

Control Panel → Display → Desktop tab → Customize Desktop → Web tab → select item → Properties → Download tab

Desktop web pages, automatic updates

Control Panel → Display → Desktop tab → Customize Desktop → Web tab → select item → Properties → Schedule tab

Desktop web pages, automatic updates (enable / disable)

Control Panel → Internet Options → Advanced tag → Browsing → Enable offline items to be synchronized on a schedule

---

Devices

See "Hardware."

Dialing

Settings relating to the initiation of a connection to the Internet with a modem over standard phone lines.

Dialing, area code settings

Control Panel → Phone and Modem Options → Dialing Rules tab → select location → Edit

Dialing, call waiting

Control Panel → Phone and Modem Options → Dialing Rules tab → select location → Edit → General tab → To disable call waiting...

Dialing, calling card

Control Panel → Phone and Modem Options → Dialing Rules tab → select location → Edit → Calling Card tab

---

Dialing, connect to the Internet when needed
Control Panel → Internet Options → Connection tab → Dial whenever / Always dial

Dialing, connect to the Internet when needed, depending on location
Control Panel → Network Connections → Advanced → Dial-Up Preferences

Dialing, default Internet connection
Control Panel → Internet Options → Connection tab → select connection → Set Default

Dialing, disconnect Internet connection when no longer needed
Control Panel → Internet Options → Connection tab → select connection → Settings

Dialing, operator-assisted dialing
Control Panel → Network Connections → Advanced → Operator-Assisted Dialing

Dig-Dis

Digital Camera, add as drive in Explorer (still camera only)
Control Panel → Scanners and Cameras → Add Device

Disconnect from Internet automatically
Control Panel → Internet Options → Connection tab → select connection → Settings

Display

Settings dealing with your monitor and video card (display adapter). See also "Desktop." A quick way to get to Control Panel → Display is to right-click on an empty area of the Desktop and select Properties.

Display, force restart after changing resolution or color depth
Control Panel → Display → Settings tab → Advanced → General tab → Compatibility section

Display, list all possible combinations of resolution and color depth
Control Panel → Display → Settings tab → Advanced → Adapter tab → List All Modes

Display, magnify portions
See "Microsoft Magnifier" in Chapter 4.

Display, refresh rate
Control Panel → Display → Settings tab → Advanced → Monitor tab → Screen refresh rate

Display, resolution
Control Panel → Display → Settings tab → Screen resolution

Display, show amount of memory installed on display adapter
Control Panel → Display → Settings tab → Advanced → Adapter tab → Adapter Information section

Task and Setting Index

Display, size

Control Panel → Display → Settings tab → Screen resolution

Display, style

Control Panel → Display → Appearance tab → Windows and buttons list

Display, style, apply to controls in web pages

Control Panel → Internet Options → Advanced tab → Browsing → Enable visual styles on buttons and controls in web pages

Display, troubleshooting

Control Panel → Display → Settings tab → Advanced → Troubleshoot tab

Display, turn off to save power

Control Panel → Power Options → Power Schemes tab → Turn off hard disks

Do-Dr

Double-click required to open icons

Control Panel → Folder Options → General tab → Double-click to open an item

Download Complete message, enable / disable

Control Panel → Internet Options → Advanced tag → Browsing → Notify when downloads complete

Drivers

See "Hardware."

DVD

Settings that affect CD and DVD drives.

DVD drive, autoplay enable / disable

Explorer → right-click DVD drive icon → Properties → AutoPlay tab

DVD drive, change drive letters

Disk Management (*diskmgmt.msc*); see "Microsoft Management Console" in Chapter 4.

Ef-Em

Effects, display settings

Control Panel → Display → Appearance tab → Effects

E-mail icon, show in Start menu (XP Start menu only)

Control Panel → Taskbar and Start Menu → Start Menu tab → Customize → General tab → E-mail

Email program, default

Control Panel → Internet Options → Programs tab → E-mail

Encrypted NTFS Files

See the "NTFS Encryption Utility" in Chapter 4.

Encrypted NTFS files, differentiate with a different color
Control Panel → Folder Options → View tab → Show encrypted or compressed NTFS files in color

Encrypted NTFS files, use with offline files
Control Panel → Folder Options → Offline Files tab → Encrypt offline files to secure data

En-Ex

Environment variables
Control Panel → System → Advanced tab → Environment variables

Error messages, font
Control Panel → Display → Appearance tab → Advanced → choose "Message Box" from the "Item" list

Error messages, sound
Control Panel → Sounds and Audio Devices → Sounds tab

Error messages, text color
Control Panel → Display → Appearance tab → Advanced → choose "Window" from the "Item" list

Error Reporting, advanced settings
Group Policy (*gpedit.msc*) → Computer Configuration → Administrative Templates → System → Error Reporting

Error Reporting, enable / disable
Control Panel → System → Advanced tab → Error Reporting

Explorer
See "Windows Explorer."

Extensions, show / hide filename extensions
Control Panel → Folder Options → View tab → Hide extensions for known file types

Favorites

These settings affect to how the items in the Favorites folder (including Internet Short-cuts in Internet Explorer) appear and are accessed.

Favorites, hide infrequently used items
Control Panel → Internet Options → Advanced tag → Browsing → Enable Personalized Favorites Menu

Favorites, show in Start menu (Classic Start menu only)
Control Panel → Taskbar and Start Menu → Start Menu tab → Customize → "Advanced Start menu options" section → Display Favorites

Favorites, show in Start menu (XP Start menu only)
Control Panel → Taskbar and Start Menu → Start Menu tab → Customize → Advanced tab → "Start menu items" section → Favorites menu

Fax

See "Fax Console" in Chapter 4.

Fax service, install support
Control Panel → Printers and Faxes → File → Set Up Faxing

Files

The following settings and tasks relate to using files. See also "Folders" and "Windows Explorer."

Files, change attributes
See "Attrib" in Chapter 4.

Files, compare
See "File Compare (fc)" in Chapter 4.

Files, differentiate encrypted or compressed NTFS files with a different color
Control Panel → Folder Options → View tab → Show encrypted or compressed NTFS files in color

Files, display size in folder tips
Control Panel → Folder Options → View tab → Display file size information in folder tips

Files, distribute to other users
See "IExpress" in Chapter 4.

Files, downloads (enable / disable)
Control Panel → Internet Options → Security tab → Custom Level

Files, drag-drop (enable / disable)
Control Panel → Internet Options → Security tab → Custom Level

Files, extensions (show / hide)
Control Panel → Folder Options → View tab → Hide extensions for known file types

Files, hidden files (show / hide)
Control Panel → Folder Options → View tab → Hidden files and folders

Files, Indexing Service
See "Indexing."

Files, list all files in use
See "OpenFiles" in Chapter 4.

Files, prepare for offline use
See "Synchronization Manager" in Chapter 4.

Files, synchronize offline files
See "Synchronization Manager" in Chapter 4.

Files, system files (show / hide)
Control Panel → Folder Options → View tab → Hide protected operating system files

Files, transfer across Internet
See "FTP" in Chapter 4.

Firewall

See "Internet Connection Firewall."

Folders

The following settings and tasks relate to using folders and folder windows. See also "Hard Disk" and "Windows Explorer." A quick way to get to Control Panel → Folder Options is to select Folder Options from the Tools menu in any open folder window.

Folders, cache settings for offline access
Explorer → right-click folder icon → Sharing → Caching

Folders, close automatically when Favorites or History folder is shown
Control Panel → Internet Options → Advanced tag → Browsing → Close unused folders in History and Favorites

Folders, columns in details view
Folder window → View → Details → View → Choose Details

Folders, display file size in folder tips
Control Panel → Folder Options → View tab → Display file size information in folder tips

Folders, group similar items
Folder window → View Arrange Icons by → Show in Groups

Folders, history settings
Control Panel → Internet Options → General tab → History section

Folders, Indexing Service
See "Indexing."

Folders, map as drive
See "Subst" in Chapter 4.

Folders, open each folder in its own window
Control Panel → Folder Options → General tab → Open each folder in its own window

Folders, open in separate process
Control Panel → Folder Options → View tab → Launch folder windows in separate process

(If this option is on and one folder window crashes, they won't all close.)

Folders, refresh view
Folder window → View → Refresh or press F5

Folders, remember individual settings
Control Panel → Folder Options → View tab → Remember each folder's view settings

Task and Setting Index

Folders, reopen all folder windows that were left open when system was last shut down
Control Panel → Folder Options → View tab → Restore previous folder windows at logon

Folders, reset default appearance to Windows default
Control Panel → Folder Options → View tab → Reset All Folders

Folders, reuse folder windows
Control Panel → Folder Options → General tab → Open each folder in the same window

Folders, reuse folder windows when launching Internet shortcuts
Control Panel → Internet Options → Advanced tag → Browsing → Reuse windows for launching shortcuts

Folders, set default appearance
Open any folder and configure it as you wish → Tools → Folder Options → View tab → Apply to All Folders

Folders, share folders from a remote computer
See "Create Shared Folder" in Chapter 4.

Folders, share on network
Explorer → right-click folder icon → Sharing → Share this folder

Folders, show / hide hidden folders
Control Panel → Folder Options → View tab → Hidden files and folders

Folders, show all shared folders
Shared Folders (*fsmgmt.msc*); see "Microsoft Management Console" in Chapter 4.

Folders, show background images
Control Panel → System → Advanced tab → Performance section → Settings → Visual Effects tab → Custom

Folders, show common tasks
Control Panel → System → Advanced tab → Performance section → Settings → Visual Effects tab → Custom

Folders, show contents of system folders
Control Panel → Folder Options → View tab → Display the contents of system folders

Folders, show Digital Camera memory as a folder (still camera only)
Control Panel → Scanners and Cameras → Add Device

Folders, show FTP site as folder in Internet Explorer
Control Panel → Internet Options → Advanced tag → Browsing → Enable folder view for FTP sites

Folders, show lines in Explorer tree view
Control Panel → Folder Options → View tab → Display simple folder view in Explorer's Folders list

Folders, show the full path in the Address Bar
Control Panel → Folder Options → View tab → Display the full path in the Address Bar

Folders, show the full path in the titlebar
Control Panel → Folder Options → View tab → Display the full path in the titlebar

Fonts

Features relating to screen fonts.

Fonts, change DPI of all screen fonts
> Control Panel → Display → Settings tab → Advanced → General tab → select "Custom setting" from the "DPI setting" list

Fonts, determine link between font filename and font screen name
> Control Panel → Fonts → View → Details

Fonts, downloads (enable / disable)
> Control Panel → Internet Options → Security tab → Custom Level

Fonts, edit
> See "Private Character Editor" in Chapter 4.

Fonts, eliminate duplicates
> Control Panel → Fonts → View → List Fonts by Similarity

Fonts, in web pages
> Control Panel → Internet Options → General tab → Fonts

Fonts, in windows, menus, and icons
> Control Panel → Display → Appearance tab → Advanced

Fonts, install
> Control Panel → Fonts → File → Install New Font

Fonts, size in applications
> Control Panel → Display → Appearance tab → Font size

Fonts, smooth edges (enable / disable)
> Control Panel → System → Advanced tab → Performance section → Settings → Visual Effects tab → Custom

Fonts, smooth edges (settings)
> Control Panel → Display → Appearance tab → Effects → Use the following method to smooth edges of screen fonts

Fonts, uninstall
> Control Panel → Fonts → delete a font file to uninstall it

Fonts, view and compare
> Control Panel → Fonts → double-click any font

FTP

The settings typically deal with accessing FTP sites in Internet Explorer. See also "FTP" in Chapter 4.

FTP, server restrictions
> Control Panel → Network Connections → right-click connection → Properties → Advanced tab → Settings → Services tab

FTP, show as folder in Internet Explorer
> Control Panel → Internet Options → Advanced tag → Browsing → Enable folder view for FTP sites

Task and Setting Index

FTP, use passive mode

Control Panel → Internet Options → Advanced tag → Browsing → Use Passive FTP

Go-Ha

Go button, show in Address Bar

Control Panel → Internet Options → Advanced tag → Browsing → Show Go button in Address Bar

Right-click on empty portion of Address Bar → Go Button

Hang up Internet Connection automatically

Control Panel → Internet Options → Connection tab → select connection → Settings

Hard Disk

The following settings and tasks relate to using hard disks, typically accessed through My Computer or Windows Explorer. See Figure 5-4. (See also "Folders.")

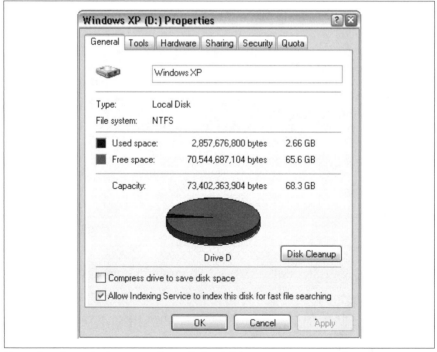

Figure 5-4. Open the Properties sheet of a hard disk to view statistics and to access certain hard disk tools

Hard Disk, cache settings for offline access

Explorer → right-click drive icon → Sharing → Caching

Hard Disk, change Chkdsk options at Windows startup

See "Chkntfs" in Chapter 4.

Hard Disk, change drive letters

Disk Management (*diskmgmt.msc*); see "Microsoft Management Console" in Chapter 4.

Hard Disk, change label

See "Label" in Chapter 4.

Hard Disk, check for errors

Explorer → right-click drive icon → Properties → Tools tab → Check Now

Hard Disk, clean up

Explorer → right-click drive icon → Properties → General tab → Disk Cleanup

Hard Disk, compress drive

Explorer → right-click drive icon → Properties → Compress drive to save disk space

Hard Disk, compression options

See "NTFS Compression Utility" in Chapter 4.

Hard Disk, convert FAT and FAT32 drives to NTFS filesystem

See "FAT to NTFS Conversion Utility" in Chapter 4.

Hard Disk, convert to dynamic disk

Disk Management (*diskmgmt.msc*) → View → Top → Disk List → right-click on drive in top pane → Convert to Dynamic Disk

Hard Disk, defragment

Explorer → right-click drive icon → Properties → Tools tab → Defragment Now

Hard Disk, enable / disable write caching

Device Manager → right-click drive → Properties → Policies tab → Enable write caching on the disk

Hard Disk, encryption options

See "NTFS Compression Utility" in Chapter 4.

Hard Disk, format (prepare for use)

See "Format" in Chapter 4.

Hard Disk, Indexing Service

See "Indexing."

Hard Disk, list volumes

Device Manager → right-click drive → Properties → Volumes tab → Populate

Hard Disk, partition

See "DiskPart" in Chapter 4.

Hard Disk, quota management

Explorer → right-click folder icon → Properties → Quota tab

Hard Disk, quota security policies

Group Policy (*gpedit.msc*) → Computer Configuration → Administrative Templates → System → Disk Quotas

Hard Disk, scan and fix errors
> See "Chkdsk" in Chapter 4.

Hard Disk, share on network
> Explorer → right-click drive icon → Sharing → Share this folder

Hard Disk, turn off to save power
> Control Panel → Power Options → Power Schemes tab → Turn off monitor

Hard Disk, view partition information
> Disk Management (*diskmgmt.msc*); see "Microsoft Management Console" in Chapter 4.

Hardware

These settings help you install, configure, and troubleshoot the various hardware devices attached to your system. For details about specific hardware, try looking up the device name (e.g., "Display" or "Hard Disk").

Hardware, change the driver for a device
> Device Manager → right-click on device → Properties → Driver tab → Update Driver

Hardware, driver information for a device
> Device Manager → right-click on device → Properties → Driver tab → Driver Details

Hardware, driver signing options
> Control Panel → System → Hardware tab → Driver Signing

Hardware, enable / disable
> Device Manager → right-click on device → Properties → General tab → Device usage

Hardware, install
> Control Panel → Add Hardware

Hardware, IRQ Steering settings
> Device Manager → Computer → right-click sole entry → Properties → IRQ Steering tab

Hardware, list devices
> System Information (*winmsd.exe*) → Components

Hardware, list drivers
> System Information (*winmsd.exe*) → Software Environment

Hardware, list installed drivers
> See "DriverQuery" in Chapter 4.

Hardware, list resources used
> System Information (*winmsd.exe*) → Hardware Resources

Hardware, places to look for drivers
> Group Policy (*gpedit.msc*) → User Configuration → Administrative Templates → System

Hardware, profile settings
> Control Panel → System → Hardware tab → Hardware Profiles

Hardware, resources in use by a device
Device Manager → right-click on device → Properties → Resources tab

Hardware, security policies
Group Policy (*gpedit.msc*) → Computer Configuration → Windows Settings → Security Settings → Local Policies → Security Options

Hardware, show all installed devices
Device Manager

Hardware, uninstall
Device Manager → right-click on device → Uninstall

Hardware, Universal Plug and Play support
Control Panel → Network Connections → Advanced → Optional Networking Components → Networking Services

He-HT

Help, pop-up help windows
See "Tooltips."

Help, show in Start menu (XP Start menu only)
Control Panel → Taskbar and Start Menu → Start Menu tab → Customize → Advanced tab → "Start menu items" section → Help and Support

Hibernation, enable / disable
Control Panel → Power Options → Hibernate tab → Enable hibernation

Hidden files and folders, show / hide
Control Panel → Folder Options → View tab → Hidden files and folders

Hourglass, change icon
Control Panel → Mouse → Pointers tab

HTML editor, default
Control Panel → Internet Options → Programs tab → HTML Editor

Icons

These settings apply to icons displayed on the Desktop, in folder windows, and elsewhere. Paint, discussed in Chapter 4, can be used to create and edit icon files.

Icons, highlight color and font
Control Panel → Display → Appearance tab → Advanced → choose "Selected Items" from the "Item" list

Icons, show shadows under icon captions
Control Panel → System → Advanced tab → Performance section → Settings → Visual Effects tab → Custom

Icons, show translucent selection rectangle when highlighting multiple icons
Control Panel → System → Advanced tab → Performance section → Settings → Visual Effects tab → Custom

Icons, single-click or double-click
Control Panel → Folder Options → General tab → Click items as follows

Icons, size on Desktop and in folders

Control Panel → Display → Appearance tab → Effects → Use large icons

Control Panel → Display → Appearance tab → Advanced → choose "Icon" from the "Item" list

Icons, spacing on Desktop and in folders

Control Panel → Display → Appearance tab → Advanced → choose "Icon Spacing (Horizontal)" or "Icon Spacing (Vertical)" from the "Item" list

Icons, underline captions

Control Panel → Folder Options → General tab → Click items as follows

Images

Settings related to image files and images shown in web pages (Internet Explorer only).

Images, edit

See "Paint" in Chapter 4.

Images, show as thumbnails in Explorer

Explorer → View → Thumbnails

Images, show in web pages

Control Panel → Internet Options → Advanced tag → Multimedia → Show pictures

Images, show placeholders in web pages (if pictures are disabled in web pages)

Control Panel → Internet Options → Advanced tag → Multimedia → Show image download placeholders

Indexing

See "Microsoft Management Console" in Chapter 4 for more information on the Indexing Service.

Indexing Service, enable / disable for individual drives

Explorer → right-click drive icon → Properties → General tab → Allow Indexing Service to index this disk for fast file searching

Indexing Service, manage indexes

Indexing Service (*ciadv.msc*); see "Microsoft Management Console" in Chapter 4.

Insertion Point, change

Control Panel → Mouse → Pointers tab → choose "Text Select" from "Customize" list

Ins-Int

Install On Demand, enable / disable

Control Panel → Internet Options → Advanced tag → Browsing → Enable Install On Demand

Internet Call, default application

Control Panel → Internet Options → Programs tab → Internet Call

Internet Connection Firewall

A new feature in Windows XP, the Internet Connection Firewall helps protect the privacy and security of your computer by limiting the types of connections, both incoming and outgoing, that can be made via your Internet connection.

Internet Connection Firewall, enable / disable

Control Panel → Network Connections → right-click connection → Properties → Advanced tab → Protect my computer and network by limiting or preventing access to this computer from the Internet

Internet Connection Firewall, logging

Control Panel → Network Connections → right-click connection → Properties → Advanced tab → Settings → Security Logging tab

Internet Connection Firewall, settings

Control Panel → Network Connections → right-click connection → Properties → Advanced tab → Settings

Internet Explorer

Internet Explorer, the default web browser included with Windows, is also responsible for the Windows Update feature, discussed later in this chapter, as well as Help and Support (discussed in Chapter 4) and several other features of Windows XP. These settings primarily affect the display of web pages in Internet Explorer as well as many of the security features of the browser. Some settings also affect the Internet connection, used by all browsers.

Internet Connection, set up

Control Panel → Internet Options → Connection tab → Setup

Internet Explorer, abbreviate link addresses in status bar

Control Panel → Internet Options → Advanced tag → Browsing → Show friendly URLs

Internet Explorer, ActiveX settings

Control Panel → Internet Options → Security tab → Custom Level

Internet Explorer, additional security policies

Group Policy (*gpedit.msc*) → Computer Configuration → Administrative Templates → Windows Components → Internet Explorer

Group Policy (*gpedit.msc*) → User Configuration → Administrative Templates → Windows Components → Internet Explorer

Internet Explorer, animated GIFs (enable / disable)

Control Panel → Internet Options → Advanced tag → Multimedia → Play animations in web pages

Internet Explorer, AutoComplete settings

See "Autocomplete."

Internet Explorer, automatically check for updates

Control Panel → Internet Options → Advanced tag → Browsing → Automatically check for Internet Explorer updates

Task and
Setting Index

Internet Explorer, automatically download linked pages for Desktop web pages

Control Panel → Display → Desktop tab → Customize Desktop → Web tab → select item → Properties → Download tab

Internet Explorer, automatically update Desktop web pages

Control Panel → Display → Desktop tab → Customize Desktop → Web tab → select item → Properties → Schedule tab

Internet Explorer, buttons and controls, use display settings

Control Panel → Internet Options → Advanced tag → Browsing → Enable visual styles on buttons and controls in web pages

Internet Explorer, cache settings

Control Panel → Internet Options → General tab → Temporary Internet Files section → Settings

Internet Explorer, cache settings for encrypted pages

Control Panel → Internet Options → Advanced tag → Security → Do not save encrypted pages to disk

Internet Explorer, cache, clear automatically when browser is closed

Control Panel → Internet Options → Advanced tag → Security → Empty Temporary Internet Files folder when browser is closed

Internet Explorer, certificates for secure sites

See "Certificates."

Internet Explorer, check to see if it is the default browser

Control Panel → Internet Options → Programs tab → Internet Explorer should check to see whether it is the default browser

Internet Explorer, colors and fonts

Control Panel → Internet Options → General tab

Internet Explorer, cookies

See "Cookies."

Internet Explorer, default home page

Control Panel → Internet Options → General tab → Home page

Internet Explorer, disable compositing effects when using Terminal Server

Control Panel → Internet Options → Advanced tag → Browsing → Force offscreen compositing even under Terminal Server

Internet Explorer, download complete notification

Control Panel → Internet Options → Advanced tag → Browsing → Notify when downloads complete

Internet Explorer, enable / disable HTTP 1.1

Control Panel → Internet Options → Advanced tag → HTTP 1.1 settings

Internet Explorer, enable / disable moving or resizing web page items on Desktop

Control Panel → Display → Desktop tab → Customize Desktop → Web tab → Lock Desktop items

Internet Explorer, enlarge picture boxes to accommodate "ALT" captions (if pictures are disabled in web pages)

Control Panel → Internet Options → Advanced tag → Accessibility → Always expand ALT text for images

Internet Explorer, explain server error messages
Control Panel → Internet Options → Advanced tag → Browsing → Show friendly HTTP error messages

Internet Explorer, fading animation when moving from one web page to another
Control Panel → Internet Options → Advanced tag → Browsing → Enable page transitions

Internet Explorer, Go button
See "Go button, show in Address Bar."

Internet Explorer, hand icon (change)
Control Panel → Mouse → Pointers tab → choose "Link Select" from "Customize" list

Internet Explorer, hide infrequently used Favorites
Control Panel → Internet Options → Advanced tag → Browsing → Enable Personalized Favorites Menu

Internet Explorer, History settings
Control Panel → Internet Options → General tab → History section

Internet Explorer, icon, change
Control Panel → Display → Desktop tab → Customize Desktop → General tab → select icon → Change Icon

Internet Explorer, icon, show on Desktop
Control Panel → Display → Desktop tab → Customize Desktop → General tab → Internet Explorer

Internet Explorer, image placeholders (if pictures are disabled in web pages)
Control Panel → Internet Options → Advanced tag → Multimedia → Show image download placeholders

Internet Explorer, Image Toolbar (enable / disable)
Control Panel → Internet Options → Advanced tag → Multimedia → Enable Image Toolbar

Internet Explorer, Java
See the topics related to Java (later in this chapter).

Internet Explorer, Link underline
Control Panel → Internet Options → Advanced tag → Browsing → Underline links

Internet Explorer, list additional settings
System Information (*winmsd.exe*) → Internet Settings → Internet Explorer

Internet Explorer, Media Bar content
Control Panel → Internet Options → Advanced tag → Multimedia → Don't display online media content in the media bar

Internet Explorer, plug-ins (enable / disable)
Control Panel → Internet Options → Advanced tag → Browsing → Enable third-party browser extensions

Internet Explorer, print background colors and images when printing web pages
Control Panel → Internet Options → Advanced tag → Printings → Print background colors and images

Task and Setting Index

Internet Explorer, profile assistant (enable / disable)
Control Panel → Internet Options → Advanced tag → Security → Enable Profile Assistant

Internet Explorer, restrict certain sites
Control Panel → Internet Options → Content tab → Content Advisor section

Internet Explorer, reuse folder windows when launching shortcuts
Control Panel → Internet Options → Advanced tag → Browsing → Reuse windows for launching shortcuts

Internet Explorer, save form data
Control Panel → Internet Options → Content tab → AutoComplete

Internet Explorer, script debugging
Control Panel → Internet Options → Advanced tag → Browsing → Disable script debugging

Internet Explorer, script error notification
Control Panel → Internet Options → Advanced tag → Browsing → Display a notification about every script error

Internet Explorer, search from the Address Bar
Control Panel → Internet Options → Advanced tag → Search from the Address Bar

Internet Explorer, show web page on Desktop
Control Panel → Display → Desktop tab → Customize Desktop → Web tab

Internet Explorer, shrink large images to fit browser window
Control Panel → Internet Options → Advanced tag → Multimedia → Enable Automatic Image Resizing

Internet Explorer, smooth scrolling
Control Panel → Internet Options → Advanced tag → Browsing → Use smooth scrolling

Internet Explorer, sounds (enable / disable)
Control Panel → Internet Options → Advanced tag → Multimedia → Play sounds in web pages

Internet Explorer, SSL settings
Control Panel → Internet Options → Advanced tag → Security

Internet Explorer, status bar shows abbreviated link addresses
Control Panel → Internet Options → Advanced tag → Browsing → Show friendly URLs

Internet Explorer, Underline links
Control Panel → Internet Options → Advanced tag → Browsing → Underline links

Internet Explorer, use passive mode in FTP
Control Panel → Internet Options → Advanced tag → Browsing → Use Passive FTP

Internet Explorer, video clips (enable / disable)
Control Panel → Internet Options → Advanced tag → Multimedia → Play videos in web pages

Internet Explorer, warning for redirected form submission
Control Panel → Internet Options → Advanced tag → Security → Warn if forms submittal is being redirected

Internet Explorer, warnings, enable / disable
Control Panel → Internet Options → Security tab → Custom Level

In-Jo

Internet icon, show in Start menu (XP Start menu only)
Control Panel → Taskbar and Start Menu → Start Menu tab → Customize → General tab → Internet

Internet Shortcuts, use same folder window or Explorer window to open web page
Control Panel → Internet Options → Advanced tag → Browsing → Reuse windows for launching shortcuts

Java, compile applets before running using the Just In Time (JIT) compiler
Control Panel → Internet Options → Advanced tag → Microsoft VM → JIT compiler for virtual machine enabled

Java, console
Control Panel → Internet Options → Advanced tag → Microsoft VM → Java console enabled

Java, logging
Control Panel → Internet Options → Advanced tag → Microsoft VM → Java logging enabled

Java, security settings
Control Panel → Internet Options → Security tab → Custom Level

Joystick settings
Control Panel → Game Controllers

Keyboard

The following settings affect the Keyboard and text entry in most applications.

Keyboard shortcuts, hide until Alt key is pressed
Control Panel → Display → Appearance tab → Effects → Hide underlined letters for keyboard navigation until I press the Alt key

Keyboard shortcuts, show in menus and windows
Control Panel → Accessibility Options → Keyboard tab → Show extra keyboard help in programs

Keyboard, choose international layout
Control Panel → Regional and Language Options → Language tab → Details

Keyboard, enable alternative device
Control Panel → Accessibility Options → General tab → Use Serial Keys

Keyboard, ignore brief or repeated keystrokes
Control Panel → Accessibility Options → Keyboard tab → Use FilterKeys

Keyboard, specify type

Control Panel → Keyboard → Hardware tab → Properties → Driver tab → Update Driver → Install from a list of specific location → Next → Don't search → Next

Keyboard, speed (repeat rate and delay)

Control Panel → Keyboard → Speed tab → Character repeat section

Keyboard, use with mouse

See "On-Screen Keyboard" in Chapter 4.

Language

These settings affect the language and regional settings used throughout Windows. See also "Country."

Language settings in web pages

Control Panel → Internet Options → General tab → Languages

Language, settings for non-Unicode applications

Control Panel → Regional and Language Options → Advanced tab → Language for non-Unicode programs

Language, settings for text entry

Control Panel → Regional and Language Options → Language tab → Details

Language, use more than one

Control Panel → Regional and Language Options → Language tab → Details → Settings tab → Add

Li-Me

Listboxes, enable / disable animation

Control Panel → System → Advanced tab → Performance section → Settings → Visual Effects tab → Custom

Log off, from the command line

See "Logoff" in Chapter 4.

Log off, show in Ctrl-Alt-Del window

Group Policy (*gpedit.msc*) → User Configuration → Administrative Templates → System → Ctrl+Alt+Del Options

Log off, show in Start menu (Classic Start menu only)

Control Panel → Taskbar and Start Menu → Start Menu tab → Customize → "Advanced Start menu options" section → Display Log Off

Log on, use Welcome screen

Control Panel → User Accounts → Change the way users log on or off → Use the Welcome screen

Log on, scripts policies

Group Policy (*gpedit.msc*) → Computer Configuration → Administrative Templates → System → Scripts

Group Policy (*gpedit.msc*) → User Configuration → Administrative Templates → System → Scripts

Log on, security policies

> Group Policy (*gpedit.msc*) → Computer Configuration → Windows Settings → Security Settings → Local Policies → Security Options

> Group Policy (*gpedit.msc*) → Computer Configuration → Administrative Templates → System → Logon

> Group Policy (*gpedit.msc*) → User Configuration → Administrative Templates → System → Logon

Magnifier, move with focus change in web pages

> Control Panel → Internet Options → Advanced tag → Accessibility → Move system caret with focus/selection changes

Mail Server, restrictions

> Control Panel → Network Connections → right-click connection → Properties → Advanced tab → Settings → Services tab

Memory, priorities

> Control Panel → System → Advanced tab → Performance section → Settings → Advanced tab → Memory usage section

Memory, show amount of memory installed on display adapter

> Control Panel → Display → Settings tab → Advanced → Adapter tab → Adapter Information section

Memory, show amount of system memory installed

> Control Panel → System → General tab

Memory, virtual memory

> See "Virtual memory, settings."

Menus

What is displayed in any given menu is up to the application, but the look and feel of the menus is constant across nearly all Windows applications and can be configured with these settings. See also "Start Menu."

Menu animation, enable / disable

> Control Panel → Display → Appearance tab → Effects → Use the following transition effect for menus and tooltips

Menus, animation (enable / disable)

> Control Panel → System → Advanced tab → Performance section → Settings → Visual Effects tab → Custom

Menus, fonts and colors

> Control Panel → Display → Appearance tab → Advanced → choose "Menu" from the "Item" list

Menus, highlight color and font

> Control Panel → Display → Appearance tab → Advanced → choose "Selected Items" from the "Item" list

Menus, shadows (enable / disable)

> Control Panel → Display → Appearance tab → Effects → Show shadows under menus

Task and Setting Index

Menus, size
> Control Panel → Display → Appearance tab → Advanced → choose "Menu" from the "Item" list

Menus, underlined keyboard shortcuts (show / hide)
> Control Panel → Display → Appearance tab → Effects → Hide underlined letters for keyboard navigation until I press the Alt key

Message Box

These settings affect generic message boxes used by Windows XP and many applications.

Message boxes, font
> Control Panel → Display → Appearance tab → Advanced → choose "Message Box" from the "Item" list

Message boxes, sound
> Control Panel → Sounds and Audio Devices → Sounds tab

Message boxes, text color
> Control Panel → Display → Appearance tab → Advanced → choose "Window" from the "Item" list

Modems

Modems can be added with the New Hardware wizard (in Control Panel). See also "Dialing."

Modems, settings
> Control Panel → Phone and Modem Options → Modems tab

Mouse

The following settings affect the look of the mouse pointer, the way the mouse moves, and other features relating to whatever pointing device you're using.

Mouse, control with keyboard
> Control Panel → Accessibility Options → Mouse tab

Mouse, double-click speed
> Control Panel → Mouse → Buttons tab → Double-click speed section

Mouse, drag without holding down buttons
> Control Panel → Mouse → Buttons tab → ClickLock section

Mouse, enable alternative device
> Control Panel → Accessibility Options → General tab → Use Serial Keys

Mouse, hide when typing
> Control Panel → Mouse → Pointer Options tab → Hide pointer while typing

Mouse, left-handed use
> Control Panel → Mouse → Buttons tab → Switch primary and secondary buttons

Mouse, move to default button when window is opened
Control Panel → Mouse → Pointer Options tab → Automatically move pointer to the default button in a dialog box

Mouse, pointer
Control Panel → Mouse → Pointers tab

Mouse, precise control enhancement
Control Panel → Mouse → Pointer Options tab → Enhance pointer precision

Mouse, shadow
Control Panel → Mouse → Pointers tab → Enable pointer shadow

Mouse, show location with animated circles when Ctrl is pressed
Control Panel → Mouse → Pointer Options tab → Show location of pointer when I press the Ctrl key

Mouse, specify type
Control Panel → Mouse → Hardware tab → Properties → Driver tab → Update Driver → Install from a list of specific location → Next → Don't search → Next

Mouse, speed
Control Panel → Mouse → Pointer Options tab → Motion section

Mouse, switch left and right buttons
Control Panel → Mouse → Buttons tab → Switch primary and secondary buttons

Mouse, trails
Control Panel → Mouse → Pointer Options tab → Display pointer trails

My Computer

The My Computer window/folder is just another view of Windows Explorer (discussed later in this chapter and in Chapter 4). These settings apply to the folder, as well as the Desktop icon that opens the My Computer folder window.

My Computer, change icon
Control Panel → Display → Desktop tab → Customize Desktop → General tab → select icon → Change Icon

My Computer, show Control Panel
Control Panel → Folder Options → View tab → Show Control Panel in My Computer

My Computer, show icon on Desktop
Control Panel → Display → Desktop tab → Customize Desktop → General tab → My Computer

My Computer, show in Start menu (XP Start menu only)
Control Panel → Taskbar and Start Menu → Start Menu tab → Customize → Advanced tab → "Start menu items" section → My Computer

My Documents

The My Documents folder is a central location on your hard disk where the documents for all of your applications are supposed to be stored. Although you can store documents anywhere, the My Documents folder is convenient because it is easily accessible from the Desktop and the Start menu and is the default folder in many File → Open and File → Save dialog boxes. Each user has his/her own My Documents folder, located at \Documents and Settings\[username]\Documents.

My Documents, change icon
Control Panel → Display → Desktop tab → Customize Desktop → General tab → select icon → Change Icon

My Documents, clear recently opened documents from Start menu (Classic Start menu only)
Control Panel → Taskbar and Start Menu → Start Menu tab → Customize → Clear

My Documents, clear recently opened documents from Start menu (XP Start menu only)
Control Panel → Taskbar and Start Menu → Start Menu tab → Customize → Advanced tab → Clear List

My Documents, show as menu in Start menu (XP Start menu only)
Control Panel → Taskbar and Start Menu → Start Menu tab → Customize → Advanced tab → "Start menu items" section → Expand My Documents

My Documents, show icon on Desktop
Control Panel → Display → Desktop tab → Customize Desktop → General tab → My Documents

My Documents, show in Start menu (Classic Start menu only)
Control Panel → Taskbar and Start Menu → Start Menu tab → Customize → "Advanced Start menu options" section → My Documents

My Documents, show recently opened on Start menu (XP Start menu only)
Control Panel → Taskbar and Start Menu → Start Menu tab → Customize → Advanced tab → "Recent documents" section

My Music

A special folder, like My Pictures, that is intended to store music files downloaded from the Internet or extracted from music CDs. See also "Sounds."

My Music, show as menu Start menu (XP Start menu only)
Control Panel → Taskbar and Start Menu → Start Menu tab → Customize → Advanced tab → "Start menu items" section → My Music

My Network Places

The My Network Places folder is the starting point for browsing the shared resources of other computers on your local network. The My Network Places replaces the Network Neighborhood found in earlier versions of Windows. See also "Network Connections" and "Windows Explorer." Right-click on the My Network Places icon and select Properties to view the Network Connections window.

My Network Places icon, change

Control Panel → Display → Desktop tab → Customize Desktop → General tab → select icon → Change Icon

My Network Places icon, show on Desktop

Control Panel → Display → Desktop tab → Customize Desktop → General tab → My Network Places

My Network Places, show in Start menu (XP Start menu only)

Control Panel → Taskbar and Start Menu → Start Menu tab → Customize → Advanced tab → "Start menu items" section → My Network Places

My Pictures

A special folder, like My Music, intended to store images that are downloaded from the Internet, scanned, or taken with a digital camera. See also "Images."

My Pictures, show as menu in Start menu (Classic Start menu only)

Control Panel → Taskbar and Start Menu → Start Menu tab → Customize → "Advanced Start menu options" section → Expand My Pictures

My Pictures, show in Start menu (XP Start menu only)

Control Panel → Taskbar and Start Menu → Start Menu tab → Customize → Advanced tab → "Start menu items" section → My Pictures

NetMeeting

See "Microsoft NetMeeting" in Chapter 4.

NetMeeting, make the default for Internet Calls

Control Panel → Internet Options → Programs tab → Internet Call

Network

The following settings and tasks relate to networking functionality, performance, and security (see Figure 5-5). See also "Network Connections," "My Network Places," and Chapter 6.

Network, add new connection

Control Panel → Network Connections → New Connection Wizard

Network, advanced adapter settings

Device Manager → right-click adapter → Properties → Advanced tab

Network, Authentication

Control Panel → Network Connections → right-click connection → Properties → Authentication tab

Network, bindings

Control Panel → Network Connections → Advanced → Advanced Settings → Adapters and Bindings tab

Control Panel → Network Connections → right-click connection → Properties → General tab → turn on or off listed protocols and services

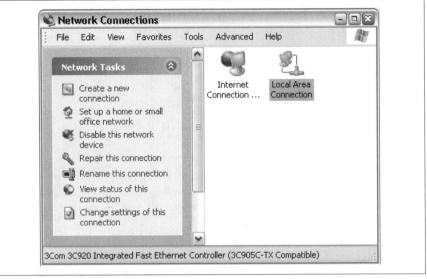

Figure 5-5. Use the Network Connections window to set up your network

Network, bridge two connections
  Control Panel → Network Connections → select two connections → Advanced → Network Bridge

Network, computer description
  Control Panel → System → Computer Name tab

Network, computer name
  Control Panel → System → Computer Name tab → Change

Network, connect to shared printer
  Control Panel → Printers and Faxes → Add Printer → Next → A network printer or a printer attached to another computer

Network, connection status
  Control Panel → Network Connections → double-click connection → General tab

Network, disconnect mapped network drive
  Explorer → Tools → Disconnect Network Drive

Network, DNS settings
  Control Panel → Network Connections → right-click connection → Properties → General tab → Internet Protocol (TCP/IP) → Properties → Advanced → DNS tab

Network, enable / disable
  Control Panel → Network Connections → right-click connection → Enable or Disable

Network, Firewall
  See "Internet Connection Firewall."

Network, include in Files or Folders search
  Control Panel → Folder Options → View tab → Automatically search for network folders and printers

Network, install a network protocol or service

Control Panel → Network Connections → right-click connection → Properties → General tab → Install

Network, IP address and other connection information

Control Panel → Network Connections → double-click connection → Support tab

Network, IP addresses

See "Windows IP Configuration" in Chapter 4.

Network, join a Windows NT domain

Control Panel → System → Computer Name tab → Change

Network, map network drive

Explorer → Tools → Map Network Drive

Network, preliminary setup

Control Panel → Network Connections → Network Setup Wizard

Network, priorities

Control Panel → Network Connections → Advanced → Advanced Settings → Provider Order tab

Network, protocol, enable or disable for a connection

Control Panel → Network Connections → right-click connection → Properties → General tab → check or uncheck entries in list

Network, security policies

Group Policy (*gpedit.msc*) → Computer Configuration → Windows Settings → Security Settings → Local Policies → Security Options

Group Policy (*gpedit.msc*) → Computer Configuration → Administrative Templates → Network

Group Policy (*gpedit.msc*) → User Configuration → Administrative Templates → Network

Network, set IP address

Control Panel → Network Connections → right-click connection → Properties → General tab → Internet Protocol (TCP/IP) → Properties → Use the following IP address

Network, set multiple IP addresses

Control Panel → Network Connections → right-click connection → Properties → General tab → Internet Protocol (TCP/IP) → Properties → Advanced → IP Settings tab

Network, share printer

Control Panel → Printers and Faxes → right-click printer → Sharing → Shared as

Network, show all shared folders

Shared Folders (*fsmgmt.msc*); see "Microsoft Management Console" in Chapter 4.

Network, show icon in Taskbar notification area when connected

Control Panel → Network Connections → right-click connection → Properties → General tab → Show icon in notification area when connected

Network, SNMP components (install / uninstall)

Control Panel → Network Connections → Advanced → Optional Networking Components → Management and Monitoring Tools

Network, TCP/IP filtering

Control Panel → Network Connections → right-click connection → Properties → General tab → Internet Protocol (TCP/IP) → Properties → Advanced → Options tab → TCP/IP filtering → Properties

Network, TCP/IP settings

Control Panel → Network Connections → right-click connection → Properties → General tab → Internet Protocol (TCP/IP) → Properties

Network, TCP/IP statistics and status

See "Active Connections Utility" in Chapter 4.

Network, uninstall a protocols or service

Control Panel → Network Connections → right-click connection → Properties → General tab → Uninstall

Network, WINS settings

Control Panel → Network Connections → right-click connection → Properties → General tab → Internet Protocol (TCP/IP) → Properties → Advanced → WINS tab

Network Connections

The Network Connections window allows you to configure your various connections to network resources, including the Internet, your local network, virtual private networking, and other types of connections. Right-click on the My Network Places icon and select Properties to view the Network Connections window.

Network Connections, automatically dial

Control Panel → Internet Options → Connection tab

Network Connections, security policies

Group Policy (*gpedit.msc*) → User Configuration → Administrative Templates → Network → Network Connections

Network Connections, show as menu in Start menu (Classic Start menu only)

Control Panel → Taskbar and Start Menu → Start Menu tab → Customize → "Advanced Start menu options" section → Expand Network Connections

Network Connections, show in Start menu (XP Start menu only)

Control Panel → Taskbar and Start Menu → Start Menu tab → Customize → Advanced tab → "Start menu items" section → Network Connections

Ne–OD

Newsgroup reader, default

Control Panel → Internet Options → Programs tab → Newsgroups

Numbers, customize display

Control Panel → Regional and Language Options → Regional Options tab → Customize → Numbers tab

ODBC data sources, restrict access

Control Panel → Internet Options → Security tab → Custom Level

Offline Files

The Offline Files feature lets you work on files over a network even when you're not actually connected. See also "Synchronization Manager" in Chapter 4.

Offline Files, action to take when network connection is lost
Control Panel → Folder Options → Offline Files tab → Advanced

Offline Files, automatic synchronization
Explorer → Tools → Synchronize → Setup → Logon/Logoff tab → Automatically synchronize the selected items...

Offline Files, automatic synchronization on idle
Explorer → Tools → Synchronize → Setup → On Idle tab → Advanced

Offline Files, compatibility with computers running on batteries
Explorer → Tools → Synchronize → Setup → On Idle tab → Advanced → Prevent synchronization when my computer is running on battery power

Offline Files, enable scheduling of Desktop web page updates
Control Panel → Internet Options → Advanced tag → Browsing → Enable offline items to be synchronized on a schedule

Offline Files, prepare
See "Synchronization Manager" in Chapter 4.

Offline Files, security policies
Group Policy (*gpedit.msc*) → User Configuration → Administrative Templates → Network → Offline Files

Offline Files, settings
Control Panel → Folder Options → Offline Files tab

Explorer → Tools → Synchronize → Setup

Offline Files, synchronize
Explorer → Tools → Synchronize

(See "Synchronization Manager" in Chapter 4.)

Ou-Pa

Outlook Express, make the default
Control Panel → Internet Options → Programs tab → E-mail or Newsgroups

Parental Control of web sites
Control Panel → Internet Options → Content tab → Content Advisor section

Passwords

These settings deal with the way passwords are handled in Windows XP. See also "Users."

Passwords, automatic logon
Control Panel → Internet Options → Security tab → Custom Level → User Authentication

(It's best to disable this feature; otherwise, another server can gain access to your username and password.)

Passwords, change
> Control Panel → User Accounts → click an account from the list → Change my password

Passwords, expiration
> Group Policy (*gpedit.msc*) → Computer Configuration → Windows Settings → Security Settings → Account Policies → Password Policy

Passwords, prevent forgotten passwords
> Control Panel → User Accounts → click an account from the list → Related Tasks section → Prevent a forgotten password

Passwords, require for exiting screensaver
> Control Panel → Display → Screen Saver tab → On resume, password protect

Passwords, require for resuming from standby mode
> Control Panel → Power Options → Advanced tab → Prompt for password when computer resumes from standby

Passwords, saving in web pages
> Control Panel → Internet Options → Content tab → AutoComplete

Passwords, security policies
> Group Policy (*gpedit.msc*) → Computer Configuration → Windows Settings → Security Settings → Account Policies → Password Policy

Passwords, show "Change Password" in Ctrl-Alt-Del window
> Group Policy (*gpedit.msc*) → User Configuration → Administrative Templates → System → Ctrl+Alt+Del Options

---

Pa-Pr

Path, show full path in folder windows
> Control Panel → Folder Options → View tab → Display the full path in the titlebar / Display the full path in the address bar

Personalized menus, Favorites
> Control Panel → Internet Options → Advanced tag → Browsing → Enable Personalized Favorites Menu

Pictures
> See "Images."

Pointer
> See "Mouse."

Pop-up help windows
> See "Tooltips."

Power Management
> See "Advanced Power Management (APM)."

Print Server settings
> Control Panel → Printers and Faxes → File → Server Properties

Printers

The printer settings in Windows typically concern installing printer drivers and managing print jobs. The drivers and the software that comes with your printer will provide more settings and features specific to your hardware (see Figure 5-6).

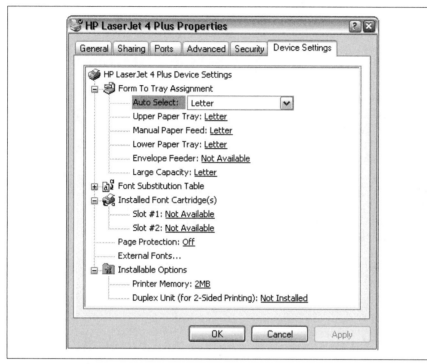

Figure 5-6. Use the Device Settings tab in your printer's Properties sheet to fine-tune your printing preferences

Printers, advanced settings
> Group Policy (*gpedit.msc*) → Computer Configuration → Administrative Templates → Printers
>
> Group Policy (*gpedit.msc*) → User Configuration → Administrative Templates → Printers

Printers, cancel printing of all documents
> Control Panel → Printers and Faxes → right-click printer → Cancel All Documents

Printers, cancel printing of one document
> Control Panel → Printers and Faxes → double-click printer → right-click document → Cancel

Printers, change settings for a single application
> Open application → File → Print or Printer Setup

Printers, change settings for all applications

Control Panel → Printers and Faxes → right-click printer → Properties

Printers, connect to a printer on your network

Control Panel → Printers and Faxes → Add Printer → Next → A network printer, or a printer attached to another computer

Printers, install

Control Panel → Printers and Faxes → Add Printer

Printers, pause printing

Control Panel → Printers and Faxes → right-click printer → Pause Printing

Printers, print background colors and images when printing web pages

Control Panel → Internet Options → Advanced tag → Printings → Print background colors and images

Printers, set default printer

Control Panel → Printers and Faxes → right-click printer → Set as Default Printer

Printers, share with other computers on network

Control Panel → Printers and Faxes → right-click printer → Sharing → Shared as

Printers, show as menu in Start menu (Classic Start menu only)

Control Panel → Taskbar and Start Menu → Start Menu tab → Customize → "Advanced Start menu options" section → Expand Printers

Printers, show in Start menu (XP Start menu only)

Control Panel → Taskbar and Start Menu → Start Menu tab → Customize → Advanced tab → "Start menu items" section → Printers and Faxes

Printers, uninstall

Control Panel → Printers and Faxes → right-click printer → Delete

Printers, view status

Control Panel → Printers and Faxes → double-click printer

Pr-Ru

Processor, priorities

Control Panel → System → Advanced tab → Performance section → Settings → Advanced tab → Processor scheduling section

Processor, show details

Control Panel → System → General tab

Profile Assistant, enable / disable

Control Panel → Internet Options → Advanced tag → Security → Enable Profile Assistant

Proxy settings

Control Panel → Internet Options → Connection tab → LAN Settings

Quick Launch toolbar, show on Taskbar

Control Panel → Taskbar and Start Menu → Taskbar tab → Show Quick Launch

Right-click on Taskbar → Toolbars → Quick Launch

Registered User, change
See Chapter 8.

Registered User, view
Control Panel → System → General tab

Remote Assistance, allow invitations to be sent
Control Panel → System → Remote tab → Remote Assistance tab

Remote Desktop Connection, invite others to connect to your computer
See "Remote Assistance" in Chapter 4.

Remote Desktop, enable incoming connections
Control Panel → System → Remote tab → Remote Desktop tab

Report crashes to Microsoft
Control Panel → System → Advanced tab → Error Reporting

Run, show in Start menu (Classic Start menu only)
Control Panel → Taskbar and Start Menu → Start Menu tab → Customize → "Advanced Start menu options" section → Display Run

Run, show in Start menu (XP Start menu only)
Control Panel → Taskbar and Start Menu → Start Menu tab → Customize → Advanced tab → "Start menu items" section → Run Command

Scheduled Tasks

The scheduled tasks feature runs applications and scripts automatically at scheduled times. See also "Scheduled Tasks" in Chapter 4.

Scheduled Tasks, add a task
Control Panel → Scheduled Tasks → Add Scheduled Task

Scheduled Tasks, choose user for a single task
Control Panel → Scheduled Tasks → right-click task → Properties → Task tab → Run as

Scheduled Tasks, choose user for At service
Control Panel → Scheduled Tasks → Advanced → At Service Account

Scheduled Tasks, command-line
See "At" in Chapter 4.

Scheduled Tasks, compatibility with computers running on batteries
Control Panel → Scheduled Tasks → right-click task → Properties → Settings tab → Power Management section

Scheduled Tasks, delete a task
Control Panel → Scheduled Tasks → right-click task → Delete

Scheduled Tasks, delete completed tasks automatically
Control Panel → Scheduled Tasks → right-click task → Properties → Settings tab → Delete the task if it is not scheduled to run again

Scheduled Tasks, enable / disable
Control Panel → Scheduled Tasks → Advanced → Stop Using Task Scheduler or Start Using Task Scheduler

Scheduled Tasks, enable / disable a single task

Control Panel → Scheduled Tasks → right-click task → Properties → Task tab → Enabled

Scheduled Tasks, log

Control Panel → Scheduled Tasks → Advanced → View Log

Scheduled Tasks, missed task notification

Control Panel → Scheduled Tasks → Advanced → Notify Me of Missed Tasks

Scheduled Tasks, pause

Control Panel → Scheduled Tasks → Advanced → Pause Task Scheduler

Scheduled Tasks, perform only if computer is idle

Control Panel → Scheduled Tasks → right-click task → Properties → Settings tab → Idle Time section

Scheduled Tasks, repeat settings for a single task

Control Panel → Scheduled Tasks → right-click task → Properties → Schedule tab → Advanced

Scheduled Tasks, schedule settings for a single task

Control Panel → Scheduled Tasks → right-click task → Properties → Schedule tab

Scheduled Tasks, security policies

Group Policy (*gpedit.msc*) → Computer Configuration → Administrative Templates → Windows Components → Task Scheduler

Group Policy (*gpedit.msc*) → User Configuration → Administrative Templates → Windows Components → Task Scheduler

Scheduled Tasks, stop hung tasks

Control Panel → Scheduled Tasks → right-click task → Properties → Settings tab → Stop the task if it runs for...

Sc-Si

Screen

See "Display."

Screensaver settings

Control Panel → Display → Screen Saver tab

Scrollbars, color

Control Panel → Display → Appearance tab → Advanced → choose "3D Objects" from the "Item" list

Scrollbars, size

Control Panel → Display → Appearance tab → Advanced → choose "Scrollbar" from the "Item" list

Search, Address Bar

Control Panel → Internet Options → Advanced tag → Search from the Address Bar

Search, include network folders and printers

Control Panel → Folder Options → View tab → Automatically search for network folders and printers

---

Shared folders, include in searches

Control Panel → Folder Options → View tab → Automatically search for network folders and printers

Shared folders, make accessible to all users

Control Panel → Folder Options → View tab → Use simple file sharing

(Turn this off to further restrict access to shared resources.)

Shift Key, make it "sticky"

Control Panel → Accessibility Options → Keyboard tab → Use StickyKeys

Single-click required to open icons

Control Panel → Folder Options → General tab → Single-click to open an item

Software

The following settings control the installation of software in Windows XP.

Software, install or uninstall

Control Panel → Add or Remove Programs

Software, install or uninstall (network components)

Control Panel → Network Connections → Advanced → Optional Networking Components

Software, installation security policies

Group Policy (*gpedit.msc*) → Computer Configuration → Administrative Templates → Windows Components → Windows Installer

Group Policy (*gpedit.msc*) → User Configuration → Administrative Templates → Windows Components → Windows Installer

Sounds

These settings involve Windows' support audio hardware. See also "Speech" and "Voice."

Sounds, default audio devices for playback, recording, and MIDI

Control Panel → Sounds and Audio Devices → Audio tab

Sounds, disable unwanted audio devices

Control Panel → Sounds and Audio Devices → Audio tab → Use only default devices

Sounds, events that trigger sounds

Control Panel → Sounds and Audio Devices → Sounds tab

Sounds, list devices

Control Panel → Sounds and Audio Devices → Hardware tab

Sounds, mute all

Control Panel → Sounds and Audio Devices → Volume tab → Mute

Sounds, play in web pages

Control Panel → Internet Options → Advanced tag → Multimedia → Play sounds in web pages

Sounds, play sounds when Caps Lock, Num Lock, or Scroll Lock is pressed
Control Panel → Accessibility Options → Keyboard tab → Use ToggleKeys

Sounds, record and edit
See "Sound Recorder" in Chapter 4.

Sounds, show visual notification
Control Panel → Accessibility Options → Sound tab

Sounds, speaker orientation
Control Panel → Sounds and Audio Devices → Volume tab → Speaker settings section → Advanced → Speakers tab

Sounds, speaker troubleshooting
Control Panel → Sounds and Audio Devices → Volume tab → Speaker settings section → Advanced → Performance tab

Sounds, speaker volume
Control Panel → Sounds and Audio Devices → Volume tab → Speaker settings section → Speaker Volume

Sounds, surround sound setup
Control Panel → Sounds and Audio Devices → Volume tab → Speaker settings section → Advanced → Speakers tab

Sounds, Volume
Control Panel → Sounds and Audio Devices → Volume tab

Speech

The speech synthesizer included with Windows XP is basically intended for use with the Narrator feature discussed in Chapter 4. See also "Accessibility," "Sounds," and "Voice."

Speech, read text on screen
See "Narrator" in Chapter 4.

Speech, recording voice
See "Voice."

Speech, select preferred audio device
Control Panel → Speech → Text to Speech tab → Audio Output

Speech, speed
Control Panel → Speech → Text to Speech tab → Voice speed section

Speech, voice selection
Control Panel → Speech → Text to Speech tab → Voice selection section

Speech, volume
Volume Control (*sndvol32.exe*) → adjust master or "Wave" controls

Start Menu

The look and feel of the Start menu, a component of Windows Explorer (discussed in Chapter 4), can be controlled with the following settings. See also "Desktop" and "Windows Explorer."

Start menu, button look and feel
Control Panel → Display → Appearance tab → Windows and buttons list

Start menu, clear list of recently opened applications
Control Panel → Taskbar and Start Menu → Start Menu tab → Customize → General tab → Clear List

Start menu, enable dragging and dropping (Classic Start menu only)
Control Panel → Taskbar and Start Menu → Start Menu tab → Customize → "Advanced Start menu options" section → Enable Dragging and Dropping

Start menu, enable dragging and dropping (XP Start menu only)
Control Panel → Taskbar and Start Menu → Start Menu tab → Customize → Advanced tab → "Start menu items" section → Enable Dragging and Dropping

Start menu, hide infrequently accessed applications (Classic Start menu only)
Control Panel → Taskbar and Start Menu → Start Menu tab → Customize → "Advanced Start menu options" section → Use Personalized Menus

Start menu, highlight newly installed programs (XP Start menu only)
Control Panel → Taskbar and Start Menu → Start Menu tab → Customize → Advanced tab → Highlight newly installed programs

Start menu, look and feel
Control Panel → Taskbar and Start Menu → Start Menu tab → "Start menu" or "Classic Start menu"

Start menu, number of recently opened applications to show (XP Start menu only)
Control Panel → Taskbar and Start Menu → Start Menu tab → Customize → General tab → "Programs" section

Start menu, open menus when hovering with mouse (XP Start menu only)
Control Panel → Taskbar and Start Menu → Start Menu tab → Customize → Advanced tab → Open submenus when I pause on them with my mouse

Startmenu, size of icons (Classic Start menu only)
Control Panel → Taskbar and Start Menu → Start Menu tab → Customize → Advanced tab → "Start menu items" section → Show Small Icons in Start Menu

Start menu, size of icons (XP Start menu only)
Control Panel → Taskbar and Start Menu → Start Menu tab → Customize → General tab → "Select an icon size for programs" section

Startup

These settings affect what happens when Windows XP is first started.

Startup, log
Control Panel → System → Advanced tab → Startup and Recovery section → Settings → System failure section

Startup, multiboot menu settings
Control Panel → System → Advanced tab → Startup and Recovery section → Settings → System startup section

Startup, sound
See "Sounds."

St-Sy

Status Bar, show in Explorer
Explorer → View → Status Bar

Style sheets, impose a single style sheet for all web pages
Control Panel → Internet Options → General tab → Accessibility → Format documents using my stylesheet

Style, apply to controls in web pages
Control Panel → Internet Options → Advanced tag → Browsing → Enable visual styles on buttons and controls in web pages

Style, enable / disable all styles
Control Panel → System → Advanced tab → Performance section → Settings → Visual Effects tab → Custom

Style, visual style of windows and buttons
Control Panel → Display → Appearance tab → Windows and buttons list

Swap File, size and location
See "Virtual memory, settings."

Synchronize
See "Offline Files."

System Restore

See also "System Restore" in Chapter 4.

System Restore, disk space usage
Control Panel → System → System Restore tab → Disk space usage section

System Restore, enable / disable
Control Panel → System → System Restore tab → Turn off System Restore

System Restore, policies
Group Policy (*gpedit.msc*) → Computer Configuration → Administrative Templates → System → System Restore

System Restore, status
Control Panel → System → System Restore tab → Status section

Task

Task, show extra task pane in folder windows
Control Panel → Folder Options → General tab → Tasks section

Task Manager, show in Ctrl-Alt-Del window
Group Policy (*gpedit.msc*) → User Configuration → Administrative Templates → System → Ctrl+Alt+Del Options

See "Task Manager" in Chapter 4 for more information.

Task Scheduler
See "Scheduled Tasks."

Taskbar

The Taskbar not only holds the Start menu button, but provides rudimentary control over running applications. See also "Taskbar Notification Area," later in this chapter, and "Task Manager" in Chapter 4.

Taskbar, group buttons by application

Control Panel → Taskbar and Start Menu → Taskbar tab → Group similar Taskbar buttons

(This setting only has meaning with applications, like word processors that can open more than one document window simultaneously, and is configured to display those windows as separate buttons on the Taskbar.)

Taskbar, hide when not in use

Control Panel → Taskbar and Start Menu → Taskbar tab → Auto-hide the Taskbar

Taskbar, keep on top of other windows

Control Panel → Taskbar and Start Menu → Taskbar tab → Keep the Taskbar on top of other windows

Taskbar, move to a different screen location

Click on an empty portion of the Taskbar and drag

Taskbar, prevent moving and resizing

Control Panel → Taskbar and Start Menu → Taskbar tab → Lock the Taskbar

Right-click on Taskbar → Toolbars → Lock the Taskbar

Taskbar, resize

Drag the border of the Taskbar to make it larger or smaller

Taskbar, sliding button animation (enable / disable)

Control Panel → System → Advanced tab → Performance section → Settings → Visual Effects tab → Custom

Taskbar, style

Control Panel → Display → Appearance tab → Windows and buttons list

Taskbar Notification Area

Commonly known as the Tray, the Taskbar Notification Area is the little box on the right-side of the Taskbar that typically holds the clock and several application status icons. These settings allow you to add and remove items from this area (see Figure 5-7).

Taskbar Notification Area, hide infrequently accessed applications

Control Panel → Taskbar and Start Menu → Taskbar tab → Hide inactive icons

Taskbar Notification Area, network icon

Control Panel → Network Connections → right-click connection → Properties → General tab → Show icon in notification area when connected

Taskbar Notification Area, power icon

Control Panel → Power Options → Advanced tab → Always show icon on the Taskbar

Figure 5-7. The Customized Notifications dialog helps reduce clutter by letting you hide the Tray icons you don't need

Taskbar Notification Area, volume control (yellow speaker)
Control Panel → Sounds and Audio Devices → Volume tab → Place volume icon in the Taskbar

Tele-Teln

Telephony settings
Control Panel → Phone and Modem Options → Advanced tab

Telnet Server, restrictions
Control Panel → Network Connections → right-click connection → Properties → Advanced tab → Settings → Services tab

Temporary Internet Files

Also known as Internet Explorer's browser cache, the Temporary Internet Files folder is used to store recently viewed web pages for quicker access. See also "Internet Explorer."

Temporary Internet Files, clear automatically when browser is closed
Control Panel → Internet Options → Advanced tag → Security → Empty Temporary Internet Files folder when browser is closed

Temporary Internet Files, policy regarding encrypted pages
Control Panel → Internet Options → Advanced tag → Security → Do not save encrypted pages to disk

Temporary Internet Files, settings
Control Panel → Internet Options → General tab → Temporary Internet Files section → Settings

Terminal Server

Terminal Server, disable compositing effects in Internet Explorer

Control Panel → Internet Options → Advanced tag → Browsing → Force offscreen compositing even under Terminal Server

Terminal Server, security policies

Group Policy (*gpedit.msc*) → Computer Configuration → Administrative Templates → Windows Components → Terminal Services

Group Policy (*gpedit.msc*) → User Configuration → Administrative Templates → Windows Components → Terminal Services

Text Cursor

The text cursor, also known as the Insertion Point, is the blinking bar shown in most text fields.

Text Cursor, blink rate

Control Panel → Keyboard → Speed tab → Cursor blink rate

Text Cursor, blink rate and size

Control Panel → Accessibility Options → Display tab → Cursor Options section

Text Cursor, change mouse "I-beam" cursor

Control Panel → Mouse → Pointers tab → choose "Text Select" from "Customize" list

The-Thu

Themes

Control Panel → Display → Themes tab

Thumbnails, cache

Control Panel → Folder Options → View tab → Do not cache thumbnails

(Disable this option to force Explorer to reread thumbnails every time.)

Thumbnails, show in Explorer

Explorer → View → Thumbnails

Time

Einstein showed us that time is relative. On your computer, however, you may desire a greater sense of consistency. The following options affect your computer's clock and they way the current time is displayed.

Time, customize display

Control Panel → Regional and Language Options → Regional Options tab → Customize → Time tab

Time, set

Control Panel → Date and Time → Date & Time tab

Time, synchronize with Internet time server automatically
> Control Panel → Date and Time → Internet Time tab

Time, time service policies
> Group Policy (*gpedit.msc*) → Computer Configuration → Administrative Templates → System → Windows Time Service

Time, time zone
> Control Panel → Date and Time → Time Zone tab

Ti-To

Titlebar, font, color, and size
> Control Panel → Display → Appearance tab → Advanced → choose "Active Title Bar" or "Inactive Title Bar" from the "Item" list

Titlebar, size only
> Control Panel → Display → Appearance tab → Advanced → choose "Caption Buttons" from the "Item" list

Toolbar, size and font for floating toolbar captions
> Control Panel → Display → Appearance tab → Advanced → choose "Palette Title" from the "Item" list

Tooltips

These settings affect the look and feel of the little yellow pop-up notes that appear from time to time.

Tooltips, animation
> Control Panel → Display → Appearance tab → Effects → Use the following transition effect for menus and tooltips

Tooltips, animation (enable / disable)
> Control Panel → System → Advanced tab → Performance section → Settings → Visual Effects tab → Custom

Tooltips, enable / disable (Desktop, Taskbar, and Explorer only)
> Control Panel → Folder Options → View tab → Show pop-up description for folder and Desktop items

Tooltips, font and color
> Control Panel → Display → Appearance tab → Advanced → choose "ToolTip" from the "Item" list

Tr-Us

Transition effects, enable / disable
> Control Panel → Display → Appearance tab → Effects → Use the following transition effect for menus and tooltips

Tray
> See "Taskbar Notification Area."

Uninstall Hardware
    Control Panel → Add Hardware

Uninstall Software
    Control Panel → Add or Remove Programs

Uninterruptible Power Supply (UPS) settings
    Control Panel → Power Options → UPS tab

User names in web pages, saving
    Control Panel → Internet Options → Content tab → AutoComplete

Users

The following settings concern user accounts, security, and user policies in Windows XP. See also "Passwords."

Users, add new user account
    Control Panel → User Accounts → Create a new account

Users, advanced account management
    Local Users and Groups (*lusrmgr.msc*); see "Microsoft Management Console" in Chapter 4.

Users, allow fast switching between users
    Control Panel → User Accounts → Change the way users log on or off → Use Fast User Switching

Users, group management
    Local Users and Groups (*lusrmgr.msc*); see "Microsoft Management Console" in Chapter 4.

Users, multiple profiles for each user account
    Control Panel → System → Advanced tab → User Profiles section → Settings

Users, passwords
    See "Passwords."

Users, registered user
    See "Registered User, change" and "Registered User, view."

Users, security policies
    Group Policy (*gpedit.msc*) → Computer Configuration → Windows Settings → Security Settings → Local Policies → User Rights Assignment

    Group Policy (*gpedit.msc*) → Computer Configuration → Administrative Templates → System → User Profiles

    Group Policy (*gpedit.msc*) → User Configuration → Administrative Templates → System → User Profiles

Users, security policies for groups
    Group Policy (*gpedit.msc*) → Computer Configuration → Administrative Templates → System → Group Policy

    Group Policy (*gpedit.msc*) → User Configuration → Administrative Templates → System → Group Policy

Task and Setting Index

Vid-Vir

Video, edit and convert

See "Windows Movie Maker" in Chapter 4.

Video, play in web pages

Control Panel → Internet Options → Advanced tag → Multimedia → Play videos in web pages

Virtual memory, settings

Control Panel → System → Advanced tab → Performance section → Settings → Advanced tab → Change

Voice

Although Windows XP doesn't include voice recognition software, these settings affect the recording of voice (through a microphone, usually) into third-party voice recognition or applications (such as Sound Recorder).

Voice, calibrate volume settings

Control Panel → Sounds and Audio Devices → Voice tab → Test hardware

Voice, playback and recording volume

Control Panel → Sounds and Audio Devices → Voice tab

Voice, speech synthesis

See "Speech."

Vo-We

Volume

See "Sounds."

Wallpaper

See "Background."

Warnings in web pages, enable / disable

Control Panel → Internet Options → Security tab → Custom Level

Web pages

See "Internet Explorer."

Web pages, set default browser

Control Panel → Internet Options → Programs tab → Internet Explorer should check to see whether it is the default browser

Web pages, set default editor

Control Panel → Internet Options → Programs tab → HTML Editor

Web Server, restrictions

Control Panel → Network Connections → right-click connection → Properties → Advanced tab → Settings → Services tab

Welcome screen, enable / disable

Control Panel → User Accounts → Change the way users log on or off → Use the Welcome screen

Windows

These settings affect the look and feel of application function;windows.

Windows, background of multiple document interface (MDI) windows
Control Panel → Display → Appearance tab → Advanced → choose "Application Background" from the "Item" list

Windows, background of non-MDI windows
Control Panel → Display → Appearance tab → Advanced → choose "Window" from the "Item" list

Windows, cascade all open application windows
Right-click on Taskbar → Cascade Windows

Windows, closing crashed applications
Task Manager (*taskmgr.exe*) → Applications tab

Windows, closing hidden applications
Task Manager (*taskmgr.exe*) → Processes tab

Windows, color of borders
Control Panel → Display → Appearance tab → Advanced → choose "3D Objects" from the "Item" list

(You can also use "Active Window Border" and "Inactive Window Border," but it will only affect a tiny stripe.)

Windows, minimize all open application windows
Windows Logo Key + D

Windows, show outline or full window when dragging
Control Panel → Display → Appearance tab → Effects → Show window contents while dragging

Windows, tile all open application windows
Right-click on Taskbar → Tile Windows Horizontally or Tile Windows Vertically

Windows, titlebar font, color, and size
Control Panel → Display → Appearance tab → Advanced → choose "Active Title Bar" or "Inactive Title Bar" from the "Item" list

Windows Explorer

Often referred to simply as "Explorer," Windows Explorer is the default interface shell in Windows XP and is responsible for the Desktop, the Start menu, and all folder windows. See also "Folders."

Windows Explorer, access digital camera memory as a drive (still camera only)
Control Panel → Scanners and Cameras → Add Device

Windows Explorer, additional security policies
Group Policy (*gpedit.msc*) → User Configuration → Administrative Templates → Windows Components → Windows Explorer

Windows Explorer, columns in details view
Explorer → View → Details → View → Choose Details

Windows Explorer, group similar items

Explorer → View Arrange Icons by → Show in Groups

Windows Explorer, refresh view

Explorer → View → Refresh or press F5

Windows Explorer, reuse window when launching Internet shortcuts

Control Panel → Internet Options → Advanced tag → Browsing → Reuse windows for launching shortcuts

Windows Explorer, show lines in tree view (Folders Explorer bar)

Control Panel → Folder Options → View tab → Display simple folder view in Explorer's Folders list

Windows Explorer, show Status Bar

Explorer → View → Status Bar

Windows Explorer, toolbar, customize

Explorer → View → Toolbars → Customize

Windows Explorer, toolbar, icon size

Explorer → View → Toolbars → Customize → Icon options

Windows Explorer, toolbar, prevent being moved

Explorer → View → Toolbars → Lock the Toolbars

Windows Explorer, toolbar, text captions

Explorer → View → Toolbars → Customize → Text options

Windows File Protection, advanced settings

Group Policy (*gpedit.msc*) → Computer Configuration → Administrative Templates → System → Windows File Protection

---

Wi...

Windows Registered User information

Control Panel → System → General tab

Windows Startup, change Chkdsk options

See "Chkntfs" in Chapter 4.

Windows Startup, multiboot configuration

See "Boot Configuration Manager" in Chapter 4.

Windows startup, selectively disable startup options

See "System Configuration Utility" in Chapter 4.

Windows Update

Internet Explorer → Tools → Windows Update

Windows Update, automatic updating

Control Panel → System → Automatic Updates tab

Windows version

Control Panel → System → General tab

Windows XP Style for screen elements

Control Panel → Display → Appearance tab → Windows and buttons list

6

The Command Prompt

The point and click graphical user interface (GUI) revolutionized the way we use computers, eliminating the need to remember cryptic commands and type them at an unfriendly prompt. However, as users become more advanced, they often rediscover the older command prompt interface and learn to appreciate how quickly and efficiently certain tasks can still be performed.

Microsoft certainly hasn't forgotten Windows' roots in the command prompt, either, as it is still an integral part of Windows XP. As explained in the beginning of Chapter 4, many of the programs that come with Windows don't have corresponding shortcuts in the Start menu, and therefore must be started with some form of the command prompt. Other applications, such as Notepad or Windows Explorer, have *command-line parameters*, special options that can be specified only if the program is started from the command prompt. And then there are programs, such as Telnet, that are still entirely command-line based.

Understanding the command prompt in all of its forms is not only helpful in getting a better idea of how Windows works, but can open up new ways of accomplishing tasks that would otherwise require repetitive pointing and clicking. Disk Operating System (DOS) was the command-line-only OS run by early PCs, and Windows was merely an application that ran on top of DOS. Windows NT, the predecessor to Windows XP, was Microsoft's first version of Windows that did not rely on DOS. However, in Windows NT, 2000, and XP, the command prompt is still made available as a standalone application.

Later in this chapter, you'll find complete documentation on MS-DOS Batch Files, which can be used to automate repetitive tasks by incorporating a list of commands into a single script that can be typed like a command at the command prompt, or even double-clicked in Explorer. Even if you don't use the Command Prompt, batch files can be a great time saver and are typically easier to write than WSH scripts (see Chapter 9).

Using the Command Line

The premise of the command prompt is simple enough: commands are typed, one at a time, at a blinking cursor. The commands are then issued when the Enter key is pressed. After the command has completed, a new prompt is shown, allowing additional commands to be typed.

Some commands are fairly rudimentary, requiring only that you type their name. Other commands are more involved and can require several options (sometimes called arguments or command-line parameters). For example, the del command (discussed later in this chapter) is used to delete one or more files; it requires that the name of the file be specified after the command, like this:

```
del /p myfile.txt
```

Here, *myfile.txt* is the filename to be deleted and /p is an extra option used to modify the behavior of del. The fact that this usage is not limited to internal commands (like del) is what makes the command line (but not necessarily the Command Prompt application) such an important part of Windows XP's design. For example:

```
notepad myfile.txt
```

is what Windows executes behind the scenes, by default, when you double-click the *myfile.txt* icon in Explorer. Notepad (discussed in Chapter 4) is effectively a "command" here. If you type the filename of any existing file at the command prompt, it instructs Windows to launch that file. This works for applications, Windows Shortcuts, batch files, documents, or any other type of file; the only requirement is that the file be located in the current working directory (see "cd or chdir," later in this chapter) or in a folder specified in the path (also discussed later in this chapter).

Specifying a filename as an argument when launching Notepad (such as *myfile.txt* in the example above) from the command prompt instructs Notepad to open that file. Throughout this book, you'll see references to a component's command line syntax that documents these otherwise hidden features. Since every program and command has its own set of command-line options, it's best to get a feel for the way they work in general rather than trying to commit them all to memory.

If you've executed a command that takes a long time to complete, such as one that displays a great deal of information on the screen, you can interrupt it by pressing Ctrl-C.

Open the control menu of any open Command Prompt window (click the little icon in the top left of the window or press Alt-Space) and select Properties to customize the look and feel of the command prompt window. An important option here is Layout → Screen Buffer Size → Height, which controls the number of lines kept in memory; this enables you to scroll up to view a history of your entire session. This is useful, for example, if you're looking at long directory listings. Note that this is not the same as Options → Buffer Size, which contains a "most frequently used" list of typed commands; use the up-and-down error keys at the prompt to cycle through them.

Copy and paste operations are also possible at the Command Prompt, but not using the traditional keyboard shortcuts: Ctrl-X, Ctrl-C, and Ctrl-V won't work here. If QuickEdit is enabled (Properties → Options → QuickEdit mode), text can be highlighted at any time with the mouse, copied to the clipboard by pressing Enter, and pasted by clicking anywhere in the window with the right mouse button. If QuickEdit is disabled (the default), right-clicking will display the Edit menu; select Mark to begin highlighting text and then go to Edit → Copy or simply press Enter to copy the text to the clipboard.

Finally, the prompt itself, known as the *caret* (>), is usually accompanied by a folder name representing the current working directory. Note that the term "directory" is synonymous with "folder," and is used throughout this chapter only because it is customary when discussing the command prompt.

See "Command Prompt" in Chapter 4 for more information on the *cmd.exe* application and its command-line parameters. Of special interest is the /e parameter, which enables or disables "command extensions," additional features documented throughout this chapter.

Command Prompt Choices

Windows XP provide three different components, all essentially different implementations of the command-line interface. These three components work similarly, but there are some important differences and limitations.

Command Prompt (cmd.exe)

Commonly known as a DOS box because of its visual and functional likeness to DOS, the Command Prompt window (see Figure 6-1) is the most complete implementation of the command prompt in Windows XP. Any program, GUI- or command-line based, can be started by typing its executable filename at the prompt. In addition, a variety of internal DOS commands (discussed later in this chapter), used primarily for file management, can be executed at the prompt.

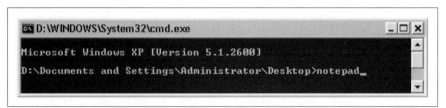

Figure 6-1. The Command Prompt window

If a command-line based program is launched, it is run in the same window. Many command-prompt applications simply display information and quit; in this case, you'd be returned to the prompt immediately after the program output.

An important distinction between the Command Prompt and the alternatives below is that the Command Prompt maintains context between commands. Each instance of the command interpreter runs in its own virtual machine, each with its own "environment." The environment includes such information as the current directory, the search path (the directories in which the command interpreter looks for the commands whose names you type), and the format of the prompt. Some commands, once issued, change the environment for subsequent commands. The most obvious example of this is when you type a sequence of commands, like this:

```
C:>cd \stuff
C:\Stuff>notepad myfile.txt
```

This command sequence couldn't be carried out at either the Run prompt or the Address Bar. Since they execute only one command at a time and then exit, the context is lost between each command. Concepts such as "change directory" therefore have no meaning.

But the Command Prompt has limitations as well. Unlike the Address Bar or Start → Run, if you type a web address (URL) or the name of a folder at the Command Prompt, you'll get a "not recognized" error.

Note that Windows XP also includes *command.com*, the Command Prompt application found in Windows 9x/Me. While visually and functionally similar to *cmd.exe*, it's included for legacy support only. *Cmd.exe* is more sophisticated and has native support for long filenames.

Start → Run

Any program can be run by typing its executable filename here, as shown in Figure 6-2, just like in a Command Prompt window. However, in the case of command-line based programs, the context is lost every time a new program is launched. Internal Command Prompt commands, such as CD and DIR, discussed later in this chapter, are not recognized here or in the Address Bar.

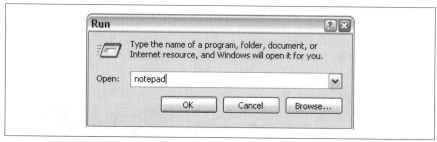

Figure 6-2. The Start → Run dialog

Unlike the Command Prompt, you can type a web address (URL) here to open it in the default web browser, or any folder name to open it in an Explorer folder window.

Start → Run is commonly used to start programs, which is an alternative to wading through Start → Programs or opening a new Command Prompt window. However, if you've enabled the Address Bar, there's little need for Start → Run, since the Toolbar is so much more convenient.

Address Bar

The Address Bar, shown in Figure 6-3, is nearly the functional equivalent of Start → Run, with a few exceptions. There are actually three different Address Toolbars: the one attached to the Taskbar, the one that's part of Windows Explorer, and the one that's part of Internet Explorer.

Figure 6-3. The Address Bar on the Taskbar

The Taskbar Address Bar can be enabled by right-clicking on an empty area of the Taskbar and selecting Toolbars → Address. This implementation is functionally identical to Start → Run.

The Address Bar can be enabled in Windows Explorer and Internet Explorer by going to View → Toolbars → Address Bar. In either of these Windows, the launching programs is handled the same way as with the Taskbar Address Bar and with Start → Run.

The various Address Bars differ only in the way folder names and web addresses are handled. If you type a folder name into either Windows Explorer or Internet Explorer, the contents of that folder will be shown in the current window (i.e., no new window will be opened). If a web address, such as *http://www.annoyances.org/*, is typed into the Taskbar Address Bar or the Windows Explorer Address Bar, that address is opened in the default web browser. If, the other hand, an address is typed into Internet Explorer's Address Bar, the page at that address is opened in IE regardless of the default browser setting.

The main difference between the Address Bar and the Start → Run prompt is in the assumptions that are made about ambiguous names and addresses. For example, if you type Notepad or http://www.annoyances.org/ into either place, Windows would launch a program or web site, respectively. If you type something that Windows won't recognize, though, like BigBadaBoom, what happens next depends on where the text was typed. If you type the text into an Address Bar, Windows XP will open a web browser to the location *http://BigBadaBoom/* and then complain that the web site doesn't exist. If you type the same text at the Start → Run prompt, you'll get an error message explaining that "Windows cannot find BigBadaBoom."

Wildcards, Pipes, and Redirection

In addition to the various command-line parameters used by each of the commands documented in this chapter (and the components documented in Chapter 4), there are certain symbols used on the command line that have special meaning. Table 6-1 shows these special symbols and what they do. They must be used in conjunction with other commands (they don't stand alone) and can be used in the Command Prompt window, in Start → Run, and in any Address Bar.

Table 6-1. Special symbols on the command line

Symbol	Description
*	Multiple-character wildcard, used to specify a group of files.
?	Single-character wildcard, used to specify multiple files with more precision than *.
.	One dot represents the current directory; see "cd or chdir."
..	Two dots represent the parent directory; see "cd or chdir."
... (three dots)	Three dots represent the grandparent directory; see "cd or chdir."
\	Separates directory names, drive letters, and filenames. By itself, \ represents the root directory of the current drive.
>	Redirects a command's text output into a file instead of the console window; existing files will be overwritten.
>>	Redirects a command's text output into a file instead of the console window, appending existing files.
<	Directs the contents of a text file to a command's input; use in place of keyboard entry to automate interactive command-line applications.
|	Redirects the output of a program or command to a second program or command (this is called a "pipe").

Examples

The following examples demonstrate some uses of wildcards, pipes, and redirection:

.

> Specify all files with all extensions.

professor*.*

> Specify all files (with filenames that begin with "professor") with any extension.

chap??.doc

> Specify all files named "chap" followed by any two characters and with the *doc* extension (e.g., *chap01.doc*, but not *chap1.doc* or *chap.doc*).

dir ..

> List all the files in the current directory's parent.

dir > c:\nutshell\mylist.txt

> List all files in the current directory and store this listing into a file called *mylist.txt* rather than displaying it in the command prompt window. If the file already exists, it will be overwritten.

> In addition to directing output to a file, you can direct to a device, such as NUL (an electronic void). This is useful if you want a command to run without sending output to the screen.

dir c:\windows >> c:\nutshell\mylist.txt

> Add the directory listing of the files in the *c:\Windows* directory to the end of the file *windows.txt*.

> If the specified file doesn't exist, one is created. If one does exist, the output from the command is added to it, unlike with the > key, where the original contents are overwritten.

echo y | del *.*

> Normally, the DEL command has no prompt. However, if you try to delete all the files in a directory, *del* will prompt you for confirmation. To automate this command, the output of the ECHO command (here, just a "y" plus a carriage return) is "piped" into the input (commonly known as STDIN) of the DEL command.

del *.* < y.txt

> Assuming *y.txt* contains only a letter "y" followed by a carriage return, this command has the same effect as the previous example.

sort /+12 < c:\nutshell\mylist.txt

> To sort the lines in a text file (*c:\nutshell\mylist.txt*) on the twelfth character, the SORT command is fed input from the file. The output is sent to the screen, not reordered in the file.

Keep in mind that not all commands handle wildcards in exactly the same way. For example, *dir ** and *dir *.** list the same thing, but *del ** will delete only files without an extension.

Alphabetical Reference to DOS Commands

Most of the following commands are not standalone applications (like those listed in Chapter 4), but rather internal functions of the Command Prompt (*cmd.exe*) application. This restricts their use only to the Command Prompt application. (They won't be recognized by the Address Bar or by Start → Run.) Some items that are standalone programs, but are normally used only in the Command Prompt window, such as *xcopy.exe* and *move.exe*, are listed here rather than in Chapter 4.

---

cd or chdir

Display the name of or change the current working directory (folder).

Syntax

```
cd [/d] [directory]
chdir [/d] [directory]
```

Description

With no arguments, cd displays the full pathname of the current directory. Given the pathname of an existing directory, it changes the current directory to the specified directory.

If *directory* is on a different drive (for example, if the current directory is *c:\dream* and you type cd d:\nightmare), the current working directory on that drive is changed, but the current working drive is not. To change the current drive, use the /d parameter, or simply type the letter followed by a colon, by itself, at the prompt (see the examples below).

Pathnames can be absolute (including the full path starting with the root) or relative to the current directory. A path can be optionally prefixed with a drive letter. The special paths .. and ... (and so on) refer to the parent and grandparent of the current directory, respectively.

Examples

If the current drive is *C:*, make *c:\temp\wild* the current directory:

```
C:\>cd \temp\wild
C:\temp\wild>
```

Note how the current working directory is displayed in the prompt. If the current directory is *c:\temp*, all that is necessary is:

```
C:\temp>cd wild
C:\temp\wild>
```

Change to the parent directory:

```
C:\more\docs\misc>cd ..
C:\more\docs>
```

Change to the grandparent (parent of the parent) directory:

```
C:\more\docs\misc>cd ...
C:\more>
```

Change to the root directory of the current drive:

```
C:\Windows\Desktop\>cd \
C:\>
```

Change to another drive:

```
C:\>cd \d d:\
D:\>
```

or simply:

```
C:\>d:
D:\>
```

Notes

- The chdir and cd commands are functionally identical.
- The "current working directory" only has meaning in the current Command Prompt session and any other Command Prompts or applications launched from that window. If you open a new Command Prompt window, it will start over with it's default (set in the properties of the Windows Shortcut).
- The current directory is shown in the prompt; see "prompt," later in this chapter, for information on changing the information displayed.

---

cls

Clear the DOS window and buffer, leaving only the command prompt and cursor.

Description

Type cls at the prompt to clear the screen and the screen buffer (see "Using the Command Line," earlier in this chapter), which is useful for privacy concerns or simply reducing clutter.

The difference between using cls and simply closing the current Command Prompt window and opening a new one, is that your working environment (such as the current directory) is preserved with cls.

---

cls is also useful in complex batch files—for clearing the screen after one set of inter-
actions or command output. The name cls (Clear Screen) refers to the old days when
DOS owned the whole screen.

copy

Copy one or more files to another location.

Syntax   copy *source destination*
               copy [/a | /b] *source* [/a | /b] [+ *source* [/a | /b] [+ ...]]
                   [*destination* [/a | /b]] [/v] [/y | /-y] [/d] [/z]

Description

copy makes a complete copy of an existing file. If another file by the same name exists
at *destination*, you will be asked if you want to overwrite it.

Omit the destination to copy the specified files to the current working directory. If the
file (or files) to be copied is in a different directory or on a different disk, you can omit
the destination filename. The resulting copy or copies will have the same name as the
original.

You can use the special device name con (or con:) in place of either the source or destination filename to copy from the keyboard to a file (or from a file to the screen).

copy accepts the following parameters and options:

/a   Specifies that the file to copy is in ASCII format

/b   Specifies that the file to copy is a binary file

/v   Verifies that new files are written successfully by comparing them with the
       originals

/y   Suppresses prompting to confirm you want to overwrite an existing destination
       file

/-y   Enables prompting to confirm you want to overwrite an existing destination file
       with the same name (default)

/d   Allow the new file to be decrypted (NTFS volumes only)

/z   Copies networked files in restartable mode

Examples

Copy the file *temp.txt* from *C:* to *d:\files* (all three examples do the same thing):

```
C:\>copy c:\temp.txt d:\files\temp.txt
C:\>copy c:\temp.txt d:\files
C:\>copy temp.txt d:\files
```

The third sample above works here because the source file is located in the current
director. Here's another way to do it:

```
C:\>d:
D:\>cd \files
D:\files>copy c:\temp.txt
```

The Command Prompt

Copy all the files from the directory *d:\Cdsample\Images* to the current directory, giving the copies the same names as the originals:

```
C:\>copy d:\cdsample\images\*.*
C:\>copy d:\cdsample\images\*.* .
```

Copy the file *words.txt* in the current directory to *d:\files*, renaming it *morewords.txt*:

```
C:\>copy words.txt d:\files\morewords.txt
```

Copy all of the files in the current directory to *d:\files* (all three examples do the same thing):

```
C:\>copy *.* d:\files
C:\>copy .\*.* d:\files
C:\>copy . d:\files
```

Notes

- The copy command is easier to use, but xcopy (discussed later in this chapter) is more powerful and flexible.

- It is also possible to use the copy command to concatenate (combine) files. To concatenate files, specify a single file for the destination, but multiple files for the source (using wildcards or *file1*+*file2*+*file3* format):

  ```
  copy mon.txt+tue.txt+wed.txt report.txt
  ```

  You can specify a relative or absolute path (including disk names and/or UNC paths) or use a simple filename. When concatenating, if no destination is specified, the combined files are saved under the name of the first specified file.

  When attempting to concatenate files, copy expects ASCII files by default, so in order to concatenate binary files, you need to use the /b option. The reason for this is that binary files typically contain one or more bytes outside the normal ASCII printable range (i.e., 32 through 127).

- The con device (console) can also be used in conjunction with copy. To create a new text file by typing its contents directly, first enter:

  ```
  C:\>copy con mystuff.txt
  ```

  then type the text to be saved into the file. When you're done, type Ctrl-Z and press Enter. All text typed from the keyboard in this example is then saved as *mystuff.txt*.

  Here's how to copy the contents of the file *mystuff.txt* to the screen (see also "type"):

  ```
  C:\>copy mystuff.txt con
  ```

- Binary file copy is assumed for normal copying, but the /b option should be used when appending one binary file to another, as in:

  ```
  C:\>copy file1+file2 newfile /b
  ```

  By default, when concatenating, both source and destination files are assumed to be ASCII format, since binary files can seldom be usefully concatenated due to internal formatting.

- You can substitute a device (e.g., COM1) for either the source or the destination. The data is copied in ASCII by default.

- copy doesn't copy files that are 0 bytes long; use xcopy to copy these files.

- copy, move, and xcopy will prompt you before overwriting an existing file, unless you specify a command line parameter instructing them to do otherwise. To change the default, set the copycmd environment variable to /y. To restore the default behavior, set copycmd to /-y. See "set" for details.

date

Display or set the system date.

Syntax   date [/t | *date*]

Description

Date is essentially a holdover from the very early days of DOS when the user was required to enter the system date and time every time the computer was started. Now it's essentially included as a way to set the data from the command line; the preferred method is to use Control Panel → Date and Time.

If you type date on the command line without an option, the current date setting is displayed and you are prompted for a new one. Press Enter to keep the same date.

Date accepts the following options:

date
> Specifies the date. Use the *mm-dd-*[*yy*]*yy* format. Values for *yy* can be from 80 through 99; values for *yyyy* can be from 1980 through 2099. Separate month, day, and year with periods, hyphens, or slashes.

/t
> Displays the current date without prompting for a new one.

Notes

- The date format depends on settings in Control Panel → Regional and Language Options.
- Windows records the current date for each file you create or change. This date is listed next to the filename in the dir directory listing.
- The date display format for most applications can be changed in Control Panel → Regional and Language Options → Regional Options tab → Customize, but this doesn't affect the output of the DOS date command.

See Also
"time"

del or erase

Delete one or more files.

Syntax   del [/p] [/f] [/s] [/q] [/a:*attributes*] *filename*
        erase [/p] [/f] [/s] [/q] [/a:*attributes*] *filename*

Description

The del command is used to delete one or more files from the command line without sending them to the Recycle Bin.

The del options are:

filename

Specifies the file(s) to delete. If you do not specify the drive or path, the file is assumed to be in the current directory. You can use standard * and ? wildcards to specify the files to delete.

/p

Prompts for confirmation before deleting each file.

/f

Forces deletion of read-only files.

/s

Delete specified files in all subdirectories (when using wildcards).

/q

Quiet mode; do not prompt if *filename* is *.*.

/a:*attributes*

Selects files to delete based on attributes (read-only, hidden, system, or archive). See "Attrib" in Chapter 4 for more information on attributes.

Examples

Delete the file *myfile.txt* in the current directory:

```
C:\>del myfile.txt
```

Delete the file *myfile.txt* in the *c:\files* directory:

```
C:\>del c:\files\myfile.txt
```

Delete all files with the pattern *myfile.** (e.g., *myfile.doc*, *myfile.txt*, etc.) in the current directory, but prompt for each deletion:

```
C:\>del c:\files\myfile.* /p
```

Notes

- The del and erase commands are functionally identical.
- Using the del command to delete a file does not move it to the Recycle Bin. In other words, you can't get a file back once you use the del command, unless you have a special "unerase" disk recovery utility.

---

dir

Display a list of files and subdirectories in a directory (folder).

Syntax   dir [*filename*] [/b] [/c] [/d] [/l] [/n] [/p] [/q] [/s] [/w] [/x]
              [/4] [/a:*attributes*] [/o:*sortorder*] [/t:*timefield*]

Description

Without any options, dir displays the disk's volume label and serial number, a list of all files and subdirectories (except hidden and system files) in the current directory,

---

file/directory size, date/time of last modification, the long filename, the total number of files listed, their cumulative size, and the free space (in bytes) remaining on the disk.

If you specify one or more file or directory names (optionally including drive and path, or the full UNC path to a shared directory), information for only those files or directories will be listed.

Wildcards (* and ?) can be used to display a subset listing of files and subdirectories.

dir accepts the following options:

/a:*attributes*

Display only files with/without specified attributes (using – as a prefix specifies "not," and a colon between the option and attribute is optional). See "Attrib" in Chapter 4 for more information on attributes.

/b

Use bare format (no heading information or summary). Use with /s to find a filename.

/c

Display compression ratio of files on *Dblspace* or *DrvSpace* drives, assuming 16 sectors/cluster.

/d

Same as /w, except files are sorted vertically.

/l

Use lowercase.

/n

List files in a "new" Unix-like display, where filenames are shown on the right.

/o:*sortorder*

List files in sorted order (using – as a prefix reverses the order, and a colon between the option and attribute is optional):

d   By date and time (earliest first)

e   By extension (sorted alphabetically)

g   Group directories first

n   By name (sorted alphabetically)

s   By size (smallest first)

/p

Pause after each screenful of information; press any key to continue.

/q

Display the owner of each file.

/s

Include all files in all subdirectories, in addition to those in the current directory.

/t:*timefield*

Control which time is used when sorting:

c   Created

a   Last accessed

w   Last modified (written)

/w

Wide list format. File and directory names are listed in five columns and are sorted horizontally. Use /d instead to sort vertically.

/x

Include the "short" 8.3 versions of long filenames. For example, *Sam's File.txt* has an alternate filename, *samsfi~1.txt*, to maintain compatibilty with older applications.

/4

Display the listed years as four digits. By default, two-digit years are displayed.

Examples

Display all files in the current directory:

    C:\>**dir**

Display all files in the current directory that end with the *.txt* extension:

    C:\>**dir *.txt**

Display all files, listing years in four digits and pausing for each screenful:

    C:\>**dir /4 /p**

Display all files, sorted by date and time, latest first:

    C:\>**dir /o-d**

Display only directories:

    C:\>**dir /ad**

List all files on disk, sorted by size, and store output in the file *allfiles.txt*:

    C:\>**dir \ /s /os > allfiles.txt**

List the contents of the shared folder *cdrom* on machine *bubba*:

    C:\>**dir \\bubba\cdrom**

Notes

- To change the default sort order, set the dircmd environment variable to the same value you'd use with the /o parameter. See "set" for details.

- When using a redirection symbol (>) to send dir output to a file or a pipe (|) or to send dir output to another command, you may want to use /b to eliminate heading and summary information.

 dir *filename* /b /s acts as a kind of "find" command, which looks in all subdirectories of the current directory. For example:

    C:\>**dir readme.txt /b /s**
    C:\Windows\readme.txt
    C:\Stuff\Misc\FAQ\readme.txt

  Unfortunately, this usage doesn't work with wildcards; you must specify an actual filename.

- One of Windows Explorer's weaknesses is that there's no way to print a directory listing or save a directory listing into a file. However, the dir command with some clever redirects will do the job.

To print out a sorted directory listing of all files in the Windows directory:

C:\>**dir c:\windows /oa > lpt1**

To create a file containing the directory listing of the same directory:

C:\>**dir c:\windows /oa > c:\myfiles\windows.txt**

Actually, dir can be used to fix this weakness of the Explorer. See *Windows 98 Annoyances* (O'Reilly) for details on how to give the Explorer a Print-Dir facility.

- Files and folders that are hidden (see "Attrib" in Chapter 4) will not show up in dir listings by default. However, if you know the name of a hidden directory, there's nothing stopping you from displaying a listing of the contents in that directory.

echo

Display a string of text; turn command echoing on or off.

Syntax   echo [on | off | *message*]

Description

Echo is typically used with other commands or in a batch file to display text on the screen. It's also used to control command echoing from batch files.

The following options can be used with echo:

on | off
> By default, each command in a batch file is echoed to the screen as it is executed. Echo on and echo off toggles this feature. To turn echoing off without displaying the echo off command, use @echo off. The @ symbol in front of any command in a batch file prevents the line from being displayed.

message
> Types the message you'd like displayed to the console (screen).

Examples

To display an ordinary message, use the following:

echo Hello World!

To display a blank line, use one of the following (all equivalent):

echo.
echo,
echo"

(Note the absence of the space between the echo command and the punctuation; you can also use a colon, semicolon, square brackets, backslash, or forward slash.)

One handy use of echo is to answer y to a confirmation prompt such as the one del issues when asked to delete all the files in a directory. For example, if you wanted to clear out the contents of the \temp directory from a batch file, you could use the following command:

echo y | del c:\temp*.*

or even:

echo y | if exists c:\temp*.* del c:\temp*.*

This construct works because the pipe character takes the output of the first command and inserts it as the input to the second.

Announce the success or failure of a condition tested in a batch file:

```
if exist *.rpt echo The report has arrived.
```

It's a good idea to give the user usage or error information in the event that they don't supply proper arguments to a batch file. You can do that as follows:

```
@echo off
if (%1) == () goto usage
. . .
:usage
echo You must supply a filename.
```

See Also

"type"

exit

End the current Command Prompt session and close the window.

Syntax   exit [/b] [*exitcode*]

Description

Typing exit has the same effect as closing the Command Prompt window with the [x] button.

dir accepts the following options:

/b   If exit is used from within a batch file, it will close the current Command Prompt window. Specify /b to exit the batch file but leave *cmd.exe* running.

exitcode
Specifies a numerical "exit code" number that is passed to the application or process that launched the Command Prompt or started the batch file. *Exitcode* is typically used when one batch file runs another batch file and wishes to report to the "parent" batch file whether successful or not.

Notes

If you start a new Command Prompt session by typing cmd in an open Command Prompt window, exit will end that session. However, since the "parent" session is still active, the window won't close until you type exit again.

find   *\Windows\Command\find.exe*

Search in one or more files for text.

To Launch   find [/v] [/c] [/n] [/i] [/offline] "*string*" [*filename*[...]]

Description

After searching the specified files, find displays any lines of text that contain the string you've specified for your search. find is useful for searching for specific words (strings) in files, but don't get it confused with Start → Search → For Files or Folders (See "Windows Explorer" in Chapter 4), which is capable of searching for text, files, directories, etc., and has many other capabilities that the find command doesn't have.

The find options are:

"string"
> The text to look for, enclosed in quotation marks.

filename
> The file(s) in which to search. Although wildcards (*, ?) are not supported, multiple filenames can be specified as long as they are separated with commas. If *filename* is omitted, find searches text typed at the prompt or piped from another command via the pipe character (|), as described in "Wildcards, Pipes, and Redirection," earlier this chapter.

/c
> Displays only the count of lines containing the string.

/i
> Ignores the case of characters when searching for the string.

/n
> Displays line numbers with the displayed lines.

/v
> Displays all lines not containing the specified string.

/offline
> Includes files with the offline attribute set (that otherwise would be skipped).

Examples

Search for "redflag" in *myemployees.txt*:

> `C:\>`**`find "redflag" myexployees.txt`**

Count occurrences of the word "deceased" in *myemployees.txt*:

> `C:\>`**`find /c "deceased" myexployees.txt`**

Search the current directory for the string "cls" in all *.bat* files and store the result in the file *cls.txt* (note that >> rather than > is necessary when redirecting the output of a for loop):

> `C:\>`**`for %f in (*.bat) do find "cls" %f >> cls.txt`**

Notes

- You can search through multiple files by specifying each file to search on the command line, but unfortunately, wildcards (* and ?) are not accepted in the filename. To search for a string in a set of files, however, it's possible to use the find command within a for loop structure. If redirecting for to a file, use >> rather than > (see the earlier example).

- If a filename is not specified, find searches the text input from the "standard" source (usually the keyboard), a pipe, or a redirected file.

  If you have a Unix background, you might be tempted to try something like:

  > `dir c:\ /s /b | find "chap"`

  to search the contents of all files with "chap" in their names, but in fact, all you'd be doing is running find on the list of filenames, not on their contents.

- find won't recognize a string that has a carriage return embedded in it. For example, if "chapter" is at the end of the line and "05" on the next, find won't report a match on "chapter 05."

md or mkdir

Create a new directory (folder).

Syntax   md [*drive:*]*path*
              mkdir [*drive:*]*path*

Description

Windows XP, like its predecessors, uses a hierarchical directory structure to organize its filesystem. On any physical disk, the filesystem begins with the root directory, signified by a lone backslash.

md and mkdir accept the following option:

[drive:]path
> Specifies the directory to create.

Examples

Create a subdirectory named *harry* in the current directory:

    C:\tom\dick>**md harry**

Create a new directory called *newdir* under the *c:\olddir* directory:

    C:\>**md c:\olddir\newdir**

If *c:\olddir* doesn't exist, it will be created as well.

Create two new directories, *c:\rolling* and *c:\stones*:

    C:\>**md rolling stones**

Create a single new directory, *c:\rolling tones*:

    C:\>**md "rolling stones"**

(Enclose directory names in quotation marks to accommodate spaces).

Notes

- The md and mkdir commands are functionally identical.
- You can also create new folders in Windows Explorer by going to File → New → Folder.
- You may indicate an absolute or relative path for the path parameter. When absolute, the new directory is created as specified from the root directory. When relative, the directory is created in relation to the current directory.

more

\windows\system32\more.com

Display the contents of a file with the output of another command, but pause the display so that only one screen of text is shown at a time.

Syntax   more /e [/c] [/p] [/s] [/tn] [+n] [*filename*]
more [/e [/c] [/p] [/s] [/tn] [+n]] < *filename*
{some other command} | more [/e [/c] [/p] [/s] [/tn] [+n]]

Description

more displays one screen of text at a time. more is often used as a filter with other commands that may send a lot of output to the screen (i.e., to read standard input from a pipe or redirected file). Press any key to see the next screenful of output. Press Ctrl-C to end the output before it is done.

more accepts the following options:

filename
> Specifies the name of a file to display.

/c Clears the screen before displaying file.

/e If the /e option is specified, the following additional extended commands are available at the -- More -- prompt:

> P*n*
> > Displays next *n* lines.
>
> S*n*
> > Skips next *n* lines.
>
> Spacebar
> > Displays next page.
>
> Enter
> > Displays next line.
>
> F
> > Displays next file.
>
> Q
> > Quits.
>
> =
> > Shows line number.
>
> ?
> > Shows help.

/p
> Expands form-feed characters.

/s
> Squeezes multiple blank lines into a single line.

/t*n*
> Expands tabs characters to *n* spaces (default 8).

/+*n*
> Starts display of the file at line *n*.

filename
> Specifies the name of a file to display.

Examples

Display the contents of \Windows\readme.txt and pause for each screenful of text (both of the following examples have the same effect):

```
C:\>more c:\windows\readme.txt
C:\>type c:\windows\readme.txt | more
```

Keep the output of dir from scrolling off the screen before you can read it:

```
C:\>dir c:\windows | more
```

Notes

Some commands (like dir) have a /p option that "pages" the output (i.e., dir | more is the same as dir /p), but many do not.

See Also

"type"

---

move

Move files and directories from one location to another.

Syntax

```
move [/y | /-y] filename[,...] destination
```

Description

move works like copy, except that the source is deleted after the copy is complete. Filename can be a single file, a group of files (separated with commas), or a single file specification with wildcards.

The move options are:

filename

Specify the location and name(s) of the file or files you want to move. Wildcards (*, ?) are supported.

destination

Specify the new location of the file. The destination parameter can consist of a drive, a directory name, or a combination of the two. When moving one file, destination may include a new name for the file.

/y Suppress prompting to confirm creation of a directory or overwriting of the destination. This is the default when move is used in a batch file.

/-y Cause prompting to confirm creation of a directory or overwriting of the destination. This is the default when move is used from the command line.

Examples

Move myfile.txt from the current directory to d:\files:

```
C:\>move myfile.txt d:\files\
```

Same, but rename the file to newfile.txt:

```
C:\>move myfile.txt d:\files\newfile.txt
```

Change the name of the directory d:\files to d:\myfiles:

```
C:\>move d:\files myfiles
```

Notes

copy, move, and xcopy will prompt you before overwriting an existing file, unless you specify a command line parameter instructing them to do otherwise. To change the default, set the copycmd environment variable to /y. To restore the default behavior, set copycmd to /-y. See "set" for details.

See Also

"ren or rename"

---

path

Set or display the command search path.

Syntax   path [*path1*][;*path2*][;*path3*][;...]

Description

When you type an executable filename at the command prompt (as opposed to an internal DOS command), Windows starts by looking in the current directory for a file that matches. If no matching file is found, Windows then looks in a series of other folders—these folders are known collectively as the path or the command search path.

The path statement is used to define additional directories to be included while searching for files. The path consists of a series of absolute directory pathnames, separated by semicolons. No spaces should follow each semicolon, and there should be no semicolon at the end of the statement. If no drive letter is specified, all pathnames are assumed to be on the boot drive.

Type path without any arguments to display the current command search path. The default path in Windows XP is *c:\windows\system32;c:\windows;c:\windows\system32\wbem*.

When you type the name of a command, DOS looks first in the current directory, and then in each successive directory specified in the path. Within each directory, it will look for executable files by their extension in the following order: *.com*, *.exe*, *.bat*. Windows searches your path for certain other file types (i.e., *.dll* or *.ocx*) as well, although most cannot be executed from the command line (see Notes for more information).

Examples

Specify the directories *c:\Stuff* and *d:\Tools* in the path:

    C:\>**path c:\stuff;d:\tools**

However, this will replace the path with these two folders. To add these folders to the existing path, type the following:

    C:\>**path %path%;c:\stuff;d:\tools**

Notes

- The path is actually an environment variable and the path command is merely a shortcut for the following:

      set path=%path%;c:\stuff;d:\tools

See "set," later in this chapter, for more information environment variables and details on setting global environment variables that don't expire when the Command Prompt window is closed.

- Unlike some earlier versions of Windows, XP recognizes long folder names in the path (e.g., *c:\Program Files*). If the folder name has a semicolon in it, you may still have to use the short names equivalent (e.g., *c:\PROGRA~1*).

- Type path ; to clear all search path settings and direct Windows to search only in the current directory.

- The order of directories in the search path is quite important. For example, you might run MKS Toolkit, a set of third-party tools that brings Unix functionality to Windows systems. MKS normally stores its files in *\MKSNT*, but if you have the path set as follows:

      path=C:\;C:\MKSNT;C:\Windows;C:\Windows\Command

  you won't be able to run a DOS command like find without typing its full pathname because the MKS find command will be found and executed first.

- Windows also searches the path for Windows shortcuts, but the usage might be nonintuitive. To launch a shortcut named Widget, for example, you'd have to type widget.lnk at the prompt.

- All of the supported file types are specified in the PATHEXT environment variable (see "set," later in this chapter). By default, Windows searches the path for the following extensions: *.com, .exe, .bat, .cmd, .vbs, .vbe, .js, .jse, .wsf,* and *.wsh.*

prompt

Change the appearance of the prompt.

Syntax   prompt [*text*]

Description

Type prompt by itself (without *text*) to reset the prompt to its default setting.

The *prompt* options are:

text

Specifies a new command prompt. *Text* can contain normal characters and the following special codes:

$_   Carriage return and linefeed

$$ Dollar sign ($)

$a   **Ampersand (&)**

$b   Pipe (|)

$c   **Left parenthesis (()**

$d   Current date

$e   Escape character (ASCII code 27)—used to provide extended formatting

$f   **Right parenthesis ())**

$g   Greater-than sign (>), commonly known as the caret

$h   Backspace (erases previous character)

$1 Less-than sign (<)

$n Current drive

$p Current drive and path

$q Equal sign (=)

$s **Space**

$t Current time

$v Windows version number

Examples

Specify the current drive and directory followed by the greater-than sign (>)—the default prompt in Windows XP:

C:\>**prompt pg**

Specify the drive and directory on one line and the date, followed by the greater-than sign (>) on another:

C:\>**prompt p_dg**

Specify the drive only, followed by the greater-than sign (>), which was the default prompt on early versions of DOS:

C:\>**prompt ng**

Notes

The current prompt setting is actually stored in the environment, and the prompt command is merely a shortcut for the following:

set prompt=pg

See "set," later in this chapter, for more information environment variables and details on setting global environment variables that don't expire when the Command Prompt window is closed.

rd or rmdir

Remove (delete) a directory.

Syntax   rd [/s] [/q] *path*
             rmdir [/s] [/q] *path*

Description

Unlike in Windows Explorer, files and folders are deleted differently; if you try to use del to delete a directory, it will simple delete all the files in the directory, but the directory itself will remain. rd is used to delete empty directories and, optionally, to delete directories and all of their contents.

rd accepts the following options:

path
    Specifies the directory to delete.

/s
    Removes all files and subdirectories of the specified directory.

/q

    Quiet mode; don't prompt when using /s.

Examples

Delete the empty subdirectory called *newdir* located in the *c:\olddir* directory:

    `C:\>rd c:\olddir\newdir`

Delete the directory *Online Services* and all of its contents within the current directory, *c:\Program Files*:

    `C:\Program Files>rd /s "online services"`

Note that quotes must be used with rd for folders with spaces in their names.

Notes

- The rd and rmdir commands are functionally identical.
- As a safety feature, attempting to delete a directory that is not empty without including the /s option will display the message, "The directory is not empty."
- rd with the /s option takes the place of the deltree command found in earlier versions of Windows, but no longer included in Windows XP.
- If you try to delete the current directory, you'll get the following error: "The process cannot access the file because it is being used by another process." In this case, you'll have to change to a different directory first.

---

ren or rename

Rename a file or directory.

Syntax   ren [*filename1*] [*filename2*]
                  rename [*filename1*] [*filename2*]

Description

Use ren to rename any file or directory. Unlike Windows Explorer, though, ren is capable of renaming several files at once (via wildcards 8 and ?).

The ren options are:

[filename1]
    The name of the existing file or directory.

[filename2]
    The new name to assign the file or directory.

Examples

Rename *myfile.txt* to *file.txt*:

    `C:\>rename myfile.txt file.txt`

Rename *chap 5.doc* to *sect 5.doc*: (the following two methods are identical):

    `C:\>ren "chap 5.doc" "sect 5.doc"`
    `C:\>ren chap?5.doc sect?5.doc`

Each of these examples represent different ways to rename files with spaces in their names. In addition to the standard quotation marks, in certain circumstances, you can use wildcards to avoid the spaces problem. Here, both *chap 5.doc* and *sect 5.doc* have spaces in the fifth character position, so the single wildcard character (?) can be used.

Rename the files *chap1.doc*, *chap2.doc*, etc. to *revchap1.doc*, *revchap2.doc*, etc.:

```
C:\>ren chap*.doc revchap*.doc
```

ren can be a convenient way to rename the filename extensions of several files at once, as well:

```
C:\>ren *.txt *.rtf
C:\>ren *.htm *.html
C:\>ren *.mpeg *.mpg
```

Notes

- The ren and rename commands are functionally identical.
- You can't move files from on directory to another with ren; use move instead.
- The file's Last Modified date is not changed when using ren.

See Also

"move"

---

set

Display, assign, or remove environment variables.

Syntax

```
set [variable[=[string]]]
set /p variable=[promptstring]
set /a expression
```

Description

The *environment* is a small portion of memory devoted to the storage of a few values called environment variables. set is used to manipulate environment variables from the command line, but since the Command Prompt's environment is reset when its window is closed, the usefulness of set is fairly limited.

To affect more permanent changes to environment variables, go to Control Panel → System → Advanced tab → Environment variables. This window should be fairly self-explanatory; the variables in the upper listing are for the current user and variables in the lower listing apply to all users. Some environment variables, such as the Temp user variable, are assigned with respect to other variables, like this:

```
%USERPROFILE%\Local Settings\Temp
```

where %USERPROFILE% (note the percent signs (%) on either side) signifies the USERPROFILE variable, which represents the path of the current user's home directory. See "path," earlier in this chapter, for another example of this usage.

In addition to providing a simple means of interapplication communication, environment variables are also useful for storing data used repeatedly in a batch file (see "MS-DOS Batch Files," later in this chapter).

Type set without options to display all of the current environment variables. Type set with only a variable name (no equal sign or value) to display a list of all the variables whose prefix matches the name.

The set options are:

variable

> Specifies the variable name. When assigning a new variable, the case used is preserved. But when referencing, modifying, or deleting the variable, *variable* is case-insensitive. If *variable* is specified by itself, its value is displayed. If *variable* is specified by itself with an equal sign, the variable is assigned an empty value and deleted. *Variable* cannot contain spaces.

string

> Specifies a series of characters to assign to *variable*. As stated above, this can contain references to other variables by surrounding them with preceding and trailing percent signs (%).

/p

> Specifies that *variable* will be assigned by text input from the user, rather than *string*. As stated above, this can contain references to other variables with preceding and trailing percent signs (%).

promptstring

> The text prompt to display when using the /p option.

/a

> Specifies that *expression* is a numerical expression to be evaluated. If used from the command prompt, set /a will display the final evaluated result of *expression*, even if you include an assignment operator (such as =) to assign a variable.

expression

> When used with the /a option, *expression* is a collection of symbols, numbers, and variables arranged so that it can be evaluated by set. The following symbols are recognized (in decreasing order of precedence):

> ( ) Parenthesis for grouping

> !~ Unary operators

> */ Arithmetic operators (multiply, divide)

> +- Arithmetic operators (add, subtract)

> << >>
> > Logical shift

> & Boolean "and"

> ^ Boolean "exclusive or"

> | Boolean "or"

> = *= /= %= += -= &= ^= |= <<= >>=
> > Assignment

> , Expression separator

> If you use /a with any of the boolean or modulus operators, you need to enclose *expression* in quotes. Any non-numeric strings in *expression* are treated as environment variable names, and their values are converted to numbers during evaluation (zero is used for undefined variables); the percent signs (%) are not used here.

Examples

Set the variable dummy to the string "not much:"

```
C:\>set dummy=not much
```

Set the dircmd variable, which instructs the dir command (discussed earlier in this chapter) to sort directory listings by size with the largest first:

```
C:\>set dircmd=/s /o-s
```

Append the directory *c:\mystuff* to the path (see "path," earlier in this chapter); note how the path variable is used on the right side of the equal sign so that its original contents aren't lost:

```
C:\>set path=%path%;c:\mystuff
```

Set the prompt (see "prompt," earlier in this chapter) to show the current time, followed by a right angle bracket:

```
C:\>set prompt=$t>
```

Display the contents of the variable named dummy (both of the following statements are equivalent):

```
C:\>set dummy
C:\>echo %dummy%
```

You can also reference environment variables with other commands:

```
C:\>set workdir=C:\stuff\tim's draft
C:\>cd %workdir%
```

Here the environment variable is used to store a long pathname for quick navigation to a frequently used directory.

Display the values of all variables that begin with the letter H:

```
C:\>set h
```

Clear the value of an environment variable, dummy:

```
C:\>set dummy=
```

Prompt the user to enter text to be inserted into the dummy variable (typically used in batch files):

```
C:\>set /p dummy=Enter text here>
```

Evaluate an arithmetic expression (the two following expressions are not the same):

```
C:\>set /a 7+(3*4)
C:\>set /a (7+3)*4
```

The results of these two expressions, 19 and 40, respectively, will be displayed. To assign the result to a variables, type the following:

```
C:\>set /a dummy=7+(3*4)
```

Even though you're assigning the result variable, the result will still be displayed (unless set is executed from batch file). To suppress the output, type this:

```
C:\>set /a dummy=7+(3*4) > nul
```

In addition to any custom environment variables you may use, Windows XP recognizes the following variables (many of which are already defined):

ALLUSERSPROFILE
The location of the All Users folder, usually *c:\Documents and Settings\All Users*.

APPDATA
The location of the Application Data folder, usually *c:\Documents and Settings\ %USERNAME%\Application Data*.

COMMONPROGRAMFILES

The location of the Common Files folder, usually *c:\Program Files\Common Files*.

COMPUTERNAME

The network name of the computer, set by going to Control Panel → System → Computer Name tab → Change.

COMSPEC

The location of the command prompt application executable, *c:\Windows\system32\cmd.exe* by default.

COPYCMD

Whether the copy, move, and xcopy commands should prompt for confirmation before overwriting a file. The default value is /-y. To stop the warning messages, set copycmd to /y.

DIRCMD

Specifies the default options for the dir command. For example, setting dircmd to /p will cause dir to always pause after displaying a screenful of output.

HOMEDRIVE

The drive letter of the drive containing the current user's home directory, usually *c:*, used with HOMEPATH.

HOMEPATH

Along with HOMEDRIVE, the path of the current user's home directory, which is usually *\Documents and Settings\%USERNAME%*.

LOGONSERVER

The name of the computer as seen by other computers on your network, usually the same as COMPUTERNAME preceded by two backslashes.

NUMBER_OF_PROCESSORS

The number of processors currently installed, usually 1. In a multiprocessor system, it can be 2 or 4.

OS

Used to identify the operating system to some applications; for Windows XP, OS is set to "Windows_NT." You may be able to "fool" an older program that is programmed not to run on an NT system by changing this variable temporarily.

PATH

The sequence of directories in which the command interpreter will look for commands to be interpreted. See "path," earlier in this chapter.

PATHEXT

The filename extensions (file types) Windows will look for in the directories listed in the path (see "path," earlier in this chapter). The default is *.COM*, *.EXE*, *.BAT*, *.CMD*, *.VBS*, *.VBE*, *.JS*, *.JSE*, *.WSF*, and *.WSH*

PROCESSOR_ARCHITECTURE

The type of processor; set to x86 for Intel-based processors (such as the Pentium 4).

PROCESSOR_IDENTIFIER, PROCESSOR_LEVEL, and PROCESSOR_REVISION

A series of values used by the processor manufacturer to identify the processor.

PROGRAMFILES

The location of the Program Files folder, usually *c:\Program Files*.

PROMPT
> The format of the command-line prompt, usually PG. See "prompt," earlier in this chapter, for details.

SESSIONNAME
> The name of the current command prompt session; usually "Console."

SYSTEMDRIVE
> The drive letter of the drive containing Windows, usually C:.

SYSTEMROOT
> The location of the Windows directory (or more specifically, the name of the folder in which the \Windows\System32 folder can be found), usually c:\windows.

TEMP and TMP
> The location where many programs will store temporary files. TEMP and TMP are two different variables, but they should both have the same value; usually set to c:\DOCUME~1\%USERNAME%\LOCALS~1\Temp (short name used to maintain compatibility with older DOS programs).

USERDOMAIN
> The name of the domain to which the computer belongs (set by going to Control Panel-System-Computer Name-Change). If no domain is specified, USERDOMAIN is the same as COMPUTERNAME.

USERNAME
> The name of the current user.

USERPROFILE
> The location of the current user's home directory, which should be the same as HOMEDRIVE plus HOMEPATH, usually c:\Documents and Settings\%USERNAME%.

WINDIR
> The location of the Windows directory, usually c:\windows.

Notes

Among the standard environment variables listed above, some represent certain system folders (such as PROGRAMFILES). These variables only reflect the corresponding settings in the Registry (and elsewhere); changing them will only affect what is reported to applications that use these variables; it won't actually change where Windows looks for these folders.

---

sort
\windows\system32\sort.exe

Sort text or the contents of text files in alphanumeric order.

Syntax
```
sort [/r] [/+n] [/m kilobytes] [/l locale] [/rec recordbytes]
     [/t [tempdir]] [/o outputfilename] [filename]
```

Description

The sort command sorts text on a line-by-line basis. Each line of the input is ordered alphanumerically and output to the screen (or optionally, stored in a file). By default, sorting starts with the character in the first column of each line, but this can be changed with the /+n option. sort is often used in conjunction with either pipes or output redirection (both discussed earlier in this chapter). That is, you might want to

The Command Prompt

sort the output of another command, and you will often want to redirect the output to a file so that it can be saved. sort takes the following options:

/r

Reverses the sort order; that is, it sorts Z to A and then 9 to 0

/+n

Sorts the file according to characters in column *n*.

/m kilobytes

Specifies amount of main memory to allocate for the sort operation in kilobytes. The default is 90 percent of available memory if both the input and output are files, and 45 percent of memory otherwise. The minimum amount of memory sort will use is 160 Kb; if the available (or specified) memory is insufficient, sort will split the operation up using temporary files.

/l locale

Overrides the system default locale (see Control Panel → Regional and Language Options). The "C" locale yields the fastest collating sequence, and in Windows XP, is the only choice.

/rec recordbytes

Specifies the maximum number of characters on a line (in a record); the default is 4,096 and the maximum is 65,535.

/t tempdir

Specifies the location of the directory used to store temporary files, in case the data does not fit in main memory (see the /m option). The default is to use the system temporary directory.

/o outputfilename

Specifies a file where the output is to be stored. If not specified, the sorted data is displayed at the prompt. Using the /o option is faster than redirecting output (with the > symbol).

filename

Specifies the maximum number of characters on a line; the default is 4,096 and the maximum is 65,535.

Examples

Display an alphabetically sorted directory (similar to dir /o):

```
C:\>dir | sort
```

Sort the contents of a file, *data.txt*, and store the sorted version in *results.txt* (the following four examples are all equivalent, although the first is the most efficient):

```
C:\>sort /o results.txt data.txt
C:\>sort data.txt > results.txt
C:\>sort /o results.txt < data.txt
C:\>type data.txt | sort > results.txt
```

Notes

- The input to sort should be ASCII text, so that each line can be considered a record of data.

- Using the /+n parameter, the lines (records) of the input text may be broken into fields, each beginning a fixed number of characters from the start of the line, facilitating a sort of third column.

- Blank lines and leading spaces will be sorted. This can result in many blank lines at the top of the sorted output; you may need to scroll down in an editor to see nonblank lines.
- If you do a lot of command-line sorting, you may want to get a Windows version of the Unix sort utility (available as part of the MKS Toolkit; *http://www.mkssoftware.com/*), which is much more powerful. The Unix sort command lets you define and sort on fields within the line, ignore upper- and lowercase distinctions, and eliminate duplicate lines, among other things.

time

Display or set the system time.

Syntax   time [/t | *time*]

Description

Like date (discussed earlier in this chapter), time is essentially a holdover from the very early days of DOS when the user was required to enter the system date and time every time the computer was started. Now it's essentially included as a way to set the data from the command line; the preferred method is to use Control Panel → Date and Time.

If you type time on the command line without an option, the current time setting is displayed, and you are prompted for a new one. Press Enter to keep the same date.

The time options are:

time
> Sets the system time without a prompt. The format of *time* is *hh*:*mm*:*ss* [A|P], where:
>
> *hh* Hours: valid values = 0–23
>
> *mm* Minutes: valid values = 0–59
>
> *ss* Seconds: valid values = 0–59
>
> A|P A.M. or P.M. (for a 12-hour format). If a valid 12-hour format is entered without an A or P, A is the default.

/t
> Displays the current time without prompting for a new one.

Notes

- The time format depends on settings in Control Panel → Regional and Language Options.
- Windows records the current time for each file you create or change. This time is listed next to the filename in the dir directory listing.
- The time display format for most applications can be changed in Control Panel → Regional and Language Options → Regional Options tab → Customize, but this doesn't affect the output of the DOS time command.
- To have Windows automatically synchronize the clock with an Internet time server, go to Control Panel → Date and Time → Internet Time tab.

The Command Prompt

See Also
"date"

---

type

Display the contents of a text file.

Syntax   type *filename*

Description

The type command is useful if you need to quickly view the contents of any text file (especially short files). type is also useful for concatenating text files, using the >> operator.

Notes

If the file is exceptionally long, you can press Ctrl-C to interrupt the display before it's finished.

See Also

"more," "echo"

---

ver

Display Windows version information.

Syntax   ver

Description

ver shows the version of Windows you're using. You can also find the Windows version at Control Panel → System → General tab, but it won't show you the revision number.

ver takes no options.

/r   This undocumented option also displays the revision number, and whether DOS is located in the high memory area (HMA; the same as DOS=HIGH).

Notes

Windows XP is known internally as Windows NT 5.1.*xxxx*, where *xxxx* is the build/revision number.

See Also

"Windows Update" in Chapter 4

---

xcopy   *\windows\system32\xcopy.exe*

Copy files and directory trees (directories, subdirectories, and their contents).

Syntax   xcopy *source* [*destination*] [/a | /m] [/d[:*date*]] [/p] [/s [/e]]
        [/v] [/w] [/c] [/i] [/q] [/f] [/l] [/g] [/h] [/r] [/t] [/u]
        [/k] [/n] [/o] [/x] [/y] [/-y] [/z] [/exclude:*filenames*]

Description

xcopy works like copy, but provides more options and is often faster.

The xcopy32 options are:

source
> Specifies the file(s) to copy; source must include the full path.

destination
> Specifies the location and/or name of new files. If omitted, files are copied to the current directory.

/a   Copies files with the archive attribute set, but doesn't change the attribute of the source file (similar to /m).

/c   Continues copying even if errors occur.

/d:*date*
> Copies only files changed on or after the specified date. If no date is given, copies only those source files that are newer than existing destination files.

/e   Copies all directories and subdirectories (everything), including empty ones (similar to /s.) May be used to modify /t.

/exclude:*filenames*
> Specifies a file (or a list of files) containing strings of text (each on its own line). When any of the strings match any part of the absolute path of the file to be copied, that file will be excluded from being copied. Contrary to what you might expect, *filenames* does not actually list the filenames to exclude.

/f   Displays full source and destination filenames while copying (unless /q is specified); normally, only filenames are displayed.

/h   Allows the copying of encrypted files to a destination that does not support encryption; otherwise, such files are skipped.

/h   Copies hidden and system files also; normally files with the hidden or system attributes are skipped (see "Attrib" in Chapter 4 for details).

/i   If a destination is not supplied and you are copying more than one file, assumes that the destination must be a directory. (By default, xcopy asks if the destination is a file or directory.)

/k   Duplicates the attributes of the source files; by default, xcopy turns off the read-only attributes (see "Attrib" in Chapter 4 for details).

/l   Displays files that would be copied given other options, but does not actually copy the files.

/m   Copies files with the archive attribute set, then turns off the archive attribute of the source file (similar to /a).

/n   Copies files using short (8.3) file and directory names (for example, *PROGRA~1* instead of *Program Files*). Use this feature to convert an entire branch of files and folders to their short names.

/o   Copies file ownership and ACL information.

/p   Prompts you before creating each destination file.

The Command Prompt

/q   Quiet mode; does not display filenames while copying.

/r   Overwrites read-only files.

/s   Copies directories and subdirectories, except empty ones (similar to /e.)

/t   Creates the directory structure, but does not copy files; does not include empty directories unless /e is specified.

/u   Copies from the source-only files that already exist on destination; used to update files.

/v   Verifies copied files by comparing them to the originals.

/w   Prompts you to press a key before copying (useful in batch files).

/x   Copies file audit settings (implies /o).

/y, /-y
     Turns off or on (respectively) the prompt for overwrites existing files.

/z   Copies networked files in restartable mode.

The following are exit codes generated by xcopy, and can be tested in batch file with ERRORLEVEL to determine if the xcopy operation was successful:

0   All files were copied without errors.

1   No files were found to copy.

2   xcopy was terminated by Ctrl-C before copying was complete.

4   An initialization error occurred. Such an error would generally be caused by insufficient memory or disk space, or an invalid drive name or syntax.

5   A disk-write error occurred.

Examples

Copy all the files and subdirectories, including any empty subdirectories and hidden files, from *c:\foobar* to the root directory of *d*:

```
C:\>xcopy \foobar d: /s /e /h
```

Notes

- copy, move, and xcopy will prompt you before overwriting an existing file, unless you specify a command line parameter instructing them to do otherwise. To change the default, set the copycmd environment variable to /y. To restore the default behavior, set copycmd to /-y. See "set" for details.

- In some earlier versions of Windows, there were to versions of xcopy: *xcopy.exe* and *xcopy32.exe*. In Windows XP, the xcopy command is equivalent to the 32-bit *xcopy32.exe* utility; there's no equivalent to the old 16-bit *xcopy.exe*, however.

- Use caution when using the /s or /e options in conjunction with /d or /u, as the results may be unpredictable.

See Also

"copy"

MS-DOS Batch Files

Most Windows books treat batch files as if they were some kind of skeleton in the closet or a crazy aunt you wouldn't want anyone to meet. While it's true that batch files are much less important than they were in DOS and earlier versions of Windows, they can still provide useful functionality.

The Windows Script Host (WSH), discussed in Chapter 9, makes it easier to use much more advanced scripting languages, such as Visual Basic, Perl, PerlScript, JavaScript, or Python. But even with WSH, batch files are not completely obsolete.

A batch file is an ASCII text file containing a series of commands, each on its own line, that will be executed one line at a time. The filename of the batch file becomes a command that can be executed at the Command Prompt, from another batch file, or even run from a Windows Shortcut.

Although any commands you can type at the command line can be used in a batch file, several additional commands can be used only in a batch file. These commands are used for loops, conditionals, and other programming functions within the batch file and are explained in detail later in this chapter.

Creating Batch Files

You can create batch files with any text editor or word processor that can save plain ASCII text files, such as Notepad. In fact, by default, you can right-click any batch file and select Edit to open that file in Notepad.

When naming a batch file, make sure you don't use a name that is already used by a DOS internal command (such as *dir*, *copy*, or *cd*) or by a *.com* or *.exe* file in your search path. The reason for this is that when DOS executes programs, it first looks for the *.com* extension and then the *.exe* extension before finally executing a file with the *.bat* extension. For instance, if you have a file called *work.exe*, and you create *work.bat* in the same directory, your batch file will not execute unless you type the filename extension as well.

 You can create and execute batch files from the current directory or any directory in your search path, or by specifying their complete pathname, as with any other command. But if you're going to use batch files a lot, it makes sense to keep them all in one place. Create a directory called \Batch and add it to your search path. See "path," earlier in this chapter, for details.

Some Rules of the Road

Here are the basics of batch file programming:

- Each command in a batch file must be on a separate line. The last command line in the file should end with a carriage return. The commands are the same as you'd type in succession at the command prompt.
- The name of the batch file itself is stored in the variable %0. This allows you to do things like have a temporary batch file that deletes itself when done. The

name is stored as it was typed at the command line, so if you had typed myfile.bat, %0 would be *myfile.bat*, but if you had typed c:\batch\myfile, %0 would be *c:\batch\myfile*.

- A batch file run from the command prompt or by double-clicking on its icon will open a command prompt window while it is executing; however, a batch file run from an existing command prompt window will run inside that window.

- Click the control menu and select Properties (see "Using the Command Line," earlier in this chapter, for details) to control the default look and feel of the Command Prompt window. To change these settings for an individual batch file, create a Windows Shortcut to the batch file, right-click the new shortcut, and select Properties.

The Properties sheet for the shortcut actually adds several options not normally available through the control menu. For example, Shortcut → Start in allows you to choose the initial working directory, and Shortcut → Run allows you to have the batch file run minimized. (Note that the option to have the window close or remain open after it completes, found in some earlier versions of Windows, is not present in Windows XP.)

- You can stop a running batch file by pressing Ctrl-Break or Ctrl-C; the following message will appear in its DOS window: "Terminate batch job (Y/N)?" Press Y to abort or N to continue running the batch file.

- By default, each command in a batch file is echoed to its DOS window. To execute a command silently, precede it with an @ symbol. Alternatively, you can turn command echo off by issuing @echo off at the beginning of the batch file.

- A batch file can contain any command that you can type at the command prompt (e.g., anything described elsewhere in this chapter or in Chapter 4). However, keep in mind that each line in the batch file is executed sequentially, so there are a couple of gotchas, especially when the batch file runs programs that pop up a separate window. When you run a Windows program and it pops up its own window, control returns immediately to the batch file and the next line is executed. This "race condition" is unfortunately unavoidable with batch files; you'll have to use a WSH script for this type of control (see Chapter 9).

- You can store temporary data in your batch file using environment variables created with the set command. To use the value of any variable with any other command or program, surround its name with % symbols.

The "Why" and "When" of Using Batch Files

This section gives a few examples of instances when you might want to use batch files.

Batch files are used to automate repetitive tasks, but can be useful for more than just issuing a sequence of commands. For example, type the names of three applications in a batch file to have them all opened in a single step. Or, write a one-line batch file that copies a directory of files onto a removable drive; instead of performing a copy manually every day before you go home from work, just double-click the batch file icon and it will be done for you.

Batch files are particularly powerful for creating and moving files and directories. For example, when starting a new project, an author might always want to create the same directory structure and put some basic files into each directory. Here's the kind of batch file you might create for this kind of housekeeping:

```
@echo off
if "%1"=="" goto skip
mkdir %1\figures
mkdir %1\sources
mkdir %1\old
copy c:\templates\mainfile.doc %1
copy c:\templates\other.doc %1
copy c:\templates\image.tif %1\figures
:skip
```

Create a new folder in the Explorer, and then drag and drop it onto this batch file (or add the batch file to the SendTo menu). Subdirectories called *figures*, *sources*, and *old* will be created inside, and three template files are copied into the new directories. Voilà—you just saved about a minute of clicking and dragging.

The construct:

```
if "%1"=="" go to skip
```

is a useful error-checking technique. You can use an if statement to test for null arguments (or other similar conditions), and if encountered, either issue an error message or simply quit. (This example will exit after jumping to the :skip label, since there are no further commands to be executed.)

You can also use batch files to work around some of the limits of Windows XP. For example, the Explorer doesn't let you print out a hardcopy listing of the contents of a folder. You can do this from the command line by typing:

```
dir > lpt1:
```

But the following batch file does even better—you can drag and drop a folder icon onto it to get a printed directory listing:

```
@echo off
if "%1"=="" goto skip
dir %1 > lpt1:
:skip
```

You could also replace lpt1: with something like c:\windows\desktop\dir-list.txt to output the directory listing to a text file instead, or construct a loop so that the batch file could repeat itself automatically for multiple directory name arguments.

Variables

Variables can be used in batch files. In fact, a variable that is assigned in one batch file can be accessed by a different batch file (in the same command prompt session), since the command prompt environment is used to store all variables. See "set," earlier in this chapter, for more information on setting, modifying, reading, and deleting variables from the environment.

A batch file can take arguments such as filenames or options. Up to nine arguments are stored in the variables %1 through %9. For example, the following line in a batch file:

```
copy %1 %2
```

would mean that the batch file would copy the filename specified in the first argument to the name specified in the second argument. Use this feature in conjunction with the if statement—for example, to display a help screen when the "user" includes the /? option. The %* variable returns a string with all arguments (e.g., %1 %2 %3 %4 %5...), which can be a convenient way to pass all a batch file's arguments to another batch file or command.

The following variable operators, a new feature in Windows XP, can also be used with variables containing filenames. They don't actually change the contents of the target variable, but they do return an expanded version of it:

%~*var*
> Expands %*var*, removing any surrounding quotes.

%~f*var*
> Expands %*var* to a fully qualified path name (useful if %*var* references a file in the current directory).

%~d*var*
> Expands %*var* to a drive letter only.

%~p*var*
> Expands %*var* to a path only.

%~n*var*
> Expands %*var* to a filename only.

%~x*var*
> Expands %*var* to a file extension only.

%~s*var*
> The expanded path contains short names only.

%~a*var*
> Expands %*var* to file attributes.

%~t*var*
> Expands %*var* to the date/time of the file.

%~z*var*
> Expands %*var* to the size of the file.

%~$*dir*:*var*
> Searches the directories listed in the *dir* variable and expands %*var* to the fully qualified name of the first one found. If *dir* is not defined, or the file is not found by the search, then an empty string is returned. If you specify path for *dir*, the command search path will be used (see "path," earlier in this chapter).

These operators are most commonly used with command-line arguments; for example, use %~z2 in a batch file to display the size of the file specified by %2. These operators can be combined; for example, %~nx1 expands %1 to the filename and extension only, and %~ftza7 expands %7 to a dir-like output line. If the variable *%var* is not defined or does not contain the filename of an existing file, an empty string will be returned.

Additional Commands Used in Batch Files

The following list contains descriptions of the commands that are used principally within batch files. These can be used in conjunction with any of the commands listed earlier in this chapter, as well as the filenames of any command prompt programs or even Windows applications.

call

Invoke a batch file from within another batch file, returning control to the original when the called file completes.

Syntax   `call [filename] [arguments]`

Description

The `call` command lets you invoke a batch file from within another batch file and wait for it to finish before continuing. Once the called file has completed its execution, the control returns to the original batch file.

 If you run another batch file from within a batch file without using `call`, the control will never be returned to the parent batch file when the child process is finished. The whole thing just quits. Of course, this fact can be put to use; for example, it helps to avoid recursion when a batch file calls itself.

The options for `call` are as follows:

filename
    Specifies the filename of the batch file to call.

arguments
    Specifies any command-line arguments to be passed to the target batch file.

Examples

The following *parent.bat* calls *child.bat*, and then returns the control back to itself:

parent.bat:

```
@echo off
cls
call child.bat First
set first=%inputvar%
call child.bat Second
set second=%inputvar%
echo You typed %first% and then you typed %second%
```

child.bat:

```
set /p inputvar=Please type the %1 option:
echo Thank you.
```

In this example, *parent.bat* launches *child.bat* twice, which illustrates how you can write modular code in batch files. *Child.bat* asks for input and then places what the user types into the environment variable inputvar. When control is returned to *parent. bat*, the variable first stores the input so that *child.bat* can be run again. At the end, *parent.bat* spits out both variables.

The next example illustrates how one of the batch file's limitations can be overcome. The if statement, discussed later in this chapter, is only capable of executing a single command, but the following is a simple workaround:

parent.bat:

```
@echo off
for %%j in (1,2,3,4,5) do call child.bat
```

child.bat:

```
set /p inputvar=Please type option #%j%:
echo You typed %inputvar% - good for you.
```

choice

The choice command found in earlier versions of Windows is no longer supported in Windows XP. The set command with the /p option is a suitable replacement.

errorlevel

See "if."

for

Repeat a specified command any number of times.

Syntax
```
for [/d] %%variable in (set) do command [arguments]
for /r [path] %%variable in (set) do command [arguments]
for /l %%variable in (start,step,end) do command [arguments]
```

(in and do are not options, but rather simply part of the syntax; if omitted, an error will occur.)

Description

Use this command to create loops in a batch file. A for loop is a programming construct that allows you to repeat a command for a list of items (such as filenames). You specify an arbitrary variable name and a set of values to be iterated through. For each value in the set, the command is repeated.

The options used by for are the following:

command [arguments]
   The command to execute or the program filename to run. This can be anything you'd normally type at a command prompt; *arguments* are the options, if any, to pass to the command.

%%variable

A one-letter variable name that is assigned, one by one, to the elements listed in *set*. Although *variable* is treated like a standard environment variable (see "set," earlier in this chapter), it's name is case sensitive (%%j is different than %%J) and can only be one letter long. Note also the use of two preceding percent signs. If the for command is issued directly from the command prompt (and not from within a batch file), use only one percent sign here.

set

The sequence of elements through which the for command cycles. Elements are separated with spaces and can be files, strings, or numbers. Wildcards can be used when specifying files. See Examples, below, for details. Use the /l option for the more traditional *start,step,end.* format.

/d   Instructs for to match against directory names instead of filenames if *set* contains wildcards. Can't be used with the /l or /r options.

/l   Specifies that *set* takes the form of *start,step,end.*, allowing you to specify a range of numbers and an increment instead of having to list each element. The /l parameter allows you to mimic the more traditional usage of for found in more advanced programming languages. See Examples, below, for details.

/r [path]

Recursively executes *command* for each directory and subdirectory in *path*. If *path* is omitted, the current directory is used. Without /r, files specified in *set* only relate to the current directory. The /r option instructs for to "walk" the directory tree rooted at *path* and repeat the entire loop in each directory of the tree encountered. If *set* is just a single period (.), for will simply list all the directories in the tree.

Examples

for can cycle through an array of strings:

```
for %%n in (rock paper scissors) do echo %%n
```

Create a set of numbered directories (e.g., ch1, ch2, ch3, ch4, and ch5):

```
for %%n in (1 2 3 4 5) do md ch%%n
```

Here's an alternate way to accomplish the same thing, using the /l option:

```
for /l %%n in (1,1,5) do md ch%%n
```

Here, the first 1 represents the beginning number, the second 1 represents the increment (or step), and the 5 represents the end. Here are some more examples of this syntax:

```
for /l %%n in (0,5,100) do echo %%n
for /l %%n in (100,-2,0) do echo %%n
```

Since the for loop works only for a single command (and it doesn't work well with goto), you need to do something like this to run multiple commands with for:

```
for %%f in (1 2 3 4 5) do call loop1.bat %%f
echo done!
```

loop1.bat might then look like this:

```
if not exist file%1 goto skip
copy file%1 c:\backup
:skip
```

The Command Prompt

Note how the %%f variable is passed to *loop1.bat* as a command-line parameter, and is then referenced with %1.

The set parameter can also contain filenames:

```
for %%j in (a.txt b.txt c.txt) do copy %%j a:
```

The following statements are equivalent:

```
for %%x in (*.txt) do type %%x
type *.txt
```

While the second example is simpler, it does illustrate a way to deal with programs or commands that don't normally support wildcards.

List all the directories (with full paths) on your hard disk

```
for /r c:\ %%i in (.) do echo %%i
```

Copy all *.doc* files in all subdirectories of *c:\Documents and Settings* to drive *D*:

```
for /r "c:\Documents and Settings" %%i in (*.doc) do copy %%i d:
```

Notes:

- When redirecting the output of a for loop to a file, you'll want to use >> (append to a file) rather than >. Otherwise, you will save only the last iteration of the loop.

- The commands executed by the for statement will be echoed to the screen unless you issue the @echo off command beforehand or precede *command* with @. See "echo," earlier in this chapter, for details.

- The for command also supports the rather arcane /f option; type for /? at the command prompt for more information.

---

goto

Branch to a labeled line in a batch program.

Syntax
```
goto label
...
:label
GOTO :EOF
```

Description

goto is typically used with the if statement to branch to a particular part of a batch file, depending on the result of the condition or user response.

Label, any string of text (no spaces) following a colon, marks the beginning of a section of a batch file and represents a target for the goto command. Only the first eight characters of *label* are used; the labels pneumonia and pneumonic are therefore equivalent. If you type goto :eof (note the colon, not normally used here), it will skip to the end of the batch file (EOF=end of file).

If your batch program doesn't contain the label you specify after goto, the batch program stops and displays the message "Label not found." However, you can specify labels that don't appear in goto commands.

Examples

Format a floppy disk in drive *a:* and display an appropriate message of success or failure:

```
@echo off
format a:
if not errorlevel 1 goto skip
echo An error occurred during formatting.
exit
:skip
echo Successfully formatted the disk in drive a!
```

See Also

"if"

---

if

Execute a command if certain conditions are met.

Syntax
```
if [not] string1==string2 command [arguments]
if [/i] string1 compare-op string2 command [arguments]
if [not] exist filename command [arguments]
if [not] errorlevel n command [arguments]
```

Description

Conditional branching lets your batch file test to see whether a condition is true, and if it is, instructs the batch file to execute a command or continue execution at another location in the batch file (via the goto command). The following options can be used with the if command:

command [arguments]

The command to execute or the program filename to run. This can be anything you'd normally type at a command prompt; *arguments* are the options, if any, to pass to the command.

not

Specifies that *command* should be carried out only if the condition is false; not valid with *compare-op*.

string1==string2

Specifies a true condition if the specified text strings match. *String1* and *string2* must be enclosed in quotation marks or parenthesis.

string1 compare-op string2

Performs a more flexible comparison than *string1==string2*, shown above. The *compare-op* term can be one of the following:

EQU   Equal

NEQ   Not equal

LSS   Less than

LEQ   Less than or equal

GTR   Greater than

GEQ   Greater than or equal

The Command Prompt

/i

Specifies a case-insensitive comparison; used only with *compare-op*.

exist *filename*

Specifies a true condition if the specified file exists.

errorlevel *n*

Specifies a true condition if the previous command or program returned an exit code equal to or greater than the number specified. Zero typically means no error; other numbers depend on the command or program.

Examples

Since batch files can accept parameters (stored in %1, %2, %3, and so on); the if statement is vital to interpreting these parameters. The following statements might appear at the beginning of such a batch file:

```
if "%1"=="" echo You didn't specify a parameter
if "%1"=="/?" goto help
if "%1"=="hullabalooza" goto doit
```

The following statements are equivalent:

```
if not "%1"=="" echo You must've typed something.
if "%1" NEQ "" echo You must've typed something.
```

The following batch file checks the current directory for the file *form.bat*. If it finds it, the message "It exists!" is displayed, and if it doesn't, "The file doesn't exist" is displayed:

```
@echo off
if exist form.bat goto jump
goto skip

:jump
echo It exists!
pause
exit

:skip
echo The file doesn't exist.
pause
exit
```

When a program exits or a command completes, it returns an integer value to the operating system called the errorlevel. Typically, errorlevel is zero (0) if the operation was successful or a higher number if there was a problem. The if errorlevel statement checks if the errorlevel value is equal to or greater than a specified number:

```
find /i "xp" c:\stuff\tips.txt
if errorlevel 2 goto error
if errorlevel 1 goto nomatch
if errorlevel 0 goto match

:match
echo A match was found!
goto end
```

```
:nomatch
echo Sorry, but a match wasn't found.
goto end

:error
echo Ack! An error has occurred!

:end
pause
```

Note that the `if errorlevel` statements are ordered so that higher numbers are checked first; if the order was reversed, the first one (`if errorlevel 0`) would always return true since the errorlevel is always greater than or equal to zero.

It's also important to account for the possibility that none of the `if` statements will encounter a true condition; in the example above, if all `errorlevel` checks failed, execution would simply continue onto the `:match` section.

The `if` statement also supports `else`, but the syntax is very strict. `else` must be the first word on the line immediately following the `if` statement, like this:

```
if exist %1 del %1
else echo Sorry, %1 was not found
```

Batch files in Windows XP also support `if...else` blocks, like this:

```
if exist %1 (
    echo I'm about to delete %1.  Are you sure?
    pause
    del %1
) else (
    echo I couldn't find %1.  To bad for you.
    exit
)
```

The indenting here isn't necessary, but it does make the code easier to read. Note the opening and closing parentheses used to enclose the blocks, and the fact that `else` must be on the same line as the closing parenthesis of the first block and the opening parenthesis of the second block.

See Also

"for," "goto"

---

pause

Suspends processing of a batch program and prompts the user to press any key to continue.

Description

Include the pause command whenever you want your batch file to stop and wait for user input, giving the user a chance to read the text on the screen, insert a floppy disk, or press Ctrl-C to abort the batch file.

The message "Press any key to continue..." is automatically displayed whenever the pause command is used; it is not affected by the echo off statement.

Examples

Prompt the user to change disks in one of the drives in a batch program:

```
@echo off
echo Insert next disk in drive A, and
pause
```

When this batch file is executed, the following message will appear:

```
Insert next disk in drive A, and
Press any key to continue ...
```

Something like this is also common:

```
@echo off
echo Press Ctrl-C to cancel, or
pause
```

---

rem   Internal to: \Windows\command.com

Insert comments ("remarks") into a batch file. Lines beginning with rem will be ignored when the batch file is executed.

Syntax

```
rem [comment]
```

Description

The comment can say whatever you want. It's a good idea to put comments in your batch file so that others (including you in the distant future) can figure out how it works.

The rem command is also useful for disabling commands. Just add rem right before the command to disable it.

Examples

A batch file that uses remarks for explanations and to disable a command:

```
@echo off
rem This batch program may one day change a directory.
rem But not until I remove the rem before the cd command.
rem It is called mydir.bat.
rem cd \batch\ch2
```

This example, if executed, would do absolutely nothing.

See Also

"echo"

---

shift

Delete the variable that holds the first command-line argument (%1) and shifts over the remaining arguments.

Syntax

```
shift
```

Description

Use the shift command when you want to cycle through all of the command-line arguments specified when the batch file was run. When a shift statement is encountered, the value stored in %2 is assigned to %1, the value stored in %3 is assigned to %2, and so on. The value stored in %1 before the shift statement is lost. This is particularly useful when processing loops.

Examples

In the following batch file, shift is used so that each of the command-line options becomes option #1 (%1) for processing within the loop. The beauty is that this works regardless of the number of arguments entered:

```
@echo off
rem MTYPE.BAT
rem example: mtype foo.txt bar.txt *.bat
:loop
if "%1"=="" exit
for %%f in (%1) do type %%f
shift
pause
goto loop
```

The if statement tests for an empty argument (meaning that shift has exhausted the supply of arguments) and ends the loop when found.

Notes

- Normally, the number of command-line arguments is limited to nine (%1 through %9), but shift makes it possible for a batch file to accommodate more.
- If you use a wildcard on the command line, it is passed to the batch file as a single argument (e.g., *.*), which can be used as is. It isn't expanded first, as with Unix shells, so you can't pick it apart in the script and use each matched filename separately.

Advanced Topics

Alphabetical Topics

7

Networking

A network is established when two or more computers are connected to each other for the purpose of exchanging data. Although networks have been common in large companies for decades, they're becoming more common in homes and small offices, not only because these environments are getting more computers, but because networking is becoming easier, cheaper, and more useful.

Among the things you can do with a simple network are the following:

File sharing
> Documents and even some applications stored on one computer can be accessed by another computer on the network, as though they were on the remote computer's hard disk. Put an end to walking floppies!

Device sharing
> Printers connected to one computer can be used by any other computer on the network. The same goes for many scanners, backup devices, and even high-speed Internet devices, such as DSL and cable modems.

Online gaming
> Networkable games can be played against other users on your local network or even over the Internet; after all, it's more fun blowing up your friends than computer-generated characters.

Communication
> Send and receive email, chat, and even videoconference across the room or the country in seconds, over any type of network connection.

Web
> The Web has become ubiquitous. Using Internet Explorer or the web browser of your choice, you can retrieve information from the other side of the world as easily as the other side of town.

Data collaboration

A network connection allows two or more users to simultaneously access the same database, useful for patient-tracking in a doctor's office, parallel development an application in a software company, or keeping track of bills and expenses at home.

Administration

Maintain and troubleshoot multiple computers over a network more easily. Using Remote Desktop Sharing (or a third-party alternative), control a remote computer as though you were sitting in front of it. Rather than spending several hours over the phone helping someone far away fix a problem with their computer, fix it yourself in a few minutes.

The ability to perform these tasks depends only on your software and the speed of your connection. Since Windows XP includes built-in support for networking, as well as starter applications that provide all of the functionality just described, all that's left is setting it up.

Fortunately, networking in Windows XP (and Windows 2000) is easier than in any previous version of Windows. The convoluted and temperamental networking subsystem in Windows 9x/Me has been completely abolished, and the cryptic networking found in Windows NT 3.x/4.x has been greatly simplified and streamlined. In this chapter, we'll cover the steps required to connect your computer to a network and use the connection to its fullest.

It's important to note at this point that when you connect your computer to a network, you can dramatically increase its exposure to hackers and viruses. See the section "Implementing Network Security," later in this chapter, for more information on safeguarding your computer.

Networking Terminology

Understanding networking terminology is essential to making sense of the software and hardware used to assemble a network. The following terms are used throughout this chapter, as well as in just about any conversation about networking:

Bandwidth

The capacity of a network connection to move information. If a network is capable of transferring data at 10 mbps, and two users are simultaneously transferring large files, each will only have about 5 mbps of bandwidth at their disposal. See "Hubs and switches," later in this list, for limitations.

Ethernet

The technology upon which the vast majority of local area networks is built. A standard Ethernet connection is capable of transferring data at a maximum of 10 mbps, and a Fast Ethernet connection can transfer data at 100 mbps. A device capable of communicating of both speeds is typically labelled "10/100."

Firewall

A layer of protection that permits or denies network communication based on a predefined set of rules. A firewall can be used to restrict unauthorized access from intruders, close backdoors opened by viruses and other malicious applications, and eliminate wasted bandwidth by blocking certain types of network applications. Windows XP includes a rudimentary firewall feature, described in "Implementing Network Security," later in this chapter.

Hubs and switches

Devices on your network to which multiple Ethernet connections (called *nodes*) are made. See Figure 7-1 for an example. The main difference between a hub and a switch is a matter of performance (and cost). A switch is capable of handling multiple, simultaneous, full-bandwidth connections, while the less expensive hub throttles all connections such that, for example, three simultaneous connections can only each use one third of the total bandwidth.

IP address

A set of four numbers (e.g., 207.46.230.218) corresponding to a single computer or device on a TCP/IP network. No two computers on a single network can have the same IP address, but a single computer can have multiple IP addresses. Each element of the address can range from 0 to 255, providing 256^4 or nearly 4.3 billion possible combinations. Network Address Translation (NAT) is used to translate an address from one network to another. This is useful, for example, when a LAN is connected to the Internet. On the Internet, dedicated machines called nameservers are used to translate named hosts, such as *www.microsoft.com*, to their respective numerical IP addresses. See "Windows IP Configuration" and "NSLookup," both in Chapter 4, for more information.

LAN

Local Area Network, a designation typically referring to a network contained in a single room or building.

MBPS

Mega-Bits Per Second, the unit of measure used to describe the speed of a network connection. Ethernet-based networks can transfer data either up to 10 mbps or up to 100 mbps. High-speed T1, DSL, and cable modem connections typically transfer data up to 1.5 mbps, while the fastest analog modems communicate at a glacial 56 kbps, or 0.056 mbps.

Since there are eight bits to a byte, you can determine the theoretical maximum data transfer rate of a connection by simply dividing by 8. For example, a 384 kbps connection transfers 384 / 8 = 48 kilobytes of data per second, which should allow you to transfer a 1 megabyte file in a little more than 20 seconds. However, there is more going on than just data transfer (such as error correction), so actual performance will always be slower than the theoretical maximum.

NIC

Network Interface Card, commonly known as an Ethernet Adapter. If your computer doesn't have built-in Ethernet, you'll need a NIC to connect your computer to a network. For Desktops, your NIC should be a PCI card; for laptops, your NIC should be a PCMCIA (PC Card) card. Universal Serial Bus (USB) based NICs can also be used with both desktops and laptops.

Ports

A number representing the type of communication to initiate. For example, web browsers typically use port 80 to download web pages, so web servers must be "listening" at port 80. Other commonly used ports include port 25 for sending email (SMTP), port 110 for retrieving email (POP3), port 443 for accessing secure web pages, port 21 for FTP, port 23 for Telnet, port 22 for SSH, port 53 for DNS, port 144 for newsgroups, and port 6699 for peer-to-peer file sharing applications (such as Napster).

PPP

Point-to-Point Protocol, a protocol used to facilitate a TCP/IP connection over long distances. PPP is used by Windows to provide an Internet connection over ordinary phone lines using an analog modem. Some DSL and cable connections use PPPoE (PPP over Ethernet), discussed later in this chapter.

Protocol

A protocol is the language, so to speak, that your computer uses to communicate with other computers on the network. These days, the TCP/IP set of protocols is the de-facto standard for local area networks, and is required for Internet connections.

TCP/IP

Shorthand notation for the collection of protocols that includes Transmission Control Protocol (TCP), Internet Protocol (IP), User Datagram Protocol (UDP), and Internet Control Message Protocol (ICMP). TCP/IP is required for all Internet connections, and is the standard protocol for most types of modern LANs.

Topology

The physical layout of your network. See the next section, "Planning Your Network," for more information on how topology comes into play.

WAN

Wide Area Network, or a network formed by connecting computers over large distances. The Internet is an example of a WAN.

Workgroup

Another name for a peer-to-peer LAN.

Planning Your Network

There are many types of networks, but for the purposes of this chapter, we will be focusing on two basic categories:

Peer-to-Peer Local Area Network (LAN)

A LAN is the connection of two or more computers in close proximity, typically in the same building or room. The term "peer-to-peer" implies that each of the computers on the network will have pretty much the same role. This is in contrast to a client/server setup, in which certain computers are intended solely to store data, handle printing, or manage user accounts.

Connection to the Internet

By connecting your computer to the Internet, you are networking your machine to the world's largest Wide Area Network (WAN).

Now, as far as Windows XP is concerned there is very little difference between these two types of network connections. The distinction is made primarily to help you visualize the topology of your environment. See Figure 7-1, Figure 7-2, and Figure 7-3 for some example setups.

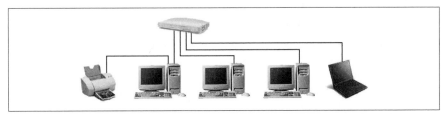

Figure 7-1. A simple network with four computers connected with a hub (or switch), one printer connected to one of the computers, and no Internet connection

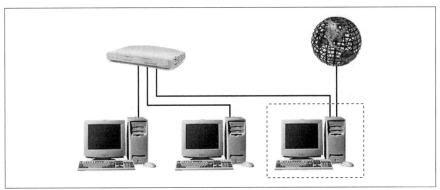

Figure 7-2. A simple network with three computers, one of which has an internet connection that can be shared; see "Sharing an Internet Connection," later in this chapter, for details

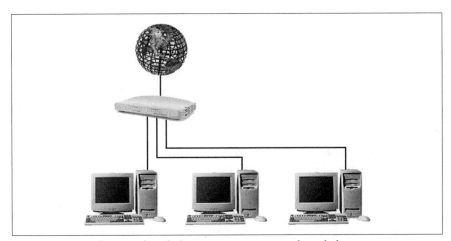

Figure 7-3. A simple network with three computers connected to a hub or router; see "Internet connection sharing," later in this chapter, for details

An especially interesting application of these technologies is how they can be mixed and matched. For example, you can connect your LAN to the Internet using Internet Connection Sharing, giving Internet access to everyone on your local network. Or, you can simulate a LAN over an Internet connection using Virtual Private Networking.

Here are some things to consider when planning your network:

- Wiring can be time consuming and frustrating. Drawing a diagram of the physical layout of the computers and devices on your network can help you visualize the topology and plan the cables, hubs, and other devices required. For example, if two more users are to share a printer, make sure the printer is in a convenient, central location.

- Wireless networking is a reality, but it is more expensive and not as fast as a wired connection. Whether the cost is worth the convenience depends on what you're using it for. For example, a IEEE 802.11b–compliant wireless network transfers data up to 5 mbps, which is plenty for a 1.5 mbps Internet connection, but may not be adequate for transferring large amounts of data when compared with a 100 mbps connection.

  It's also important to realize that you don't have to commit solely to one technology or another. For instance, you can mix and match wireless and wired networks, which may mean only purchasing wireless equipment for laptops, or those computers that would otherwise be very difficult to wire.

- When assigning roles to different computers, think about how often they'll be used. For example, a computer that provides an Internet connection for your network must be on for the connection to be active, so it's best to hook up your Internet connection to the computer that is most likely to be turned on at any given time. And a computer hosting a shared printer or shared files will not only need to be turned on, but should also be a fast system with lots of memory so that it can handle the extra load.

- Windows XP includes firewall and Internet connection-sharing functionality right out of the box, but these can be somewhat limited when compared with extra-cost hardware alternatives.

- Some printers can be hooked up directly to the network, eliminating the need for a dedicated computer to host them. While this typically adds cost, it means that any computer on the network can print without first having to turn on another computer. If this option is not available for your printer, you can still hook it up to a separate print server device.

Configuring Network Connections

The central interface used to configure the networking features in Windows XP is the Network Connections window, introduced in Chapter 4. Right-click the My Network Places icon on your Desktop and select Properties, or use Control Panel → [Network and Internet Connections] → Network Connections to open the Network Connections Window.

Figure 7-4 and Figure 7-5 show two different views of the Network Connections window. Depending on your Windows Explorer settings (discussed in Chapters 3 and 4), your view may be different, but all the required components are still there. If you haven't done so already, select Details from the View menu to see all the pertinent information.

Figure 7-4. If common tasks (Tools → Folder Options) are enabled, the Network Setup Wizard and New Connection wizard are accessible through the tasks pane on your left

Figure 7-5. If common tasks are not shown, the Network Setup Wizard and New Connection Wizard appear as icons in your Network Connections window

As its name implies, Network Connections lists all of the networking connections configured on your computer. Windows doesn't care how many computers are on your network, whether you're using a hub or a switch, or even what type of cabling you've used. Rather, the only thing you need to worry about in the context of this window is the individual connections attached to this computer.

In Figure 7-4 and Figure 7-5, two network connections are shown, one for each network adapter installed in the machine. In the right-hand computer in Figure 7-2, a dotted rectangle shows the same setup graphically. Here, we have a single computer with two networking connections: one used to connect to the Internet, and one used to connect to the hub and the rest of the LAN. (See "Sharing an Internet Connection," later in this chapter, for more information on why two connections are required to share an Internet connection with the other computers on a LAN.)

You should have a connection icon for each network adapter (NIC) installed in your system; install a new network adapter, and (if properly installed) it will show up automatically in the Network Connections window. You might also have one or more connection icons for so-called "soft" connections, such as dial-up connections (for your analog or ISDN modem), PPPoE connections (for certain types of DSL and cable modems), and Virtual Private Networking (VPN) connections.

To add a new connection (all types except those that correspond to physical network adapters), open the New Connection Wizard (or click Create a new connection if you have the Common Tasks pane enabled). See "New Connection Wizard" in Chapter 4 for more information on this feature. Throughout the rest of this chapter, you'll see several examples of how and when this wizard is used.

A similar-sounding feature, called the Network Setup Wizard (click "Set up a home or small office network" if you have the Common Tasks pane enabled), is used to automatically configure your Internet connection and local network settings based on one of several predefined scenarios. See "Network Setup Wizard" in Chapter 4 as well as several sections throughout the rest of this chapter for more details.

Right-click a connection icon and select Properties to configure any existing network connection. Depending on the type of connection, you'll see one of several different types of Properties sheets.

LAN or High-Speed Internet connection properties

The Properties window for LAN or High Speed Internet connections is divided into three tabs: General (as shown in Figure 7-6), Authentication, and Advanced (as shown in Figure 7-7).

Figure 7-6. The Authentication Tab allows you to set security features

The use of these tabs is as follows:

General

The General tab allows you to configure the main aspects of the connection. The Connect using box shows the hardware adapter with which this connection is associated; click Configure to open the device's properties window, which is the same one you'll get through Device Manager (see Chapter 4).

Next is the list of installed networking components; the checked items represent the services and protocols to be used with the connection. See "Protocols and Services," later in this chapter, for details.

Finally, the "Show icon in notification area when connected" option allows you to toggle the tray icon; if the connection is always active, you can reduce clutter by turning this off.

Authentication

The settings on this page are used to implement certain security features, mostly used in conjunction with wireless networks. Most users will never need to adjust these settings. If you have a wireless network, and you're concerned about unauthorized users accessing your network with their own wireless equipment, look up "Authentication" in the Help and Support Center. (See Chapter 4 for more information.)

Advanced

The Advanced settings are simple, but powerful. These options allow you to control the Internet Connection Firewall and Internet Connection Sharing, both discussed later in this chapter.

Dial-up / Broadband connection properties

For dial-up broadband connections (such as PPPoE), the Properties window (shown in Figure 7-7) has the following tabbed pages:

General

The General tab allows you to configure the main aspects of the connection.

The Connect using box (Dial-Up connections only) shows the currently selected modem; click Configure to open the device's properties window, which is the same one you'll get through Device Manager (see Chapter 4). Below, you can change the phone number or even add additional phone numbers, through which Windows will cycle if the first one is busy or unavailable.

The Service name box (Broadband connections only) should be left blank, unless instructed otherwise by your service provider.

Finally, the "Show icon in notification area when connected" option allows you to toggle the tray icon; turning this option on will allow you to disconnect the connection more easily (by right-clicking on the tray icon).

Options

The settings in the Options page affect dialing properties, such as when and how many times to redial, and whether Windows should prompt for information before attempting a connection.

Figure 7-7. The Advanced tab controls the firewall and Internet Connection Sharing

Security

> The Security settings allow you to control how your username and password are transmitted to the server; most users will want to leave these settings unchanged. Contact your service provider for more information on supported security protocols.

Networking

> The first box is a drop-down list containing all of the supported connection types for the connection. For dial-up connections, you'll usually want PPP; for broadband connections, you'll usually want PPPoE. Like some of the other settings in this window, your service provider will inform you if you need to change any of these settings.

> Next is the list of installed networking components; the checked items represent the services and protocols to be used with the connection. See "Protocols and Services," later in this chapter, for details.

Advanced

> The Advanced tab is the same as the Advanced tab for standard network connections; these options allow you to control the Internet Connection Firewall and Internet Connection Sharing, both discussed later in this chapter.

Other connection actions

In addition to Properties, there are other items available on the connection icons' context menus (depending on the connection type):

Enable/Disable
> This allows you to selectively enable or disable permanent connections, such as LAN or High-Speed Internet connections. Disabling a connection is effectively the same as pulling out the cable; a red X will appear over the icon of a disabled connection.

Connect/Disconnect
> Connect establishes a temporary connection, and Disconnect breaks that connection. For Dial-up connections, these commands dial and hang up, respectively. For Broadband connections, these commands login and logout, respectively.
>
> If the "Show icon in notification area when connected" option is enabled in the connection's properties window, you can also access Disconnect by right-clicking the connection icon that appears in the Taskbar tray. You can also open the connection's Status window (see Figure 7-8) and click Disconnect.

Status
> This is the default action for all connections; double-click any connection to view its Status window. (See Figure 7-8.) The Status window shows the amount of time the connection has been active, the number of TCP packets sent and received, and even the IP address of the connection (in the Support tab). Also available are buttons for the other actions where applicable, such as Enable / Disable, Connect / Disconnect, Properties, and Repair.

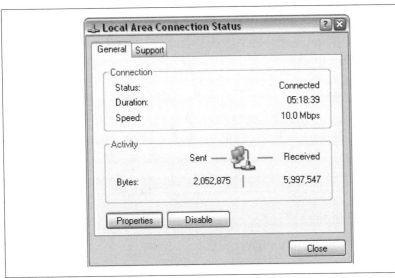

Figure 7-8. The Status window displays information about the current network connection

If you suspect that a connection is down, check the packets sent and received in the Activity section of the Status window; if the numbers change when you, say, try to open a web page or check your email, the connection is still active.

Repair

Repair reinstalls the drivers associated with the connection. If a connection does not appear to be working, try disabling it and then reenabling it (or disconnecting and then reconnecting, if applicable). If that doesn't work, then try Repair.

Set as Default Connection/Cancel as Default Connection

Available only for temporary connections, such as Dial-up connections and Broadband connections. If a connection is set as the default connection, and Windows is configured to dial automatically (through Control Panel → [Network and Internet Connections] → Internet Options), it will be connected automatically when needed. If you have more than one connection of this type, use Set as Default Connection to determine which one gets connected automatically.

A black checkmark in a circle will appear over the connection icon for any connection that is set as the default.

Bridge Connections

Simply put, this allows data to be transferred between two (or more) different networks. In effect, a bridge turns you computer into a hub of sorts, but with the advantage of allowing you to combine two otherwise incompatible networks. Windows XP supports only one bridge at any given time, but a single bridge can contain as many different connections as you want.

Select at least two connection icons, right-click, and select Bridge Connections (or go to Advanced → Bridge Connections) to create a network bridge between the connections.

Create Copy

Any network connection that can be added with the New Connection Wizard can be copied. Create a copy of a Dial-up connection, for example, to have two connection profiles without having to enter all the information twice. Create Copy is also handy for creating a backup of a connection so that you can experiment with different settings without loosing a working profile.

Note that if you want to add only alternate phone numbers, you can right-click the connection, select Properties, and click Alternates.

Protocols and Services

When you view the Properties window for a connection (see Figure 7-6, earlier in this chapter), you'll see the "This connection uses the following items" list (either in the General tab or the Networking tab, depending on the connection type). This list, also accessible via Network Connections → Advanced → Advanced

Settings, shows all of the installed protocols and services. You can selectively choose which protocols and services are supported by any specific connection with the checkboxes in the list.

If you need to add support for a protocol or service not shown in the list, click Install to add it. If a protocol or service is shown but you're certain it's not used by any of your connections, you can uninstall it. If you install or uninstall a protocol or service, the change will take effect for all existing connections.

Probably the most useful button, however, is Properties. Depending on the service or protocol currently selected, Properties allows you to set many of the advanced options for a connection. The following list shows common services and protocols available in Windows XP:

Client for Microsoft Networks
An essential component for connecting to a Microsoft Network. This entry should always be present and enabled, unless you specifically need to connect to a non-Microsoft network (such as NetWare). This entry has one setting in its Properties window, and most users will have no need to modify it.

File and Printer Sharing for Microsoft Windows
The service responsible for sharing files and printers over a Microsoft Network; see "Sharing Resources," later in this chapter, for more information. This component should be enabled for LAN connections, and disabled for Internet connections. The Properties window is unavailable for this entry.

Internet Protocol (TCP/IP)
The TCP/IP protocol, introduced in the beginning of this chapter, is the protocol used by all Internet connections, as well as most LAN connections. Unless you specifically don't want TCP/IP support for some reason, the Internet Protocol (TCP/IP) entry should be enabled for all of your connections.

Select Internet Protocol (TCP/IP) and click Properties to view and change the connection's TCP/IP settings. The Internet Protocol (TCP/IP) Properties window, shown in Figure 7-9, is where you set the IP address of your connection (if you have a static IP address), as well as the subnet mask, gateway, and DNS server addresses. If the connection has a dynamic IP address (assigned randomly every time you connect), choose the "Obtain and IP address automatically" option.

Click Advanced to configure multiple IP addresses and multiple gateways, use more than two DNS servers, set up WINS, and enable NetBIOS over TCP/IP. Choose the Options tab to configure TCP/IP filtering, which allows you to selectively permit or deny communication based on the port (described at the beginning of this chapter). Note that this is somewhat like a firewall, described in "Implementing Network Security," later in this chapter.

NWLink IPX/SPX/NetBIOS Compatible Transport Protocol
Enable this entry to add support for the IPX/SPX (Internetwork Packet eXchange/Sequenced Packet eXchange) protocol. IPX/SPX is used by Novell NetWare networks, as well as some old DOS games and some network printers. Unless you know specifically that you need IPX/SPX support, you probably don't need this protocol.

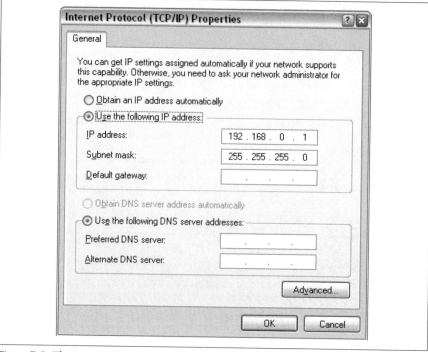

Figure 7-9. The Internet Protocol Properties Window

NWLink NetBIOS

Use this protocol to connect to a NetWare server running Novell NetBIOS. If you use only Microsoft-compatible networks, you'll have no use for this protocol. This entry has no properties.

General Procedures

The preceding sections of this chapter outline the fundamentals of networking and the various components that make up Windows XP's built-in support for networking. As stated earlier, Windows is really only concerned with the connections directly attached to the computer, so building a network essentially means configuring the connections for each computer involved.

The following sections explain the procedures for building and connecting to different types of networks. It's important to realize that there are limitless combinations of networking hardware and software, and it's obviously impossible to cover them all.

Setting Up a LAN

Connecting two computers to form a basic peer-to-peer workgroup is fairly easy with Windows XP, as long as you have the proper equipment, drivers, and an hour or two. Ideally, you should be able to set up a functioning workgroup in less than ten minutes, but that doesn't include fishing for drivers, resolving hardware conflicts, or running a cable through your attic.

We'll start with a basic peer-to-peer workgroup consisting of two computers. Here's what you'll need:

- Two computers, each presumably running Windows XP. Although you can connect a Windows machine to a machine running any networkable operating system (Windows 9x/Me, Windows NT/2000, Mac, Unix, etc.), for the sake of simplicity, we'll assume that both machines are running Windows XP.

- At least one network adapter (see NIC in "Networking Terminology," earlier in this chapter) installed in each computer. NICs are cheap and readily available, and are even built-in to many higher-end systems.

  If you're not sure what to get, just purchase a standard, plug-and-play 10base-T Ethernet adapter with an RJ45 connector. If you have a Desktop system, get a PCI card; if you have a laptop, get a PC Card (PCMCIA) adapter. You can also get a USB-based NIC (useful if you don't want to take your Desktop apart), although these tend to be slower and a little more temperamental than true Ethernet adapters.

- Finally, you'll need a hub (or switch) and two category-5 patch Ethernet cables. Alternately, you can use just a single category-5 crossover Ethernet cable and skip the hub, but this will limit your network to only two computers. Figure 7-1 shows a simple workgroup of four computers connected to a hub (or switch).

  An alternative to the cables and hub is to use wireless equipment. Although more expensive, and a little slower (see "Planning Your Network," earlier in this chapter), it allows you to eliminate some or all of the cabling. Instead, simply install a wireless network adapter in each of your computers, and, as long as they're in close enough proximity, a network will be established. You can even connect a DSL or cable modem to your wireless network with a wireless router. (See "Sharing an Internet Connection," later in this chapter, for details.) You can even mix and match wired and wireless networks. Figure 7-10 shows a simple wired workgroup extended with a wireless notebook adapter and a wireless access point plugged into the hub.

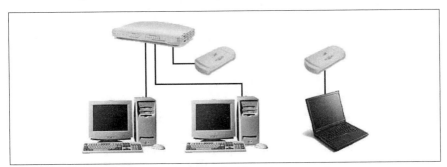

Figure 7-10. A network supporting both wired and wireless connections

Once you have all of the components, you can begin with the following procedure. Naturally, different types of hardware will require a modified procedure, but the methodology is the same.

1. Plan your network by drawing a quick diagram similar to the ones shown in Figure 7-1, Figure 7-2, Figure 7-3, and Figure 7-10.

2. Install a network adapter in each computer, according to the instructions that accompany your hardware. If you're using Plug-and-Play adapters, Windows should automatically install and configure the drivers for the adapters.

   A connection icon labeled "Local Area Connection" should appear in your Network Connections window for each installed adapter; check for this in each computer. Select Details from the View menu to show the Type and Status columns; the connections should be enabled and of type "LAN or High-Speed Internet." If the icons don't show up, make sure Windows recognizes your network cards in Device Manager (see Chapter 4) and doesn't report any problems with the devices.

3. Next, hook up your cables. Nearly all network adapters, hubs, and switches have lights next to their RJ45 ports. When a cable is properly plugged in to both ends, the light goes on. If the lights don't go on, you're either using the wrong type of cable, you've plugged the cable into the wrong port, or the cable is defective. Until the lights are lit, don't go any further. Hint: use a different color cable for each computer to make troubleshooting easier.

   Make sure to use only category-5 patch cables, except under the following conditions. A category-5 crossover cable can be used instead to connect two computers directly (if you don't have a hub or switch) and can also be used to connect two hubs together. In some cases where a Digital Subscriber Line (DSL) adapter or cable modem connects directly to a computer with a patch cable, a crossover cable is required to connect either of these devices to a hub. (Naturally, consult the documentation to be sure.)

4. Go to Control Panel → [Performance and Maintenance] → System to open the System Properties window (described in Chapter 4), and choose the Computer Name tab.

5. Click Network ID to run the Network Identification Wizard. Click Next on the first page, choose "This computer is for home use and not part of a business network," click Next, and then click Finish.

6. Next, click Change to open the Computer Name Changes window (see Figure 7-11), and enter both a Computer name and Workgroup name. The Workgroup name should be the same for all computers on your local network, but the Computer name must be different for each computer.

7. Click OK when you're done; if Windows informs you that you need to restart your computer, do so now. Repeat steps 4–6 for the other computers on your network.

8. Your connection should now be active. Determine the IP address of each computer using the connections' Status windows (see "Other connection actions," earlier in this chapter).

Figure 7-11. Set the Computer Name and Workgroup Name on the Computer Name Changes Window

9. Test your connection with Ping (described in Chapter 4). By default, Windows will assign IP addresses in the following way: the first computer will be 192.168.0.1, the second will be 192.168.0.2, and so-on. (See the following section, "What to Do if Your Connection Doesn't Work," for more information on manually assigning IP addresses.) Assuming your network is similar, pick a computer, go to Start → Run, and type ping *address*, where *address* is the IP address of the other computer. For example, from the 192. 168.0.2 computer, you would type:

```
ping 192.168.0.1
```

If the network is working, you'll get something like this:

```
Pinging 192.168.0.1 with 32 bytes of data:
Reply from 192.168.0.1: bytes=32 time=24ms TTL=53
Reply from 192.168.0.1: bytes=32 time=16ms TTL=53
```

On the other hand, if you get this result:

```
Pinging 192.168.0.1 with 32 bytes of data:
Request timed out.
Request timed out.
```

it means the network is not functioning.

10. If your network is functioning, you can proceed to set up the various services you need, such as file sharing, printer sharing, and Internet Connection Sharing (all described later in this chapter). Otherwise, look through the checklist in the following section.

What to do if your connection doesn't work

The following tips should help you get around most of the common hurdles you'll encounter when setting up a LAN:

- Run the Network Setup Wizard, as described in Chapter 4. While this step isn't always required, it does occasionally fix errant settings that otherwise would prevent a network from working properly.

- Check your cables and make sure the appropriate lights are lit. If you're unsure which lights to look for, try unplugging a cable from a device. If a light on the device goes out and then goes back on when the cable is plugged in, that's the light you're concerned with. Such lights are often labelled "Link."

- Windows XP is designed to implement most changes to the network without restarting. However, if you encounter problems, try restarting one or all of your machines to force them to recognize the new network.

- Make sure no two computers on your network are attempting to use the same Computer name or IP address.

- Make sure you have the latest drivers for your NIC (network adapter); check with the manufacturer for details. Note that hubs, routers, and switches typically don't require any special drivers.

- Right-click the connection icon in the Network Connections window, and select Repair. Note that this feature reinstalls some drivers, but doesn't necessarily investigate your network settings.

- The instructions in the previous section assume the network settings for your connections haven't been tampered with. If you suspect that your settings might be wrong, open Device Manager, right-click the entry corresponding with your network adapter, and select Uninstall. (Note that it's not necessary to physically remove the device from your system.) When you restart Windows, the adapter will be redetected, and the drivers will be installed with their default settings.

Sharing Resources

There's little point in setting up a network if you don't take advantage of the connection by sharing files and printers. Once you've established a network connection with another Windows computer and verified that the connection is working (as described in the previous two sections), you can set up resources to be shared over your network.

A shared resource is a folder on your hard disk or a printer physically attached to your computer, which you would like made accessible by other computers on your network. If you share a printer, others on your network can print to it; if you share a folder, others on your network can access the files and folders contained therein as though they were stored on their own hard disks.

Whenever you share a resource, you are opening a backdoor to your computer. It's important to keep security in mind at all times, especially if you're connected to the Internet. Otherwise, you may be unwittingly exposing your personal data to intruders looking for anything they can use and abuse. Furthermore, an insecure system is more vulnerable to viruses and other malicious programs.

The first thing you should do is go to Control Panel → [Appearance and Themes] → Folder Options → View tab, and turn off the "Use simple file sharing" option. See "Folder Options" in Chapter 4 and "Implementing Network Security," later in this chapter, for more information on the problems with this feature.

Sharing resources is easy. Simply right-click a folder or printer icon, select Sharing and Security (or select Properties and choose the Sharing tab), and choose the appropriate options. Figure 7-12 shows a sharing window for a user's *Desktop* folder. (Sharing printers is discussed later).

Note that under some circumstances, the dialogs shown in Figures 7-12, 7-13, 7-15, and 7-16 may look different. For example, in Windows XP Home Edition, if you're not using the NTFS file, or if you have the "Use Simple File Sharing" option enabled in Windows XP Professional Edition, you may see simpler dialogs with fewer options. The concepts discussed still hold, but some of the advanced options relating to permissions will be unavailable.

Figure 7-12. Use the Sharing tab of a file or folder to set its access privileges

Choose the "Share this folder" option to enable sharing for the selected item. (Note that if you're sharing a disk and Sharing already appears to be active, you may be looking at an Administrative Share, discussed later in this chapter.) The name you typed in the "Share name" field is what users of other computers will see when they try to access the folder; the Comment field is optional.

At this point, you can click OK to begin sharing the folder (and all of its contents) over your network. When a folder or drive is shared, a small hand appears over its icon. Note that it's best to share only those folders that you need others to access.

However, you need to make sure that your user accounts are in order before others on your network are able to access your shared resources. Simply put, every user who wishes to access data on your computer remotely (that is, through the network connection) must have a user account on your computer. For example, if you're logged in as "Lenny," you'll only be able to access resources on other computers that also have an account called "Lenny" and that have the same password configured for that account. If you have two Windows XP machines, one with a "Lenny" account and one with a "Lenny" and a "Karl" account, a user logged in as "Karl" will only be able to access resources on the second machine.

Once a folder has been shared, and assuming the user accounts are set up properly, you can access the folder from another computer by using My Network Places. My Network Places is available as an icon on your Desktop and as a folder in the Windows Explorer tree. See Figure 7-13 for an example of how a shared folder called *Desktop* located on the computer called *Karl*, is accessed over the network. Files and folders can be dragged to and from this location as though it was just another folder on your hard disk.

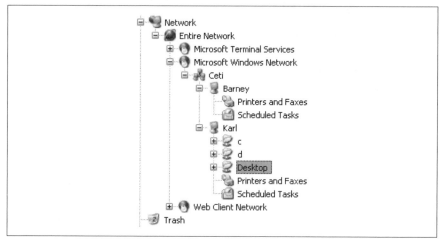

Figure 7-13. My Network Places gives access to shared folders on other machines

The full path to a network resource (called a UNC path, for "Universal Naming Convention") looks a little different than a standard path. The path to a folder called *Desktop*, located on a computer called *Barney*, will look like this:

    \\Barney\Desktop

Note that only the Share name (*Desktop*) is shown here, even though the folder may have a long path on its host computer (e.g., *c:\Documents and Settings\ Barney\Desktop*).

Mapping drives

Although generally considered passe, you can also access shared resources by mapping them to a network drive. Select Map Network Drive from Windows Explorer's Tools menu to display the window shown in Figure 7-14. Here, if we choose an unused drive letter, such as *N:*, and specify the path to an existing network resource, such as *\\Barney\Desktop*, we can then access the files in that folder by navigating to *N:* in Explorer.

Drive mapping was used more commonly several years ago when most applications didn't support UNCs like *\\Barney\Desktop*, but happily accessed files off of a fictitious drive *N:*. Today, it is preferred to simply create a Windows Shortcut to a commonly accessed network resource rather than going to the trouble of mapping a drive. However, if you still rely on an old application or even a DOS program, you may still need to resort to drive mapping.

Figure 7-14. Mapping a network drive

Administrative shares

In Windows XP Professional, every drive is automatically shared by default. However, this is for administrative purposes and is not intended for general file sharing. (Unfortunately, there's no way to disable the administrative shares. For most intents and purposes, though, this does not pose a significant security risk, as the shares can be accessed like normally shared resources.) Figure 7-15 shows the "Default Share" for a drive; the dollar sign in the Share name signifies the administrative share. To initiate the type of file sharing most users will need, click the New Share button at the bottom at of the window to display the New Share window (see Figure 7-16).

Here, you can type the Share name and a comment, if desired, as described earlier in this section. The Share name you've typed, as well as the default share (here, D$), will then appear in a drop-down list; you can subsequently select the desired Share name from this list to configure or remove it.

Networking

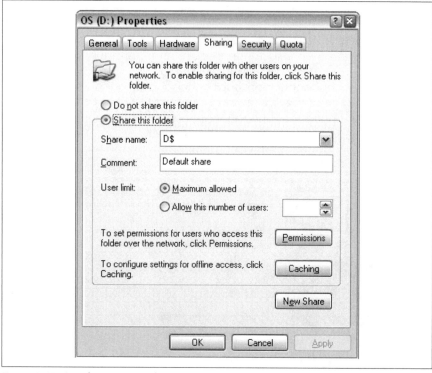

Figure 7-15. An administrative share

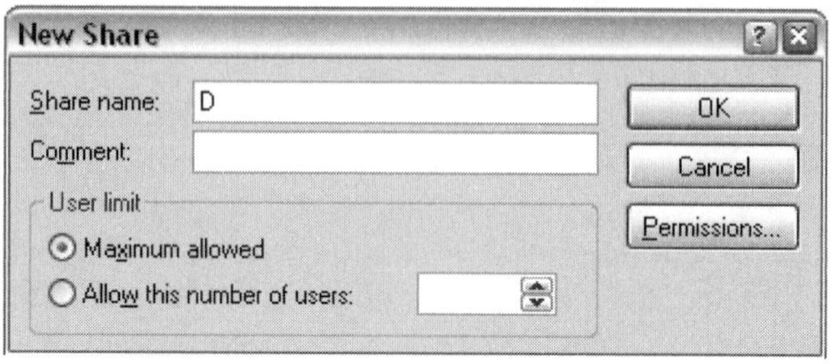

Figure 7-16. The New Share window

Permissions

If you're using Windows XP Professional and the NTFS filesystem, you'll be able to control who can view your files and who cannot; click Permissions in the Sharing window to see the Permissions dialog shown in Figure 7-17. By default, a single entry, "Everyone," is shown in the top list. If you want to selectively allow and disallow access to various users, first click all the checkboxes in the Deny column. Then, click Add to configure the access rights for other configured users. Figure 7-18 shows the Select Users or Groups window, which configures permissions for user accounts on your machine and other machines on your network.

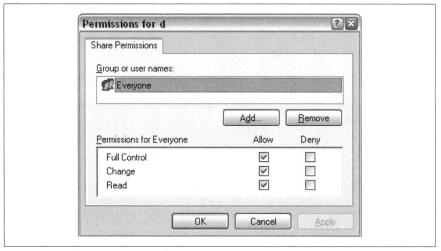

Figure 7-17. The Permissions window

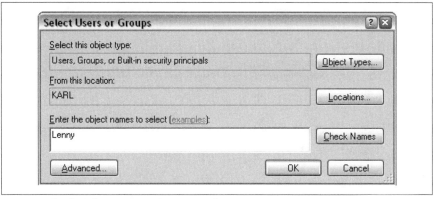

Figure 7-18. The Select Users or Groups window

When a new user has been added to the Permissions window, highlight the user-name, and selectively click Allow for the various permissions available.

In Figure 7-17, we have three choices:

Full Control
    Allows a user to read, modify, and delete files and folders, and add new files and folders. If allowed, the Change and Read options are also enabled.

Change
    Allows a user to modify a file. If allowed, the Read option is also enabled.

Read
    Provides basic read-only access to a file or folder. Remote users can view folder listings and open files, but aren't allowed to make any changes, including deleting files or adding new files to protected folders.

Networking

Permissions are inherited, which means if you configure the permissions for a folder, those permissions will be active for all subfolders and their contents. However, you can set rather liberal permissions for, say, a drive, and then selectively restrict access for the more sensitive folders contained therein.

Sharing printers

Printers are shared much in the same way that folders are (described in the previous sections), with two exceptions. First, there's really only one option on the Printer Sharing window (see Figure 7-19): the Share name. Second, printers aren't accessed through the My Network Places folder.

Figure 7-19. The Printer Sharing window

Here's how to share a printer:

1. On the computer physically connected to the printer, go to Control Panel → [Printers and Other Hardware] → Printers and Faxes.

2. Right-click on the printer icon to share, and select Sharing.

3. Choose the "Share this printer" option, verify that the Share name is as close to the original printer name as possible, and click OK.

4. Then, go to another computer on your network, and open Control Panel → [Printers and Other Hardware] → Printers and Faxes.

5. Double-click the Add Printer icon (or, if you have common tasks enabled, click "Add a printer" in the Printer Tasks pane).

6. Click Next on the first page, select "A network printer, or a printer attached to another computer" on the second page, and then click Next.

7. Leave the default setting of "Browse for printer" selected, and click Next.

8. You'll then be presented with a rather strange-looking collapsible tree (see Figure 7-20). Although it doesn't look or feel much like the tree in Windows Explorer, it works in somewhat the same way. Double-click any branch to expand it; when you've found the printer, click Next. If the printer does not appear under the computer to which it's attached, either the computer is not properly hooked up to the network or the printer driver does not support network sharing.

 Some printer drivers don't support being shared over a network, especially those for cheaper printers. However you may still be able to share your printer by purchasing a separate print server. Note that it may be less expensive to simply purchase a new printer, but that's up to you.

9. When you complete the wizard, a new icon will appear in the Printers and Faxes window for the newly shared printer, and you'll be able to print to that printer from any Windows application is not physically attached to the computer. Note that the computer that *is* physically attached to the printer must be turned on in order to print.

10. Repeat steps 4–9 for all other computers on your network that you need to print from.

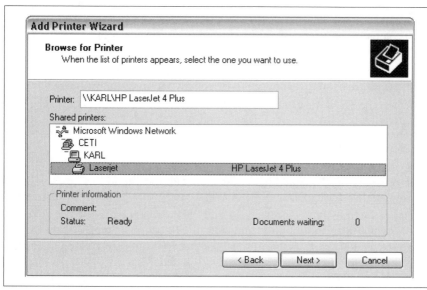

Figure 7-20. Browsing for a Shared printer

Connecting to the Internet

There are four basic ways to connect to the Internet in Windows XP. The one you choose depends on the type of connection you wish to establish:

- DSL, cable, or other high-speed connection with a static IP address
- DSL, cable, or other high-speed connection via PPPoE
- Connection provided by another computer or router via Internet Connection Sharing
- Dial-up connection, including analog modems over standard phone lines

If your connection doesn't fit neatly into one of these categories, your setup may still be similar to one of the following sections. Otherwise, you'll need to contact your service provider for specific instructions and software for Windows XP.

If you have a single Internet connection and more than one computer, see "Sharing an Internet Connection" later in this chapter.

Once you've successfully connected to the Internet, see "Implementing Network Security," later in this chapter, for more steps to protect your computer and data.

DSL, cable, or other high-speed connection with a static IP address

High-speed connections with static IP addresses are very easy to set up in Windows XP. (A static IP address means you have the same IP address every time you start your computer.) No additional software is typically required for such a connection. If you're not sure if you have such a connection, check to see if your connection requires a username and password to log on; if so, you most likely have a PPPoE connection (see the next section). Otherwise, proceed with these steps:

1. Connect your network adapter directly to your Internet connection. (This assumes your Internet connection is properly set up and functioning.)

2. Open the Network Connections window, locate the connection icon corresponding to your network adapter, and rename it to "Internet Connection." Then, right-click the newly named Internet Connection icon and select Properties.

3. Under the General tab, only Client for Microsoft Networks, and Internet Protocol (TCP/IP) should be checked (see "Protocols and Services," earlier in this chapter, for details).

4. Select Internet Protocol (TCP/IP) and click Properties. Click the "Use the following IP address" option and enter the IP address, Subnet mask, Default gateway, and the Preferred (primary) DNS server and Alternate (secondary) DNS server addresses provided by your Internet service provider.

5. Click OK, then click OK again; the change should take effect immediately. Test your connection by loading a web page or using Ping (see Chapter 4).

Notes:

If Windows ever prompts you to connect to the Internet after completing these steps, go to Control Panel → [Network and Internet Connections] → Internet Options → Connections tab, and click "Never dial a connection."

DSL, cable, or other high-speed connection via PPPoE

PPPoE is the protocol used to establish temporary, dynamic IP connections over high-speed Internet connections. If your connection provides a dynamic IP address, it means your Internet service provider assigns a different IP address every time you connect to the Internet. The PPPoE (PPP over Ethernet) protocol facilitates this connection by sending your username and password to your provider. If your ISP provides special software that connects to the Internet (such as Efficient Networks' NTS Enternet 300 utility or RASPPPoE), you can abandon it in favor of Windows XP's built-in support for PPPoE.

One of the differences between this type of connection and the static IP connection discussed in the previous section is that PPPoE connections must be initiated every time you start Windows or every time you wish to use the Internet, which is somewhat like using old-fashioned dial-up connections (discussed later).

Here's how to set up a PPPoE connection in Windows XP:

1. If you have PPPoE software (such as Enternet 300) installed, remove it from your system now. This is typically accomplished by going to Control Panel → Add or Remove Programs. Refer to the documentation that came with the software for details.

2. Open the Network Connections window and start the New Connection Wizard (or click Create a new connection if you have the Common Tasks pane enabled).

3. Click Next to skip the introductory page, choose the "Connect to the Internet" option, and click Next.

4. Choose the "Set up my connection manually" option, and click Next.

5. Choose the "Connect using a broadband connection that requires a username and password" option, and click Next.

6. Type a name for this connection; a good choice is the name of your ISP or just "DSL" or "cable," and click Next.

7. Enter your username and password, choose the desired options (if you're not sure, turn them all on), and click Next.

8. Click Finish to complete the wizard.

9. To start the connection, double-click the icon you just created in the Network Connections folder. If you elected to create a Desktop shortcut in the wizard, double-click said Desktop icon.

10. The "Connect" box can be disabled by clicking Properties, selecting the Options tab, and changing the "Prompt for name and password, certificate, etc." option. You can return to this window by right-clicking the new connection and selecting Properties.

Notes

- To have Windows connect automatically whenever the connection is needed, first right-click the connection icon and select Set as Default Connection. Then, go to Control Panel → [Network and Internet Connections] → Internet Options → Connections tab and click "Always dial my default connection."

Networking

- To have Windows connect automatically when you first start your computer, place a shortcut to the connection in your Startup folder. You'll also need to make sure that the "Prompt for name and password, certificate, etc." option is turned off as just described.

- If you need to make more than one PPPoE connection quickly, right-click an existing PPPoE connection icon and select Create Copy. Then, right-click the new connection icon and select Properties to modify it.

- If you're having trouble getting your new PPPoE connection to work, check your DSL or cable modem first to see if the correct lights are lit (refer to your documentation). Sometimes, turning off the adapter, waiting several minutes, and then turning it back on solves the problem.

Connection provided by another computer or router via Internet Connection Sharing

If you're using Internet Connection Sharing, the setup for the clients (all the computers on your network, other than the one with the physical Internet connection) is a snap. This procedure is also appropriate if you're using a router to share an Internet connection.

This procedure assumes you've already set up your Internet connection, as described in "Sharing an Internet Connection," as well as a properly functioning peer-to-peer workgroup, as described in "Setting up a LAN," discussed earlier in this chapter.

Follow these steps to connect a computer to an existing shared Internet connection:

1. Open the Network Connections window, right-click the connection icon corresponding to your network adapter, and select Properties.

2. Under the General tab, make sure Client for Microsoft Networks and Internet Protocol (TCP/IP) are checked (see "Protocols and Services," earlier in this chapter for details). Other protocols and services may be checked here as well, depending on your needs.

3. Select Internet Protocol (TCP/IP) and click Properties. Here, there are two possibilities.

   - If you're not using fixed IP addresses on your LAN (which will be the most common case), select both the "Obtain an IP address automatically" and the "Obtain DNS server address automatically" options, and click OK.

   - If you've set up your network with fixed IP addresses such as 192.168.0.1, 192.168.0.1, and so on (see "Setting Up a LAN," earlier in this chapter), click the "Use the following IP address" option and enter the IP address of the machine. Then type 255.255.255.0 for the subnet mask. For the gateway, enter the IP address of the computer hosting the shared Internet connection. If you're using a router to share your Internet connection, refer to the instructions that come with the router for the proper gateway settings. Finally, type the Preferred (primary) DNS server and Alternate (secondary) DNS server addresses provided by your Internet service provider. Click OK when you're done.

4. Click OK to close the connection properties window; the change should take effect immediately. Test your connection by loading a web page or using Ping (see Chapter 4).

5. If the connection doesn't work at this point, run the Network Setup Wizard (or click "Set up a home or small office network" if you have the Common Tasks pane enabled). Click Next at the first two pages, and on the third page, choose "This computer connects to the Internet through another computer..." Then click Next. Depending on your network configuration, the remaining pages will vary here; answer the questions the best you can and complete the wizard.

Notes

- If Windows ever prompts you to connect to the Internet after completing these steps, go to Control Panel → [Network and Internet Connections] → Internet Options → Connections tab, and click "Never dial a connection."

- If you're able to view some web sites but not others from the client computers, see *http://www.annoyances.org/exec/show/article04-107*.

Dial-up connection, including analog modems over standard phone lines

If you have a standard analog modem and you connect to the Internet by dialing a phone number, follow these steps to set up your connection. You can have as many connections as you like, which is especially useful if you travel; just repeat these steps for each subsequent connection.

1. Open the Network Connections window, and then start the New Connection Wizard (or click Create a new connection if you have the Common Tasks pane enabled).

2. Click Next to skip the introductory page, choose the "Connect to the Internet" option, and click Next.

3. Choose the "Set up my connection manually" option, and click Next.

4. Choose the "Connect using a dial-up modem" option, and click Next.

5. Type a name for this connection; a good choice is your ISP name, or perhaps something like "Analog connection at my sister's house," and click Next.

6. Type the phone number here, and click Next.

   If your ISP provides two or more phone numbers, you have the option of creating multiple connections (one for each phone number), or creating a single connection that cycles through a list of phone numbers until a connection is established. If you choose the latter, you'll have the opportunity to enter additional phone numbers for the connection later on.

7. Enter your username and password, choose the desired options (if you're not sure, turn them all on), and click Next.

8. Click Finish to complete the wizard.

9. To start the connection, double-click the icon you just created in the Network Connections folder. If you elected to create a Desktop shortcut in the wizard, double-click said Desktop icon.

Networking

10. The "Connect" box can be disabled by clicking Properties, selecting the Options tab, and changing the "Prompt for name and password, certificate, etc." option. You can return to this window by right-clicking the new connection and selecting Properties.

Notes

- To have Windows connect automatically whenever the connection is needed, first right-click the connection icon and select Set as Default Connection. Then, go to Control Panel → [Network and Internet Connections] → Internet Options → Connections tab, and click "Always dial my default connection."

- To have Windows connect automatically when you first start your computer, place a shortcut to the connection in your Startup folder. You'll also need to make sure that the "Prompt for name and password, certificate, etc." option is turned off.

- To enter additional phone numbers for this connection, right-click the new connection icon, select Properties, choose the General tab, and click Alternates. See Figure 7-21 for an example.

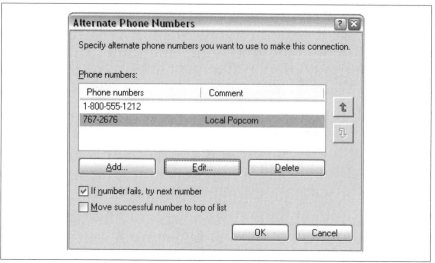

Figure 7-21. Adding alternate phone numbers

- If you need to make more than one dial-up connection, a quick way is to right-click an existing dial-up connection icon and select Create Copy. Then, right-click the new connection icon and select Properties to modify it.

- If you're using America Online, MSN, or some other proprietary service, these instructions may not apply to you. Contact your service provider for setup instructions for Windows XP.

Sharing an Internet Connection

It obviously makes sense to share a single Internet connection among all the computers in your home or office, rather than investing in a separate connection for each machine. Fortunately, Windows XP comes with an Internet Connection Sharing (ICS) feature built right into the operating system. Additionally, there are third-party hardware and software products that provide similar functionality, each with its own advantages and disadvantages. See "Alternatives to Internet Connection Sharing," later in this chapter, for details.

Setting up Internet Connection Sharing

Internet Connection Sharing is a system by which a single computer with an Internet Connection acts as a gateway, allowing other computers on the LAN to use the connection. The computer that is connected directly to the Internet is called the *host*; all the other computers are called *clients*.

In order to get ICS (Internet Connection Sharing) to work, you'll need the following:

- At least two computers, each with an Ethernet card properly installed and functioning. It is assumed you've already set up your local network, as described in "Setting up a LAN," earlier in this chapter. Your Internet connection can be shared with as many clients as your LAN will support.

- One of the computers must have an Internet connection properly set up, as described in "Connecting to the Internet," earlier in this chapter. The instructions that follow assume that the computer handing the Internet connection is running Windows XP; if you need to set up a computer running another version of Windows as the ICS host, visit *http://www.annoyances.org/exec/show/ics*.

  You do not need a special type of Internet connection, nor do you need to pay your Internet service provider extra fees to use Internet Connection Sharing. The whole point of ICS is to take a connection intended for a single computer and share it with several other machines.

  There is no minimum connection speed, but you should keep in mind that when two users are downloading using the shared connection simultaneously (the worst-case scenario), each user will experience half of the original performance. In other words, you probably don't want to bother sharing a 14.4k analog modem connection; see the discussion of bandwidth at the beginning of this chapter for more information.

  If your Internet connection is provided by a router or you've allocated multiple IP addresses, you don't need Internet Connection Sharing; see "Alternatives to Internet Connection Sharing," later in this chapter, for details.

- If you're sharing a DSL, cable modem, or other high-speed, Ethernet-based Internet connection, the computer with the Internet connection must have two Ethernet cards installed. See Figure 7-2 for a diagram of this setup.

The first step in setting up ICS is to configure the host, the computer with the Internet Connection that will be shared.

1. Open the Network Connections window. Here, you should have at least two connections listed: one for your Internet Connection, and one for the Ethernet adapter connected to your Local Area Network (LAN). If they're not there, your network is not ready; refer to the earlier topics in this chapter, and try again.

   For clarity, I recommend renaming the two connections to "Internet Connection" and "Local Area Connection," as shown in Figure 7-4 and Figure 7-5.

2. If you haven't already done it, select Details from the View menu.

3. Right-click the connection icon corresponding to your Internet connection and select Properties. In most cases, it will be the Ethernet adapter connected to your Internet connection device.

   However, if you're using DSL or cable with PPPoE, the icon to use is the "Broadband" connection set up in "Connecting to the Internet: DSL, cable, or other high-speed connection via PPPoE," earlier in this chapter.

4. Choose the Advanced tab, and turn on the "Allow other network users to connect through this computer's Internet connection" option, as shown in Figure 7-22. Click OK when you're done.

   For more information on the Firewall option shown here, see "Implementing Network Security," later in this chapter.

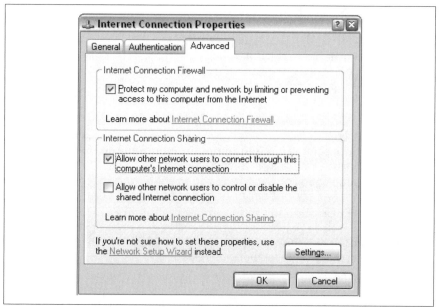

Figure 7-22. Allowing ICS via the Advanced tab of a network connection's properties

5. Verify that Internet Connection Sharing is enabled; it should say "Enabled, Shared" in the Type column of the Network Connections window, as shown in Figure 7-4 and Figure 7-5.

6. Verify that the Internet connection still works on the host by attempting to open a web page or by using Ping (see Chapter 4). If the Internet connection doesn't work on the host, it *definitely* won't work on any of the clients.

7. That's it! The change should take effect immediately.

The next step is to configure each of the client computers to use the shared connection. The only requirements of the client machines are that they are running an operating system that supports networking, and that their network connections are properly set up. The clients can be running Windows 2000, Windows Me, Windows 9x, Windows NT, Windows 3.x for Workgroups, or even MacOS, Unix, Linux, or FreeBSD.

See "Connecting to the Internet," earlier in this chapter, and follow the instructions under "Connection provided by another computer or router via Internet Connection Sharing." While the instructions are specific to Windows XP, the settings explained therein can be adapted to any OS; refer to your operating system's documentation for more information.

Troubleshooting Internet Connection Sharing

Here are some tips that should help you fix the problems you might encounter with Internet Connection Sharing:

- If the Internet is accessible by one client machine, it should work for them all. If none of the clients work, the problem is with the host; if some of the clients work, and others don't, it's a problem with the clients.

  ICS works over existing network connections, so those connections must be functioning before ICS will operate. Refer to "Setting Up a LAN" and "Connecting to the Internet," earlier in this chapter, for more troubleshooting details.

- Check to see if you have any firewall software installed on the host or clients that might be interfering with the connection. The Internet Connection Firewall included with Windows XP (discussed later in this chapter) shouldn't pose any problems, though.

- The ICS host must have the IP address for the connection to the LAN set to 192.168.0.1, which means that no other computers can be using that address. If you can't get ICS to work with the default Windows XP configuration, try assigning a fixed IP address to each of your clients: 192.168.0.2 for the first, 192.168.0.3 for the second, and so on. Refer to "Setting Up a LAN," earlier in this chapter, for details on setting IP addresses

  You can determine any computer's IP address with the "Windows IP Configuration" utility discussed in Chapter 4, or with each connection icon's Status window, discussed in "Configuring Network Connections," earlier in this chapter.

- If you're experiencing poor performance, it's important to realize that whatever bandwidth is available though a given Internet connection will be shared among all of the computers using the connection. The worst-case scenario is when two or more users download large amounts of data simultaneously; in this case, they would each receive only half the total connection bandwidth.

Most of the time, though, this bandwidth sharing will have little noticeable effect, because two or more users on a small workgroup will rarely consume a great deal of bandwidth at the same time.

- If you're using special connection software for use with your DSL or cable (such as Efficient Networks' NTS Enternet 300 software), it's best to remove it and use Windows XP's built-in support for PPPoE (described earlier in this chapter).

- If you're using PPPoE and find that you can access some web sites but not others from the client machines, see this article: *http://www.annoyances.org/exec/show/article04-107*.

Alternatives to Internet Connection Sharing

The Internet Connection Sharing feature built into Windows XP has it's limitations. For example, the host computer must be on and connected to the Internet for the other computers to have Internet access. If you don't want your network's Internet connection to rely on any single computer, there are alternatives to ICS.

The cheapest and most flexible way to share an Internet connection is to use ICS, but it's worth investigating the alternatives to see if they make sense for you.

Use a router

A router works similarly to a hub or switch, both discussed at the beginning of this chapter, except that it is also capable of connecting a single Internet connection directly to a LAN. The advantages of a router over ICS is that no single computer must be on for the other computers to have Internet access. Among the disadvantages are the added cost, the potentially more complicated setup, and the support for only certain types of high-speed Internet Connections. Figure 7-3 shows a setup that uses a router.

If you're looking for a router, make sure to get one that supports both DSL and cable connections, as well as PPPoE connections (if that's what your service provider uses). Refer to the documentation that comes with the router for basic setup instructions, and see the "Connection provided by another computer or router via Internet Connection Sharing" section earlier in this chapter for instructions on connecting a Windows XP system to a router.

Use multiple IP addresses

Some ISPs may provide, at extra cost, multiple IP addresses, with the specific intent that Internet access be provided for more than one computer. Instead of using software or hardware to share a single connection (as described in the preceding sections), each computer has its own IP address and, therefore, effectively has its own Internet connection.

Refer to the instructions in the "DSL, cable, or other high-speed connection with a static IP address" section earlier in this chapter to set up each of your computers to access the Internet. The only thing to keep in mind is that each computer must have a different IP address.

The advantages of multiple IP addresses over ICS or using a router, as described above, is that the setup is very easy, and no additional hardware or software is required. The downside is that Internet connections with multiple

IP addresses are often much more expensive than standard Internet connections. In fact, the added monthly cost will most likely exceed the one-time cost of a router.

Implementing Network Security

Security is a very real concern for any computer connected to a network or the Internet. There are three main categories of security threats:

A deliberate, targeted attack through your network connection
Ironically, this is the type of attack most people fear, but realistically, it is the least likely to occur, at least where home and small office networks are concerned. It's possible for a so-called hacker to obtain access to your computer, either through your Internet connection or from another computer on your local network.

An automated invasion by a virus or robot
A virus is simply a computer program that is designed to duplicate itself with the purpose of infecting as many computers as possible. If your computer is infected by a virus, it may use your network connection to infect other computers; likewise, if another computer on your network is infected, your computer is vulnerable to infection. The same goes for Internet connections, although the method of transport is typically an infected email message.

There also exist so-called robots, programs that are designed to scan large groups of IP addresses and look for vulnerabilities. The motive for such a program can be anything from exploitation of credit card numbers or other sensitive information to the hijacking of computers for the purpose of distributing spam or viruses.

A deliberate attack by a person sitting at your computer
A person who sits down at your computer can easily gain access to sensitive information, including your documents, email, and even various passwords stored by your web browser. An intruder can be anyone, from the person who steals your computer to a co-worker casually walking by your unattended desk. Naturally, it's up to you to determine the actual likelihood of such a threat, and to take the appropriate measures.

Windows XP includes several features that will enable you to implement a reasonable level of security without purchasing additional software or hardware. Unfortunately, Windows is not configured for optimal security by default. Before you proceed with any of the solutions in this section, complete the following steps:

1. A feature called Simple File Sharing, which could allow anyone, anywhere, to access your personal files, is turned on by default in Windows XP. Go to Control Panel → [Appearance and Themes] → Folder Options → View tab, and turn *off* the "Use simple file sharing" option.

2. If you need to share files or folders with other computers on your network, see "Sharing Resources," earlier in this chapter. It's wise to share only those folders that need to be shared; also, make sure none of your sensitive data is stored in shared folders or folders located on shared drives. You can see exactly which folders are shared by navigating to My Network Places → Entire Network →

Microsoft Windows Network → the name of your workgroup → the name of your computer. Figure 7-23 shows an example of this folder.

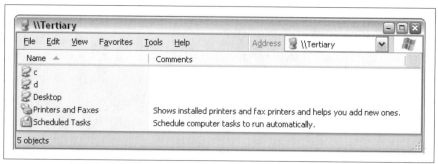

Figure 7-23. Showing which files and folders your computer is sharing

3. Open the Network Connections window, and right-click on the icon corresponding to your Internet connection. If you have more than one, repeat this procedure for each Internet connection.

4. In the General tab, clear the checkmark next to the "File and Printer Sharing for Microsoft Networks" entry. The only connection for which this option should be enabled is the connection to your LAN (if you have one). See "Services and Protocols," earlier in this chapter, for more information.

Read through the remaining topics in this chapter for additional security features in Windows XP.

Using the Internet Connection Firewall

A firewall is a layer of protection that permits or denies network communication based on a predefined set of rules. These rules restrict communication so that only certain applications are permitted to use your network connection. This effectively closes backdoors to your computer that otherwise might be exploited by viruses, hackers, and other malicious applications.

To enable the Internet Connection Firewall (ICF) on your computer, follow these steps:

1. Open the Network Connections window, and, if you haven't already done so, select Details from the View menu.

2. Right-click the connection icon corresponding to your Internet connection, and select Properties. In most cases, it will be the Ethernet adapter connected to your Internet connection device.

   However, if you're using DSL or cable with PPPoE, the icon to use is the "Broadband" connection set up in "Connecting to the Internet: DSL, cable, or other high-speed connection via PPPoE," earlier in this chapter.

3. Choose the Advanced tab, and turn on the "Protect my computer and network by limiting or preventing access to this computer from the Internet" option, as shown in Figure 7-22 (earlier in this chapter). Click OK when you're done.

For more information on the Internet Connection Sharing option shown here, see "Sharing an Internet Connection," earlier in this chapter.

4. Verify that Internet Connection Sharing is enabled; it should say "Enabled, Firewalled" or "Enabled, Shared, Firewalled" in the Type column of the Network Connections window, as shown in Figure 7-4 and Figure 7-5.

5. Verify that the Internet connection still works on the host by attempting to open a web page or by using Ping. (See Chapter 4.)

As you use your computer, you may find that a particular program no longer works. Verify that the firewall is causing the problem by temporarily disabling the Internet Connection Firewall, and trying again. If indeed the firewall is the culprit, you can add a new rule to permit the program to communicate over your Internet Connection.

1. Open the Network Connections window, right-click the firewalled connection icon corresponding to your Internet connection, and select Properties.

2. Choose the Advanced tab, click Settings, and choose the Services tab.

3. If the program or service you wish to use is on the list, place a checkmark next to it. Otherwise, click Add to display the Service Settings window as shown in Figure 7-24.

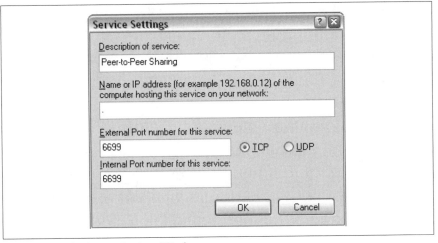

Figure 7-24. The Service Settings Window

4. The Description of service is simply a name you assign to the new service; it can be anything that doesn't already exist on the list. The description should be clear and easily recognizable, such as "Peer-to-Peer Sharing" or "Whiteboard software."

5. The "Name or IP address" field can be somewhat confusing. If you're connecting to a service provided by a single, specific computer, enter the IP address or network name of the computer here. Otherwise, simply type a period. (The field can't be left blank.)

6. Port numbers, described at the beginning of this chapter, are how ICF distinguishes one service from another. You may need to consult the documentation

of the particular software or service to determine the appropriate port number. Type the external and internal port numbers in the two remaining fields; in most cases, both of these values will be the same. And unless you specifically need to specify UDP ports, leave the TCP option enabled.

7. Click OK when you're done. Place a checkmark next to the newly added service, as well as any other services you wish to permit, and click OK. Finally, click OK to close the properties window.

8. Test the newly permitted service. You may have to experiment with different firewall rules until your software or service works properly.

Notes

- There are third-party firewall solutions available that might provide a higher level of security or more options, but the Internet Connection Firewall that comes with Windows XP should provide an adequate level of protection for most home and small office computers and networks.

- The Internet Connection Firewall only protects Internet connections; if you need a firewall between your computer and others on your local network, you'll need to use a third-party solution.

- If you're using Internet Connection Sharing, you can protect your entire network by simply enabling the Internet Connection Firewall for the single shared Internet Connection on the host computer.

- By default, Windows XP does not log communication blocked by the Internet Connection Firewall. To enable firewall logging, open the Advanced Settings window, and turn on the "Log dropped packets" option. The default location of the log is \Windows\pfirewall.log, which is a text file that can be opened in Notepad.

Protecting your data with passwords and encryption

Most users consider passwords to be a monumental nuisance. After all, we use passwords to access our email, place orders from online stores, access our bank accounts, and bid on all of those priceless artifacts on eBay. However, if it weren't for passwords, anyone could read our email, abuse our credit cards, steal from our accounts, and place bids on all sorts of annoying little ceramic figurines, all without our knowledge or authorization.

Windows XP has a rather robust security subsystem, allowing you to deny access to your computer to anyone who does not know your password. If you're using Windows XP Professional, you can also protect your data from other, less-privileged users on the same machine or on your network.

See "User Accounts" in Chapter 4 for more details on adding and removing users, as well as assigning passwords to existing user accounts. Although Windows NT permits user accounts to be created without a password (it's actually the default), you should ensure that each user on your machine is assigned a unique password. Even if you're not the least bit worried about a family member or co-worker accessing the data on your computer, a password-less account is vulnerable to attacks over your network or Internet connection.

Assigning a password doesn't necessarily mean that you have to log in every time use your computer, however. If you're the only one who uses your computer, you can use TweakUI I (discussed in Appendix D) to set Windows XP to log in with your username and password automatically.

Suppose you have three different people who all use the same computer, and you don't want other users to be able to read or modify your personal files. Now, any user with administrator privileges has unrestricted access to every file and folder on your computer, but less-privileged users can easily be selectively locked out of any folder on your hard disk. While Windows XP Home Edition only supports administrator accounts, XP Professional supports several levels of users, and is therefore required for this type of security. See the section on Permissions in "Sharing Resources," earlier in this chapter, for details on setting permissions.

Finally, Windows XP supports file encryption, an additional layer of security that scrambles your sensitive data, making it totally unreadable for anyone without the proper authorization. See the "NTFS Encryption Utility" in Chapter 4 for more information.

Additional security tips

The following tips should help you make your computer more secure and less vulnerable to the types of security threats present today:

- Close all of the applications and stop all of the services that you don't need running. For example, Windows Messenger (discussed in Chapter 4) opens yet another backdoor to your computer, potentially allowing outside users to obtain information about your network connection. By default, Windows Messenger is run every time you start Windows XP, but it should certainly be disabled immediately if you don't use it. This advice applies to Yahoo Messenger and AOL Instant Messenger as well.

- Go to Control Panel → [Performance and Maintenance] → System → Remote tab, and turn off both of the options in this window. Otherwise, another user could connect to your computer over a network or Internet connection and use it as though they were sitting in front of it. See "Remote Desktop Connection" and "Remote Assistance," both in Chapter 4, for more information.

- Viruses are probably the biggest threat to computer security. A virus can automatically disable certain security features on your computer, and even open backdoors, allowing additional viruses and other more malicious attacks. The vast majority of viruses come through email attachments. Fortunately, it's extremely easy to protect yourself from email viruses: just don't open them. They can't activate themselves; a virus contained in a Word document will remain dormant until the document is opened in Word.

  The downside is that it's not always obvious which files are viruses and which are not. Sometimes, of course, it's easy: if you receive an attachment with an email advertisement to make money fast, visit a porn site, or enlarge a portion of your anatomy, delete the attachment immediately *without* opening it. However, other times, an email attachment may come from someone you know; the file may be clean, or it may be infected. It may have even been sent without the sender's knowledge, as some viruses are capable of hijacking your email program and sending infected attachments to everyone in your contact list. Most of these types of viruses are targeted to Outlook users; not only are Microsoft Outlook and Outlook Express both very common, they are also both especially vulnerable. One way to protect yourself is to use a different email program, such as Eudora (available at *http://www.eudora.com*).

The best defense against such an attack is an up-to-date antivirus utility, such as Norton Antivirus (available from *http://www.symantec.com*). But as useful and beneficial as antivirus software can be, don't let it lull you into a false sense of security. The majority of serious virus infestations I've seen have been on computers with full-blown antivirus software; the infestations are invariably caused by negligence by the user.

- Don't write your password on a Post-It note stuck to your monitor. Instead, if you have trouble remembering all of your passwords, there are a number of password-management programs available for Windows (such as Keypack, available at *http://www.magellass.com/prod-kp.html*, and Password Pro, available at *http://cmbsoftware.com/passpro.htm*). Instead of remembering twenty different username and password combinations, you only need to remember one: the password required to open your password manager!

In addition, your web browser can be instructed to remember passwords for your various secure web sites. Both Internet Explorer (see Chapter 4) and Mozilla (available at *http://www.mozilla.org*) can not only save usernames and passwords, but will type them for you automatically the next time you visit those sites.

- Finally, take security seriously, even if your computer is not on a network, if for no other reason than to save the massive headache you'd otherwise get when you had to format your hard disk and reinstall Windows after a virus attack.

8

The Registry

The Windows Registry is a database of settings used by Windows XP and the individual applications that run on it. Knowing how to access and modify the Registry effectively is important for troubleshooting, customizing, and unlocking hidden features in Windows XP.

An amazing amount of what one might assume to be "hardwired" into Windows—the locations of key directories, the titles of on-screen objects such as the Recycle Bin, and even the version number of Windows XP reported in Control Panel—is actually the product of data stored in the Registry. Change a setting in the Registry and key parts of your system can be affected; for this reason, Microsoft passively discourages tampering by providing only minimal user documentation on the Registry Editor, and no documentation at all on the structure of the Registry itself.

 Despite the enormous potential for harm, the Registry is fairly robust, and for every entry that you can wreak havoc by changing, there are hundreds that you can change with impunity. Nonetheless, you should back up the Registry files before making significant changes with Registry Editor. See "Backing Up the Registry," later in this chapter, for details.

The Registry is normally consulted silently by the programs (such as Explorer) that comprise the Windows user interface, as well as by nearly all applications. Programs also commonly write varying amounts of data to the Registry when they are installed, when you make changes to configuration settings, or just when they are run. For example, a game like FreeCell keeps statistics in the Registry on how many games you've won and lost. Every time you play the game, those statistics are updated. For that matter, every time you move an icon on your Desktop, its position is recorded in the Registry. All of your file type associations are stored in the Registry, as well as all of the network, hardware, and software settings for

Windows and all of the particular configuration options for most of the software you've installed. The settings and data stored by each of your applications and by the various Windows components vary substantially, but more often than not, a given Registry setting will appear in plain English, making it relatively easy to decipher. There are also several advanced techniques that not only help to identify more obscure settings, but allow you to use undocumented settings to uncover hidden functionality.

Microsoft provides the Registry Editor (*regedit.exe*), which is used to view and modify the contents of the Registry. Don't confuse the Registry with the Registry Editor; the Registry Editor merely reads and writes data in the Registry like any other Windows application. When you start Registry Editor, you'll see a window similar to the one in Figure 8-1.

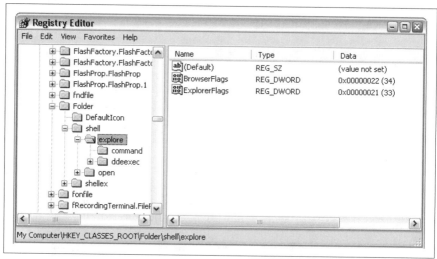

Figure 8-1. The Registry Editor uses a familiar interface to manipulate unfamiliar data

The organizational structure of the Registry is hierarchical, so Microsoft chose an interface familiar to anyone who has used Windows Explorer. As in Explorer, there are two panes: the folders (keys) are displayed in a cascading tree on the left, and the contents of the currently selected key appear on the right. Use the small plus (+) and minus (-) icons to expand and collapse the branches, respectively; cursor keys also work here.

While the interface elements might appear familiar, the data that is manipulated with Registry Editor is nothing like the files and folders we deal with in Explorer. Although you can certainly dive in and begin wading through the thousands of keys and values in the Registry, you're not likely to find anything of value until you arm yourself with a basic understanding of the way data is stored and organized in the Registry. And, of course, this is the focus of the next few sections.

What's in the Registry

Data in the Registry is stored in individual pieces called *values*. Every value has a name and is capable of holding one of several types of data. Values are grouped and organized in *keys*, which are represented by Folder icons in Registry Editor. Keys can also contain other keys, thereby forming the basis for the hierarchy in the Registry. Like Explorer, Registry Editor arranges the keys in a collapsible tree structure, allowing you to navigate through the branches to locate a particular key, and hence, all the values contained therein.

Often, in order to view or modify a certain key or value, one must follow a *Registry path*. A path is merely a series of key names, separated by backslashes (\), used to specify an absolute location in the Registry. For example, to navigate to HKEY_CURRENT_USER\Control Panel\Keyboard, simply expand the HKEY_CURRENT_USER branch by clicking on the plus sign (+) next to it, then expand the Control Panel branch, and finally click on the Keyboard key name to display its contents. The path leading to the currently highlighted key is always shown at the bottom of the Registry Editor window.

 It's easy to get confused about keys and values. In fact, value names sometimes appear at the end of a path, although this is mostly a holdover from the early days of the Registry. It's important to realize that only values can contain data, while keys are only used to organize values—just like files and folders in Explorer, respectively. Note that unlike folders in Explorer, keys never appear in the right pane of the Registry Editor window, even though keys can contain other keys.

Every key contains a value named (Default). If the default value contains no data, you'll see (value not set), as in Figure 8-2. If a given key contains other values, they will be listed below the default value. To modify the data stored in a value, simply double-click on the value name, or highlight it and select Modify from the Edit menu. To rename a value, which is not the same as changing its data, highlight it and press F2 or right-click it and select Rename.

For example, if I wanted to change the location of my Word Startup Folder, I could navigate to HKEY_CURRENT_USER\Software\Microsoft\Office\8.0\Word\Options, double-click on the Startup-Path value, and use the edit dialog box shown in Figure 8-2 to type new data.

The data stored in the Startup-Path value is a string of text, which means that Startup-Path is a *string value* (the most common type). There are seven types of values in all, each having a common name and a symbolic name (shown in parentheses in the following list). While all value types can be viewed and modified in Registry Editor, only three can be created.

String values (REG_SZ)
String values contain *strings* of characters, more commonly known as text. Most values of interest to us are string values; they're the easiest to edit and are usually in plain English. In addition to standard strings, there are two far less common string variants, used for special purposes:

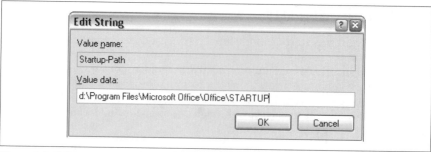

Figure 8-2. Editing a string value to change Microsoft Word Startup directory

String array value (REG_MULTI_SZ)

Contains several strings (usually representing a list of some sort), concatenated (glued) together and separated by null characters (ASCII code 00). You can't create these in the Registry Editor, but you can edit them. The dialog used to modify these values is the same as for binary values. Note that the individual characters in REG_MULTI_SZ keys are also separated by null characters, so you'll actually see three null characters in a row between multiple strings.

Expanded string value (REG_EXPAND_SZ)

Contains special variables into which Windows substitutes information before delivering to the owning application. For example, an expanded string value intended to point to a sound file may contain %SystemRoot%\media\startup.wav. When Windows reads this value from the Registry, it substitutes the full Windows path for the variable, %SystemRoot%; the resulting data then becomes (depending on where Windows is installed) c:\windows\media\startup.wav. This way, the value data is correct regardless of the location of the Windows folder. You can't create these in the Registry Editor, but you can edit them.

Binary values (REG_BINARY)

Similarly to string values, binary values hold strings of characters. The difference is the way the data is entered. Instead of a standard text box, binary data is entered with hexadecimal codes in an interface commonly known as a *hex editor*. Each individual character is specified by a two-digit number in base-16 (e.g., 6E is 110 in base 10), which allows characters not found on the keyboard to be entered. See Figure 8-3 for an example. Note that you can type hex codes on the left or normal ASCII characters on the right, depending on where you click with the mouse.

Binary values are often not represented by plain English and, therefore, should be left unchanged unless you either understand the contents or are instructed to do so by a solution in this book.

DWORD values (REG_DWORD)

Essentially, a DWORD is a number. Often, the contents of a DWORD value are easily understood, such as 0 for no and 1 for yes, or 60 for the number of seconds in some timeout setting. A DWORD value is used only where numerical digits are allowed; string and binary types allow anything.

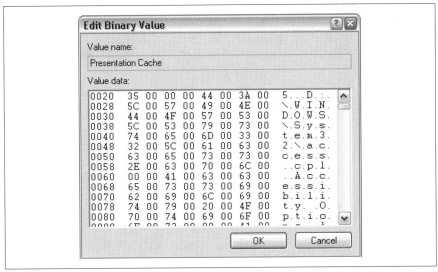

0020	35 00 00 00 44 00 3A 00	5...D.:.
0028	5C 00 57 00 49 00 4E 00	\.W.I.N.
0030	44 00 4F 00 57 00 53 00	D.O.W.S.
0038	5C 00 53 00 79 00 73 00	\.S.y.s.
0040	74 00 65 00 6D 00 33 00	t.e.m.3.
0048	32 00 5C 00 61 00 63 00	2.\.a.c.
0050	63 00 65 00 73 00 73 00	c.e.s.s.
0058	2E 00 63 00 70 00 6C 00	..c.p.l.
0060	00 00 41 00 63 00 63 00	..A.c.c.
0068	65 00 73 00 73 00 69 00	e.s.s.i.
0070	62 00 69 00 6C 00 69 00	b.i.l.i.
0078	74 00 79 00 20 00 4F 00	t.y. .O.
0080	70 00 74 00 69 00 6F 00	p.t.i.o.

Figure 8-3. Binary values are entered differently from the common string values, but the contents are sometimes nearly as readable

In some circumstances, the particular number entered into a DWORD value is actually made up of several components, called bytes. The REG_DWORD_BIGENDIAN type is a variant of the DWORD type, where the bytes are in a different order. Unless you're a programmer, you'll want to stay away from these types of DWORD values.

The DWORD format, like the binary type, is a hexadecimal number, but this time in a more conventional representation. The leading 0x is a standard programmer's notation for a hex value, and the number is properly read from left to right. The equivalent decimal value is shown in parentheses following the hex value. What's more, when you edit a DWORD value, the edit dialog box gives you a choice of entering the new value in decimal or hex notation.

In general, if a value is stored in binary or DWORD format, you can guess that it was either programmatically generated or the program's author wished to make the value a little more obscure and difficult to edit. However, if you know what you are doing, you can edit binary or DWORD values almost as easily as you can string values. For example, if I want to lie to my friends to tell them I've won 435 games of FreeCell rather than just one, I simply need to double-click on "won" and edit the value as shown in Figure 8-4.

Even if you're not a programmer, you can figure out hexadecimal values pretty easily with the Windows Calculator (*calc.exe*; see Chapter 4). Just enter the number you want to convert and click the Hex radio button to see the hexadecimal equivalent; 435 decimal is equal to 1B3 hex. Note, however, that hex values stored in binary Registry values are displayed in a somewhat unconventional format, in which the lowest-order digits appear first, followed by the next-higher pair of digits, and so on. In other words, the digits in a binary value are paired, and their order reversed: the hex value 1B3 thus needs to be entered as B3 01. If you want to convert a binary value shown in Registry Editor to decimal, you'll have to reverse this notation. For example, to find the decimal equivalent of 47 00 65 6e, set Calculator to hexadecimal mode and enter 6e650047, and then switch to decimal mode to display the decimal equivalent, 1,852,112,967.

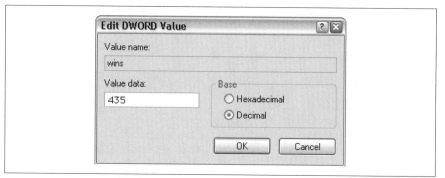

Figure 8-4. Editing a DWORD value to alter the number of games won in FreeCell

If you aren't sure about the meaning of a specific Registry value, don't be afraid to experiment. Experimenting might include editing a value with Registry Editor, but it might be easier or safer to work from the other end: open the application whose data is stored there (e.g., a Control Panel applet), change a setting, and watch how the Registry data changes. In this way, you can derive the meaning of many binary-encoded values. Note that while the Registry data will often change immediately, you may need to press F5 (Refresh) to force Registry Editor to display the newly affected data.

It's a good idea, though, to make a backup copy of a Registry key before making any changes. See "Adding and Deleting Registry Keys and Values" and "Exporting and Importing Registry Data with Patches" later in this chapter for details.

Figure 8-4 shows an additional value, called New Value #1, which I entered into the FreeCell key using Registry Editor → Edit → New → DWORD Value. This example illustrates a very important point: a Registry entry is superfluous unless a program actually reads it. You can enter new keys and values all you like, with the only consequence being that you've bloated your Registry. (Note that there are sometimes undocumented Registry values that are meaningful to a program but that are not normally present; adding them to the Registry can make useful changes; see *Windows Me Annoyances* by David Karp (O'Reilly) for several examples.) The chief concern is in deleting or modifying existing entries; the odds of randomly creating a value that an application might be looking for are extremely small.

I take advantage of this fact by occasionally leaving myself notes in new Registry values. For example, before modifying a value, I might place a backup of its data in a new value in the same key. The application will ignore it, and it has sure come in handy for me to have a record of the original value!

A final note: any changes made in Registry Editor are saved automatically and immediately; there's no "undo" command in Registry Editor, and the automatic Registry backups made by Windows are of little use when small changes are made. The saving grace is the use of Registry patches, discussed later in this chapter.

Adding and Deleting Registry Keys and Values

The Registry Editor, as mentioned earlier, is the primary tool for viewing, modifying, and deleting data in the Registry. And as you'll see later in this chapter, it also allows you to conveniently import and export data (via Registry patches), which can be thought of as another form of data entry.

Basic data entry in Registry Editor is fairly simple. In order to type data, you must first create a value to hold it. Depending on your goal, you may also need to create a new key in which to place the value.

To create a new key or value, use Edit → New. The key or value then appears within the currently selected key, with the name New Key or New Value #1, respectively. A new string value will have the null string as its value; a new binary value will show the following message in parentheses: "(zero length binary value)." A new DWORD value will show up as zero: 0x00000000 (0). You can then edit that value (see later in this chapter) to change it. New keys aren't created empty, either. They all contain the (Default) value described in the previous section.

To delete a key or value, select it and click Edit → Delete, or simply press the Del key. But be warned, there's no undelete, so you might want to first write out the branch containing the key you're about to delete as a *.reg* file (see "Backing Up the Registry" and "Exporting and Importing Registry Data with Patches," later in this chapter). Or, you can use Edit → Rename to rename the value or key. Since applications access values and keys by their names, renaming has the effect of disabling or "hiding" the item from the application that uses it, while preserving its data.

To edit a value, double-click on its icon or name, or highlight it and use Edit → Modify. You will see an edit box appropriate to the value type. When editing a string value, Registry Editor provides a standard text box, in which you can type text, as well as copy and paste (by right-clicking on the text, or by using Ctrl-C, Ctrl-X, and Ctrl-V). Binary values have a more complicated and less familiar edit dialog, which allows data entry via ASCII codes on the left, or plain text on the right. Finally, DWORD values have a simpler edit interface, providing only for entry of a single number (either in Hex or Decimal format). Cut, Copy, and Paste work in DWORD and Binary dialogs as well. See the previous section, "What's in the Registry," for more details on the different types of values.

Unfortunately, automation in Registry Editor is virtually nonexistent. For example, you can't copy and paste whole keys or values like you might expect (given the familiar Explorer-like interface), but you can copy key and value *names* to the clipboard by pretending you're going to rename them, and then pressing Ctrl-C to copy. Another useful tool is the Copy Key Name command on the Edit menu, which copies the full path to the selected key to the Clipboard (very handy for writing this book, for example). It doesn't copy the contents of the key, nor does it include the selected value, however.

If you want to duplicate an existing value, double-click it and select all of the data in the Edit window, as shown in Figure 8-5.

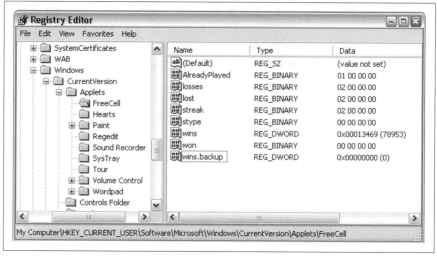

Figure 8-5. Copying an existing Registry value

Ctrl-C will copy the data to the clipboard. Then create a new value, being sure to match the type (string, binary, or DWORD) of the original value. Type the desired value name, double-click the new value to edit it, and then use Ctrl-V to paste the copied data into the edit window.

Duplicating values can be handy not only when using an existing value as a template for a new value, but also whenever you're going to make changes to an existing value. You can make little "inline backups" by creating a new value (*whatever*.bak, for instance) and pasting in the old value data before you change it. This might seem a little tedious, but it might prevent future headaches if you're about to change a complex value whose format you aren't completely sure you understand, or even if you anticipate having to roll back a value to its previous state for some reason.

Unfortunately, there's no easy way to copy a key and all of its contents in Registry Editor. If you want to copy an entire key and all its values, you'll have to do it one value at a time. It's usually much easier to export the key, edit the resulting file with a text editor, and then import the edited file. (See "Exporting and Importing Registry Data with Patches" later in this chapter.)

In addition to the Edit menu, you may find Registry Editor's context menus convenient. Right-clicking on a key in the left pane gives a context menu with Expand or Collapse, New, Find, Delete, Rename, and Copy Key Name. (Expand displays a key's subkeys. It will be grayed out if there are no subkeys to display, and it will be replaced with Collapse if said subkeys are already showing.) Right-clicking with a value selected in the right pane gives a context menu with Modify, Delete, and Rename. Right-clicking in the right pane with no value selected gives a context menu with New (to create a new string, binary, or DWORD value). Press Shift-F10 to open a context menu without having to use the mouse.

Organization of the Registry

The Registry is enormous and complex; a full Registry might easily contain 15,000 keys and 35,000 values. Entire books have been written about it, and we can't do it justice here. Our purpose in this section is to arm you with a basic understanding of how the Registry is organized, not to document individual values in detail or suggest changes you might want to make with Registry Editor.

 David A. Karp's book *Windows Me Annoyances* provides many tips and tricks that rely on the Registry. If you can still find Ron Petrusha's out-of-print book, *Inside the Windows 95 Registry*, you'll find lots of useful information there. While aimed primarily at software developers and covering Windows 95, it contains several chapters aimed at experienced users. In particular, see Chapters 1 to 3, which give a good overview of the Registry and a detailed description of how to use Registry Editor. Also see Chapter 8.

As shown in Figure 8-1, the top level of the Registry is organized into five main *root* branches. By convention, the built-in top-level keys are always shown in all caps, even though the keys in the Registry are not case-sensitive. (For example, HKEY_CURRENT_USER\SOFTWARE\MICROSOFT\Windows is identical to HKEY_CURRENT_USER\ Software\Microsoft\Windows.) Their purposes and contents are listed in the following summaries. Note that the root keys are sometimes abbreviated for convenience in documentation (although never in practice); these abbreviations are shown in parentheses. Subsequent sections go into the contents of the root keys in more detail.

HKEY_CLASSES_ROOT (HKCR)
> Contains file types, filename extensions, URL protocol prefixes, and registered classes. The information in this branch can be thought of as the "glue" that binds Windows with the applications and documents that run on it. It is critical to drag-and-drop operations, context menus, double-clicking, and many other familiar user interface semantics. The actions defined here tell Windows how to react to every file type available on the system.
>
> This entire branch is a mirror (or symbolic link) of HKEY_LOCAL_MACHINE\ SOFTWARE\Classes, provided as a root key purely for convenience.

HKEY_CURRENT_USER (HKCU)
> Contains user-specific settings for the currently logged-in user. This entire branch is a mirror (or symbolic link) of one of the subkeys HKEY_USERS (see below). This allows Windows and all applications to access and store information for the current user without having to determine which user is currently logged in.
>
> An application that keeps information on a per-user basis should store its data in HKEY_CURRENT_USER\Software, and put information that applies to all users of the application in HKEY_LOCAL_MACHINE\SOFTWARE. However, it is somewhat arbitrary what Windows applications seem to consider user-specific and what is for all users on the machine. Like many aspects of Windows, the Registry

provides a mechanism for applications to store configuration data, but does little to enforce any policies about how and where it will actually be stored.

HKEY_LOCAL_MACHINE (HKLM)

Contains information about hardware and software on the machine not specific to the current user.

HKEY_USERS (HKU)

Stores underlying user data from which HKEY_CURRENT_USER is drawn. Although several keys will often appear here, only one of them will ever be the active branch. See the discussion of HKEY_USERS, below, for details.

HKEY_CURRENT_CONFIG (HKCC)

Contains hardware configuration settings for the currently loaded hardware profile. This branch works similarly to HKEY_CURRENT_USER, in that it is merely a mirror (or symbolic link) of another key. In this case, the source is HKEY_LOCAL_MACHINE\SYSTEM\CurrentControlSet\Hardware Profiles\XXXX, in which *XXXX* is a key representing the numeric value of the hardware profile currently in use. On a system with only a single hardware profile, its value will most likely be 0001.

HKEY_CLASSES_ROOT (HKCR)

At first glance, Windows XP seems very object-oriented. Files, folders, and devices are represented by icons that respond differently to various actions such as single or double-clicks, right-clicks, and left-clicks. But in a true object-oriented system, the object itself contains the knowledge of how to respond to events such as mouse clicks.

By contrast, Windows XP performs much like the Wizard of Oz, not with true object-oriented magic, but with a complex machinery hidden behind a screen. The knowledge of how the Explorer should treat each object is stored in the Registry in a complex chain of interrelated keys.

Much of the system's behavior depends on filename extensions. A *filename extension*, the string of letters that appear after the last dot in a filename, is the primary mechanism Windows uses to determine a file's type. Therefore it's essential that each filename extension accurately reflect the file type. For example, a file named *stuff.txt* will be treated by Windows as a text file. If one were to rename the file to *stuff.old*, it would still be a text file, but Windows would treat it differently: it would have a different icon in Explorer, a different description in Explorer's Details view, and a different action when double-clicked. (The exceptions are certain Microsoft Office documents, which are handled by Windows in a consistent manner regardless of the filename extension.) This illustrates how fragile and fallible Windows' file types system is, how some applications can so easily register themselves as the default for any given file type, and how stupid it is that filename extensions are hidden in Explorer by default.

When you open HKEY_CLASSES_ROOT, the first thing you'll see is a very long list of file extensions known to the system, from something like *.ai* (Adobe Illustrator Document) to *.zip* (Zip archive). What follows is a list of *document type keys*, which typically contain the actual file type information. These two sets of keys make up the file types in Windows XP.

Here's how it works: a file extension key (one which has a dot at the beginning of its name) has its default value set to the name of a document type key (and thus "points" to that key). For example, HKEY_CLASSES_ROOT\.txt, which corresponds to all files with the *.txt* extension, has its default value set to txtfile. Lower down, the HKEY_CLASSES_ROOT\txtfile key contains several keys that describe files of this type, and instruct Windows how to handle double-clicks, right-clicks, and other operations.

You also may notice that HKEY_CLASSES_ROOT\.log key also has its default value set to txtfile; in this way, many extension keys can point to a single file type key, and hence, a single file type can encompass several different filename extensions.

Applications frequently add new file types to the Registry, registering themselves with certain filename extensions. In the case of the txtfile file type, Notepad is registered as the default application when Windows XP is first installed; thus, when one double-clicks on a *.txt* file or a *.log* file, the file is opened in Notepad.

A common conflict occurs when two or more applications find themselves fighting to be the default application. For example, should a file with the *.htm* extension be opened by Netscape Navigator or Microsoft Internet Explorer? If you use Navigator, the *.htm* key might have the value name (Default) with the data NetscapeMarkup. If you use Internet Explorer, the value name (Default) will have the value data htmlfile. If you then look at either of those two class definition keys (NetscapeMarkup or htmlfile), you'll see a different chain of subkeys. While both Navigator and Internet Explorer know how to handle HTML files, they use a different set of internal instructions for figuring out how to display or edit the files, which icon to display for the file, and so on.

The detailed subkeys and values that appear under the class definition and document type keys start to get really confusing. (See *Windows Me Annoyances* for an in-depth examination of file types.)

Because each program may record and retrieve different keys, it's very hard to generalize about them. The best we can do is mention some of the kinds of keys you might see associated with a particular file extension subkey or class definition subkey. Here are some of the most common keys and values you may find in HKEY_CLASSES_ROOT, sorted alphabetically:

CLSID

Class identifier for an ActiveX component, a unique, 16-bit 16-byte number in the following format: {aaaaaaaa-bbbb-cccc-dddd-ffffffffffff}, in which each letter represents a hexadecimal digit. (That's a sequence of eight, four, four, four, and twelve hex digits, with a hyphen between each group of digits and the whole thing enclosed in curly braces.)

CLSID appears both as a subkey of many file type definition keys and as a class definition key in its own right. That is, the key HKCR\NetscapeMarkup might have a subkey CLSID with the data value {61D8DE20-CA9A-11CE-9EA5-0080C82BE3B6}, but there's also a key called HKCR\CLSID with the subkey {61D8DE20-CA9A-11CE-9EA5-0080C82BE3B6}, which in turn has the data value Netscape Hypertext Document. The first entry is simply a pointer to the second, which contains the actual class data. You must always be on the lookout for this kind of indirection.

CLSID keys don't necessarily correspond to filename extensions or file types. The HKEY_CLASSES_ROOT\CLSID branch, for example, contains a huge list of class ID keys, which each represent a different component. Most of the components are of little interest to mere mortals, but some correspond to visual elements in Windows XP. If you search for "Recycle Bin" here, for example, you'll find the key that describes the Recycle Bin Desktop icon. Try changing the contents of the Default value to "Trash," refresh your Desktop, and see what happens!

Content Type

The data in this value is the Multipurpose Internet Mail Extension (MIME) descriptor for the corresponding file type. This key will typically appear in the file type key for Internet-related file types such as GIF and JPEG. It's used by email programs that support attachments and web browsers, such as Netscape Navigator and Internet Explorer, to help them identify downloaded files.

DefaultIcon

The location (usually a pathname and an optional "icon index" within the file) of the file containing the default icon to use for a file type or CLSID. If you see the value data "%1", it means that the file will act as its own icon (a neat effect when used with BMP files).

Note that there may be more than one default icon for a given file type. A good example is the Recycle Bin, which shows a different icon when it is empty and when it is full. In cases like this, the program knows to copy its icon for the appropriate state to the DefaultIcon (Default) value. In other cases, though, a DefaultIcon may be specified in more than one place (e.g., under a document type key and under an associated CLSID key).

Shell

Contains subkeys that define actions (open, edit, print, play, and so forth) appropriate to the object. These actions appear on the context menu for the associated file type, among other things. The easiest way to edit these actions is with the File Types dialog in Explorer (Tools → Folder Options → File Types), but you sacrifice a pretty interface for increased flexibility.

A common structure that uses the Shell key is Shell\Open\Command, where the default value in the Command key is the executable filename for a registered application. The command line often ends with "%1" (including the quotes), which represents a command-line parameter passed to the application (familiar to those who use batch files). For example, when you double-click on a *.txt* file (say, *c:\stuff\junk.txt*), Windows replaces "%1" in the command line with the name of the file, resulting in the following command being run: notepad c:\stuff\junk.txt. If you were to select Run from the Start menu, and type that command, Notepad would appear and open the file. Note that the quotes around the %1 accommodate any spaces in the filename; otherwise, Windows would interpret a single filename with a space as two distinct filenames, and you'd get an error.

You might also find the key, Shell\Open\ddeexec, which contains information necessary for a DDE (Dynamic Data Exchange) conversation. DDE is the mechanism with which Windows communicates with applications that are already open. For example, Windows might send a DDE message to an application to tell it to print a file after opening it. Microsoft insists that DDE is obsolete, but you'd never know it from the important role DDE plays in Windows file types.

You'll see the same split between command-line options and DDE using the Explorer interface to file associations, via Tools → Folder Options → File Types. Some actions will list a command line; others will use DDE. If you're not a programmer with access to the DDE documentation for a particular application, you may find this difficult to follow at times.

You may find that a particular Shell branch doesn't contain all the actions for a particular file type. This is because these items may be specified in three other places. First, the ShellEx key contains more advanced actions. Second, the HKEY_CLASSES_ROOT* key contains additional actions that apply to all file types.Third, some actions available to all files, such as the Delete and Properties actions, can't be removed, and therefore don't appear in this key.

ShellEx

This is short for Shell Extensions. These keys contain entries that supplement a file's context menu (via the ContextMenuHandlers subkey), a file's Properties sheet (via the PropertySheetHandlers subkey), and a file's drag-drop behavior (via the CopyHookHandlers subkey). These extra features are too complex to be simple Shell\Command structures; instead, these keys simply point to registered CLSIDs (described earlier) and special programs that perform advanced features. For example, if you install the WinZip utility (*http://www.winzip. com*), all ZIP files will have extra items in their context menus (click with the right mouse button) and their drag-drop menus (drag with the right mouse button) that handle certain ZIP operations. Also, movie files (*.avi, .asf*, and *. mpg*) and Word Documents (*.doc*) all have an extra Summary tab in their Properties sheets that displays additional information about the contents of the file.

ShellNew

Defines whether the file type will appear on Explorer's New menu. If the ShellNew key is present inside a file type or file extension key, the file type will appear in the list when you select New from Explorer's File menu. In most cases, this key will be empty, if it exists at all. (Contrast the enormous number of file types defined in the Registry with the much smaller number that appear on the New menu.) ShellNew can also contain one or more of the following values:

Command

Contains a command line to create the new file, used only for Briefcases and Windows Shortcuts (the *.bfc* and *.lnk* extensions, respectively), as well as any other file type that can't be created merely by copying a template (see next).

Filename

Contains the name of a file "template" to copy to the new location. Its value data may contain a complete pathname, but if it's just a filename (e.g., *netscape.html, winword.doc*, or *winword8.doc*), it will be found in the directory *Windows\ShellNew*. If the Filename value is not present, Windows will create an empty, zero-byte file.

Nullfile

If present, instructs Windows not to create the file at all, but instead to launch a program that will create the file when first saved. Some file types (such as *.bmp* files, which may contain data in any one of a number of related formats, as specified by binary header data within the file itself) are described by the NullFile value. NullFile has the empty string ("") as its value data.

Data

Contains binary data that needs to be written to the new file. This might, for example, be some kind of binary header data.

Before leaving HKEY_CURRENT_USER, two other keys are worthy of note.

HKCR* contains information that will be applied to all files, regardless of their extension.

HKCR\Unknown describes, via its Shell\OpenAs\Command subkey, what will happen to a file whose type is unknown, either because the file has no extension, or because the particular extension has not yet been registered with Windows. By default, if you double-click on a file Windows categorizes as unknown, the Open With dialog appears, allowing you to choose a new association for the filename extension, thereby automatically creating new file type keys in the Registry. box. Here you find the *rundll32* command line to bring up that dialog box. *runndll32* is merely a program that allows a particular function in a *.dll* or *.exe* file to be run via a command-line interface.

HKEY_CURRENT_USER (HKCU)

The Registry separates settings specific to individual users from global Windows settings applicable to all users. In the FreeCell example earlier in this chapter, each user of the machine can have his or her own separate won/lost statistics because the program keeps these statistics in the HKEY_CURRENT_USER branch of the Registry. If it instead used HKEY_LOCAL_MACHINE, all users would share the same statistics.

This entire branch is a mirror (or symbolic link) of HKEY_USERS\.*DEFAULT* (see below), and its contents always correspond to those of the currently logged-in user.

By default, there are twelve top-level subkeys in HKCU: AppEvents, Console, Control Panel, Environment, Identities, Keyboard Layout, Printers, RemoteAccess, SessionInformation, Software, UNICODE Program Groups, and Volatile Environment.

HKCU\AppEvents

The associations between events and system sounds are kept here. (See "Sounds" in Chapter 5.) There are two branches: EventLabels and Schemes. EventLabels contains the labels that will be used for the sounds; Schemes contains the pointers to the actual sounds.

Schemes has two main subkeys: Apps and Names.

Applications that use sounds can create their own subkey under Schemes\ Apps, or they can add sounds into the default list, which is kept in the subkey Apps\.Default. If they add their own subkey, the sounds will show up in a separate section of the sounds list in Control Panel → Sounds. So you might see a subkey such as Mplayer or Office97, since these applications add some of their own sound events in addition to the default sounds. Note that unless Windows or an application is specifically designed to look for an event listed here, any new events you might add will have no effect.

Schemes\Names is where Windows stores the settings for each of the sound schemes, such as Utopia. When you change the sound scheme using the drop-down Scheme list on Control Panel → Sounds, the appropriate scheme is copied into .Default.

HKCU\ControlPanel

Data from several of the Control Panel applets is stored here, particularly Accessibility and some of the Display settings. The names don't match up cleanly to the names used in the Control Panel, but you can usually figure out what's what by going back and forth between Registry Editor and the target Control Panel applet. For example, HKCU\ControlPanel\Accessibility maps directly to Control Panel → Accessibility, but HKCU\ControlPanel\Cursors maps to Control Panel → Mouse → Pointers.

As is typical in the convoluted world of the Registry, some entries point somewhere else entirely. For example, HKCU\ControlPanel\International simply defines a Locale value, such as 00000409, which is the standard code for what the Control Panel calls "English (United States)." If you use Registry Editor's Find function to trace this value, you'll eventually find the scattered locations of many of the individual values that Control Panel → Regional Settings brings together in one place.

This example illustrates a key point: there's usually little reason to poke around in the Registry for values that have a convenient user interface in the application. The exception is where the interface has limited which values can be entered, making the Registry a tool you can use for greater control (at the expense of the convenience of a user interface), as well as where there is simply no interface for some of the more obscure settings.

HKCU\Environment

The *environment* is a small chunk of memory devoted to storing a few system-wide settings, primarily for use with older Windows and DOS applications, but still used by Windows XP. In Windows 9x and Windows Me, information was added to the environment via the *AUTOEXEC.BAT* file (now obsolete). Like Windows 2000, Environment variables in Windows XP are set via Control Panel → System → Advanced → Environment Variables. The upper section of this dialog box (user variables for *username*) is where user-specific variables are entered, and are thus stored in the HKCU\Environment Registry key. The lower box (system variables) is for system-wide, user-independent variables and is stored in HKLM\SYSTEM\CurrentControlSet\Control\SessionManager\Environment. Note also the HKCU\Volatile Environment key, which contains temporary environment variables, resets each time Windows is started.

`HKCU\keyboard layout`

This key is used only if you have installed more than one keyboard layout via Control Panel → Keyboard → Language. A Preload subkey lists a separate subkey for each installed language, with subkey 1 specifying the default language.

`HKCU\RemoteAccess`

This key lists various types of information used by Dial-Up Networking, including the default connection to be used by Internet applications. The Implicit subkey lists the UNC path of any shared folders or printers that are accessed over a particular Dial-Up Networking connection. The Profile subkey stores information specific to each connection, such as the saved login name that will be supplied automatically when you make the connection.

`HKCU\Software`

Probably the most useful key in `HKEY_CURRENT_USER`, this key contains subkeys for each vendor whose software is loaded onto the machine, and, within each vendor's area, subkeys for each product. The keys stored here are supposed to contain only user-specific settings for each software application. Other settings, which are common to all users of software on the machine, are stored in `HKLM\SOFTWARE`.

The structure of this branch (and particularly of the `Microsoft\Windows\CurrentVersion` branch under both) is described later in this chapter, in the section "HKCU\Software and HKLM\SOFTWARE."

HKEY_LOCAL_MACHINE (HKLM)

HKLM contains hardware settings and global software settings that apply to all users. It has five top-level subkeys: HARDWARE, SAM, SECURITY, SOFTWARE, and SYSTEM. Each of these keys is stored in a separate hive file (see "Hives," earlier in this chapter).

`HKLM\HARDWARE`

The data stored in this branch is used by Windows XP to load drivers and initialize resources for the various hardware components of your computer. All of the settings here are more easily accessible through Device Manager (Control Panel → System → Hardware → Device Manager); there's little need to edit them directly. However, you may find it interesting to snoop around in this branch and see the various pieces of information that are stored for your CD Writer, your scanner, your hard disk, and your processor. The `HKLM\HARDWARE\DESCRIPTION\System\CentralProcessor\0` key tells me that my CPU is "GenuineIntel." I hope the thought police aren't checking this key.

`HKLM\SAM`

This key stores data for the Security Accounts Manager (SAM), used only if your Windows XP system is providing domain services. You'll find little reason to ever mess with the settings in this branch, and as most of the data is in binary format, you'll have a hard time deciphering it anyway. The information stored in this key is managed primarily through the User Manager for Domains (on NT Server) and User Manager (on NT Workstation). All of the settings here can be accessed through the Local Security Policy Editor (*secpol.msc*).

HKLM\SECURITY

The Security branch is where Windows stores the local security policy, which includes user accounts, permissions, passwords, and group membership information. Like HKLM\SAM, there is little reason to mess with this key. All of the settings here can be accessed through Control Panel → User Accounts.

HKLM\SOFTWARE

Probably the most useful key in HKEY_LOCAL_MACHINE, this key contains subkeys for each vendor whose software is loaded onto the machine, and, within each vendor's area, subkeys for each product. The keys stored here are supposed to contain global system settings for each application, common to all users on the machine. Other settings, specific to each user, are stored in HKCU\SOFTWARE.

The structure of this branch (and particularly of the Microsoft\Windows\CurrentVersion branch under both) is described later in this chapter, in the section "HKCU\Software and HKLM\SOFTWARE."

HKLM\SYSTEM

The settings in this branch primarily handle multiple hardware profiles. Windows uses this data together with HKLM\HARDWARE to handle drivers and Plug-&-Play management for all hardware on the system. All of the settings stored in this branch are accessible via Control Panel → System → Hardware → Hardware Profiles.

HKCU\Software and HKLM\SOFTWARE

As noted earlier, both HKEY_CURRENT_USER\Software and HKEY_LOCAL_MACHINE\SOFTWARE are structured similarly. Each of these areas has a branch for each manufacturer who has software installed on the system, and most vendors will have keys that appear in both areas. In each manufacturer key, there will be one or more subkeys, corresponding to each of that manufacturer's applications that are installed. For example, under the Adobe key, you might see an entry for Photoshop and one for Illustrator, assuming both of those applications are installed on your system.

In theory, the HKCU branch should include information that is configurable on a per-user basis (which is the case, for instance, with a software package with a per-user license or per-user customization). The HKLM branch should include software that is standard for all users. In practice, though, it doesn't seem to be as consistent as that. Some data might seem to be placed in wrong branch, while other data might be placed in both branches. Fortunately, this doesn't pose much of a problem in practice, partly because the vast majority of systems will only have a single user account, but more importantly, because the only practical rule as to the location and organization of data in the Registry is that it is consistent with the application that uses it. For example, since WordPerfect knows where to look for its own settings, it doesn't really matter that they aren't in a place the casual user would expect. Basically, if you're looking for something, look in both branches (HKLM and HKCU).

Because this is a book about Windows XP and not about the third-party applications that might be installed in it, the primary focus of this discussion is on the Microsoft\Windows\CurrentVersion branch, located in both HKCU and HKLM. There is a ton of information in these two areas, and the following keys represent the more useful and intelligible data:

..\Microsoft\Windows\CurrentVersion

> This key contains a dozen-or-so values describing some basic Windows settings, such as the folder location for Program Files, and the 20-digit Product ID number. Note the use of REG_EXPAND_SZ values, described earlier in this chapter.

..\Microsoft\Windows\CurrentVersion\App Paths *(HKLM only)*

> This branch lists a path for many application executables (Microsoft and otherwise) that are installed in nonstandard locations (i.e., not in \, \ *Windows*, or *\Windows\Command*). It is the reason why you can successfully type a command name like excel or winword at the Run prompt, but not at the Command prompt, unless you add *\Program Files\Microsoft Office\Office* to your search path. They have listed their path individually under this key.

 If you have an application that installs a shortcut on the Start menu, but doesn't let you type its name at the Run prompt, add a key for it in the App Paths key (using an existing entry as a template). For example, I added a *PHOTOSHOP.EXE* key, with the values:

```
(Default)    "C:\Program Files\Adobe Photoshop\Photoshop.exe"
Path    "C:\Program Files\Adobe Photoshop"
```

The end result is something like the Path environment variable, except that the target is a specific executable rather than an entire folder.

..\Microsoft\Windows\CurrentVersion\Explorer\ShellFolders
..\Microsoft\Windows\CurrentVersion\Explorer\User Shell Folders

> Specifies the locations of many of the standard Windows system folders, including Desktop, Programs, Send To, Start Menu, Startup, and Templates.

> This branch really brings home the extent of Windows' mutability. Even the directory names that Explorer relies on, such as *\Windows\Desktop*, are not hard-wired. So Explorer doesn't know anything about *c:\Windows\Desktop*. All it knows is that it can get the name of the folder it's supposed to use as the Desktop from the Registry. Most of these values probably shouldn't be changed.

> The ShellFolders and User Shell Folders keys each exist in the HKCU and HKLM branches. If you're looking for a particular setting, make sure you look in all four keys; whenever a key seems to be duplicated in more than one place, it's good practice to make changes in both places. Note also the use of the REG_EXPAND_SZ data type (explained earlier in this chapter) is used for some of the values.

`..\Microsoft\Windows\CurrentVersion\Explorer\Desktop\NameSpace`

Contains keys named with the CLSID of system icons that appear on the Desktop such as the Recycle Bin, My Documents, and My Network Places. Since these are simply pointers to objects defined elsewhere in the Registry (like Windows Shortcuts), they can be safely deleted (one method of removing the respective icons from your Desktop).

`..\Microsoft\Windows\CurrentVersion\Explorer\DontShowMeThisDialogAgain`

Every time you click the "Don't show me this again" option on some warning dialogs, Windows records your choice in this key. If you'd like to restore a warning you've previously dismissed, you can remove the corresponding value here. Too bad you can't add new values here to get rid of all the annoying Windows messages!

`..\Microsoft\Windows\CurrentVersion\Explorer\FindExtensions`

Contains keys corresponding to the various entries in the Start menu's Search menu and in the Explorer Search Bar. While you can't indiscriminately add items here (unless you're a programmer), you can remove unwanted entries.

`..\Microsoft\Windows\CurrentVersion\Explorer\MyComputer`

Contains several keys that relate to the My Computer window. The NameSpace subkey, for example, contains keys pointing to CLSIDs of various optional components that might appear in your My Computer window. To identify any unlabeled CLSID that shows up here or anywhere else, copy the entire CLSID string to the clipboard and paste it into Registry Editor's search box.

`..\Microsoft\Windows\CurrentVersion\Explorer\StartMenu` *(HKLM only)*

Contains several keys that relate to the seemingly hardcoded entries that appear in the Start Menu → My Computer window. The NameSpace subkey, for example, contains keys pointing to CLSIDs of various optional components that might appear in your My Computer window. To identify any unlabeled CLSID that shows up here or anywhere else, copy the entire CLSID string to the clipboard and paste it into Registry Editor's search box.

`..\Microsoft\Windows\CurrentVersion\Internet Settings`

Contains a whole slew of settings for Internet Explorer and the Internet Options dialog in Control Panel. You'll find settings in this key for just about everything from Passport settings to the filename of the bitmap used for the background of Internet Explorer's toolbar.

`..\Microsoft\Windows\CurrentVersion\Run` *(HKLM only)*
`..\Microsoft\Windows\CurrentVersion\RunOnce`

In these keys, you'll find a list of programs that Windows loads at start up. Note that these aren't the same as those found in the Startup folder in your Start menu, but they work similarly. The format is simple enough: the data in each value contains the full path and filename of a program to be launched, and the name of the value is merely a reminder as to the purpose of the entry. You can safely add any program you like, or remove entries you'd like to stop loading automatically. Note that values placed in either of the RunOnce keys (HKCU or HKLM) will only be run the next time Windows starts, and will be deleted immediately thereafter. There are several advantages of these keys over the Startup folder. For example, they're more concealed, and therefore more tamper-resistant. Also, items placed here (HKLM only) are run before the login screen appears, while items in the Startup folder are run only after a user logs in.

In addition to the previous specific keys, there are a few paradigms that show up again and again, such as the following:

../MRU

Stands for Most Recently Used. Any time Windows shows you a "history" of the last few things you've typed into a field, such as the Start menu's Run dialog, those items are stored in an MRU key in the Registry. A quick search for MRU in the Registry Editor will yield dozens of instances.

Knowing the location and use of a particular MRU list has several advantages. For example, you can write a script to clear a given list to erase your "footprints," so to speak. Or, perhaps you could create a Registry patch that would preload the Find drop-down list with a set of long names you wanted to search for repeatedly.

In MRU keys, the value names are a series of letters; there is also a value called MRUList that specifies the order in which the entries should be displayed. That is, if you've just typed in the filenames *.dll and *.exe into the Find dialog box, they might appear as items h and i in the list. But then, if you picked *.dll again from the list, the MRUList would show ijabcdefgh. The list is updated only when you actually execute a find, not when you type in a new filename to search for or pick an item from the drop-down list. In addition, when you quit Find, value j, which always contains an empty string, rotates to the front of the list.

../Namespace

Keys named Namespace usually contain values or subkeys that point to CLSIDs (16-bit identifiers to registered program components), which, in effect, instructs Windows to load those components. For example, if a CLSID for the Recycle Bin is listed under the Desktop\Namespace key, it corresponds to the Recycle Bin object appearing on the Desktop. Sometimes, removing these entries will have the effect of removing the corresponding objects, but not always. I recommend experimentation with some degree of caution.

HKEY_USERS (HKU)

Despite its name, this branch does not contain the Registry entries for all users configured on the system. This is because user information is loaded when a user logs in, and only one user can be logged in at any given time. Rather, it contains only information for the currently logged-in user as well as a template for new user profiles. (For those of you familiar with this key in Windows 9x and Windows Me, it does not quite work in the same way in Windows XP.)

This branch contains several keys, although only one of them is mirrored as HKEY_CURRENT_USER (discussed above). Usually, it's the one that looks like S-x-x-xx-xxxxxxxxxx-xxxxxxxxxx-xxxx, where the long string of x's is the Windows serial number. If it's not clear which key is the active one, just create a new key or value in one of the branches called test. Then, move up to HKEY_CURRENT_USER, and press F5 to refresh the view. If the test entry you just added shows up here as well, you've found the active key; if not, delete test and try again in a different key.

The .DEFAULT key is used as a template for creating new users, and unless you want to affect new user settings, you should leave this key alone. In fact, there's little reason to ever play with the HKEY_USERS branch, as all applicable settings for the active user are more easily accessible through HKEY_CURRENT_USER.

This design prevents one user from easily viewing or changing another user's settings.

HKEY_CURRENT_CONFIG (HKCC)

As noted earlier, HKCC is mirrored from the HKEY_LOCAL_MACHINE\SYSTEM\ CurrentControlSet\Hardware Profiles\XXXX, in which *XXXX* is a key representing the numeric value of the hardware profile currently in use. On a system with only a single hardware profile, its value will most likely be 0001. This branch contains hardware configuration settings for the currently loaded hardware profile, but there's little reason to edit this branch directly. Instead, go to Control Panel → System → Hardware → Hardware Profiles.

Hives

HKEY_USERS and HKEY_LOCAL_MACHINE can be thought of as the only true root keys, since the Registry's three other root keys are simply symbolic links, or mirrors, of different portions of these two. This means that these two branches are the only ones that actually need to be stored on your hard disk, and this is where *hives* come into play.

For every branch in HKEY_LOCAL_MACHINE, a corresponding hive file is stored in your \Windows\System32\config folder. For example, HKEY_LOCAL_MACHINE\Software is stored in a file called *software* (no filename extension). Since new branches can be added to HKEY_LOCAL_MACHINE, new hives can be generated at any time. Most systems will have the following hives: *sam*, *security*, *software*, and *system*.

Not all Registry data is stored on your hard disk, however. Some keys are dynamic, in that they are held only in memory, and are forgotten when you shut down. An example of a dynamic branch is HKEY_LOCAL_MACHINE\HARDWARE, which is built up each time Windows is started (an artifact of plug-and-play). Only non-dynamic branches are stored in hives, so you won't see a hive called *hardware*.

The branches in HKEY_USERS, one for each configured user, are similarly stored in hives. The hive file for each user is called *ntuser.dat*, and is located in \Documents and Settings\{username}. For example, the hive for the Administrator user is stored in the file \Documents and Settings\Administrator\ntuser.dat.

Knowing which files comprise the Registry is important only for backup and emergency recovery procedures (see "Backing Up the Registry," next), and for troubleshooting (and so you don't accidentally delete them). The storage mechanism is quite transparent to the Registry Editor and the applications that use the Registry; there's no reason to ever edit the hive files directly. If you want to migrate a key or a collection of keys from one computer to another, don't even think about trying to copy the hive files. Instead, use Registry patches, discussed later in this chapter.

Backing Up the Registry

Given that the Registry is an essential component of Windows, and a damaged Registry can make Windows totally inaccessible, a good backup of the Registry is one of the most important safeguards you can employ.

Unlike Windows 98 and Windows Me, Windows XP does not come with a distinct mechanism that automatically backs up the Registry, which means you'll have to implement one of your own to fully safeguard your Windows environment.

The Registry is stored in certain files (see "Hives" earlier in this chapter) on your hard disk, so you can create a backup by simply copying the appropriate files to another location.

When you start Windows, the information in the Registry is loaded into memory. While Windows is running, some changes may not be physically written to the Registry files until you shut down your computer; others, such as those made by the Registry Editor, are usually written immediately. For this reason, if you've made any substantial changes to the contents of the Registry, you may want to restart Windows *before* backing up the Registry to ensure that the files on the disk reflect the most recent changes.

The other consequence of using the Registry files is that you may not be able to simply use Explorer to copy them while Windows is running, and you certainly won't be able to overwrite them. The workaround is to attempt these measures when Windows isn't running, which means starting with the Emergency Recovery Console or with a set of boot disks, and then using DOS commands or a DOS batch file to copy the files (see Appendix C for details).

Although it's very useful to make backups of the Registry on your hard disk, it certainly can't prepare your computer for an actual disaster. If your hard disk crashes or gets infected with a virus or if your computer is stolen or dropped out of a eight-story building, those Registry backups on your hard disk won't do you much good. The most effective Registry backup is simply a matter of making a copy of all hives on your hard disk and keeping that copy somewhere other than inside your computer.

If you back up your entire system regularly, such as to a tape drive or other backup device, you should ensure that the backup software you use specifically supports safeguarding the Registry. Although your Registry certainly won't be compact enough to fit on a single floppy, it will fit easily on a removable drive (recordable CD, Zip disk, etc.). In addition, most modern backup software, such as the Backup utility that comes with Windows XP (see Chapter 4), includes a feature to back up the Registry.

One useful shortcut is a *local backup*. If you plan on modifying a specific value or key, it's wise to back up just that key, because restoring it in the event of a problem is much less of a hassle than attempting to restore the entire Registry. See the subsequent section for details.

Exporting and Importing Registry Data with Patches

Hives have an arcane format, making direct editing all but futile. Fortunately, the Registry Editor conveniently supports the importing and exporting of any number of keys and values with *Registry patches*. Patches (*.reg* files) are ordinary ASCII text files that can contain anything from a single key to a dump of the entire Registry.

Registry patches can be created with Registry Editor or a standard text editor, such as Notepad. You can also use Notepad to view and modify patches, and then use Registry Editor to reimport the patch.

Patches have many practical uses, including creating local backups of portions of the Registry as a preventative measure before editing keys (see the previous section). You can create a Registry key on one computer and apply it on another, useful for migrating a single setting or a whole group of settings to any number of Windows systems. Patches can allow easier editing than with Registry Editor, and certainly afford quicker and more flexible searches.

To create a Registry patch, highlight the key you want to export and select File → Export. Once you've chosen a filename, the selected key, any subkeys, and all their values and respective data will be saved in a single file with the *.reg* extension. In most cases, you wouldn't want to select My Computer to export the entire Registry, since, for no other reason, HKLM is enormous and you wouldn't want to reimport it in any case.

Before making any changes to a Registry key, do a quick backup by exporting the key. Depending on what changes you've made, the Registry might not be identical after reimporting the key, but at least you'll have a record of what the key looked like before the changes.

Importing *.reg* files isn't quite as simple as creating them, partly because of the concept of merging, and partly because of the potential for harm. It's important to note that the contents of a Registry patch are merged with existing keys; they don't simply overwrite them. So, if a given key contains four keys (apple, pear, banana, and peach), and you apply a Registry patch (pointing to the same key) that contains four keys (apple, pear, banana, and pomegranate), the resulting key will have five keys (apple, pear, banana, peach, and pomegranate). The existing values and keys will indeed be overwritten with those in the patch, but any additional values and keys in the Registry will remain intact.

The format of *.reg* files is similar to *.ini* files, rather than anything resembling the way data is displayed in Registry Editor. A section begins with the full path of a key in square brackets, like this: [section name]. This is followed by any number of values, each of the format name="data" (the default value appears as @="value").

The Registry

Stop! Do Not Double-Click on This File!

The default action for double-clicking on a *.reg* file is not to edit the file, as you might expect, but to merge it into the Registry. Registry Editor does warn you before committing a patch, and then informs you that the patch was successful (both messages can be turned off with the /s command-line parameter—see Appendix A). However, if you work with Registry patches often, and are concerned about accidentally applying one, you may want to change the default action so that *.reg* files are edited when double-clicked. Open the File Types dialog (Control Panel → Folder Options → File Types), highlight REG|Registration Entries in the list of file types, and click Advanced. Highlight the Edit action, click Set Default (making it appear bold), and click OK.

Then, the next key (if any) is listed, followed by all the values *it* contains. The order of the keys, as well as the order of the values in each key, is irrelevant. However, if you were to move a key from one section to another, it would, in effect, be moving the value from one key to another.

The quotes around value data are only used for string values; binary values and REG_EXPAND_SZ values are prefixed with the keyword hex: and appear without quotes. Similarly, DWORD values are preceeded by dword: and appear without quotes. Any backslashes in value data (found most often in folder paths and Registry paths) are doubled to distinguish them from the backslashes in key names.

Lastly, the first line in every Registry patch created in Windows XP and Windows 2000 will be Windows Registry Editor Version 5.00, followed by a blank line. Patches created in Windows 95, 98, and Me will instead begin with Registry Editor4, also followed by a blank line. There doesn't appear to be any difference in the treatment of these two types of patches by Registry Editor.

Here is an excerpted Registry patch:

```
Windows Registry Editor Version 5.00

[HKEY_CURRENT_USER\Software\mozilla.org\Mozilla\0.9.2 (en)\Main]
"Program Folder Path"="C:\\Documents and Settings\\All Users\\Start Menu\\
Programs\\Mozilla\\"
"Install Directory"="C:\\Program Files\\Mozilla\\"

[HKEY_CURRENT_USER\Software\Microsoft\Internet Explorer\Main]
"NoUpdateCheck"=dword:00000001
"Show_ChannelBand"="No"
"Display Inline Images"="yes"
"Show_ToolBar"="yes"
"Check_Associations"="no"
"SmoothScroll"=dword:00000001
"Play_Animations"="yes"
"Play_Background_Sounds"="yes"
"Display Inline Videos"="yes"
"Print_Background"="no"
```

You may notice that these two keys are in different manufacturer branches, and wouldn't appear next to one another in the Registry. If you think about the way Registry patches are created, you'll realize that the one shown above couldn't have been created in a single step. Instead, two different Registry Patches were created, and the contents of one were cut and pasted into the other using a plain text editor. As long as you remove the redundant header, this is perfectly acceptable. In fact, it can be a very convenient way to implement several Registry changes in one step.

Extra credit question: given the structure of file types discussed earlier in this chapter, how would you create a single Registry patch that contains all the necessary information to register a new file association on any computer? Could you use such a patch to restore your preferred file type settings if another application were to ever overwrite them?

Ten Cool Things You Can Do in Your Registry

Armed with your new understanding of the Windows XP Registry, you're no doubt ready to get in there and start exploring. Hopefully, this chapter has provided the "lay of the land" you need to get and keep your bearings in the otherwise confusing wilderness of the Registry. While we don't have the kind of room in this book it takes to make you an expert, we would like to send you on your way by pointing out some interesting landmarks; i.e., ten cool changes you can make in your own Registry.

1. *Expand the scope of IE's AutoComplete feature.*

    In Internet Explorer, you can enter an incomplete URL (i.e., *oreilly* instead of *www.oreilly.com*) and IE will attempt to complete the address itself by searching for all instances. However, IE only searches the *.com*, *.edu*, *.net*, and *.org* top-level domains (TLDs) by default, and only tries the *www* prefix. To add new domain suffixes and prefixes to search, go to:

    ```
    HKEY_LOCAL_MACHINE\SOFTWARE\Microsoft\Internet Explorer\Main\UrlTemplate
    ```

    By default, this key has four values in Windows XP: 1, 2, 3, and 4, set to www. %s.com, www.%s.net, www.%s.org, and www.%s.edu, respectively. The value names (the numbers) specify the search order (lower numbers take precedence), and the data specifies the format. Feel free to rearrange the existing items, remove unwanted items, or add new TLDs, like *.gov* (for US government websites), *.co.nz* (for commercial web sites in New Zealand), or *.store* (one of the newly proposed TLDs, still on the drawing table at the time of this writing).

2. *Roll back any single setting to the Windows default.*

    An entire branch in the Registry is used as a template with which to create new user profiles. As described earlier in this chapter, the path:

    ```
    HKEY_USERS\.DEFAULT
    ```

    is duplicated for each new user that is created in Windows XP. If, down the road, you trace a certain problem to an incorrect Registry setting, you can just visit this branch and obtain the default value. For example, I recently ran into a problem caused by incorrect data in the UserPreferenceMask value, located in HKEY_CURRENT_USER\Control Panel\Desktop. I looked up the corresponding value in `HKEY_USERS\.DEFAULT\Control Panel\Desktop`, and copied its data into the active `UserPreferenceMask` value. Problem solved!

Another use of this key, especially for those who need to configure a large number of users, is that any change made to the `.DEFAULT` branch will appear in each new user that is added to the system (existing users won't be affected). This can be a great way, for example, to disable the system sounds for each student account on a classroom computer.

3. *Disable the Shut Down command.*

   If you're running a kiosk or demo system (or if you just don't want people shutting down your machine), you can disable the Shut Down command by going to:

   ```
   HKEY_CURRENT_USER\Software\Microsoft\Windows\CurrentVersion\Policies\
   Explorer
   ```

   Create a new DWORD value in this key and name it `NoClose`. Double-click the new value, and set its data to 1. You'll have to log out and log back in (or restart Windows) for this change to take effect. Note that in order to shut down now, you'll have to press Ctrl-Alt-Del, and click Shut Down. To undo this change, just delete the `NoClose` value.

4. *Registry Editor remembers where you were.*

   Each time you open the Registry Editor, it automatically expands the branch you had open the last time Registry Editor was used, but no others. So, if you find yourself repeatedly adjusting a particular setting and then closing Registry Editor (such as when implementing the previous tip), make sure the relevant key is highlighted just before Registry Editor is closed, and that key will be opened next time as well.

   Note also the Favorites menu, which works very much like the one in Internet Explorer, allows you to bookmark frequently accessed Registry keys. While it's useful, I personally find the existence of such a feature in a trouble-shooting tool like Registry Editor to be more than a little eerie.

5. *Change the registered user and company names for Windows XP.*

   When Windows XP is installed, a user and company name are entered. Unfortunately, there is no convenient way to change this information after installation. Surprise—you can do it in the Registry! Just go to:

   ```
   HKEY_LOCAL_MACHINE\Software\Microsoft\Windows NT\CurrentVersion
   ```

   The values you need are `RegisteredOwner` and `RegisteredOrganization`, both of which can be changed to whatever you'd like. You may notice that the Registry key containing these values is in the Windows NT branch, rather than the more commonly used Windows branch. Don't worry, both branches are used in Windows XP. The less-used Windows NT branch contains more advanced settings, mostly those that differentiate the Windows 9x and Windows NT lines of operating systems (as described in Chapter 1).

6. *Change your default installation path.*

   When you install Windows XP, the path to your installation files is set in the Registry. Unfortunately, this setting is not updated when drive letters change or when you point to a different location when optional components are added or removed. To change the default setup path, making subsequent configuration changes more convenient, go to:

```
HKEY_LOCAL_MACHINE\Software\Microsoft\Windows\CurrentVersion\Setup
```

Start by changing the SourcePath value to either the root directory of your CD drive (e.g. *d:*), or to a path on your hard disk or network containing the Windows XP installation files. Note also the Installation Sources entry, which is a REG_MULTI_SZ value (see "What's in the Registry," earlier in this chapter, for details on this value type). It contains a list of all the folders displayed in Windows' drop-down list, allowing you to quickly point to any one of several favorite installation paths.

7. *Try something new with My Computer.*

   Double-click the My Computer icon, and the My Computer window appears. It doesn't have to be this way. The program launched when you double-click My Computer is simply another value in the Registry. Start by navigating to:

   ```
   HKEY_CLASSES_ROOT\CLSID\{20D04FE0-3AEA-1069-A2D8-08002B30309D}
   ```

   (See the following tip for an easy way to locate this key)

   You'll notice that the structure of this key is very similar to standard file type keys (discussed earlier in this chapter), which means we can treat this object like a file type and create new actions for it. Open the Shell subkey, and create a new key named open; in the new Open key, create a new key named command. You should then be here:

   ```
   HKEY_CLASSES_ROOT\CLSID\{20D04FE0-3AEA-1069-A2D8-08002B30309D}\shell\
   open\command
   ```

   Double-click on the default value of that new Command key and type the full path and filename of the program you wish to open. For example, I find it handy to have the My Computer icon open an Explorer window; to do this, just type explorer.exe for the value data. You'll have to log out and log back in for the change to take effect.

8. *Some handy Registry navigation shortcuts.*

   The previous tip involved navigating to the Registry key associated with the My Computer icon on the Desktop, which is located in the HKCR\CLSID branch. If you visit this branch, you'll notice hundreds of Class ID keys, all sorted alphabetically (so to speak), which makes finding a single key rather laborious. Luckily, there are a few alternatives that will greatly simplify this task.

   First, you can simply search the Registry for "My Computer." Start by highlighting the key at the top of the tree (coincidentally named "My Computer"), which instructs Registry Editor to begin searching at the beginning. Then, use Edit → Find, type My Computer, make sure that all the "Look at" options are checked, and click Find Next. The first instance it finds will probably be the key you're looking for, although it won't always be this easy.

   Another shortcut is to use the keyboard. Like Explorer, when you press a letter or number key, Registry Editor will jump to the first entry that starts with that character. Furthermore, if you press several keys in succession, they will all be used to spell the target item. For example, to navigate to:

   ```
   HKEY_CLASSES_ROOT\CLSID\{20D04FE0-3AEA-1069-A2D8-08002B30309D}
   ```

The Registry

start by expanding the HKEY_CLASSES_ROOT key. Then, press C + L +S quickly in succession, and Registry Editor will jump to the CLSID key. Next, expand that key by pressing the (+) button, or by pressing the right arrow key, and press { + 2 + 0 (the first three characters of the key name, including the curly brace), and you'll be in the neighborhood of the target key in seconds.

9. *Permanently remove many unwanted system tray icons.*

In the "HKCU\Software and HKLM\SOFTWARE" section, earlier in this chapter, the HKLM\SOFTWARE\Microsoft\Windows\CurrentVersion\Run key is described as listing many programs that are run automatically when Windows starts. Some of these entries are included in order to install icons in the system tray (the area on your Taskbar, by the clock). Since most of the tray icons that come with Windows can be toggled on and off in Control Panel, the more bothersome ones are usually installed by third-party programs. To disable one or more of these tray icons, preventing them from loading the next time Windows starts, you'll have to delete the corresponding value in this key (renaming isn't sufficient). Use caution, and certainly make a Registry patch to back up the entire key before fiddling with it.

10. *Alphabetize your Start menu in one step.*

The Windows XP Start menu allows you to rearrange shortcuts by dragging and dropping them; the unfortunate consequence of this feature is that new shortcuts and folders that appear when applications are installed are added to the end of the list. Now, you can sort a single Start Menu folder alphabetically by right-clicking any shortcut and selecting Sort by Name, but this can get tedious very quickly. The solution to this is in the Registry; just navigate to:

    HKEY_CURRENT_USER\Microsoft\Windows\CurrentVersion\Explorer\MenuOrder\
    Start Menu

and you'll see subkeys and values that determine the sort order of the contents of the Start menu (and the Favorites menu, next door). Simply delete the entire Start menu key to sort all of the folders in your Start menu alphabetically, or selectively delete the desired subkeys to sort corresponding folders. Note that the next time you drag-drop a shortcut in the Start menu, Windows will recreate these keys automatically, so you may wish to write a WSH script (see Chapter 9) to automatically delete this key, say, every time Windows is started.

9

The Windows Script Host

One of the features that has distinguished operating systems like Unix and Linux from Windows is that they've made it relatively easy to write scripts that automate repetitive tasks. Since doing the same thing over and over again is one of the basic labor-saving benefits of a computer, the lack of robust scripting capabilities has always been one of the great weaknesses of Windows.

Originally released as part of Windows 98, the Windows Script Host (WSH) is Microsoft's answer to this problem and a replacement for the remarkably limited batch file language (see Chapter 6). The addition of WSH to the Windows platform represents a major step forward in Windows' role in the networking world.

WSH provides a way to automate Windows-based graphical applications using any one of several, powerful, full-featured scripting languages. WSH provides a set of objects that allow you to interact with the network, Registry, files and folders, and even other applications, using scripting languages such as VBScript and Microsoft JScript (a JavaScript-like language). Third-party add-ons that provide the same functionality in other scripting languages, such as Perl, Tcl, REXX, and Python, are also available.

WSH scripts can be used to create network login scripts that are more complex than those that are built into Windows, and can be used to automate local Desktop tasks. The resulting scripts can be run from the Desktop, from the command line, or via the Explorer's Scheduled Tasks. WSH scripts can also be embedded in HTML files, which in turn can be used as part of the Active Desktop.

Unfortunately, while WSH is powerful, it is not for the faint-hearted. If you do not already know a scripting language such as VBScript, JavaScript, or Perl, you should get a good book on the language of your choice before starting out. *Learning VBScript*, by Paul Lomax; *JavaScript, The Definitive Guide*, by David Flanagan; and *Learning Perl on Win32 Systems*, by Randal Schwartz, Erik Olson, and Tom Christiansen, are three useful books available from O'Reilly.

This chapter shows how to run WSH scripts, gives a brief introduction to VBscript programming, and describes the syntax of the objects provided by WSH. It also describes how to use the Object Browser to discover information about system and application objects, and concludes with some practical examples that illustrate the power of WSH scripts.

 Scripts created on Windows XP can be run on other versions of Windows, as long as they have the Windows Script Host component installed (it's an option on some earlier versions.) Note also that the version of WSH that comes with Windows XP may be more recent than the ones included with previous versions of Windows, so you may need to obtain updates from *http://www.microsoft.com* and install them on any target machines.

What Is WSH?

So what is WSH? A language? As the name implies, WSH "hosts" a language and provides a shell to run scripts in. Scripts can be created in the language of your choice (provided it's available).

By default, WSH supports VBScript and Jscript as available scripting languages. But other popular scripting languages, such as Perl, have been implemented in the WSH environment. (To obtain Perl, which many people regard as the most powerful and versatile scripting language available on any platform, visit *http://www.activestate.com.*)

The capabilities provided in WSH, such as network and registry access, are provided by ActiveX Component Object Model (COM) objects. A COM object is a component that performs one or more specific tasks. This may vary from something as simple as displaying a message to running large applications. All Office applications are COM objects and can be manipulated through WSH. Internet Explorer is also a COM object. WSH itself provides a number of COM objects, and there are also objects associated with some parts of the system, such as the filesystem. Other functionality provided by COM objects includes file access, messaging (email), and database access.

The ability to use COM objects opens a whole world of possibilities that were once available only in dedicated programming environments such as C++ or Visual Basic. Once an object is created, it exposes information and functionality to the programming environment (in this case, WSH). Think of an object as a black box that performs specific operations. The box exposes information and functionality through a predefined set of commands. Since WSH has implemented core functionality using COM objects, it doesn't rely on language-specific features; many of the concepts discussed in this chapter are applicable to any scripting language implemented through WSH.

Additional Resources

Table 9-1 lists additional resources available on the Internet.

Table 9-1. Additional Windows Script Host resources

Link	Description
http://cwashington.netreach.net	Excellent WSH resource web site, including chat groups, scripts, and COM objects.
http://communities.msn.com/windowsscript/	Discussion forum for WSH developers.
http://msdn.microsoft.com	Microsoft's developer site. Contains current versions of WSH, scripting engines, documentation, and tutorials.

Executing Scripts

Windows XP supplies two programs used to run WSH scripts (whatever language they are written in). *Wscript.exe* is used to run WSH scripts from the Windows graphical environment, and *cscript.exe* is used to run them from the command line or from within batch files. Both programs are fully documented in Chapter 4.

Using wscript.exe

Using *wscript.exe*, you can run scripts under Windows in the following ways:

- Double-click on script files or icons listed in My Computer, Windows Explorer, the Find window, the Start menu, or on the Desktop.

   If you double-click a script file whose extension has not yet been associated with *wscript.exe*, an Open With dialog box appears asking which program you would like to use to open the file. After choosing WScript, check the "Always use this program to open this file" checkbox, and WScript is registered as the default application for all files with the same extension as the one you double-clicked.

- Enter wscript, followed by a script name at the Run command on the Start menu or at any command prompt. You must enter the full name of the script, including the file extension and any necessary path information.

Although the *wscript.exe* application has several command-line parameters (see "Windows Script Host" in Chapter 4), it's more convenient to use the Properties window of a script file (right-click the file and select Properties). Options are set in the usual way, but the properties are not saved in the script file or in the Registry as you might expect; instead, a new file with the *.wsh* extension is created (the filename prefix is the same as the original script file). The file is a plain text file with the familiar *.ini* format, and can be edited with a text editor such as Notepad.

Figure 9-1 shows the Script tab of the properties for a script file. You can choose whether the script should time out, what the timeout for the script should be, and whether the script logo should be displayed when the script is run.

A sample *.wsh* file might look like this:

```
[ScriptFile]
Path=C:\Scripts\MyScript.vbs
[Options]
Timeout=30
DisplayLogo=1
BatchMode=0
```

The Windows
Script Host

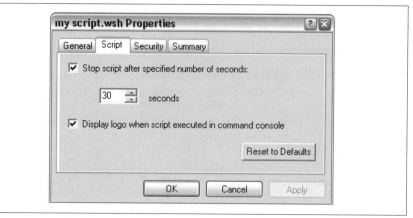

Figure 9-1. The Script tab in a .wsh property sheet

The Path setting in the [ScriptFile] section identifies the script file that the *.wsh* file is associated with. The keys in the [Options] section correspond to settings on the Script tab.

A *.wsh* file can be treated as if it were a Windows Shortcut; you can run a *.wsh* file directly by double-clicking on it, or by using it as the script name parameter with *wscript.exe* or *cscript.exe*. If you delete the *.wsh* file, the original script will be unaffected. The *.wsh* files are very useful for administration purposes. Since you can run a *.wsh* file directly (rather than invoking the script itself), you can use a text editor to create multiple *.wsh* files for the same script, each containing different parameters but the same script name.

Using cscript.exe

Using *cscript.exe*, you can run command-line based WSH scripts from the command prompt. In most circumstances, you'll want to use the Windows-based *wscript.exe*. However, *cscript.exe* is more appropriate when used with command prompt applications or when you need the script to use STDOUT (standard output), such as when writing CGI scripts for web servers. This is illustrated by the *Wscript.Echo* method described in "Object Model" later in this chapter.

Like *wscript.exe*, *cscript.exe* has several command-line parameters documented in "Windows Script Host" in Chapter 4.

Creating a Script

Scripts are stored in an ASCII (plain text) format. Any text editor, such as Notepad, can create text files. If you choose a program such as Word or Wordpad to create scripts, you must save the file as a text file and not their native format.

To put it simply, a script is simply a list of commands, one-on-a-line, and then saved into a file. There are no prerequisites in script filenames except the file extension. The file extension relates to the language the script is created in. For VBScript scripts, this is *.vbs*, while for JScript, it is *.js*.

VBScript

While WSH is language-independent, in this chapter we use Visual Basic Script (VBScript) for demonstrating its capabilities. This section provides a basic introduction to VBScript programming.

The concepts explained in this section, especially those related to the creation and manipulation of objects, apply to all scripting languages implemented in WSH. Even if you have worked with other languages such as Perl but have limited exposure to the concept of objects, you should read through it.

Scripting languages such as VBScript are interpreted. That is, the commands in a script are translated into a low-level computer language and executed at the same time. This differs from standard applications (*.exe* files), which are compiled by the designers long before being executed. Although interpreted scripts are inherently slower than compiled applications, interpretations provide the advantage of not requiring a compiler or any type of specialized authoring environment.

A script is composed of a number of elements. Variables are created to temporarily store values and object information. Commands, known as functions or methods, are executed to perform various predefined operations. Complex routines are built up with the aid of programming statements (such as conditional statements that are used to determine if a certain operation is to be executed based on a condition), and loops (which allow operations to be repeated a set number of times).

Comments

It is important to add comments to your scripts, especially larger ones. Comments document the operation of the script, but are ignored when the script is executed. To add a comment in VBScript, add a single quote (') on a new line followed by text, which is the comment. You can add comments at the end of other statements by adding the single quote followed by the comment. For example:

```
'this is a comment on its own line
strName="Fred"    'this comment is at the end of a statement
```

Continuation Character

If a statement is longer than one line, it can be continued onto another line by using an underscore as the last character on the line. For example:

```
Wscript.echo "This is an unnecessarily very long message" & _
            " to the reader."
```

Variables

And you thought you were done with variables when you finished algebra. A variable is used to store information for use during the processing of the script. This might be text information such as a name, number, date, or a reference to an object.

A variable is identified with a name. A variable name can be any combination of letters or numbers, but cannot contain spaces. An example of a name could be startdate or employeewage.

Variable names do not have to be descriptive, but it's good practice to create human-readable names. If you open up a script you wrote six months ago, you'll want to be able to understand what's going on. Variable names are case-insensitive; that is, shoesize, ShoeSize, and SHOESIZE are all identical.

The usual practice is to prefix variable names with a few characters to identify the type. This is not required, but it does make it easier to remember what type of data a given variable holds. There is no standard naming convention for variables, but it's best to be consistent.

Table 9-2 lists the prefixes that are used throughout this chapter to identify data types.

Table 9-2. Common variable name prefix types and examples

Prefix	Type	Example
str	String or text. This can be any combination of letters or numbers, including any character that can be entered from your keyboard.	strName
date	Date.	datStartDate
b	Boolean. A boolean variable is a switch or flag variable; its value is either True (−1)[a] or False (0).	bFlag
num	Number	numSalary
obj	Object.	objMailMessage
int	Integer. Whole number, no decimals.	intCounter
any	Any type. Can be any of the above mentioned data types.	

[a] True is defined as −1, but any positive number will also be interpreted at True.

You do not have to explicitly declare variables in VBS. This means that when you create a script, you do not have to tell the script about the existence of a variable, or declare what type of data a variable will hold, before using it. This is contrary to other programming languages, such as C++. However, it is always wise to declare variables before using them for clarity and debugging purposes. To declare a variable, use the Dim directive followed by the variable name:

    dim variablename

To force the explicit declaration of variables, add the statement Option Explicit at the beginning of your script. This will cause VBScript to generate an error if it encounters a variable that hasn't been declared with dim. Why would you want to do this and create more work for yourself? Because of typos. If you misspell a variable name and you're not using Option Explicit, VBScript won't catch it; instead the script simply won't work as expected, and you'll have to carefully comb through the script file looking for errors.

To assign a value to a variable in VBScript, enter the variable name followed by an equals sign and the value you wish to assign:

    variablename = value

Different types of data are assigned in different ways.

Text values, which are referred to as strings in programming jargon, need to be surrounded by quotes:

```
strEmpoyeename = "Fred Smith"
```

Numeric values don't need to be surrounded by anything, but should not include formatting characters such as commas:

```
intEmployeeage = 45
numEmployeesalary = 35000.50
```

Dates must be surrounded by hash symbols (#):

```
datBirth = #1/5/69#   'date format interpreted depending on system
                      'settings
datBirth = #January 5, 1999#
datBirth = #5-Jan-1999#
```

When assigning values to variables, you can perform calculations that involve other values or variables:

```
intAge = intAge + 1 'increase the intAge variable by one
numTotal = intQuantity * numPrice 'multiply quantity by price
```

You can concatenate (combine) strings using the ampersand operator:

```
strFirstName = "Fred"
strLastName = "Smith"
strFullName = strFirstName & " " & strLastName
```

Since all variables in VBScript are the same type (they're all "variants" for VB programmers), the ampersand operator can also combine different types of data in one string:

```
'combine a string and a number
strNameAndAge = strFullName & " is " & intAge & " years old"
```

Note (in both of the previous examples) how spaces are used to ensure that text doesn't run together.

Object Variables

Objects are also stored in variables. Objects are assigned values just like other variable types, but you must use the Set statement when assigning an object a value:

```
Set objectA = objectB
```

As mentioned earlier, an object is similar to a black box. This black box exposes functions and information to the environment in which it is created. When you create an object, it is referred to as an instance of the object. You can have multiple instances of any given object. Each object instance is independent of other instances of the same object.

For example, we have a mail message object. This object stores information and performs email-related operations. It would store information such as the message body, subject, and recipients. It would also contain the code to instruct your email program to send the message.

Each instance of an object stores its own set of variables. These variables are known as object properties.

To access a property, use the object instance's name followed by a period, then the name of the property:

```
objMailmessage.subject= "Message subject"  'set the message subject
objMailmessage.text = "This is a message to fred"  'set message body
```

An object property might only allow you to read a value (read-only), write (write-only), or both. For example, the size of a mail message is a read-only value.

```
intSize = objMailmessage.size  'show the size of the message
```

Object actions are performed using methods. A method performs a specific operation. When you execute or call a method, it is referred to as invoking the method. To invoke a method, enter the object name followed by a period and the method name (no equal sign).

```
objMailMessage.Send( ) ' invoke the send method
```

Before you can do any object-related operations, you must first create an instance of an object. Any scripting language implemented in the WSH environment automatically creates an instance of one object, the Wscript object. The Wscript object exposes a couple of basic methods, one of which is CreateObject.

Here is the syntax of the CreateObject method:

```
Set objInstance = Wscript.CreateObject(strObjectname)
```

For example, create a network object instance:

```
Set objMail = Wscript.CreateObject("Wscript.Network")
```

Another method available through the Wscript object is the Echo method:

```
Wscript.Echo anyValue
```

The Echo method displays information specified in the anyValue parameter:

```
Wscript.Echo "Hello World"
```

The Wscript object model, its methods, and its properties will be covered in more detail later in the chapter.

Conditional Statements

When creating scripts, it is often necessary to check for a certain condition. If it is met, perform specific operations; if not, do something else or nothing at all.

A condition is the comparison of one or more expressions. The comparisons are made using standard mathematical operators: =, >, <, >=, >=, and <>. A condition evaluates to True if the condition is met; otherwise, it's False.

```
4>5  → false
5>4  → true
"Fred" = "Joe"  → false
10<=10  → true
```

You might need to test more than one condition at a time. For example, in a personnel application, you might want to perform an operation only if the age is greater than 50 and the employee earned $40,000 or more dollars a year. To check multiple conditions, use the Boolean AND and/or OR operators (see Table 9-3 and Table 9-4). These operators combine two conditions, and the outcome of the operation returns either True or False.

Table 9-3. AND operator condition examples and results

Age	Salary	A > 50	Salary >= 40000	A > 50 AND Salary >= 40000
45	35000	False	False	False
52	39000	True	False	False
30	42000	False	True	False
56	43000	True	True	True

Table 9-4. OR operator condition examples and results

Age	Salary	A > 50	Salary >= 40000	A > 50 OR Salary >= 40000
45	35000	False	False	False
52	39000	True	False	True
30	42000	False	True	True
56	43000	True	True	True

The following set of conditions will return True if the age is greater than 40, the salary is greater than or equal to 50000, or the title is Manager.

```
Age>40 Or Salary>50000 Or Title ="Manager"
```

The following set of conditions will return True only if the age is greater than 40, the salary is greater than or equal to 50000, and the title is Manager.

```
Age>40 And Salary>50000 And Title="Manager"
```

You can also combine any number of AND and/or OR conditions. When doing so, you have to be careful of the order in which you write the conditions. As in algebra, there is a precedence as to what operator is performed first. In the mathematical expression 1+2*3, the multiplication is performed before the addition and the result is 7. With Boolean operators, AND has precedence over the OR operator.

The following condition will return True if the salary is greater than 50000 and the title is Manager, or the age is greater than 40.

```
Age>40 Or Salary>50000 And Title ="Manager"
```

This is not quite what you'd expect. What if you wanted the condition to return True if the age is greater than 40 or the salary is greater than 50000, and the title had to be Manager? Going back to our math example, 1+2*3, what if we wanted the 1+2 to be executed before the 2*3? We would surround the 1+2 in parentheses: (1+2)*3=9. The same applies to conditional expressions. Any expressions surrounded in parentheses are executed first.

```
(Age>40 Or  Salary>50000) And  Title ="Manager"
```

To test a condition in a script, use the If Then Else statement.

```
If condition Then
  'do something if true
End If
```

If a condition is met, the code after the Then statement is executed. The following example displays a message if the value of the intAge variable is greater than 10:

```
intAge= 5
If intAge > 10 Then
    Wscript.Echo "The person is older than 10 years old"
End If
```

If you wish to perform an operation if the statement is not true, include the Else statement after the Then statement and before the End If statements.

```
intAge= 5
numSalary = 65000
strTitle = "Manager"
If (Age>40 Or numSalary>50000) And strTitle ="Manager" > 10 Then
    Wscript.Echo "A Manager either over 40 or earns over 50000"
Else
    Wscript.Echo "Either not a manager" & _
                 " or less than 40 with lower salary"
End If
```

Functions and Subroutines

When creating scripts and with programming in general, it is important to break up larger programs into smaller parts and create reusable functions wherever possible. Large scripts can be unwieldy and difficult to read and debug.

To break up scripts into smaller parts, you can create subroutines and functions.

Subroutines allow smaller script elements to be created. To create a subroutine, enter the Sub statement, followed by a list of parameters (if required). Then add all of the statements to be executed within the subroutine, followed by an End Sub:

```
Sub subname([parameter1, parameterX])
    statements...
End Sub
```

All of the code that belongs to the subroutine is contained between the Sub and End Sub routine statements.

```
Sub HelloWorld( )
    Wscript.Echo "Hello World"
End Sub
```

To execute a subroutine from somewhere else within the script, just type its name like you would a built-in command. For example, to execute the HelloWorld routine above, add HelloWorld on its own line anywhere in your script.

Subroutines can also have parameters passed to them. Include all parameters within the parentheses on the subroutine declaration. Separate the parameters with commas:

```
Sub showhello(strMessage, strMessage2)
    Wscript.Echo strMessage & " " & strMessage2
End Sub
ShowMessage("Hello", "World")
```

A function is basically the same as a subroutine, except that it is capable of returning a value. The value returned is based on a calculation of parameters passed to the function:

```
Function Squared(numValue)
    Squared = numValue * numValue
End Function
Wscript.Echo Squared(5)
```

It's up to you to choose whether you want to make something a subroutine or function; some programmers create functions exclusively and just ignore the returned values of the functions that don't have them.

While you can create your own functions, VBScript has hundreds of built-in functions that perform certain operations, such as mathematical, string, and logic operations:

```
datToday= Date( ) 'return todays date
strName = Ucase(strName) ' convert string to upper case
```

For more information on VBScript's built-in functions, see "Additional Resources," earlier in this chapter.

Variable Scope

When you start declaring variables in different routines, you will encounter scope issues. These scope issues can cause problems if you are not careful how and where you declare your variables.

Both subroutines and functions can have variable declarations inside the routines; these variables have no meaning outside of the routines, and are considered "local." This is useful for larger scripts where it is not practical to declare all variables in one spot, as well as for debugging purposes.

If you create a variable in a subroutine, you cannot access the variable outside of the subroutine. However, if you create several "local" variables with the same name, but in different routines, they will be treated like separate variables and won't cause a conflict. Variables that are declared in the main portion of the script (outside of subroutine and function blocks) are considered "global" and have meaning in all parts of the script.

```
Option Explicit 'force explicit declaration of variables
Dim strGlobal, strSameName

strGlobal = "I can see everywhere"
strSameName = "Global local"
```

```
Wscript.Echo strLocal 'this won't work - error will occur

Sub one
    Dim strLocal, strSameName
    strSameName = "Inside one "
    Wscript.Echo strGlobal 'this works
End Sub
```

Loops

Often a script needs to repeat an operation a set number of times. The For...Next
statement provides this ability. Its syntax is as follows:

```
For intVariable = start To end
    [Exit For]
Next
```

The code between the For and Next statements is executed the number of times
specified between the start and end values:

```
For intCounter = 1 To 10
    intValue = intValue * 2   'multiply the variable intValue by two
Next
```

The Do While Loop provides the ability to repeat operations a set number of times
based on a condition.

```
Do While condition
    [Exit Do]
Loop
```

The code between the Do While and Loop statements is repeatedly executed while
the condition is true.

```
Do While intCounter < 100
    Wscript.Echo intCounter
    intCounter = intCounter + 1
Loop
```

The Exit For and Exit Do statements are used to leap out of the loops before the
loops conclude, and while they can appear anywhere, they're typically used in
conjunction with the if statement.

Collections

An object exposes methods and properties to the programming environment. The
properties can be of any data type, including an object. This can include a special
type of an object known as a *collection*. A collection is an object that contains a
list of related objects.

Table 9-5 lists a number of default properties that a collection object always
exposes.

Table 9-5. Object collection properties

Property	Description
Count	Returns the number of items contained in the collection.
Length	Same as the Count property. Not all collections use this property.
Item	Returns a specified item from the collection.

We will use a fictitious Persons collection to demonstrate how to reference values from a collection. The Persons collection contains Person objects. The Persons object contains Name, Social Security, and PhoneNumber properties.

objPersons is an instance of a Persons collection object:

```
'list the number of Person objects in the Collection
Wscript.Echo objPersons.Count
```

To get an object stored in a collection, reference the Items property. The Items property returns the *n*th item in the collection:

```
objPerson =objPersons.Item(0)    'returns the first item
```

Many collections will return an item based on a key value used to identify objects within the collection:

```
anyValue = objCollection.Item(strKey)
```

For example, in the case of the Persons collection, we can reference Person objects based on the social security number, since it would uniquely identify the object within the collection. This method of referencing depends on how the object was implemented; not all collections will support this.

```
objPerson = objPersons("123-456-789")
For intCounter = 0 To objPersons.Count - 1
    Wscript.Echo objPersons(intCounter).Name
Next
```

VBScript's special version of the For statement, For Each, can be used to iterate through a collection:

```
For Each objObject In objObjects Next
'list the name for all of the Person objects in the collection.
For Each objPerson In objPersons
    Wscript.Echo objPerson.Name
Next
```

Note that most collections start with a zero offset, so the first item is referenced as zero (0), the second is referenced as one (1), and so on.

Error Handling

When you are executing a script, there is always the potential of running into errors. Errors may be due to bugs in your script as well as bugs in external objects or programs you reference.

When an error occurs in WSH, the script will terminate execution and display the error message. This may not be desirable, especially in scripts where you want to continue executing even if certain errors occur.

In order to implement error handling, we need to be able to have a script continue processing. This is done using the On Error Resume Next statement. Any errors encountered after this statement in a script are ignored.

Errors can then be "trapped" by checking the Err object. The Err object returns a nonzero value if an error occurs. The Err object also exposes a Description property, which contains a description of the last error:

```
On Error Resume Next
intValue = 5
numDiv = intValue/0 'this will generate an error
If Err Then
    Wscript.Echo "Error# " & Err & " occurred. " _
        & "Description " & Err.Description
End If
```

Constants

When creating a script, you may want to store some values using symbolic names. These are called *constants*.

Constants are similar to variables, but you cannot modify a constant during the execution of the script. You can represent string and numeric values using constants.

It's often wise to define constant values at the start of your program, rather than repeatedly entering the same value when you're writing your script. This way, if you later need to change the value, you only need to change it in one place, rather than searching through the program for multiple instances of the value.

To create a constant, enter the Const statement followed by the constant name and an assigned value:

```
Const Pi = 3.14
Const MyFolder = "d:\Shared Documents\Milhouse"
Const CompanyName = "Acme Inc"
Const StartDate = #1/1/99#
```

Constants are referred to in the same way as other variables:

```
Wscript.Echo "Company is " & CompanyName
```

Object Model

WSH includes a number of objects that provide access to Windows system-related operations. Table 9-6 lists the main objects and the operations they perform.

Table 9-6. WSH objects and their functionality

Object	Functionality provided
Wscript	Create new objects, output data, and process command-line arguments
WSHShell	Registry, shortcut, and environment variable manipulation; ability to execute external executables
WSHNetwork	Network directory and printer resource enumeration and manipulation
FileSystem	Text file manipulation and file maintenance operations such as creating, deleting, and moving files

The main objects expose additional objects. For example, the FileSystem object exposes a Drives collection object. These objects and their uses are covered next.

The object reference presented in this chapter covers the most important features of the objects listed in Table 9-6, but is not a complete reference. For more information, see "Additional Resources," earlier in this chapter.

Conventions

The next section provides a reference to the core WSH objects, describing their methods and properties.

Like the rest of this book, the convention for the objects' methods is that any parameter surrounded by square brackets is optional. For example, in the syntax for the method PrintName:

```
PrintName strName, [strAddress]
```

the *strName* parameter is required, but the *strAddress* parameter is optional since it's surrounded with square brackets. Words in monospace are to be typed exactly as shown, but *italicized words* are to be replaced with your own values.

Wscript Object

The Wscript object is a built-in object. You do not have to create an instance of this object in your scripts; it is created automatically. The Wscript object provides the ability to create new objects, output basic info, and exit a script.

Table 9-7 lists a number of properties the Wscript object exposes.

Table 9-7. Wscript object properties

Full name	Name and path of executable
Interactive	Identifies if script is running in interactive (Wscript) or batch (Cscript) mode
Name	Name of the WSH (e.g., Windows Script Host)
Path	Path where WSH executables reside
ScriptFullName	Full name and path of script
ScriptName	Name of script
Version	Version of WSH

Echo Method

The Echo method outputs data to the screen. If you are running the script using *cscript.exe*, the information will be output to the command prompt window from which the script was run, while *wscript.exe* will output the data as a Windows message box. Its syntax is:

```
Wscript.Echo [anyArg1, anyArg2...anyArgX]
```

CreateObject Method

The CreateObject method creates a new instance of a specified COM object. Once the object has been successfully created, you can access any properties or call any methods the object exposes. Its syntax is:

```
Set objObject = Wscript.CreateObject(strObjectId)
```

The strObjectId parameter identifies which component to create. This is unique for each type of COM object. The values will be provided in the documentation for each object.

Arguments Collection

The Arguments collection contains the parameters passed to the script. This is useful for scripts that perform operations based on information specified in command-line parameters.

You can access a specific argument by specifying the parameter number as it appears on the command line. The argument count starts at 0.

The following example lists all parameters passed to the script:

```
Wscript.Echo Wscript.Arguments(0) 'output the first parameter
For Each arg in Wscript.Arguments 'output all parameters
    Wscript.Echo arg
Next
```

The following example sets the file attribute on a file specified in the command line to Hidden:

```
Dim objFileSystem, objFile
'check if parameter count is a single parameter.
'If not, show the command syntax
If Wscript.Arguments.Count<>1 Then
    Wscript.Echo " Syntax: HideFile FileName " & vbCrLf & _
            " Filename: is valid path to file you wish to hide"
Else
    'create FileSystem object
    Set objFileSystem = CreateObject("Scripting.FileSystemObject")
    On Error Resume Next
    'get the file specified in command line
    Set objFile = objFileSystem.GetFile(Wscript.Arguments(0))
    'check if error occured - file not found
    If Err Then
        Wscript.Echo "File:'" & Wscript.Arguments(0) & "' not found"
```

```
        Else
            objFile.Attributes = 2
        End If
    End IF
End IF
```

Quit

The Quit method forces the script to stop execution. Execution will terminate even if the script is in the middle of a loop or subroutine. Its syntax is:

```
Wscript.Quit([intExitValue])
```

The parameter intExitValue is the value returned to the calling program. This is useful, for example, if the script is being called from a batch file (see "if" in Chapter 6). Batch files can access the results using the ErrorLevel variable.

```
scriptname.vbs
If ErrorLevel 5 Goto skip
```

Shell Object

The WSH Shell object provides the ability to create Windows shortcuts, read environment variables, manipulate registry settings, and run external programs.

To create an instance of the WSH Shell object, pass the argument Wscript.Shell to the Wscript.CreateObject method:

```
Set objShell = Wscript.CreateObject("Wscript.Shell")
```

ExpandEnvironmentVariables Method

Environment variables are information stored by the Windows operating system. You can list the environment variables currently set by executing the DOS *Set* command from the command prompt. You can interpolate their values into your script using the ExpandEnvironmentVariables method of a Shell object. Its syntax is:

```
strValue = objShell.ExpandEnvironmentVariables(strString)
```

Any strings in the *strString* parameter that are enclosed with % symbols will be expanded using the corresponding environment variable value.

```
Set objShell = Wscript.CreateObject("Wscript.shell")
Wscript.Echo _
    objShell.ExpandEnvironmentStrings( _
    "Your temp directory is %TEMP%")
```

Run Method

The Run method executes an external program. This can be any Windows executable or command-line program. If you don't specify an explicit path to the application, the Run method will search the paths specified in the PATH environment variable. The following example executes Notepad:

```
Set objShell = Wscript.CreateObject("Wscript.shell")
objShell.Run ("Notepad.exe")
```

SpecialFolders Collection

The SpecialFolders collection returns the path to a specified system folder:

```
strPath = objShell.SpecialFolders(strFolderName)
```

The *strFolderName* parameter can be any one of the following values: Desktop, Favorites, Fonts, MyDocuments, NetHood, PrintHood, Programs, Recent, SendTo, StartMenu, Startup, and Templates.

```
Set objShell = Wscript.CreateObject("Wscript.shell")
strDesktop = objShell.SpecialFolders("Desktop")
```

Registry Routines

The Shell object provides Windows Registry access through the RegRead, RegWrite, and RegDelete methods.

When accessing a Registry key, you must specify the path. The path is built from the Registry hive name (the name of one of the major Registry branches described in Chapter 8), followed by the path to the key separated by backslash characters. Table 9-8 lists the hive names.

Table 9-8. Registry parameters

Short	Long
HKCU	HKEY_CURRENT_USER
HKLM	HKEY_LOCAL_MACHINE
HKCR	HKEY_CLASSES_ROOT
	HKEY_USERS
	HKEY_CURRENT_CONFIG
	HKEY_DYN_DATA

For example, the path to the Windows version number would be represented as HKLM\Software\Microsoft\Windows\CurrentVersion\VersionNumber.

One way to easily get the path for registry values is to use the RegEdit application to search for Registry information and copy the key path to the clipboard using Edit → Copy Key Name. The Registry routines do not provide the ability to list any values under a particular key, so you need to know the path to any Registry values you wish to reference.

RegRead

RegRead reads the registry value from the specified Registry path:

```
strVal = objShell.RegRead(strKeyPath)
```

strKeyPath is a path to the Registry value you wish to read.

```
Set objShell = CreateObject("Wscript.Shell")
Wscript.Echo "Your Windows Version Number is " _
    & objshell.RegRead _
( "HKLM\Software\Microsoft\Windows\CurrentVersion\VersionNumber")
```

RegWrite

RegWrite writes a value to a specified key value or creates a new key:

```
objShell.RegWrite strPath, anyValue [,strType]
```

The *strPath* parameter is the path to the key to write. If the Registry path ends with a backslash, then RegWrite attempts to create a new key.

Table 9-9 lists the possible values for the optional *strType* parameter.

Table 9-9. Registry data types

Registry type value	Description
REG_SZ	String value. This is the default value.
REG_EXPAND_SZ	Expandable string.
REG_DWORD	Integer value.

```
'change the default document directory for Word 97
Set objShell = CreateObject("Wscript.Shell")
objShell.RegWrite _
    "HKCU\Software\Microsoft\Office\8.0\Word\Options\Doc-Path" _
    , "H:\Data\Word"
'create new registry key
objShell.RegWrite _
    "HKCU\Software\Microsoft\Office\8.0\Word\Options\NewPath\" _
    , ""
```

RegWrite will create a Registry path if it does not already exist.

RegDelete

RegDelete deletes an existing Registry key or value:

```
objShell.RegDelete strPath
```

The *strPath* parameter is the path to the value or key you want to delete. If the Registry path ends with a backslash, then RegDelete will attempt to delete the specified key; otherwise, it assumes it's a value.

If you specify a key to delete, RegDelete will delete all child values and keys, so exercise caution.

```
'delete the Newpath key. This will delete the NewPath key and all
'values and keys under it
objShell.Delete _
    "HKCU\Software\Microsoft\Office\8.0\Word\Options\NewPath\"
    , ""
```

Shortcuts

The Shell object provides the ability to create shortcuts via the CreateShortCut method. This method returns a WshShortCut object:

```
objShortCut = objShell.CreateShortcut(strPath)
```

Once you have created a Shortcut object, you can set properties for it. This object provides the same settings that are available when creating shortcuts using Explorer.

Table 9-10 lists the properties that can be set for the shortcut.

Table 9-10. Shortcut object properties

Parameter	Type	Description
Description	String	Shortcut description.
Hotkey	String	Hotkey used to execute shortcut. The easiest way to get a hotkey is to use Windows Explorer to create a shortcut and copy the hotkey settings used by the shortcut.
IconLocation	String	Path to file containing icons to use in shortcut.
TargetPath	String	Path of the application or document to execute.
WindowStyle	Integer	Type of Window to display application in. 1 for normal, 2 for minimized, and 3 for maximized Window.
WorkingDirectory	String	Default working directory for application to use.

Once you have set the parameters for the shortcut, invoke the Save method to save and update the shortcut.

```
'create a shortcut on desktop linked to hello script
Set objShell = CreateObject("Wscript.Shell")
strDesktop = objShell.SpecialFolders("Desktop")   'get path to desktop
Set objShortcut = objShell.CreateShortcut(strDesktop & "\nlink.lnk")
objShortcut.TargetPath = "D:\heh.vbs"  'script to execute
objShortcut.Save    'save and update shortcut
```

Popup

The Popup method displays an interactive Windows popup message and returns a value depending on which button was selected (see Table 9-11):

```
intButton = object.Popup(strMessage, [numSecondsToWait], _
    [strTitle], [intType])
```

Table 9-11. Popup parameters

Parameter	Description
strMessage	Message to display.
numSecondsTo-Wait	Optional parameter. If specified, popup waits indicated number of seconds and then closes.
strTitle	Optional title for popup window.
intType	Optional numeric value that decides the number of buttons and icons to show. This is determined by combining a value from Table 9-12 and Table 9-13. For example, the value of 65 displays an OK button and the Information icon.

Popup returns an integer value depending on which button was selected. Tables 9-12, 9-13, and 9-14 list the button selection values, the icon types, and the return values.

```
'display a popup with yes/no buttons and question mark icon
Set objShell = CreateObject("Wscript.Shell")
intValue = objShell.Popup("Do you wish to continue?", , , 36
'test if the Yes button was selected
If intValue = 6 Then
    'do something
End I
```

Table 9-12. Button selection values

Value	Buttons shown
0	OK
1	OK and Cancel
2	Abort, Retry, and Ignore
3	Yes, No, and Cancel
4	Yes and No
5	Retry and Cancel

Table 9-13. Icon types

Value	Icon to show
16	Stop Mark
32	Question Mark
48	Exclamation Mark
64	Information

Table 9-14. Popup return values

Value	Description
1	OK button
2	Cancel button
3	Abort button
4	Retry button
5	Ignore button
6	Yes button
7	No button

Network Object

The Wscript Network object provides access to network resources and information. The ID for the object is Wscript.Network.

To create an instance of the Wscript Network object, pass the argument Wscript. Network to the Wscript.CreateObject method:

```
Set objNetwork = Wscript.CreateObject("Wscript.Network")
```

Table 9-15 lists the Network object properties

Table 9-15. Network object properties

Property	Description
ComputerName	Name of computer
UserName	Name of user logged into the machine
UserDomain	Name of domain user is currently logged into

The following example displays the name of the user logged into the machine:

```
Set objNetwork = CreateObject("Wscript.Network")
Wscript.Echo "You are logged on as " & objNetwork.UserName
```

EnumNetworkDrives

EnumNetworkDrives returns a collection of the currently connected network drives. The collection that is returned is a special WSH collection; it doesn't operate the same way as other object collections.

For each connected drive, the collection contains an item for the drive letter and another item for the connected share name. If you have three connected network drives (*K:*, *S:*, and *Y:*), the collection contains six elements, the first element being the *K:* drive, the second being the share to which *K:* is connected, and so on.

```
Set objNetwork = Wscript.CreateObject("Wscript.Network")
Set objShares = objNetwork.EnumNetworkDrives()
Wscript.Echo "Drive " & objShares(0) & " is connected to " & objShares(1)
```

The following example returns the next available network drive. If all drives are connected, it returns a blank string. It assumes your network drives start at *F:*.

```
Function ReturnNextDrive()
Dim nF, objNetwork, objShares, intNextDrive

Set objNetwork = Wscript.CreateObject("Wscript.Network")
Set objShares = objNetwork.EnumNetworkDrives()

intNextDrive = 0
For nF = 0 To objShares.Count - 1 Step 2
   If intNextDrive <> Asc(objShares(nF)) - 70 Then
      ReturnNextDrive = Chr(intNextDrive + 70) & ":"
      Exit Function
   End If
   intNextDrive = intNextDrive + 1
Next

ReturnNextDrive = ""
End Function
```

MapNetworkDrive

The MapNetworkDrive method connects a drive to a network share:

```
objNetwork.MapNetworkDrive strDrive, strRemoteShare, _
    [bUpdateProfile], [strUser], [strPassword]
```

Table 9-16 lists the parameters for the MapNetworkDrive method.

Table 9-16. MapNetworkDrive parameters

Parameter	Description
strDrive	The local drive letter to connect the network share to.
strRemoteShare	Name of remote share using UNC format; e.g., \\server\sharename.
bUpdateProfile	Optional Boolean parameter that indicates if drive connection is remembered for next session.
strUser	Optional username to use when connecting to remote share.
StrPassword	Optional password to use when connecting to remote share. This is used with the strUser parameter.

If you attempt to connect to a drive that is already connected to a share, an error will occur. Therefore, the On Error Resume Next statement is required beforehand to ensure the script is completed.

Usually when users log on, they are connected to their home share. This is usually identified by their network user ID. The following example connects the *H:* drive to the user's home share:

```
Set objNetwork = Wscript.CreateObject("Wscript.Network")
objWshNetwork.MapNetworkDrive "H:", _
        "\\THOR\" & objWSHNetwork.UserName & "$" , True
```

RemoveNetworkDrive

The RemoveNetworkDrive method disconnects a specified network share:

```
objNetwork.RemoveNetworkDrive strName, [bForceDisconnect], _
    [bUpdateProfile]
```

The RemoveNetworkDrive method has two optional parameters, the first being a Boolean ForceDisconnect flag. If set to True, it will forcefully disconnect the drive, even if it is currently in use. The second parameter specifies whether the user's profile is to be updated.

If there is a possibility of a drive being mapped to another network connection and you wish to connect it to a different network share, first delete the existing connection using the RemoveNetworkDrive method.

The following (forcefully) removes the *T:* drive connection:

```
objWshNetwork.RemoveNetworkDrive "T:", True, True
objWshNetwork.MapNetworkDrive "P:", _
        "\\THOR\PublicArea", True
```

Network Printer-Related Functions

WSH provides access to connected network printers in a similar fashion to network drives. You can enumerate (list), add, and remove network printer connections. The network printers are connected to a specified printer port, such as LPT1.

 These connected printers are not the same as printers added using Control Panel settings, so they are not accessible to Windows applications and are therefore of limited use. The SetDefaultPrinter method uses the Control Panel printer settings. Future versions of WSH will support manipulation of Windows printers.

EnumPrinterConnections

The EnumPrinterConnections method returns a special WSH collection with a format similar to the one described for the EnumNetworkDrives method. It lists the printer port and connected network printer information.

```
Set objNetwork = CreateObject("Wscript.Network")
Set objPrinters = objNetwork.EnumPrinterConnections()
'loop through and display all connected printers
For nF = 0 To objPrinters.Count - 1 Step 2
    Debug.Print objPrinters(nF) & _
            " is connected to " & objPrinters(nF + 1)
Next
```

AddPrinterConnection

The AddPrinterConnection method connects a port to a specified shared network printer.

```
objNetwork.AddPrinterConnection(strPrinterPort, strRemoteName, _
        [bUpdateProfile], [bUserName], [bPassword])
```

Table 9-17 lists the parameters for the AddPrinterConnection method.

Table 9-17. AddPrinterConnection parameters

Parameter	Description
strPrinterPort	Local drive letter to connect the network share to; e.g., LPT1:.
strRemoteName	Name of remote shared printer in UNC format; e.g., \\server\printername.
bUpdateProfile	Optional Boolean parameter that indicates if printer connection is remembered in future sessions.
strUser	Optional username to use when connecting to remote printer.
strPassword	Optional password to use when connecting to remote printer. This is used with the strUser parameter.

For example:

```
Set objNetwork = CreateObject("Wscript.Network")
objNetwork.AddPrinterConnection "LPT2", "\\training_06\laserjet"
```

SetDefaultPrinter

The `SetDefaultPrinter` method sets the default Windows printer. This method uses the printers specified under the Printers icon under Control Panel, not the printers connected using the `AddPrinterConnection` method. Its syntax is:

```
objNetwork.SetDefaultPrinter(strPrinterPort)
```

The `strPrinterPort` parameter specifies the UNC path of the printer you wish to make the default printer. This printer must be defined under Control Panel → Printers.

```
objNetwork.SetDefaultPrinter "\\thor\laserjet"
```

RemovePrinterConnection

The `RemovePrinterConnection` method disconnects connected network printers:

```
objNetwork.RemovePrinterConnection strName, [bForceDisconnect],
    [bUpdateProfile]
```

The `RemovePrinterConnection` method has two optional parameters, the first being a Boolean `bForceDisconnect` flag. If set to True, it will attempt to forcefully disconnect the printer. The `bUpdateProfile` parameter specifies whether the user's profile is to be updated.

FileSystem Object

The default WSH scripting languages (VBScript and JScript) do not have any native file manipulation capabilities. This functionality is provided by the COM object `FileSystem`.

The `FileSystem` object (FSO) exposes a number of separate objects that provide the ability to perform file-related operations. Table 9-18 lists the objects exposed by the `FileSystem` component

Table 9-18. FileSystem objects

Object	Description
Folders	A collection that contains a list of folders for a specified folder
Folder	Exposes folder information such as size, attributes, and date information and methods to move, delete, and copy
Files	A collection that contains a list of files for a specified folder
File	Exposes file information such as size, attributes, and date information and methods to move, delete, and copy
Drives	Collection object that contains a list of available drives on the local machine
Drive	Exposes drive information, such as size and type
TextStream	Provides text file manipulation

The FSO exposes methods and properties that perform file manipulation operations. Before you can reference any of the objects listed in Table 9-18, you must create an instance of the FSO object:

```
'create an instance of an FSO object
Set objFSO = CreateObject("Scripting.FileSystemObject")
```

The FSO object exposes a number of file manipulation methods and properties. The following commands are a few of the most useful FSO-related methods and properties. See "Additional Resources," earlier in this chapter, for additional documentation. The book, *Windows Me Annoyances* (O'Reilly) provides a great deal of ready-to-use subroutines that perform all sorts of FSO-based file operations.

GetTempName Method

The GetTempName method generates a temporary filename.

```
strTempName = objFSO.GetTempName()
```

FileExists/FolderExists Methods

The FileExists/FolderExists methods return True if the specified path exists, False otherwise.

Drives Collection

The Drives collection contains a list of drives available to the local machine. This includes any drive visible to the system, including fixed hard, removable floppy, CD-ROM, or network drives. This collection is returned from the FSO object. The information for each object in the collection is exposed as a Drive object.

```
Set objFSO = CreateObject("Scripting.FileSystemObject")
Set objDrive = objFSO.Drives(0) 'get the first drive in collection
Set objDrive = objFSO.Drives("C") 'get a reference to the C drive
```

Table 9-19 contains Drive object properties. All properties are read-only unless otherwise specified.

Table 9-19. Drive object properties

Property	Description
AvailableSpace, FreeSpace	Free space on drive in bytes. These properties return the same operation.
DriveLetter	Drive letter associated with drive.
DriveType	Type of drive: Unknown=0, Removable=1, Fixed=2, Remote=3, CD-ROM=4, RamDisk=5.
FileSystem	Filesystem drive utilities, e.g., FAT, NTFS, CDFS, etc.
IsReady	Returns True if drive is ready, False otherwise. Useful for removable media such as floppy and CD-ROM drives to determine if there is media in the drive.
RootFolder	Returns root folder for drive.
SerialNumber	Serial number uniquely identifying the drive.
ShareName	Displays share name if network drive.
TotalSize	Total size in bytes.
VolumeName	Name of drive. This is read/write, so you can set a drive's volume name.

The following example displays the percentage of space used by each drive:

```
Dim objFSO, objDrive
Set objFSO = Wscript.CreateObject("Scripting.FileSystemObject")
For Each objDrive In objFSO.Drives
    'check if drive is ready
    If objDrive.IsReady() Then
        Wscript.Echo objDrive.Name & " is " & _
        Fix(((objDrive.TotalSize - objDrive.FreeSpace) _
            / objDrive.TotalSize) * 100) & "% used"
    Else
        Wscript.Echo objDrive.Name & " is not ready"
    End If
Next
```

Folders Collection

The Folders collection contains list of a Folder objects for a specified folder. To get a reference to a Folders collection, use the FSO object's GetFolder method to return a Folder object, and then use the folder's SubFolders property to return the Folders collection. Its syntax is:

```
Set objFolder = objFSO.GetFolder(strFolderPath)
```

The *strFolderPath* parameter identifies which folder to reference.

Table 9-20 lists Folder object properties. Properties are read-only unless otherwise indicated.

Table 9-20. Folder properties

Attributes	Attributes
Attributes	Directory attributes. Numeric value is comprised of one or more directory attribute types. The following attribute values are added together to form the directory Attributes property and Read/Write property: Normal=0, Hidden=2, System=4, Volume=8, Archive=32, Compressed=2048.
DateCreated/ DateLastAccessed/ DateLastModifed	Returns file created, last accessed, and modified date for file.
Drive	Drive object folder resides on.
Files	Files collection containing all files in folder.
IsRootFolder	True if Folder object is folder directory root.
Name	Filename.
ParentFolder	Folder object with folder's parent folder.
Path	Full path to folder.
ShortName/ShortPath	DOS short name for folder and path, respectively.
Size	Size of all files and folders in folder, including all subfolders.
Type	Folder type, e.g., File or Subscription folder.

For example:

```
Dim objFSO, objFolder, objSub
Set objFSO = Wscript.CreateObject("Scripting.FileSystemObject")
Set objFolder = objFSO.GetFolder("C:\Windows")
For each objSub In objFolder.SubFolders( )
    Wscript.Echo "Folder " & objSub.Name & " is " & objSub.Size _
    & " bytes"
Next
```

The folder object provides methods to copy, move, and delete a Folder object.

Copy/Move Methods

The Copy and Move methods copy or move the contents of the Folder object, including all subfolders and their contents, to a specified destination folder:

```
objFolder.Copy strDestination, [bOverWriteFiles]
objFolder.Move strDestination
```

Both methods require a destination folder parameter. The Copy method has an optional bOverWriteFiles parameter. This parameter is set to True by default, but if it is set to False, the copy operation will generate an error if a file already exists in the destination folder.

```
Dim objFSO, objFolder, objSub
Set objFSO = Wscript.CreateObject("Scripting.FileSystemObject")
Set objFolder = objFSO.GetFolder("C:\LocalData")
'copy items from folder to network folder
objFolder.Copy("H:\Data")
```

Delete Method

The Delete method deletes the folder object and its contents. The folder does not have to be empty, and any subfolders and their contents will be deleted when the method is invoked:

```
objFolder.Delete [bForce]
```

The Delete method has an optional *bForce* parameter that will attempt to delete the folder and its contents if there is a situation such as a locked file that prevents it from being deleted normally. However, there are situations even when using the *bForce* parameter where the folder and its contents will not be deleted.

Files Collection

The Files collection contains a list of File objects for a specified folder:

```
Set objFSO = Wscript.CreateObject("Scripting.FileSystemObject")
Set objFolder = objFSO.GetFolder("C:\Windows")
Set objFiles = objFolder.Files
```

Once you have a Files collection, you can enumerate the individual File objects in the collection. Table 9-21 lists File object properties. The properties are read-only unless otherwise indicated.

Table 9-21. File object properties

Attributes	Description
Attributes	File attributes. Numeric value comprised of one or more file attribute types. The attribute values are added together to form the directory Attributes property and the Read/Write property: Normal=0, Hidden=2, System=4, Volume=8, Archive=32, Compressed=2048.
DateCreated/ DateLastAccessed/ DateLastModifed	Returns file created, last accessed, and modified date for file.
Drive	Drive object file resides on.
Name	Filename.
ParentFolder	Folder object containing file's parent folder .
Path	Full path to file.
ShortName/ShortPath	DOS short name for folder and path, respectively.
Size	Size of all files and folders in folder, including all subfolders.
Type	File type description, e.g., Text Document.

The File object for an individual file can be referenced using the FSO object's GetFile method:

```
For each objFile In objFolder.Files( )
    Wscript.Echo objFile.Name & " is " & objFile.Size & " bytes"
Next
```

Copy/Move Methods

The Copy and Move methods copy or move the file to a specified destination folder. (This is the same method for copying or moving folders; it is described here a second time in the context of manipulating files instead of folders.) These methods use the following syntax:

```
objFolder.Copy strDestination, [bOverWriteFiles]
objFolder.Move strDestination
```

Both methods require a destination folder parameter. The Copy method has an optional *bOverWriteFiles* parameter. This parameter is set to True by default, but if it is set to False, the copy operation will generate an error if a file already exists in the destination folder.

```
Dim objFSO, objFolder, objSub
Set objFSO = Wscript.CreateObject("Scripting.FileSystemObject")
Set objFolder = objFSO.GetFolder("C:\LocalData")
'copy items from folder to network folder
objFolder.Copy("H:\Data")
```

Delete Method

The Delete method deletes a file:

```
objFolder.Delete [bForce]
```

The Delete method has an optional *bForce* parameter that will attempt to force a delete of the file if there is a situation such as a locked file that prevents it from being deleted normally. Using *bForce* does not guarantee that a locked file will be deleted.

TextStream Object

The TextStream object provides powerful text file creation and manipulation abilities. To create a new TextStream object, invoke the FSO object's CreateTextFile method:

```
Set objText = objFSO.CreateTextFile(strFileName, _
    [bOverwrite],[bUnicode])
```

The *strFileName* parameter identifies the new filename. The optional *bOverwrite* parameter will overwrite any existing files with same name if True. The default value is True. The optional *bUnicode* parameter will create a Unicode file if True. The default is False.

The following example creates a new text file:

```
Set objFSO = Wscript.CreateObject("Scripting.FileSystemObject")
Set objTextFile = objFSO.CreateTextFile("C:\Data\data.txt")
```

Once you have created a TextStream object, you are ready to write data to it. The Write or WriteLine method will write data to the file:

```
objTextStream.Write(strText)
objTextStream.WriteLine(strText)
```

The *strText* parameter is the text that will be written to the file. The difference between the Write and WriteLine methods is that the WriteLine method writes an end-of-line character at the end of the line.

Whenever you are done performing operations on a TextStream object, invoke the Close method. The Close method closes the object and flushes any updates to the file.

```
Dim objFSO, objTextFile

Set objFSO = CreateObject("Scripting.FileSystemObject")
Set objTextFile = objFSO.CreateTextFile("D:\data.txt")

objTextFile.WriteLine "Write a line with end of line character"
objTextFile.Write "Write string without new line character"

objTextFile.Close
```

To open an existing text file, invoke the FSO object's OpenTextFile method:

```
Set objText = objFSO.OpenTextFile(strFileName, intIOMode, bCreate,
intTrisState)
```

Table 9-22 lists the OpenTextFile method parameters.

Table 9-22. OpenTextFile parameters

Parameter	Description
strFileName	Filename to open.
intIOMode	Optional. Specifies whether file is to be opened for Reading=1 or Appending=2. Default is reading.
bCreate	Optional. If set to True, a new text file will be created if it is not found. Default is False.
TriState	Optional. If -2, then open using filesystem settings; if -1, then use Unicode; and if 0, use ASCII. Default is 0, ASCII file.

If you have opened the file for read access, you can read in parts or the whole file.

There are three methods for reading data. The ReadAll method returns the whole text file as a string. ReadLine reads the line up to the end-of-line character sequence. The Read method reads a specified number of characters.

```
strData = objTextFile.ReadLine( ) 'read a single line
strData = objTextFile.Read(10) 'read 10 characters
strData = objTextFile.ReadAll( ) 'read the whole file
```

If you are reading the file either character by character using the Read method or line by line using the ReadLine method, you need to be able to determine when you hit the end of the file.

The following example opens the *data.txt* file and lists the contents of it:

```
Set objFSO = CreateObject("Scripting.FileSystemObject")
Set objTextFile = objFSO.OpenTextFile("D:\data.txt")

Do While Not objTextFile.AtEndOfStream
    strData = strData & objTextFile.ReadLine & vbCrLf
Loop

objTextFile.Close
```

Object Browser

It is easy to be overwhelmed by the number of objects and what they do. It's equally overwhelming when you realize the number of objects that might be available to your machine without your being aware of it.

Microsoft Office 97, 2000, and XP provide a powerful programming environment based on the Visual Basic for Applications language (similar to VBScript). Within this environment, there is an object browser, which allows you to browse objects installed on your system and investigate the methods and properties associated with them. You do not actually have to write any code to take advantage of the Object Browser.

 If you aren't familiar with the Visual Basic Environment, the Object Browser can be a little intimidating. See *Learning Word Programming* or *Writing Excel Macros*, both by Steve Roman (O'Reilly), for an introduction.

From either Microsoft Word or Excel:

1. Select Tools → Macro → Visual Basic Editor. This will start the VBA environment.
2. Select Tools → References. The dialog box shown in Figure 9-2 will appear.

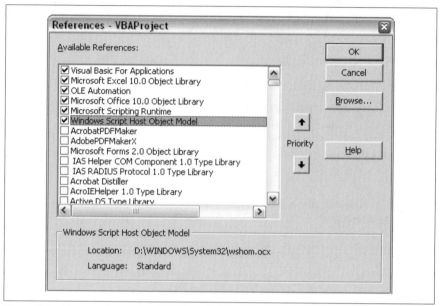

Figure 9-2. Object References dialog box

Select the library references you wish to use. The reference name for the WSH Wscript object is Microsoft Windows Script Host Object Model, and the File-System object is Microsoft Scripting Runtime.

Once you have selected the libraries you wish to reference, select the OK button.

Now press the F2 key. This will display the object browser window.

Select the object you wish to browse from the drop-down list in the upper left-hand corner. The Classes window on the left lists all objects related to the component, while the right window lists all methods and properties related to the selected object. Figure 9-3 shows the Object Browser viewing the FileSystem object.

Database Example

VBScript does not provide native database access. As with other functions provided in the WSH environment, this is implemented using a COM object. ActiveX Data Objects (ADO) is a COM object that provides database access.

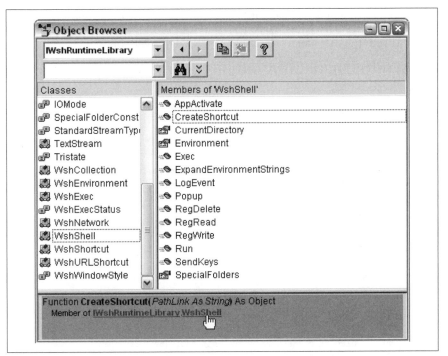

Figure 9-3. Object Browser

The following example uses the "Northwind" sample database that is shipped with Microsoft Access. This sample assumes that an ODBC entry called Northwind exists for the database.

```
Const adCmdText = 1
Dim objRst, objConn
Set objConn = CreateObject("ADODB.Connection")
objConn.Open "Northwind"
'execute the query against the provider
Set objRst = objConn.Execute("Select * From Customers",, adCmdText)

Do While Not objRst.Rst
    Wscript.Echo objRst("CompanyName")
Loop
objRst.Close
objConn.Close
```

Messaging

Messaging services (email) can be accessed using CDO (Collaborative Data Objects). This COM object contains a large and powerful selection of objects.

CDO is a powerful but complex object model. The web site, CDO Live, at *http:// www.cdolive.com*, is an excellent resource to get you started working with CDO.

The following example will log on to your default messaging profile and send a message. This assumes you are using an Exchange or Outlook client that has been set up to send Internet email. This will not work with Outlook Express.

```
Dim objSession, objMessage, WshShell, sPrf, objRecipient

Set WshShell = CreateObject("WScript.Shell")

'create a MAPI session
Set objSession = CreateObject("MAPI.Session")

'check if the OS string contains NT
'set the profile string. This will read your default setting
sPrf = "HKCU\Software\Microsoft\Windows Messaging Subsystem\Profiles"

'log on using the default profile name
objSession.Logon WshShell.RegRead(sPrf)

'create a new message, setting the subject to Hello There
Set objMessage = _
        objSession.Outbox.Messages.Add("Hello There")

objMessage.Text = "This is the body of the message"

'send to Joe Blow
Set objRecipient = objMessage.Recipients.Add("Joe Blow", _
        "SMTP:joeb@abc.com")
objRecipient.Resolve 'resolve the address

'send the message
objMessage.Send

objSession.Logoff
```

IV

Appendixes

A

Installing Windows XP

Some of you will be fortunate enough to never have to endure the installation of an operating system. After all, a large number of Windows XP users will obtain the OS preinstalled on new PCs. Others, however, may be confronted with one of the scenarios listed in this appendix.

Windows XP can be installed from within Windows XP, Windows 2000, Windows NT, Windows Me, and Windows 9x.* It can be installed from DOS, or even on a system with no operating system. The procedure is somewhat different in each of these scenarios, as are the programs that are used and the components of Windows that end up being installed. The following sections outline the steps required to install Windows XP in each of these scenarios. Refer also to Appendix B for additional issues that may complicate the process.

Note that if you're installing Windows XP on a hard disk that has data on it, you're strongly encouraged to back up your entire system before you proceed. Make sure you use backup software that you'll be able to run from within Windows XP; otherwise, your backup will be worthless. See Appendix B for more information on backup software.

Installation on a New (Clean) System

The Windows XP installation CD is bootable, which means that (assuming your PC supports bootable CDs) you can put it in the drive, turn on your computer, and the installation process will start automatically.

---

* If you have the upgrade version of Windows XP Home, you can install only from Windows 98, Windows 98 SE, or Windows Me. If you have the upgrade version of Windows XP Professional, you can install only from Windows 98, Windows 98 SE, Windows Me, Windows NT 4.0, Windows 2000 Professional, or Windows XP Home Edition.

To configure your computer to boot off a CD, you'll need to use your system's BIOS setup utility. When you first power on your machine, you'll see a text screen with a summary of your motherboard, processor, and installed memory. (If you see only a logo, try pressing the Esc or Tab keys.) Here, you typically press F2, Del, or some other key combination to "Enter Setup." (Refer to your PC's documentation for specifics.) Once you've entered the BIOS setup utility, go to the boot section, and change the "boot device priority" or "boot sequence" so that your CD drive appears before your hard disk. Exit the BIOS setup screen when you're finished.

If you have a SCSI-based CD drive, look in your SCSI controller's BIOS setup screen and enable support for bootable CDs. If your SCSI controller is built into your motherboard, you'll probably need to both specify your SCSI controller as a boot priority over your hard disk, and enable bootable CDs in your SCSI BIOS.

If you're unable to boot off the Windows XP CD, you'll need to use a bootable floppy, either one made from a previous version of Windows (see "Installation from DOS (or a Windows 9x/Me Boot Disk)" later), or one that comes with the full version of Windows XP.

After a lengthy initialization process, you'll finally be presented with several choices. The first screen instructs you to press Enter to set up Windows XP now, or press R to repair a Windows XP installation using the Recovery Console. The Recovery Console, covered later in this appendix, is an advanced diagnostic and repair tool. Unless you specifically need to use the Recovery Console, press Enter to continue (even if you need to repair Windows).

At this point, setup will look for an existing Windows XP installation. If found, you'll have the opportunity to repair it now, which is usually preferred over using the Recovery Console. The repair process essentially involves reinstalling Windows XP, and is what you'll want to do if you're unable to start Windows. If you don't need to repair Windows XP, press Esc to continue.

The next screen will allow you to choose a drive and partition on which to install Windows; in most cases, you'll have only a single drive and a single partition. Here, you'll have the option of installing onto an existing drive or making changes to your partition table. This effectively replaces the FDISK utility used when installing some earlier versions of Windows on a clean system. To partition your hard disk after you've installed Windows XP, use PartitionMagic (*http://www. powerquest.com*). It's important to note that if you delete a partition that has data on it, all of the data will be erased.

If you're installing on a clean system (with a new, empty hard disk), you'll want to create a new partition using all of the available space (or several partitions, as desired). In most cases, you'll want to choose the NTFS filesystem, which is more robust and secure than the now-obsolete FAT32 filesystem. NTFS also supports encryption, compression, and permissions. Use FAT32 only if you need to share data with a Windows Me/9x installation.

If you're installing on a hard disk with data on it, and you don't want to erase the data, simply select the desired partition (usually the first one, C:\). Note that if you've backed up your data, you have the option of deleting your partition, creating a new one, and installing fresh. Although this does require the additional work involved in restoring your data, it does result in a cleaner, usually faster, and more reliable installation.

The rest of the installation process should be fairly straightforward; if you run into a problem, see "Potential Problems During Setup," later in this appendix.

Upgrade from a Previous Version of Windows

The preferred way to upgrade Windows XP from a previous version is to install from within Windows. With Windows running, insert the Windows XP CD into your drive. If you have AutoPlay disabled, or Setup doesn't start automatically for some reason, open Windows Explorer, navigate to your CD drive, and double-click *setup.exe*. When Setup starts, you'll be given four choices, as shown in Figure A-1.

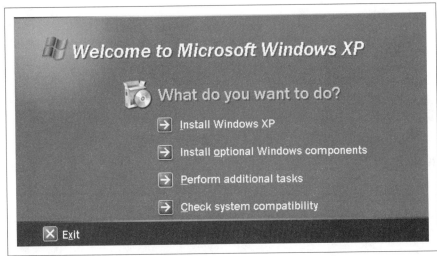

Figure A-1. Setup options for the Windows XP upgrade

Install Windows XP

> This opens the main Windows Setup program. When it starts, your first choice will be between "Upgrade (Recommended)" and "New Installation (Advanced)." Choose Upgrade only if you want to install Windows XP over your existing installation, replacing your current OS with Windows XP and migrating all your settings and applications in one step.

> On the other hand, you may wish to choose New Installation if you want to set up a dual-boot system (discussed later in this appendix), or if you want to install on another partition or on a clean hard disk (see "Installation on a New (Clean) System," earlier in this appendix).

Install optional Windows components

> This is the same as going to Control Panel → Add or Remove Programs → Add/Remove Windows Components. Place a checkmark next to components you want installed, or clear the checkmark next to components you want removed.

Perform additional tasks

This page contains links to several, mostly self-explanatory, tasks. Click "Set up Remote Desktop Connection" to install the Remote Desktop Connection software on another computer; see "Remote Desktop Connection" in Chapter 4 for details. Click "Set up a home or small office network" to run the Network Setup Wizard, also discussed in Chapter 4. Finally, click "Transfer files and settings" to run the Files and Settings Transfer Wizard, additionally discussed in Chapter 4.

Check system compatibility

This runs the Microsoft Windows Upgrade Advisor, which looks for potential problems, such as incompatible software and hardware. The Upgrade Advisor is also run automatically at Windows setup. When the Upgrade Advisor finds a potential incompatibility, it lists it in a report along with any available information.

The report contains two types of alerts: if an alert is marked with a red circle and an X, it's a critical problem that will prevent setup from completing. These items, typically incompatible software, must be dealt with before setup will continue. The other type of alert is marked with a yellow triangle that, while not requiring immediate attention, should be resolved soon. See Appendix B for additional issues.

The rest of the installation process should be fairly straightforward. If you run into a problem, see "Potential Problems During Setup," later in this appendix.

Installation from DOS (or a Windows 9x/Me Boot Disk)

DOS (Disk Operating System) is the now-obsolete, command-line based operating system upon which Windows 9x and Windows Me were based. If you need to install Windows XP on a new system, and you are unable to boot off the CD, you can optionally install from DOS. Start by creating a boot disk by going to Control Panel → Add/Remove Programs in Windows 95, Windows 98, or Windows Me. Then, insert the floppy in your A: drive, and power on your computer. If it's a Windows 98 or Windows Me floppy, it should contain all the necessary drivers for your CD drive; otherwise, you'll need to obtain DOS drivers from the manufacturer of your CD drive and install them according to the included instructions.

When you get to the DOS prompt (A:\>), change to your CD drive by typing D: or E: (depending on the letter with which the drive is installed), and then type \i386\ winnt.exe to start the DOS-based setup utility. The setup utility will copy the necessary boot files to your hard disk, reboot your computer, and run the same installer discussed in "Installation on a New (Clean) System," earlier in this appendix.

Setting Up a Dual-Boot System

Windows XP has built-in support for a dual-boot system. With a dual-boot (or multiboot) setup, you can install multiple operating systems side-by-side, and choose which one to use every time you start your computer.

Why would you want to do this? If you rely on some software or hardware that will not operate in Windows XP, you may wish to keep your old OS around until another solution is found. Or, you may wish to set up a dual-boot with Windows

XP if you're not certain if XP will meet your needs. That way, you won't have to commit your system to XP until you're sure it will do everything you need it to do.

The dual-boot feature (called the Boot Manager) is installed automatically when you install Windows XP. If, at the end of the installation, Windows XP is the only operating system on your computer, it will boot automatically without giving you a choice. Otherwise, you'll see a menu of installed operating systems, from which you can choose the OS for the current session.

So, if you're installing Windows XP on a system with another OS, such as Windows 9x/Me, Windows 2000/NT, Unix, Linux, FreeBSD, or even NeXT, and you don't replace it with Windows XP (instead, you choose a new installation in a different directory or partition), you'll get a dual-boot system without even trying.

The boot manager of the last operating system installed is the one that will be used. Some other operating systems, such as FreeBSD and Windows 2000, also have boot managers, and they can be installed at any time (before or after XP). If, however, you want to set up a dual-boot system with, say, Windows XP and Windows 98, you'll need to install Windows 98 first, as neither Windows 9x nor Windows Me have boot managers.

One word about the filesystem: Windows XP supports both the NTFS and FAT32 filesystems. If you need to set up a dual-boot machine with Windows 9x/Me and Windows XP, you'll need to use FAT32 on any drives that you want to access from the older Windows, as only Windows 2000, NT, and XP support NTFS.

Re-Installation over an Existing Windows XP Install

You may find yourself in a position in which you'll need to reinstall Windows XP, either to solve a configuration problem or to repair a damaged installation. The procedure you choose depends on the current state of your computer.

If you're able to start Windows, you'll definitely want to install from within Windows. See "Upgrade from a Previous Version of Windows," earlier in this appendix, for details.

Otherwise, you'll need to repair your current installation by installing from the bootable CD (see "Installation on a New (Clean) System," earlier in this appendix) or by using the Recovery Console (discussed later).

Potential Problems During Setup

Fully documenting all of the problems that could occur during the installation of Windows XP would require a book ten times the size of this one. Luckily, about 95 percnet of the problems you're likely to encounter can be covered by the following tips:

- The most common thing that will cause a failed installation of Windows XP is an out-of-date BIOS. Fortunately, nearly all motherboards made in the last decade have software-upgradable flash BIOSes. Contact the manufacturer of your system or motherboard for any BIOS updates they have available, but don't bother unless a BIOS upgrade is absolutely necessary. (A failed BIOS upgrade will make your motherboard unusable.)

- Next to an incompatible BIOS, the most common stumbling block to Windows XP setup is your video card (display adapter). If setup stops with an unintelligible error message, hangs at a blank screen, or reboots unexpectedly during setup, your video card may be at fault. If replacing the video card permits Windows XP to install, your video card should be discarded (no pun intended). Note that many video cards have upgradable flash BIOSes (like your motherboard), although I've never seen an instance where a BIOS upgrade can solve this type of incompatibility.

- Windows XP is a little more touchy about improper hardware configurations than previous versions of Windows. If, for example, your memory (RAM) is not all the same rated speed, is not the correct type for your motherboard, or is malfunctioning in some way, it will prevent Windows XP from installing or running. Other potential problems include insufficient processor cooling, incorrect SCSI termination, improper jumpers on your IDE devices, bad cables, and even an older power supply.

- Windows XP attempts to install drivers for all of the hardware on your computer. If Setup crashes at the same point each time (towards the end of the process), try removing all extraneous devices (unneeded drives, cards, and external peripherals) until setup is complete.

- See Appendix B for additional tips involving hardware and software that will need to be updated or removed before you install Windows XP.

The Windows Recovery Console

Among the growing pains that many users will experience when upgrading to Windows XP is the complete abandonment of DOS. Now, don't get me wrong—I'm as happy to see DOS disappear as anyone else, but DOS has always been the reliable and easy-to-use last resort for repairing a Windows 9x/Me system. In Windows XP, you can't boot into DOS because DOS isn't there. And if you're using the NTFS filesystem (recommended for most users), you won't be able to see your hard disk at all if you boot off a DOS diskette.

Enter the Windows XP Recovery Console, the command-line based troubleshooting and repair utility for Windows XP. Although it looks like DOS (and the Command Prompt in Windows XP; see Chapter 6), some of the familiar Command Prompt commands will not work, nor will you be able to start any DOS or Windows programs. Instead, a small set of commands is used to accomplish the following tasks:

- Copy, rename, delete, or replace operating system files.
- Enable or disable services or devices for the next time Windows is started.
- Repair the filesystem boot sector or the Master Boot Record (MBR).
- Create and format hard drive partitions.

There are two ways to start the Windows Recovery Console. If you start Windows XP setup by booting off the CD, as described at the beginning of this appendix, you'll be given an option to load the Recovery Console. Since it's use is rather limited, this option is probably suitable for most users.

The alternative is to install the Recovery Console on your hard disk. This option, which will add it to the Boot Manager menu (see "Setting Up a Dual-Boot System," earlier in this appendix), is useful if you find that you need the Recovery Console frequently or you're unable to boot off a CD. Go to Start → Run and type the following:

d:\i386\winnt32.exe /cmdcons

where *d:* is the drive letter of your CD drive.

Using either method, once you boot to the Recovery Console, you'll get the following message:

```
Windows NT(TM) Boot Console Command Interpreter.

WARNING:
This is a limited function command prompt intended only as a system recovery
utility for advanced users. Using this utility incorrectly can cause serious
system-wide problems that may require you to reinstall Windows to correct
them.

Type 'exit' to leave the command prompt and reboot the system.

1: C:\WINDOWS

Which Windows installation would you like to logon to (enter to abort)?
```

Your options may be different. Choose 1, or whatever number corresponds to the Windows installation you wish to repair, and log in using your Administrator account and password. Once you've logged in, you'll see a Command Prompt-style interface, with which the following commands can be used. Note that although similar to their Command Prompt counterparts, the commands listed here are typically more limited, so not all parameters documented elsewhere in this book will be applicable in the Recovery Console.

attrib [+r|-r] [+a|-a] [+s|-s] [+h|-h] [*filename*]
> Changes the attributes of a file or directory; see "Attrib" in Chapter 4. The /s and /d parameters documented in Chapter 4 are not supported here.

batch *filename [outputfile]*
> Runs a batch file (see "MS-DOS Batch Files" in Chapter 6), where *filename* is the name of the batch file to run, and *outputfile* is the name of an optional file into which the output from the job is stored. Note that you can't execute batch files simply by typing the filename, as you can in the true Command Prompt.

bootcfg /*command*
> Starts the Boot Manager configuration file (*boot.ini*) configuration and recovery. *command* can be any of the following:

add
> Add a Windows installation as a new entry.

copy
> Create a backup of the *boot.ini* configuration file.

default
> Set the default boot entry.

disableredirect
> Disable redirection instigated by redirect.

list
> Display the entries currently specified in *boot.ini*.

rebuild
> List all of the Windows installations, and rebuild the boot menu by selectively adding entries. Note: it is recommended that you use bootcfg/copy to backup *boot.ini* before using rebuild.

redirect [*port baudrate* | useBiosSettings]
> Enable redirection of the boot loader output to the specified serial port, using the specified baudrate. Alternately, specify bootcfg /redirect useBiosSettings to use the default COM port settings in the system bios.

scan
> Scan your hard disk for all Windows installations and display a list of the results.

cd (or chdir) [*directory*]
> Displays the name of the current directory or changes the current directory; see "cd or chdir" in Chapter 6.

chkdsk [/p] [/r]
> Checks a disk and displays a status report; see "Chkdsk" in Chapter 4.

cls
> Clears the screen; see "cls" in Chapter 6.

copy *source* [*destination*]
> Copies a single file to another location; see "copy" in Chapter 6.

del (or delete) *filename*
> Deletes one or more files; see "del or erase" in Chapter 6.

dir *filename*
> Displays a list of files and subdirectories in a directory; see "dir" in Chapter 6.

disable [*service* | *device_driver*]
> Disables a system service or a device driver. See enable for details.

diskpart [/add | /delete] [*device* | *drive* | *partition*] [*size*]
> Creates and deletes partitions on your hard drives.* Omits all parameters to use the interactive mode. Here's an example of creating a partition by specifying *device* (*size* is the size of the partition to create, in megabytes):

> ```
> diskpart /add \Device\HardDisk0 1500
> ```

> Uses the map command to display all *device*s. Here's an example of deleting a partition, either by specifying *drive* or by specifying *partition* (respectively):

> ```
> diskpart /delete g:
> diskpart /delete \Device\HardDisk0\Partition3
> ```

---

* This takes the place of FDISK, found in some earlier versions of Windows.

---

enable *service* | *device_driver* [*startup_type*]

Starts or enables a system service or a device driver. Available services and device drivers are listed with the listsvc command. *startup_type* can be SERVICE_BOOT_START, SERVICE_SYSTEM_START, SERVICE_AUTO_START, or SERVICE_DEMAND_START.

exit

Exits the Recovery Console and restarts your computer.

expand *source* [/f:*filename*] [*destination*] [/d] [/y]

Extracts a file from a compressed file; see "File Expansion Utility" in Chapter 4.

fixboot [*drive*]

Writes a new partition boot sector onto the specified partition, in which *drive* is the drive letter. Omit *drive* to use the current partition. Use this command if the partition boot sector has been damaged.

fixmbr [*device*]

Repairs the master boot record of the specified disk. Use the map command to display the entries for *device*. Omit *device* to use the default boot device, upon which your primary operating system is installed. Use this if the boot record has been damaged, typically by a virus or a failed installation of another operating system.

format [*drive*:] [/q] [/fs:*filesystem*]

Formats a disk; see "Format" in Chapter 4.

help

Displays a list of the commands you can use in the Recovery Console.

listsvc

Lists the services and drivers available on the computer, for use with enable and disable.

logon

Logs on to a Windows installation. Note that only an administrator can use the Recovery Console. Use logon to log onto a different Windows installation without having to reboot and re-enter the Recovery Console.

map

Displays the drive letter mappings, for use with several other commands listed here.

md (or mkdir) *directory*

Creates a directory; see "md or mkdir" in Chapter 6.

more *filename*

Displays a text file (similar to type) one page at a time; see "more" in Chapter 6.

net use [*share_path* [/user:*user*] *password*] | [*drive*:] [/d]

Connects an unused drive letter, *drive*, to a shared network folder, *share_path*. See "Net" in Chapter 4 and "Mapping drives" in Chapter 7.

`ren` (or `rename`) *filename1 filename2*

Renames a single file (wildcards * and ? are not supported here); see "ren or rename" in Chapter 6.

`rd` (or `rmdir`) *directory*

Deletes a directory; see "rd or rmdir" in Chapter 6.

`set` [*variable*=[*string*]]

Displays and sets environment variables. Although it works much like the `set` command discussed in Chapter 6, it allows you to display or modify only these four environment variables (the default for all four is False):

> AllowWildCards = True | False

Turn this on to allow wildcards in commands that support them, such as `del` and `copy`.

> AllowAllPaths = True | False

Turn this on to permit access to all directories, not just the Windows directory.

> AllowRemovableMedia = True | False

Turn this on to permit access to removable drives, such as CDs and floppies.

> NoCopyPrompt = True | False

Turn this on to disable the copy overwrite prompt.

`systemroot`

Changes the current directory (like *cd*) to the "systemroot" directory, typically *c:\windows*, of the operating system to which you are currently logged on.

`type` *filename*

Displays a text file (similar to `more`); see "type" in Chapter 6.

B

Migrating to Windows XP

For those of you who have moved to Windows XP from an earlier version of Windows, or are planning to do so, there are several migration issues that warrant attention, both before and after the transition is made.

Before Upgrading to Windows XP

As with the move to any new operating system, there are some software and hardware components that either aren't compatible with the new version, or must be updated to work with the new version. In the case of Windows XP, any versions of the following products not specifically designed to work with Windows XP must be updated or removed:

- Antivirus software and disk utility software. Examples include Norton Utilities, Norton SystemWorks, and Norton Antivirus.

- Tape backup software. Examples include Veritas Backup (all versions) and Seagate Backup Exec. Note that if you back up your system before you upgrade to Windows XP, make sure you'll be able to read your backup media *from within* Windows XP as well.

- CD burner software not designed specifically for Windows XP may interfere with the built-in CD burner features in Windows XP, or may stop functioning because of said features. Examples include Roxio Easy CD Creator (Versions 5.0 and earlier) and Adaptec DirectCD.

- Any software that works with settings specific to any single version of Windows, such as Microsoft TweakUI (Versions 1.33 and earlier). See Appendix D for details.

- Games, especially the more graphic-intensive and 3D-accelerated ones, frequently have problems with newer versions of Windows, particularly those based on Windows NT (such as Windows 2000, and, yes, Windows XP). You'll need to contact the manufacturers of each game for any patches, updates, or special settings required for their games to run on Windows XP.

- Any software that requires you to boot directly into DOS will not function on a Windows XP system, as DOS is no longer part of the operating system. Furthermore, many older DOS programs (including games) may not function from within Windows XP. If you rely on such software, you may need to set up a dual-boot system (discussed in Appendix A).

- Drivers and accompanying software for any of the less-common peripherals, such as webcams, TV and radio cards, video capture devices, audio cards, flash memory readers, scanners, input devices, synchronization cradles for handheld computers, oddball printers, CD changers, DVD decoders, SCSI cards, and older network hardware and software.

While this list is far from complete, it should give you an idea of the *types* of products that may cause problems with Windows XP (or any new operating system, for that matter). If you haven't yet upgraded to Windows XP, it's best to check with the manufacturers of each and every card, drive, printer, input device, and other peripheral you use to make sure they support your devices under Windows XP.

Another option is to run the Microsoft Windows Upgrade Advisor, described in Appendix A. This scans your system and compares it with a list of devices and software known to cause problems with Windows XP. While it's far from complete as well, it will certainly warn you of any incompatibilities of which Microsoft is aware.

The Microsoft Windows Upgrade Advisor is available on the Windows XP CD (click "Check system compatibility" in the main Setup screen), or from Microsoft's web site (*http://www.microsoft.com/windowsxp/pro/howtobuy/upgrading/*).

After Upgrading to Windows XP

Assuming you've taken care of the various incompatibilities mentioned in the first section of this appendix, two main migration issues remain: making Windows XP look and feel more like previous versions, and finding the features that have been moved (or removed) from previous versions.

Visual style of windows and dialog controls
Make Windows XP look more like previous versions of Windows by going to Control Panel → [Appearance and Themes] → Display → Appearance tab, and choose "Windows Classic style" from the "Windows and buttons" list.

Visual style of Start menu
To revert to the simpler single-column Start menu found in earlier versions of Windows, go to Control Panel → [Appearance and Themes] → Taskbar and Start Menu → Start Menu tab, and select the "Start menu" option.

Dial-up networking
Dial-up connections are now located alongside standard network connections in the Network Connections window.

Network Neighborhood
This is now called "My Network Places."

My Computer icon on the Desktop
By default, the My Computer icon isn't shown on the Windows XP Desktop, but it's there if you need it. Go to Control Panel → [Appearance and Themes] → Folder Options → View tab, and turn on the "Show Control Panel in My Computer" option.

Control Panel in My Computer
By default, Control Panel no longer appears in the My Computer window, but it's available in the Start menu. Confusingly, it still appears under the My Computer branch in Windows Explorer. Go to Control Panel → [Appearance and Themes] → Folder Options → View tab, and turn on the "Show Control Panel in My Computer" option.

Behavior of single-folder windows
When you click a folder icon, a new folder window may appear, or the contents of the current window may be replaced with the contents of the new folder (unless the folder icon was on the Desktop). All versions of Windows, from Windows 95 to Windows XP, allow you to configure this setting, but different releases of Windows have had different defaults. To change this setting to your liking, go to Control Panel → [Appearance and Themes] → Folder Options → General tab, and make a choice in the "Browse folders" section.

Animation and other eye candy
The animation and other eye candy used with windows, menus, lists, and even your mouse cursor is more prevalent in Windows XP than any previous version of Windows. Curbing this behavior not only simplifies the interface, but can improve the performance of your system as well. These settings are located in two places. Go to Control Panel → [Appearance and Themes] → Display → Appearance tab → Effects, or go to Control Panel → [Performance and Maintenance] → System → Advanced tab, and click Settings in the Performance section.

Categories in Control Panel
The categories in Control Panel, which are somewhat superfluous, can be removed by opening the Control Panel window (not the Control Panel menu in the Start menu, nor the Control Panel folder in Windows Explorer, however) and clicking "Switch to Classic View" in the Common Tasks pane. If Control Panel appears as a menu, simply right-click the Control Panel item and select Open. If you don't have a Common Tasks pane, see the next topic.

Common Tasks pane in folder windows
The Common Tasks pane shows links to additional programs and features, but can be removed if you prefer the simpler, cleaner folders found in earlier versions of Windows. Go to Control Panel → [Appearance and Themes] → Folder Options → General tab, and click "Use Windows classic folders."

File type associations
Whenever you upgrade to a new version of Windows, the Windows setup program will claim a bunch of different file type associations without asking. For example, your default applications for *.html* files (web pages), *.jpg* images, and *.zip* files (archives) are all forgotten in favor of Microsoft's

replacements. The fact that Windows doesn't preserve your associations, or at least ask before overwriting them, should be considered a total embarrassment and complete failure on the part of Microsoft's developers.

Fortunately, you can choose new associations by going to Control Panel → [Appearance and Themes] → Folder Options → File Types tab. The two exceptions are *.zip* files and image files (*.jpg*, *.gif*, etc.), for which the default applications don't follow your settings in the File Types dialog.* Fix them using one of two types of files:

Image files

Regardless of the application you choose as the default for all of your image files, Windows XP will always launch the "Windows Picture and Fax Viewer" when they're double-clicked. To fix this, launch the Registry Editor (see Chapter 8), and navigate to HKEY_CLASSES_ROOT\ CLSID\{e84fda7c-1d6a-45f6-b725-cb260c236066}\shellex. Delete the MayChangeDefaultMenu key here, and close the Registry Editor when you're done. (The "Preview" action will still appear in your files' context menus, but it won't be activated when you double-click on the files.)

ZIP files

Even if you install your own program for handling ZIP files, Windows XP will still open *.zip* files like standard folders. To fix this, go to Start → Run, type regsvr32 /u %windir%\system32\zipfldr.dll at the prompt, and click OK. You'll have to restart Windows for this change to take effect.

Desktop icons

The icons used for the standard Desktop items, such as My Computer and the Recycle Bin, have a new look in Windows XP. To use the icons found in earlier versions of Windows, go to Control Panel → [Appearance and Themes] → Display → Desktop tab → Customize Desktop. Most of the older icons can be found in the file *\Windows\System32\SHELL32.dll*.

DOS is history

Unlike some earlier versions of Windows (such as Windows 95, Windows 98, and Windows Me), Windows XP does not rely on DOS. This means that you can no longer boot directly into DOS on a Windows XP system, even with a floppy. If you attempt to boot your computer with a Windows 9x/Me startup diskette, possibly in the hopes of effecting repairs or copying files (a common practice on older computers), you probably won't even be able to see the hard disk.† If you're unable to start Windows XP, you'll need to "repair" the installation using the original CD, either with the Recovery Console or by using the Windows setup (both described in Appendix A).

Additional topics like these can be found at *http://www.annoyances.org*.

---

* This type of thing makes me furious (Microsoft does it all the time), and is one of the primary motivations for the Annoyances.org web site and the various Annoyances books.

† This is due to the fact that Windows 9x/Me isn't compatible with the NTFS filesystem, used predominantly on Windows XP systems. See Chapter 4 for more information on NTFS.

C

Keyboard Shortcuts

This appendix lists many useful keyboard accelerators. The listings are organized both by keystroke (alphabetically within groups such as function key, Alt-key combination, and so forth) and then by function or context (during startup, in the Recycle Bin, for managing windows, and so forth). The first section lists the key, and then the function. The second section lists the desired function, and then the required key(s).

Note that in addition to the standard keyboard accelerators, you can define additional accelerators of your own. For example, you can define a Ctrl-Alt combination to invoke any shortcut, whether it's on the Desktop, in the Start menu, or in any other folder. Right-click any Windows shortcut icon (even those right in your Start menu), select Properties, choose the Shortcut tab, and in the Shortcut key field, type the key (not including Ctrl and Alt) to which the shortcut should be linked. For example, to assign Ctrl-Alt-Z to the current shortcut, simply type Z in the field. You can use any key except Esc, Enter, Tab, the Spacebar, PrintScreen, Backspace, or Delete. If it conflicts with an accelerator used by any existing application, the accelerator you've just defined will usually override the existing accelerator (test it to make sure). To clear an existing shortcut's accelerator, just empty the Shortcut key field on the shortcut's Properties sheet. These instructions apply to Windows Shortcuts only. Internet Shortcuts don't support keyboard accelerators.

Keyboard Accelerators Listed by Key

Tables C-1 through C-7 list keystrokes that will work in Windows Explorer and most of the components that come with Windows XP. However, some applications (including Microsoft applications) don't always follow the rules.

Table C-1. Function keys

Key	Action
F1	Start Help (supported in most applications).
F2	Rename selected icon or file in Windows Explorer or on the Desktop.
F3	Open a Search window (in Windows Explorer or on the Desktop only).
F4	Open a drop-down list (supported in many dialog boxes)—for example, press F4 in a File Open dialog to drop down the Look In list.
F5	Refresh the view in Windows Explorer, on the Desktop, in the Registry Editor, and some other applications.
F6	Move focus between panes in Windows Explorer.
F10	Send focus to the current application's menu.

Table C-2. Miscellaneous keys

Key	Action
Arrow keys	Basic navigation: move through menus, reposition the text cursor (insertion point), change the file selection, and so on.
Backspace	Move up one level in folder hierarchy (Windows Explorer only).
Delete	Delete selected item(s) or selected text.
Down Arrow	Open a drop-down listbox.
End	Go to end of line when editing text, or else to the end of file list.
Enter	Activate highlighted choice in menu or dialog box, or insert a carriage return when editing text.
Esc	Close dialog box, message window, or menu without activating any choice (usually the same as clicking Cancel).
Home	Go to beginning of line (when editing text), or else to the beginning of file list.
Page Down	Scroll down one screen.
Page Up	Scroll up one screen.
PrintScreen	Copy entire screen as a bitmap to the Clipboard.
Spacebar	Toggle a checkbox that is selected in a dialog box, activate the command button with the focus, or toggle the selection of files when selecting multiple files with Ctrl.
Tab	Move focus to next control in a dialog box or window (hold Shift to go backwards).

Table C-3. Alt key combinations

Key(s)	Action
Alt (by itself)	Send focus to the menu (same as F10).
Alt-x	Activate menu or dialog control, where letter *x* is underlined.
Alt-double-click (on icon)	Display Properties sheet.
Alt-Enter	Display Properties sheet for selected icon in Windows Explorer or on the Desktop. Also switches Command Prompt between windowed and full screen display.
Alt-Esc	Drop active window to bottom of pile, which, in effect, activates next open window.
Alt-F4	Close current window; if Taskbar or Desktop has the focus, exit Windows.
Alt-hyphen	Open the current document's system menu in an MDI (multiple document interface) application.

Table C-3. Alt key combinations (continued)

Key(s)	Action
Alt-numbers	When used with the numbers on the numeric keypad only, inserts special characters corresponding to their ASCII codes into many applications. For example, type Alt-0169 for the copyright symbol. See "Character Map" in 4 for details.
Alt-PrintScreen	Copy active window as a bitmap to the Clipboard.
Alt-Shift-Tab	Same as Alt-Tab, but in the opposite direction.
Alt-Spacebar	Open the current window's system menu.
Alt-Tab{+Tab}	Switch to the next running application—hold Shift while pressing Tab to cycle through running applications.
Alt-M	When the Taskbar has the focus, minimize all windows and move focus to the Desktop.
Alt-S	When the Taskbar has the focus, open the Start menu.

Table C-4. Ctrl key combinations

Keys	Action
Ctrl-A	Select all; in Windows Explorer, selects all files in the current folder. In word processors, selects all text in the current document.
Ctrl-Alt-x	User-defined accelerator for a shortcut, in which x is any key (discussed at the beginning of this appendix).
Ctrl-Alt-Del	Show the logon dialog when no user is currently logged on; otherwise, switch to the Windows Security dialog, which provides access to Task Manager and Shut Down, as well as allows you to change your password or lock the computer. Use Ctrl-Alt-Del to access Task Manager when Explorer crashes or your computer becomes unresponsive.
Ctrl-arrow key	Scroll without moving selection.
Ctrl-click	Use to select multiple, noncontiguous items in a list or in Windows Explorer.
Ctrl-drag	Copy a file (see Chapter 2).
Ctrl-End	Move to the end of a document (in many applications).
Ctrl-Esc	Open the Start menu; press Esc and then Tab to then move focus to the Taskbar, or press Tab again to move focus to the Desktop.
Ctrl-F4	Close a document window in an MDI application.
Ctrl-F6	Switch between multiple documents in an MDI (multiple document interface) application; similar to Ctrl-Tab; hold Shift to go in reverse.
Ctrl-Home	Move to the beginning of a document (in many applications).
Ctrl-Spacebar	Select or deselect multiple, noncontiguous items in a listbox or in Windows Explorer.
Ctrl-Tab	Switch between tabs in a tabbed dialog, or between multiple documents in an MDI (multiple document interface) application (similar to Ctrl-F6, except that Ctrl-Tab doesn't work in most word processors); hold Shift to go in reverse.
Ctrl-C	Copy the selected item or selected text to the Clipboard. Also interrupts some command-prompt applications (see Chapter 2).
Ctrl-F	Open a Search window (in Windows Explorer or on the Desktop only).
Ctrl-V	Paste the contents of the Clipboard (see Chapter 2).
Ctrl-X	Cut the selected item or selected text to the Clipboard (see Chapter 2).
Ctrl-Z	Undo; for example, erases text just entered, and repeals the last file operation in Windows Explorer.

Table C-5. Shift key combinations

Key(s)	Action
Shift	While inserting a CD, hold to disable AutoPlay.
Shift-arrow keys	Select text or select multiple items in a listbox or in Windows Explorer.
Shift-click	Select all items between currently selected item and item on which you're clicking; also works when selecting text.
Shift-click Close button	Close current folder and all parent folders (Windows Explorer in single-folder view only).
Shift-Alt-Tab	Same as Alt-Tab, but in reverse.
Shift-Ctrl-Tab	Same as Ctrl-Tab, but in reverse.
Shift-Ctrl-Esc	Open Task Manager (see Chapter 4).
Shift-Del	Delete a file without putting it in the Recycle Bin.
Shift-double-click	Open folder in two-pane Explorer view.
Shift-Tab	Same as Tab, but in reverse.

Table C-6. Windows logo key (WIN) on some keyboards

Key(s)	Action
WIN	Open the Start menu.
WIN-F1	Start Help and Support Services (see Chapter 4).
WIN-Tab	Cycle through Taskbar buttons without activating the applications (Alt-Tab is more convenient, though).
WIN-Pause/Break	Display System Properties dialog.
WIN-B, Spacebar	Open Date and Time Properties (see Chapter 4).
WIN-D	Minimize all windows and move focus to Desktop.[a]
Shift-WIN-D	Undo Minimize All.
WIN-E	Start Windows Explorer.
WIN-F	Search for Files or Folders.
Ctrl-WIN-F	Search for a computer on your network.
WIN-L	Lock computer, requiring password to regain access.[b]
WIN-M	Minimize current window.
Shift-WIN-M	Undo minimize current window.
WIN-R	Display Run dialog (same as Start → Run).
WIN-U	Open the Utility Manager (see Chapter 4).

[a] This has been known to be buggy on some systems; if your Desktop turns gray, use Task Manager to close *Explorer.exe*.
[b] You can also lock your computer by pressing Ctrl-Alt-Del and clicking Lock Computer.

Table C-7. Command Prompt keyboard accelerators

Key(s)	Action
Left/Right arrow	Move cursor back/forward one character.
Ctrl + Left/Right arrow	Move cursor back/forward one word.
Home/End	Move cursor to beginning/end of line.
Up/Down arrow	Scroll up (and back) through list of stored commands (called the Command Buffer or History). Each press of the up key recalls the previous command and displays it on the command line.

Table C-7. Command Prompt keyboard accelerators (continued)

Key(s)	Action
Page Up/Down	Recall oldest/most recent command in buffer.
Insert	Toggle insert/overtype mode (block cursor implies overtype mode).
Esc	Erase current line.
F1	Repeat text typed in previous line, one character at a time.
F2 + key	Repeat text typed in previous line, up to first character matching *key*.
F3	Repeat text typed in previous line.
F4 + key	Delete characters from present character position up to (but not including) *key* (note: does not work reliably in Windows XP).
F5	Change the template for F1, F2, and F3 (described above) so that earlier commands are used as the template; press F5 repeatedly to cycle through the entire command buffer.
F6	Place an end-of-file character (^Z) at current position of command line.
F7	Show all entries in command buffer (history).
Alt-F7	Clear all entries in command buffer (history).
chars + F8	Entering one or more characters *chars* followed by F8 will display the most recent entry in the command buffer beginning with *chars*. Pressing F8 again will display the next most recent matching command, and so on. If no characters are specified, F8 simply cycles through existing commands in buffer.
F9 + command#	Display designated command on command line; use F7 to obtain numbers.
Ctrl-C	Interrupt the output of most Command Prompt applications.

Keyboard Accelerators Listed by Function

Table C-8 lists keys that operate in most contexts—i.e., on the Desktop, in the Explorer, and within most applications and dialogs. Functions are listed alphabetically, except where a logical order might make more sense.

Note also that there are essentially a limitless combinations of keystrokes that can be used to activate any particular feature in a given application, all of which can be formed by combining the various keystrokes listed in this appendix. For example, you can press Alt-F to open an application's File menu, then press P to Print, then press Enter to begin printing. Or, press Ctrl-Esc to open the Start menu, Alt-Enter to open Taskbar and Start Menu Properties, Ctrl-Tab to open the Taskbar tab (if necessary), and Alt-L to lock (or unlock) the Taskbar

Table C-8. Keyboard accelerators listed by function

Key(s)	Action
Shift (while inserting CD)	AutoPlay, disable temporarily
Spacebar	Checkbox, toggle on or off
Ctrl-C	Clipboard, copy
Alt-PrintScreen	Clipboard, copy current window as a bitmap
PrintScreen	Clipboard, copy entire screen as a bitmap
Ctrl-X	Clipboard, cut
Ctrl-V	Clipboard, paste
Ctrl-F4	Close current document

Table C-8. Keyboard accelerators listed by function (continued)

Key(s)	Action
Alt-F4	Close current window
Esc	Close dialog box, message window, or menu
Spacebar	Command button, click
Shift-F10, or context menu key on some keyboards	Context menu, open
Tab (hold Shift to go in reverse)	Controls, cycle focus on a dialog box
Ctrl-C	Copy selected item or selected text to the Clipboard
Ctrl-X	Cut selected item or selected text to the Clipboard
Windows Logo Key-B, Spacebar	Date and Time Properties, open
Shift-Del or Shift-drag item to Recycle Bin	Delete a file without putting it in the Recycle Bin
Del	Delete selected item
Ctrl-Esc (or Windows Logo Key), then Esc, Tab, Tab, Tab	Desktop, activate
Windows Logo Key-D, or click empty portion of Taskbar and press Alt-M	Desktop, activate by minimizing all windows
Tab (hold Shift to go in reverse)	Dialog box, cycle through controls
Ctrl-Tab (hold Shift to go in reverse)	Dialog box, cycle through tabs
Ctrl-F4	Document, close
Ctrl-Home	Document, move to the beginning
Ctrl-End	Document, move to the end
Ctrl-F6 or Ctrl-Tab	Document, switch between
Down Arrow or F4	Drop-down listbox, open
Alt-F4	Exit an application
Ctrl-Esc, then Alt-F4	Exit Windows
Shift-Del	File, delete without moving to Recycle Bin
Windows Logo Key-F (or F3 or Ctrl-F in Windows Explorer or on the Desktop)	File, search
Ctrl-Windows Logo Key-F	Find a computer on your network
Windows Logo Key-F (or F3 or Ctrl-F in Windows Explorer or on the Desktop)	Find Files or Folders
Tab (hold Shift to go in reverse)	Focus, move between controls on a dialog box
Shift-click Close button	Folder, close current and all parents (Windows Explorer in single-folder view only)
Right and left arrows	Folder, expand and collapse folders in tree
Shift-double-click	Folder, open in two-pane Explorer view
Windows Logo Key-F (or F3 or Ctrl-F in Windows Explorer or on the Desktop)	Folder, search
F1	Help (in most applications)
Windows Logo Key-F1	Help and Support Services, open
Down Arrow or F4	Listbox, drop-down
Ctrl-click	Listbox, select multiple items
Ctrl-Spacebar	Listbox, select or deselected items
Windows Logo Key-L (or press Ctrl-Alt-Del and then Spacebar)	Lock computer

Table C-8. Keyboard accelerators listed by function (continued)

Key(s)	Action
Alt-x if menu doesn't have focus, x by itself if menu has focus	Menu, activate specific item with letter x underlined
Arrow keys	Menu, basic navigation
Esc	Menu, close
F10 or Alt (by itself)	Menu, move focus to
Shift-F10, or context menu key on some keyboards	Menu, open context menu
Windows Logo Key-D, or click empty portion of Taskbar and press Alt-M	Minimize all windows and move focus to Desktop
Windows Logo Key-M (hold Shift to undo)	Minimize current window
F6	Panes, move focus between
Backspace	Parent folder, move to (in Windows Explorer)
Ctrl-V	Paste the contents of the Clipboard
Alt-double-click, or select and then press Alt-Enter	Properties, display for an icon
F5	Refresh (in Windows Explorer, on the Desktop, and some other applications)
F2	Rename selected icon or file in Windows Explorer or on the Desktop
Windows Logo Key-R	Run (same as Start → Run)
Alt-PrintScreen	Screenshot, copy current window as a bitmap to the clipboard
PrintScreen	Screenshot, copy entire screen as a bitmap to the clipboard
Page Down	Scroll down one screen
Page Up	Scroll up one screen
Ctrl-arrow key	Scroll without moving selection
Ctrl-Windows Logo Key-F	Search for a computer on your network
Windows Logo Key-F	Search for Files or Folders
F3 or Ctrl-F	Search for Files or Folders (in Windows Explorer or on the Desktop only)
Ctrl-A	Select all
Alt-drag file	Shortcut, create
Windows logo key or Ctrl-Esc	Start menu, open
Alt-Tab or Ctrl-Esc (hold Shift to go in reverse)	Switch to next application
Ctrl-F6 or Ctrl-Tab (hold Shift to go in reverse)	Switch to next document window
Alt-hyphen	System menu, show for current document
Alt-Spacebar	System menu, show for current window
Windows Logo Key-Pause/Break	System Properties, open
Ctrl-Tab (hold Shift to go in reverse)	Tabs, switch between tabs
Shift-Ctrl-Esc (or press Ctrl-Alt-Del and click Task Manager)	Task Manager, open
Ctrl-Esc, then Alt-Enter	Taskbar and Start Menu Properties, open
Windows Logo Key-Tab	Taskbar buttons, cycle through
Ctrl-Z	Undo
Alt-Tab (hold Shift to go in reverse)	Window, activate next

Table C-8. Keyboard accelerators listed by function (continued)

Key(s)	Action
Alt-F4	Window, close
Alt-Esc	Window, drop to bottom of pile
Windows Logo Key-M (hold Shift to undo)	Window, minimize
Windows Logo Key-D (hold Shift to undo)	Window, minimize all
Alt-Tab (hold Shift to go in reverse)	Window, switch to
Windows Logo Key-E	Windows Explorer, open
F6	Windows Explorer, switch between panes

D

Power Toys and TweakUI

Since the release of Windows 95, Microsoft has made available a set of "Power Toys," which is a suite of extra little utilities that Microsoft feels power users would appreciate. A new set of Power Toys has been released especially for Windows XP and can be downloaded for free.

You can download the entire Power Toys package from *http://www.microsoft.com/windowsxp/pro/downloads/powertoys.asp* and install them selectively. (If this link becomes unavailable for whatever reason, the Power Toys package will always be available at *http://www.annoyances.org.*) Power Toys for Windows XP comes with the following tools:

Tweak UI

> This Power Toy gives you access to system settings that are not exposed in the Windows XP default user interface, including mouse settings, Explorer settings, Taskbar settings, and more. By far the most useful component of the Power Toys package, TweakUI is discussed further in the subsequent section.

> Note that TweakUI 1.33, which was designed for Windows 2000, Windows Me, and Windows 9x, will also work on Windows XP, but it won't provide the XP-specific settings available in Version 2.0.

Super-Fast User Switcher

> If you find yourself frequently switching between multiple user accounts, and aren't concerned with security, use this Power Toy to instantly switch between users without having to go through the Logon screen.

Open Command Window Here

> This Power Toy allows you to right-click any folder and select "Open Command Window Here" to open a Command Prompt window (as described in Chapter 6), with the current directory set to the selected folder.

> You can also implement this feature manually with the Registry Editor (see Chapter 7). Navigate to HKEY_CLASSES_ROOT\Directory\shell, and create a new

key called cmd. Open the new key, double-click the (default) value, and type Open Command Window Here. Then, create a new key called command. Open this key, double-click the (default) value, and type cmd.exe /k "cd %L".

Alt-Tab Replacement
This Power Toy adds a preview of each window to the Alt-Tab window. Although it's a little more awkward than the standard Alt-Tab window, it can be particularly helpful when multiple sessions of an application are open.

Power Calculator
This enhanced calculator is an alternative to the standard Calculator (discussed in Chapter 4), and adds expression solving, graphing, unit conversions, and customizable constants.

Image Resizer
This Power Toy (see Figure D-1) allows you to quickly resize a group of image files to one of several predefined sizes, or to a custom size you specify.

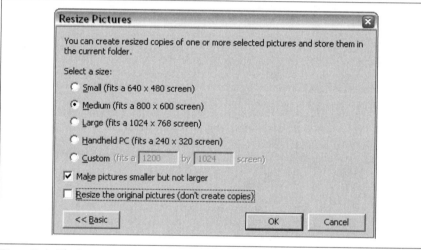

Figure D-1. The Image Resizer

CD Slide Show Generator
You can view images stored on a CD as a slide show with this Power Toy.

Virtual Desktop Manager
The Virtual Desktop Manager doubles or quadruples your Desktop area. More accurately, it simply allows you position application windows off screen and easily view or hide them.

Taskbar Magnifier
Use this Power Toy to magnify part of the screen from the Taskbar. See "Microsoft Magnifier" in Chapter 4 for a similar tool.

HTML Slide Show Wizard
This wizard generates a series of HTML files, allowing you to create a web-based slide show of your digital pictures.

Webcam Timershot
> The Webcam Timershot takes pictures with your webcam at specified time intervals, and saves them to any location. The images can then be uploaded to a web server with a WSH script (see Chapter 9), or simply saved on a folder for later viewing.

Inside TweakUI

TweakUI is a handy tool that provides more control over a wide variety of Windows settings than is available through the standard Windows XP interface. The tips are arranged into the following categories:

About
> The Tips subsection lets you peruse the collection of Windows tips that, by default, are displayed every time you start Windows XP. These tips can be edited by opening the Registry Editor (*regedit.exe*) and going to HKEY_LOCAL_ MACHINE\SOFTWARE\Microsoft\Windows\CurrentVersion\Explorer\Tips.
>
> The Policy subsection simply provides a link to the Group Policy editor discussed in Chapter 4.

General
> Among the more interesting settings in this category are options that allow you to turn off the PC Speaker beep (which doesn't always work), selectively disable certain types of animation, and keep Windows from stealing the focus while you're working.

Mouse
> Move the Menu Speed control all the way to the left (Fast) to eliminate the delay when opening menus. The other options allow you to fine-tune how Windows responds to double-clicks, mouse hover, and the mouse wheel.

Explorer
> The settings in this category allow you to hide additional entries from the Start menu, disable the Documents history, turn off the "Shortcut to" prefix for new shortcuts, program your keyboard's navigation keys, and even revert the Search tool to the "classic" style found in Windows 2000/Me.

Common Dialogs
> This extremely useful category (see Figure D-2) lets you customize the "Places Bar" shown in most File Open and File Save dialog boxes. Just select "Custom places bar" and type your five most frequently used folders in the spaces provided.
>
> See *http://www.annoyances.org/exec/show/article08-804* for a similar procedure involving Microsoft Office file dialogs.

Taskbar
> Selectively hide certain applications from the Frequently Used Programs section of the XP-style Start menu, as well as fine-tune the grouping of similar Taskbar buttons.

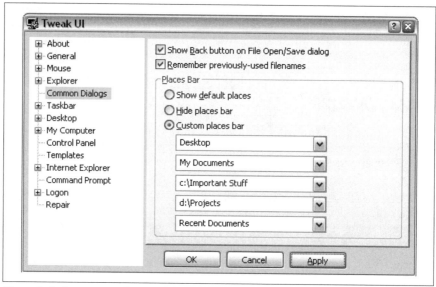

Figure D-2. Common Dialogs

Desktop

Selectively show or hide certain built-in Desktop icons, and choose whether the My Documents or My Computer icon appears first when auto-sorting Desktop icons.

My Computer

Show or hide drives and other icons in the My Computer window. Additionally, the AutoPlay subcategory allows you to control or even disable the feature that plays CDs and DVDs automatically when they're inserted in your drive.

Control Panel

Hide unused icons in your Control Panel.

Templates

Selectively remove unwanted items from Explorer's New menu, or add new entries and even specify blank files (templates) to use.

Internet Explorer

Choose bitmap backgrounds for the toolbars in Internet Explorer and Windows Explorer, add new web sites to search for keywords typed into the Address Bar, and choose the text editor used for Internet Explorer's View Source feature.

Command Prompt

Control the filename and directory completion for the Command Prompt window.

Logon

The Autologon subcategory allows you to save a username and password, eliminating the need to log in manually every time you start Windows XP. This functionality was built into Windows 2000, but removed in Windows XP.

Note that using TweakUI to bypass the logon screen in Windows XP is known to cause boot-up delays of up to several minutes on some computers.

Repair

If you find that certain Desktop icons seem to be broken, your Fonts folder (see Chapter 4) isn't behaving, the unread mail count appears to be wrong, or certain information is missing from the Registry Editor, use the options in this category to affect repairs.

E

Keyboard Equivalents for Symbols and International Characters

Among the programs included in Windows XP is the Character Map utility (described in Chapter 4), which allows you to place special characters and symbols in your documents that can't otherwise by typed from the keyboard. The collection of 1185 characters and symbols shown in Character Map is the Unicode set, a character encoding standard developed by the Unicode Consortium, intended to represent nearly all of the written languages of the world.

A subset of the Unicode set is the ASCII character set (American Standard Code for Information Interchange); while only a mere 255 characters, this character set includes the numbers, upper- and lowercase letters, and standard symbols (!, @, #, $, %, [,], and so on) found on any standard keyboard. The symbols and international characters shown in Table E-1 are also part of the ASCII character set.

What sets the members of the ASCII set apart from the larger Unicode set is every single one of the ASCII characters can be typed from the keyboard, even the extended characters shown here. To type a character listed in Table E-1, hold the Alt key and type the four-digit number shown on the right using the numeric keypad, including the initial zero. For example, for the copyright symbol, type Alt+0169. Note that the standard number keys (above the alphabet) won't work, so those with abbreviated laptop keyboards may not be able to use these at all.

Table E-1. Common symbols and characters and their keyboard shortcuts

Char	Code	Char	Code	Char	Code	Char	Code
ª	0170	©	0169	À	0192	à	0224
º	0176	®	0174	Á	0193	á	0225
°	0186	™	0153	Â	0194	â	0226
¹	0185	Æ	0198	Ã	0195	ã	0227
²	0178	æ	0230	Ä	0196	ä	0228
³	0179	ß	0223	Å	0197	å	0229
¼	0188	Œ	0140	Ç	0199	ç	0231

Table E-1. Common symbols and characters and their keyboard shortcuts (continued)

Char	Code	Char	Code	Char	Code	Char	Code
½	0189	œ	0156	È	0200	è	0232
¾	0190	Ð	0208	É	0201	é	0233
‰	0137	þ	0254	Ê	0202	ê	0234
±	0177	Þ	0222	Ë	0203	ë	0235
×	0215	?	0259	Ì	0204	ì	0236
÷	0247	µ	0181	Í	0205	í	0237
Ø	0216	…	0133	Î	0206	î	0238
ø	0248	´	0180	Ï	0207	ï	0239
‹	0139	'	0145	Ñ	0209	ñ	0241
›	0155	'	0146	Ò	0210	ò	0242
«	0171	"	0147	Ó	0211	ó	0243
»	0187	"	0148	Ô	0212	ô	0244
¦	0166	•	0149	Õ	0213	õ	0245
€	0128	·	0183	Ö	0214	ö	0246
¢	0162	¤	0164	Š	0138	š	0154
£	0163	-	0173	Ù	0217	ù	0249
¥	0165	–	0150	Ú	0218	ú	0250
§	0167	—	0151	Û	0219	û	0251
ƒ	0131	¬	0172	Ü	0220	ü	0252
†	0134	¯	0175	Ý	0221	ý	0253
‡	0135	¿	0191	Ÿ	0159	ÿ	0255
¶	0182	¨	0168	Ž	0142	ž	0158

F

Common Filename Extensions

This appendix lists many of the most common filename extensions that you'll find on your system, that you might download, or have sent to you over the Internet.

Extensions were universally used on DOS and Windows 3.1 files, but Microsoft has gone to some difficulty to hide them in Windows XP. This is unfortunate, since they play a major role in the way Windows decides what application will be used to open a file, as well as which files will be visible when opening files in a given application. While direct associations are made between some files without extensions and the applications needed to open them, in most cases, the association is between an extension and a Registry setting that tells the system what application to use. To enable the display of filename extensions, go to Control Panel → [Appearance and Themes] → Folder Options → View tab, and turn off the "Hide extensions for known file types" option.

If you double-click on an unknown file type, the Open With dialog box (see "Folder Options" in Chapter 4) appears, allowing you to make a new association. To subsequently change an association once it has been made, right-click on the file and select Open With, or select Properties and then click Change.

We've tried to list the most common system extensions in Table F-1, but there are literally thousands of file formats used by third party applications. And you might be thrown off by an improperly named file, or an application using a standard filename extension for a nonstandard purpose.

Many of these file types can be opened only if you have the appropriate application. However, especially with the growth of the Web, there are often viewers available that allow you to at least view the contents of the file, even if you can't change them. Your web browser and the Windows Picture and Fax Viewer are capable of reading several formats. Paint Shop Pro (*http://www.jasc.com*) can read and convert nearly any image (graphics) format. And any modern word processor (WordPerfect, Word, etc.) will be able to read just about any text-based document and convert it to a more usable format. If all else fails, you can open just about any file in Notepad; while nontext files will look mostly like jibberish, you may get clues in some of the excerpts of readable text you'll see.

If you still can't find a file's type from it's extension, there are several more good sources:

- Microsoft has put together a simple "extension finder" web site, intended for use with the "Use the Web service to find the appropriate program" feature that appears when you try to open a file with an extension that Windows doesn't recognize. The address for this site is:

  http://shell.windows.com/fileassoc/0409/xml/redir.asp?Ext={your extension}

  where *{your extension}* is the filename extension (without the dot) that you wish to learn more about. For example, to find out about the *.sit* extension, you'd go to:

  http://shell.windows.com/fileassoc/0409/xml/redir.asp?Ext=sit

- Use an ordinary search engine such as Google (*http://www.google.com*) to search for references to the filename extension. For example, to find out about the *.hqx* extension, try searching for "hqx file" (with the quotes).

- For more details on dealing with downloads and file formats found on the Net, see *Internet in a Nutshell*, by Valerie Quercia (O'Reilly). For details on the internals of many graphics file formats, see *The Encyclopedia of Graphics File Formats* by James Murray and Bill van Ryper (O'Reilly).

Table F-1. Common filename extensions

Extension	Description
.$$$	Temporary file
.1st	ASCII text file (e.g. READ.1ST)
.3ds	3D Studio File
.3fx	CorelChart Effect
.3gr	Windows Video Grabber Data file
.8m	PageMaker Printer font with Math 8 extended character set
.8u	PageMaker Printer font with Roman 8 extended character set
.abf	Adobe Binary Font
.abk	CorelDRAW Automatic backup file
.abm	photo album
.abs	MPEG audio sound file
.aca	Microsoft Agent Character File
.ace	Ace Archiver compressed file
.acf	Microsoft Agent Character File
.ad	AfterDark Screen saver
.adi	AutoCAD Graphics
.adn	Lotus 1-2-3 Add-in
.adx	Archetype Designer Document
.afi	Truevision bitmap graphics

Table F-1. Common filename extensions (continued)

Extension	Description
.afm	ATM - many Type 1 font metric ASCII data for font installer
.ai	Adobe Illustrator Vector graphics
.all	WordPerfect for Win General printer information
.alt	WordPerfect Library Menu file
.ans	Ansi graphics; character animation
.aps	MS Visual C++ file
.arc	Compressed file archive
.arf	Automatic Response File
.arj	Compressed file archive created by ARJ
.asc	Ascii text file
.ascx	Microsoft ASP.NET user control file
.asd	Lotus 1-2-3 Screen driver
.asd	Word for Windows Autosave file
.asf	Lotus 1-2-3 Screen font
.asm	Assembly source code file
.asmx	Microsoft .NET Web Service file
.asp	Microsoft Active Server Page
.aspx	Microsoft ASP.NET file
.asx	Microsoft Windows Media Active Stream Redirector file
.asx	Windows Media Streaming video shortcut
.at2	Aldus Persuasion 2.0 Auto template
.atm	Adobe Type Manager data/info
.au	Audio file used on older web pages
.avi	Video for Windows Audio Video Interleaved movie clip
.awm	Animation Works Movie
.b3d	3D Builder file
.bak	Backup file (generic)
.bas	Basic source code file
.bat	DOS Batch file
.bco	Bitstream Outline font description
.bdr	MS Publisher Border
.bez	Bitstream Outline font description
.bga	Bitmap graphics
.bib	Bibliography (ASCII)
.bin	Binary file
.bit	Bitmap X11
.bk!	WordPerfect for Win Document backup
.bkf	Microsoft Backup File
.bkw	FontEdit Mirror image of font set
.blk	WordPerfect for Win Temporary file
.bm	Bitmap graphics

Table F-1. Common filename extensions (continued)

Extension	Description
.bmf	Corel Image file
.bmp	Windows Bitmap
.bpt	CorelDRAW Bitmap fills file
.bsc	MS Fortran Pwbrmake object file
.bup	Backup file (generic)
.c	C source code file
.c++	C++ source code file
.cab	Microsoft installation archive Cabinet File
.cas	Comma-delimited ASCII File
.cc	C++ source code file
.ccb	Visual Basic Animated Button Configuration
.cch	CorelChart Chart
.ccx	Corel PrintHouse file
.cdr	CorelDRAW native format Vector graphics
.cdt	CorelDraw 4.0 Data
.cel	Autodesk Animator - Lumena Graphics
.cfg	Configuration file
.cfl	CorelFLOW Chart
.cgi	Common Gateway Interface script
.cgm	Computer Graphics Metafile vector graphics
.chd	FontChameleon Font descriptor
.chk	ChkDsk Recovered data
.chk	WordPerfect for Win Temporary file
.cif	Caltech Intermediate Format graphics
.cif	Easy CD Creator CD Image File
.clp	Quattro Pro Clip art graphics
.cls	C++ class definition file
.cmf	Creative Music File FM-music file
.cmp	CorelDRAW Header file for PostScript printer files
.cmp	MS Word for DOS User dictionary
.cmv	CorelMove CorelDraw 4.0 Animation
.cnt	Helpfile contents
.cnv	Word for Windows Data conversion support file
.cnv	WordPerfect for Win Temporary file
.col	Autodesk Animator - many Color palette
.col	MS Multiplan Spreadsheet
.cph	Corel Print House image
.cpi	Colorlab Processed Image bitmap graphics
.cpi	DOS Code Page Information file
.cpp	C++ source code file
.cps	Colored postscript files

Table F-1. Common filename extensions (continued)

Extension	Description
.cpx	Corel Presentation Exchange Compressed Drawing
.crf	MS MASM - Zortech C++ Cross-reference
.crs	WordPerfect 5.1 File Conversion Resource
.csv	Comma Separated Values text file format (ASCII)
.ctx	Microsoft online guides Course TeXt file
.ctx	Pretty Good Privacy RSA System Ciphertext file
.cvp	WinFax Cover page
.cvs	Canvas Graphics
.dat	Data file (generic)
.dbg	MS C/C++ Symbolic debugging information
.dcr	Shockwave file
.dcs	CYMK format Bitmap graphics
.ddb	Bitmap graphics
.dev	Device driver (old)
.dfv	Word Printing form
.dib	Device-Independent Bitmap Bitmap graphics
.dic	Lotus Notes / Domino dictionary file
.dip	Graphics
.dis	CorelDraw Thesaurus
.diz	Description In Zip Description file
.dld	Lotus 1-2-3 Data
.dlg	MS Windows SDK Dialog resource script file
.dll	CorelDRAW Export/import filter
.doc	Microsoft Word Document
.dot	CorelDRAW Line-type definition file
.dot	Word for Windows Template
.drs	WordPerfect for Win Display Resource
.drv	Device driver (old)
.dsr	WordPerfect for Win Driver Resource
.dvc	Lotus 1-2-3 Data
.dvp	AutoCAD Device parameter file
.dwg	AutoCAD Drawing database
.dxf	AutoCAD Drawing Interchange File Format vector graphics
.dyn	Lotus 1-2-3 Data
.eeb	WordPerfect for Win Button bar for Equation Editor
.emf	Enhanced Metafile graphics
.eml	MS Outlook Express Electronic Mail
.end	CorelDRAW Arrow-head definition file
.env	WOPR Enveloper macro
.env	WordPerfect for Win Environment file
.eps	Adobe Illustrator Encapsulated PostScript vector graphics

Table F-1. Common filename extensions (continued)

Extension	Description
.eqn	WordPerfect for Win Equation
.evt	Event log
.evy	WordPerfect Envoy Document
.exe	Executable program
.f77	Fortran 77 source code file
.faq	Frequently Asked Questions text file
.fax	Incoming Fax
.fd	MS Fortran Declaration file
.feb	WordPerfect for Win Button bar for Figure Editor
.ff	Agfa Compugraphics Outline font description
.ffl	Microsoft Fast Find File
.ffo	Microsoft Fast Find File
.ffx	Microsoft Fast Find File
.fh3	Aldus FreeHand 3.x Vector graphics
.fh4	Aldus FreeHand 4.x Vector graphics
.fi	MS Fortran Interface file
.fif	Fractal Image Format file
.fil	WordPerfect Overlay
.flc	Autodesk Animator Animation
.fli	Autodesk Animator Animation
.flm	AutoCAD/AutoShade Film Roll
.fm	FrameMaker Document
.fm1	Lotus 1-2-3 release 2.x Spreadsheet
.fm3	Lotus 1-2-3 release 3.x Spreadsheet
.fmb	WordPerfect for Win File Manager Button bar
.fnt	Font file
.fon	Windows 3.x font library Font file
.fot	Windows Font Installer Installed Truetype font
.frf	FontMonger Font
.frm	Visual Basic Form
.frs	WordPerfect for Win Screen Font Resource
.fsx	Lotus 1-2-3 Data
.fts	Windows Help Full-Text Search Index file
.fxs	WinFax Fax Transmit Format graphics
.gcd	Graphics
.gly	MS Word Glossary
.gph	Lotus 1-2-3/G Graph
.gwi	Groupwise File
.gz	GNU zip Compressed file archive created by GZIP
.h	Header file (used with .c source code)
.h++	C++ Header file

Table F-1. Common filename extensions (continued)

Extension	Description
.hdf	Help Development Kit Help file
.hdx	AutoCAD - Zortech C++ Help index
.hgl	Hp Graphics Language graphics
.hh	C++ header file
.hlp	Help information
.hpf	PageMaker Hp LaserJet fonts
.hpg	AutoCad - Harvard Graphics HPGL plotter file vector graphics
.hpj	MS Help Compiler Help project
.hqx	Compressed Macintosh file archive created by Binhex
.htm	HyperText Markup Language document
.html	HyperText Markup Language document
.htt	Hypertext template
.hwd	Hollywood Presentation
.hxx	C++ header file
.hyc	WordPerfect Data
.hyd	WordPerfect for Win Hyphenation dictionary
.icb	Bitmap graphics
.icn	Icon source code file
.ilk	MS ILink incremental linker Outline of program's format
.imp	Lotus Improv Spreadsheet
.imz	Compressed floppy image
.inc	Include file (programming)
.inf	Information text file
.inf	Install script / Driver information
.ini	Initialization file
.ink	CorelDRAW Pantone reference fills file
.ins	WordPerfect Data
.ion	File description (e.g. descript.ion)
.ipl	CorelDRAW Pantone Spot reference palette file
.irs	WordPerfect Resource
.isr	MS Streets & Trips Route file
.jar	Java archive file
.jas	Graphics
.jav	Java source code file
.jff	JPEG File Interchange Format Bitmap graphics
.jpg	JPEG Image File
.jsp	Java Server page
.jtf	JPEG Tagged Interchange Format Bitmap graphics
.kar	Midi file with karaoke word track
.key	Keyboard macros
.lbm	DeluxePaint Bitmap graphics

Table F-1. Common filename extensions (continued)

Extension	Description
.lbr	Lotus 1-2-3 Display driver
.lcn	WordPerfect Lexicon
.ldb	MS Access Data
.lex	Lexicon
.lha	Compressed file archive created by LHA/LHARC
.lib	Library file (programming)
.lif	Compressed file archive
.lin	AutoCAD Line types
.lnk	Windows Shortcut
.log	Log file (ASCII)
.lrf	MS C/C++ Linker response file
.lrs	WordPerfect for Win Language Resource File
.lsl	Lotus Script Library
.ltm	Lotus Forms Form
.lwz	MS Linguistically Enhanced Sound File
.lzh	Compressed file archive created by LHA/LHARC
.lzs	Compressed file archive created by LARC
.lzx	Compressed file archive
.mak	Makefile
.mak	Visual Basic Project file
.man	Command manual
.map	Color palette
.map	Linker map file
.mat	Matlab Data file
.mbx	Eudora Mailbox
.mda	MS Access Data
.mdb	MS Access Database
.mdl	3D Design Plus Model
.mdt	MS ILink incremental linker Data table
.me	ASCII text file (e.g. READ.ME)
.meb	WordPerfect Library Macro Editor bottom overflow file
.med	WordPerfect Library Macro Editor delete save
.mem	WordPerfect Library Macro Editor macro
.meq	WordPerfect Library Macro Editor print queue file
.mer	WordPerfect Library Macro Editor resident area
.mes	WordPerfect Library Macro Editor work space file
.met	WordPerfect Library Macro Editor top overflow file
.mex	WordPerfect Library Macro Editor expound file
.mht	MS MHTML Document
.mic	Microsoft Image Composer file
.mif	FrameMaker Maker Interchange Format

Table F-1. Common filename extensions (continued)

Extension	Description
.mim	MIME file (used for email attachments)
.mk	Makefile
.mke	MS Windows SDK Makefile
.mmf	MS Mail Mail message file
.mnd	AutoCAD Menu Compiler Menu source
.mnx	AutoCAD Compiled menu
.mny	MS Money Account book
.mov	AutoCAD AutoFlix Movie
.mp2	Mpeg audio or video file
.mp3	MPEG Layer 3 Audio file
.mpc	MS Project Calender file
.mpd	MS Project database file
.mpg	Mpeg movie
.mpm	WordPerfect Library Mathplan macro
.mpp	MS Project Project file
.mpv	MS Project View file
.mrb	MS C/C++ Multiple Resolution Bitmap graphics
.mrs	WordPerfect for Win Macro Resource file
.msc	MS C makefile
.msi	Windows Installer file
.mso	MS FrontPage file
.msp	Microsoft Paint Bitmap graphics
.mst	MS Windows SDK Setup script
.msw	MS Word Text file
.mu	Quattro Pro Menu
.mvf	AutoCAD AutoFlix Stop frame file
.mvi	AutoCAD AutoFlix Movie command file
.mxt	MS C Data
.nfo	Info file (ASCII)
.nlm	Netware Loadable Module
.nsf	Lotus Notes / Domino database
.nt	Windows NT Startup files
.ntf	Lotus Notes / Domino template file
.nws	Info text file
.nxt	NeXT format Sound
.ofm	Adobe font
.oft	MS Outlook Item Template
.old	Backup file (generic)
.org	Lotus Organizer Calendar file
.ost	Microsoft Outlook Offline file
.out	Output file (ASCII)

Table F-1. Common filename extensions (continued)

Extension	Description
.p65	Adobe PageMaker v6.5
.pab	Microsoft Outlook personal address book
.pak	Compressed file archive created by PAK
.pal	Color palette
.pas	Pascal source code file
.pat	AutoCAD - Photostyler Hatch patterns
.pat	CorelDRAW Vector fill files
.pb	WinFax Pro Phonebook
.pbi	MS Source Profiler Profiler Binary Input
.pbm	Portable Bit Map graphics
.pbo	MS Source Profiler Profiler Binary Output
.pbt	MS Source Profiler Profiler Binary Table
.pcc	PC Paintbrush Cutout picture vector graphics
.pcd	Kodak PhotoCD Graphics
.pcf	MS Source Profiler Profiler Command File
.pch	MS C/C++ Precompiled header
.pcl	HP Printer Control Language HP-PCL graphics data
.pcx	PC Paintbrush Bitmap graphics
.pda	Bitmap graphics
.pdd	Adobe PhotoDeluxe Image
.pdf	Adobe Portable Document Format
.peb	WordPerfect Library Program Editor bottom overflow file
.ped	WordPerfect Library Program Editor delete save
.pem	WordPerfect Library Program Editor macro
.peq	WordPerfect Library Program Editor print queue file
.per	WordPerfect Library Program Editor resident area
.pes	WordPerfect Library Program Editor work space file
.pet	WordPerfect Library Program Editor top overflow file
.pfb	Type 1 font file
.pfm	Type 1 font metric file
.pgm	Portable Grayscale bitMap graphics
.pgp	Pretty Good Privacy RSA System Support file
.ph	MS C/C++ Phrase-table
.ph	Perl header file
.pic	PC Paint Bitmap graphics
.pka	Compressed file archive created by PKARC
.pkg	NeXT Installer script
.pl	Perl source code file
.pl1	3D Home Architect Room plan
.pln	WordPerfect for Win Spreadsheet
.plt	AutoCAD Hpgl plotter file vector graphics

Filename
Extensions

Table F-1. Common filename extensions (continued)

Extension	Description
.pm3	PageMaker 3 Document
.pm4	PageMaker 4 Document
.pm5	PageMaker 5 Document
.png	Portable Network Graphics Bitmap
.pnm	Graphics file (Portable aNy Map)
.pov	Persistence Of Vision Raytraced graphics image
.ppb	WordPerfect for Win Button bar for Print Preview
.ppd	Acrobat PostScript Printer Description
.ppm	Portable Pixel Map graphics
.pr2	Aldus Persuasion 2.x Presentation
.pr3	Aldus Persuasion 3.x Presentation
.prc	Palm Pilot resource file
.prj	Project
.prn	Lotus 1-2-3 - Symphony Text file
.prs	WordPerfect for Win Printer Resource eg. fonts
.ps	Postscript file
.psd	Photoshop Image
.pst	Microsoft Outlook personal folder
.pt3	PageMaker 3 Template
.pt4	PageMaker 4 Template
.pub	MS Publisher Page template
.pub	Pretty Good Privacy RSA System Public key ring file
.pwl	Password List
.py	Python script file
.pyc	Compiled PYTHON script file
.qbw	QuickBooks for Windows Spreadsheet
.qdat	Quicktime Installer Cache
.qdb	Quicken data file
.qdf	Quicken for Windows data file
.qdt	Quicken data file
.qfl	Quicken Family Lawyer file
.qfx	QuickLink Fax
.qic	Backup set for Microsoft Backup
.qif	Quicken Interchange Format
.qlb	MS C/C++ Quick library
.qlp	QuickLink Printer driver
.qrs	WordPerfect for Win Equation Editor support file
.qt	Quicktime movie
.qxd	QuarkXPress Document
.qxl	QuarkXPress Element library
.r00, .r01	Compressed file archive created by RAR (supplemental to .rar)

Table F-1. Common filename extensions (continued)

Extension	Description
.ra	RealMedia file
.ram	RealMedia shortcut
.rar	Compressed file archive created by RAR
.ras	Sun Rasterfile graphics
.rc	MS C/C++ - Borland C++ Resource script
.rcg	Netscape newsgroup file
.rdp	Remote Desktop Connection Profile
.ref	Cross-reference
.reg	Corel programs Registration
.res	MS C/C++ - Borland C++ Compiled resource
.ri	Lotus 1-2-3 Data
.rib	3DReality Graphics in Renderman format
.rif	Fractal Design Painter Riff bitmap graphics
.rl4	Bitmap graphics
.rl8	Bitmap graphics
.rlc	Graphics 1bit/pixel scanner output
.rnd	AutoCAD AutoShade Rendering Slide
.rs1	Route 1 Pro Script
.rtf	Windows Word Rich Text Format text file (Word)
.rtf	Windows Help file script
.rvp	MS Scan Configuration file
.sav	Configuration file
.sav	Backup file
.sbi	Creative Labs Sound Blaster Instrument file
.sco	High score
.sdf	System Data Format (ASCII)
.sea	Self-Extracting compressed Macintosh file Archive
.sec	Pretty Good Privacy RSA System Secret key ring file
.sfi	HP LaserJet landscape Printer font
.shb	CorelShow Background
.shm	WordPerfect Library Shell macro
.shp	AutoCAD Shape file and source file for text fonts
.shw	WordPerfect Presentations Slide show
.shx	AutoCAD Shape entities
.sif	Windows NT Setup Setup Installation Files info
.sit	Compressed Macintosh archive created by STUFFIT
.slb	AutoCAD Slide library
.sld	AutoCAD Slide
.sng	midi sound Song
.som	Quattro Pro Network serial numbers
.spc	MS Multiplan Program

Table F-1. Common filename extensions (continued)

Extension	Description
.spc	WordPerfect for Win Temporary file
.spm	WordPerfect wp{wp}.spm Data
.srp	QuickLink Script
.ssm	RealPlayer Standard Streaming Metafile
.sts	MS C/C++ Project status info
.sup	WordPerfect for Win Supplementary dictionary
.svd	MS Word Autosave file for document
.svg	MS Word Autosave file for glossary
.svs	MS Word Autosave file for stylesheet
.swf	ShockWave Flash object
.syn	MS Word 5 Synonym file
.sys	DOS System file - device driver or hardware configuration info
.tar	Compressed file archive created by TAR
.taz	Compressed file archive created by TAR and COMPRESS (equiv. to .tar.Z)
.tga	Truevision Targa bitmap graphics
.tgz	Compressed file archive created by TAR and GNUzip (equiv. to .tar.gz)
.thm	Microsoft Clipart Gallery database
.ths	WordPerfect for Win Thesaurus dictionary
.tif	Tagged Image File Format bitmap graphics
.tis	MahJongg 3.0 Tile set
.tlb	Visual C++ Type library
.tmf	WordPerfect for Win Tagged Font Metric file
.tmp	Temporary file
.toc	Eudora Table Of Contents
.tpz	Compressed file archive created by TAR and GNUzip (equiv. to .tar.gz)
.trn	Quattro Translation support file
.tst	WordPerfect for Win Printer test file
.ttf	Truetype Font file
.txt	Text file
.tym	PageMaker 4 Time Stamp
.tz	Compressed file archive created by TAR and COMPRESS (equiv. to .tar.Z)
.uhs	Universal Hint System
.uif	WordPerfect for Win Long prompts for windows
.uu	Compressed ASCII file archive created by UUEncode/UUDecode
.uue	Compressed ASCII file archive created by UUEncode/UUDecode
.vbs	Visual Basic Visual Basic Script file
.vbx	Visual Basic Visual Basic eXtension (custom control)
.vcf	VCard file
.vcw	MS Visual C++ Visual workbench information
.vda	Bitmap graphics
.vmc	Acrobat reader Virtual memory configuration

Extension	Description
.vnc	VNC connection profile
.voc	Creative Voice file Digitized samples
.vrm	QuattroPro Overlay file
.vrs	WordPerfect Video Resource eg. video device driver
.vue	3D Studio Animation
.vxd	Virtual device driver
.wab	Outlook (Windows Address Book) File
.wad	Doom Game File
.wav	Waveform audio file
.wb1	Quattro Pro Notebook
.wb2	Quattro Pro Spreadsheet
.wba	Winace Zip file
.wba	WindowBlinds Compressed Skin for Windows XP
.wbk	WordPerfect for Win Document/workbook
.wcd	WordPerfect for Win Macro token list
.wcm	MS Works Data transmission file
.wcm	WordPerfect for Win Macro
.wcp	WordPerfect for Win Product information description
.wdb	MS Works Database
.wdl	Windows XP Watchdog Log file
.wfn	CorelDRAW Font
.wfx	WinFax Data file
.wg1	Lotus 1-2-3/G Worksheet
.wg2	Lotus 1-2-3 for OS/2 Worksheet
.wiz	MS Publisher Page wizard
.wk1	Lotus 1-2-3 version 2.x - Symphony 1.1+ Spreadsheet
.wk3	Lotus 1-2-3 version 3.x Spreadsheet
.wk4	Lotus 1-2-3 version 3.4 Spreadsheet
.wkb	WordPerfect for Win Document
.wke	Lotus 1-2-3 educational version Spreadsheet
.wkq	Quattro Spreadsheet
.wks	Lotus 1-2-3 version 1A - Symphony 1.0 - MS Works Spreadsheet
.wma	Microsoft Windows Media Active Streaming file
.wmc	WordPerfect for Win Macro file
.wmf	Windows MetaFile vector graphics
.wmv	MS Active Streaming file
.wn	NeXT WriteNow Text
.wnf	CorelDRAW native format Outline font description
.wp	WordPerfect 4.2 Text file
.wp5	WordPerfect 5.x Document
.wpd	WordPerfect 6.0 - PFS:WindowWorks Document

Filename Extensions

Table F-1. Common filename extensions (continued)

Extension	Description
.wpf	WordPerfect Form
.wpg	DrawPerfect WordPerfect Graphics vector graphics
.wpk	WordPerfect for Win Macros
.wpm	WordPerfect Macros
.wps	MS Works Text document
.wq!	Quattro Pro Compressed spreadsheet
.wq1	Quattro Pro Spreadsheet
.wri	Windows Write Text file
.wrl	VRML file
.wrml	VRML file
.wrs	WordPerfect for Win Windows Resource eg. printer driver
.wsz	WinAmp Skin Zip file
.wwb	WordPerfect for Win Button bar for document window
.wwk	WordPerfect for Win Keyboard layout
.xla	MS Excel Add-in macro sheet
.xlb	MS Excel Data
.xlc	MS Excel Chart document
.xll	MS Excel Excel Dynamic Link Library
.xlm	MS Excel Macro sheet
.xlr	MS Works file
.xls	MS Excel Worksheet
.xlt	Lotus 1-2-3 - Symphony - Procomm Plus Translation table
.xlt	MS Excel Template
.xlw	MS Excel Workbook
.xmi	Compressed extended midi music
.xnk	Microsoft Exchange Shortcut
.xwk	Crosstalk Keyboard mapping
.xwp	Crosstalk Session
.z	Compressed file ASCII archive created by COMPRESS
.z3	Infocom game module
.zip	Compressed ZIP file archive
.zoo	Compressed file archive created by ZOO

G

Services

Table G-1 lists the background services installed by default in Windows XP Professional. Note that some of the following may not be present in your system (depending on your Windows edition or installed components), and you may see some services on your own computer that aren't listed here (which may have been added after you installed Windows XP).

One of the advantages of services over standard applications and drivers is that they are run when Windows starts, but before a user logs in. So, for example, you could have an FTP daemon or VNC server service running even when nobody is logged in.

Services can be started, stopped, and configured to automatically start with the Services utility (*services.msc*). By default, most of the services listed in Table G-1 will remain dormant (stopped) until started by the user. For more information on services, see the "Microsoft Management Console" in Chapter 4.

Table G-1. Services in Windows XP

Name	Filename	Description
Alerter	*svchost.exe*	Notifies selected users and computers of administrative alerts. If the service is stopped, programs that use administrative alerts will not receive them. If this service is disabled, any services that explicitly depend on it will fail to start.
Application Layer Gateway Service	*alg.exe*	Provides support for third-party protocol plug-ins for Internet Connection Sharing and the Internet Connection Firewall.
Application Management	*svchost.exe*	Provides software installation services such as Assign, Publish, and Remove.
ATM ARP Client Protocol	*atmarpc.sys*	ATM ARP Client Protocol.
Automatic Updates	*svchost.exe*	Enables the download and installation of critical Windows updates. If the service is disabled, the operating system can be manually updated at the Windows Update web site.
Background Intelligent Transfer Service	*svchost.exe*	Uses idle network bandwidth to transfer data.

Name	Filename	Description
ClipBook	*clipsrv.exe*	Enables ClipBook Viewer to store information and share it with remote computers. If the service is stopped, ClipBook Viewer will not be able to share information with remote computers. If this service is disabled, any services that explicitly depend on it will fail to start.
COM+ Event System	*svchost.exe*	Supports System Event Notification Service (SENS), which provides automatic distribution of events to subscribing Component Object Model (COM) components. If the service is stopped, SENS will close and will not be able to provide logon and logoff notifications. If this service is disabled, any services that explicitly depend on it will fail to start.
COM+ System Application	*dllhost.exe*	Manages the configuration and tracking of Component Object Model (COM)+–based components. If the service is stopped, most COM+–based components will not function properly. If this service is disabled, any services that explicitly depend on it will fail to start.
Computer Browser	*svchost.exe*	Maintains an updated list of computers on the network and supplies this list to computers designated as browsers. If this service is stopped, this list will not be updated or maintained. If this service is disabled, any services that explicitly depend on it will fail to start.
Cryptographic Services	*svchost.exe*	Provides three management services: Catalog Database Service, which confirms the signatures of Windows files; Protected Root Service, which adds and removes Trusted Root Certification Authority certificates from this computer; and Key Service, which helps enroll this computer for certificates. If this service is stopped, these management services will not function properly. If this service is disabled, any services that explicitly depend on it will fail to start.
DHCP Client	*svchost.exe*	Manages network configuration by registering and updating IP addresses and DNS names.
Direct Parallel	*raspti.sys*	Direct Parallel.
Direct Parallel Link Driver	*ptilink.sys*	Direct Parallel Link Driver.
Distributed Link Tracking Client	*svchost.exe*	Maintains links between NTFS files within a computer or across computers in a network domain.
Distributed Transaction Coordinator	*msdtc.exe*	Coordinates transactions that span multiple resource managers, such as databases, message queues, and filesystems. If this service is stopped, these transactions will not occur. If this service is disabled, any services that explicitly depend on it will fail to start.
DNS Client	*svchost.exe*	Resolves and caches Domain Name System (DNS) names for this computer. If this service is stopped, this computer will not be able to resolve DNS names and locate Active Directory domain controllers. If this service is disabled, any services that explicitly depend on it will fail to start.
Error Reporting Service	*svchost.exe*	Allows error reporting for services and applications running in non-standard environments.
Event Log	*services.exe*	Enables event log messages issued by Windows-based programs and components to be viewed in Event Viewer. This service cannot be stopped.
Fast User Switching Compatibility	*svchost.exe*	Provides management for applications that require assistance in a multiple user environment.
Fax	*fxssvc.exe*	Enables you to send and receive faxes, utilizing fax resources available on this computer or on the network.
Generic Packet Classifier	*msgpc.sys*	Generic Packet Classifier.
Help and Support	*svchost.exe*	Enables Help and Support Center to run on this computer. If this service is stopped, Help and Support Center will be unavailable. If this service is disabled, any services that explicitly depend on it will fail to start.

Name	Filename	Description
Human Interface Device Access	*svchost.exe*	Enables generic input access to Human Interface Devices (HID), which activates and maintains the use of predefined hot buttons on keyboards, remote controls, and other multimedia devices. If this service is stopped, hot buttons controlled by this service will no longer function. If this service is disabled, any services that explicitly depend on it will fail to start.
IMAPI CD-Burning COM Service	*imapi.exe*	Manages CD recording using Image Mastering Applications Programming Interface (IMAPI). If this service is stopped, this computer will be unable to record CDs. If this service is disabled, any services that explicitly depend on it will fail to start.
Indexing Service	*cisvc.exe*	Indexes contents and properties of files on local and remote computers; provides rapid access to files through flexible querying language.
Internet Connection Firewall (ICF) / Internet Connection Sharing (ICS)	*svchost.exe*	Provides network address translation, addressing, name resolution and/or intrusion prevention services for a home or small office network.
IP in IP Tunnel Driver	*ipinip.sys*	IP in IP Tunnel Driver.
IP Network Address Translator	*ipnat.sys*	IP Network Address Translator.
IP Traffic Filter Driver	*ipfltdrv.sys*	IP Traffic Filter Driver.
IPSEC Services	*lsass.exe*	Manages IP security policy and starts the ISAKMP/Oakley (IKE) and the IP security driver.
IPX Traffic Filter Driver	*nwlnkflt.sys*	IPX Traffic Filter Driver.
IPX Traffic Forwarder Driver	*nwlnkfwd.sys*	IPX Traffic Forwarder Driver.
Logical Disk Manager	*svchost.exe*	Detects and monitors new hard disk drives and sends disk volume information to Logical Disk Manager Administrative Service for configuration. If this service is stopped, dynamic disk status and configuration information may become out of date. If this service is disabled, any services that explicitly depend on it will fail to start.
Logical Disk Manager Administrative Service	*dmadmin.exe*	Configures hard disk drives and volumes. The service runs only for configuration processes and then stops.
Messenger	*svchost.exe*	Transmits net send and Alerter service messages between clients and servers. This service is not related to Windows Messenger. If this service is stopped, Alerter messages will not be transmitted. If this service is disabled, any services that explicitly depend on it will fail to start.
MS Software Shadow Copy Provider	*dllhost.exe*	Manages software-based volume shadow copies taken by the Volume Shadow Copy service. If this service is stopped, software-based volume shadow copies cannot be managed. If this service is disabled, any services that explicitly depend on it will fail to start.
NDIS Usermode I/O Protocol	*ndisuio.sys*	NDIS Usermode I/O Protocol.
Net Logon	*lsass.exe*	Supports pass-through authentication of account logon events for computers in a domain.
NetBIOS Interface	*netbios.sys*	NetBIOS Interface.
NetMeeting Remote Desktop Sharing	*mnmsrvc.exe*	Enables an authorized user to access this computer remotely by using NetMeeting over a corporate intranet. If this service is stopped, remote Desktop sharing will be unavailable. If this service is disabled, any services that explicitly depend on it will fail to start.
Network Connections	*svchost.exe*	Manages objects in the Network and Dial-Up Connections folder, in which you can view both local area network and remote connections.

Services

Name	Filename	Description
Network DDE	*netdde.exe*	Provides network transport and security for Dynamic Data Exchange (DDE) for programs running on the same computer or on different computers. If this service is stopped, DDE transport and security will be unavailable. If this service is disabled, any services that explicitly depend on it will fail to start.
Network DDE DSDM	*netdde.exe*	Manages Dynamic Data Exchange (DDE) network shares. If this service is stopped, DDE network shares will be unavailable. If this service is disabled, any services that explicitly depend on it will fail to start.
Network Location Awareness (NLA)	*svchost.exe*	Collects and stores network configuration and location information, and notifies applications when this information changes.
NT LM Security Support Provider	*lsass.exe*	Provides security to remote procedure call (RPC) programs that use transports other than named pipes.
Performance Logs and Alerts	*smlogsvc.exe*	Collects performance data from local or remote computers based on preconfigured schedule parameters, then writes the data to a log or triggers an alert. If this service is stopped, performance information will not be collected. If this service is disabled, any services that explicitly depend on it will fail to start.
Plug and Play	*services.exe*	Enables a computer to recognize and adapt to hardware changes with little or no user input. Stopping or disabling this service will result in system instability.
Portable Media Serial Number	*svchost.exe*	Retrieves the serial number of any portable music player connected to your computer.
Print Spooler	*spoolsv.exe*	Loads files to memory for later printing.
Protected Storage	*lsass.exe*	Provides protected storage for sensitive data, such as private keys, to prevent access by unauthorized services, processes, or users.
QoS RSVP	*rsvp.exe*	Provides network signaling and local traffic control setup functionality for QoS-aware programs and control applets.
RAS Asynchronous Media Driver	*asyncmac.sys*	RAS Asynchronous Media Driver.
Rdbss	*rdbss.sys*	Rdbss.
Remote Access Auto Connection Driver	*rasacd.sys*	Remote Access Auto Connection Driver.
Remote Access Auto Connection Manager	*svchost.exe*	Creates a connection to a remote network whenever a program references a remote DNS or NetBIOS name or address.
Remote Access Connection Manager	*svchost.exe*	Creates a network connection.
Remote Access IP ARP Driver	*wanarp.sys*	Remote Access IP ARP Driver.
Remote Access NDIS TAPI Driver	*ndistapi.sys*	Remote Access NDIS TAPI Driver.
Remote Access NDIS WAN Driver	*ndiswan.sys*	Remote Access NDIS WAN Driver.
Remote Access PPPOE Driver	*raspppoe.sys*	Remote Access PPPOE Driver.
Remote Desktop Help Session Manager	*sessmgr.exe*	Manages and controls Remote Assistance. If this service is stopped, Remote Assistance will be unavailable. Before stopping this service, see the Dependencies tab of the Properties dialog box.
Remote Procedure Call (RPC)	*svchost*	Provides the endpoint mapper and other miscellaneous RPC services.

Name	Filename	Description
Remote Procedure Call (RPC) Locator	*locator.exe*	Manages the RPC name service database.
Remote Registry	*svchost.exe*	Enables remote users to modify registry settings on this computer. If this service is stopped, the registry can be modified only by users on this computer. If this service is disabled, any services that explicitly depend on it will fail to start.
Routing and Remote Access	*svchost.exe*	Offers routing services to businesses in local area and wide area network environments.
Secdrv	*secdrv.sys*	SafeDisc driver.
Secondary Logon	*svchost.exe*	Enables starting processes under alternate credentials. If this service is stopped, this type of logon access will be unavailable. If this service is disabled, any services that explicitly depend on it will fail to start.
Security Accounts Manager	*lsass.exe*	Stores security information for local user accounts.
Server	*svchost.exe*	Supports file, print, and named-pipe sharing over the network for this computer. If this service is stopped, these functions will be unavailable. If this service is disabled, any services that explicitly depend on it will fail to start.
Shell Hardware Detection	*svchost.exe*	Provides notifications for AutoPlay hardware events.
Smart Card	*SCardSvr.exe*	Manages access to smart cards read by this computer. If this service is stopped, this computer will be unable to read smart cards. If this service is disabled, any services that explicitly depend on it will fail to start.
Smart Card Helper	*SCardSvr.exe*	Enables support for legacy nonplug and play smart-card readers used by this computer. If this service is stopped, this computer will not support legacy reader. If this service is disabled, any services that explicitly depend on it will fail to start.
SSDP Discovery Service	*svchost.exe*	Enables discovery of UPnP devices on your home network.
System Event Notification	*svchost.exe*	Tracks system events such as Windows logon, network, and power events. Notifies COM+ Event System subscribers of these events.
System Restore Service	*svchost.exe*	Performs system restore functions. To stop service, turn off System Restore from the System Restore tab in My Computer → Properties.
Task Scheduler	*svchost.exe*	Enables a user to configure and schedule automated tasks on this computer. If this service is stopped, these tasks will not be run at their scheduled times. If this service is disabled, any services that explicitly depend on it will fail to start.
TCP/IP NetBIOS Helper	*svchost.exe*	Enables support for NetBIOS over TCP/IP (NetBT) service and NetBIOS name resolution.
TCP/IP Protocol Driver	*tcpip.sys*	TCP/IP Protocol Driver.
Telephony	*svchost.exe*	Provides Telephony API (TAPI) support for programs that control telephony devices and IP-based voice connections on the local computer and, through the LAN, on servers that are also running the service.
Telnet	*tlntsvr.exe*	Enables a remote user to log on to this computer and run programs, and supports various TCP/IP Telnet clients, including Unix-based and Windows-based computers. If this service is stopped, remote user access to programs might be unavailable. If this service is disabled, any services that explicitly depend on it will fail to start.
Terminal Services	*svchost.exe*	Allows multiple users to be connected interactively to a machine as well as the display of Desktops and applications to remote computers. The underpinning of Remote Desktop (including RD for Administrators), Fast User Switching, Remote Assistance, and Terminal Server.

Services

Name	Filename	Description
Themes	*svchost.exe*	Provides user experience theme management.
Uninterruptible Power Supply	*ups.exe*	Manages an uninterruptible power supply (UPS) connected to the computer.
Universal Plug and Play Device Host	*svchost.exe*	Provides support to host Universal Plug and Play devices.
Upload Manager	*svchost.exe*	Manages synchronous and asynchronous file transfers between clients and servers on the network. If this service is stopped, synchronous and asynchronous file transfers between clients and servers on the network will not occur. If this service is disabled, any services that explicitly depend on it will fail to start.
Volume Shadow Copy	*vssvc.exe*	Manages and implements Volume Shadow Copies used for backup and other purposes. If this service is stopped, shadow copies will be unavailable for backup and the backup may fail. If this service is disabled, any services that explicitly depend on it will fail to start.
WAN Miniport (L2TP)	*rasl2tp.sys*	WAN Miniport (L2TP).
WAN Miniport (PPTP)	*raspptp.sys*	WAN Miniport (PPTP).
WebClient	*svchost.exe*	Enables Windows-based programs to create, access, and modify Internet-based files. If this service is stopped, these functions will not be available. If this service is disabled, any services that explicitly depend on it will fail to start.
WebDav Client Redirector	*mrxdav.sys*	WebDav Client Redirector.
Windows Audio	*svchost.exe*	Manages audio devices for Windows-based programs. If this service is stopped, audio devices and effects will not function properly. If this service is disabled, any services that explicitly depend on it will fail to start.
Windows Image Acquisition (WIA)	*svchost.exe*	Provides image acquisition services for scanners and cameras.
Windows Installer	*msiexec.exe*	Installs, repairs and removes software according to instructions contained in *.MSI* files.
Windows Management Instrumentation	*svchost.exe*	Provides a common interface and object model to access management information about operating systems, devices, applications and services. If this service is stopped, most Windows-based software will not function properly. If this service is disabled, any services that explicitly depend on it will fail to start.
Windows Management Instrumentation Driver Extensions	*svchost.exe*	Provides systems management information to and from drivers.
Windows Time	*svchost.exe*	Maintains date and time synchronization on all clients and servers in the network. If this service is stopped, date and time synchronization will be unavailable. If this service is disabled, any services that explicitly depend on it will fail to start.
Wireless Zero Configuration	*svchost.exe*	Provides automatic configuration for the 802.11 adapters.
WMI Performance Adapter	*wmiapsrv.exe*	Provides performance library information from WMI HiPerf providers.
Workstation	*svchost.exe*	Creates and maintains client network connections to remote servers. If this service is stopped, these connections will be unavailable. If this service is disabled, any services that explicitly depend on it will fail to start.

Index

We'd like to hear your suggestions for improving our indexes. Send email to *index@oreilly.com*.

More Titles from O'Reilly

Power Users

Windows Me: The Missing Manual

By David Pogue
1st Edition September 2000
423 pages, ISBN 0-596-00009-X

In *Windows Me: The Missing Manual*, author David Pogue provides the friendly, authoritative book that should have been in the box. It's the ideal user's guide for the world's most popular operating system.

Outlook 2000 in a Nutshell

By Tom Syroid & Bo Leuf
1st Edition May 2000
660 pages, ISBN 1-56592-704-4

Outlook 2000 in a Nutshell fills the need for an up-to-date and comprehensive reference book for sophisticated users who want to get all they can out of this powerful and versatile program.

PC Hardware in a Nutshell, 2nd Edition

By Robert Bruce Thompson
& Barbara Frichtman Thompson
2nd Edition Jun 2002 (est.)
696 pages (est.), ISBN 0-596-00353-6

Fully updated and expanded, *PC Hardware in a Nutshell*, 2nd Edition is a comprehensive guide to buying, building, upgrading, troubleshooting and repairing Intel-based PCs. Features include how-to advice for specific components, ample reference material, and a complete case study for building a PC using separate components. Although this book serves a number of audiences, from novice to expert, its focus is often on professionals who service and support computers frequently.

Word 2000 in a Nutshell

By Walter Glenn
1st Edition August 2000
520 pages, ISBN 1-56592-489-4

Word 2000 in a Nutshell is a clear, concise, and complete reference to the most popular word-processing program in the world. This book is the first choice of the Word power user who needs help completing a specific task or understanding a command or topic. It's also an invaluable resource that uncovers Word 2000's undocumented features and shares powerful time-saving tips.

Excel 2000 in a Nutshell

By Jinjer Simon
1st Edition August 2000
606 Pages, ISBN 1-56592-714-1

Excel 2000 in a Nutshell is a one-stop reference to every one of Excel's menu options and functions, for both professional and power users of Excel 2000. In typical Nutshell fashion, information is organized for quick and easy access, providing readers with everything they need to know about the premier spreadsheet application.

Dreamweaver MX: The Missing Manual

By David McFarland
1st Edition July 2002 (est.)
750 pages (est.), ISBN 0-596-00349-8

Dreamweaver MX: The Missing Manual is the ideal companion to this complex software. The book begins with an anatomical tour of a web page, and then walks users through the process of creating and designing a complete web site. Armed with this book, both first-time and experienced web designers can easily use Dreamweaver to bring stunning, interactive web sites to life. In addition, users new to Ultra Dev and database-driven web sites will be given an overview of the technology and a brief primer on using these new additions to Dreamweaver.

O'REILLY®

TO ORDER: 800-998-9938 • order@oreilly.com • www.oreilly.com
ONLINE EDITIONS OF MOST O'REILLY TITLES ARE AVAILABLE BY SUBSCRIPTION AT safari.oreilly.com
ALSO AVAILABLE AT MOST RETAIL AND ONLINE BOOKSTORES

Power Users

PalmPilot: The Ultimate Guide, 2nd Edition

By David Pogue
2nd Edition June 1999
624 pages, Includes CD-ROM
ISBN 1-56592-600-5

This new edition of O'Reilly's runaway bestseller is densely packed with previously undocumented information. The bible for users of Palm VII and all other Palm models, it contains hundreds of timesaving tips and surprising tricks, plus an all-new CD-ROM (for Windows 9x, NT, or Macintosh) containing over 3,100 PalmPilot programs from the collection of palmcentral.com, the Internet's largest Palm software site.

Windows Me Annoyances

By David A. Karp
1st Edition March 2001
472 pages, ISBN 0-596-00060-X

Based on the author's popular Annoyances.org web sites, *Windows Me Annoyances* is an authoritative collection of techniques for customizing Windows Me. Packed with creative and seldom-documented ways to quickly identify and fix a particular annoyance or customize Windows for individual needs, it's the definitive resource for dealing with crashes, unintelligible error messages, unwanted icons, and much more.

Windows 2000 Pro: The Missing Manual

By Sharon Crawford
1st Edition August 2000
450 pages, ISBN 0-596-00010-3

In *Windows 2000 Pro: The Missing Manual*, best-selling Windows NT author Sharon Crawford provides the friendly, authoritative book that should have been in the box. It's the ideal (and desperately needed) user's guide for the world's most popular corporate operating system.

Windows 2000 Quick Fixes

By Jim Boyce
1st Edition December 2000
304 pages, ISBN 0-596-00017-0

Windows 2000 Quick Fixes provides fixes to common problems in a clear, well-organized fashion. It extensively troubleshoots both the Windows 2000 Professional and the Windows 2000 Server editions, taking power users through installation, complex networking configuration problems, and important backup and security concerns. When the pressure is on and there's no time to waste hunting for Windows 2000 solutions, this is the book to reach for.

MP3: The Definitive Guide

By Scot Hacker
1st Edition March 2000
400 pages, ISBN 1-56592-661-7

MP3: The Definitive Guide introduces the power user to just about all aspects of MP3 technology. It delves into detail on obtaining, recording, and optimizing MP3 files using both commercial and open source methods. Coverage is complete for four platforms: Windows, Macintosh, Linux, and BeOS. Readers will learn how to test their equipment, evaluate their playback options, control and organize a collection, even burn their own CDs or distribute their own music to a massive worldwide audience over the Internet. Everything you need to know to enjoy MP3 today and tomorrow is contained in this single volume.

O'REILLY®

TO ORDER: 800-998-9938 • order@oreilly.com • www.oreilly.com
ONLINE EDITIONS OF MOST O'REILLY TITLES ARE AVAILABLE BY SUBSCRIPTION AT safari.oreilly.com
ALSO AVAILABLE AT MOST RETAIL AND ONLINE BOOKSTORES

How to stay in touch with O'Reilly

1. Visit our award-winning web site

http://www.oreilly.com/

★ "Top 100 Sites on the Web"—PC Magazine
★ CIO Magazine's Web Business 50 Awards

Our web site contains a library of comprehensive product information (including book excerpts and tables of contents), downloadable software, background articles, interviews with technology leaders, links to relevant sites, book cover art, and more. File us in your bookmarks or favorites!

2. Join our email mailing lists

Sign up to get email announcements of new books and conferences, special offers, and O'Reilly Network technology newsletters at:

http://www.elists.oreilly.com

It's easy to customize your free elists subscription so you'll get exactly the O'Reilly news you want.

3. Get examples from our books

To find example files for a book, go to:

http://www.oreilly.com/catalog

select the book, and follow the "Examples" link.

4. Work with us

Check out our web site for current employment opportunites:

http://jobs.oreilly.com/

5. Register your book

Register your book at:

http://register.oreilly.com

6. Contact us

O'Reilly & Associates, Inc.
1005 Gravenstein Hwy North
Sebastopol, CA 95472 USA
TEL: 707-827-7000 or 800-998-9938
        (6am to 5pm PST)
FAX: 707-829-0104

order@oreilly.com
For answers to problems regarding your order or our products. To place a book order online visit:

http://www.oreilly.com/order_new/

catalog@oreilly.com
To request a copy of our latest catalog.

booktech@oreilly.com
For book content technical questions or corrections.

proposals@oreilly.com
To submit new book proposals to our editors and product managers.

international@oreilly.com
For information about our international distributors or translation queries. For a list of our distributors outside of North America check out:

http://international.oreilly.com/distributors.html

O'REILLY®

*TO ORDER: **800-998-9938** • **order@oreilly.com** • **www.oreilly.com***
*ONLINE EDITIONS OF MOST O'REILLY TITLES ARE AVAILABLE BY SUBSCRIPTION AT **safari.oreilly.com***
ALSO AVAILABLE AT MOST RETAIL AND ONLINE BOOKSTORES